JOHN VRBANCIC

W9-BBY-928

Commerce Server 2000: Building eBusiness Solutions

Gopal Sreeraman

201 West 103rd St., Indianapolis, Indiana, 46290 USA

Commerce Server 2000: Building eBusiness Solutions

Copyright © 2002 by Sams Publishing

All rights reserved. No part of this book shall be reproduced, stored in a retrieval system, or transmitted by any means, electronic, mechanical, photocopying, recording, or otherwise, without written permission from the publisher. No patent liability is assumed with respect to the use of the information contained herein. Although every precaution has been taken in the preparation of this book, the publisher and author assume no responsibility for errors or omissions. Nor is any liability assumed for damages resulting from the use of the information contained herein.

International Standard Book Number: 0-672-32220-x

Library of Congress Catalog Card Number: 00-109563

Printed in the United States of America

First Printing: August 2001

04	03	02	01		4	3	2	1

Trademarks

All terms mentioned in this book that are known to be trademarks or service marks have been appropriately capitalized. Sams Publishing cannot attest to the accuracy of this information. Use of a term in this book should not be regarded as affecting the validity of any trademark or service mark.

Warning and Disclaimer

Every effort has been made to make this book as complete and as accurate as possible, but no warranty or fitness is implied. The information provided is on an "as is" basis. The author and the publisher shall have neither liability nor responsibility to any person or entity with respect to any loss or damages arising from the information contained in this book or from the use of programs accompanying it.

ASSOCIATE PUBLISHER
Linda Engelman

ACQUISITIONS EDITOR
Karen Wachs

DEVELOPMENT EDITOR
Chris Zahn

MANAGING EDITOR
Charlotte Clapp

PROJECT EDITOR
Elizabeth Finney

COPY EDITOR
Bart Reed
Rhonda Tinch-Mize

INDEXER
Chris Barrick

PROOFREADER
Teresa Stephens

TECHNICAL EDITOR
Henry Winkler
Alex Kruchkov

TEAM COORDINATOR
Chris Feather

INTERIOR DESIGNER
Anne Jones

COVER DESIGNER
Aren Howell

PAGE LAYOUT
Lizbeth Patterson

Contents at a Glance

Introduction **1**

Part I **Commerce Server Fundamentals** **9**

1 Overview **11**

2 Planning and Installation **25**

3 Creating the Store Foundation **39**

4 From the Business Desk **59**

5 Understanding the Site Architecture **73**

Part II **Advanced Topics** **115**

6 Catalog Management **117**

7 User Management **187**

8 Personalization and Targeting **217**

9 Commerce Server Pipelines **249**

10 Order-Processing Pipelines **277**

11 Direct Mailer and Content Selection Framework Pipelines **323**

12 Running Ads and Auctions **363**

13 Building and Customizing Pipelines **395**

14 Extending the Business Desk **441**

15 Data Warehouse, Reports, and Prediction **485**

16 Integration with BizTalk Server **533**

Part III **Appendixes** **569**

A Commerce Server Objects: A Quick Reference **571**

B Pipeline Components: A Quick Reference **591**

C Retail Store Helper Routines: Where to Find What **603**

D Migrating from Site Server 3.0 to Commerce Server 2000 **613**

Index **621**

Table of Contents

Introduction   1

PART I   Commerce Server Fundamentals   9

1   Overview   11

Business and the WWW 12

The Case for Electronic Commerce 13

The Virtual Marketplace 14

Components of an E-Commerce Store 16

    Catalogs 16

    Shopping Cart 16

    Shopper Registration 17

    Order 17

    Personalization 17

    Store Back End 18

    A Management System 18

What Does Commerce Server 2000 Provide? 19

    Speedy Time to Market 20

    Efficient Administration 20

    Ease of Deployment 21

    Ease of Extension 21

    Core Systems 22

    Business Management 22

    New Vision 23

Summary of Key Commerce Server Features 23

2   Planning and Installation   25

Business Requirements 26

Technical Requirements 27

    Hardware Requirements 28

    Software Requirements 30

Installing Commerce Server 32

    Single-Server Scenario 32

    Multiple-Server Scenario 34

Maximizing Performance 36

Summary 36

3   Creating the Store Foundation   39

Creating IIS Web sites 41

Unpack with Site Packager 44

    Resources 47

    CS Resources 53

    Explore the Changes 56

Summary 58

4   From the Business Desk   59

What is the Business Desk? 60

Installing Business Desk 60

What Can You Do With Business Desk? 62

Using the Business Desk 63

Creating an Ad-hoc Catalog 64

Summary 71

5   Understanding the Site Architecture   73

Initializing the Site Application 74

Configuration Settings 76

Inside the Global Files 78

Starting with the Home Page 82

Standard Include Files 84

Header File 84

Site Constants 84

HTML Rendering Routines 85

Standard Libraries 85

Page to Setup the Environment 86

Browsing Catalogs 89

Catalog.asp: The Core File 89

Navigating Product Categories 91

The Category Page 91

Caching Is Good 94

Testing Caches 96

Viewing Product Details 97

The Shopping Basket 101

Adding Items Using _additem.asp 101

Specify Shipping and Billing Addresses 104

Choosing a Shipping Method 105

The Order Summary 108

Pay for Your Purchase 110

Order Confirmation 112

Summary 113

PART II   Advanced Topics   115

6   Catalog Management   117

Basics of a Commerce Server Catalog 119

Property Definitions 120

Product Definitions 127

Category Definitions 130

Creating Catalogs 133
Creating a Category 133
Creating a Product 135
Catalog Refresh 140
Catalog Sets 141
Custom Catalogs 143
Summary of Steps in Catalog Creation 147
Importing and Exporting Catalogs 148
File Formats 148
Exporting a Catalog in XML Format 148
Exporting a Catalog as CSV 152
Importing a CSV File 153
About Product Variants 156
Creating Product Variants 157
COM Objects for the Catalog System 161
CatalogManager 162
CatalogSets 162
ProductCatalog 162
Category 163
Product 163
Simulating Catalog Browsing In Estore 163
Showing Related Products 168
Searching the Catalogs 174
Free Text Search 174
Specification Search 176
Summary 184

7   User Management   187
Fundamentals 188
GetUserInfo() 190
EnsureAccess() 191
Tickets and Ticket Modes 192
Determining Ticket Mode 192
Generating a Profile 192
Profile Schemas 194
The UserObject Profile 195
Generating a Ticket 198
Cookies-less Browsing 200
User Registration 201
Sending the MSCSAuth Ticket 203
A Little Personalization 206
Managing Users from the Biz Desk 208
Summary of the Profile System 212
The Authentication Filter 212
Summary 216

8   Personalization and Targeting   217

Methods of Profiling 218
Methods of Targeting 219
Catalog Sets 220
Campaigns 223
Applying a Site Wide Discount 224
    Creating the Customer 225
    Creating the Campaign 225
    Creating the Discount 227
    Publishing the Campaign 232
Targeting Discounts 233
    Modifying the User Profile 234
Catalog Expressions and Target Expressions 244
    Creating a Catalog Expression 244
    Adding the Catalog Expression 246
Target Group 248
Summary 248

9   Commerce Server Pipelines   249

What Is a Pipeline? 250
The Pipeline Editor 251
Pipeline Stages and Components 251
Modifying a Pipeline 257
Standard Pipelines 259
Pipelines in Brief 260
    Content Selection Pipeline 260
    Order Processing Pipelines 263
    The Direct Mailer Pipeline 271
High Precision in Currency 276
Summary 276

10   Order-Processing Pipelines   277

Global Initialization 278
The Product Page 279
    Add Item Script 280
The Basket Page 286
    Inside basket.asp 287
    Error Handling in Pipelines 294
    The Check-out Button 298
    The total.pcf Pipe 304
    Display of Summary Page 310
Checkout Processing 312
    Purchase Check Stage 313
    Payment Stage 314
    Accept Stage 317
Summary 321

11   Direct Mailer and Content Selection Framework Pipelines   323

The Direct Mailer 324

Global Resource 324

Direct Mailer Database 325

What Can It Do? 326

List Manager 327

Importing a Mailing List from a CSV File 328

Creating a Direct Mail Campaign 330

Sending a Test Mail 331

The Mail Drop 332

Sending a Personalized Page 333

Creating a Dynamic E-mail List 334

The Personalized Mail Campaign 335

ASP Page for Personalization 337

Opt-out List 337

Direct Mailer Pipeline 339

Direct Mailer as Standalone 342

Troubleshooting Tips 343

Other Sources of E-mail Lists 343

Content Selection Framework 344

Components of the Content Selection Framework 344

Content Cache 345

Content Context 347

Content Selector 349

Content Selection Pipelines 350

Event Processing Pipeline 359

Summary 361

12   Running Ads and Auctions   363

The Advertising Infrastructure 364

Concepts to Know 366

The Case of StarTrek Travels 367

Define Ad Metadata 369

Creating a Customer 372

Creating the Ad Campaign 373

Creating an Ad 374

Using the ContentSelector Object 378

Troubleshooting Ad Campaigns 381

Recording Ad Delivery 383

Enabling Auctions 385

Adding Message Strings 385

Preparing the Biz Desk 385

Preparing the Site 388

The Sample Auction Page 390
The Bid Page 391
Summary 392

13   Building and Customizing Pipelines   395
Customizing a Pipeline: E-mail on Order Confirmation 396
Preparing the E-mail with a Scriptor Component 397
Inserting the SendSMTP Component 399
Verifying Order Confirmation 400
The Component Object Model (COM) 401
A Pipeline Component 402
Building a Pipeline Component Using VB 403
Installing the VB Pipeline Component Wizard 404
Building an Order-level Discount for Visa Corp 404
Using the VB Pipeline Wizard 404
Checking the Generated Code 406
Modifying the Configuration Interface 408
Modifying IPipelineComponent_Execute 408
Setting Values Read and Written 411
Compiling and Building the Component 411
Registering Pipeline Components 411
Inserting the Component in the Pipeline 413
Setting Configuration Values 413
Reporting the Discount 414
Testing the VisaDiscount Component 415
Debugging Pipelines 416
Dumping the Order Form 416
Logging Pipeline Execution 418
The Micropipe 419
Ready for Production? 422
Building Pipeline Components with Visual C++ 422
Creating the Project 423
Using the ATL Pipeline Wizard 423
Inserting the Property Page UI 424
Writing the Code 426
Fleshing Out IPipelineComponent::Execute 427
Working with the Property Page 430
Code for Registering the Component 438
Tips on Building the Component 439
Summary 440

14   Extending the Business Desk   441

Understanding the Architecture 442

HTML Application 443

The Visual Framework 444

Business Desk Configuration 448

The Master Configuration File 449

Module Configuration File 452

The List Page 456

XML Data Islands 457

Metadata Island 458

Action Page Overview 459

Action Page Details 459

Edit Page 462

Securing Modules 464

Building a Module 464

Design Decisions 465

Inserting Order Status Codes 465

Creating the Module Folder 466

Creating the Module Configuration 466

Updating the Master Configuration 467

Creating List and Edit Pages 467

Restarting the Biz Desk Application 468

Modifying the Module Configuration 469

Modifying the List Page 472

Debugging Business Desk 476

Modifying the Edit Page 477

Summary 482

15   Data Warehouse, Reports, and Prediction   485

Introduction to Data Warehousing 486

OLTP Versus OLAP 486

OLAP Structures 487

The Data Store 488

OLAP Storage 489

Multidimensional Expressions 489

Data Mining 490

Data Warehouse Resources 490

Commerce Server Data Warehouse 491

SQL Server and OLAP Databases 492

Cubes, Measures, and Dimensions 492

Logical Schema 496

Importing Data 498

Importing Web Logs 501

Populating the Cubes 505

Workflow Between Tasks 506

Analysis Reports 507

Working with a Dynamic Report 508

Working with Static Reports 513

Creating Custom Reports 515

Prediction in Commerce Server 518

The Predictor Resource 518

Analysis Models 519

Data for a Model 519

The Transactions Configuration 521

Building a Predictor Model 523

About the Scores 526

Using the PredictorClient Object 527

Segment Models 530

Segment Viewer 530

Tips on Extending the DW 531

Summary 532

16   Integration with BizTalk Server   533

About BizTalk Server 534

Messaging Manager Objects 535

Integration Between Commerce Server and BizTalk Server 536

Building a Partner Site 537

Unpacking a Retail Site 538

Installing BizTalk Server 539

Exchanging Catalogs with Partners 539

Configuring AppDefaultConfig 540

Creating Messaging Manager Objects 541

Creating the Source Organization 541

Creating the Destination Organization as Partner 543

Creating a Document Definition 544

Scenario 2: Partner Has Different Infrastructure 545

Creating a Messaging Port 545

Creating a Channel 547

Sending the Catalog 550

Tips for Troubleshooting 551

The Vendor Picker 551

Scenario 1: Partner Has Similar Infrastructure 553

Modifying the Messaging Port 553

Modifying the Channel 554

Sending the Catalog 555
Tips for Troubleshooting 556
Fulfilling Orders Through Partners 557
Integrating with Partner for Order Fulfillment 558
Configuring AppDefaultConfig Properties 558
Creating Messaging Manager Objects 558
Modifying the Organizations 559
Creating a Purchase Order Definition 559
Creating the Messaging Port 559
Creating the Channel for PurchaseOrder 561
Associating a Catalog with a Vendor 562
The Checkout Pipeline 562
Sending the Order to BizTalk 563
Receiving the Order 565
Testing the Integration 567
Summary 568

PART III   Appendixes   569

A   Commerce Server Objects: A Quick Reference   571
List of Commerce Server Objects 572
Methods and Properties of Frequently Used Objects 578
AuthManager 578
CacheManager 579
MessageManager 580
CatalogManager 581
OrderForm 583
OrderGroup 584
ProfileService 586
ContentSelector 587
AppConfig 587
Category 588
MtsPipeline 589
ProfileObject 590

B   Pipeline Components: A Quick Reference   591
Reference by Type or Pipeline and Stage 592
Order Processing Pipelines 592
Content Selection Framework Pipeline 598
Direct Mailer Pipeline 599
Other Pipeline Components 600
Reference By Component Names 600

C   Retail Store Helper Routines: Where to Find What   603

D   Migrating from Site Server 3.0 to Commerce Server 2000   613

SSCE Features That Migrate to CS2K 614

SSCE Features That Migrate to Other Products 615

SSCE Features That Do Not Migrate 615

Getting Ready to Migrate 615

SFW/SBW to Site Packager 615

Starter Site to Solution Site 616

Site Manager to Business Desk 616

Online Store to Catalog System 616

P&M to User Profiles 617

Ad Server/Ad Manager to CSF/Campaigns Manager 618

Analysis: Data Import and Reports 618

Predictor 619

Content Deployment and Replication 619

Site Vocabulary and Rule Builder 619

Pipelines 619

Direct Mail 620

Search 620

B2B Pipelines 620

Migration Approaches 620

Summary 620

Index   621

Foreword

In his 1995 book, *The Road Ahead*, Bill Gates articulated a vision of how computers and the Internet would transform common personal and business experiences in the near future. One of the concepts Bill introduced was *friction-free capitalism*—the notion that ubiquitous communication, standardized protocols, and new software services would soon combine to revolutionize the way trade is conducted in the twenty-first century.

In mid-1999, I was given the opportunity to lead the engineering team working on the next generation of Microsoft's e-commerce server software. Bill's original vision still resonated with me, and I saw in Commerce Server the potential to solve many of the problems traditionally associated with conducting business online.

Our priorities for this next-generation server product were all about making it easier for companies to build, deploy, and manage business-oriented sites. We had three primary themes for this release:

- *Provide rich infrastructure and functionality critical to any company wanting to conduct trade over the Internet.*

  The Trade Trinity: Objects and associated runtimes for handling people, products, and payment. Without a way to create and manage any one of these, you simply could not conduct commerce.

  Business Intelligence: A system for deriving the key metrics and trends affecting the online business. Provide a decision support system for the site business manager.

  Targeting System: Essentially a rules engine and set of associated applications that made it easy for the site manager to target (advertise, up-sell, cross-sell, and so on) customers, making the site increasingly relevant to the visitor, with resulting increased sales.

- *Reduce time to market. Make it much easier for the developer to build and deploy Web-based businesses.*

  Solution Sites: Production viable, prebuilt starter sites for retail and sell-side e-business scenarios.

  An extensible, COM/ASP/SQL Server–based framework that makes it easy for developers with an existing understanding of Microsoft technologies to rapidly learn and customize.

- *Empower the business manager. Provide more capabilities directly to nontechnical business users, allowing them fine-grained control over day-to-day site activities.*

  Business Desk: A centralized application console, with modules for managing users, catalogs, orders, reports, campaigns, and much more.

From these themes, Microsoft Commerce Server 2000 was born—and released to manufacturing on November 13, 2000. The feedback from early adopters and recent customer wins underscores our success: This product delivers against the release themes we set for it.

Speaking for the entire product unit at Microsoft, we are very excited about Commerce Server 2000. Further, this book, *Commerce Server 2000: Building eBusiness Solutions*, provides valuable information of interest to anyone involved with building or managing e-businesses. Gopal Sreeraman's use of a single, detailed example to drill down to the essence of the product platform provides an excellent mechanism for learning key concepts that are immediately applicable to real-world deployments. The release of Commerce Server 2000 and the publication of this book represent important steps towards enabling the vision of the new economy—friction-free capitalism.

Michael Nappi

Product Unit Manager

Commerce Server

Microsoft Corp.

About the Author

Gopal Sreeraman is a Senior Consultant in the Emerging and Integrating Technologies service line of PricewaterhouseCoopers, LLP's Management Consulting Services. He routinely works with challenging projects for many Fortune 500 clients. However, he remembers consulting for quite a few small companies, too, during the boom! Gopal's recent engagements have been focussed around content management, portal infrastructure, and custom Internet applications. He also contributes to IEEE journals in the area of Systems Engineering. In his spare time, he is probably watching one of the original 80 Star Trek episodes for the nth time while the fight for the remote continues at home!

About the Technical Editors

Henry Winkler is a Senior Consultant with Microsoft Consulting Services in Denver, Colorado. His primary responsibility is designing and developing commerce solutions for Microsoft's strategic customers in the Rocky Mountain region. Prior to joining Microsoft, he spent seven years working for Andersen Consulting. He enjoys mountain biking, skiing, playing with his two children, and catching Rockies games at Coors Field.

Andrey Kruchkov is a chief consultant on e-commerce and network security for Quarta Technologies, a Microsoft Gold-Certified Partner that specializes in developing complex e-commerce solutions in Russia for European and U.S. clients. Andrey has been working on e-commerce projects on Microsoft's platform since the first beta of Microsoft Merchant Server 1.0.

You can find Andrey's articles about Windows NT security in *Windows 2000 Magazine* and hear him at all of Microsoft's events in Russia talking about the platform and e-commerce. Andrey is one of the founders, and an active member, of the Russian Windows NT User Group. When he is not at work, he spends his time with his family or traveling to see *Phantom of the Opera* in theaters all over the world.

Dedication

To Amma, Appa and Sangeetha.

Acknowledgments

Let me start by acknowledging Karen Wachs, Acquisitions Editor, and Chris Zahn, Development Editor. They have made this book possible from start to finish. Many thanks to Karen for being patient, understanding, and helpful. She has certainly run with me and the project to see that this book optimally covers a large product. Chris is the main reason why each word, sentence, and paragraph is connected with the others in the book. Credit goes to him where you find the chapters readable, logical, and unambiguous. I need to acknowledge the valuable contributions made to the book by Elizabeth Finney, Bart Reed, Rhonda Tinch-Mize in their roles as Project Editor and Copy Editors, respectively. Thanks are also due to Henry Winkler of Microsoft and Andrey Kruchkov of Quarta Technologies for criticisms, as well as encouragement, in their technical reviews.

Last but not least, kudos to Sangeetha, who helped me handle the pressures of working for a Big Five firm, writing on a big product, and watching the big adventures of the starship Enterprise, all at the same time!

Tell Us What You Think!

As the reader of this book, *you* are our most important critic and commentator. We value your opinion and want to know what we're doing right, what we could do better, what areas you'd like to see us publish in, and any other words of wisdom you're willing to pass our way.

As an Associate Publisher for Sams Publishing, I welcome your comments. You can fax, email, or write me directly to let me know what you did or didn't like about this book—as well as what we can do to make our books stronger.

Please note that I cannot help you with technical problems related to the topic of this book, and that due to the high volume of mail I receive, I might not be able to reply to every message.

When you write, please be sure to include this book's title and author as well as your name and phone or fax number. I will carefully review your comments and share them with the author and editors who worked on the book.

Fax: 317-581-4770

Email: feedback@samspublishing.com

Mail: Linda Engelman
             Associate Publisher
             Sams Publishing
             201 West 103rd Street
             Indianapolis, IN 46290 USA

Introduction

At the turn of the new millennium, the world is at the crossroads of technology. In a time like this we look to anything that would lead the way forward, particularly to the proven leaders of the recent past. Microsoft is one such giant in the short history of technology. It came as no surprise when a Microsoft product was awarded the Best E-Commerce Platform at the annual Crossroads Conference in March 2001. The Crossroads awards chooses new technologies that are promising for the future, and Microsoft's Commerce Server 2000 was placed in the A-List award category.

In fact, Microsoft has already made its intentions clear for the new Internet-enabled world. In the year 2000, the .NET strategy was unveiled to the millions of companies, developers, and consumers of Microsoft technology throughout the world. The .NET strategy is aimed at revolutionizing the way technology is used and incorporates industry standards such as XML and SOAP. A crucial part of the .NET family of Enterprise Servers is Commerce Server 2000 (CS2K). CS2K is not just a version upgrade of the successfully adopted Site Server 3.0 Commerce server, but it has morphed itself to be the e-commerce platform of choice for B2C and B2B. CS2K has been critically acclaimed for its speed-to-market development, convenient tools for managers, and ease of administration. It provides a comprehensive, functional platform for managing catalogs, users, orders, personalization, targeting, marketing, data warehouse analysis, and reports. Developers will find extending CS2K easy and powerful for implementing unique site requirements.

CS2K integrates well with BizTalk Server, another .NET Enterprise Server, for enabling B2B transactions with partners and external entities. The user profile system provides an aggregated store of user information from disparate data stores, such as an Active Directory or SQL Server. The personalization and targeting engine exposes a manager-friendly interface to build rules for targeting ads, discounts, mail, and content to users. CS2K takes advantage of the security and performance capabilities of the Windows 2000 platform and the COM+ infrastructure. All these strengths of CS2K have made it an early e-commerce platform for adoption by companies such as Hewlett Packard Co., Ford Motor Co., J.D. Edwards & Co., Radio Shack Corp., Starbucks Coffee Co., and Clarus Corporation. Further, over 30,000 independent software vendors (ISVs) are ready to support Microsoft technologies across a broad spectrum of products and services available today.

By being a reader of this book, you are one of the early adopters of the technologies for tomorrow. This book provides you with the basic grounding and advanced analysis skills needed to implement Commerce Server either to meet your company's or your clients' needs.

Target Audience

This book is intended for anyone interested in rapidly building a scalable, enterprise-class commerce site with most of the standard features built within CS2K. You might be currently involved or may become involved with a project that is laying the e-commerce infrastructure of a company. Here is a brief list of people who will be reading this book:

- A manager evaluating CS2K for the current and future infrastructure of a company.
- An ISP wishing to serve a growing base of e-commerce clients who would want an e-commerce site on CS2K.
- An architect currently evaluating or implementing e-commerce architecture who wants to extend and integrate CS2K to meet requirement challenges.
- A developer experienced with Site Server 3.0 and related Microsoft technologies. (This is the right book to upgrade the knowledge and skills needed for customizing CS2K.)
- A project leader or a developer who hasn't worked with Site Server so far. (This book provides the right concepts and examples to master this platform.)

Prerequisites

This is a solution-oriented book, as compared to a concepts-only volume. Therefore, I would say concepts versus application are laid out at sort of 40:60 rate in most of the chapters. If you are a developer or a project leader, you will use the entire book. But to do that, I assume you have a working knowledge of Active Server Pages (ASP), VBScript/JavaScript, SQL Server, Data Access Objects, and IIS. In fact, one chapter requires a working knowledge of Visual Basic, Visual C++, and COM.

However, if you are a manager or a non-developer, you will still enjoy the concepts in each chapter. These concepts lay out the architecture, philosophy, and integration aspects of each functional area in Commerce Server. Be warned, though: Some of the chapters might induce you to become a techie!

Software You'll Need to Complete the Examples

Because the book is solution oriented, there will be quite a few examples that need to be executed in order to successfully complete a chapter. At the minimum, you will need Windows 2000 Server or Advanced Server running SQL Server 7.0 or 2000 on the machine. Also, if you need to run the management modules, the manager's workstation should be loaded with Internet Explorer 5.5. Chapter 2, "Planning and Installation," gives more information on the software requirements for running CS2K.

How This Book Is Organized

The entire book is organized around a thread example called eStore.com. It is highly recommended that you start building this site as each chapter progresses. However, if you are in a hurry, each chapter by itself should provide sufficient information to extend an existing site. The organization of this book is designed based on a typical project implementation, where each phase builds on the earlier ones. The following sections provide a rundown of each chapter.

Chapter 1: Overview

This chapter talks about the virtual marketplace and how e-commerce has come to stay. We discuss some of the generally accepted e-commerce elements, such as the shopping basket, online catalogs, shopper registration, online ordering, credit card processing, personalization aspects, and integration with external systems. You will then see how these standard features can be achieved with the capabilities of Commerce Server and what more CS2K has to offer.

Chapter 2: Planning and Installation

In this chapter, we cover the planning and installation of CS2K in the context of typical project plans. There are discussions about business and technical requirements—specifically the minimum hardware and software requirements for running Commerce Server. This chapter also illustrates two typical scenarios: one for development and the other for production. References to installation resources can be found in this chapter.

Chapter 3: Creating the Store Foundation

Chapter 3 gets you started with unpacking a solution site using the Site Packager. We walk through the process of unpacking a commerce site application along with its associated business desk. The various resources that form the foundation for a site are discussed while they are installed for a site. Finally, we analyze the changes after unpacking a site in terms of the database, Web server configurations, and the files installed.

Chapter 4: From the Business Desk

This chapter gives you a simple introduction to the business desk application installed to manage a commerce site. It walks you through the conceptual workings of the business desk, installation of the client software on a workstation, and finally the creation of a product catalog for the site unpacked in the previous chapter.

Chapter 5: Understanding the Site Architecture

Often the size of a new product is overwhelming for developers, making it difficult to visualize the start and end of it. This chapter takes a use-case approach and provides you with an under-the-hood view of a commerce site's architecture. You will see how Commerce Server objects are initialized globally. Then you will walk through the pages of the site for a typical use case, from catalog to order confirmation. During each of the stages in the process, we stop to take a look at what's happening behind the scenes, what objects are used on a page, and so on. This chapter has the right level of detail to prepare you for diving deep into individual pages and objects in the following chapters.

Chapter 6: Catalog Management

Catalogs are the soul of an online business, and a considerable amount of effort goes in to designing, creating, populating, and maintaining product catalogs. In this chapter, you will find the basic philosophy of catalog organization and schemas in Commerce Server. Then we will move on to create catalogs, categories, products, and variants for the sample site. We will also delve deep into integrating the CS2K catalog system with external systems to import and export catalogs. We use the business desk modules for creating everything necessary to publish an online catalog. A major portion of the chapter is dedicated to discussing the various COM objects available in the Catalog API to programmatically access and manage catalogs on a site. We then discuss some advanced functionality, such as product relations, variants, and catalog searches. All these come with examples, so the even the harder concepts are easier to understand once you run through the examples on your server.

Chapter 7: User Management

Users are the main reason why a site is built. Commerce Server provides an effective profile system, and in this chapter we discuss how to authenticate, authorize, and manage user sessions using the profile system. This chapter provides a basic grounding in the profile system and how it can be used to manage user profiles. Authentication filters, cookies, and cookie-less browsing are also part of the discussions. Also, throughout the examples, we stop and take note of various COM objects used by the site page to access the profile system. You'll also see a brief example of personalization and how the site is equipped with the necessary infrastructure to personalize content.

Chapter 8: Personalization and Targeting

This chapter helps you in understanding how the profile system can be used to personalize and target content to site users. You'll see how easily catalogs can be delivered based on the user or organization profile. We run through an example of creating targeted discounts, and in the process you'll see how to extend the user profile to gather personalization information that a site requires. Managers as well as developers can read this chapter to know how content can be personalized and targeted—and to know how the profile system can be extended to aid personalization.

Chapter 9: Commerce Server Pipelines

Pipelines are becoming a standard software infrastructure in many of the Microsoft products. In this chapter, you will be introduced to the philosophy, concepts, and workings of pipelines in Commerce Server. We discuss the stages, components, configurations, and COM objects that make up a business-processing pipeline. Then we move on to take a look at all the pipelines provided by Commerce Server for order processing, content selection, and direct mail. You also get introduced to the Pipeline Editor and ways to modify a pipeline configuration by inserting or removes stages and components. This chapter should give you a thorough grounding on pipelines and how ASP pages on the site use them.

Chapter 10: Order-Processing Pipelines

This chapter is completely about understanding how a commerce site processes orders using the order-processing pipelines (OPPs) and associated infrastructure. We take the use-case approach and go behind the scenes at each stage of the purchase process, including checking out the basket, specifying a shipping method, entering credit card information, and showing order confirmation. You see in detail the various stages and components used in the OPP, specifically the Plan and Purchase pipeline configurations. This chapter also introduces you to the OrderForm object, which is the electronic equivalent of a purchase order. Other COM objects and their methods related to order processing are discussed in detail.

Chapter 11: Direct Mailer and Content Selection Framework Pipelines

This is a chapter that goes into detail about the Content Selection Framework (CSF) in CS2K, which is a core infrastructure for personalizing and targeting content to users effectively. First, we talk about the Direct Mailer pipeline and how it can be used to send personalized direct mail to users. Here, you will learn more about the ListManager and Direct Mailer, how to create highly targeted e-mail lists, and how to process recipients and send emails with opt-out options. Next, in the section on CSF, we discuss content caches, Content Selection pipelines, and the stages in selecting content for delivery. We run through the various stages and components as well as the global infrastructure used for delivering content and recording content delivery.

Chapter 12: Running Ads and Auctions

Building on the earlier chapter on CSF, this chapter demonstrate how to schedule and run advertisements for an imaginary client. In this chapter, we take a detailed look at how ads are filtered, scored, selected, and formatted for delivery to the user. You'll see how to use the ContentSelector object to get content from the CSF. Debugging tips and examples are also provided. In the next section, we take a brief look at the auction infrastructure provided by Commerce Server. We use the Auction object to develop site pages that serve auctions on the site.

Chapter 13: Building and Customizing Pipelines

This chapter should be a developer's delight! First, it shows how to customize an existing pipeline to send an order confirmation e-mail. Then the technical architecture and concepts related to pipeline components are discussed. We then move on to create a pipeline component using Visual Basic, to calculate an order-level discount for the site. This exercise gives step-by-step instructions on how to create a VB project, implement the required COM interfaces, and register the component. Similarly, we walk through the ATL Wizard in Visual C++ to build the same component for high performance. This chapter also discusses various ways in which a pipeline can be debugged.

Chapter 14: Extending the Business Desk

The business manager no longer needs to depend on the technical team to get each and every task done in order to affect changes on a site. Using the business desk modules, nontechnical members of company can access the commerce site's database conveniently. The developers can extend the default modules provided with a site's business desk. This chapter gives a detailed picture of the business desk architecture and includes a step-by-step guide to adding modules to the "biz desk." This chapter, again, is indispensable to developers responsible for extending the business desk.

Chapter 15: Data Warehouse, Reports, and Prediction

Data warehousing requires specialized and dedicated study, but this chapter attempts to give you a broad overview of data warehousing. You'll see how the Commerce Server data warehousing is organized and learn how the different built-in tasks can be used to import site data into OLAP cubes.

Chapter 16: Integration with BizTalk Server

BizTalk Server is another important part of the .NET server family. CS2K has pretty good integration with BizTalk for exchanging catalogs and purchase orders with partners. This chapter walks you through the necessary procedures to integrate CS2K with BizTalk. The examples take into account scenarios of similar as well as different infrastructures between partners.

Appendixes

The appendixes provide handy information while you work with a Commerce Server project. Appendix A, "Commerce Server Objects: A Quick Reference," contains a brief list of the CS2K objects frequently used throughout the site pages. Appendix B, "Pipeline Components: A Quick Reference," gives a comprehensive reference of pipelines, stages, and components used in a commerce site. Appendix C, "Retail Store Helper Routines: Where to Find What," gives information about helper routines and where to find them in the solution site's library files. Appendix D, "Migrating from Site Server 3.0 to Commerce Server 2000," describes the migration possibilities between Site Server 3.0 Commerce Edition and Commerce Server 2000.

Conventions Used in This Book

The following typographic conventions are used in this book:

- Code lines, commands, statements, variables, and any text you type or see onscreen appears in a monospace typeface. **Bold monospace** typeface is often used to represent the user's input.

- Placeholders in syntax descriptions appear in an *italic mono* typeface. Replace the placeholder with the actual filename, parameter, or whatever element it represents.

- *Italics* highlight technical terms when they're being defined.

- The ➥ icon is used before a line of code that is really a continuation of the preceding line. Sometimes a line of code is too long to fit as a single line on the page. If you see ➥ before a line of code, remember that it's part of the line immediately above it.

Commerce Server Fundamentals

IN THIS PART

1 Overview   11

2 Planning and Installation   25

3 Creating the Store Foundation   39

4 From the Business Desk   59

5 Understanding the Site Architecture   73

Overview

IN THIS CHAPTER

- Business and the WWW   12

- The Case for Electronic Commerce   13

- The Virtual Marketplace   14

- Components of an E-Commerce Store   16

- What Does Commerce Server 2000
  Provide   19

Of all that people living today have seen and heard, no single phenomenon has influenced everyday life as the Internet has. The world's largest network is a place where millions of humans go every day to read news, send mail, buy products, place ads, look up neighbors' phone numbers, and search for deals. We are no longer backward compatible with the pre-information Stone Age.

Even amid the frenzy of technological changes happening at the start of this millennium, the course of the future appears to be clear: Man is going to break down the archaic structures that mostly he himself created, including societal, cultural, legal, and geographic boundaries. Commerce has been the one structure that has lent itself most readily to the onslaught of the next wave on the Internet.

Business and the WWW

The Internet grew rapidly from being a narrow, private network of government and large corporations to a wire that reaches far into homes and offices worldwide. Thanks mainly to the rapid adoption of international standards such as HTTP and TCP/IP, Internet use grew rapidly in university and corporate settings. However, it was really the HTML and the WWW technologies that opened this amazing information maze to the public. The *World Wide Web (WWW)* is essentially a visual interface to the millions of information sources on the Internet; it uses the *Hypertext Markup Language (HTML)* to paint a uniform picture. The HTML marked up document is served by a Web Server and viewed using a Browser. Even though numerous individual and educational entities started to build HTML Web sites early on, it was again the business and commerce section of society that fueled the growth and innovation on the Web.

Companies initially built Web sites that would host plain HTML pages, containing information about the company, its products and prices, and a 1-800 number to call to place orders. The Web was used mainly as a communication medium, serving its purpose of information delivery. But with the advent of *Common Gateway Interface (CGI)* and server-side scripting technologies, the Web pages became more interactive. It became possible to accept user input to store in a database or to retrieve information from a database to be displayed over the WWW.

As businesses moved from static to dynamic information interchange, the Internet morphed itself into a powerful commercial channel. This altered the way companies had been traditionally doing business and gave rise to tremendous opportunities to those in both the business and the consumer sectors. In the comfort of the home, the consumer can browse catalogs of various companies, compare prices, and place orders for the best possible deal. Businesses can sell directly to consumers at a much lower price than possible through traditional channels because of the absence of physical intermediary overheads. The World Wide Web also is a transparent window to the entire world, so businesses can have a larger customer base and consumers can look for shops beyond those on the street.

The Case for Electronic Commerce

Let us consider the case of a company in the early 1990s. Flowers & Flowers, a firm founded in 1988 to sell high-quality, fresh-cut flowers via direct mail demonstrates the complex nature of IT-enabled interorganizational relationships in that period. Figure 1.1 shows how Flowers & Flowers tried to change the dynamics in the industry using its IT infrastructure.

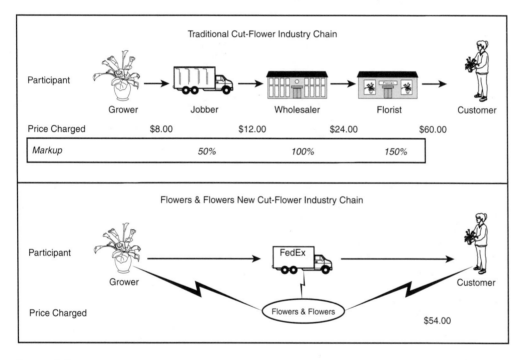

FIGURE 1.1
Economics in IT driven business.

Each intermediary in the traditional cut-flower industry—jobbers who buy directly from growers, wholesalers who buy from jobbers, and retailers who sell to the end customer—typically takes a hefty markup, reflecting their "added value" in the chain. Figure 1.1 shows clearly how a dozen roses bought from the florist used to cost $60. Then in the Flowers & Flowers model, customers who buy from the catalog get the dozen roses for $54.00. The customer definitely benefited as well as the growers who were paid more by Flowers & Flowers.

The case so far describes an example of economics obtained when businesses are able to come close to the ultimate consumer. The advent of the Internet and the WWW have made us think of ways to interact directly with the customer. By now you must have had the question "What if the grower sells directly to the customer?" These are the exciting possibilities thrown open to companies in the world of electronic commerce on the WWW. We can only approximate what the grower will charge for the dozen roses in his catalog on the Web site, but definitely both the grower and the customer are bound to gain in the model shown in Figure 1.2

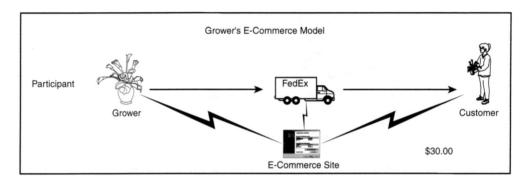

FIGURE 1.2

An e-commerce case.

Experts even feel that electronic commerce has the potential to play a greater role in the entire world's supply-demand curve and wealth creation.

The Virtual Marketplace

The previously illustrated case demonstrates another reality of electronic commerce: partnerships. Similar to how Flowers & Flowers, an online florist, partnered with FedEx for logistics, companies build relationships with other businesses for outsourcing services such as customer credit authorization, supply-side management, and advertisement. This is a *business-to-business (B2B)* paradigm, as compared to a *business-to-consumer (B2C)* relationship.

Flowers & Flowers accepts an order on its Web site for a bouquet. That is a B2C transaction. The system then places a shipment order automatically, including the item information, customer address, and other details, with the FedEx database. This is a B2B transaction. After the information technology revolution that started in the 1960s, companies, including consumer-oriented ones, have tried to use technology to maintain efficient business relationships with upstream and downstream businesses. For instance, a large automobile company might have many suppliers around the world. To automate its purchasing, billing, and logistics, a private *wide area network (WAN)* might connect the systems of these suppliers with those of the company. Interbusiness electronic commerce is mostly done using these proprietary *Electronic Data Interchange (EDI)* networks.

Because private networks are highly expensive, only medium to large companies have the opportunity to do B2B transactions using these networks. But with open Internet standards such as *Secure Sockets Layer (SSL)*, *Secure Multipurpose Internet Mail Extensions (SMIME)*, and *(eXtensible Markup Language) XML*, even small companies can venture into electronic commerce with business partners, thereby adding value to the supply chain. This paradigm of using the public infrastructure (the Internet) to conduct B2B transactions is achieved through setting up an extranet using such open technologies.

The openness and cost-effective nature of the WWW has resulted in an enormous flood of "click-and-mortar" stores. These are Web sites that conduct e-commerce only and that do not have a real-world enterprise. A good example of an online-only business is Amazon.com, one of the pioneers in electronic commerce. Amazon.com was started with the business model of a virtual bookstore on the Internet. Its virtual shelves house more than 4.5 million volumes, compared to the 200,000 titles housed at the largest physical Barnes & Noble bookstore in the United States. Competition from Amazon has forced real-world big booksellers such as Barnes & Noble and Borders to start selling books online. With the reach and efficiency of the Web, start-up companies are capable of threatening the positions of large, established corporations. This has led most of the businesses in the world to consider electronic commerce as an inevitable business strategy for the present and the future.

There have been major successes in the "pure-play" Internet companies, even among many burnouts. These companies owe their existence to the Web, and their business models are based on subscriptions, referrals, advertisements, and the like. For example, Yahoo!, which initially was successful as a free Internet e-mail service provider, has become the favorite portal for many resources such as travel, jobs, entertainment, health, shopping, auctions, and so on. Another virtual e-commerce business is eBay.com, a major auction site that is thought of as a *consumer-to-consumer (C2C)* business model.

The broad acceptance of WWW technologies has resulted not only in Internet and extranet applications, but also in intranet software. Companies want to use a single infrastructure to do business with customers and partners, as well as to share information with employees. Thus, in this standards-based infrastructure, applications can be plugged in from specialized vendors for the Internet, intranet, and extranet needs of a company. EBusiness is considered to be the strategy and infrastructure that would support electronic transactions within and outside the business corporation.

Components of an E-Commerce Store

Whether it be the latest "click-and-mortar" store on the block or an established "brick-and-mortar" shop setting up a e-tail presence, there seems to be a commonly accepted fundamental structure for organizing an e-commerce store. The functioning of the virtual store closely reflects the process that we go through while shopping at a real-world store. For example, we browse the product aisles, putting things that we choose into the shopping cart, move the cart to the payment counter, and do the payment using, say, a credit card. E-Commerce Web sites offer this basic functionality and much more. They go beyond the limitations of physical store space and time requirements. Although different e-commerce stores are doing a variety of business, the basic components discussed in the following sections characterize many of them.

Catalogs

Similar to the print version, these online catalogs carry the products or services offered by the company. For example, Dell.com allows users to browse various units that make up a computer. Customers can pick and choose the configurations that they like. Some companies sell "soft goods" over the Internet rather than ship physical goods. Aberdeen Group, a research organization, makes it possible for customers to read through various industry reports that can be bought and downloaded online. Key information contained in a typical catalog for a product includes the item number, name, description of the item, price, and discounts available; a picture of the item usually also appears, if applicable.

Furthermore, other value additions to the catalog are made possible with the Internet. For example, shoppers might be able to read reviews about the item from other shoppers, or to view items that are related to the one that the shopper is browsing. If you are looking at a printer on Epson's Web site, for instance, Epson's related products, such as ink cartridges, printer cables, and printer papers, are also shown. This provides tremendous up-sell and cross-sell opportunities to a business marketer. Shoppers also have the convenience of searching for specific items instead of having to browse through entire catalogs. Thus electronic catalogs make it easier for both the shopper as well as the business.

Shopping Cart

The functionality of a shopping cart is carried over from the real world: It provides the facility of accumulating items that a shopper has chosen. The virtual cart usually contains individual lines for each item, and each line shows details such as the quantity ordered and the total price.

> **NOTE**
>
> Most of the e-commerce stores allow any unknown user in the world to access their catalogs and to add items to the virtual shopping cart. This anonymous shopper can behave much like a window-shopper who might just like to look at the items without deciding to buy anything. Usually shopping carts are deleted after anonymous users leave the store.

Shopping carts for officially registered site users are preserved for an extended period of time. In fact, it is not uncommon for sites to send discount e-mails to registered users who haven't decided to check out their carts. Registered users can come back and add, modify, or delete items in their cart.

Shopper Registration

Anonymous users can go only so far; they can browse items and fill their carts. Beyond that, a customer must be a valid user registered with the e-commerce store to proceed to the checkout. Typical information required from the user includes name, e-mail address, postal address, and credit cart details. Other details optionally captured are user interests in travel, computers, magazines, movies, music, and so on. Registered users log in using either a name or an e-mail address that they provide. Most of the sites allow users to update their personal information as needed.

Order

When a user decides to buy the items in the cart, he simply clicks a button to initiate the purchase order or checkout process. In the case of physical items, the user is required to enter a shipping address because the e-commerce store must ship them. On the order page, the user is shown the individual items and their prices, along with the total cost of the order. Typically, shipping and handling charges are added to this order subtotal. Finally, tax is added if applicable, to arrive at the order total.

The user is also allowed to verify the credit card and billing address for this transaction. When the user accepts the details, the system generates and displays an order confirmation, with the order number as a key detail. Sites also give customers the capability to track orders.

Personalization

The automation of the shopping process gives rise to many possibilities made possible by the "intelligent" capabilities of a computer system. Because the system knows various personal information about the user from the registration profile, content that matches user interests could be displayed. For example, an apparel store might mix in a lot of Atlanta Braves t-shirts while displaying items to a user from Atlanta who likes baseball. Similarly targeted marketing e-mails can be sent frequently to bring the shopper back to the site. Also a lot of Web sites automatically fill in details such as billing address and credit card information once the shopper has registered his profile with the site.

Store Back End

Most of the successful e-commerce stores have a strong back end that enables them to fulfill their front-end promises. The *back end* in an e-commerce store refers to applications and systems that feed from or to the Web application. These could be the company's internal applications or an external partner's systems.

Imagine what would happen to Amazon.com if it did not have an effective inventory system. Even out-of-stock books would be shown as in stock. Add to that a poor shipping system, and customers would never get a book that was ordered. In fact, a considerable number of dot-com difficulties have had to do with the incapability to fulfill promises because of insufficient back-end systems, an inefficient business model, or both.

Multiple systems, such as *Enterprise Resource Planning(ERP)*, *Customer Relationship Management(CRM)*, and legacy applications can be implemented in an enterprise. Your Web application should have the capability to integrate with them meaningfully. We also know that a company must work with many business partners on a continuing basis. For example, if a shipping company promises overnight delivery, it must get the required information—say, a shipping order—as soon as possible to make this happen. Even in the case of a nonconsumer company that doesn't deal with physical goods, timely and effective interchange of documents is essential to business success. For instance, Reuters, an international news agency that caters to many print and online newspapers, has a system that syndicates content based on its business agreement terms with individual downstream news producers, on time.

Figure 1.3 depicts a simplified case of an Internet-enabled e-commerce business utilizing many of the components discussed so far.

A Management System

To manage these components effectively, a good management and administration system should be in place. Investments in maintenance or expansion are usually considered on the *return on investment(ROI)* that these activities bring in. For example, the sales manager would like to know the outcome of an advertisement, in terms of shopper visits and sales. Therefore, analysis and feedback are very important to keep the system sustainable.

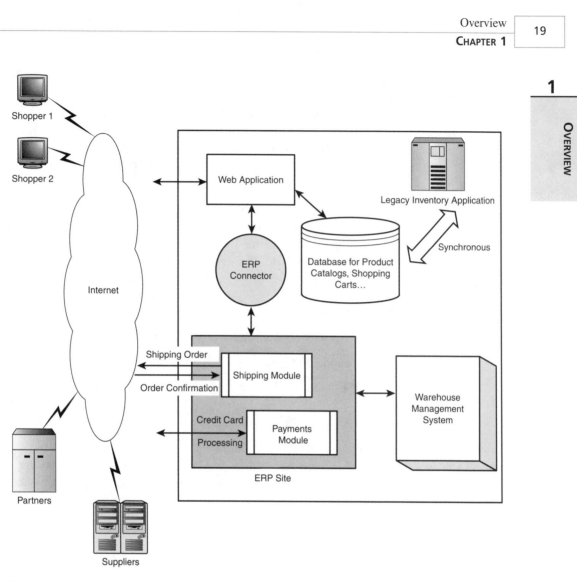

FIGURE 1.3

An Internet-enabled e-commerce system.

What Does Commerce Server 2000 Provide?

Even after achieving huge success in areas such as operating systems, office suites, databases, and Internet software, Microsoft has been nimble enough to attack the e-commerce and Internet applications market with offerings such as Site Server and *Site Server Commerce Edition (SSCE)*. SSCE version 3.0 was accepted immediately by the Active Server Pages and COM world as a platform from which to build Web applications for e-commerce. SSCE relieved developers from having to build Web applications from scratch and also introduced designers to the extensibility of pipelines with COM components. The Site Server suite provided for integration with directory services using *Lightweight Directory Access Protocol (LDAP)*, search systems, content replication, and Web usage analysis. All these features, coupled with developer tools that are integrated with various Microsoft and third-party products, have made SSCE a successful platform for companies as diverse as Dell, 1-800-FLOWERS, Barnes & Noble, and Compaq.

Commerce Server 2000 (Commerce Server) is the successor to SSCE 3.0. Commerce Server was designed as a platform made of out-of-the-box features and associated tools to build, deploy, and manage commerce applications for the Web. This book is all about understanding, building, and deploying e-commerce systems with Commerce Server. The next sections cover the highlights of Commerce Server in a nutshell.

Speedy Time to Market

Commerce Server comes with four solution sites that can be used to jump-start your development:

- **Retail**—Can be used to build a B2C retail site
- **SupplierActiveDirectory**—Can be used to build a B2B supplier site that uses an Active Directory service
- **Blank**—Has the basic resources to build a custom site

Using these initial sites, you can build a ready-made commerce site quickly with only a few tweaks in the look and feel and business rule extensions. The initial site will have most of the components of a standard e-commerce site, such as product catalogs, prices, a shopping basket, order-processing capabilities, payment-processing capabilities, and user profiles.

Efficient Administration

The administrators can centrally manage the various resources implemented by many different sites across a Web remotely, using the Commerce Server Manager. *Commerce Server Manager(CSM)* is a typical Microsoft Management Console (MMC) application; it provides a view that can be used to manage various resources that make up the Web application. Such resources include the following:

- Global resources such as Predictor and Direct Mail, used by all sites
- Site-specific resources such as Web Server(s), ASP pages, and COM objects
- General resources such as SQL servers, Active Directory, performance logs, and Event Viewer

NOTE

The snap-ins for the general resources are installed by default within the CSM even though they are individual applications and have their own administrative consoles. For instance, SQL Server can be managed with its own Enterprise Manager. But Enterprise Manager is available as a snap-in with the CSM. This facilitates operational convenience in managing these different resources.

Ease of Deployment

A tool called Site Packager gives developers and administrators the ability to pack all the resources that make up an entire site into a single file with a .PuP extension. This .PuP file can be unpacked, and the entire site can be installed on another computer. This is convenient when moving, say, a completely developed application from the development to the production environment.

Ease of Extension

Commerce Server's Pipeline mechanism allows managers and developers to easily add or modify the business rules by using any of the provided COM objects or by building custom components. A pipeline is a framework in Commerce Server that allows modeling business processes conveniently. Pipelines are run at different stages in various site pages. For instance, order-processing pipelines are run during the purchase process, whereas content-selection pipelines are used in pages that display targeted content. Commerce Server provides certain standard pipelines out-of-the box:

- Order Processing pipelines, such as Product, Plan, and Purchase, relating to a retail B2C store

- Order Processing pipelines for a B2B, such as Corporate Purchasing Plan and Corporate Purchasing Submit

- Content Selection pipelines that are used to select content, advertisements, or discounts, and to rate events such as clicks on the served ads

Pipelines contain one or more COM objects that are executed sequentially on invoking the pipeline. The components in these pipelines are COM components that can be built and plugged in easily to implement custom business rules. Commerce Server also provides pooled pipelines that can run in a COM+ object-pooling environment. This improves the scalability and response times of the pages that run these pipelines.

Core Systems

In Commerce Server, core systems provide great functionality and add value to your applications. A few of them are listed here:

- **The Profiling System**—Use this system to collect desired information to form a profile of any entity, such as site visitors (registered and anonymous), organizations, or even context information such as date and time of a specific transaction.

- **The Product Catalog**—Use this system to manage the catalogs of the company. It's now possible to import catalogs in standard formats such as XML or comma-separated values (CSV). This will help in migrating catalogs in, say, a legacy database to your Commerce Server product catalog database. The system also allows exporting of the product catalog into standard formats that enable integrating with other applications or exchange catalogs with business partners.

- **The Targeting System**—This system contains expressions that can be configured as rules to serve advertisements, content, and discounts to shoppers based on the profiling information. Specific campaigns serve this content based on the rules they contain. Using the Direct Mailer and List Builder, a site can send targeted e-mails to user groups.

- **The Business Analytics**—This system is a combination of features that allow better reports and enable managers to take action based on analysis. The BIA includes a data warehouse consisting of imported data repository and OLAP database; the Analysis module, to generate reports from these various data sources; and the Predictor service, to segment and model your site's users and user behavior.

All the core systems have programming interfaces so that developers can extend their functionality. These core features and many other elements of Commerce Server functionality are available and exposed as modules in a tool called the Business Desk.

Business Management

Commerce Server is also designed to give business managers the power to actively participate in the online business. For a long time now, business managers had to depend on administrators or technical analysts to get reports on transactions and to change business data. There was always a time gap between what users got and what the business wanted users to get. Managers did not have the essential tools to fine-tune the Web business based on customer behavior. With companies fighting to add and retain customers, this gap is something that has been difficult to bridge in a timely manner. With a tool called BizDesk, managers now can close that gap themselves without knowing anything about ASP or HTML. For instance, they can launch advertisement campaigns targeted at specific user profiles, generate reports out of transactions, customize product catalogs for specific groups, and take actions based on the site performance. Microsoft calls this process "closing the loop." BizDesk has more than 20 predefined modules to manage catalogs, ad campaigns, orders, users, and much more.

Developers can build custom modules to be integrated with BizDesk for easy management.

New Vision

Commerce Server is not intended to be merely a follower of an earlier version in terms of added features and functionality. Instead, it is designed to fit in a much larger vision of Microsoft, called the Microsoft.NET platform. The Microsoft.NET platform is based on services made available on the Web; it uses a highly scalable network of .NET Enterprise servers. This will fundamentally change the way Windows programmers develop and use applications.

Commerce Server 2000 is one of the initial set of .NET Enterprise servers released, including Application Center 2000, BizTalk Server, Host Integration Server, and SQL Server 2000, so Commerce Server has strong integration capabilities with these servers. For instance, Commerce Server can be configured to send catalogs, orders, and various documents to BizTalk Server, which then can engage in external B2B transactions using these documents.

.NET

For more information on the Microsoft .NET platform visit www.microsoft.com/net.

Summary of Key Commerce Server Features

The key Commerce Server features include the following:

- **Business Desk**—Tool for managers to update product catalogs, prices, and discounts; manage orders; and generate reports to fine-tune the site as soon as possible.

- **Site Packager**—Tool for easy packing and unpacking of an entire site between different environments as a .PuP file.

- **Solution Sites**—Tool that provides a foundation for building sites and that speeds up development.

- **Product Catalog**—System that has the capability to import and export catalogs.

- **Profiling System**—System to collect and store profile data on different site users in Active Directory or SQL Server.

- **Targeting System**—System Tool that has tools such as List Builder, Direct Mailer, Segment Viewer, and Expression Builder to target content, advertisements, and discounts based on profile data such as user profiles and context profiles.

- **Business Analytics**—System that consists of a Data Warehouse that makes use of SQL Server and OLAP Databases for storing and manipulating data. Analysis module for generating standard and customized reports.

- **Pipelines**—Mechanism for B2C order processing, content selection, direct mailing, and B2B corporate purchasing. Enhanced pipelines for using COM+ object pooling.

- **Commerce Server Manager**—MMC application to administer all resources of a site from a single place.
- **Integration**—Commerce Server integrates with BizTalk Server for an XML-based document interchange with external partners.
- **COM Objects**—Objects to extend and add custom functionality easily for developers.

Commerce Server Tool is too comprehensive a product for us to be able to analyze everything theoretically before we do anything practically. Therefore, I will move to the next chapter right away so that you can learn some of the system requirements needed to make Commerce Server work.

Planning and Installation

IN THIS CHAPTER

- Business Requirements   26
- Technical Requirements   27
- Installing Commerce Server   32
- Maximizing Performance   36

Planning is an important activity in any project, whether it be for development or production environments. It is even more so when a large feature-rich product such as Commerce Server is being implemented. It takes considerable time and effort to complete the fit and gap analysis based on business requirements. Once business requirements are solidified, technical architects and managers start putting together a technical framework that satisfies identified business needs. The technical framework is then broken down into technical requirements. Developers, administrators, and technical managers complete work on these technical requirements, testing the integrated units of the requirements. Finally, Quality Assurance, and in some cases the legal department, pass the version of the site, which is then published to the production environment.

In order to meet the business and technical requirements, a product has to integrate and work along with other systems. Commerce Server 2000 (CS2K) belongs to the family of .NET Enterprise Servers and hence integrates with many other enabling technologies that are common to Microsoft products. Also, because CS2K is based on many of the Internet-standard technologies, such as HTTP, SSL, and XML, third-party products can also be conveniently integrated. However, before any development work can start, invariably there is a requirements-identification stage in the overall project plan. We will start this chapter by discussing typical business requirements that the e-commerce site you build may have to satisfy. It might help to read through Chapter 1, "Overview," as well, to have a general understanding of how e-commerce sites work and to enable better functional and technical analysis of the requirements.

Business Requirements

Identifying the business requirements mostly follows product identification (that is, after the decision is made to implement the product/platform). Once the strategic-level decision has been made, it is now up to the tactical managers to carry out the vision and objectives for which the project budget has been secured. Functional analysts and subject matter experts are assembled to produce the business requirements document. The analysis-gathering phase generates various questions, depending on the objectives, size, and other factors of a company. Here is a sample list:

- What are the immediate and long-term goals to be achieved by this project?
- What are the timelines, budgets, and constraints related to this project? (Scoping is really a balancing act between functionality, resources, and schedules.)
- Who are the stakeholders and approvers in the project phases? What are the established milestones?
- Does the site cater primarily to internal or external users (employees or customers)? Do business partners need to use the site?
- Is this site to be built from scratch or is it to be built on an existing site?

- Do any existing business processes have to be changed because of this project? What existing processes must be part of the site application?

- What are the integration requirements for the site? Does it need to integrate with, say, ERP, LDAP, or BizTalk?

- How many users are estimated to visit the site regularly? What are their most common activities (browsing, registering, logging in, ordering, and so on)?

- What is the level of security required for the site?

- Who will administer the site? Who will be responsible for managing the catalog system and the user profiles?

- Do users need to be trained to use the system for administration?

- Does the site require internationalization or localization?

- Who will manage or administer various resources of Commerce Server? What are the service-level agreements with support teams for required services?

- What should be the design of the product catalog? How will initial loading be accomplished? Is the catalog to be exchanged with business partners?

- How do pricing requirements influence catalog design? Is an existing pricing schema difficult to implement with the CS2K product catalog system?

- What information is to be collected in a user profile? How complex are the personalization requirements for serving content?

- Is the site going to sell advertisements?

- Do managers require customized reports to analyze various aspects of the site performance?

Note that the preceding list is really a small sample of the questions analysts ask at the beginning of a project. There are more questions that relate to functionality, usability, administration, and technical capabilities that need to be incorporated into the technical requirements. Let's look at some of the typical technical requirements that one might encounter on a Commerce Server project.

Technical Requirements

After the strategic vision is sold to all stakeholders in a company and business requirements are gathered, detailed technical requirements are prepared. Often, business and technical requirements have a many-to-many mapping to each other. For example, a requirement that the site will be initially available to existing customers might mean that the servers need to handle a limited amount of traffic initially. This would provide you with enough time to analyze user behavior and then open the site to the public. Once the estimated amount and type of initial customers are known, the hardware- and software-acquisition tasks on the project plan will detail how many hardware components and software licenses need to be acquired. Similarly, a technical requirement of linking up a catalog server via the company's VPN would solve multiple business requirements, such as the capability to remotely administer the server and perform catalog updates via a geographically distributed sales team.

Technical requirements can be broadly divided into hardware and software requirements. In the next two sections, we discuss both kinds of requirements for a Commerce Server implementation.

Hardware Requirements

Hardware requirements are related to the need for reasonably advanced machines for providing speed and stability to the planned online business. These needs are most often for larger amounts of memory (RAM), multiple processors (CPUs), high-speed connections (say, T1 or better), and so on. The hardware also needs to be scalable for future growth. This type of capacity planning is dependent on the performance and scalability goals. The high end of these systems will vary from one implementation to another because of the unique needs of each company. However, there are minimum hardware requirements that need to be met in order to install and successfully run a Commerce Server site for a business. These minimum requirements are as follows:

- 400MHz or faster Pentium-compatible CPU.
- 256MB of RAM. (The Microsoft documentation states that 128MB of RAM is adequate for a development environment.)
- At least 100MB of hard disk space.
- CD-ROM drive.
- Network adapter card.
- VGA or Super VGA monitor.
- Microsoft Mouse or compatible pointing device.

These are the minimum requirements considered essential for running Commerce Server "alone." Practically speaking, though, you will also be running a SQL Server, the IIS Web Server, BizTalk Server (if integrated), and many other .NET Enterprise servers. These servers could run on dedicated machines in a distributed fashion or on a single machine. Therefore, you will definitely need much higher-end hardware components than those that meet the minimum requirements for a production environment.

As you know, managers can connect to a commerce site's database for activities such as updating catalogs, generating reports, and sending product catalogs to partners. All these can be done conveniently from within the Business Desk, a software framework that houses individual worker modules. To run Business Desk, client computers don't require higher-end machines. Here are the minimum requirements:

- 266MHz or faster Pentium-compatible CPU
- 5MB of hard disk space
- CD-ROM or DVD-ROM drive
- VGA or higher-resolution monitor set to 800×600 pixels resolution or higher
- Microsoft Mouse or compatible pointing device

Here are some other associated requirements:

- Hubs
- Routers
- Connectivity (such as a T1 line)
- Load balancers (software and hardware)
- Firewalls
- Backup devices
- SCSI disks with RAID technology
- Terminal switches
- Uninterruptible power supplies (UPS)

Planning for the right hardware is both a science and art. It requires estimations and performance data. For example, Microsoft has published many scientific results based on tests. If you know that a single server can handle 1,000 concurrent user requests for an ASP page, you would require that many servers to handle the estimated number of concurrent users.

Scalability and Availability

The hardware requirements are also based on the software that needs to run for the site. Some of the software products are memory intensive, whereas others are I/O intensive. For example, Commerce Server itself relies heavily on data-caching to boost site performance. Therefore, the larger the available memory, the faster the access. Products such as SQL Server are I/O intensive, requiring faster disk access to store and retrieve data frequently. Companies are known to scale their hardware either vertically or horizontally. *Vertical scaling* means adding more processing power to a machine in terms of multiple CPUs, increased RAM, multiple network cards, and high-speed disk arrays. Remember that the throughput of a machine should justify the cost because it is proven fact that adding multiple resources brings diminishing returns beyond a certain point.

Scaling horizontally involves adding more machines to build a Web farm. Most companies do some form of load balancing using multiple Web servers to manage heavy traffic. The number of such individual machines again depends on the performance requirements of the site. Many companies use IP switching, DNS Round Robin, Cisco Local Director, Microsoft Network Load Balancer, and other such technologies to balance the traffic. You would distribute software such as COM components on multiple machines to service the load-balanced user requests.

Load balancing not only ensures scalability but also could provide high availability. You would normally cluster servers and thus avoid a site going down because of just one server's problem. In a cluster, if a server (say, a database server) goes down, the other servers in the cluster stand in for the lost server. You can use the Windows Cluster Service Configuration Wizard to configure clusters.

The recent history of the WWW is fraught with site outages during busy periods. The opportunity cost as well as loss in business is dreaded by any company that has a Web presence. Therefore, architects and technical executives rely on several methodologies to aid in hardware capacity planning that would make sites available 365 days a year, 7 days a week, 24 hours a day. There have been many advances in CPU speed, disk-access rates, and network bandwidth. Hardware selection is a balancing act, based on the budget, performance requirements, and future growth. Let's now discuss some of the software requirements for running a Commerce Server site.

Software Requirements

As mentioned earlier, Commerce Server is a part of the .NET Enterprise Server family, and it uses the Microsoft Distributed Internetworking Architecture (DNA) elements. CS2K works with SQL Server, BizTalk Server, Host Integration Server, MDAC, and IIS to name a few. Also, because of the openness in its technologies, CS2K can be integrated with third-party systems such as ERP. One would know the software requirements clearly once the business requirements state the expectations of the project. However, installing and running CS2K requires the following software at a minimum:

- Microsoft Windows 2000 Server or Advanced Server
- Windows 2000 Service Pack 1
- Windows 2000 hot fixes
- SQL Server 2000 or 7.0 (SP2 for 7.0)
- Microsoft Data Access Components (MDAC) 2.6
- Internet Explorer 5.5 for Business Desk Clients

Apart from these minimum requirements, you might need various other tools and products to assist in site development. For example, developers might be comfortable with using Visual InterDev for ASP development, Visual Basic for prototyping pipeline components, and so on. We will now look briefly at the minimum software requirements.

Windows 2000

CS2K requires Windows 2000 Server or Advanced Server to run. These servers automatically install the basic software needed to access the Internet and provide Internet-related services, such as IIS 5.0, SMTP Server, and Microsoft Search. Also, remember that the operating system comes with a variety of other services that may or may not be required for running CS2K. To improve performance, services that are not required need to be turned off. For example, it would be prudent not to have CS2K on a Windows 2000 server that also acts as the domain controller. Not only would this scenario result in lower site performance, but it also would expose your domain to the outside world. No one in his right mind would do this! Firewalls secure the internal resources of a company. Additionally, you want to make sure that the server on which the CS2K site runs has only the bare essentials and nothing more.

Another requirement is the installation of Service Pack 1 and hot fixes for 2000. It is always good to install the most recent service packs and hot fixes so that your server is updated with many critical bug fixes and security patches. For the most recent information on service packs and hot fixes for Windows 2000, visit the Microsoft site at `http://www.microsoft.com/windows2000`.

Microsoft SQL Server

CS2K uses SQL Server as its database. You can install either SQL Server 7.0 or 2000. The requirement is that both CS2K and SQL Server be on the same network. Further, if you choose to use the Direct Mailer provided by CS2K, then SQL Server and CS2K must be installed on the same machine. Also, for data access, CS2K depends on the Microsoft Data Access Components (MDAC). Both versions of SQL Server install MDAC 2.6 on the server. You need to install MDAC on the Web server if SQL Server is installed on a separate server. You also need to install the SQL Server client tools to manage the server. CS2K provides the necessary objects to manage a data warehouse for the site. Therefore, if you decide to have data warehousing capabilities for the site, you need to install OLAP Services for SQL Server 7.0 or Analysis Services for SQL Server 2000, as is the case. Again, to manage the OLAP server, the client tools need to be installed. As with any enterprise-level software, look for the most recent service packs for the version of SQL Server required. For more information about the SQL Server service packs, visit the site `http://www.microsoft.com/sql`.

Your SQL Server installation will probably hold a number of databases, such as those for orders, catalogs, Direct Mailer, and Predictor resources. To provide high availability, more than one machine is set up with SQL Server. This type of arrangement is called a *server cluster*, which will ensure high availability if any server fails for some reason.

Internet Explorer

The Business Desk for a commerce site provides a convenient GUI to manage the site's catalogs, campaigns, users, and orders as well as to generate analysis reports. The biz desk application uses the IE behaviors and features available only in version 5.5. Therefore, in order to access business desk, a workstation should have IE 5.5 installed. IE 5.5 can be found on the CS2K CD, itself, or it can be downloaded from http://www.microsoft.com/ie. Also, some of the modules in biz desk use client-side components, such as PivotChart and PivotTable, which are available in Microsoft Office Web Components or SQL Server 2000 Client Tools. Therefore, either of these components is required for proper working of biz desk modules.

Having made sure of the hardware and software requirements, we will look at typical development and production environments and the steps involved in installing CS2K.

Installing Commerce Server

Depending on the functional and performance requirements (and, of course, the budget), you should have the final design of the required hardware and software for the site. The installation could range from a single machine that holds all the software to multiple machines that comprise a Web server farm, database clusters, a data warehouse server, a dedicated machine for Predictor and Direct Mailer, a catalog server, and so on. We will look at sample installations of both extremes just to give you an idea of what is involved.

If you don't yet have the Commerce Server CD or are only looking to evaluate the product, you can download a working 120-day evaluation copy from the Microsoft site http://www.microsoft.com/commerceserver.

To install Commerce Server, double-click the Setup.exe program in the installation CD or the Commerce Server 2000.msi Windows installer package. The installation itself should be pretty simple because it is guided by an easy-to-follow wizard.

Single-Server Scenario

No serious site on the Web can afford to have only a single machine to host the site and face the traffic. This is precarious even for the simplest of static content, let alone complex sites that host e-commerce, dynamic content, and so on. However, many small and medium-sized organizations put up their single development server loaded with all required software, with appropriate backup systems, for the initial development phase. They may also do this simply for proof of concept as well as for demonstration of a product, as is the case with my server for this book. For these situations, a single machine might be sufficient. In such a scenario, you would install all the CS2K features on the single server, as shown in Figure 2.1.

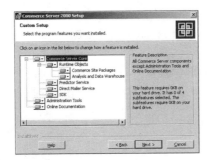

FIGURE 2.1
Choosing to install all CS2K features on a single machine.

Note the different features that can be installed using this wizard. Commerce Server Runtime objects are the COM objects that are used by CS2K to run sites. Installing Commerce Site Packages will provide for a package called Blank that can be unpacked using Site Packager. You can also download the Retail and SupplierActiveDirectory solution sites from http:// www.microsoft.com/commerceserver/downloads/solutionsites.asp. An unpacked site can be used as a starting point for developing your site. The Analysis and Data Warehouse component will enable creation of OLAP and data warehouse databases on the server and use a Data Warehouse global resource for a commerce site. Having a Predictor resource will enable building analysis models that use data gathered in the data warehouse. The Direct Mailer Service provides the ability to construct and send personalized e-mails to a list of users. The Administrator Tools, such as the Commerce Server Manager, are a necessity to administrators. Finally, the SDK and Online Documentation components are essential for developers to extend and customize CS2K.

The wizard proceeds with the installation, stopping a couple of times to get more information. One such piece of information involves specifying the SQL Server computer for hosting CS2K's administration database. The Administration Database Configuration screen asks for the SQL Server computer as well as the login name and password credentials to connect to the database. As you know, these credentials (such as "sa") should have enough permissions to create and modify databases. The installation creates the administration database with the name MSCS_Admin.

Another input that the installation asks for is the accounts for starting up the Commerce Server 2000 services. The services are Direct Mailer, List Manager, and Predictor. You could give a different Windows account for running each of these services or use a single account for all.

The wizard installs all the chosen objects, after which the Finish button should be clicked to complete the installation. After that, you can use the Site Packager to unpack the Retail solution site and create a starter solution site to start development. You can now use the shortcut

Start, Programs, Microsoft Commerce Server 2000 to access the Administration Tool Commerce Server Manager as well as the SDK and Documentation components.

Multiple-Server Scenario

Figure 2.2 shows an illustration of a sample configuration designed for a large-scale site in production.

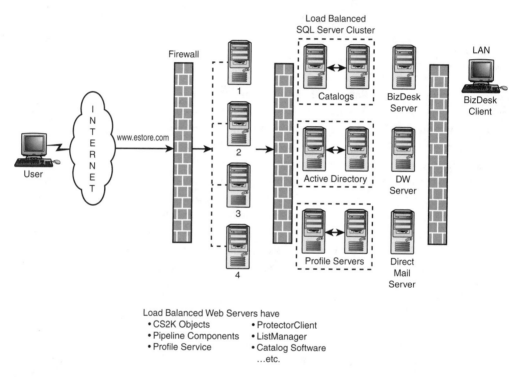

FIGURE 2.2

Commerce site configuration for scalability.

The site visitor types the address (say, http://www.estore.com) to visit the commerce site. The request passes through many of the gateways on the Internet before arriving at the Load Balancer of the site eStore. As already mentioned, there are many types of solutions—hardware and software—to provide for the load balancing of servers. For example, a machine can be put in front of the four Web servers and Microsoft Network Load Balancer can be installed to balance the requests and route to one of the four servers. The common IP address presents a unified face of the site for the underlying four Web servers. The Web servers are fairly powerful machines with advanced hardware components, and they have basic software, such as Windows 2000 Server, with all the SPs and hot fixes. These Web servers have the CS2K objects and services such as Predictor, Profile Service, and the Product Catalog resource. The IIS sites on these servers host the ASP pages that act as the front tier in this architecture. Further categorization of Web servers is possible based on static or dynamic content and CPU-intensive processing, such as pipeline components.

The databases for the site are in the demilitarized zone (DMZ), housed in separate servers to boost performance and clustered to provide availability. For example, two SQL Server computers have the catalog database of the site, and the servers are part of a load-balanced cluster. Therefore, a Web server trying to access a catalog would be connecting to a virtual IP address, ultimately resolving to one of the catalog servers. Also note that the Active Directory can be used to authenticate site users (username and password), whereas profile data is ideally maintained in a separate SQL Server cluster. In a server cluster, servers are configured to provide fail-over capabilities. You could also utilize data-partitioning techniques so that, for example, user profiles for users with last names starting with A–K would be accessed from one server and last names starting with L–Z would be stored on another server.

Also, the Business Desk application for the site is on a separate server. In short, the four web servers contain absolutely essential objects to enable faster processing of user requests. The application architecture should be such that the site can be scaled easily by adding resources.

For example, while installing CS2K on one of the Web servers, you would choose the components to install, as shown in Figure 2.3.

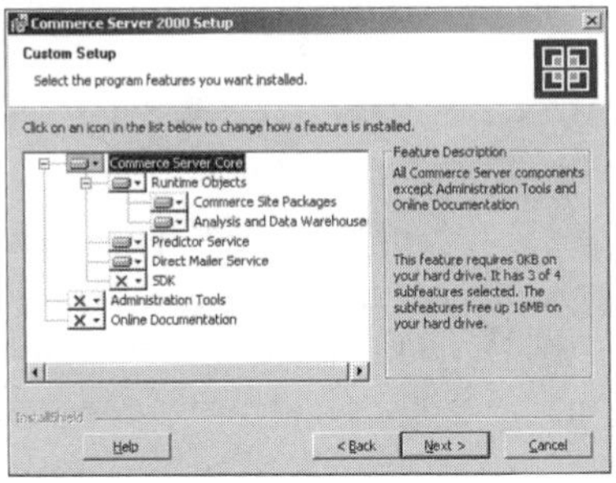

FIGURE 2.3

Choosing installation options on a production Web server.

How do you move the site from the development environment to production? The Site Packager can be used to package a completely developed site in to a PuP file. This file can then be unpacked on a Web server to install the ASP pages and resources that were developed for the site. Just note that the database connection strings and other machine-dependent parameters need to be verified again after being moved from development to production.

Maximizing Performance

Apart from vertically and horizontally scaling hardware to meet performance requirements, you can remove many bottlenecks by fine-tuning certain software configurations and parameters. Here are a few common tweaks can be performed to improve scalability:

- *Session management.* Disable IIS session management and avoid using session variables on application pages. Because session values are stored in a computer's RAM, the greater the number of concurrent users, the greater the amount of memory consumed to maintain session variables. Therefore, maintenance of the session values in memory quickly becomes a drain on the performance of the system with increasing concurrent users. Another problem with session values is that sessions are local to a machine. Therefore, in a load-balanced environment, session values on one machine are not available on other machines, thus leading to many issues.

- *Caching.* Caching commonly queried data will increase the speed of responses to user requests. Most of today's ASP pages go overboard in querying a database for fetching relatively static content. For example, a legal disclaimer, even though maintained in a database, can be generated as HTML and cached for inclusion in ASP pages. Use Dictionary or LRUCache objects with the Commerce Server CacheManager to maintain as many caches as needed.

- *Asynchronous processing.* As far as possible, process asynchronously any transactions that can be batched up. For example, some sites make the user wait for nearly a minute for processing credit cards with a credit card processor such as CyberCash. On the other hand, other sites, such as Amazon, process credit cards later in batches and send confirmation e-mails to users. You can use BizTalk, Message Queuing, or an existing ERP system to accomplish this type of batch processing.

- *Application fine-tuning.* Separation of static and dynamic content might help in speeding up responses. As already mentioned, analyzing user behavior, such as catalog browsing, ordering, logging in, registering, and searching, reveals frequently performed site operations. Therefore, putting the content for these activities on separate servers might improve performance.

Summary

A Commerce Server project will essentially be a collective effort of team members to gather business and technical requirements. The requirements boil down to hardware and software requirements based on various factors, such as site features, time schedules, budgets, and performance expectations. However, CS2K itself has certain minimum software and hardware requirements that need to be met. The entire planning phase in the project plan goes hand in hand with estimates, measures, and constraints.

Commerce Server 2000 seems to have avoided a lot of the installation issues that plagued Site Server 3.0 Commerce Edition. CS2K can be installed relatively comfortably using the CS2K Wizard. Depending on the purpose of the machine on which CS2K is being installed, CS2K objects and components can be selectively chosen. Therefore, you can install combinations of CS2K objects and the Direct Mailer, Predictor, Data Warehouse, SDK, and Documentation components on a single machine or multiple machines. Once installation completes successfully, you can use the Site Packager to unpack a solution site and get started with developing a commerce site.

2

PLANNING AND INSTALLATION

Creating the Store Foundation

IN THIS CHAPTER

- Creating IIS Web sites   41
- Unpack with Site Packager   44

One of the strengths of Commerce Server as a platform is faster time to market. Imagine having to build from scratch all the ASP files starting with the home page, the associated database elements for storing and retrieving information such as products, prices, and orders, and the middle-tier business logic components. Add to this the reporting capability that is essential for any e-commerce site, and it could be quite an effort! Commerce Server provides a set of pre-built sites called the Solution Sites that can be used to jump-start the development of your site. When you generate a site that is based on one of the solution sites, the site will contain the basic functionality of catalogs, shopping baskets, order processing, and user profile management. However, it will most probably be the initial site and not the final e-commerce site that was planned for. This is because the solution sites are designed to provide basic functionality and therefore will not satisfy the unique requirements of very many sites. Therefore, many customizations will be needed, starting with look and feel, before the site can be rolled over into production.

The Commerce Server installation provides for the solution site *Blank*. Blank just provides a couple of files such as global.asa and a default.asp home page to an application built using it. Blank is ideal if you want to use Commerce Server functionality but want to build all the other pages for your e-commerce site from scratch. Even in that case, it will be highly educational to know how the typical pages are built using other solution sites. The other solution sites are *Retail* and *SupplierActiveDirectory*. Retail provides the capability to build a B2C retail site, whereas SupplierActiveDirectory is meant to start B2B sites. In this chapter, we will create a site based on the Retail solution site. I suggest that you follow the example in a step-by-step manner and create the basic site on your server. This way, not only will you get a working knowledge of the basics of commerce server, but you will also be able to build on this (site) as we discuss advanced topics later in the book.

On the Microsoft Web Site

The solution sites Retail and SupplierActiveDirectory are also available as separate installations from the Microsoft Web site www.microsoft.com/commerceserver/ solutionsites.

We have seen that Commerce Server provides a Business Desk application to manage an e-commerce site. This application is also a part of the solution sites. Therefore, the Site Packager can be used to unpack both the applications so that we can create an e-commerce site as well as a business desk application for that site. The two essential steps in creating a commerce site using the Retail solution site are as follows:

- Creating Web sites to host the e-commerce and business desk applications.
- Unpacking the Retail site applications, using Site Packager, into the corresponding Web sites.

Creating IIS Web sites

In this chapter, you will learn how to create a Commerce Server e-commerce site and a Business Desk (BizDesk) site that manages the e-commerce application. We'll call the e-commerce site Estore and the Web-based application to manage that site EstoreBizDesk. It is good to have both these applications as separate *Internet Information Server (IIS)* sites because of security, scalability, and reliability requirements. The first step in creating a Web site would be to set up the folder in which we want to install the application files for the site. Perform the following steps:

1. Create two folders using the Windows Explorer, and name them **Estore** and **EstoreBizDesk**, respectively.

2. Launch the Commerce Server Manager by clicking Start, Programs, Microsoft Commerce Server 2000, Commerce Server Manager.

> **NOTE**
>
> The Commerce Server Manager is a *Microsoft Management Console (MMC)* application that provides centralized access to many servers and applications including IIS and SQL Server.

3. Navigate to the Internet Information Services snap-in and choose the server that will host the site. Right-click to create a new Web site, as shown in Figure 3.1.

4. Click the Next button on the Web Site Creation Wizard screen. Type **Estore** as the description in the Web Site Description screen, as shown in Figure 3.2.

5. Click the Next button to configure your IP address and port settings. On the Web Site Home Directory screen, type in the pathname for the Web site's home directory or browse to the directory created for Estore (see Figure 3.3).

Commerce Server Fundamentals

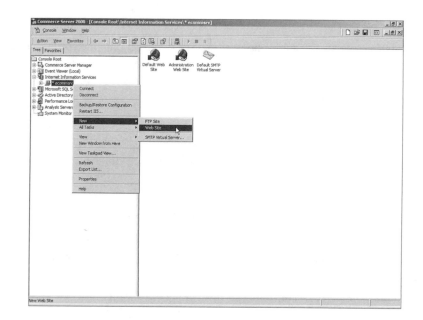

FIGURE 3.1

Creating a new IIS Web site.

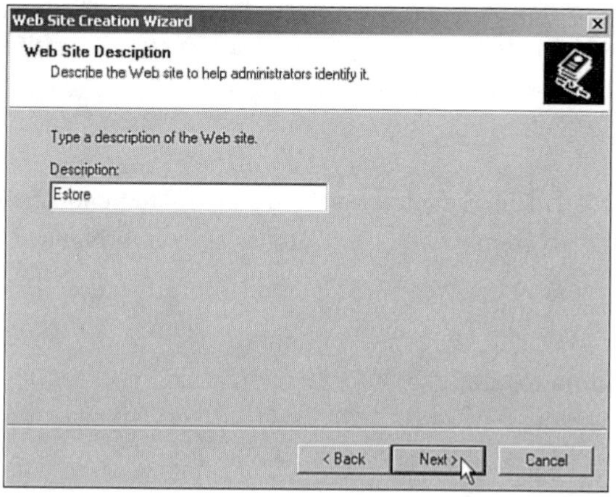

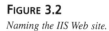

FIGURE 3.2

Naming the IIS Web site.

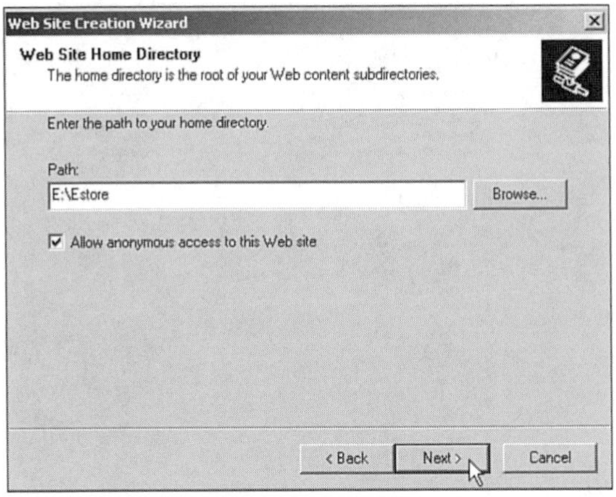

FIGURE 3.3
Physical directory of the IIS Web site.

6. Then click the *Next* button and accept the default access permissions. Finally click the Finish button to let the wizard create the Web site.

> **NOTE**
>
> If you had accepted the default TCP Port(80), you might have needed to change the TCP Port of the Default Web Site to some other port. Then only the Web site Estore can be started.

Repeat the preceding steps to create a Web site for EstoreBizDesk that will be on a different port, say 81. After they are created, both sites will appear under the Internet Information Services node in the MMC as shown in Figure 3.4 in detailed view.

If you click both the Estore and EstoreBizDesk sites, you will observe that they are empty. These sites are just placeholders for the commerce application files that will be unpacked in to them soon. You are now ready to create a B2C application and its managing BizDesk site.

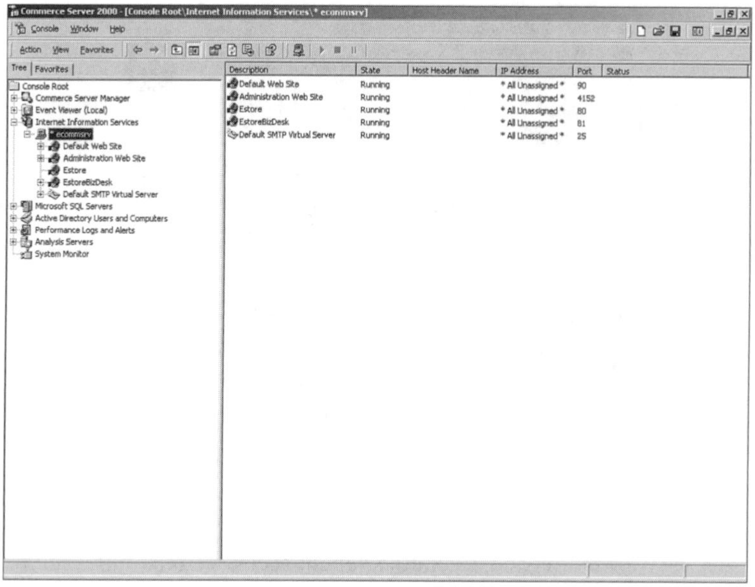

FIGURE 3.4

After creating the IIS Web sites.

Unpack with Site Packager

Its time to create your first commerce site using Commerce Server. Navigate to the Commerce Sites node under Commerce Server Manager. Right-click the Commerce Sites folder and choose New, Unpack Site (see Figure 3.5).

The Unpack Site From dialog box allows the user to choose one of the solution sites. The solution sites are installed by default under the PuP Packages folder in the Microsoft Commerce Server installation directory. Note that the default installation doesn't insert any PuP files except a Blank file. The other PuP files are downloaded from the Web site discussed earlier. After downloading and installing the solution sites, Retail and SupplierActiveDirectory PuP files should be available along with Blank. For this example, choose Retail and then click the Open button (see Figure 3.6).

After a few seconds, the Site Packager (see Figure 3.7) shows the Unpack screen, which will allow you to quickly unpack the solution site into one of the predefined Web sites. This quick unpack will install both the e-commerce site as well as the BizDesk application under the same IIS Web site. To avoid this, as well as to explore detailed unpacking options, select the Custom Unpack option. Then click Next.

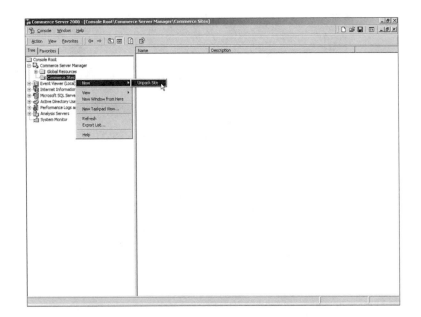

FIGURE 3.5
Starting to unpack a site.

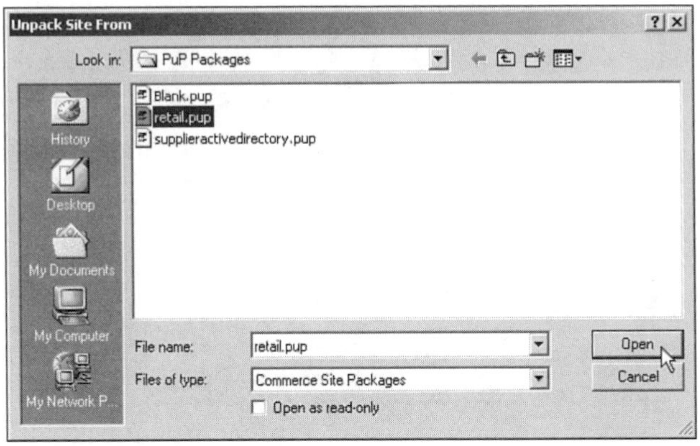

FIGURE 3.6
Choosing the solution site Retail for unpacking.

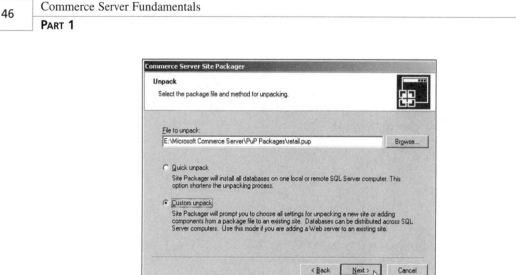

FIGURE 3.7

Performing a custom unpacking.

In the Unpack Method screen, select the Create a New Site option and click Next (see Figure 3.8).

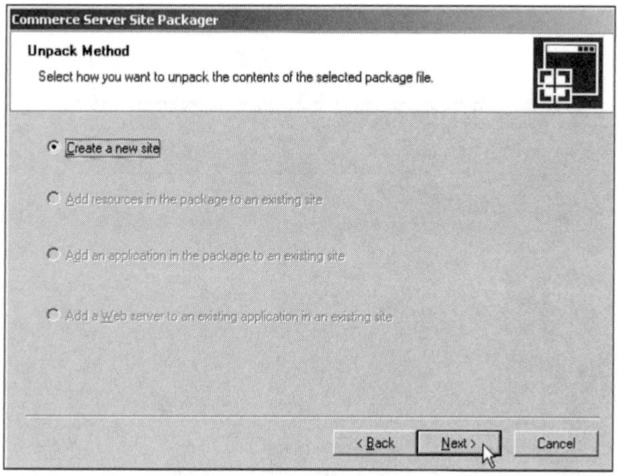

FIGURE 3.8

Creating a new commerce site.

The Site Name screen asks the user to name the e-commerce site (see Figure 3.9). Call it Estore. Thus in the example, the names of the Commerce Server site and the Web site are the same for the sake of convenience. Go on to the next stage of the Site Packager by clicking the Next button.

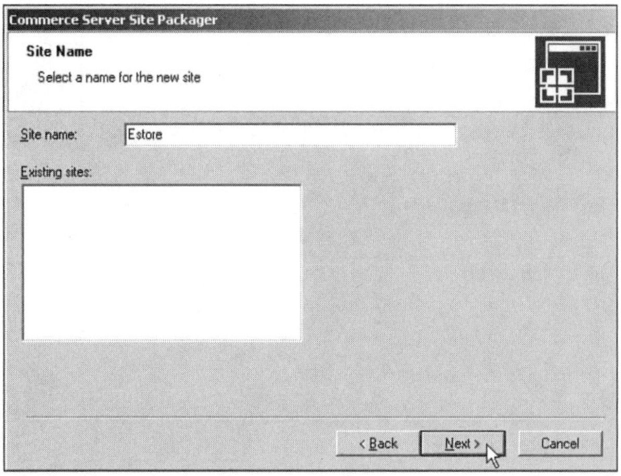

FIGURE 3.9

Naming the commerce site.

Resources

The Select Resources screen (see Figure 3.10) gives the user the option to choose resources that will be used by this site. In Commerce Server terminology, a *resource* is an entity that provides functionality to the applications in a Commerce Server site. A resource is typically a COM based object whose services are used within the ASP pages of the application. For example, Direct Mailer runs as a service (DMLService.exe) and exposes COM interfaces to be used by applications to send mail. Resources are mainly classified into two types: global and site specific. Global resources are available to all the commerce server sites, whether the sites are on one or more servers. Site specific resources are really local to a site. If you want to know a little more about CS resources at this stage, feel free to jump to the section "CS Resources."

Continuing the exercise of unpacking the Retail solution site (refer to Figure 3.10), you can see that the items to the right side are resources that will be used for the site being installed. Keep all the resources selected in the Resources to Unpack box on the right side. Click the Next button. The Global Resource Pointers screen (see Figure 3.11) shows the mapping between the site-specific resources and global resources, if any.

If there is no global resource instance to map to, a new one will be created. If there already is a global resource instance, the user has the option to choose that instance. For example, we don't yet have a global resource instance for CS Authentication. Therefore an instance, CS Authentication (Estore), will be created at the global level. There would also be a site-level resource CS Authentication (Estore), which is just a pointer to the global resource. If we create another new site, the CS Authentication resource for Estore will be listed as being used. Thus, two sites could share the same global resource instance.

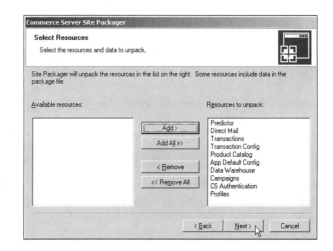

FIGURE 3.10

Selecting resources to be used.

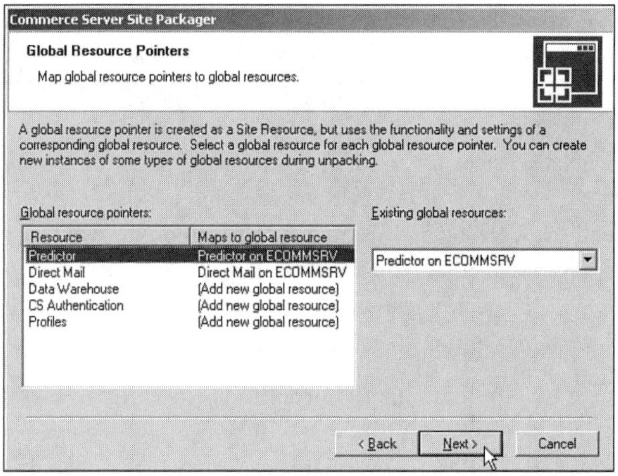

FIGURE 3.11

Mapping to global resources—existing and new.

Clicking the Next button will bring up the Database Connection Strings screen, which creates the databases and connection strings for various resources we have chosen so far (see Figure 3.12).

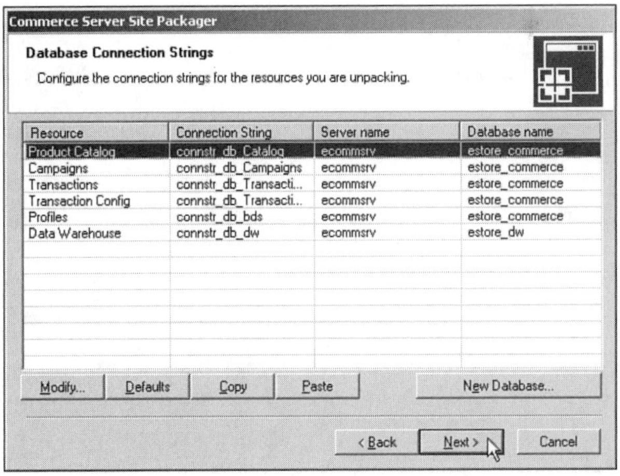

Commerce Server Site Packager

Database Connection Strings

Configure the connection strings for the resources you are unpacking.

Resource	Connection String	Server name	Database name
Product Catalog	connstr_db_Catalog	ecommsrv	estore_commerce
Campaigns	connstr_db_Campaigns	ecommsrv	estore_commerce
Transactions	connstr_db_Transacti...	ecommsrv	estore_commerce
Transaction Config	connstr_db_Transacti...	ecommsrv	estore_commerce
Profiles	connstr_db_bds	ecommsrv	estore_commerce
Data Warehouse	connstr_db_dw	ecommsrv	estore_dw

Modify...   Defaults   Copy   Paste   New Database...

< Back   Next >   Cancel

FIGURE 3.12

Resources and their database.

As we can see from the screen (Figure 3.12), the datastore for resources can all be on a single database or split across different databases. Here we have chosen to have all resources, except Global Data Warehouse, on a single database called estore_commerce. Global Data Warehouse will be on a separate database.

The next input box asks you for the username and password for the master database. After you pass on the right values, Site Packager gives the list of applications that are in the solution site. Typically it will be the Retail site and the associated RetailBizDesk applications as shown in Figure 3.13.

Make sure that both the applications are chosen and then click the Next button. The Select IIS Web Sites and Virtual Directories screen is where you specify the Web sites for each of the applications. Choose the Retail application first and choose Estore as the Web site from the drop-down box. Also name the IIS application path as Estore (see Figure 3.14). This creates a virtual directory called Estore under the Estore Web site. If you choose to install the application files at the root of the site, you can leave this input box blank.

Similarly, choose the RetailBizDesk application to change its Web site to EstoreBizDesk and the IIS application path also to EstoreBizDesk. After this input, Site Packager goes into a frenzy of action for some time before it asks you for some data warehouse information that your site will use (see Figure 3.15)

3

CREATING THE STORE FOUNDATION

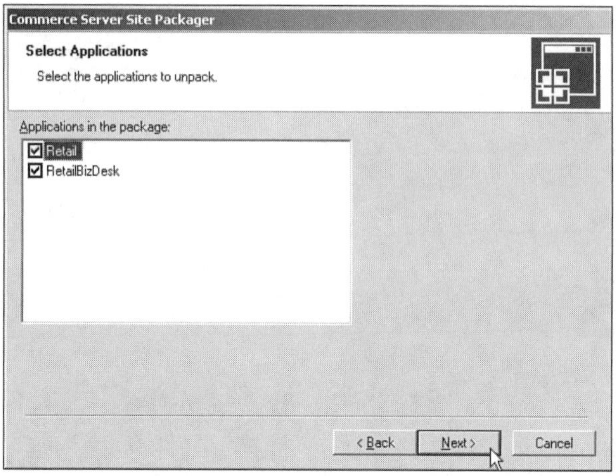

FIGURE 3.13

Available applications in a packed solution site.

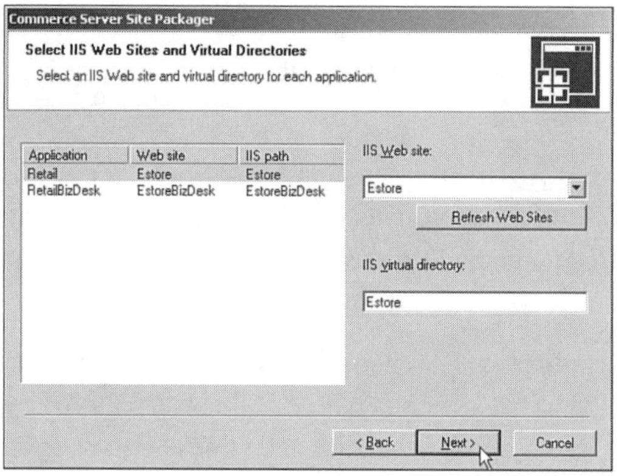

FIGURE 3.14

Commerce Server site and IIS site mapping.

Give a meaningful name, such as Data Warehouse_Estore, to the site's data warehouse. Accept the default value of ESTORE_DW for the database name on the OLAP Server for the data warehouse. The OLAP Server is the server running the Analysis Service.

Click the OK button after giving the data warehouse details, and the Profiling System screens ask for schema definitions as shown in Figures 3.16 and 3.17. These XML files contain the definitions for creating the Profiles and Site Terms schema. The database schema, as well as initial data population, also can be accomplished by custom scripts using these screens.

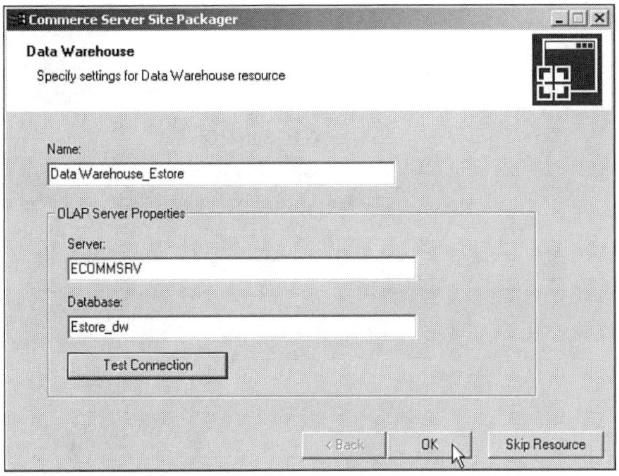

FIGURE 3.15

Data warehouse settings.

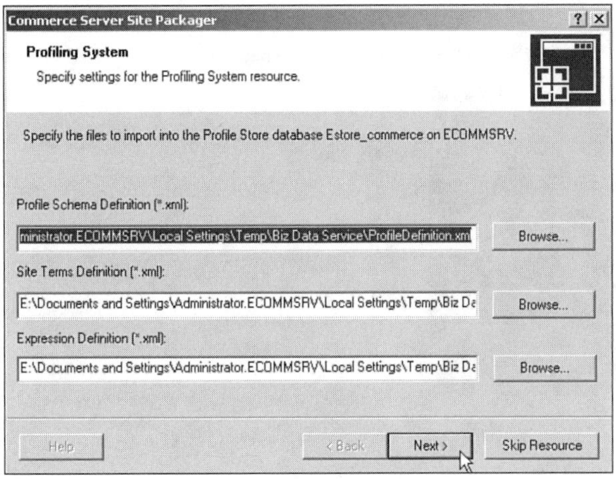

FIGURE 3.16

First schema definition screen.

For one last time, Site Packager does the extraction and installation activity to install various resources and databases. The unpacking is complete and can be verified with the final screen of the process (see Figure 3.18). It gives information about the applications and databases created. Also, the entire unpacking process is written to a log file named Pup.log.

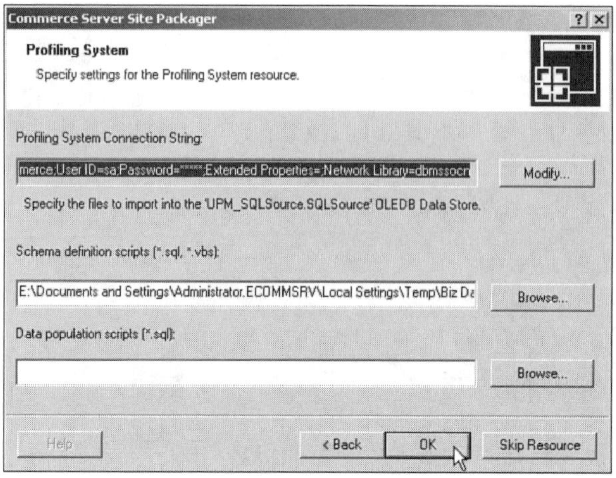

FIGURE 3.17
Second schema definition screen.

FIGURE 3.18
End of unpacking the solution site.

You can click the View Selected Application button in the final screen to launch either Estore or the EstoreBizDesk application. Before doing that, you will discover what Site Packager has accomplished as a result of unpacking and creating your starter applications.

CS Resources

Commerce Server resources are part of the core infrastructure from which a CS e-commerce site functions.

Table 3.1 lists the resources that are provided by Commerce Server.

TABLE 3.1 Available Resources

Global Level	Site Level
Direct Mailer	App Default Config
Predictor	Campaigns
Profiles Service	Product Catalog
Data Warehouse	Transaction Config
CS Authentication	Transactions

These resources store their data in the Commerce Server admin database as well as the site-specific database, depending on the resource. In the Commerce Server Manager, the global resources are visually organized under the Global Resources folder, whereas the site-specific resources are listed under Site Resources for each of the sites. I will discuss this after you have completed the unpacking with Site Packager. Also it is possible for a developer to create and add custom resources both at the global and site levels.

Even though we will deal with each of the resources in detail at appropriate places throughout the book, it would now be good to have a general understanding of each of these Commerce Server provided resources at this point.

Global Resources

Although there are only five distinct types of global resources, there could be more than one instance of a global resource. For instance, there could be a CS Authentication resource instance for Site 1, as well as a separate CS Authentication resource instance for Site 2. We will look at each of these resources more closely.

Direct Mailer

Direct Mailer (DM) runs as a Windows 2000 service (DMLService.exe). DM uses SQL Server 2000 or SQL Server 7.0 as its database and requires SQL Agent to be running in order to process e-mail jobs. Note that both DM and its database should be on the same computer. DM uses the services of Collaboration Data Objects(CDO), again a Windows 2000 object, to compose, format, and send mails using a *Simple Mail Transfer Protocol (SMTP)* server.

You can use the DM to send personalized and general e-mails to site users. A list of recipients could be generated from List Manager, a Commerce Server module, or by using a custom built query on your SQL Server database. The body of the e-mail message can be derived in many ways including Web pages, flat files, or an SQL Server database. DM can be run at the command line as well as called from ASP pages. A separate pipeline called the Direct Mailer Pipeline gives the capability to process the details of the e-mail in stages. The pipeline can be integrated with other modules of Commerce Server and also can be customized with third-party components.

Predictor

Predictor runs as a Windows 2000 service (PredServ.exe) and uses a Data Warehouse configured on the server. The Predictor resource is used to build various models for analysis such as Predictor and Segment models. These models essentially establish a relationship between statistical data in your data warehouse. After a relationship is established, we could run through the model with minimum inputs to predict user behavior. Models use Cases, which are basically name/value pairs representing user profile data such as purchase history and clicks made. The schema for these models are called Model Configurations, and Commerce Server provides you with a default configuration called Transactions. It is possible to build new analysis model configurations with the Predictor schema.

After these models are built, ASP pages could use the Predictor Client object, a COM object, to access these models and get predictions based on a limited set of real-time inputs that are available about the current context.

Profiles Service

Profiles is a Commerce Server 2000 object that manages two concepts in Commerce Server, namely Profiles and Site Terms. Profiles are aggregate information about your site that can be used in analysis of the site. Profile definitions are the schema for information to be collected either implicitly or explicitly from the Web site. For instance, you could define a user profile to collect site visitor information such as name, age, e-mail, and mailing address. When profiles are defined, they can be collected and stored in the data warehouse for analysis. The business desk module Profile Designer can also be used to manage profile definitions.

In order to make analysis and personalization more effective, you can make elements of a profile accept restricted values. If a site term called My Interests is defined with values such as Acrobatics, Movies, Food, and Baseball, this site term can be attached to a user profile called Interests. The Web site users will have to choose from the values that were defined for the site term.

Data Warehouse

The data warehouse in Commerce Server consists of a data warehouse SQL Server database for each commerce site, an OLAP database, and frequent processes that import data from various sources. Some of the sources of information about your site are Web site log files, user profiles, and transaction data. These can be imported into the data warehouse SQL Server database using *Data Transformation Services (DTS)*. In the DTS task, you would define from where and what data to import.

From the data warehouse database, again DTS tasks are run to export a portion of data into an OLAP database. The OLAP database has structures called *cubes* into which data is stored and organized. The Commerce Server data warehouse has a logical schema that taps into the physical SQL Server and OLAP databases. You can build analysis models and run reports against the data warehouse.

Data warehousing is a specialized field of study in itself. However, we will look in more detail about data warehousing and analysis in a later chapter.

CS Authentication

Commerce Server Authentication builds security on top of IIS authentication methods. CS installs an *Internet Server API (ISAPI)* filter called AuthFilter on the application Web sites. The AuthFilter can be configured to authenticate users against the Active Directory or made to look up against a custom data source. Also you can choose to automatically authenticate users by using the Autocookie feature of the AuthFilter.

CS also provides a COM object called `AuthManager` that can be used in ASP scripts to gather more information about the user and make decisions on content security. The `AuthManager` can also be used to validate users who don't accept cookies, thus enabling cookie-less browsing for your site visitors.

Site Resources

The site-specific resources affect the operations of their concerned sites and will not effect other sites on the server. We will take a brief look at what these resources provide to the sites.

App Default Config

This resource maintains the operational configuration of a commerce site and its associated business desk. It holds information that is used throughout the site such as the currency symbol, payment options accepted, and integration with BizTalk server. All of these are configurable according to the unique requirements of a site.

Other Resources

The other four site-specific resources define the database connection string for the commerce site. For example, the Campaigns resource defines the connection string to the database containing campaign data for the site, whereas the Transactions resource defines the information to connect to various transaction data of the site. These resources are used by many components of the site including the Business Desk.

If you had come to this section in the middle of the unpacking process, you could continue with the process and finish it (see Figure 3.10). If you have already unpacked the retail site, it's time to see what has been accomplished.

Explore the Changes

Commerce Server is tightly integrated with the products that form the Windows *Distributed interNet Applications Architecture (DNA)*. Commerce Server applications are actually exposed as IIS Web sites. SQL Server is used to store information for the e-commerce site as well as for Commerce Server administration itself. OLAP Server is used to store the data warehouse requirements of a site. Further Commerce Server's COM objects operate using the COM+ infrastructure. Let's take a look at some of the key system changes that have happened after the unpacking and creation of our first store.

The nodes in Commerce Server Manager can be expanded as shown in Figure 3.19 to analyze the changes.

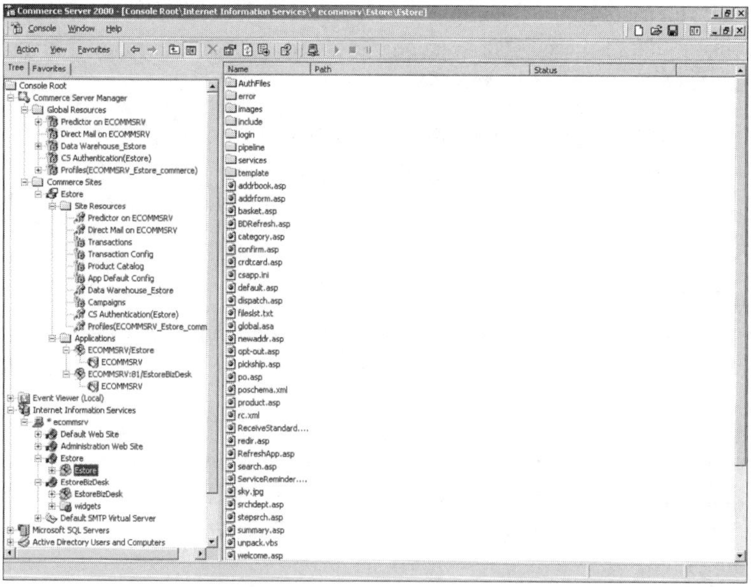

FIGURE 3.19
Changes after solution site unpacking is completed.

The IIS Sites

Because Commerce Server generated applications are Web sites under IIS, we should be able to see the Estore and EstoreBizDesk sites under the node for the Internet Information Services snap-in. In the example, these sites were created as virtual directories. We can also see the application files under Estore as well as EstoreBizDesk sites. These are the files that are served by the Web server in response to requests from browsers.

Commerce Server Manager

The commerce site Estore is added under the Commerce Sites folder. Each commerce site has its site-specific resources grouped under the Site Resources folder. For example, the App Default Config, Campaigns, and Product Catalog are found under that folder. Some of the site-specific resources such as Data Warehouse, Biz Data Service, and CS Authentication are also listed as Global Resources. When the site uses some of the global resources such as Predictor and Direct Mail, they are also listed under the Site Resources folder for the site. In short, all resource and commerce site uses will be listed under a single Site Resources folder for that site. In CSM, these global resource pointers are represented with a red arrow in the icon at the node.

Another folder to notice under the commerce site Estore is Applications. It lists all applications for that commerce site including the business desk. Because an application can run on one or more Web servers, the servers are listed under each application. In the example, Estore is a commerce application that runs on the physical Web server called ECOMMSRV. In a production environment, it is typical to have more than one Web server that runs a site. It is possible to add more servers in the Commerce Server Manager to start managing the application on a Web farm.

SQL Server Objects

Commerce Server creates a database called MSCS_Admin, which it uses to store administration information such as sites, resources, and Web servers. For each commerce site that is created using the Site Packager, a database is created with the naming convention <*sitename*>_commerce. This database holds all the database objects such as tables, stored procedures, triggers, and so on for the entire commerce site application. As already mentioned, high volume sites would typically create an application's database objects across multiple databases and servers.

If data warehouse is also part of the site resources, the data warehouse SQL Server database is also created using the name <*sitename*>_dw. In the example, these two databases are Estore_commerce and Estore_dw. For the data warehouse analysis, default OLAP cubes and dimensions are also created. This can be seen using the Analysis Manager. The Analysis Manager is available as a snap-in inside the CSM. Expand the node Analysis Servers (see Figure 3.20).

3

CREATING THE
STORE
FOUNDATION

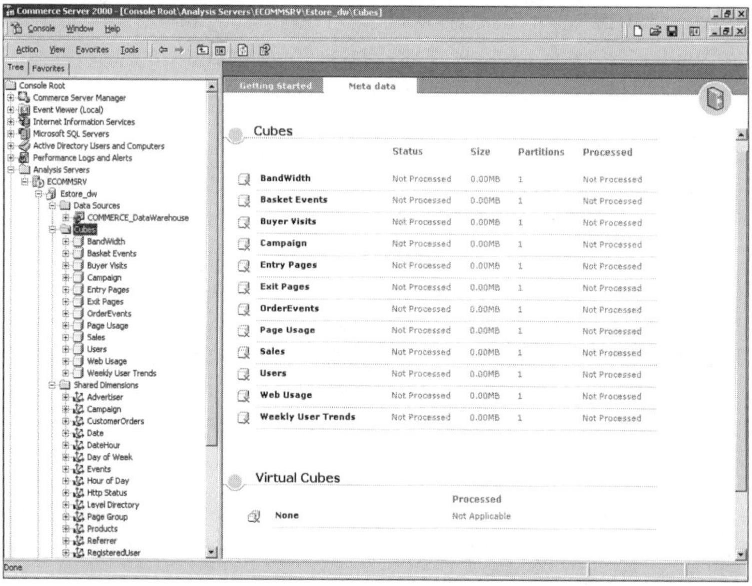

FIGURE 3.20

The OLAP server after unpacking the solution site.

Summary

In this chapter, you learned to create a B2C site using the Commerce Server solution site Retail. You also learned to create a Business Desk site to manage this commerce site. Finally, we explored the changes made by Site Packager due to the unpacking process. The site now contains the required ASP pages for typical e-commerce elements such as a catalog, products, baskets, orders, and user profiles. However, the site is not ready for transactions because we don't yet have the data needed to display our products. In Chapter 4, "From the Business Desk," you will learn how to use the Business Desk for this site to add product information and manage other characteristics of the site.

From the Business Desk

IN THIS CHAPTER

- What is the Business Desk? 60
- Installing Business Desk 60
- What Can You Do With Business Desk? 62
- Using the Business Desk 63
- Creating an Ad-hoc Catalog 64

Every business has an objective irrespective of whether it is a pure online shop or an e-commerce site of a real-world store. Most of the stakeholders in an e-commerce business such as investors, shareholders, and employees expect the business to succeed and achieve its strategic goals. With the proliferation of online strategies, managers have to deal with the *Return on Investment (ROI)* among various business analysis factors in their quarterly reports. Managers have to contend with the fact that e-commerce systems are no longer the same old information-only Web sites of yore. If online stores have to achieve their business objectives, there should be a way for business managers to analyze their performance and fine-tune the business.

Maintaining business data and analyzing transactions in any IT system has been done mostly with the help of input from technical people. Managers have to wait until the reports are ready and also have to depend on others for updating strategic policies in the system. For example, if a sales executive wants to offer a discount on one of the products, she has to pass this information on to the administrator. By the time the administrator gets a chance to update the prices, other factors might have changed so much that this discount could actually produce a per unit loss. The sales executive obviously is not in a position to analyze the dynamic changes in business and fine-tune policies of the online business. To close this loop between technology and business, Commerce Server provides you with a framework called the Business Desk tool. In this chapter, you will learn how to install and work with a Business Desk.

What is the Business Desk?

Business Desk is a tool that provides a visual interface for managers to analyze activities on the site and to effect changes to the site based on the analysis. It is essentially a centralized structure that houses individual modules to manage users, update products, target ads, generate user lists, or view analysis reports. It is possible for developers to develop custom modules that manage specific areas of the site and integrate the modules with the Business Desk.

The Business Desk application is a combination of client- and server-side functionality. That means it requires installation as a Business Desk client, whereas the Business Desk server is the application site on the Web server. Continuing with the Estore site example from Chapter 3, "Creating the Store Foundation," the EstoreBizDesk is the Business Desk application site to which managers will connect to manage the Estore site. Because the Business Desk client for a commerce site can be installed on any workstation, managers can work from anywhere after installing the client software.

Installing Business Desk

Following are the requirements for installing a Business Desk client:

- Microsoft Internet Explorer(IE) 5.5 and
- Office 2000 Web Controls or

- Client Tools for SQL Server 2000 or Client Components of SQL Server 7.0, depending on the version of SQL Server used on the database server

After these requirements are met, the Business Desk client can be installed. The first time a client browser connects to the Business Desk site, the client setup starts automatically and the setup wizard for installation guides the user. Basically, the setup downloads ActiveX controls necessary for installing and running the Business Desk. The Business Desk is implemented using *HTML Components (HTC)* whose functionality is supported by the *Document Object Model (DOM)* of IE 5.5. You will be shown the Business Desk architecture in detail while dealing with customizations in Chapter 13, "Extending the Business Desk."

In order to connect to the Business Desk application, a user has to launch IE and point to the URL of the site that houses the application. Because the EstoreBizDesk application is already installed, connect to that site. The form of the URL is typically `http://<server_name>:<port_number>/IIS_application_path`. In this case, the URL is `http://ECOMMSRV:81/EstoreBizDesk`. Note that the application was installed on port 81 on the Web server. As soon as this site is accessed, the Business Desk Client Setup Program screen tries to download ActiveX components. A standard security warning dialog box is launched asking for permission to download the components. Click Yes to begin installation. There might be more than one such warning box. Click Yes to accept all the downloads. The next screen asks the user to browse for a folder on her local machine to install the HTML application. After choosing a folder, click the OK button to continue installation. When installation is over, the browser displays the status message about the setup, as shown in Figure 4.1.

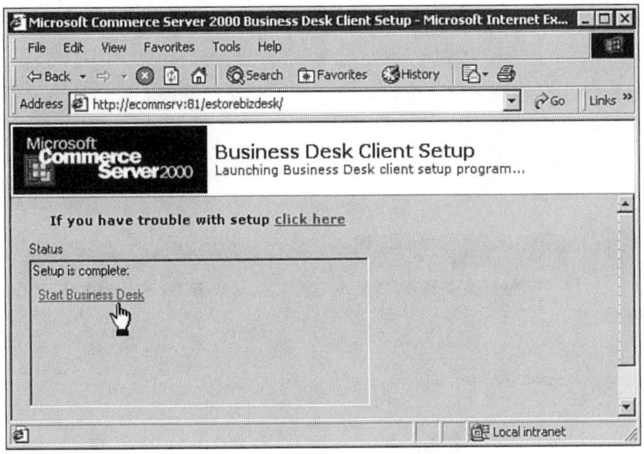

FIGURE 4.1
After the Business Desk client setup is complete, you will see this screen.

You could click on the Start Business Desk link on the page (shown in Figure 4.1) to launch the Business Desk immediately. The setup also creates two links to the Business Desk program: one is on the user's Windows desktop, and the other is on the Start menu. These two shortcuts can be used any time to launch Business Desk. Note that these shortcuts are for a specific instance of Business Desk. The two shortcuts created for the example had the name Estore Business Desk (ECOMMSRV-81). It is easy to recognize the naming convention used by the setup program, which is *<commerce_site_name>* Business Desk(*<server_name>-<port number>*).

What Can You Do With Business Desk?

The Business Desk interface is visually divided in to two main frames. The left pane is used for navigation and contains links to the individual modules. The right pane is where these modules interact with the user. The Business Desk is shown in Figure 4.2.

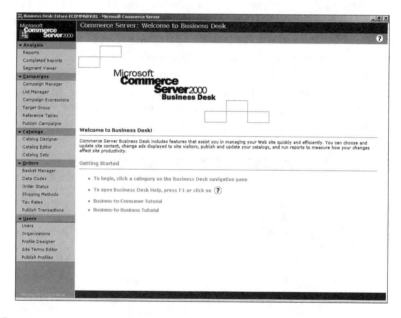

FIGURE 4.2
The main interface of Business Desk with navigation and module panes.

As soon as a module opens in the right pane, there will be a toolbar for tasks to be performed that are specific to the module. Most of the modules open with a page that lists summary details. From this page, the user can navigate to other edit pages for the module using the tool bar.

As you can see, individual modules are grouped under categories. Each module is designed to manage a different aspect of the e-commerce site. For instance, the Basket Manager module is grouped under the Orders category, and is used to find details about shopping baskets that are stored for the site. About 23 modules are provided by Commerce Server itself by default, and they are organized within five categories as evident from the navigation pane in Figure 4.2. This information is summarized in Table 4.1.

TABLE 4.1 Business Desk Categories and Modules

Category	Modules	Used For
Analysis	Reports Completed Reports Segment Viewer	These are canned as well as configurable reports that use the OLAP database and Prediction models to generate reports about site activity.
Campaigns	Campaign Manager List Manager Campaign Expressions Target Group Reference Tables Publish Campaigns	The Personalization and Marketing policies can be implemented as campaigns for ads, discounts, and mailings aimed at target users and groups.
Catalogs	Catalog Designer Catalog Editor Catalog Sets	These can create and update information on catalogs, products, prices, and other product data.
Orders	Basket Manager Data Codes Order Status Shipping Methods Tax Rates Publish Transactions	These are used to analyze baskets, manipulate order information, and update shipping and tax rates.
Users	Users Organizations Profile Designer Site Terms Editor Publish Profiles	These can manage registered and anonymous users, create profiles based on users and organizations, and maintain site wide vocabulary.

Using the Business Desk

Having created a starter site Estore, you have yet to see what became available on the site after Site Packager created it based on the Retail solution site. To browse the commerce site, the following URL convention is used:

```
http://<server_name>:<port_name>/<site_name>
```

In the example, I have to go to `http://ECOMMSRV/Estore` to reach the home page of the site. Because I have installed the Estore site on the default port 80, I don't need to specify the port number in the URL. The resulting page is shown in Figure 4.3.

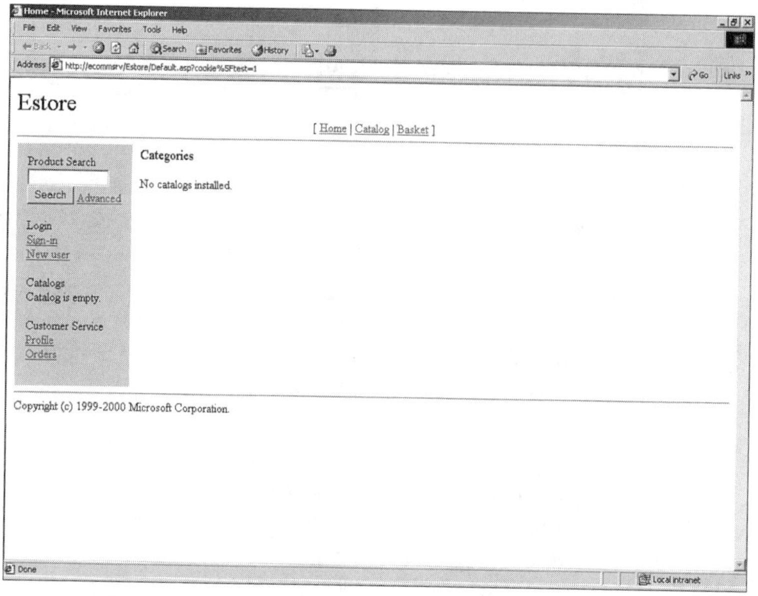

FIGURE 4.3

The home page of the e-commerce site generated from the Retail solution site.

The basic site comes with the application (ASP, XML, and Pipeline files), the database objects such as tables and stored procedures, and some initial data in the database. After browsing the home page of this basic site (refer to Figure 4.3), it seems that no product catalog is defined, and hence there is nothing to buy from our site. Also note at this point that you are an anonymous user to the site because you aren't signed in yet. We will populate our site with a catalog of products for users to browse and buy. We will use the Business Desk to do so.

Creating an Ad-hoc Catalog

In Commerce Server, a catalog holds products that can be grouped into logical categories. This is explained in Table 4.2.

TABLE 4.2 Catalogs Contain Categories that Contain Products

Catalog	Computer Accessories
Category 1	Printers
Product 1	HPDeskjet 970cxi

TABLE 4.2 Continued

Catalog	Computer Accessories
Product 2	Lexmark 3200 Color
Category 2	Scanners
Product 1	Umax Astra 200U
Product 2	Epson 1200U

We will create the catalog for the example shown in Table 4.2. In the Business Desk for Estore, click the Catalog Editor module under Catalogs in the navigation pane. Because the site has been newly created, no catalogs are defined. To create a new catalog, choose New Catalog from the toolbar button as shown in Figure 4.4.

FIGURE 4.4
Using Catalog Editor to create a new catalog.

The edit page for entering new catalog information takes a few seconds to load. In the Catalog: New page (see Figure 4.5), enter **Computer Accessories** as the name of the catalog under the Catalog Properties section. Give a valid Start and End date to the catalog. Select Name from the Product Unique ID drop-down list, and select SKU from the Product Variant Unique ID drop-down list. Note that fields with a red diamond next to them are mandatory. Save the catalog by clicking the Save button as shown in Figure 4.5.

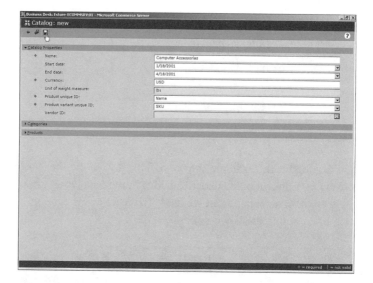

FIGURE 4.5

Creating and saving the catalog.

So far you have created and saved the catalog Computer Accessories, which is empty right now. The next step will be to create two categories in the catalog called Printers and Scanners. Expand the categories section by single-clicking on the arrow (refer to Figure 4.5) next to the Categories section. Then click the New button (see Figure 4.6).

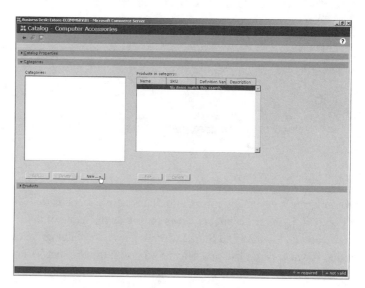

FIGURE 4.6

Adding a new category to a catalog.

The Catalog Editor asks you to choose a category schema based on which schema you want to use to create the category. Choose the Department schema, which is provided by default, and click the Continue button (see Figure 4.7).

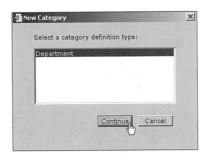

FIGURE 4.7
Choosing a schema based on which new category is to be created.

In the Category Properties section in the page that comes up, enter **Printers** for the Name field and **All types of printers for home use.** in the Description field. Also enable the Searchable field. Then click the Save and Return to the Catalog Properties button in the toolbar (see Figure 4.8).

FIGURE 4.8
Creating a category to hold products.

Similarly, enter **Scanners** as a new category in the name field, and enter **All types of scanners to scan photos at home.** as the description. Be sure to enable it to be searchable. Now we've got the categories ready. All that's left is to create products and add them to these categories. You will do that next.

In the Catalog Editor—Computer Accessories page, expand the Products section and click the New button (see Figure 4.9) to enter products.

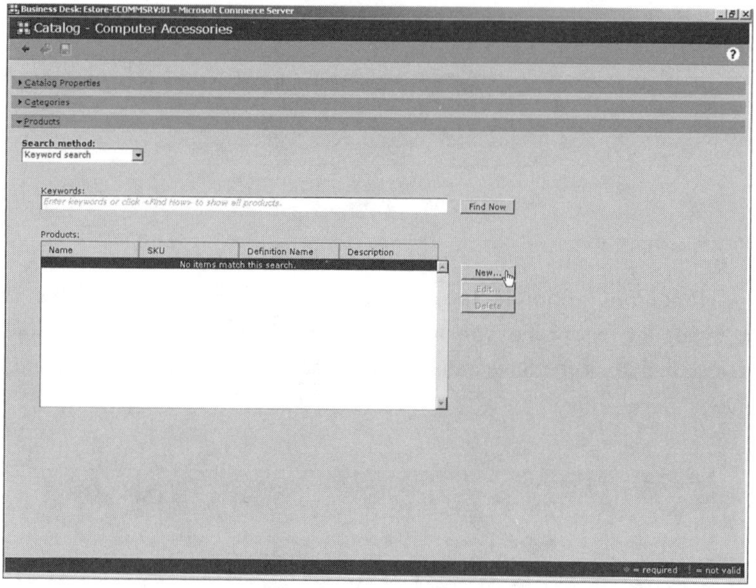

FIGURE 4.9
Creating a new product in a catalog.

The New Product dialog box prompts the user to choose a product schema that will be used to create the product. Choose Printer and click the OK button (see Figure 4.10).

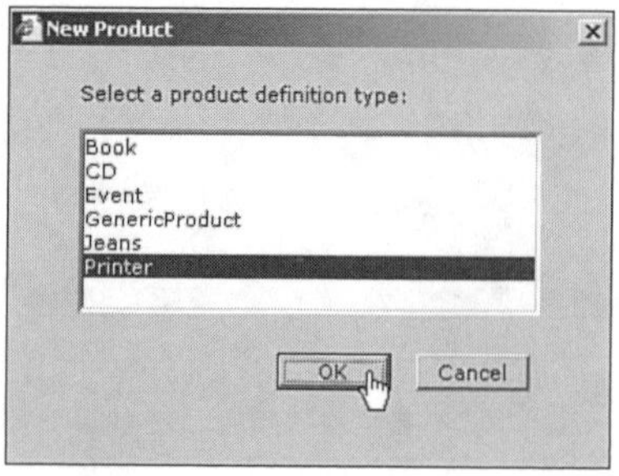

FIGURE 4.10
Choosing a schema based on which product will be created.

Depending on the product schema chosen, the next input form displayed will prompt for specific product details to be entered. In the Product Properties section (see Figure 4.11) enter values for Name, Description, and Price. Also, because we are creating a product of type Printer, we would want to add this product to the Printers category. Therefore in the Assigned Categories section, choose Printers from Available Categories text box and press the Add button to add it to the Assigned Categories list. Then click the Save and Back to Category Properties buttons on the toolbar.

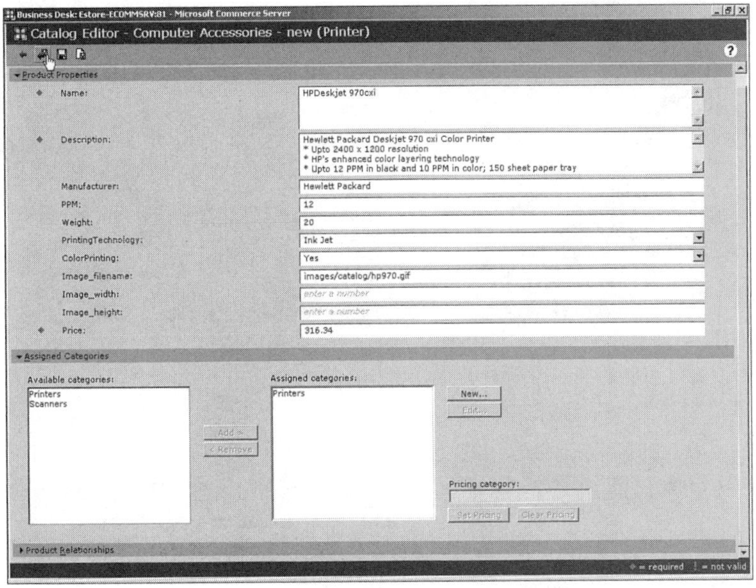

FIGURE 4.11

Entering product details and grouping products in categories.

At this point, you have successfully created a catalog called Computer Accessories, which has categories called Printers and Scanners. Also, a printer product was created and listed under the Printers category. It is time to check whether these changes are available to the end user at our e-commerce site Estore.

Catalogs are fetched and stored in a cache, which will be discussed in detail in a later chapter. The site application accesses the catalogs to display from the cache. Therefore, it is necessary to refresh the cache after any updates to catalogs. To refresh all catalog caches, navigate to the Catalogs list view. Click on the toolbar icon as shown in Figure 4.12.

By accessing the commerce site Estore once again, you can see that Printers and Scanners are now listed under Categories. If the Printers link is clicked, it opens up the page that lists the HPDeskjet 970cxi product that you just added (see Figure 4.13).

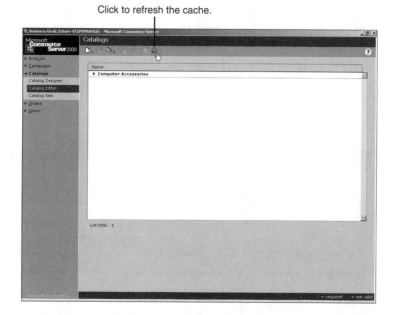

FIGURE 4.12

Refreshing the catalog cache.

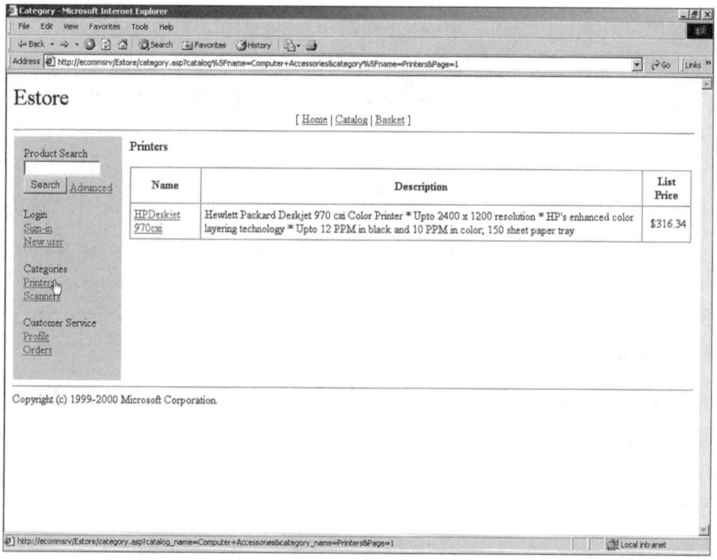

FIGURE 4.13

Web site changes effected by the Business Desk.

The site visitor would click the HPDeskjet 970cxi link to finally buy the product.

Summary

In this chapter, you learned how to install the Business Desk client on a manager's workstation. We also briefly explored how Business Desk is a framework for working with individual modules and that modules are grouped under categories in the visual interface. Finally, the Business Desk module Catalog Editor was used to populate a site with catalogs that contain products grouped into product categories.

If some of the concepts of Catalogs weren't very clear while working with the Catalog Editor, don't be discouraged. This chapter is just meant to make you understand how a Business Desk can be used to update site content dynamically. You have seen only one of the more than 23 modules available with the Business Desk. We will work with the remainder of them while dealing with other areas of Commerce Server as well as while building custom modules for the Business Desk.

Your understanding of the Site Packager-generated basic site is not complete unless we look under the hood, which we will do in Chapter 5, "Understanding the Site Architecture." That is a vital step in understanding Commerce Server as a whole before sharpening your development tools and delving deeper into customizations and extensions.

4

FROM THE
BUSINESS DESK

Understanding the Site Architecture

IN THIS CHAPTER

- Initializing the Site Application   74
- Starting with the Home Page   82
- Standard Include Files   84
- Browsing Catalogs   89
- Navigating Product Categories   91
- Caching Is Good   94
- Viewing Product Details   97
- The Shopping Basket   101
- Specify Shipping and Billing Addresses   104
- Choosing a Shipping Method   105
- The Order Summary   108
- Pay for Your Purchase   110
- Order Confirmation   112

It would almost be a cliche if I say again that one of the *Unique Selling Points (USP)* of Commerce Server 2000 is its faster time to market. This is achieved by providing prebuilt solution sites that can be used to quickly start and build the end-solution needs. You have already seen how to use the Site Packager to unpack a solution site and create a starter site. This starter site will, of course, be the starting point of your e-commerce site built using Commerce Server. Some users might perform only a little tweak here and there to bring the site up to meet their requirements, whereas others would alter most of the site including default functionality. Therefore, understanding the site and its architecture is paramount before you start customizing the site and integrating it with external systems.

In this chapter, you will go through the starter site as if you were an end user. Typically you will begin at the home page of the site, browse for products, add to a basket, and place an order. In working through this process flow, at each of the key stages, we will look at the various elements of the site infrastructure that are helping to execute the stage successfully. These elements can be broadly divided in to three types: user interfaces, middle tier, and back end. *User interface* elements are those that provide the Web site visitor with an interface to the system. Examples are ASP pages that generate HTML code to accept login.

I will refer to *middle tier* elements as those that provide services to the user interface elements directly or indirectly. For instance, an intermediate verification ASP page, called by a front-end login page, will redirect user to an error page on failure or to a specified URL on successful login. Also the COM component that is called by this intermediate page belongs to the middle tier discussion. Then at the other end, I will refer to back end activities as those affecting our database. Because Commerce Server provides complete encapsulation of database objects through the COM objects, you will only take a momentary look just to know what tables are being involved.

Initializing the Site Application

Remember that your e-commerce site is actually an IIS Web site. Therefore, the file that gets accessed first at the start of the IIS application is global.asa. Global.asa is the script that instantiates many of the Commerce Server's COM objects and makes them available for use throughout the site's ASP pages. Even though global.asa is the starting point for the application, this file doesn't contain all the code to accomplish things. All the object initializations and functions at the global level are encapsulated in subroutines in individual ASP files. These include files serve as a library of subroutines that are called from global.asa. The starting point of all global action practically starts with the Call Main() statement in the *Application_OnStart* event handler in global.asa. The subroutine Main() is defined in the file global_main_lib.asp. This routine instantiates, initializes, and sets at the application scope references to CS objects to be used throughout the application. How does Main() accomplish all this? It does so

with the help of routines defined in various specialized include files. A snippet from global.asa
is presented in the following:

```
...
...
<SCRIPT LANGUAGE=VBScript RUNAT=Server>
Option Explicit
....
....
Sub Application_OnStart()
    Application("MSCSEnv") = MSCSEnv
    Call Main()
    Application("MSCSErrorInGlobalASA") = False
End Sub
</SCRIPT>
...
...
<!—#include file="include/global_addressbook_lib.asp" —>
<!—#include file="include/global_cache_lib.asp" —>
<!—#include file="include/global_catalog_lib.asp" —>
<!—#include file="include/global_creditcards_lib.asp" —>
<!—#include file="include/global_csf_lib.asp" —>
<!—#include file="include/global_data_lib.asp" —>
<!—#include file="include/global_forms_lib.asp" —>
<!—#include file="include/global_internationalization_lib.asp" —>
<!—#include file="include/global_main_lib.asp" —>
<!—#include file="include/global_messagemanager_lib.asp" —>
<!—#include file="include/global_predictor_lib.asp" —>
<!—#include file="include/global_profile_lib.asp" —>
<!—#include file="include/global_siteconfig_lib.asp" —>
<!—#include file="include/global_siteterms_lib.asp" —>
<!—#include file="include/global_ui_lib.asp" —>
<!—#include file="include/std_dates_lib.asp" —>
<!—#include file="include/std_util_lib.asp" —>
<!—#include file="services/include/global_service_lib.asp" —>
```

Thus global.asa just calls the Main() routine in global_main_lib.asp and from there it is
global_main_lib.asp that acts as the global file for object instantiation and initialization. For
example, the CatalogManager object is instantiated, initialized, and placed in an Application
scope as shown in the following fragments of code in the Main() subroutine in
global_main_lib.asp:

```
...

Dim MSCSCatalogManager
```

```
...

Set MSCSCatalogManager = InitCatalogManager()

...

...

Set Application("MSCSCatalogManager") = MSCSCatalogManager
```

The InitCatalogManager function is actually defined in global_catalog_lib.asp and is listed as follows:

```
Function InitCatalogManager()
    Dim mscsCatalogMgr

    Set mscsCatalogMgr = Server.CreateObject("Commerce.CatalogManager")
    Call mscsCatalogMgr.Initialize(dictConfig.s_CatalogConnectionString,
    ➥ADO_CONNECTION_STRING)

    Set InitCatalogManager = mscsCatalogMgr
End Function
```

The declaration of the variable MSCSCatalogManager, calling the InitCatalogManager function, and setting a reference to the CatalogManager object at application scope are all done in Main() in global_main_lib.asp. The actual code needed in the InitCatalogManager function to do the work is defined in global_catalog_lib.asp.

Any ASP file that deals with catalogs will use the reference to the CatalogManager object stored in the application variable Application("MSCSCatalogManager").

Similarly, all other object instantiation and initialization are called from global_main_lib.asp while the actual work is done in functions defined in library files such as global_catalog_lib.asp, global_cache_lib.asp, and so on.

Configuration Settings

Before you start with analyzing more of the global files, it would be worth a look at the application configurations generated for the site after using the Site Packager. A file called csapp.ini is created in the root folder of the application. This ini file contains very basic site information such as the name of site and the date created. Here are the contents of the csapp.ini file for the Estore example:

```
SiteName=Estore
AddressKeyName=Estore
RelativeURL=Estore
```

```
CreatedBy=Author
CreatedDate=1999.04.02 00:00:00
Version=4.0.0000
```

The main operating configuration information for the site is stored in the App Default Config resource for the site. To take a look at some of the default settings for Estore, open Commerce Server Manager and navigate to the node corresponding to the App DefaultConfig resource. Right-click and choose Properties (see Figure 5.1).

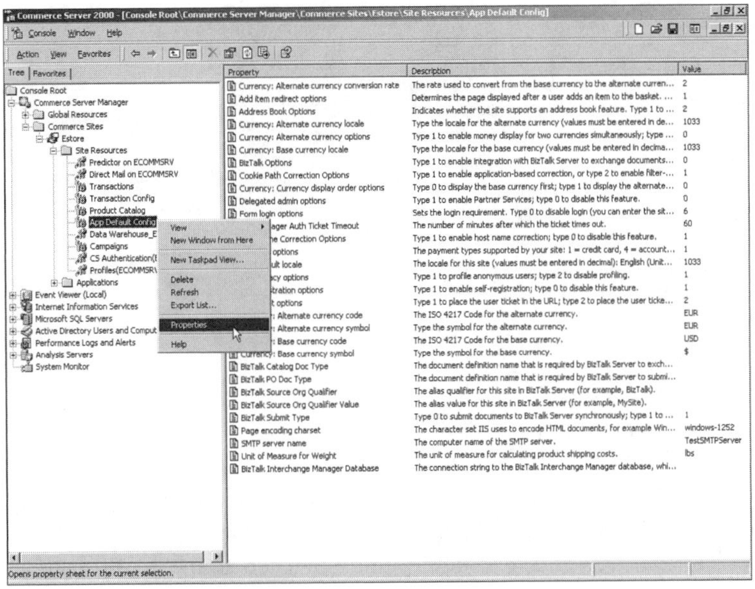

FIGURE 5.1
Accessing the App Default Config resource.

The App Default Config Properties dialog box (see Figure 5.2) displays all configuration settings for the site.

For instance, by clicking on the `Currency:Base Currency Symbol` property, you can find out what symbol will be displayed in front of money values. The description of each property appears in the Description box as soon as you click on the property. If you want to change the base currency symbol or currency code, you can update them from this dialog box. Take a moment to just glance through the property list. You will see how these properties influence customization in Part II, "Advanced Topics." All these properties effect the basic functioning of the site and can be modified easily from the Commerce Server Manager.

5

UNDERSTANDING
THE SITE
ARCHITECTURE

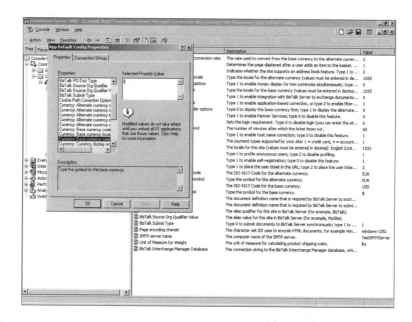

FIGURE 5.2
The site configuration stored in App Default Config.

Inside the Global Files

Having seen how to view as well as change site configuration settings, we will delve in to the global.asa file. Recollect that inside global.asa, in the `Application_OnStart` event handler, a call to `Main()` is made. Now code execution control transfers to the `Main()` subroutine defined in the global_main_lib.asp file that also resides in the include directory along with other library files. Here are some of the key activities that take place from there:

- Site and application names—The site name and application name are retrieved from csapp.ini and stored in the Application variables `Application("MSCSCommerceSiteName")` and `Application("MSCSCommerceAppName")`, respectively.

- Expression evaluator—An instance of the object `Commerce.ExpressionEvaluator` is created and connected to the site's database where expressions are stored. Then this instance is given Application scope in `Application("MSCSExpressionEvaluator")`. The `ExpressionEvaluator` object is used to evaluate expressions against a context whenever you need to deliver ads or discounts based on their respective context information.

- `GetSitePages()`—The names of the ASP pages used across the site are stored in `Application("MSCSSitePages")` as a dictionary with key/value pairs pointing to the pages. For instance, the login key in the dictionary has the value `"login/login.asp"`. Therefore to get a reference to the login page, it would suffice to use `Application` `("MSCSSitePages").Login`. This reference is returned by the `GetSitePages()` function defined in global_siteconfig_lib.asp.

- `InitProfileService()`—An instance of the `Commerce.ProfileService` object is instantiated and initialized to point to the site's profile database. It is stored in the variable `Application("MSCSProfileService")`. The `ProfileService` object is used to access and manage instances of Profile objects. For example, to access the `Zipcode` property of a user profile inside one of the ASP pages, first the reference to the Profile object instance is obtained using say,

  ```
  oProfileObject = oProfileService.GetProfile("someone@somewhere.com",
  ➥ "UserObject")
  ```

  Then the property is accessed using

  ```
  oProfileObject.Fields("Address").Value("Zipcode")
  ```

  This reference is returned by the function `InitProfileService()` defined in global_profile_lib.asp. We will see more of the `ProfileService` object when we deal with User Profiles in Chapter 7, "User Management."

- ADODB Connection—An instance of the `ADODB.Connection` object is created and stored in the variable `Application("MSCSAdoConnection")` using the `oGetOpen ConnectionObject()` function defined in global_profile_lib.asp. The ADO connection refers to the commerce site's database and is stored for easy lookup. Because the Commerce Server–provided COM objects encapsulate the backend storage and are used to access the site database, the `MSCSAdoConnection` is used in only a few profiles-related pages such as get_profiles.asp, save_all_profiles.asp, and delete_profiles.asp.

- `InitSitePipelines()`—Pipelines are configurations of sequential COM components designed to work on a business object such as `OrderForm`. Pipelines are called at different site stages such as basket, checkout, and purchase. Pipeline information for the site is stored in `Application("MSCSPipelines")`. It is a dictionary with key-value pairs such as `"Product"-"\pipeline\product.pcf"`, each key pointing to the location of the pipeline file for the site. This aids in an easy reference to the pipeline files using their mnemonics such as Product for product.pcf, wherever the file is physically installed. The worker routine `InitSitePipelines()` defined in global_siteconfig_lib.asp accomplishes this mapping. You will see more on Pipelines starting with Chapter 9, "Commerce Server Pipelines."

- `GetSiteStyles()`—Another dictionary representing HTML styles is stored in the variable `Application("MSCSSiteStyle")`. The key-value pairs are something similar to `"MenuTable"-"BORDER='0' CELLSPACING='10'"`, and so on for various styles to be used throughout the site while displaying HTML content to the browser. This dictionary is generated by the call to the `GetSiteStyles()` function defined in global_ui_lib.asp.

- `GetMessageManagerObject()`—An instance of the object `Commerce.MessageManager` is instantiated and stored in `Application("MSCSMessageManager")`. The `MessageManager` object is initialized with application error messages that are loaded from a file called rc.xml, present in the application root. It is an XML file that contains all the error messages for the application. An entry in the message file would resemble the following:

```
<Entry Name="pur_badsku" Type="_Basket_Errors">
<Value Language="English">Please note that one or more items were removed
➥ from your order because the product is no longer sold.</Value>
</Entry>
```

  Each of these messages is stored in a dictionary object with the key being `Name` and the value equal to the message found between the Value tags in the XML file. Basically the `MSXML.DOMDocument` object is used to parse the XML file. The site pages would access the initialized `MessageManager` object to retrieve error messages to display to the user when errors occur. The `GetMessageManagerObject()` function that does all the work is defined in the file global_messagemanager_lib.asp.

- `InitDataFunctions()`—An instance of `Commerce.DataFunctions` is created and initialized using the site's default locale setting. In your App Default Config resource, this property is `Site Default Locale` and typically has a default value of `1033`, which stands for U.S. Locale. The `DataFunctions` object is basically used to validate or convert data that is locale specific such as date, time, and currency. The helper routine that gets this reference is `InitDataFunctions()` and is defined in global_data_lib.asp.

- `InitCacheManager()`—An instance of `Commerce.CacheManager` is created and stored in the variable `Application("MSCSCacheManager")`. `CacheManager` helps to maintain a collection of data caches, which are implemented as either `Dictionary` or `LRUCache` Objects. Each data cache is created for various elements of the site pages such as product list, static section of default page, tax, shipping, and so on. The site pages would access the caches to retrieve values quickly and display to the user. The function `InitCacheManager()` defined in global_cache_lib.asp helps in creating the reference to the `CacheManager` object. You will see more about the `CacheManager` object in Chapter 11, "Direct Mailer and Content Selection Pipelines."

- `InitAltCurrencyDisp()`—An instance of the `Commerce.EuroDisplay` object is created and stored in the variable `Application("MSCSAltCurrencyDisp")`. The `EuroDisplay` object is initialized with a list of various international currency symbols and conversion rates. The `InitAltCurrencyDisp()` function that accomplishes this is defined in global_internationalization_lib.asp.

- `InitCatalogManager()`—An instance of the `Commerce.CatalogManager` object is created and stored in the variable `Application("MSCSCatalogManager")`. The

`CatalogManager` is initialized with the connection string to the database in which catalogs for the site are stored. Site pages that are concerned with displaying catalog and product information to users will use the `CatalogManager` object. Using the `CatalogManager`, access is gained to the `Category` and `Product` objects. Further, the `CatalogManager` object can be used to manage catalog activities such as creating, deleting, importing, exporting, and searching catalogs. The reference is created by a call to the `InitCatalogManager()` function, which is defined in global_catalog_lib.asp.

- `InitPredictor()`—An instance of the `Commerce.PredictorClient` object is created and stored in the variable `Application("MSCSPredictor")`. The `PredictorClient` will be called by ASP pages to load predictor models and be asked for a prediction based on the models. The models are built using the Predictor service. For example, the `PredictorClient` returns a list of recommended products that can be displayed on the basket page. A reference to the `PredictorClient` object is created and returned by the `InitPredictor()` defined in global_predictor_lib.asp. I will discuss prediction in depth in Chapter 15, "Data Warehouse, Reports, and Prediction."

- `InitCSF()`—Initializes the Content Selection Framework(CSF) for ads, discounts, and events by loading their respective pipelines(advertising.pcf, discounts.pcf, and recordevent.pcf). These are again placed in Application level variables that will act as global context for use in ASP pages. The CSF is essentially based on the *Content Selection Pipelines (CSP)* and provides the infrastructure to target and deliver content. `InitCSF()` is defined in global_csf_lib.asp. You will see more about the CSF and the CSP in Chapter 11.

- `GetFormDefinitions()`—All the HTML forms that are to be displayed to the users are stored in the variable `Application("MSCSForms")`. This effectively holds a dictionary that contains a key for each of the forms such as Login, Registration, Credit Card, Purchase Order, and so on. The value of the keys, in turn, contains a list of input controls for the form and associated attributes of controls. The `GetFormDefinitions()` function is defined in global_forms_lib.asp.

In addition to all the previous major objects, there are other object references created and stored in global.asa.

Global.asa is very central to the application and simplifies the instantiation and usage of middle tier COM objects throughout the site. The `Application_OnStart` event handler, in which all the previous instantiations are made, is executed the first time that the Web application is accessed. The various object instantiations stored in Application variables are then available throughout the site at all times. It is worth taking at least a cursory glance through global.asa to digest what has been discussed so far as well as to see how the global objects are instantiated for sitewide use.

The diagram in Figure 5.3 should help you recapitulate most of the global initialization architecture for the Estore site.

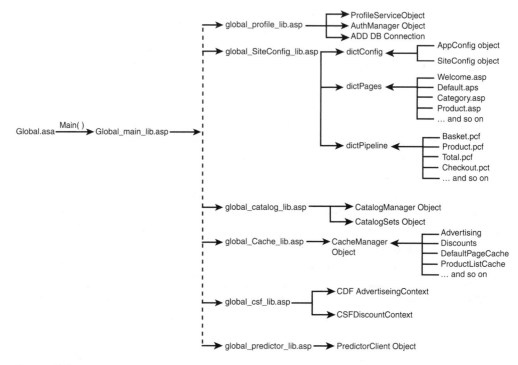

FIGURE 5.3
Global initialization of a site application.

Starting with the Home Page

The home page of the starter site is default.asp. This is usually the page from which users begin navigation for activities such as shopping, checking orders, and updating their profiles. Figure 5.4 shows a few of the navigation possibilities along with the typical shopper flow.

Notice what happens when the site is visited for the first time ever, after the application was started. Figure 5.5 shows the page that is displayed at the browser in Estore.

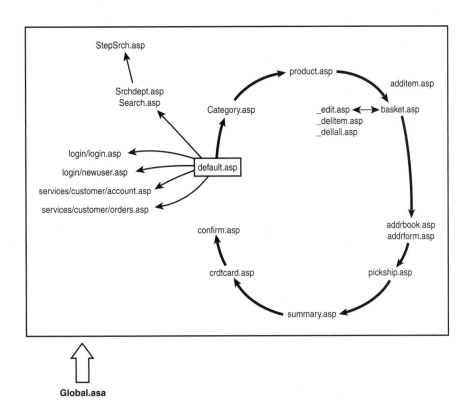

FIGURE 5.4

The site flow from the end user's point of view.

We will analyze behind-the-scenes activities while the default.asp file is getting processed. The default.asp file has many include files in it to get things done. Some of the include files are present in most of the ASP files on the site to provide the basic functionality needed by the pages. Some of those common includes found in default.asp are the following:

```
<!— #INCLUDE FILE="include/header.asp" —>
<!— #INCLUDE FILE="include/const.asp" —>
<!— #INCLUDE FILE="include/html_lib.asp" —>
<!— #INCLUDE FILE="include/catalog.asp" —>
<!— #INCLUDE FILE="include/std_access_lib.asp" —>
<!— #INCLUDE FILE="include/std_cache_lib.asp" —>
<!— #INCLUDE FILE="include/std_cookie_lib.asp" —>
<!— #INCLUDE FILE="include/std_profile_lib.asp" —>
<!— #INCLUDE FILE="include/std_url_lib.asp" —>
<!— #INCLUDE FILE="include/std_util_lib.asp" —>
<!— #INCLUDE FILE="include/setupenv.asp" —>
<!— #INCLUDE FILE="template/layout1.asp" —>
```

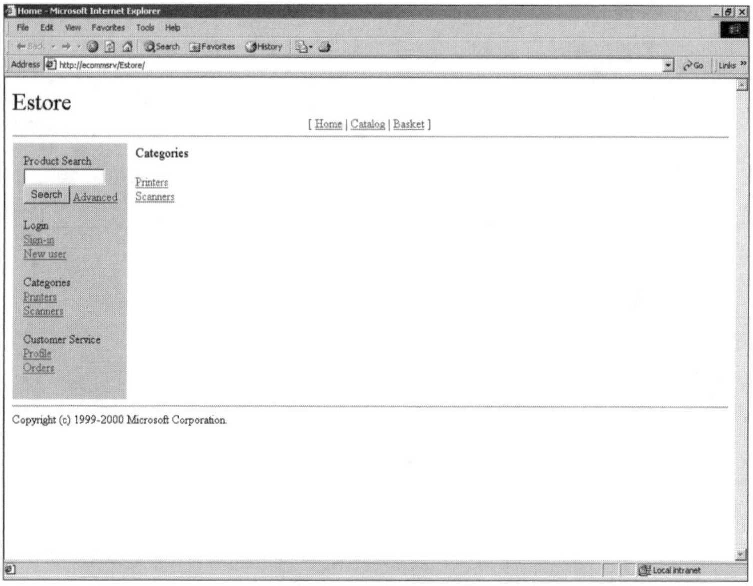

FIGURE 5.5
The home page of a starter site.

Standard Include Files

The following sections contain brief descriptions of the functionality that each of the include files provide to the default page and other pages in which they are included.

Header File

This is a simple file that helps set certain properties of the Response object to enable buffering and avoid caching of pages by a client browser. Here is a sample of the file contents:

```
<%
Response.Buffer = True

Response.CacheControl = "no-cache"
Response.AddHeader "Pragma", "no-cache"
Response.Expires = -1
%>
```

Site Constants

The file const.asp suggests that site constants would be defined in that file. This release doesn't contain anything in this file. Instead, all standard constants used throughout the site pages are available with the `AppConstants` object. The `AppConstants` object is instantiated in global.asa as follows:

```
<!—METADATA TYPE="TypeLib" NAME="AppConsts 1.0 Type Library" UUID="
➥{8F151887-1EFD-42F3-844E-A66453AF19FF}" —>
```

You can open up appconsts.idl file in the <MSCS Installation Folder>SDK/Samples/Solution Sites folder and look at various constants that will be used throughout the site. When you customize site pages or add new ones, you might need custom constants. Const.asp would be a good place to collect all such constants.

HTML Rendering Routines

The Html_lib.asp file contains a library of functions that help in rendering HTML content. These functions are pretty generic and can be called from any ASP page conveniently. Some of the functions are `RenderTextBox`, `RenderPasswordBox`, `RenderRadioButton`, `RenderCheckBox`, `RenderListBox`, and so on. As an example, the following is a function that returns the HTML code required to display a password box when called with appropriate parameters.

```
Function RenderPasswordBox(ByVal sName, ByVal sValue, ByVal iSize, ByVal
➥ iMaxLength, ByVal sAttList)
    RenderPasswordBox = "<INPUT TYPE=""PASSWORD"" NAME=""" & sName & """
➥VALUE=""" & sValue & """ SIZE=""" & iSize & """ MAXLENGTH=""" &
➥iMaxLength & """" & sAttList & ">"
End Function
```

Standard Libraries

A set of six files contain libraries of subroutines to give information that is specific to the site. These are

- std_access_lib.asp
- std_cache_lib.asp
- std_cookie_lib.asp
- std_profile_lib.asp
- std_url_lib.asp
- std_util_lib.asp

Numerous helper routines are in these files that deal with the following:

- Retrieval of current user information and profile
- Retrieval of site configuration properties
- Reading and writing cookies

- Determining user access to a page
- Getting IIS specific information such as application name and authentication type
- Manipulating order forms
- Converting generic functions such as list to array and getting array counts.
- Reading from and writing to caches
- Handling errors and logging them

Page to Setup the Environment

All the ASP files including default.asp contain a subroutine called Main that will be the entry point of execution for that page, after all include files have been processed. The file that calls this Main routine is the included file setup_env.asp. Setup_env.asp fetches various COM object instances stored in Application variables. The previous section on global.asa explains how these instances are initialized and stored. The setup_env.asp script fetches all those instances and stores them for local use by an ASP page.

For example, in setupenv.asp, the application level `MSCSAppConfig` object is used to get the site options set using the App Default Config resource.

```
Set dictConfig = Application("MSCSAppConfig").GetOptionsDictionary("")
```

The dictionary `dictConfig` is used throughout the site pages to get the properties set for the site. For instance, crdtcard.asp uses the key

```
dictConfig.s_BaseCurrencyCode
```

to get the base currency code set for the site. Similarly the connection string for the `OrderGroup` initialization is retrieved from this dictionary in std_ordergrp_lib.asp:

```
Call mscsOrderGrpMgr.Initialize
➥(dictConfig.s_TransactionsConnectionString)
```

Keys on the dictionary are used to store site settings. By looking at tables ExtendedProps and ResourceProps in the MSCSAdmin database, you can find out how each key is named such as i_BizTalkOptions and so on.

After getting these application-level environment values into local variables, this script calls the subroutine Main. Control now goes to the Main subroutine in the concerned ASP page; after which it returns to the last include file called layout1.asp, which takes care of laying out and displaying the various sections of the HTML page such as the banner, footer, body, navigation, and menu.

The Layout Page

As explained previously, layout1.asp is the file that acts as a template to display HTML to the client browser. In fact this script is found under the templates directory of the root site folder. Standard sitewide content such as the banner, footer, navigation bar, and menu bar are generated in this file as server side includes. An example is the following:

```
<! — #INCLUDE FILE="banner.inc" —> ' For the banner
<! — #INCLUDE FILE="navbar.inc" —> ' The navigation bar on top
<! — #INCLUDE FILE="menu.asp"  —>    ' The hyperlink menus
<! —#INCLUDE FILE="footer.inc" —>  ' The standard footer
```

The preceding sections are common to all the pages that include layout1.asp. Because the includes take care of most of the static content of a page, only page-specific dynamic content need to come from individual pages as a result of executing the Main subroutine. The Main subroutine stores that dynamically generated content to be displayed in a variable called htmPageContent, which is made use of by layout1.asp to write to the output stream.

Thus setup_env.asp sets up CS object references for local use, default.asp (or any other ASP file that has user interface) generates its own content, and layout1.asp displays the content. In Figure 5.6, we can see that default.asp includes the setup_env.asp and layout1.asp files.

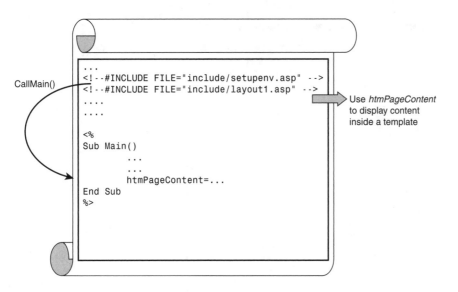

FIGURE 5.6
The relationship among setup_env.asp, layout1.asp, and default.asp.

The purpose of having a single file, layout1.asp, is to control the site's visual layout from a single place. Therefore, sitewide changes can be effected easily by just changing the layout in layout1.asp.

As illustrated in Figure 5.6, setup_env.asp, after fetching the application values defined in global.asa into local variables, finally issues a `Call Main()` statement. Hence the control now goes to the subroutine Main in default.asp. Main fetches catalogs to be displayed and builds the HTML content in the variable `htmPageContent`. At the end of the Main subroutine, control again transfers back to the next include file, layout1.asp. Layout1.asp now uses the variable `htmPageContent` to finally display the content to the browser.

This sequence of control flow is common to all site pages; that is, setupenv.asp calls `Main()`. `Main()` is defined in the page in which setupenv.asp is included. Therefore, control immediately transfers to the `Main()` routine on the page. After completing execution for the intended functionality of the page, control comes out of `Main()` and returns to the statement just after the location in which `Main()` was called. The statement just after Main is the processing of the include file layout1.asp. At this time, the page variable `htmPageContent` has the required HTML content to be displayed as a result of the `Main()` execution. Thus, layout1.asp puts the content stored in the `htmPageContent` variable on to the generated page sent to the browser.

Figure 5.7 will help you understand how the final HTML content is rendered by layout1.asp.

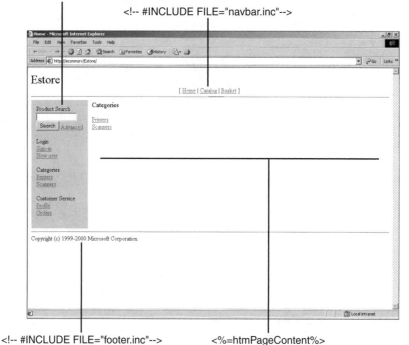

FIGURE 5.7

Layout1.asp is the template that writes the final HTML content.

The functions of the include files discussed so far are common across all site pages. Now we will examine what is unique to default.asp.

Browsing Catalogs

As you have seen so far, default.asp—the home page—is also the page that displays available catalogs to the user. Therefore, it has another file included to facilitate access to the product catalogs in the system, called catalog.asp. The server side include for that is the following:

```
<!— #INCLUDE FILE="include/catalog.asp" —>
```

Catalog.asp: The Core File

This file contains functions to return catalogs for a user and to display categories and information on products. This file will be included in many pages, such as products.asp, that need to access the catalog database of the site. Here is a brief list of catalog related functions that this library provides:

- Returns the default catalog set for the user
- Retrieves catalogs from a catalog set
- Lists the categories defined in a catalog
- Retrieves a list of products from a catalog or category
- Performs a free text search on catalogs
- Renders formatted HTML content to display catalogs, categories, and products

You will learn more about catalogs in the next chapter. For now, Figure 5.8 shows a brief layout of how products are organized.

Computer Accessories	**Catalog 1**
Printers	**Category 1**
HPDeskjet 970cxi	Product 1
Lexmark 3200 Color	Product 2
Scanners	**Category 2**
Umax Astra 200U	Product 1
Epson 1200U	Product 2
Books	**Catalog 2**
Computers	**Category 1**
ASP Fundamentals	Product 1
Programming SQL Server	Product 2
Business	**Category 2**
The Road Ahead	Product 1
Business @ the Speed of Thought	Product 2

FIGURE 5.8

Example of Catalogs, Categories, and Products.

NOTE

Estore doesn't contain all the products illustrated in Figure 5.8. This example is just to describe how catalogs, categories, and products are organized in Commerce Server.

Default.asp makes use of functions in catalog.asp and intelligently fetches the catalog hierarchy. On the home page, it lists catalog information based on the following algorithm:

```
Fetch Ids of catalogs that are available to the user
If there are no catalogs available to the user then
    Display no catalogs message
else
If there are more than one catalog(Ids) available to the user then
list the catalog names
else
    if there is only one catalog available to the user then
        if categories are defined in the catalog then
            list the categories
        else
if products are defined then
    list the products
else
    Display no products message
end if
        end if
    End if
End if
End if
```

In the Estore example, there is a single catalog with categories Printers and Scanners. The default page lists both the categories in the body of the page (refer to Figure 5.4). If there were more than one catalog, it would have listed catalog names first, with links to categories for each of them, and so on.

It is also interesting to know how the first step of fetching the catalog IDs for the Web site visitor is accomplished. The profile for the user is determined and analyzed to see if there are any catalogs attached to this profile. This is found out by retrieving the value in the user_catalog_set property of the AccountInfo dictionary of the user's profile object. In code, the following statement achieves it:

```
objUserProfile.Fields.Item("AccountInfo. user_catalog_set").Value
```

A catalog set is a named collection of catalogs available in the database. After individual catalogs are grouped in to catalog sets, the catalog sets can be assigned to a user's profile, based on the user's personalization information. If there are no catalogs found in the user's profile, one of two default catalog sets are used. By default, the visitor is either one of two User profiles: anonymous or registered. There is a default catalog set associated with each of these profiles. They are `AnonymousUserDefaultCatalogSet` and `RegisteredUserDefaultCatalogSet`, respectively.

In the Estore case, the user is anonymous and no custom catalogs are attached to the anonymous user profile. Therefore, it is determined that the user should be shown the catalogs from the `AnonymousUserDefaultCatalogSet`, which is basically to show all available catalogs that aren't part of any custom catalog set. For more about catalogs see Chapter 6, "Catalog Management."

Navigating Product Categories

After having dealt with the default page, it should be much simpler to understand what happens in the rest of the pages in the example flow (the dark lines in Figure 5.3) because all the ASP pages use a lot of common functions we have already discussed. You will see in brief the two interface pages that facilitate browsing of the products: category.asp and product.asp.

The Category Page

When the user clicks the category link on the home page, she is taken to the category page, which is served by category.asp. Similar to default.asp, this ASP page also has includes to all those libraries and constants discussed earlier. So you need to find out what is ultimately stored in the `htmPageContent` variable that will be displayed in the body section of the generated page.

As with every Main subroutine in all ASP pages of the commerce site, the function `EnsureAccess()` is called to ascertain whether the current user has access to this page, depending on the user type and user access. The user should not only have access to the page, but also to the catalog being requested. To ensure that, the function `EnsureUserHasRightstoCatalog` is called. This function is defined in the include file catalog.asp. Then the `querystring` values passed on from the default page for catalog name and category name are retrieved. These are combined to generate a cache key in the statement

```
sCacheKey = sCatalogName & sCategoryName & iPageNumber
```

The querystring `Page` is stored in `iPageNumber`.

Then the `ProductListCache` cache is searched using this key. If found, the value of the key, the HTML content, is stored in the `htmPageContent` variable. If the key wasn't found, the page uses functions such as `htmRenderCategoryPage`, defined in catalog.asp, to fetch results from the data base and generate HTML content. The content is stored in the cache under the same key without fail.

> **NOTE**
>
> The function `htmRenderCategoryPage` implements the algorithm discussed after Figure 5.8. That is, if the key isn't found in the cache, it means that this is the first time the catalog is accessed for this key combination. Thereafter `htmRenderCategoryPage` looks up the database for this key combination to fetch the records for the product.

Figure 5.9 shows how the content is delivered by category.asp for the Printers category in Estore.

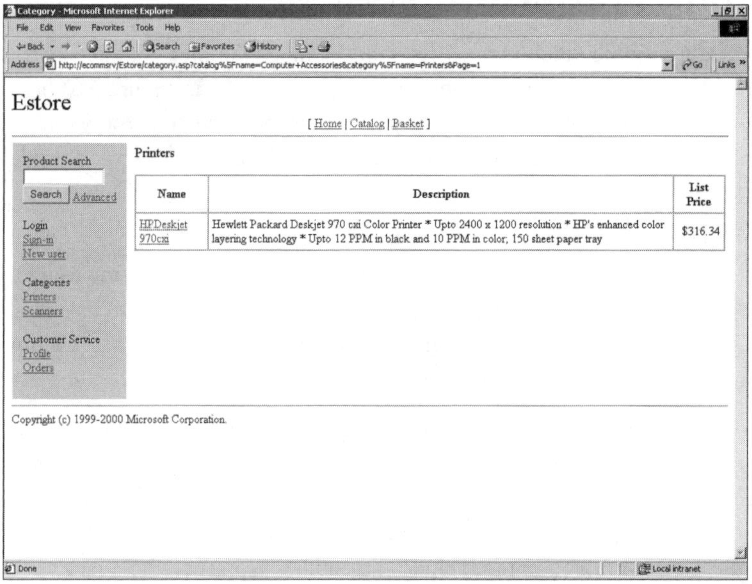

FIGURE 5.9

Category.asp actually gives product summaries.

The functions in category.asp use the `CatalogManager`, `CatalogSets`, and `Category` objects extensively to fetch information in the catalogs. These objects are part of the Product Catalog API. You will find that it is simpler to work with these objects to access the catalog database instead of having to access the database using ADO. The catalog API provides for rich functionality that can be exploited conveniently.

Given the inputs to this page, for instance, the following code segments illustrate the activity on this page that generates what you see:

```
....
' Get a reference to the ProductCatalog object
Set oCatalog = MSCSCatalogManager.GetCatalog(sCatalogName)


.....

' Get a reference to the Category object
set oCategory = oCatalog.GetCategory(sCategoryName)


.....

' Get the recordset of products in this category
rsProducts = oCategory.Products( , _
                                    sSortColumn, _
                                    nStartingRecord, _
                                    PRODUCTLIST_PAGE_SIZE, _
                                    NoutRecordsTotal)


....

' Get the name,description and cy_list_price attributes
'Loop through the rsProducts record set to render formatted HTML While Not

rsProducts.EOF
sProductName   = rsProducts.Fields("Name")
sProductDescription = rsProducts.Fields("description")
cyProductPrice  = rsProducts.Fields("cy_list_price")


.....

htmProduct = RenderProductLink(sCatalogName, sCategoryName, sProductName,
➥CStr(sProductID), MSCSSiteStyle.Body)


....

Wend


.....
```

All this functionality is neatly wrapped in catalog.asp. Fetching and rendering categories and products in a category are accomplished by numerous helper functions. The preceding segment should give you an idea of how these functions wrap some of the bare-bone statements.

Now when the user clicks on a product link, control goes to the product.asp page.

Caching Is Good

Before leaving the discussion on the category.asp page, another important topic to be discussed here is the use of caching. Commerce Server provides support for caching dynamic site content through the COM object Cache Manager, whose ProgID is `Commerce.CacheManager`. Remember that in global.asa, many caches were created and initialized in the `InitCacheManager()` function. By default, caches are provided for

- Advertisements as advertising
- Discounts as discounts
- Shipping as `ShippingManagerCache`
- Product List as `ProductListCache`
- QueryCatalogInfo as `QueryCatalogInfoCache`
- Default.asp as `DefaultPageCache`
- Product.asp as `ProductPageCache`
- Menu.asp as `StaticSectionsCache`
- Srchdept.asp as `SearchDeptPageCache`
- Stepsrch.asp as `StepSearchPageCache`
- Search.asp as `FTSearchPageCache`

Of course, you can create your own caches for custom purposes. A cache defined with the `CacheManager` is either a Dictionary object or an LRUCache object that is stored in the server's memory. The first time data is retrieved directly from the database, the results are stored as disconnected ADO recordsets in some cases; but in most cases, only the displayable HTML stream is saved in the cache. You will learn more about individual caches in various chapters ahead. Thus after content is cached, for subsequent queries the cache is looked up to fetch the results. A direct database access is necessary only when information cannot be found in the cache.

After a cache is set up with the Cache Manager, ASP pages can access a particular cache using the `GetCache` method. `GetCache` returns a reference to the Dictionary or LRUCache object. Each cache also has a component defined to populate the cache, called the `LoaderProgId` for the cache. Optionally, there is another component configured as `WriteProgId`—defined for the cache to write data that has been accumulated since the last refresh. Here is a snippet of code found in global_cache_lib.asp that is required to create a cache for the various static sections in menu.asp:

```
Set oCacheManager = Server.CreateObject("Commerce.CacheManager")

Set dictStaticSectionsConfig = Server.CreateObject("Commerce.Dictionary")
    dictStaticSectionsConfig("ConnectionString") =
    ➥dictConfig.s_TransactionConfigConnectionString
    dictStaticSectionsConfig("CacheSize") = 10000
    dictStaticSectionsConfig("TableName") = "CatalogCache_Virtual_Directory"
    dictStaticSectionsConfig("CacheName") = "CatalogCache"
    dictStaticSectionsConfig("AppUrl") = GetBaseURL()
oCacheManager.RefreshInterval("StaticSectionsCache") = 60 * 60
    oCacheManager.RetryInterval("StaticSectionsCache") = 5 * 60
    oCacheManager.CacheObjectProgId("StaticSectionsCache") =
    ➥"Commerce.LRUCache"
    oCacheManager.LoaderProgId("StaticSectionsCache") =
    ➥"Commerce.LRUCacheFlush"
    Set oCacheManager.LoaderConfig("StaticSectionsCache") =
    ➥dictStaticSectionsConfig
```

The RefreshInterval property is set to the number of seconds between refreshes for a cache. If you want to disable automatic refreshes, this value should be set to 0 and so on.

After the cache is created as previously shown, menu.asp uses it to retrieve stored information for its various sections such as search section, login section, customer service section, and so on. The code in menu.asp to render the search section is as follows:

```
htmSearchSection = LookupCachedFragment("StaticSectionsCache", "SearchSection")
    If IsNull(htmSearchSection) Then
        htmSearchSection =
        ➥htmRenderSearchSection(MSCSSiteStyle.Body, MSCSSiteStyle.Body,"")
        Call CacheFragment
        ➥("StaticSectionsCache", "SearchSection", htmSearchSection)
    End If

.....
    RenderMenu = RenderMenu & htmSearchSection
```

The LookupCachedFragment function, defined in std_cache_lib.asp, gets the cache using the GetCache method of CacheManager. After it has a reference to the StaticSectionsCache, which is an LRUCache object, it uses the Lookup method of the LRUCache object in the form:

```
oLRUCache.Lookup("key")
```

To retrieve the cache content for the search section, the following statement is used:

```
oLRUCache.Lookup("SearchSection" & sLanguage & "COOKIEMODE")
```

Continuing with the previous menu.asp code snippet, if there were no content returned from the cache for the search section, that is

```
If IsNull(htmSearchSection) ...,
```

Then the content is generated manually using the `htmRenderSearchSection` function. After that, this content is inserted in to the cache using the `CacheFragment` function, for future use. Basically the `CacheFragment` function does an insert in to the LRUCache object as follows:

```
Call oLRUCache.Insert(sCacheItemName & sLanguage & "COOKIEMODE", htmlString)
```

where `htmlString` is the content generated manually by the function `htmRenderSearch Section`. The same concept of caching is applied to database fetches for product list, shipping methods, and so on. Basically, the algorithm is as follows:

```
Get the cache
If content is found in cache retrieve and display
Else
    Retrieve content and display
    Insert content in cache for future use
End if
```

Testing Caches

To concretize what has been discussed about caching, let us leave some debugging code in std_cache_lib.asp inside a function that is used to fetch content from a cache.

In std_cache_lib.asp, inside the function `LookupCachedFragment`, add the following piece of code (if the code is already available, uncomment it) just before the `End Function` statement:

```
'If Not IsNull(LookupCachedFragment) Then
'    LookupCachedFragment = "<TABLE BORDER=1><TR><TD>Cached: " & sCacheName &
➡BR & sCacheItemName& sLanguage & "</TD></TR><TR><TD>" &
➡LookupCachedFragment & "</TD></TR></TABLE>"
'End If
```

After making this change and saving the file, unload your Web site application by right-clicking on the site in IIS. Then use the Properties page and click the Unload button for the site application. Now visit the site again. The application will be started again automatically after the first visit. But because this was the first visit, contents won't be fetched from cache, and the resulting page will be the same (refer to Figure 5.5). Now do a refresh or visit the default page again, and you will see from the debugging code that the content was indeed fetched from cache and was delivered very quickly (see Figure 5.10).

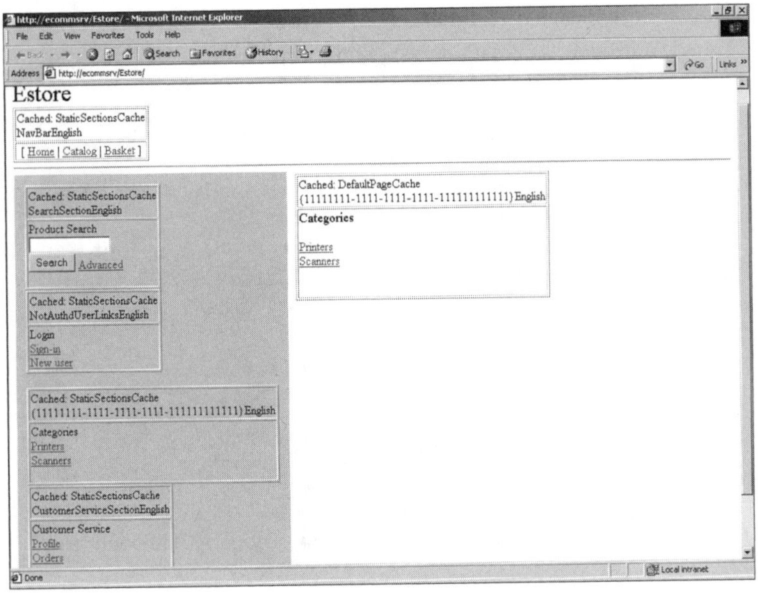

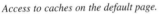

FIGURE 5.10

Access to caches on the default page.

It is no surprise that the catalog section is cached as the *Globally Unique Identifier(GUID)* {11111111-1111-1111-1111-111111111111} because it is the *identifier (ID)* for the catalog set Anonymous User Default CatalogSet in the database. Thus the first time the page was visited, the database was accessed to fetch both the catalog set ID and the HTML content generated for display. But it was saved in the cache under the GUID, and thus the page had to simply look up the GUID in the cache to fetch the HTML content.

Viewing Product Details

This ASP page is used to display detailed information about a product. The inputs (query-strings) to this page are catalog_name, category_name, and product_id. Apart from the usual common includes, the specific includes used by this page are catalog.asp and discount.asp. If the product had more than one variant, there would be another querystring for variant_id. The cache key for this page is formed as follows:

```
sCacheKey = sCatalogName & sCategoryName & sProductID & sVariantID
```

The HTML content for this page is stored in the cache ProductPageCache. So as usual, the page tries to look up this key in this cache. If found, the product page is there. Otherwise, the ASP script has to do a manual lookup at the database content using the Commerce Server

5

UNDERSTANDING
THE SITE
ARCHITECTURE

objects associated with the catalog just mentioned. Here is the typical algorithm used by wrapper functions found in product.asp, catalog.asp, and discount.asp.

```
....

'Get a reference to the specific ProductCatalog object
Set mscsCatalog = MSCSCatalogManager.GetCatalog(sCatalogName)
....
' Get a referene to the specific instance of the Product object
Set mscsProduct = mscsCatalog.GetProduct(sProductID)
....
' Get the recordset of the product
Set rsProperties = mscsProduct.GetProductProperties
' Get the attributes of the product like product_name and render HTML

sProductName = rsProperties.Fields("name").Value
....


'Display variants if defined for the product by looping through the
attributes.

' Determine if the product has variants
Set rsVariants = mscsProduct.Variants


....


' Iterate thru all variants and render each as a table row.
    While Not rsVariants.EOF
        bSelected = False

        If sSelectedVariantID =
    ➥rsVariants.Fields(sIdentifyingVariantProperty).Value Then
            bSelected = True
        End If

        arrDataCols(0) = RenderRadioButton("variant_id",
        ➥ rsVariants.Fields(sIdentifyingVariantProperty).Value,
        ➥ bSelected, MSCSSiteStyle.RadioButton)
....

        For i = 0 to listProps.Count - 2
            arrDataCols(i + 1) = rsVariants.Fields(listProps(i)).Value
        Next
...
```

```
        htmRows = htmRows & RenderTableDataRow(arrDataCols, arrAttLists,
        ➥ MSCSSiteStyle.TRMiddle)
rsVariants.MoveNext
    Wend
....


' Insert the generated HTML for the product details in 'ProductPageCache
Set oLRUCache = GetCache("ProductPageCache")
oLRUCache.Insert(sCacheKey & sLanguage & "COOKIEMODE", htmPageContent)


....


' Generate the HTML form elements for specifying Quantity and Add to basket
➥ button
htmFormContent = htmFormContent &
➥RenderText(mscsMessageManager.GetMessage
➥("L_Specify_Product_Quantity_HTMLText", sLanguage), MSCSSiteStyle.Body)
            htmFormContent = htmFormContent &
            ➥RenderTextBox(PRODUCT_QTY_URL_KEY, 1, 3, 3,
            ➥ MSCSSiteStyle.TextBox)

            sBtnText = mscsMessageManager.GetMessage("L_Add_To_Basket_Button",
            ➥ sLanguage)
            htmFormContent = htmFormContent &
            ➥RenderSubmitButton(SUBMIT_BUTTON, sBtnText,
            ➥ MSCSSiteStyle.Button)


....



' Get the discount info from DiscountProductInfo cache if available, 'this is
' to show a discount banner. Here' sCachekey is built using the following
' strings - sThisPage & ":" & sCatalogName & ":" & sCategoryName & ":" &
' sProductID & ":" & nPageNumber

Set oLRUCache = GetCache("DiscountProductInfo")
Set oCacheValue = oLRUCache.LookupObject(sCachekey)

' If discounts are not in cache get them
 using the ContentSelector object
....

Set oCSO = Server.CreateObject("Commerce.ContentSelector")
Set Discounts = oCSO.GetContent( Application("CSFDiscountContext") )
....
```

```
Set Discounts = oCSO.GetContent(Application("CSFDiscountContext"))
    For Each Discount In Discounts
        RenderDiscounts = RenderDiscounts & Discount
    Next
```

. . . .

> **NOTE**
>
> The previous code is the flow required to generate the product page. The actual execution takes place across multiple functions in various include files. But the main thread of processing resides in product.asp. Therefore, I have illustrated the generation of the product page as if all the work were done in a single page. However as previously mentioned, the core work for generating the product page is contained in product.asp, catalog.asp, and discount.asp. Thus, the product page is generated and displayed (see Figure 5.11).

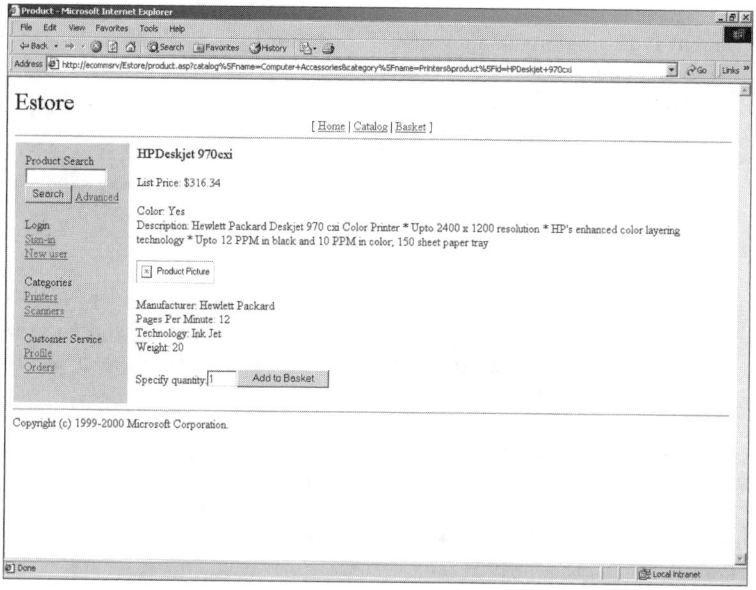

FIGURE 5.11

The product details fetched by product.asp.

Then the user enters a quantity to buy and clicks the Add to Basket button.

The Shopping Basket

The Shopping Cart Web page in an e-commerce site is the equivalent of a real-world shopping cart in which shoppers accumulate items at a single place. When the Add to Basket button is clicked in the previous page (refer to Figure 5.10), the form is actually submitted to an ASP script called _additem.asp, which after adding the item to the shopper's basket, redirects to the basket.asp page. The following section provides an overview of what happens in _additem.asp.

Adding Items Using _additem.asp

This page has an include to analysis.asp and std_ordergrp_lib.asp apart from the regular include files. Analysis.asp contains some simple wrapper functions to log events in the IIS log file, whereas std_ordrgrp_lib.asp has routines that deal with OrderForm and OrderGroup objects.

This file, _additem.asp ,creates and uses two important objects in Commerce Server: OrderGroup and OrderForm. An OrderGroup object is a container for individual OrderForm objects. In effect, each individual order is an OrderForm object, and an OrderGroup object contains a collection of OrderForm objects. The order forms contain their own product price, discount, and total price information, whereas the order group aggregates the individual order forms and contains the shipping, handling, and tax elements of the final order. Here is a code snippet that uses the OrderGroup and OrderForm objects.

```
'Get a reference to an OrderGroup object.
Set mscsOrderGrp = Server.CreateObject("Commerce.OrderGroup")
    Call mscsOrderGrp.Initialize(dictConfig.s_TransactionsConnectionString,
    ➥ UserID)
'loads the OrderGroup object in memory
 Call mscsOrderGrp.LoadBasket()


'Collect the basket information in a dictionary
Set dictItem = Server.CreateObject("Commerce.Dictionary")
dictItem.product_catalog = sCatalogName
dictItem.product_id = sProductID
dictItem.Quantity = iProductQty


'Create an OrderForm object. Now we have one each of OrderGroup and OrderForm
' objects
Call mscsOrderGrp.AddItem(dictItem) 'creates an OrderForm object with id as
➥ "default"


'Save the OrderGroup object as a basket
Call mscsOrderGrp.SaveAsBasket()
```

```
'Log this as a commerce server event("cevent") of type "AIBSK" in the IIS log
sString = "&CEVT={T=" & sCatalogName & sProductID & sVariantID & ...
Response.AppendToLog sString

'May redirect to basket.asp page or product.asp
```

This is what was written to my IIS log file after the item was added to the basket:

```
http://ecommsrv/Estore/product.asp?catalog%5Fname=
➡Computer+Accessories&category%5Fname=Printers&product%5Fid=
➡HPDeskjet+970cxi
2000-10-06 09:02:49 127.0.0.1 - 127.0.0.1 80 POST /Estore/_additem.asp
➡&CEVT={T=AIBSK,PRID="Computer+Accessories%3BHPDeskjet+970cxi"}
➡ 302 89 990 Mozilla/4.0+(compatible;+MSIE+5.5;+Windows+NT+5.0)
MSCSProfile=4DBD5F5E2ED46E9B9327CB027AB23D7A49E5AB4A35ED304714BBDD450377681C2D
➡2E5B7B1F246B273FB5EE21DF06C2E156EEE0A0CDBC9A1756B5A6C932FD53ECE09B7149
➡B5F7EBAC352723908EE5F083E5DE24765834DA4D629B1037EF82CF748F74D49AB97495
➡FE294B077CA01D0F88F515BADB05578C2564A15D665D43A2821D2CBBD6720FE0B7;
➡+CIHistory=;+ProfileVersion=10%2F5%2F2000+2%3A24%3A03+PM;
➡+ASPSESSIONIDQGQQQWAC=ILBPMNKCBPFHGDDPGDLJMCIC
```

Depending on the site configuration Add Item Redirect option, _additem.asp redirects to either basket.asp or back to product.asp. If the redirected page is product.asp, you can click on the Basket link in the navigation bar to go to the shopping basket page.

Basket.asp starts with executing an important concept in Commerce Server: pipelines. A *pipeline* is conceptually a sequential execution flow in which components work on an input object. The pipeline will have many stages and many components (COM) at each stage. The object that goes into the pipe (beginning of pipeline execution) is modified at the end of the pipe (end of pipeline execution). In basket.asp, the OrderGroup object is run through a pipeline that's configuration is set in basket.pcf. This pipeline typically calculates discounts, shipping, handling charges, and taxes and writes to each of the OrderForm object values such as order_subtotal as well as values such as taxes and order_total to the OrderGroup object.

The basket.pcf pipeline configuration file is loaded and run as shown:

```
iErrorLevel = mscsOrderGrp.RunPipe("pipeline/basket.pcf",
➡ "Commerce.PooledPipeline", dictContext)
if iErrorLevel is not 0 then there were some basket errors; display them
```

The errors that occurred while the pipeline was run can be logged to a file for debugging purposes. After the pipeline is run, the OrderGroup and OrderForm items will be updated with calculations such as discounts, subtotals, and so on. If a line item had a discount applied, the basket page will display columns to indicate the discount and effective price. If there were no discounts applicable, the basket page typically appears as shown in Figure 5.12. You will see in depth details about the OrderForm, OrderGroup, and Pipelines starting with Chapter 9, "Commerce Server Pipelines."

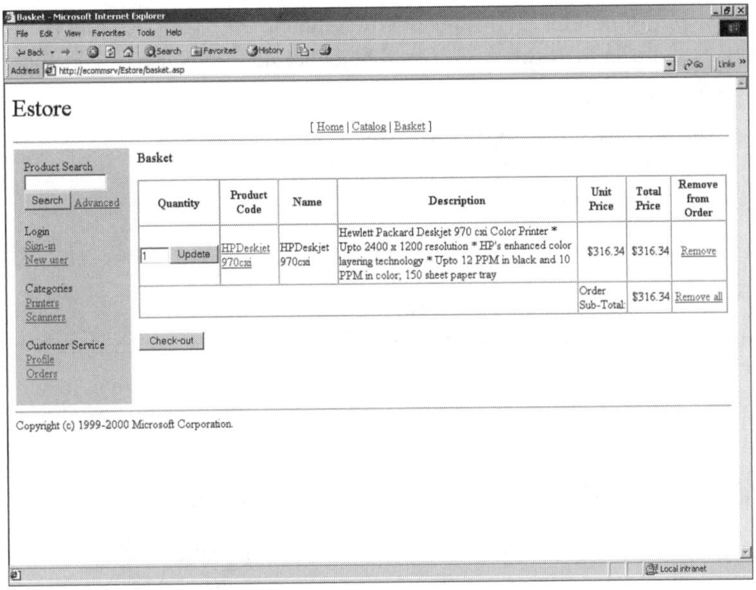

FIGURE 5.12
The basket details.

This page has a call to the Predictor object to get product recommendations. For example,

```
Set oPredictor = Application("MSCSPredictor")
oPredictor.Predict dCase, slToPredict, arPredictedProps, arPredictedVals,
➥ lMaxPredictions
```

Given the cases from the aggregate column and values to predict, the Predictor will return a number of values up to the number specified by lMaxPredictions in key and value pairs in the array variables arPredictedProps and arPredictedVals, respectively.

The specialized area of datawarehousing and predictions are covered in Chapter 15.

The basket page also has quite a few other useful areas of functionality, including the following:

- Editing the quantity for a line item
- Removing a line item
- Removing all items in the basket

Intermediate ASP pages that achieve these functions are

- _editqty.asp
- _delitem.asp
- _delall.asp

A form with a single submit button is generated on the basket page to enable the checkout process. The action attribute of this form could be either addrbook.asp or addrform.asp, depending on the following algorithm:

```
If the site visitor is an authorized user then
    If the AddressBookOption is enabled then
        Generate the submit button with action URL = addrbook.asp
    Else
        Generate the submit button with action URL = addrform.asp
    End if
Else
    Generate the submit button with action URL = addrform.asp
End if
```

Now we will go ahead and check out the basket to place an order.

Specify Shipping and Billing Addresses

In the Estore example, the shopper is an anonymous user, and hence addrform.asp is the page used to collect address information for the order (see Figure 5.13). In other cases, the addrbook.asp would be the action URL, which would display the address book for the current user. The user would then choose an address from the book or prefer to add new addresses. Continuing with Estore, observe that the form shown requires the user to first enter the shipping address for the order.

If both the shipping and billing addresses are the same, the user can check the appropriate check box provided for that purpose. If it is unchecked, addrform.asp is called again with a querystring of "address_type=2", which makes it show the input form for the billing address for the order. You can experiment with it without checking the option. But the form's action URL is always the page itself; that is, addrform.asp.

The page has a server side include to html_lib.asp, which contains a library of functions such as to render the form for shipping or billing address, find if the form was submitted to this page, get the form values, and validate the values in form fields.

If there are errors in the submitted form values, addfrm.asp renders the form with the previously entered values along with appropriate error messages. This form rendering and validation repeats as long as the form has errors. When there are no errors in the submitted values, addrfrm.asp inserts the address value in the OrderForm object using the following statement:

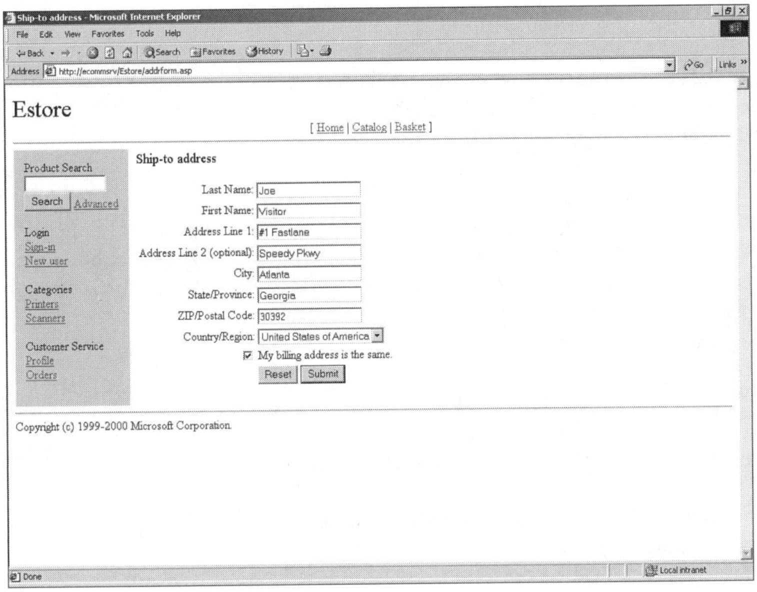

FIGURE 5.13
Address information collected for the order.

```
'sAddrID is a GUID, dictFldVals is a Dictionary object containing the address
➥ values.

Call mscsOrderGrp.SetAddress(sAddrID, dictFldVals)

'Save the mscsOrderGrp object changes from memory to database
Call mscsOrderGrp.SaveAsBasket()

'Redirect to the shipping methods page
urlRedirect = GenerateURL(MSCSSitePages.ShippingMethods, Array(), Array())
Response.Redirect urlRedirect
```

Choosing a Shipping Method

If no shipping methods are defined, the purchase process cannot be completed. Therefore, make sure that you have added at least one shipping method using the Shipping Methods module in the bizdesk. I have created two shipping methods called Overnight Delivery and Standard shipping, both as Charge By Subtotal type of charges. On being called, here is what pickship.asp does:

```
....

' Load in memory, the basket for the user which is essentially a ' '
'saved OrderGroup object. SOrderID is the user ID
Set mscsOrderGrp = LoadBasket(m_UserID)
....


' Get the Shipping Method is already specified, get it. This happens when
' users go till choosing a shipping method but dont complete the purchase.
' In that case the key shipping_method_id holds the method they had selected.

sSelectedMethodID = dictItem.Value("shipping_method_id")

....


'Try to get the shipping methods from the cache

htmCachedShippingMethods = LookupCachedFragment
➥("StaticSectionsCache", "ShippingMethods")


'If shipping methods are not found in cache get from the database using the
' ShippingMethodManager object.

Set mscsShipMgr = Server.CreateObject("Commerce.ShippingMethodManager")
    Call mscsShipMgr.Initialize(dictConfig.s_TransactionConfigConnectionString)

    arrCols = Array("shipping_method_id", "shipping_method_name",
"description")

    Set rsGetShippingMethods = mscsShipMgr.GetInstalledMethodList
    ➥("enabled=1", "shipping_method_name", arrCols)

....


'Now render the shipping methods and cache the methods

htmPageContent = htmRenderShippingMethods(mscsOrderGrp, rsMethods)
Call CacheFragment("StaticSectionsCache", "ShippingMethods", htmPageContent)

....
Make the first method selected or show the method if previously selected.

If IsNull(sSelectedMethodID) Then
                ' Set the default shipping method to the first available
                ' shipping method.
```

```
    htmPageContent = Replace(htmPageContent, "_checked", "_checked
➥ CHECKED", 1, 1, vbBinaryCompare)
Else
    ' Set the default shipping method to method user selected last
    ' time.
    htmPageContent = Replace(htmPageContent, sSelectedMethodID &
➥"_checked", sSelectedMethodID & "_checked CHECKED", 1, 1,
➥ vbBinaryCompare)
End If
```

....

The pick_ship.asp for Estore that currently has two shipping methods is shown in Figure 5.14.

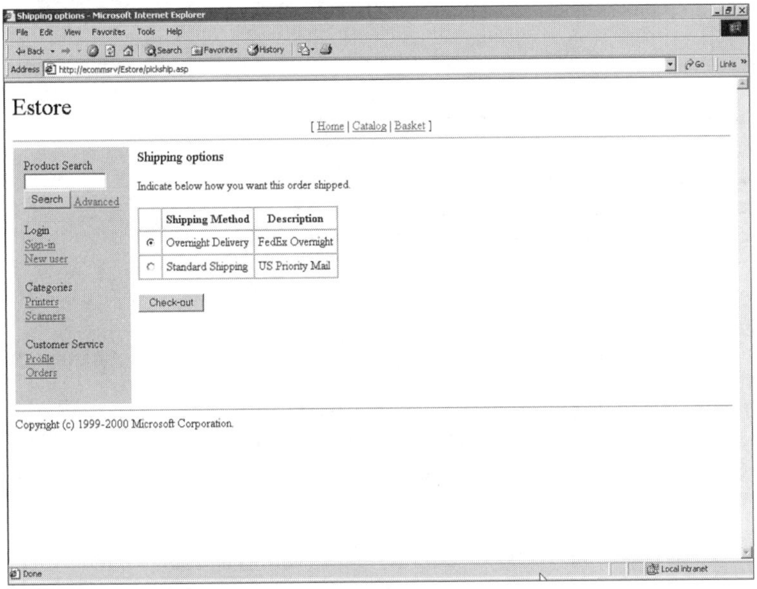

FIGURE 5.14
Choosing a shipping method.

The Checkout submit button is rendered with the action URL as _setship.asp. This intermediate page _setship.asp just puts the chosen shipping method information in the basket before redirecting the user to the order summary page:

```
....
'Put the shipping method id and name in the OrderGroup object
Call mscsOrderGrp.PutItemValue(SHIPPING_METHOD_KEY, sSelectedMethodID, True)
    Call mscsOrderGrp.PutItemValue(SHIPPING_METHOD_NAME, sSelectedMethodName,
➥ True)
```

```
'Save the mscsOrderGrp changes back to database
    Call mscsOrderGrp.SaveAsBasket()

'Redirect to summary.asp
Response.Redirect(GenerateURL(MSCSSitePages.OrderSummary, Array(), Array()))

....
```

The Order Summary

The Order Summary page is where the user sees the total cost of the order after shipping, handling, and taxes are added to the order subtotal. The order subtotal, in turn, is the sum of the effective price of each product in the basket. The helper routines for this page's functionality come mainly from payment.asp and catalog.asp. Here are the key activities in the work flow for summary.asp:

```
....
'Load the basket(OrderGroup) into memory

Set mscsOrderGrp = LoadBasket(m_UserID)
' Get all payment methods applicable to user.
    Set listMethods = GetPaymentMethodsForUser()

....

'run the basket.pcf pipeline on the OrderGroup to calculate prices, discounts
' etc to arrive at the subtotal for the order.
iErrorLevel = RunMtsPipeline(MSCSPipelines.Basket,
➥ GetPipelineLogFile("Basket"), mscsOrderGrp)iErrorLevel =
➥mscsOrderGrp.RunPipe("pipeline/basket.pcf", "Commerce.PooledPipeline",
➥ dictContext)
....
'if there is an error redirect to basket page for the user to correct problems.
If iErrorLevel > 1 Then
        Response.Redirect(GenerateURL(MSCSSitePages.Basket, Array(), Array()))
    End If
....

'run the total.pcf pipeline on the OrderGroup to add shipping, handling and
' taxes to arrive at the Order total.
iErrorLevel = RunMtsPipeline(MSCSPipelines.Total, GetPipelineLogFile("Total"),
➥ mscsOrderGrp)
' Add discount footnote symbols to each lineitem
    Call AddDiscountMessages(mscsOrderGrp)

....
```

```
'render the HTML code for displaying the order summary in a table
htmPageContent = htmRenderSummaryPage(mscsOrderGrp, mscsAnyOrderForm,
➥ dictAnyItem, listMethods, bBadVerify)
```

. . . .

If the Web site visitor is anonymous, allow only Credit Card as a valid payment method. This is her default and only payment method. If the visitor is a registered user, all payment methods included explicitly in the site configuration are allowed. The first payment method is usually chosen as the default method. Depending on the default payment method for the user, an action URL is selected for the Checkout button. If the method is Credit Card, the URL is crdtcard.asp; if it is the purchase order payment method, it will be po.asp. The summary page is shown in Figure 5.15.

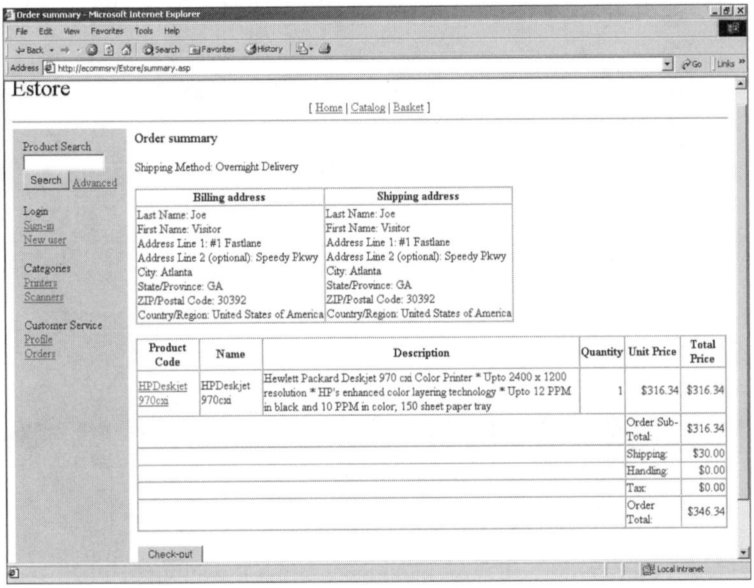

FIGURE 5.15

The Order Summary page.

The user now has a chance to verify and confirm the items in the order before proceeding to the checkout by specifying a payment method.

As I said earlier, depending on the payment method, the control goes to either crdtcard.asp or po.asp. In the example, clicking the Checkout button takes the user to the crdtcard.asp that collects credit card information.

Pay for Your Purchase

Similar to the addrform.asp page that was discussed earlier, crdtcard.asp acts as both the script to generate the credit card input form as well as the script to process the form. The first time crdtcard.asp is called as a result of doing a checkout from the summary page, it basically renders the Credit Card form (see Figure 5.16) with Name on Card filled in from the billing address. The action URL of the form is set to crdtcard.asp. The main helper functions for credit card processing are defined in payment.asp.

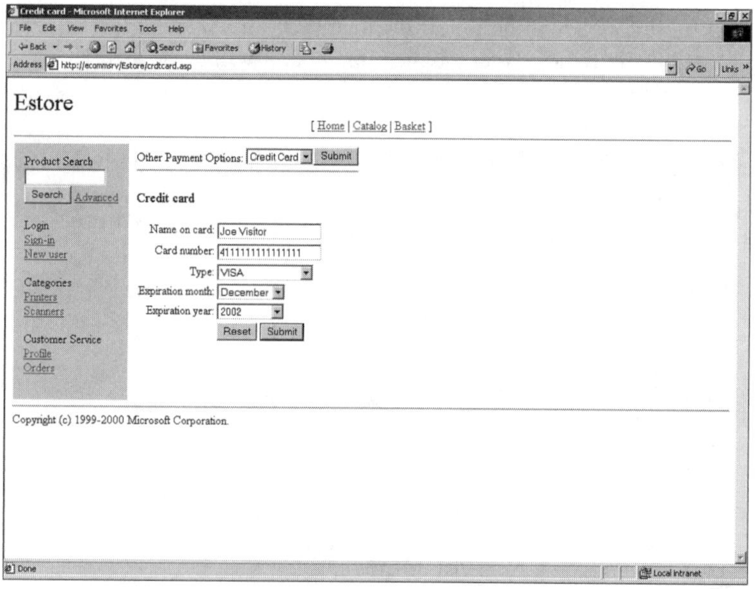

FIGURE 5.16

The Credit Card form.

When the user enters the credit card information and clicks the Submit button, control goes once again to crdtcard.asp. Now a check is made in crdtcard.asp to detect whether the form was submitted. If so, the values of the credit card form are accessed and validated. Remember that the form contains fields for credit card number, credit card type, name on the card, and so on.

```
....
Set dictFldVals = GetSubmittedFieldValues(listFlds)
iErrorLevel = ValidateSubmittedCreditCardData(mscsOrderGrp, listFlds,
➡ dictFldVals, dictFldErrs, listFrmErrs, sVerifyWithTotal)
....
```

In the `ValidateSubmittedCreditCardData` function, the fields of the credit card form are validated against standard rules such as maximum length, minimum length, valid characters, and so on. If the fields of the form passed the validations, the OrderForm is run through the checkout.pcf pipe to perform order form–level validations. But before that, the credit card form details are added to the order form, inside the `SetKeyOnOrderForms` functions, which are called by the SetCreditCardInfo function:

```
....
For Each sOrderFormName In mscsOrderGrp.Value.OrderForms
        Call mscsOrderGrp.PutOrderFormValue(sKey, sValue, sOrderFormName)
    Next
....
```

After the credit card details are set on the order form, the `CheckOut` function runs the basket, total, and checkout pipelines on the order form:

```
....
iPipeErrorLevel = CheckOut(mscsOrderGrp, sVerifyWithTotal)
....
```

You will see in detail the internals of pipeline execution in later chapters dedicated to Commerce Server pipelines.

Basically if `iPipeErrorLevel` is `0`, it means that the order form was successfully run through the pipes without errors. Then the function `SaveBasketAsOrder` is called to save the order from the basket to the order status. Here is the `SaveBasketAsOrder` function:

```
Sub SaveBasketAsOrder(mscsOrderGrp)
    Dim mscsOrderGrpMgr

    ' Remove any addresses from the orderform which are not referenced
    Call mscsOrderGrp.PurgeUnreferencedAddresses()

    Call mscsOrderGrp.SaveAsOrder()

    ' Submit appropriate OrderForms using BizTalk
    Call InvokeBizTalk(mscsOrderGrp)

    Set mscsOrderGrpMgr = GetOrderGroupManager()
    Call mscsOrderGrpMgr.DeleteOrderGroupFromDisk(m_UserID)

    Call Analysis_LogSubmitOrder(mscsOrderGrp.Value(ORDERGROUP_ID))
    'Do this last, as it can't be rolled back

End Sub
```

5

UNDERSTANDING THE SITE ARCHITECTURE

The statement that does save the order is the `SaveAsOrder()` method of the `OrderGroup` object. I will talk more about this method and the various database changes in Chapter 10, "Order-Processing Pipelines." Similarly, it is sufficient to understand now that the `InvokeBizTalk` function is is used to submit the order to the BizTalk server when Commerce Server and BizTalk are integrated. I will cover BizTalk integration in Chapter 16, "Integration and Development." The last statement dealing with Analysis also warrants special discussion in Chapter 15.

After the `SaveAsOrder` function, the user is ultimately redirected to the confirm.asp page.

Order Confirmation

This is a simple script that typically marks the end of a shopping process. It loads the order to know the order ID or number. The order number is displayed in the page for the shopper's reference (see Figure 5.17).

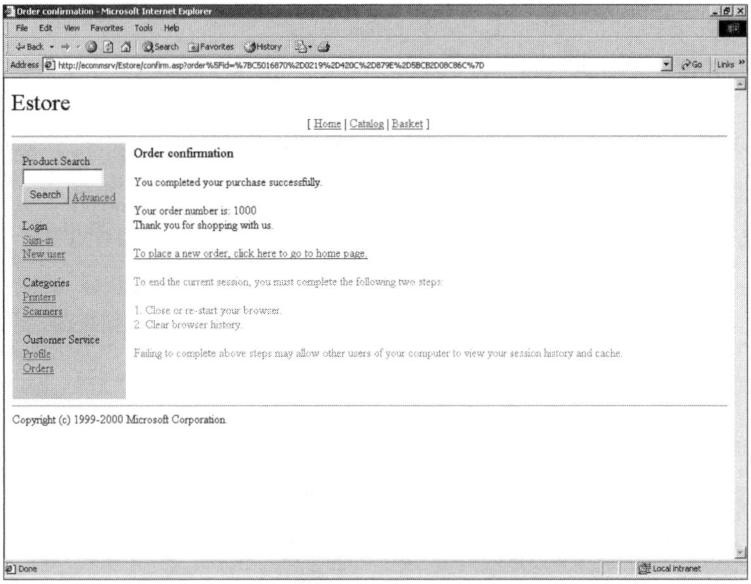

FIGURE 5.17

Order confirmation.

Summary

In this chapter, we analyzed the basic site generated by Site Packager. We took a typical user interaction with the site as a case and looked behind the scenes as the application processed the various Commerce Server elements such as ASP pages and COM objects. Specifically, we covered the helper files that are included commonly in most of the ASP pages throughout the site. These files contain constants, libraries of functions, and subroutines that will be used by ASP pages. Then we also looked at special include pages such as catalog.asp, payment.asp, analysis.asp, and form_lib.asp, which are included in pages that perform specialized functions for the site such as accessing catalogs, processing a credit card form, and so on. We also had the chance to look at some of the intermediate ASP scripts such as _additem.asp and _setship.asp that actually perform vital functions but don't interact directly with a browser. Finally we took a peek at many of the key Commerce Server COM objects such as `CatalogManager`, `CacheManager`, `OrderGroup`, `AppConfig`, and `Predictor`.

Given the fact that Commerce Server contains a wide range of services and objects to support many facets of e-commerce, this chapter doesn't bog you down with many details. Instead, I gave you an overview of the bare bones Commerce Server site so that you can get your feet wet before diving into the depths of Commerce Server. Catalog Management is next.

5

UNDERSTANDING
THE SITE
ARCHITECTURE

Advanced Topics

PART

II

IN THIS PART

6 Catalog Management 117

7 User Management 187

8 Personalization and Targeting 217

9 Commerce Server Pipelines 249

10 Order-Processing Pipelines 277

11 Direct Mailer and Content Selection Framework Pipelines 323

12 Running Ads and Auctions 363

13 Building and Customizing Pipelines 395

14 Extending the Business Desk 441

15 Data Warehouse, Reports, and Prediction 485

16 Integration with BizTalk Server 533

Catalog Management

IN THIS CHAPTER

- Basics of a Commerce Server Catalog   119
- Creating Catalogs   133
- Importing and Exporting Catalogs   148
- About Product Variants   156
- COM Objects for the Catalog System   161
- Showing Related Products   168
- Searching the Catalogs   174

Business organizations around the world are trying to reach many different objectives. However, from the financial angle, the primary objective remains the same: that is, to increase the net worth of the company by increasing revenues and profits. In the e-tail environment, this amounts to selling more and more products or services on your company Web site to the consumer. In the early days of the Internet, the Web sites of companies were just "brochure wares." These Web sites were only an online replica of the printed catalogs that a company used to send by snail mail. With the arrival of new technologies, these static catalog pages have become active product pages, with the possibility of personalizing products and prices. But the fundamental feature of an electronic catalog still mirrors a printed catalog in terms of content. A product purchasable online contains a unique item number called the *Stock Keeping Unit (SKU)*: It has a list price, a dated discount option, shipping charges, and so on.

The only difference between printed and online catalogs is the fact that customers might visit physical stores after seeing catalogs, whereas such an opportunity might not be available with online stores. This differentiation of online versus printed catalogs not only applies to online-only shops such as Amazon.com, but also to dual sales channel stores such as Office Depot. Even though Office Depot still has printed catalogs, its online catalogs have the power to present more information and be more interactive. Also, there are many unique advantages only a virtual store can give, such as central inventory and reduced overheads. Therefore, increasingly many companies treat their dot.coms as separate divisions. Hence, most of the time for an e-Commerce site, the catalogs are the store and the store represents browsing the catalogs. The catalogs give the site visitor the virtual shopping experience, which could make shopping a pleasure or a "cyber-nightmare," depending on how conveniently or complex the catalog is served to the browser.

Managing online catalogs hasn't been always easy. Designers have had to keep in mind the varying structure of products and variants, as well as presenting the products in catalogs for easy accessibility. Managers had to worry about maintaining appropriate prices and offering discounts in a timely manner. Further, catalogs could be coming from suppliers and had to be sent to upstream value-added sellers. Finally, site administrators had to do whatever was necessary to make the current updated catalog available to site visitors as soon as possible. Commerce Server provides you with a comprehensive Catalog Management system, complete with extensible components such as the database store, BizDesk modules to manage catalogs conveniently, and COM objects in the catalog *application program interfaces (API)* of Commerce Server that can integrate catalogs with external systems.

First you will learn the fundamentals of the catalog architecture in Commerce Server. Then you will create schema definitions as well as products to demonstrate the creation of a complete catalog. After that you will move on to look at ways to integrate the catalog system by importing from or exporting to external catalogs. Finally, you will look at the commonly used COM objects in the Commerce Server Catalog API.

Basics of a Commerce Server Catalog

In a Commerce Server site, a catalog essentially contains products organized under appropriate categories. The Catalog Management System consists of the data store to hold the information and also the necessary COM objects to interact with the data store. The diagram (see Figure 6.1) shows a symbolic view of the catalog system.

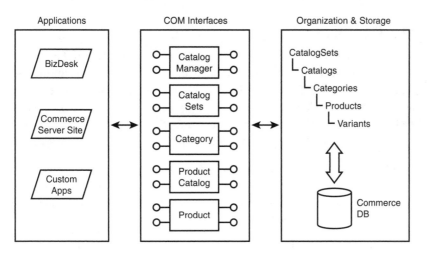

FIGURE 6.1
Commerce Server Catalog System: The Big Picture.

In the Estore example, the catalog was named as Computer Accessories and it contained the Printers category. Under the Printers category was a product named HPDeskjet 970cxi that didn't have any variants. When we used the Business Desk to create the catalog, category, and product, specific information was collected for each of these elements. For instance, in creating a catalog, properties such as name, currency, start date, end date, and unit of weight were entered. While creating a category, values of properties such as name and description were keyed in and saved.

Similarly, a lot of values relating to the product such as name, description, price, and manufacturer were saved for the product. How does Business Desk know what information to collect for each of these elements? The answer is that a definition, also called a *schema*, defines what values describe these elements in the catalog system. The categories and products that are placed in it define a catalog. A category is defined by a Category Schema and a product by a Product Schema. The property definitions such as name, description, manufacturer, and so on are defined individually and then can be attached to the category or product schemas. Therefore, the three main definitions that are fundamental to creating a catalog are

- Property definitions
- Product definitions
- Category definitions

These three types of definitions will be addressed in the next three sections.

Property Definitions

A *property* is an attribute that describes the element to which it is attached. For example, when the property Name is included in the definition of a category, its value indicates the name of the category. Similarly the name of a product is also captured using the Name property, which is included as a part of the product definition. Thus a property can be defined once and in turn can be used by any number of category or product definitions. What does a property definition contain? You can find out by looking at a predefined property using the Business Desk.

Launch the Business Desk, navigate to the Catalogs menu, and click the Catalog Designer. The Catalog Designer module is used to create and manage all three types of definitions mentioned earlier. Because you want to look at a typical property definition, click the toolbar option to view Property Definitions (see Figure 6.2).

The launched page contains the first 20 property definitions that are stored in the catalog system. Note that the page displays the List Total as the total number of properties in the catalog and the Page *N of M* formatted value. This helps in navigating to the property that you want to view or edit. Remember the *Pages Per Minute (PPM)* value that was entered as a part of the product information for the HPDeskjet printer? Look at the definition of this property. To do so, browse to the second page of the list by clicking the Next Page arrow button at the bottom right corner just below the Properties list (see Figure 6.3).

On clicking the Next Page button, Business Desk loads the next set of property lists. To view the property definition details of the property PPM, highlight PPM, and click the toolbar button for Open Property Definition or press ALT+O (see Figure 6.4). You will see that the basic type of this property is a number.

The schema for the property PPM is shown in Figure 6.5.

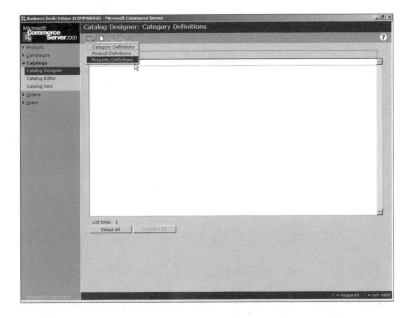

FIGURE 6.2

The Property Definitions menu option.

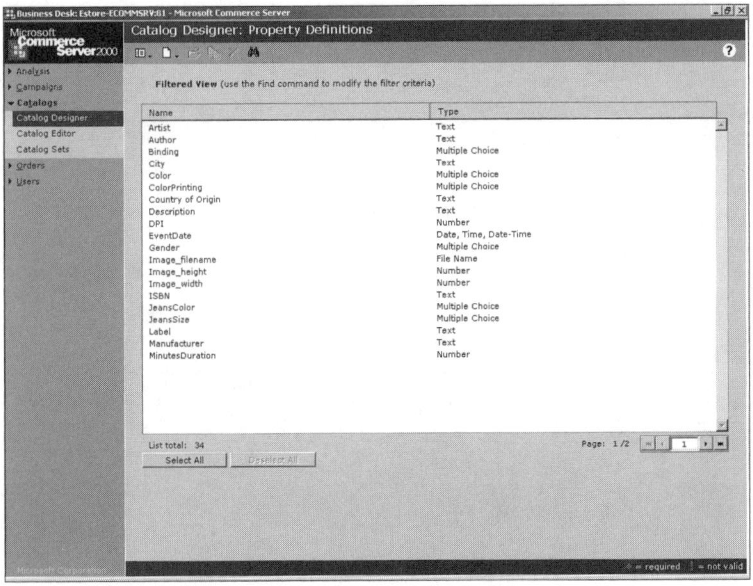

FIGURE 6.3

Browsing the Properties list.

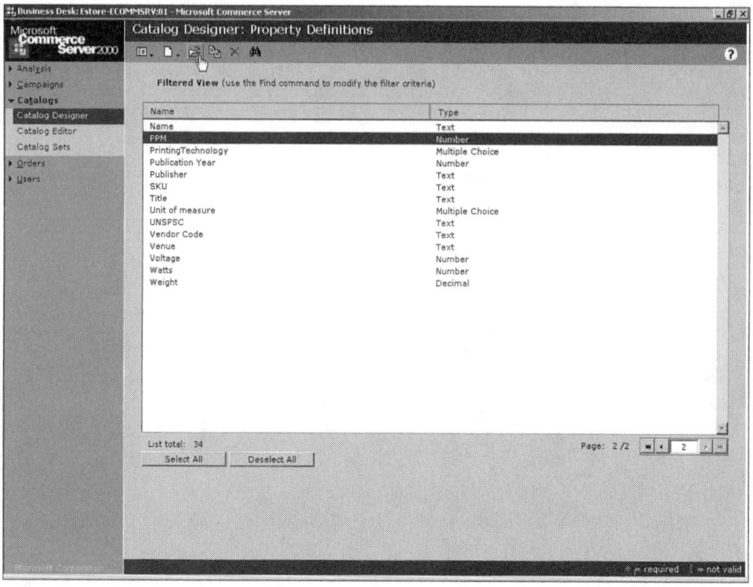

FIGURE 6.4

The PPM property type.

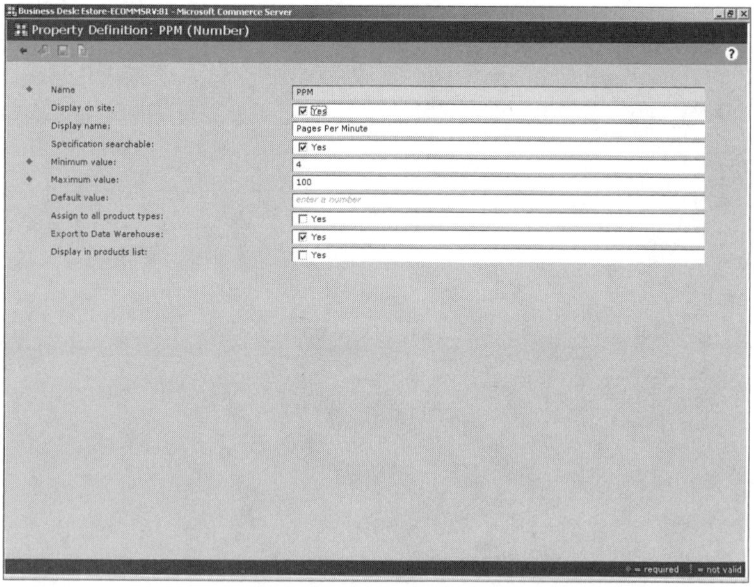

FIGURE 6.5

A property definition.

Every property has a name defined for it as well as certain field validations built into the defin-ition. The name of the pages per minute property is PPM. The minimum value that will be enforced while collecting the value of this property is 4 and the maximum value is 100. Of course, these values could be changed according to the company's requirements. The other attributes of this property, such as Default value and Specification Searchable, give additional characteristics to the property. The fields marked with a red diamond symbol are mandatory. While creating a product whose schema includes the PPM property, all these rules will be enforced when specifying the value of the PPM property for the product. For example, in the Estore example, a value of 12 was the pages per minute for the HPDeskjet printer product. Similarly, we created the Printers category by setting the Name property of the category as the value Printer.

In effect, a property definition describes the data type, the allowable values, and additional attributes of the property. This property can then be included as part of either a product defini-tion or a category definition (see Figure 6.6).

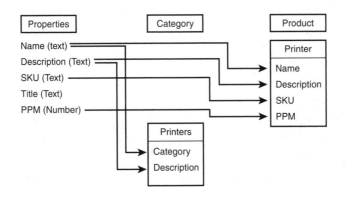

FIGURE 6.6

Properties are used in category and product definitions.

Creating a Property Definition

In addition to the Printers category in the Estore example, assume that you are adding a Scanners category to the Computer Accessories catalog. A scanner is described by certain attributes such as name, *dots per inch (DPI)*, ColorDepth, and so on. Common attributes such as name and DPI are already provided by Commerce Server as property definitions. So, say that you have to define the schema for ColorDepth. We can further assume that ColorDepth is a property of the scanner that will typically have a range of values between 8 and 42 bits. Therefore, your objective is to create a property definition with the following attributes:

Name:	ColorDepth
Type:	Multiple choice (values between 8 and 42)
Available:	To all product schemas
Searchable:	In free text searches

In the Catalog Designer module, click the New Property Definition toolbar button (or press the ALT+N) and choose Multiple Choice as the property type (see Figure 6.7).

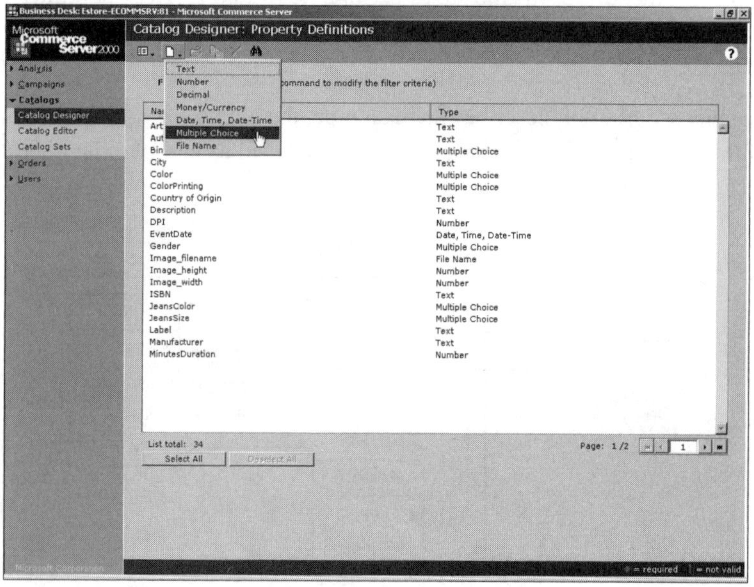

FIGURE 6.7

Choosing a type for a property.

In the edit form that comes up, enter the values and choices as shown in Figure 6.8. The name of the property is ColorDepth, and it will be displayed on the site as Color Depth. Note the options that could be checked to make this property searchable in both free-text as well as step searches. (These will be discussed later in the chapter.) Finally, the Default value list for the property has to be populated so that when the user enters values for this property while creating a product, one of the listed values can be chosen conveniently. To enter those values as part of the property schema, click the browse button next to the Default value list box (see Figure 6.8).

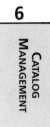

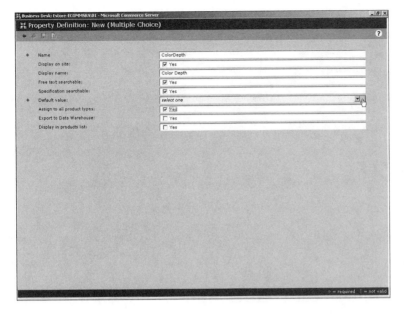

FIGURE 6.8

Default value for a multiple-choice property.

After clicking the browse button, the Multiple Choice dialog box launches, which will be used to enter the range of values that this property can have. In the New Value text box, enter the values and press the Add button for each of the values entered. These values will then be listed in the Values box. After entering the values, click the OK button (see Figure 6.9).

After the values are entered, you can choose a default value that will be displayed in the Catalog Editor for the ColorDepth attribute when a product of type Scanner is being created. Choose 32-bit from the drop-down list box and click the toolbar for Save and Back to Property Definitions List or press ALT+K (see Figure 6.10).

Now you should see ColorDepth as one of the properties in the Property Definitions list with its type being Multiple Choice.

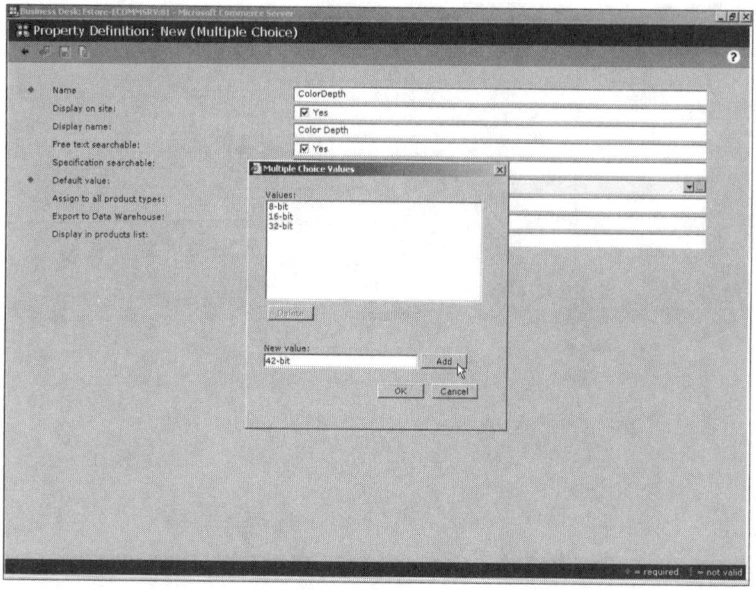

FIGURE 6.9

Values for a multiple-choice property.

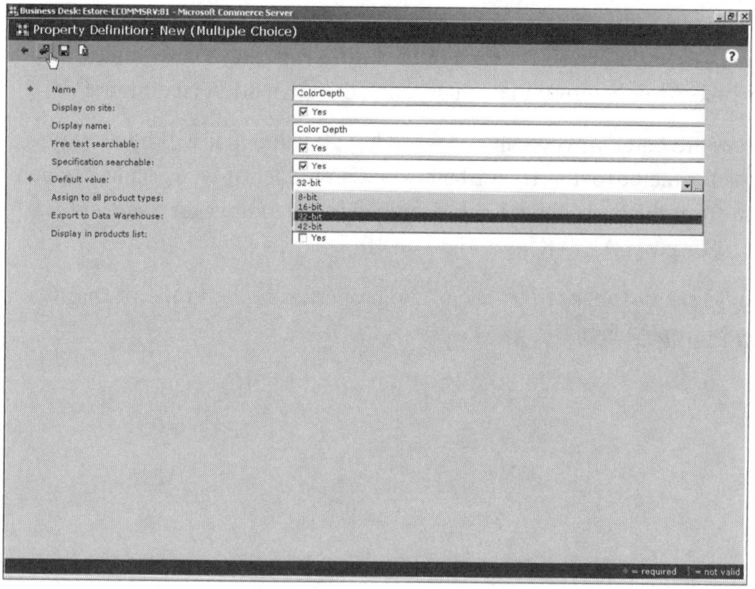

FIGURE 6.10

Setting default value for a multiple-choice property.

Product Definitions

Because I believe at this point that we have enough properties to describe a scanner, I will now define a product schema (or scheme a product definition) that will represent a scanner. To reinforce your understanding, the Catalog Designer module is used to define schemas whereas the Catalog Editor is used to create values based on the schemas. Further, a product definition is created by including properties (that were defined already) that describe the product. A definition for a scanner is shown in Figure 6.11.

NOTE

A definition for a product needs to exist before an actual product of that type can be entered into the catalog using the Business Desk.

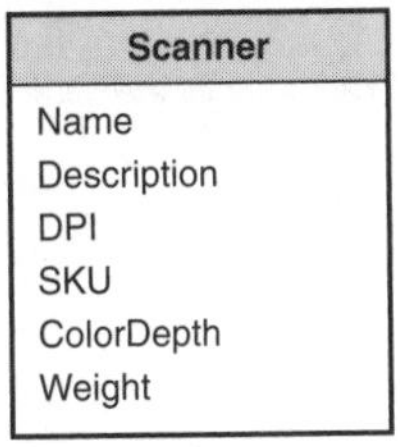

FIGURE 6.11

Product definition for a scanner.

Before you begin to create a product definition, look at the existing product definition for a printer that was used to create a product called HPDeskjet 970cxi for your catalog.

In the Catalog Designer, click the toolbar button View Catalog Definitions or press ALT+V. Then choose Product Definitions. A list of product definitions in the catalog system is displayed. Double-click the definition for Printer. You will see the properties that describe a printer and are part of the product definition for a printer (see Figure 6.12).

You can double-click other product definitions also and check out the properties that are included in each product. Curiously, the property ColorDepth, which was defined earlier, is also found in all the product definitions.

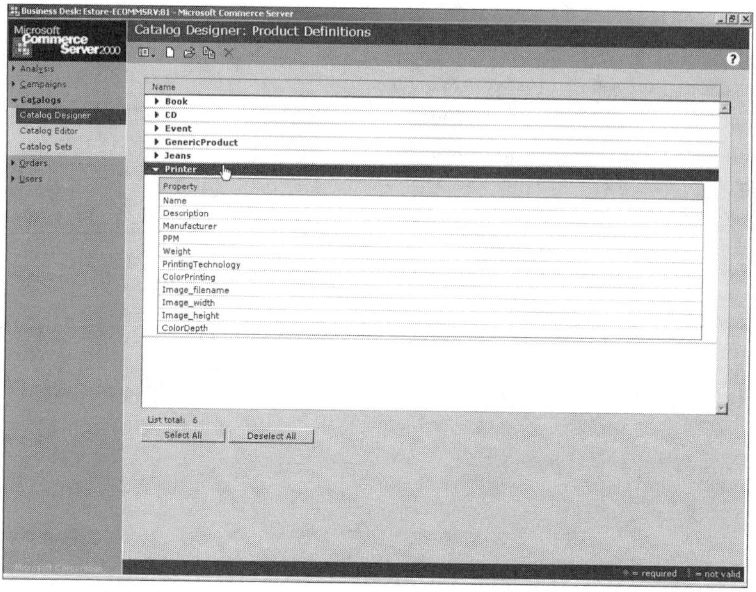

FIGURE 6.12

A product definition list view.

CAUTION

You checked the Assign to All Product Types check box (refer to Figure 6.10) when creating the property definition ColorDepth earlier. Automatically, this property was then added to all product definitions, which you might or might not have intended. At this point, even if you unchecked this status, the property is only omitted from new product definitions because the status still exists in current ones. The only way to remove this property is to remove it individually from each product definition. Therefore, use caution while defining property definitions. You don't want to add them to existing product definitions!

If you want to either delete a property or update some other element in a product definition, click the Open Product definition (the open folder icon) toolbar button or press ALT+O after choosing the product definition in the list. To modify the product definition for Printer, highlight it and press ALT+O or click the toolbar button. Give the product definition a name such as Printer and assign properties to the definition from a list of available properties. To add more properties to the product, choose Properties in the Available Properties list box and press Add, which places them in the Assigned Properties list box (see Figure 6.13). In order to remove the `ColorDepth` property from the Printer product definition, choose the `ColorDepth` property in the Assigned Properties list box and press Remove. Then press ALT+K or click the Save and back to Product Definitions List toolbar button to save the changes and return.

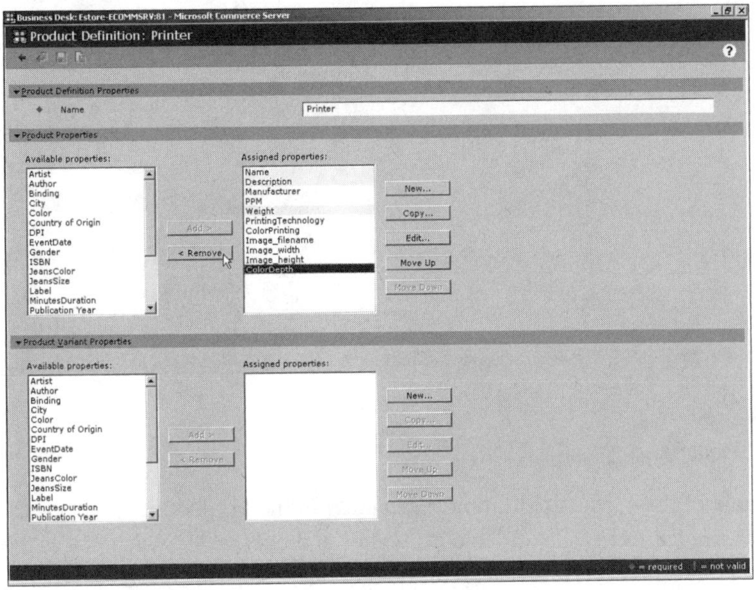

FIGURE 6.13
Detailed definition of a product.

Now if you double-click Printer in the product definitions list, the `ColorDepth` property will no longer be attached to the product definition. If you aren't able to delete the property, it is probably being treated as mandatory similar to Name, Description, and Weight. You can find mandatory properties with a colored background in the Assigned Properties box. (The colored background appears as grayscale in Figure 6.13.)

Creating a Product Definition

Its time to create your product schema for Scanner with the properties designed as per our discussion earlier (refer to Figure 6.11). In the Product Definitions page of the Catalog Designer module, press ALT+N or click the New Product Definition toolbar button. The page that loads is very similar to the one you saw when modifying the product definition for Printer. Enter the definition for Scanner as shown in Figure 6.14.

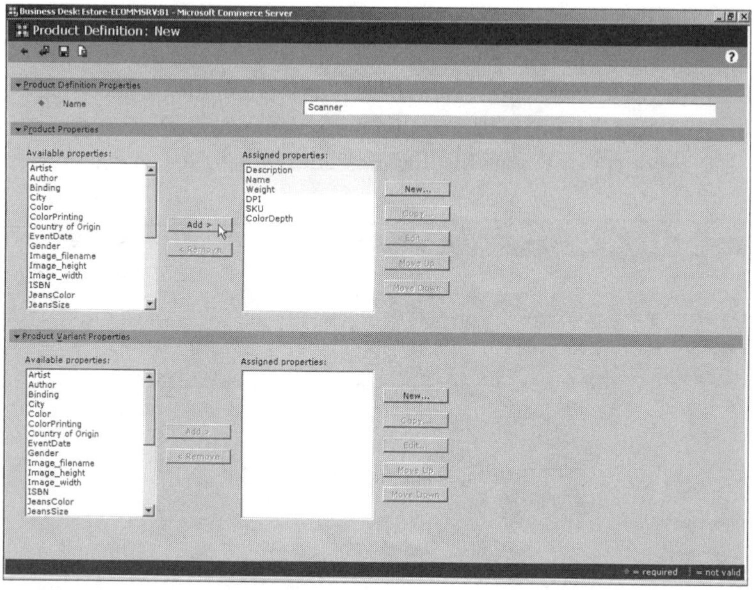

FIGURE 6.14

Defining a Scanner product.

Enter the Name of the product definition as Scanner. In the Product Properties section, choose the properties needed from the Available Properties and click Add, which places them in the Assigned Properties text box. You can save the product definition by either pressing ALT+K or clicking the appropriate toolbar button. Then return to the product definitions list, where you should see the definition for Scanner. When you expand the arrow symbol, its assigned properties should be visible (see Figure 6.15).

You have successfully defined a product schema that you will use while creating a scanner product for your Estore catalog.

Category Definitions

Recall that a category is a container to hold products. In Estore, there is a product called HPDeskjet 970cxi in the category Printers. It will be easier for users to find and navigate to products if they are organized according to common classifications. Therefore, it would be logical to organize printers under a category called Printers, and individual scanners would be organized under a category called Scanners. Also, a product could be made part of many categories if it needed to be. Similar to a product definition, a category has its own definition that consists of properties. For instance, the properties, Name and Description, which are of type Text can be part of a category schema to define the category name and description. These very same properties could also be part of a product definition for describing the product name and description. In short, a property definition could be made use of by either product or category definitions.

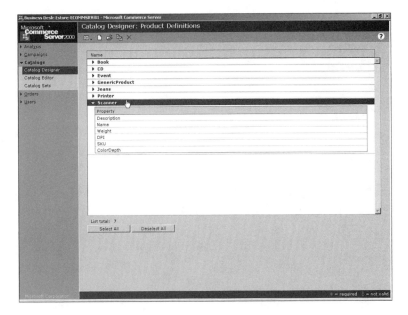

FIGURE 6.15
A list view of the Scanner definition.

Creating Category Definitions

Next, we will define the category Scanners by how we want to organize individual scanner products. For the sake of simplicity, assume that the schema for a scanner category is the same as that shown in Figure 6.16.

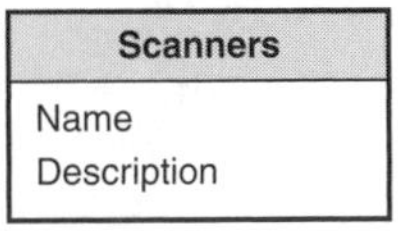

Scanners
Name
Description

FIGURE 6.16
Definition for Scanners category.

Click the Category Definitions menu option from the Catalog Designer module to go to the Category Definitions page. You will see the category called Department, which is provided by default installation. Double-click on the category to check the properties that are included as part of the category definition. Now click the New Category Definition toolbar button or press ALT+N to load the category definition page (see Figure 6.17).

In the New Category Definition page, enter the name of the category as **ScannersCategDefn** and choose the Description property to be included for the category. Then press ALT+K or click the toolbar button to save and return (see Figure 6.18).

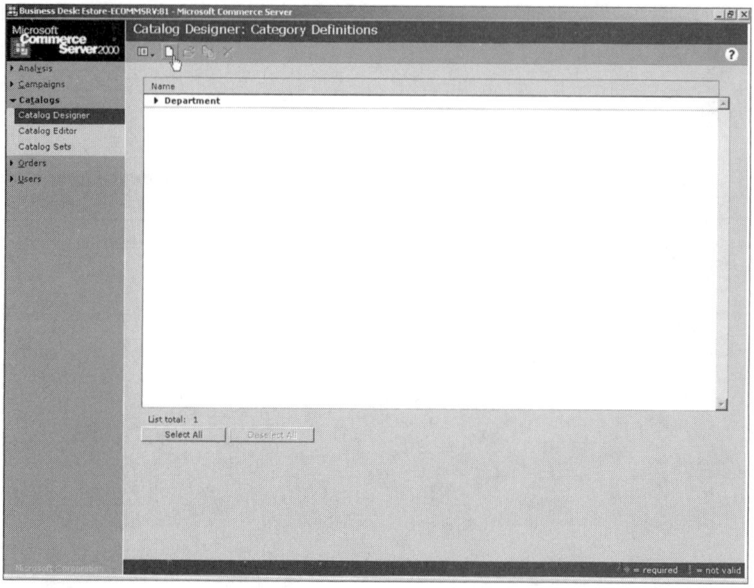

FIGURE 6.17

The button to create a new category.

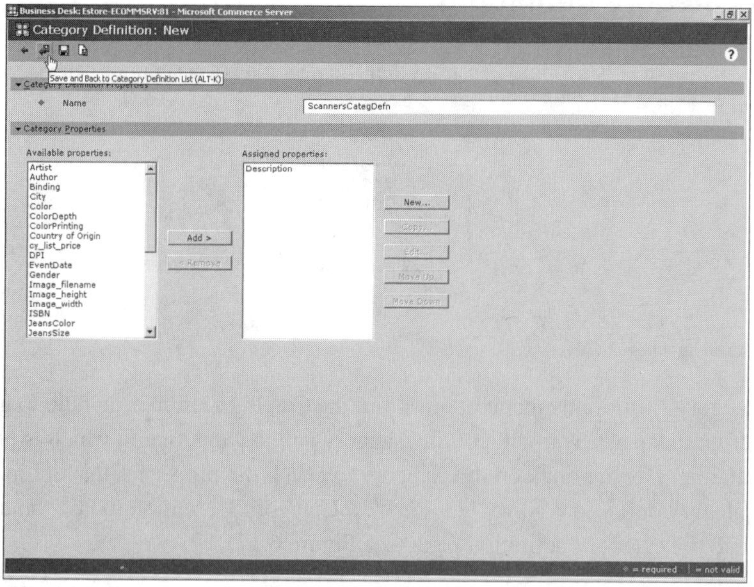

FIGURE 6.18

Defining a category.

In the Category Definitions page, you should be able to see the newly defined category ScannersCategDefn.

Creating Catalogs

In Commerce Server, a catalog is a high-level container that holds categories and products. Catalogs need to be defined in order for your e-Commerce site to display products. You have seen that there need to be definitions for properties, products, and categories. The actual values are called *instances* of this definition or schema. HPDeskjet 970cxi is an instance of the product schema Printers, whereas the value of 12 for PPM is an instance of the property schema PPM.

For a catalog, there is no such schema requirement that at least the Commerce Server developer can manipulate. The catalog is a predefined element that just allows categories and products to be added to it. The Business Desk module Catalog Editor can be used to create catalogs and add actual products and categories to it. In the Estore example, you already created a catalog called Computer Accessories and saw how to add a printer (HPDeskjet 970cxi) under the Printers category. You will use the same catalog to list scanners under the Scanners category.

Click on the Catalog Editor module link in the navigation bar of the Business Desk. The list page on the right pane lists all the catalogs created in the catalog system. Click and highlight Computer Accessories and press ALT+O or click the Open Catalog toolbar button. The Catalog—Computer Accessories page loads. This page has three sections: Catalog Properties, Categories, and Products. The Catalog Properties section contains information about the catalog, such as name of the catalog, currency used for the catalog, start and end dates for catalog availability, and so on (see Figure 6.19).

Expand the Categories section. You will see that Printers is already part of the categories in this catalog (see Figure 6.20). Clicking on a category such as Printers will load the Products in Category box with the products in that category. The product named HPDeskjet 970cxi is in the category Printers, assuming that you have the Estore example. First we will create the category called Scanners; then a scanner will be added and assigned to it.

Creating a Category

In the edit form for the Computer Accessories catalog, click the New button under the Categories section.

In the New Category box, choose the definition type ScannersCategDefn and click the Continue button (see Figure 6.21). At this point, remember that a category called Scanners is to be created using the schema called ScannersCategDefn.

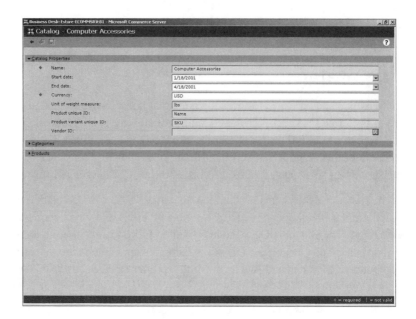

FIGURE 6.19

Catalog Creation—Catalog properties.

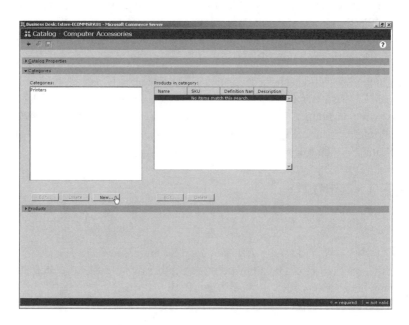

FIGURE 6.20

Creating a new Category in a catalog.

FIGURE 6.21
Choosing a Category Schema to base category creation.

The page that is loaded for creating the new category has three sections: Category Properties, Assigned Categories, and Category Relationships. The Category Properties section has the name and description of the category because these were the properties present in the category definition for Scanners. The other properties such as Price and Searchable are automatically part of a category without having to be defined in a schema. The next two sections discuss standard parts of a category creation page.

The Assigned Category section is used to define a hierarchical parent-child relationship between categories. For instance, the Scanners category could have child categories called Monochrome and Color. The Category Relationships section is used to tie category-to-category or category-to-product in some sort of a relationship, which can be used to display related products to the shopper. Later in this chapter, we will explore in detail the last two sections on the page. For now, type in the Name as `Scanners` and Description as `All types of scanners to scan photos at <b>home!</b>`. Check the Searchable box to include this category in searches. Leave the Price field blank because we don't intend to have category level pricing (see Figure 6.22). Either press ALT+K or click the toolbar button to save and return to the Catalog Properties page.

Back in the catalog page (Computer Accessories), you can see that Scanners is now a category, and when clicking it, you see that no product is assigned to it yet. You will now create a product and assign it to the Scanners category.

Creating a Product

A product is created based on a product definition. Create a scanner based on the product definition Scanner and assign it to the Scanners category created a moment ago. To accomplish this, expand the Products section in the Computer Accessories catalog page and click the New button as shown in Figure 6.23.

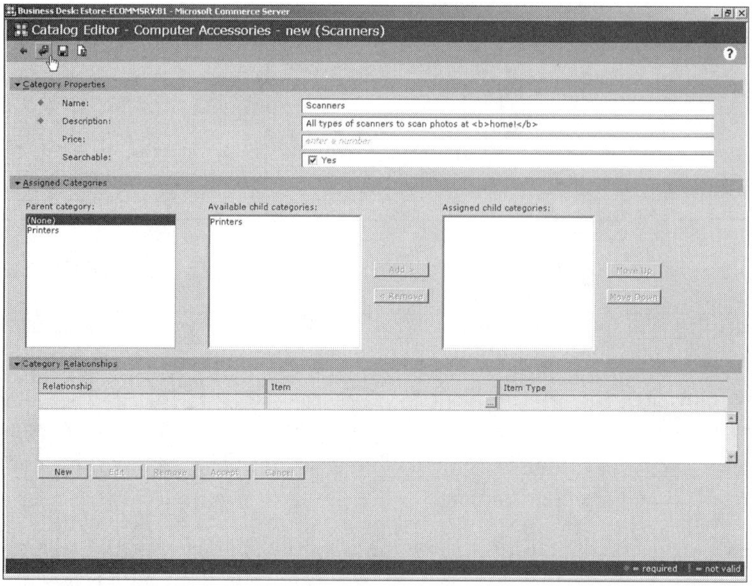

FIGURE 6.22

Creating a Category in a catalog.

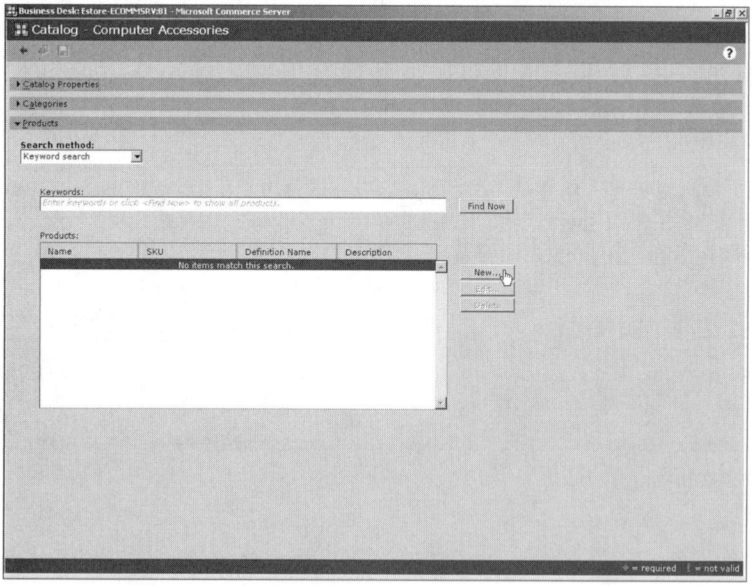

FIGURE 6.23

Creating a new product in a catalog.

In the New Product box, choose the definition for a scanner and click the OK button (see Figure 6.24).

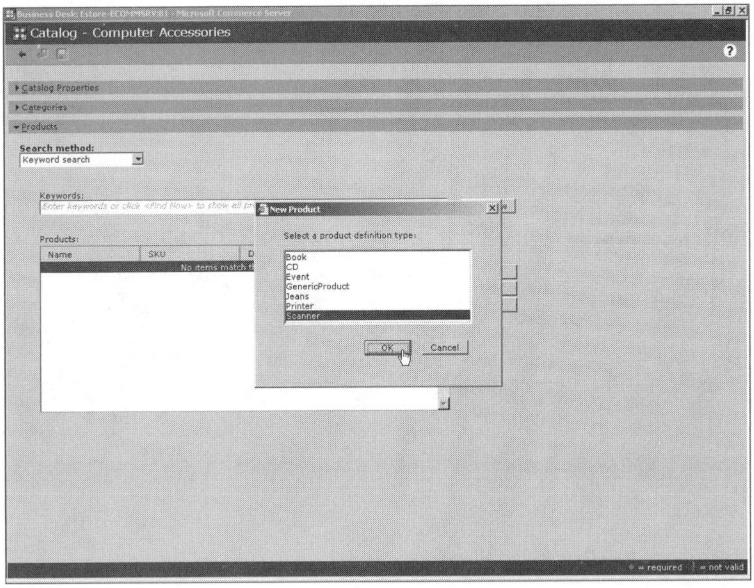

FIGURE 6.24
Creating a product based on the definition Scanner.

In the new product form, there are three sections that can be filled out: Product Properties, Assigned Categories, and Product Relationships. I will not discuss Product Relationships until later. Start entering values for fields in the section Product Properties (see Figure 6.25).

> **NOTE**
>
> The ColorDepth field is indeed an instance of the `ColorDepth` property definition, and it is a drop-down box with a defined range of values. The text entered in the description field can contain HTML tags.

After entering values for the product properties, click the Add button to add Scanners to the Assigned Categories box from the Available Categories box. Then press ALT+K or click the toolbar button to save and return to the catalog page. To verify that it was added, click the Scanners category under the Categories section in the catalog page. It should appear in the category box.

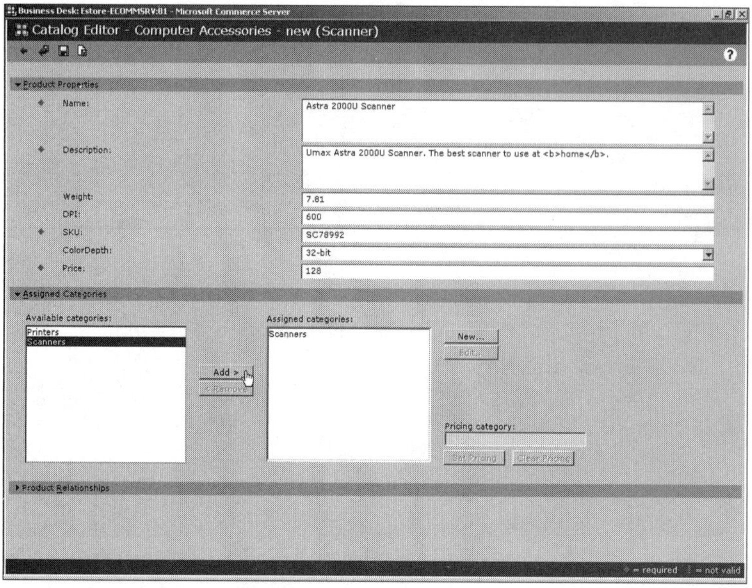

FIGURE 6.25

Create a scanner and assign it to the category Scanners.

Simple Product Searches

As products grow in number, the catalog becomes large. Therefore, it is difficult to find and modify product characteristics such as price, assign/re-assign products to categories, and so on. Using the Business Desk module Catalog Editor, the Products section in a catalog page can be used to search for products.

Open the properties page of the Computer Accessories catalog and expand the Products section. Two methods are used to search for products: Keyword and Properties. As an example of a keyword search, choose Keyword search from the Search Method drop-down box. In the Keywords text box, type **HP** and click the Find Now button. The printer product HPDeskjet 970cxi is found as shown in Figure 6.26.

After the product is listed, you can click and highlight the line and use the buttons Edit or Delete to modify product attributes or permanently delete the product itself.

You can also search for products by filtering the properties. Choose Search by Properties as the Search method, which brings up a new filter box that can be used to build a target expression. Click New to create a new condition. Choose ColorDepth as the product property from the first drop-down box, is equal to as the operator in the second box and 32-bit as the value for the third box. Then click the Find Now button. Observe that the scanner added previously has the ColorDepth equal to 32-bit, and hence is shown as a result (Figure 6.27).

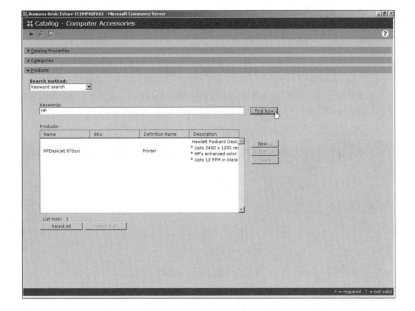

FIGURE 6.26
Searching for a product from Business Desk.

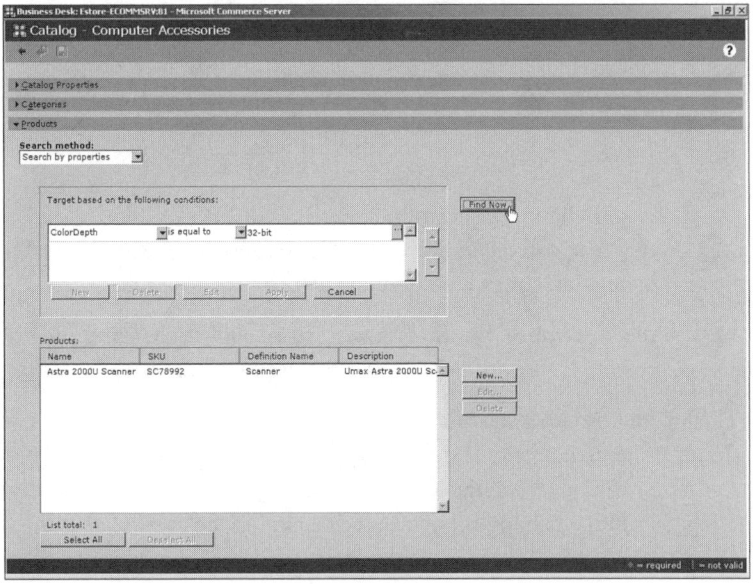

FIGURE 6.27
Searching for products based on property filters.

Catalog Refresh

Because the catalog is cached after the first retrieval, subsequent queries for a catalog from the pages of your e-Commerce site won't show the updated catalog unless the catalog cache is manually refreshed or is automatically refreshed on expiry of an update interval. To update the catalog cache manually, go to the Catalog Editor module. From the toolbar, click the button that appears as the refresh icon as shown in Figure 6.28.

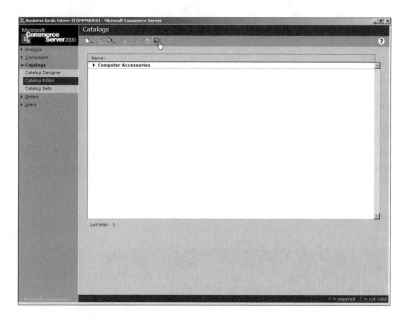

FIGURE 6.28
Refreshing the catalog cache.

To verify that the catalog is updated and now available to users, go to the Estore Web site and click Scanners listed under Categories (see Figure 6.29).

Observe that home in the description for the product Astra 2000U Scanner are in boldface, which is because of the HTML tags entered during the product creation.

Creation of a catalog and products alone doesn't make the catalog browsable by site visitors. A catalog is visible to a site visitor only if the catalog was made available to the site visitor account or the group profile to which the site visitor belongs. Catalogs are made available by grouping them together into a catalog set and in turn enabling the catalog set for a user or group.

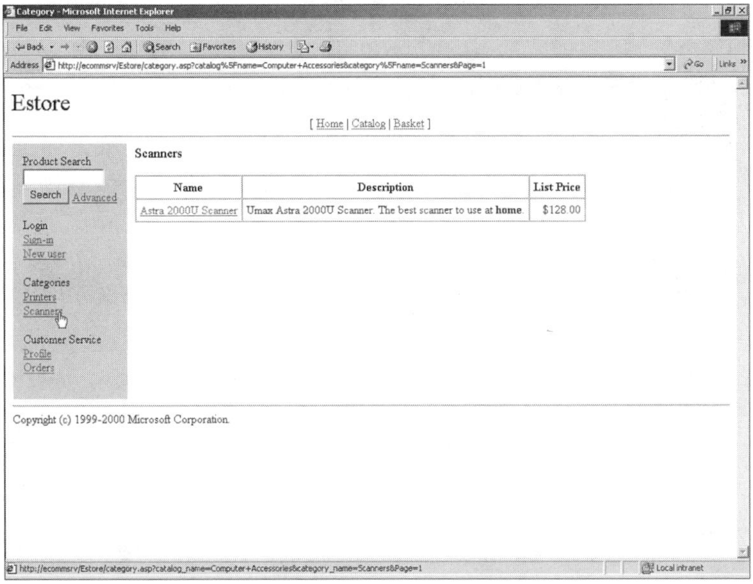

FIGURE 6.29
Verification of catalog changes at the Web site.

Catalog Sets

A catalog set is another high-level container that holds one or more catalogs. These catalog sets are then assigned to users whereby users get access to the contained catalogs. For instance, in the Estore example, we have been browsing the site as anonymous users without logging in. The Computer Accessories catalog, as well as the Printers and Scanners categories, was visible because the catalog was assigned to a catalog set called Anonymous User Default CatalogSet. This set is being used by site pages to serve catalogs to anonymous users. The general idea is to create catalogs and make them available selectively, based on class of users, by using catalog sets. To see how to assign a catalog to a catalog set, navigate to the Catalog Sets module. You will see a list of the catalog sets defined in the catalog system (see Figure 6.30)

Click on the catalog set named Anonymous User Default CatalogSet and then click the Open Catalog Set button (refer to Figure 6.30). Looking at the properties of this catalog set, you can see that any new catalog being created will be added to this catalog set because the Add all Catalogs check box underneath the Available Catalogs box is checked (see Figure 6.31).

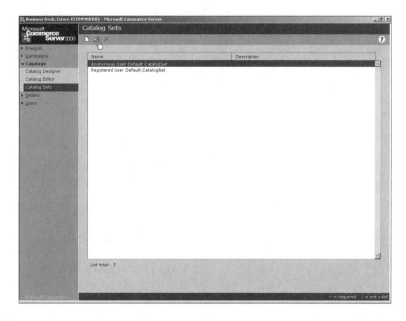

FIGURE 6.30

Catalog sets.

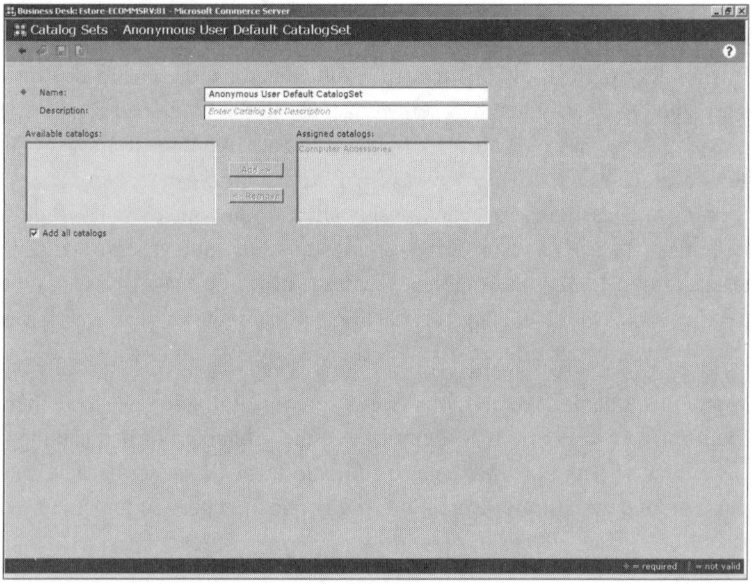

FIGURE 6.31

Modifying a catalog set.

To remove this catalog for anonymous users, uncheck the check box and click the catalog Computer Accessories in the Assigned Catalogs box. Then click Remove. Save and get back to the catalog sets list. For the changes to take effect, go to the Catalog Editor module and refresh the catalog. Then if the Estore site is accessed by an anonymous user, the messages such as `Catalog is empty` and `No catalogs installed` are displayed when the anonymous user tries to browse the catalog.

However, the catalog Computer Accessories is available to the registered users via the Registered User Default CatalogSet. To verify that, you have to log in to the site as a registered user. To create a new user, click the New User link on the left menu bar. (You could create a user called `joe` with a simple password.) Immediately after creating the user or any time after signing in, you will be able to see the categories and products under the Computer Accessories catalog.

New catalog sets can be created using the Catalog Sets module and categories assigned to it as previously discussed. You will see in a later chapter how to associate these catalog sets with a user or group profile and thus make the catalogs available or unavailable.

Custom Catalogs

Along with the notion of grouping catalogs into catalog sets for a bit of personalization in delivering catalogs, there is another way of personalizing catalogs to specific sets of users. This can be achieved by creating *custom* catalogs and assigning them to users via catalog sets. The Computer Accessories catalog from the example is called a *base* catalog. A custom catalog is derived from a base catalog with the only difference being that prices can be different between the two. The only change that can be made while creating a custom catalog is the price for selected categories in the underlying base catalog. The price in a custom catalog can be an exact flat amount, a percentage of the price specified in the base catalog, or a change by an exact amount from the base catalog price. After a custom catalog is created, it is added to the catalog sets very much the same as base catalogs are.

Say that you want to offer a 10% discount on all scanners to all registered users. You will create a custom catalog called Scanner Deals and assign it to the Registered User Default CatalogSet. Follow these steps:

1. In the Business Desk, navigate to the Catalog Editor module and bring up a list of the Catalogs. From the toolbar, choose New Custom Catalog as shown in Figure 6.32.

2. In the New Custom Catalog dialog box, choose Computer Accessories as the base catalog and click OK (see Figure 6.33).

3. In the New Custom Catalog edit page, enter the Name of the catalog as **Scanner Deals**. In the Custom Pricing section, choose the Scanners category and check the Use Custom Pricing box (see Figure 6.34)

FIGURE 6.32

The New Custom Catalog option.

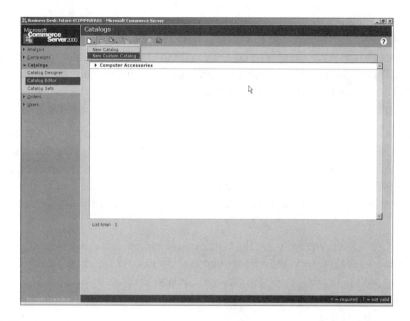

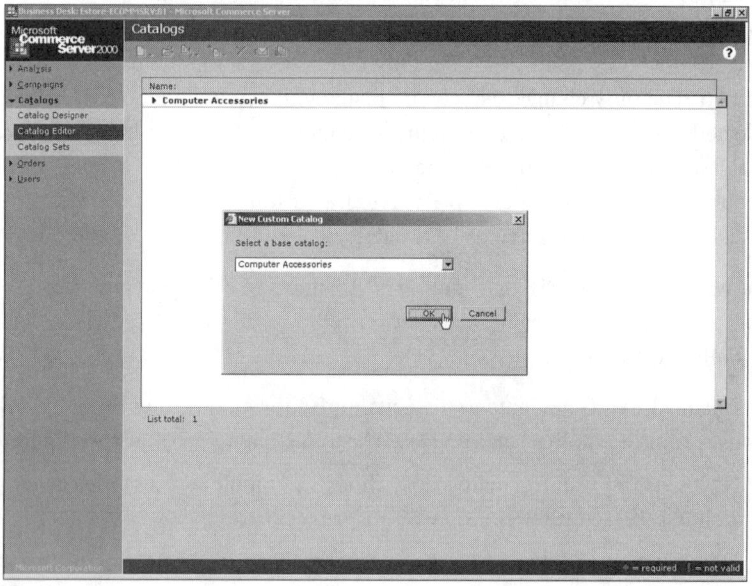

FIGURE 6.33

Specifying a base catalog for a custom catalog.

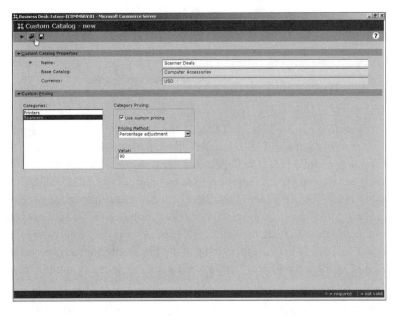

FIGURE 6.34

Customizing prices through custom catalogs.

4. Choose Percentage Adjustment as the Pricing Method and in the Value text box, enter **90** because you are giving a 10% discount. Table 6.1 shows the effect of the different pricing methods.

Table 6.1 Example of Different Pricing Methods

Pricing Method	Value	Base Price	Custom Price
Percentage Adjustment	90	100	90
Fixed Adjustment	-10	100	90
Set Price	90	100	90

The examples in Table 6.1 demonstrate how to get the custom price of $90 using each of the three pricing methods. Custom price is the effective price that is available to the browsers of the custom catalog. After completing the form, press ALT+K or click a toolbar button to save and go back to the catalogs list. If you double-click on the corresponding base catalog, you will be able to see the custom catalog defined based on the base catalog.

NOTE

The only difference between a custom catalog and a base catalog is the applicable pricing rule, so all other product information remains the same.

After creating the custom catalog Scanner Deals, it should be assigned to the Registered User Default CatalogSet to make the special pricing available to the registered users. To do this, click the Catalog Sets module link. Then click on Registered User Default CatalogSet and then the Open Catalog Set toolbar button. You won't see the new custom catalog unless the catalog cache is refreshed because the Business Desk application also uses the catalog cache to retrieve catalog information. Make sure that the custom catalog Scanner Deals is in the Assigned Catalogs box in the Registered User Default CatalogSet. After making this change, refresh the catalog cache and then verify the custom catalog at the Estore site for a registered user. As usual, press ALT+P or click the toolbar button to refresh catalog caches in the Catalog Editor module.

Sign in to the Estore site using the login created in the section "Catalog Sets." On the Home page, both Computer Accessories and Scanner Deals are listed under Catalogs. If you access the Astra 2000U Scanner via the Computer Accessories catalog, the price is $128. If the same product is accessed via the Scanner Deals catalog, the listed price is $115.20, which is a 10% discount from the base catalog price (see Figure 6.35).

Because Scanner Deals is a replica of the Computer Accessories catalog except for the reduced pricing for scanners and it is available to registered users, it would make sense to remove Computer Accessories from the catalog set for registered users. Prior to adding the Scanner Deals catalog, the Web page directly listed the Printers and Scanners categories at the first level. Now it lists the catalogs instead of the categories. Remember from Chapter 5, "Understanding the Site Architecture," that the default code for fetching catalog information goes top down starting from catalogs. If there were only one catalog, the categories are listed on the page. If there were more than one catalog, those catalogs are first listed with links to their individual category pages, and so on. As a corollary, if you remove the Computer Accessories catalog from the Registered User Default CatalogSet, the catalog page for registered users will list the categories under Scanner Deals at the first level itself. A structural representation of a catalog is shown in Figure 6.36.

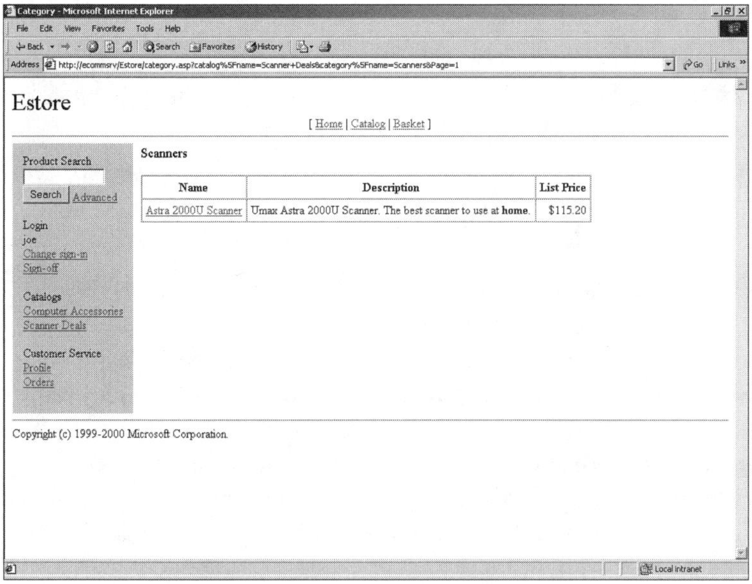

FIGURE 6.35

Verifying a discount through a custom catalog.

FIGURE 6.36

Representation of a catalog's structure.

Summary of Steps in Catalog Creation

To summarize the creation of catalogs using the Business Desk, here are the main steps:

1. Design the schema definition for Properties, Products, and Categories, depending on requirements.

2. Implement the definitions for Properties, Products, and Categories using the Catalog Designer module.

3. Using the Catalog Editor module, create catalogs, categories in catalogs, and products/variants assigned to categories in catalogs.

4. Using the Catalog Sets module, create a named catalog set and assign the required catalogs, including custom catalogs, to the catalog set.

5. Using the Users module of the Business Desk, assign the catalog set to users.

Importing and Exporting Catalogs

So far the examples used the Business Desk catalog pages to create or modify catalog elements. This method is fine for making minor changes once in a while. What if you had to bring an entire external catalog into the Commerce Server catalog system? What if you want to send a catalog to your up-stream value added sellers? Commerce Server provides you with ways to import and export catalogs conveniently. One method is to use the Business Desk module Catalog Editor to import or export entire catalogs. Also you can use the COM objects provided by Commerce Server to programmatically do the same, meeting custom requirements. Because I am speaking of an interaction with an external entity here, it is necessary for you to understand the language or format of that entity.

File Formats

The Commerce Server catalogs can be exported in two different formats:

- EXtended Markup Language(XML) format
- Comma Separated Values(CSV) format

Similarly, catalogs to be imported into the Commerce Server catalog system should be in XML or CSV format, so the external file could be in one of these formats. However, there is a difference in functionality between these two files. A Commerce Server catalog in an XML form will have all the catalog information, including the schema and product data. As soon as an XML import is complete, the catalog can be made available to the Web site without doing any additional tasks except to refresh the catalog caches. On the other hand, a CSV file has product data only. It doesn't include the schema of the catalog. So it is necessary to do some more work after the CSV file import such as creating a category, adding products to a category, and changing prices.

Exporting a Catalog in XML Format

To better understand the XML schema used for a Commerce Server catalog, export the Computer Accessories catalog to an XML file. In the Catalog Editor module, navigate to the Catalogs list page, click on Computer Accessories, and then choose the Export XML menu option from the toolbar (see Figure 6.37).

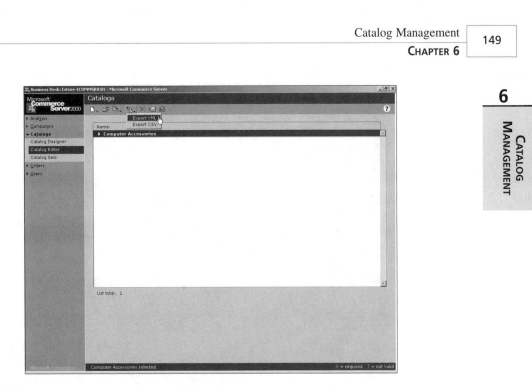

FIGURE 6.37
Exporting a catalog as XML.

In the Export XML Catalog dialog box, enter the file path where you want the catalog to be exported. There should be no spaces in the file path, otherwise the export will fail. This is true for imports too. I named the file as E:\CompAcc.xml. You could name it similarly depending on the drive assignment on the server. Click OK to start the export (see Figure 6.38).

After a while, a message box appears with the message "Catalog Export process has been started successfully". Click the OK button. This message means that the export has been initiated, and you can return to the Business Desk for other work. Essentially the export is an asynchronous process and hence doesn't tie up the user with the task. But how do you know if there were any problems with the process? The process writes to the Windows Event Viewer whether it was a success or failure. One way an export or import process could fail is if there were spaces in the file path, which was discussed earlier.

If the export process completed successfully, you should be able to see the XML file in the browser (see Figure 6.39). This is the rendering of the entire catalog schema and product data in XML format.

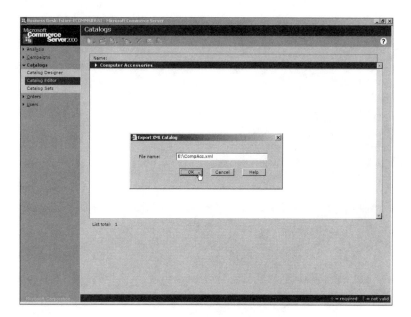

FIGURE 6.38

File path of the exported catalog.

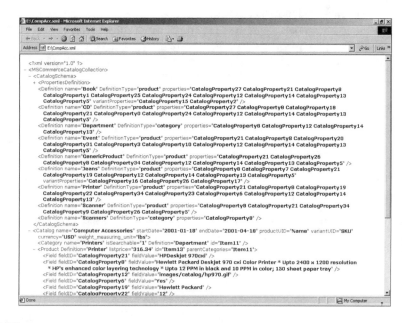

FIGURE 6.39

The XML catalog with the appropriate DTD.

As you can see, the browser renders the catalog in XML format organized in to various nodes. At the root is the `<MSCommerceCatalogCollection>` node, which holds the entire catalog, including schema and data. The next node is the `<CatalogSchema>` node that holds the entire catalog schema including property, product, and category definitions. The property definitions are under the `<PropertiesDefinition>` node, whereas the product and category definitions are under the `<Catalog>` node. The `<Definition>` tag has a `DefinitionType` that identifies whether this definition is for a Product or a Category. After the `</CatalogSchema>` tag, the `<Catalog>` tag starts and holds the data for the catalog. This node contains the tags for `<Category>` and `<Product>` for the categories and products, respectively. Inside each of these tags, `<Field>` tags are used to describe the attributes of categories or products. From the CompAcc.xml file, you can see how the Computer Accessories catalog, including the schema and data, is stored.

In general, the structure of a Commerce Server catalog in XML format will conform to the following schema:

```
<MSCommerceCatalogCollection >
   <CatalogSchema>
      <AttributeDefinition name dataType id />
      <PropertiesDefinition>
         <Property name dataType minValue maxValue displayName id HelpText />
         </Property>
         <Property name dataType minValue maxValue defaultValue id>
            <Attribute name value />
            <PropertyValue displayName />
         </Property>
      </PropertiesDefinition>
      <Definition Name DefinitionType Properties VariantProperties id />
      <Definition Name DefinitionType Properties id />
   </CatalogSchema>
   <Catalog name locale startDate endDate productUID variantUID currency
➥weight_measuring_unit>
      <Category name Definition isSearchable id>
         <Relationship name description relation />
         <Field fieldID fieldValue />
      </Category>
      <Product Definition listprice id parentCategories>
         <Relationship name description relation />
         <Field fieldID fieldValue />
         <ProductVariant listprice>
            <Field fieldID fieldValue />
         </ProductVariant>
      </Product>
   </Catalog>
</MSCommerceCatalogCollection>
```

The detailed schema for a Commerce Server catalog is defined in the file CatalogXML Schema.xml found under the MSCS installation folder. This schema file provides the DTD for a catalog exported in the XML format. You were able to look at the exported catalog CompAcc.xml using the browser because the CatalogXMLSchema.xml file was present as expected by the exported XML file. In case you didn't have the DTD, the browser wouldn't have opened the XML catalog successfully (see Figure 6.40).

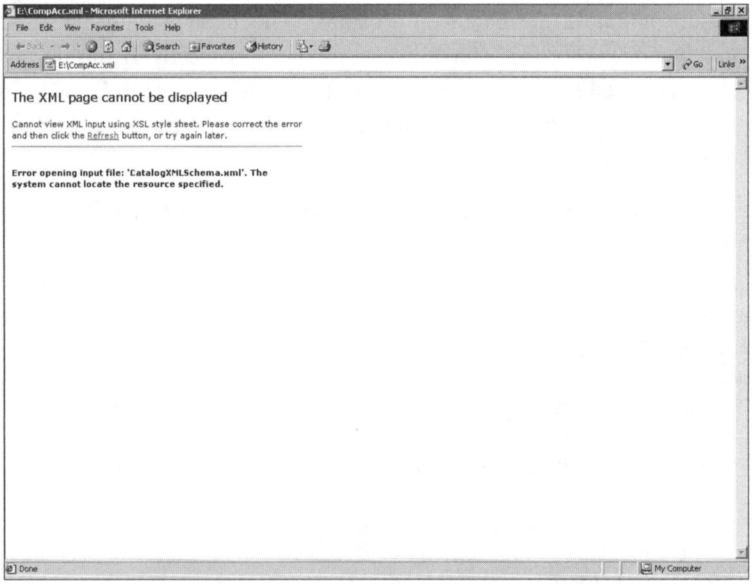

FIGURE 6.40
The XML catalog without the appropriate DTD.

To know more about the comprehensive list of elements and attributes of the catalog structure, you can browse through the CatalogXMLSchema.xml file by opening it in any browser.

Exporting a Catalog as CSV

Now you will learn how a catalog is exported in CSV format. Repeat the same steps used to export the catalog as XML, but choose the Export CSV menu option and give the file path as something similar to E:\CompAcc.csv. The export process is started successfully, and you can check the Event Viewer for any errors. If the export was successful, open the CompAcc.csv file using a text editor such as Wordpad. Figure 6.41 shows how the exported catalog looked in my csv file.

```
CompAcc.csv - WordPad
File  Edit  View  Insert  Format  Help

IsSearchable,cy_list_price,Name,SKU,Description,Image_filename,Image_height,Image_width,ColorPrinting,Manufacturer,PPM,Printin
,316.34,HPDeskjet 970cxi,,Hewlett Packard Deskjet 970 cxi Color Printer
* Upto 2400 x 1200 resolution
* HP's enhanced color layering technology
* Upto 12 PPM in black and 10 PPM in color; 150 sheet paper tray,images/catalog/hp970.gif,,,Yes,Hewlett Packard,12,Ink Jet,20,
,128,Astra 2000U Scanner,SC78992,Umax Astra 2000U Scanner. The best scanner to use at <b>home</b>.,,,,,,,,7.81,32-bit,600,

For Help, press F1
```

FIGURE 6.41
The CSV file that holds an external catalog.

If you turn off word wrap in your editor, the file should be clear in terms of what is being exported. The first line gives the name of the fields of products separated by commas. For example, cy_list_price is the price of the product, Name denotes the name field, and so on. Therefore, the first line gives what fields and in which sequential order they are exported. The subsequent lines are product details that are one product per line. For instance, the line starting with `,316.34,HPDeskjet 970cxi. . .` represents details for the printer product HPDeskjet 970cxi and the line starting with `,128,Astra 2000U Scanner. . .` is the scanner product, the Astra 2000U Scanner. The Description for the printer has multiple lines; that's why product details are on more than one line, even when word wrap is turned off. The entire second line is for the scanner product with the IsSearchable blank, list price being $128, the SKU is SC78992, and so on. All values are separated by commas and in the same sequential order as the field names in the first line.

If there were a third product in the catalog, it would have been the fourth line in the CSV file, and so on. Now that we have covered exporting, you will create a CSV file that contains products to be uploaded in to the Estore catalog system.

Importing a CSV File

Assume that you just received a catalog from a supplier partner who specializes in winter apparel, your supplier's system isn't the same as yours, and hence runs some application server other than Commerce Server. The supplier's systems don't integrate with your system via the Commerce Server's catalog XML format. You have asked your supplier to provide the catalog in at least a comma separated values format, and the supplier has generated a CSV file out of its custom catalog database.

Now you will simulate the supplier's csv file by creating one from scratch. Open a text editor such as Wordpad and enter five products. Save the file as E:\WinterApparel.csv. Remember the requirement for a csv file to be imported in to a catalog: the first line defines the fields of the products, and subsequent lines contain data. Here is what my WinterApparel.csv file will contain:

```
list_price,SKU,Description,Name
9.95,AP76092,Infant Hat. This precious acryclic fleece beanie features a rolled
➥brim that can be tied under the chin. Imported.,Infant Hat-Winter Beanie,
49.99,AP21985,The Blizzard Classic Winter Boot is a great boot for all aspects
➥of winter use.,Sorel Blizzard Classic Winter Boots Mens,
```

There are two products in the CSV file with their details such as name, description, list_price, and SKU as per the definition in the first line. To begin importing this file, click on the Catalog Editor module link. The Catalogs list page is loaded by default. Click on the Import Catalog toolbar button or press ALT+I. Then choose the Import CSV menu option. In the Import CSV Catalog dialog box, enter the values as shown in Figure 6.42.

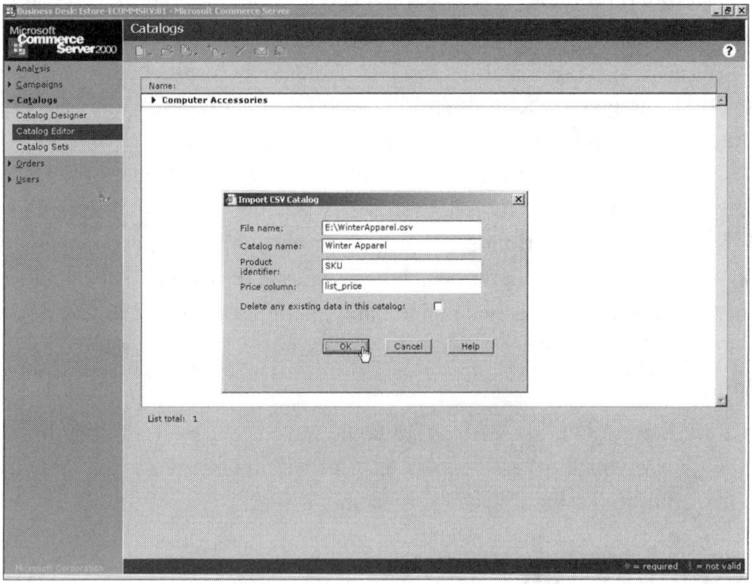

FIGURE 6.42
Importing a CSV file.

You haven't checked the Delete any existing data in this catalog box because you are creating a new catalog called Winter Apparel. Click the OK button, and a message saying "Catalog Import process has been started successfully" should appear. Because you are importing just two products in this example, the process should be really quick. In real-life scenarios, catalogs might contain large number of products, and the import process could take time. That's why the process is asynchronous; to allow you to work with other Business Desk modules while the import takes place.

Now check with the Event Viewer to verify whether the process had any errors. If everything was ok, you should see the Winter Apparel catalog listed in the Catalogs list page when you click the Catalog Editor module link. When navigating to the Product Definitions in the Catalog Designer, you can see that a product definition called Winter Apparel has been added. Thus the Catalog Editor module adds a product definition as well as property definitions for catalogs imported from csv files. Even though the csv file doesn't contain the complete schema such as the XML formatted catalog file, the import process creates a product definition out of the csv file contents. However, there are no category definitions and hence the Winter Apparel catalog contains these five products at its root. This can be found by visiting Estore and browsing the Winter Apparel catalog (see Figure 6.43). Remember to refresh the catalog cache after importing and creating the new catalog. This is automatically assigned to the registered users catalog set only, so you should sign in to view the catalog. It is added to the registered users catalog set because the Add all catalogs checkbox is still selected for the catalog set. Make sure that it is so in your settings too.

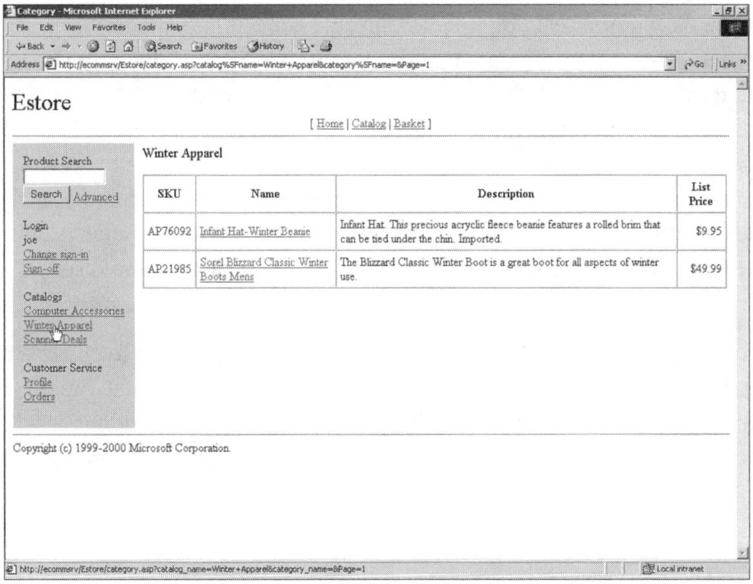

FIGURE 6.43

The Web site with the imported catalog.

What if your supplier sends more products for the Winter Apparel catalog? Simply import them into the existing catalog without choosing to delete data in the catalog.

You could build catalogs even more quickly using the Business Desk to import catalogs in bulk. The Catalog Editor also makes it possible to export catalogs to be shared with business partners and other systems. Finally, Commerce Server requires that in order to import or export catalogs, the external files be in either XML or CSV formats.

About Product Variants

You know that a SKU is the lowest level of identification that leads to a saleable product. In the real world, different classification schemes can identify products. For example, a catalog might contain Levi Strauss Jeans as the product identifier. But there are so many property variations of the jeans such as for male, regular, denim, blue color, and so on. In order to conveniently identify a saleable item, all such unique property variations of the same product are given a SKU to serve as the Variant ID. For instance, although Levi Strauss Jeans might still be the Product ID, specific jeans sold might have a SKU of LEVI98765 to uniquely identify the piece. SKU LEVI98765 might refer to jeans for female, style comfort, corduroy, brown color, and so on. Thus, each unique combination of product properties can be identified by a SKU. Normally the variant ID is a SKU, but it might be anything else as well. In short, a product in a catalog will have a unique Product Identifier, and for variations within the product, each variation would have a unique Variant Identifier.

In the Computer Accessories catalog in Estore, Name is the product identifier and SKU is the variant identifier. Whereas for the imported catalog Winter Apparel, the product identifier is SKU, but there isn't a variant identifier. To add variants to a product, the catalog should have a variant identifier. It is possible to have variants for products in Computer Accessories, but not in Winter Apparel. You can confirm whether a catalog supports variants by looking at the Product Variant Unique ID field in the Catalog Properties section of a catalog. If the field is empty, products with variants cannot be added to the catalog. Use the Catalog Editor module and open both the catalogs in Estore at this point to verify what has been discussed about variant identifiers.

Apart from the catalog supporting variants, the product definition used to create a product must also have Product variant properties assigned, in order to create a product variant. For example, using the Catalog Designer module and in Product Definitions, click on Jeans and press the Open Product Definition task bar button. The Jeans product definition shows properties assigned as variant properties (see Figure 6.44).

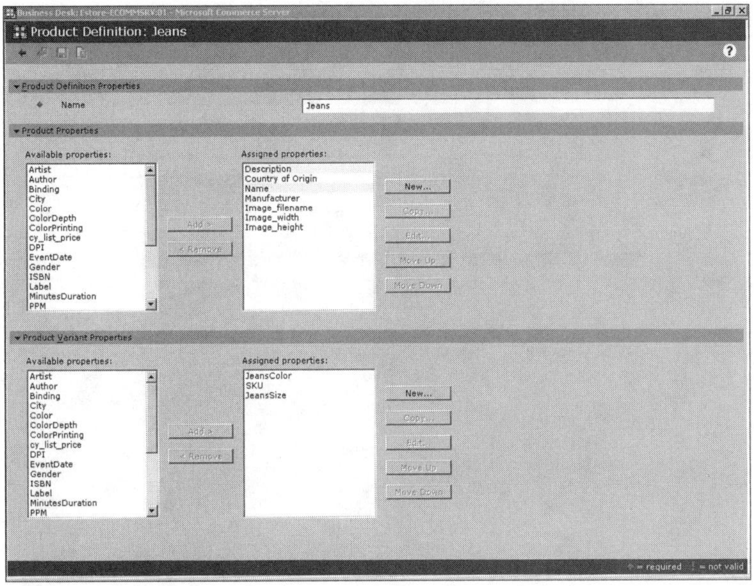

FIGURE 6.44

A Product definition that has variants.

Creating Product Variants

Suppose that Estore wants to create a catalog called Summer Catalog, which would hold jeans, and the product identifier for jeans would be the manufacturer name such as Levi Strauss. The variant identifier would be SKU, an identifier given to a specific combination of the variant properties of the product. Because the product definition Jeans is enabled for variant properties, you just need to create the Summer Catalog and assign a property such as SKU as the variant identifier.

Creating a Variant-enabled Catalog

The process is much similar to the process used for creating Computer Accessories. Figure 6.45 shows the catalog properties for Summer Catalog.

Enter the Name of the catalog as **Summer Catalog**. Make the Product Unique ID as Manufacturer because the catalog is going to be based on brands. Choose SKU as the Product Variant Unique ID. Then click the Save Catalog(or press ALT+S) task bar icon to create the new catalog.

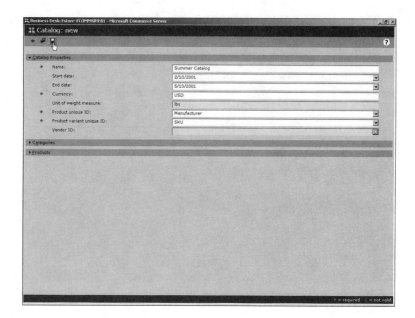

FIGURE 6.45
A catalog with a defined variant identifier.

Creating the Product and Variants

Having created the Summer Catalog, expand the Products section and click the New button to create a product for this catalog. In the New Product dialog box that pops up, choose the product definition type as Jeans. Then click the OK button. In the edit page for the product, enter the Manufacturer as **Levi Strauss** and Name as **Levi's Original Jeans**. Enter an appropriate description as you prefer and then click the Save Product(or press ALT+S) task bar button, and then save the new product to the database (see Figure 6.46).

After saving the catalog, expand the Product Variants section. Then click the New button. For the SKU, enter say LEVI98765. Choose the value for the JeansColor property as Faded Blue. Choose JeansSize as 30. Then assign a Variant Price of 34. Click the Done button (see Figure 6.47).

Click the New button again and repeat the same steps to create a second variant for the product with the following information:

SKU:	LEVI56789
JeansColor	Black
JeansSize	32
Variant Price	39

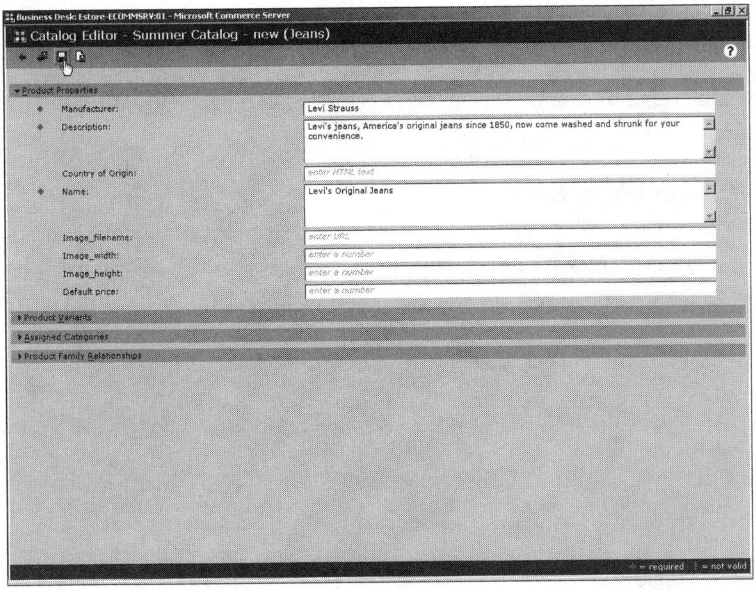

FIGURE 6.46

Creating a catalog that has product variants.

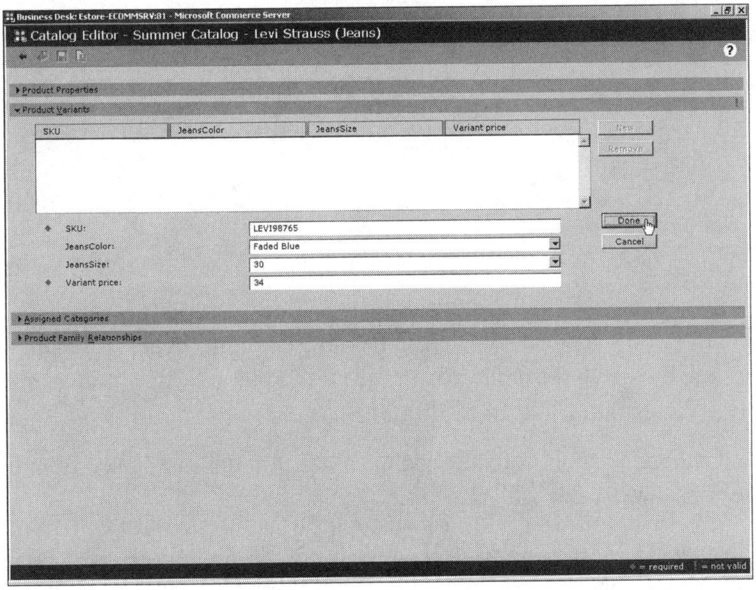

FIGURE 6.47

Adding product variants.

Make sure that you click the Done button after entering the details. Finally click the Save Product(or press ALT+S) task icon to save the added variants to the product database.

Return to the Catalogs Editor module and refresh the catalog cache to update the site with the catalog changes.

Viewing Product Variants

Now sign in as a registered user to browse the catalog Summer Catalog. As you click the catalog, the added product is shown immediately under the catalog (see Figure 6.48) because there is no category in the catalog.

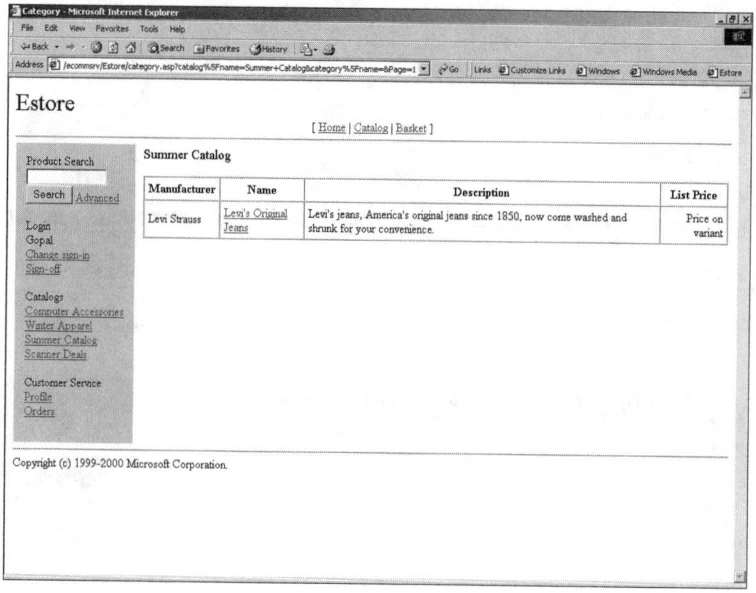

FIGURE 6.48

Displaying a product that has variants.

The Name property of the product still has the link to the product details. Clicking the Levi's Original Jeans link brings up the product.asp page that displays the details about the product and variants (see Figure 6.49).

The user would choose a variant and then add the product to the basket, and from there the shopping process is the same as with a product without variants.

Having seen how the Estore site shows the Commerce Server catalog system elements such as catalogs, categories, products and variants, you will next use the Catalog API directly in a standalone page to simulate most of the Estore's catalog functionality. First you need to understand the COM objects in the Catalog API.

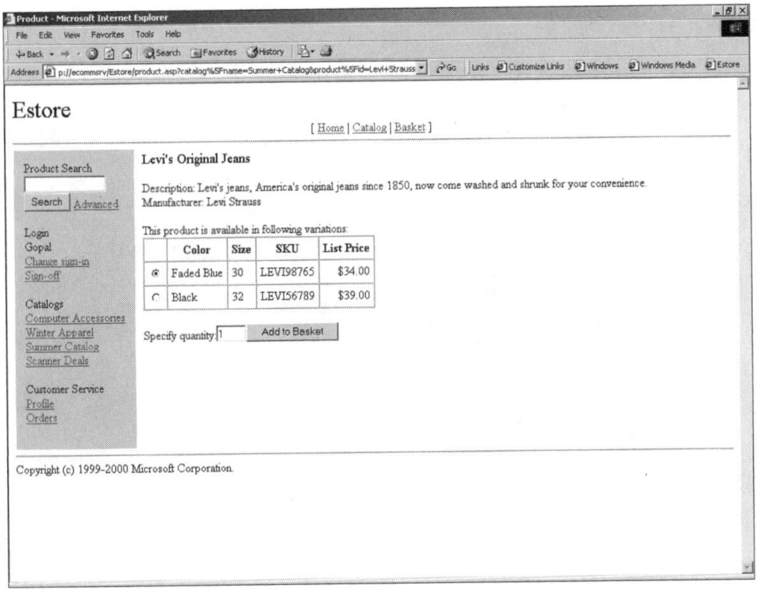

FIGURE 6.49

Browsing product variants as usual.

COM Objects for the Catalog System

Commerce Server provides important COM objects that are related to managing catalogs. The collection of all these objects form the Commerce Server Catalog API set. So far in this chapter, you have worked with the Business Desk modules for managing Catalogs. These modules are HTML Applications that, in turn, use the COM objects to interact with the catalog data store. Also the ASP pages of a Site Packager–generated e-commerce application site, such as Estore, uses these COM object interfaces for catalogs. Thus all applications, Web site as well as Business Desk, can conveniently access catalogs using these objects. These COM objects make it possible to write your own programs that can manage the catalogs based on custom needs (refer back to Figure 6.1).

I will discuss briefly what these COM objects can do. Then using these objects, you will customize some of the pages in Estore.

Commerce Server comes with two builds of these COM objects. One build is meant to be used from Visual Basic/VBScript programs, whereas the other build can be invoked from C++ programs. In terms of functionality, both the builds are identical; hence we will use the VB/VBScript set of objects for illustration purposes in this chapter and throughout the book. The main catalog related COM objects are discussed in the following sections.

CatalogManager

Create this object using the ProgID `Commerce.CatalogManager`. This object is central to the catalog management system and can be used to

- Create and delete definitions for properties, categories, and products
- Create and delete base and custom catalogs
- Retrieve schema definitions for properties, categories, and products
- Retrieve base and custom catalogs
- Import and export catalogs in the XML or CSV format
- Perform free text searches against multiple catalogs
- Perform SQL–based queries against multiple catalogs

CatalogSets

Create this object instance using the ProgID `Commerce.CatalogSets`. This object helps in grouping catalogs into sets and offer different sets to different users. Using this object, you can conveniently write scripts to

- Create, delete, and update catalog sets
- Retrieve catalog sets available for all or particular users
- Retrieve catalogs for all or particular users based on their available catalog sets

ProductCatalog

Create a reference to this object by using either the `GetCatalog` or `CreateCatalog` method of the `CatalogManager` object. Whereas the `CatalogManager` object helps to work at the higher level of a catalog, the `ProductCatalog` object is used to work at an in-depth level with catalogs. Use the `ProductCatalog` object if you want to

- Create and delete categories and products for a catalog
- Create custom catalogs based on base catalogs
- Assign custom pricing to categories
- Retrieve categories and products at the root of a catalog
- Retrieve categories, products, and custom prices
- Retrieve categories that are specification searchable
- Perform specification searches in the catalog
- Rebuild the free-text search index for a catalog

Category

Create a reference to this object by using either the `GetCategory` or `CreateCategory` method of the `ProductCatalog` object. The `Category` object is used to work closely with category hierarchy, parent-child relationships between categories, and relationships between categories and products. Use this object if you have to programmatically

- Add or delete parent/child categories
- Add or delete a product to/from a category
- Create or delete a relationship between a category and a product
- Create or delete a relationship between a category and a category
- Retrieve a parent or a child to a category
- Retrieve all products descending from this category including products under child categories
- Retrieve products that are specifically assigned to this category but not to child categories
- Retrieve categories and products that are related to a category

Product

Create a reference to this object by using either the `GetProduct` or `CreateProduct` method of the `ProductCatalog` object. This object is used mainly to work directly at a detailed product or variant level. Use the Product object to

- Create or delete product variants and update their values
- Create or delete relationship with other products
- Create of delete relationship with categories
- Get the catalog and categories to which a product is assigned
- Retrieve products or categories related to a product
- Retrieve variants of a product
- Retrieve the pricing details of a product or variant

For the actual signatures of the COM object interfaces, refer to Appendix A

Simulating Catalog Browsing In Estore

The solution site uses catalog-related functions in various pages such as default.asp, category.asp, product.asp, and catalog.asp. To comprehend the usage of the COM objects in the Catalog API, you will create a file called browsecatalog.asp and place it in the Estore folder. This file will simulate the Microsoft provided solution site in terms of showing catalogs to users, showing categories based on a chosen catalog, displaying the products for a chosen category, and so on. Here is sample code to aid you in understanding the basic flow of using these objects together to access the catalog system. Comments are provided along with the code.

```asp
<!-- #INCLUDE FILE="include/header.asp" -->
<!-- #INCLUDE FILE="include/html_lib.asp" -->
<!-- #INCLUDE FILE="include/catalog.asp" -->
<!-- #INCLUDE FILE="include/std_access_lib.asp" -->
<!-- #INCLUDE FILE="include/std_cache_lib.asp" -->
<!-- #INCLUDE FILE="include/std_cookie_lib.asp" -->
<!-- #INCLUDE FILE="include/std_profile_lib.asp" -->
<!-- #INCLUDE FILE="include/std_url_lib.asp" -->
<!-- #INCLUDE FILE="include/std_util_lib.asp" -->
<!-- #INCLUDE FILE="include/setupenv.asp" -->
<!-- #INCLUDE FILE="template/layout1.asp" -->
<%
Sub Main()
    '**Declare the variables used for holding objects, recordsets and query
    'strings**
    Dim objCatalogMgr,objCatalogSets,objCatalog,objProfileService,objCategory,
    ➥objProduct
    Dim sCatalogName,sCategoryName,sProductID
    Dim rsRootCategories,rsRootProducts,rsUserCatalogs,rsProductList,
    ➥rsProductProperties,rsChildCategories

    '**We hard code the values here; in a real site these values are a result
    'of the user browsing the catalogs.**
    sCatalogName = "Computer Accessories"
    sCategoryName="Cables"
    sProductID = "hp parallel printer cable"

    '<!--This piece of code lists catalogs for a user--->

    '**Get a reference to an instance of the CatalogManager object**
    Set objCatalogMgr = Server.CreateObject("Commerce.CatalogManager")

    '**Initialize the CatalogManager object with the connection string for the
    'catalog database.**
    'Here dictConfig is a dictionary that contains the AppConfig.**
    Call objCatalogMgr.Initialize(dictConfig.s_CatalogConnectionString,TRUE)

    '**Get a reference to an instance of the CatalogSets object**
    Set objCatalogSets = Server.CreateObject("Commerce.CatalogSets")

    '**Initialize the CatalogSets object with the connection string for the
```

```
'catalog and transaction configuration
'data stores.**
Call objCatalogSets.Initialize(dictConfig.s_CatalogConnectionString,
➥ dictConfig. s_TransactionConfigConnectionString)

'**The first parameter to the GetCatalogsForUser method is a reference to
'the ProfileService object,
'the second is the user id and the third is a catalog set which will be
'used if there were no catalog sets defined in the user profile**
Set rsUserCatalogs=
objCatalogSets.GetCatalogsForUser(MSCSProfileService,m_UserID,
dictConfig.s_AnonymousUserDefaultCatalogSet)



'**Now rsUserCatalogs contains a RecordSet of all the catalogs assigned to
' a user through various catalog sets and can be iterated through and
'written to the page**
While NOT rsUserCatalogs.EOF
    htmPageContent = "<b>Available catalogs for the current user</b><br>"
    htmPageContent= htmPageContent & rsUserCatalogs("CatalogName")
    rsUserCatalogs.MoveNext
Wend

'<!—This piece of code lists categories and products at the root of a
'catalog —>

'**Assume that the user has chosen a catalog out of those listed and we
'know the name of the catalog the user clicked on. Get a reference to the
' ProductCatalog object for the catalog**

htmPageContent = htmPageContent & "<br><br> <u><i>Assuming the user chose
➥ the catalog :</i></u> " & sCatalogName & "<br><br>"
Set objCatalog = objCatalogMgr.GetCatalog(sCatalogName)

'**Get the products and categories directly under the root of the
'catalog **
Set rsRootCategories= objCatalog.RootCategories
Set rsRootProducts= objCatalog.RootProducts

'** Now you can iterate through the RecordSet objects to list the products
' and categories that are at the root of the catalog **
htmPageContent = htmPageContent & "<b>The Products at the root of the
➥catalog </b> " & sCatalogName & "<br><br>"
While NOT rsRootProducts.EOF
```

```
        htmPageContent= htmPageContent & rsRootProducts("ProductID") & "<br>"
        'response.write rsUserCatalogs(1)
        rsRootProducts.MoveNext
    Wend

    htmPageContent = htmPageContent & "<b>The Categories at the root of the
    [ic:cccc] catalog </b> " & sCatalogName & "<br><br>"
    While NOT rsRootCategories.EOF
        htmPageContent= htmPageContent & rsRootCategories("CategoryName")
        ➡ & "<br>"
        'response.write rsUserCatalogs(1)
        rsRootCategories.MoveNext
    Wend


    '<!—This piece of code lists products under a category —>

    '** Assume that the user has clicked on a category link. Now we know the
    ' name of the category the user clicked on.
    'Get a reference to the Category object for the category **
    htmPageContent = htmPageContent & "<br><br> <u><i>Assuming the user chose
    ➡ the category :</i></u> " & sCategoryName & "<br><br>"
    Set objCategory = objCatalog.GetCategory(sCategoryName)

    '** Get the products under this category. Also get any sub-categories if
    ' defined under this category. Note that the Products property has many
    ' optional parameters, here we have indicated to sort the product lists
    ' by name. **
    Set rsProductList = objCategory.Products(,"name")
    Set rsChildCategories= objCategory.ChildCategories

    '** Now the rsChildCategories RecordSet contains all the categories
    'directly under this category. This can be iterated through to write
    'the category name **
    htmPageContent = htmPageContent & "<b>The Child categories under the
    ➡ category </b> " & sCategoryName & "<br><br>"
    While NOT rsChildCategories.EOF
        htmPageContent= htmPageContent & rsChildCategories("CategoryName")
        ➡ & "<br>"
        rsChildCategories.MoveNext
    Wend

    '** Now the rsProductList RecordSet contains all the properties of all
    ' products under this category. This can be iterated through to write the
    ' product properties like product id, name , price etc out to the HTML
    ' stream **
    htmPageContent = htmPageContent & "<b>The Products under the  category
```

```
➥</b> " & sCategoryName & "<br><br>"
While NOT rsProductList.EOF
    htmPageContent= htmPageContent & rsProductList("ProductID") & "<br>"
    rsProductList.MoveNext
Wend


'<!—This piece of code lists product details of a product —>

'** Assume that the user has clicked a product link. Now we know the id of
' the product the user clicked on. Get a reference to the Product object
'for the product **
htmPageContent = htmPageContent & "<br><br> <u><i>Assuming the user chose
➥ the product :</i></u> " & sProductID & "<br><br>"
Set objProduct = objCatalog.GetProduct(sProductID)

'** Get all the properties of the product inlcuding user defined(using
' product definition) as well as built-in properties. **
Set rsProductProperties = objProduct.GetProductProperties

'** Now the rsProductProperties RecordSet contains all the properties of
' the product like name, description, sku, price, image and so on. Write
' these properties to the HTML stream as needed. This page is usually
' where the user chooses to add this product to the basket **
htmPageContent = htmPageContent & "<b>The product details for : </b> " &
➥ sProductID & "<br>"
htmPageContent= htmPageContent &  rsProductProperties("Description") &
➥"<br>"
htmPageContent= htmPageContent & rsProductProperties("cy_list_price") &
➥ "<br>"
htmPageContent= htmPageContent & "<img src='" &
➥rsProductProperties("Image_Filename") & "'><br>"
end sub
%>
```

When you access this file from the browser, it will list the catalogs available for the user. After that, you can assume that the user chooses the Computer Accessories catalog, the Cables category, and finally the HP parallel printer cable product to display details. Also you must have noticed that I am using the infrastructure provided by the solution site itself for accessing page variables from setupenv.asp, writing the content to the variable htmPageContent and leaving it to layout1.asp to display the content generated by this page. Thus, if you take the time to create and run through this example, it would be a good exercise in understanding the Commerce Server–provided solution site elements. Figure 6.50 shows the output that the browsecatalog.asp page generates in my browser.

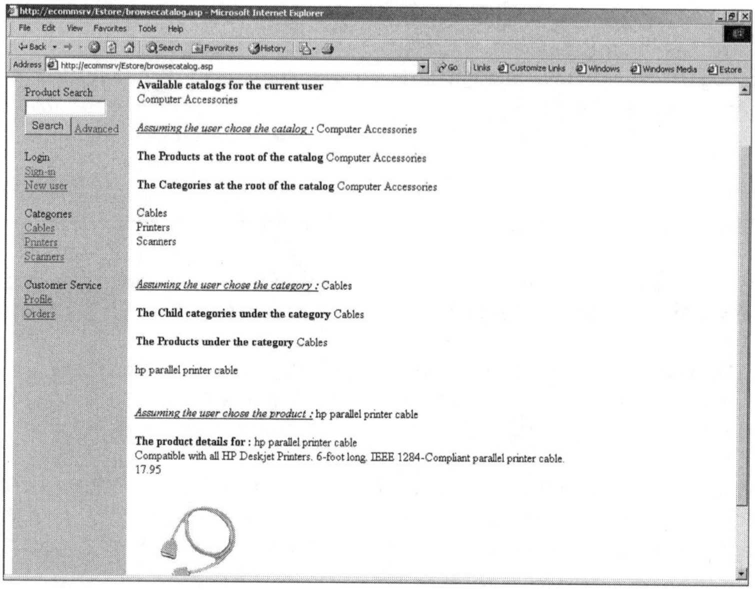

FIGURE 6.50

The output generated by browsecatalog.asp.

Now that you've seen how to program using the catalog-related objects, use this knowledge and explore another area of product catalogs—relationships.

Showing Related Products

With the reality of e-commerce as a business strategy, marketers have started using the Web site as a potential promotion medium. Nowadays it isn't uncommon to see other products being suggested when you are browsing the details of a specific product. These other products might be something related to the product you are browsing or totally unrelated and based on other shopper's recommendations. This strategy aids in increasing impulse purchases as well as generating supplemental orders. Practically speaking, shoppers often browse related products and are more likely to order items that are useful to their main purchase. For example, it would be useful to show a user who is shopping for a printer details about related items such as ink cartridges, printer cables, printing paper, and so on.

Commerce Server provides the infrastructure to maintain relationship between elements in the catalog system. You already know about the category-to-category parent/child relationship, which is necessarily a container relationship to aid meaningful browsing of the catalog. Apart from that, a business manager can establish a relationship between different elements based on business acumen. The relationships supported by default in Commerce Server are

- Category-to-category
- Category-to-product
- Product-to-product

In this section, you will implement a real-life scenario of a product-to-product relationship to understand how you can relate catalog elements for custom purposes. In the Computer Accessories catalog, there is a printer product HPDeskjet 970cxi. Suppose that a printer cable is also in the catalog. The design is to add the printer cable as a related item while showing the printer details to the shopper. Before implementing this scenario in Estore, take a look at the printer product in the browser, as shown in Figure 6.51.

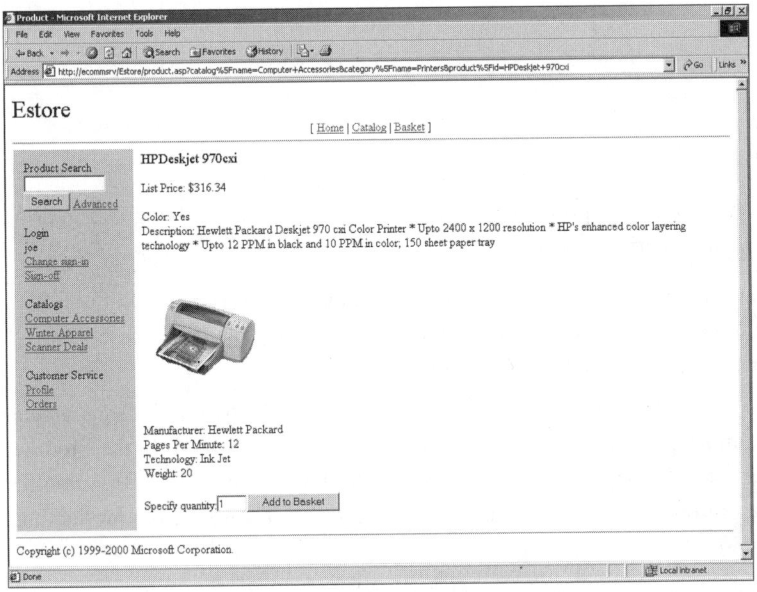

FIGURE 6.51

A product without a related item.

You know that product.asp displays the product details, and it is the page in which you want to display related items. The following steps are needed:

1. In the Computer Accessories catalog, create a category called Cables. By now, you should be familiar with adding categories and products to a catalog. Create the Cables category based on the Department category definition and create the product based on the GenericProduct product definition. Assign the product to the Cables category. Create a product with the details shown in Figure 6.52 and assign it to the Cables category.

GenericProduct	
Name	hp parallel printer cable
Description	Compatible with all HP DeskJet Printers. 6-feet long. IEEE 1284-compliant parallel printer cable.
Price	17.95
SKU	CB887766

FIGURE 6.52

A cable created based on the GenericProduct definition.

Figure 6.53 shows how the product edit page might look in the Catalog Designer module for the Computer Accessories catalog.

2. After adding the printer cable to the catalog, the next step is to edit the HPDeskjet 970cxi product and establish a relationship with the cable. If necessary, search for the printer and edit the product (see Figure 6.54).

   In the Product Relationships section, type the name of the relationship as **Accessory** for this example and click the Browse button under the Item field. In the Product Picker dialog box, choose the hp printer cable and click the OK button (see Figure 6.55). Click the Accept button in the Product Relationships section. Then save the product and return to the catalog.

3. Now a relationship has been established with the printer cable. It's time to use some of the COM object interfaces to get the related item and display on the product.asp page.

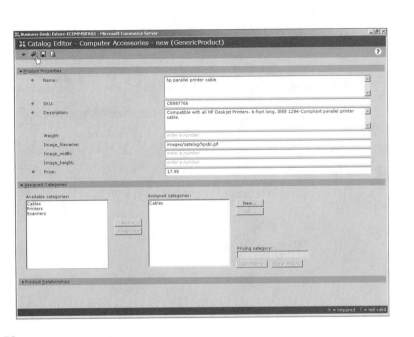

FIGURE 6.53

Creating a new product.

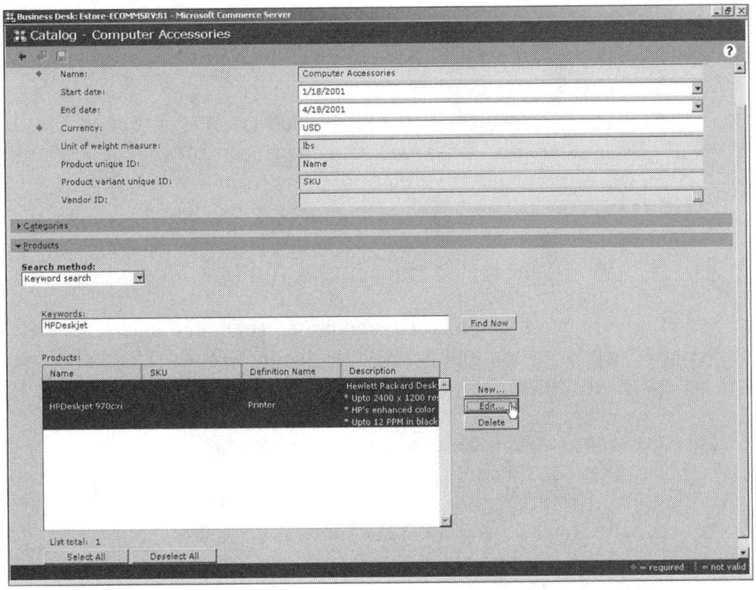

FIGURE 6.54

Edit an existing product.

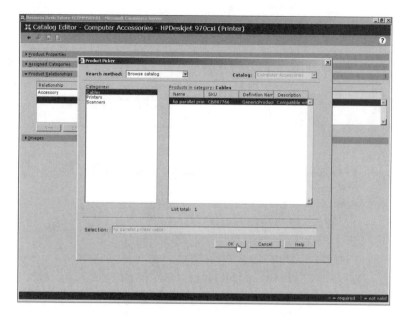

FIGURE 6.55

Choosing a product to establish a relationship.

In the product.asp file, add the following code just before the Call CacheFragment statement (comments included) and save the file.

```
'<!— Added related-item code —>
        '**Declare variables**
        Dim rsRelatedProducts,objRelatedProduct,sRelatedProductID,
        ➡rsRelProductProps,htmRelatedProduct,sRelatedProductName

        '** Get a list of related products. MscsProduct is a reference
        'to this product **
        Set rsRelatedProducts = mscsProduct.RelatedProducts

        '**If there exists related products then proceed. Seems to be
        'buggy, gives a recordset for a product even if there are no
        'related products. **

        If (Not rsRelatedProducts is Nothing) and
        ➡(Not rsRelatedProducts.EOF) then

        '**Get the id for the related product. All products in a catalog
```

```
' have the same property as the product identifier. Keep in mind
'that in our Computer Accessories catalog it is Name.**
        sRelatedProductID = rsRelatedProducts.Fields
        ➥(mscsCatalog.IdentifyingProductProperty).Value

'**Get a reference to the related product**
        Set objRelatedProduct=mscsCatalog.GetProduct
        ➥(sRelatedProductID)

'**Get all the properties of the related product**
        Set rsRelProductProps =
        ➥objRelatedProduct.GetProductProperties

'**Get the value of the property Name of the related product. In
' our case it should return "hp parallel printer cable" for the
'product HPDeskjet 970cxi.**
        sRelatedProductName =
        ➥rsRelatedProducts.Fields("Name").Value

'**Use the Commerce Server provided function RenderProductLink
'to generate the HTML content needed to display the product
'name as a link. This function is defined in one of the
'include files.**
        htmRelatedProduct = RenderProductLink(sCatalogName, "",
        ➥ sRelatedProductName, CStr(sRelatedProductID),
        ➥ MSCSSiteStyle.Body)

'**Add the generated HTML fragment to the page's main content**
        htmContent = htmContent & CRLF & "<b>Related Items</b>"
        ➥ & CRLF & htmRelatedProduct
    End if
    '<!— Added related-item code —>
    htmPageContent = htmTitle & CRLF & htmContent
    Call CacheFragment("ProductPageCache", sCacheKey, htmPageContent)
```

4. Refresh the catalog cache and browse to the detailed product page (product.asp) of
   HPDeskjet 970cxi. There you will find the related item to display, as shown in
   Figure 6.56.

Of course, you need to add more code to handle multiple related products as well as any error
conditions. This example shows how easy it is to extend Commerce Server functionality using
the COM objects.

FIGURE 6.56
A product with a related product in the catalog.

Searching the Catalogs

In order to give the power of searching to shoppers, Commerce Server provides two types of search capabilities to a site: free text search and specification search.

By using the CatalogManager object's FreeTextSearch method, it is possible to search multiple catalogs for a specific phrase entered in the *free text* search box. CatalogManager in turn depends on the full-text indexing of SQL Server and the search capability of Microsoft Search service.

Another way to search catalogs is using specification search supported by the ProductCatalog object. In *specification* search, the COM object tries to refine the records that are fetched based on successive inputs the user chooses from the provided results at the previous level. I will discuss briefly various ways to search for products on the site.

Free Text Search

When a user enters free text in the Product Search box on the site and clicks the Search button, the form is posted to the file search.asp. As with many other pages, the search.asp page tries to retrieve results from the cache FTSearchPageCache, if available. The key that it searches for in the cache is made up of the combination-catalog set ID of the user and the search text entered.

In search.asp, the function `bFullTextResultsAreCached` is used to find whether the cache has the results for this search:

```
...
sCatalogSetID = mscsUserCatalogsetID()
        sCacheKey = sCatalogSetID & sSearchPhrase
....
```

Note how `sCacheKey` is formed as a combination of catalog set ID of the user and the search text entered. This is important because the search should be performed only on the catalogs that are available to the current user.

If the key isn't found in the cache, search.asp calls the function `rsFreeTextSearch`, which is defined in catalog.asp.

The function `rsFreeTextSearch` basically uses the `FreeTextSearch` method of the `CatalogManager` object to return a `RecordSet`:

```
Function rsFreeTextSearch(ByVal sPhrase, ByVal iStartingRecord,
➡ ByVal iRecordsToRetrieve, ByRef iRecordCount)
   Dim sPropertiesToReturn, sPropertiesToSortOn, rsResult, iClassType,
    ➡ sCatalogsToSearch

    ' "name" and "description" are required product properties and cannot have
    ' null values.
    sPropertiesToReturn = PRODUCT_NAME_PROPERTY_NAME & "," & _
                          PRODUCT_DESCRIPTION_PROPERTY_NAME & "," & _
                          CATALOG_NAME_PROPERTY_NAME & "," & _
                          CATEGORY_NAME_PROPERTY_NAME & "," & _
                          CATALOG_PRODUCTID_PROPERTY_NAME & "," & _
                          CATALOG_VARIANTID_PROPERTY_NAME & "," & _
                          DEFINITION_TYPE_PROPERTY_NAME

    ' "name" is a required product property and cannot have null value.
    sPropertiesToSortOn = CATEGORY_NAME_PROPERTY_NAME & "," & _
                          PRODUCT_NAME_PROPERTY_NAME

    ' iClassType determines the type of entities to search.
    ' (See FreeTextSearch documentation)
    iClassType = cscProductFamilyForVariantsClass Or _
                 cscProductClass Or _
                 cscCategoryClass

    sCatalogsToSearch = sUserCatalogsAsString()

    Set rsFreeTextSearch = MSCSCatalogManager.FreeTextSearch( _
                                            sPhrase, _
                                            sCatalogsToSearch, _
```

```
                                    iClassType, _
                                    sPropertiesToReturn, _
                                    sPropertiesToSortOn, _
                                    True, _
                                    iStartingRecord, _
                                    iRecordsToRetrieve, _
                                    iRecordCount _
                        )
End Function
```

Some of the values for the `FreeTextSearch` method come from the search.asp page. For example, `sPhrase`, `iStartingRecord`, and `iRecordsToRetrieve` might have values as jeans, 1, and 50, respectively. The `iRecordCount` parameter is an out parameter that will have the number of records in the returned recordset. The names of catalogs to search is passed in the parameter `sCatalogsToSearch`, which—as you can see from the previous code—is a comma-separated string containing available catalogs for the current user. To search all catalogs, you would pass an empty string in `sCatalogsToSearch`. The parameters `sPropertiesToReturn` and `SPropertiesToSortOn` are very straightforward to understand. The `iClassType` parameter specifies where to search inside a catalog; whether inside a category, product, a combination of category and product, and so on. The enumerated values for the class parameter can be found from the AppConsts.idl file or from the Commerce Server documentation for the `CatalogManager` object.

The recordset returned by the `FreeTextSearch` method is iterated through and written to the HTML stream by the function `htmRenderFullTextSearchResults` in search.asp. The resulting page is shown in Figure 6.57.

Recall that categories can be made searchable by setting the `IsSearchable` property to `True`. While creating a category, check the Searchable check box. Similarly, while creating property definitions, there are two check boxes: Free Text Searchable and Specification Searchable. Now that you have learned about the free text search, you will learn about the specification search in the next section.

Specification Search

If you had visited the Microsoft site or google.com, you would have observed the ability to search within previously returned results. This method is conceptually a drill-down of the content item you are searching. The initial recordset might return more records, but as you progressively specify additional constraints or filters, the number of records returned gets reduced when more search criteria is added. Specifying additional criteria as results are returned is also called as *step* search. The `ProductCatalog` object in Commerce Server provides the ability to perform this step search on a catalog while a shopper searches for her preferred item.

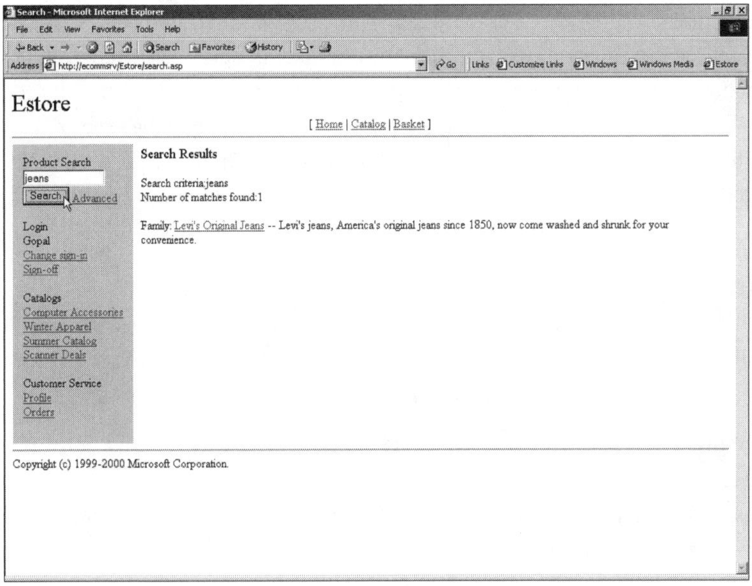

FIGURE 6.57
A Free Text search on the site.

Specification searches can be done on a single catalog only. Inside a catalog, a search can be made on categories and properties that are defined as searchable. Because a catalog must be chosen for a specification search, the root of the search starts with categories. One of the site pages, for example, srchdept.asp, displays all the catalogs available to the current user. Under each catalog, all the searchable categories are also listed. The user chooses a category under a catalog, say Denim under Summer Catalog. Now a specification search begins on the chosen catalog and category, using the method `BeginSpecificationSearch`. If the number of records (products and variants) for the category is more than a predefined display limit, a list of all searchable properties (and their values) of all products under the category is shown to the shopper in list boxes. At this point, the shopper can either see the resultset or choose to narrow down the search by specifying constraints. To narrow down the resultset, choose property values and continue the search again. The property values chosen by the user are the constraints for the specification search and are added using the method `AddSpecificationSearchClause`. After a property is chosen as part of the search clause, it is removed from the list available to the user.

The specification search is executed using the method `PerformSpecificationSearch`. This method knows which catalog and category to search for as well as the accumulated constraints. The number of records returned as compared to the predefined display limit will determine whether to display the results or allow the user to decide. The user might again decide to refine the search and choose more search constraints. This process of adding search clauses to the specification search continues until the returned recordset is below the predefined display limit, or the user chooses to view the results at any point. Also if during any search no records are returned for the specified constraints, another method called `GuaranteedSpecificationSearch` is used to return records to guarantee a resultset. `GuaranteedSpecificationSearch` removes constraints that were applied, one at a time in reverse order, until a recordset is obtained for the search.

Demonstrating Specification Search

The solution site already has code built to perform fundamental specification searches. This could be customized as required for a site. I will demonstrate the specification search on Estore and briefly discuss the methods of the ProductCatalog used for this purpose.

As previously discussed, specification search is an interactive process that helps the site user reduce the resultset until the desired results are fetched. This ability is essential for a site with large catalogs with hundreds of products per catalog. Because there aren't many in Estore, I created some more products and variants for Summer Catalog so that a specification search can be demonstrated.

I created two categories called JeansWear and Denim under the Summer Catalog. Then I added products for manufacturers Lee and Newport. For each of the products, I added many variants for combination of JeansColor and JeanSize. Figure 6.58 shows the Newport product information.

Go ahead and create as many such products as you want for Summer Catalog: the more variants and products the better for demonstrating specification search. These products are all under the newly created Denim category.

Before actually seeing the search work, you might want to make a couple of changes to the stepsrch.asp file, which executes the methods related to specification search. This file is also located under the root folder of Estore. Open the file for editing and look for the constant definition `SEARCH_THRESHOLD`. By default, it has a value of 5, meaning that the shopper gets to refine a search if the results displayed are more than five records. You might want to adjust this number depending on the number of products in your catalog. I set the value to 2 so that even if I have fewer products in the Summer Catalog catalog, the working of specification search can be seen conveniently.

Next, disable the cache lookup because it might be irksome during the development process. You want the search to access the database every time. To do that, go to the `Main()` routine inside the file stepsrch.asp and comment the following line:

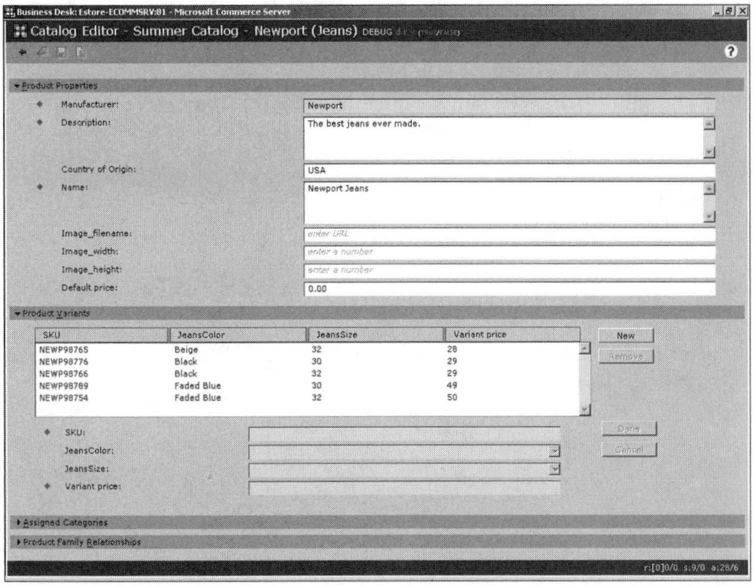

FIGURE 6.58
Creating products and variants for the example.

```
'If Not bIsStepSearchPageCached(sCategoryName, sCatalogName, htmPageContent,
➥sCacheKey) Then
'Call CacheFragment("StepSearchPageCache", sCacheKey, htmPageContent)

'End If
```

Thus, accessing the cache for reading or writing is avoided.

Next go to the routine `PerformSpecificationSearch` defined inside stepsrch.asp and add `cscProductVariantClass` to the `iSearchType` variable so that search is performed on variants also:

```
iSearchType = cscProductClass + cscProductFamilyClass + cscProductVariantClass
```

Similarly, in the `ShowSearchMatches` routine, add `cscProductVariantClass` to the case statement:

```
Case cscProductClass, cscProductFamilyClass,cscProductVariantClass
```

Finally, save the stepsrch.asp file. Now you will see how the user would implement specification search on the catalog. On the Estore site, click the Advanced link in the Product Search menu section. This link directs the user to the page srchdept.asp. This file is located at the root of the Estore folder. This page is pretty simple; it fetches all the available catalogs for the user and displays all the searchable categories under the catalogs, as shown in Figure 6.59.

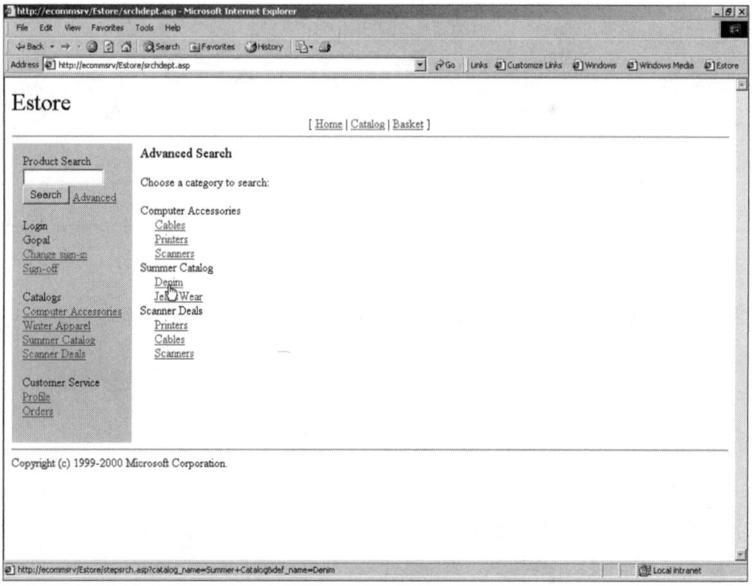

FIGURE 6.59

Srchdept.asp displays searchable categories.

From the searchable categories, click the category Denim. As you can see, the link on Denim points to the file stepsrch.asp.

Inside stepsrch.asp, many tasks such as fetching the category name chosen, getting available catalogs for the user, and so on are performed.

Beginning the Search

The initialization of the specification search is done mainly by the following call:

```
Call PrepareSpecificationSearch(sCategoryName, sCatalogName, oCatalog,
➡ bViewResults, rsFields, rsResults, sSearchHandle, iMatchesFound,
➡ iConstraintFieldsCount, iNonConstraintFieldsCount, arr1, arr2,
➡ bNoValues, bClosestMatches)
```

This routine is defined inside stepsrch.asp, and in turn it calls the `ProductCatalog` method `BeginSpecificationSearch` to initialize the search:

```
sSearchHandle = oCatalog.BeginSpecificationSearch(sCategoryName, rsFields,
➡ iMatchesFound)
```

The third parameter supplied has the number of records returned by the method. The return value of this method is a `String` that contains the state of the search. For example the return value might be `"[Summer Catalog][Denim]"`. This value is used as a handle to be passed to the method `AddSpecificationsSearchClause`.

BeginSpecificationSearch

This is the first method that should be called to initialize a specification search. The first parameter is the input to the method, or the category in which to search for. The second parameter is a pointer to a recordset returned by the method. This is a single-row recordset, each field containing a SAFEARRAY for one searchable property for the specified category. Only properties that are defined as Specification Searchable are returned in this recordset. For instance, the recordset might return properties such as JeansColor, JeansSize, Manufacturer, and so on with their values in the SAFEARRAY. Field one of the returned recordset might be for JeansColor. The field in turn contains a SAFEARRAY of values Beige, Black, Faded Blue, and so on.

You can use the following code snippet to get these values:

```
If Not (rsFields Is Nothing) Then
    For Each objField In rsFields.Fields
        dim i,a
        a = objField.Value
        For i=0 to UBOUND(objField)
            Response.Write a(i) & "<br>"
        Next
    Next
End if
```

The preceding code isn't part of the stepsrch.asp file. It's given here just for illustrating the access to the returned recordset and the SAFEARRAY.

The third parameter supplied has the number of records returned by the method. The return value of this method is a String that contains the state of the search. For example the return value might be "[Summer Catalog][Denim]". This value is used as a handle to be passed to the method AddSpecificationsSearchClause.

Adding Constraint Clauses

When the search is initialized, the handle sSearchHandle returned by the BeginSpecificationSearch method can be used to add search clauses. The routine GetSpecificationSearchClauses in stepsrch.asp is called after the search is initialized. The search clause is built using the properties and values chosen by the user to refine the search. The search clause finally might resemble the following:

```
[JeansColor] IN ("Beige")
```

Then the call is made to the AddSpecificationSearchClause method of the ProductCatalog object to add this search clause to the search:

```
Call oCatalog.AddSpecificationSearchClause(sSearchClause, sSearchHandle)
```

Adding the search clause is done in a loop one clause at a time, so all properties chosen by the user are added to the search. After all clauses are added, this is what ultimately is fed by the ProductCatalog object to SQL Server.

```
AND [JeansColor] IN ("Beige") AND [Country of Origin] IN ("India") AND
➥ [Manufacturer] IN ("Levi Strauss")
```

AddSpecificationsSearchClause

As you can see, a call to this method would pass the restrictive clause to be added to the search as the first parameter. The second parameter is the search handle that was returned by the BeginSpecificationSearch method, pointing to the search initiated by the user.

Executing the Search

After the clauses are added to the search, the routine PerformSpecificationSearch defined in the same page, stepsrch.asp, is called to perform the search. That routine in turn calls the following routine of the ProductCatalog object to execute the search:

```
Set rsResults = oCatalog.PerformSpecificationSearch(sSearchHandle, iSearchType
➥, , iMatchesFound, rs, sColList)
```

PerformSpecificationSearch

This method has many parameters. The first parameter to this method is the search handle you have been dealing with so far for the particular search. All parameters except the first are optional. The second parameter,ISearchType, is an enumerated value that indicates whether the search should include products, categories, product families, and variants individually or in certain combinations.

In the example, the search type includes products, product families, and product variants as set by the statement:

```
iSearchType = cscProductClass + cscProductFamilyClass +
➥cscProductVariantClass
```

The execution of the method returns a recordset rsResults. In case the search clauses were too constraining, this method wouldn't return a result. In a situation such as this, the GuaranteedSpecificationSearch method is used to execute the search again:

```
Set rsResults = oCatalog.GuaranteedSpecificationSearch(sSearchHandle,
➥ iSearchType, , iMatchesFound, rs, sColList)
```

GuaranteedSpecificationSearch is similar to PerformSpecificationSearch except that it removes the search clauses one by one from reverse, until a result is returned. For example, assume that the user chose JeansColor as Beige, JeanSize as 32, and Manufacturer as Levi Strauss. The GuaranteedSpecificationSearch method removes the Manufacturer clause and tries to fetch the result. If not successful, the method then removes the JeanSize clause, tries to execute the query, and so on. Thus it guarantees that there would be something returned that closely matches if not exactly, the users search criteria.

Ultimately, this recordset is passed on to the routine htmRenderStepSearchPageContent to render the results on the page. This routine checks if the matches found exceeded the predefined threshold. If so, a refined search page is generated and displayed to the user.

```
If (iMatchesFound > SEARCH_THRESHOLD) And (iNonConstraintFieldsCount > 0) And _
        (bViewResults = False) Then
        Call ShowRefinedSearch (sCatalogName, sCategoryName, rsFields,
        ➥ arr1, arr2, _iMatchesFound, iConstraintFieldsCount,
        ➥iNonConstraintFieldsCount, bNoValues, htmContent)
End If

....
```

The ShowRefinedSearch routine displays all the properties and values of all products in the category. Figure 6.60 shows what the stepsrch.asp file generated as I clicked the Denim link in the srchdept.asp page.

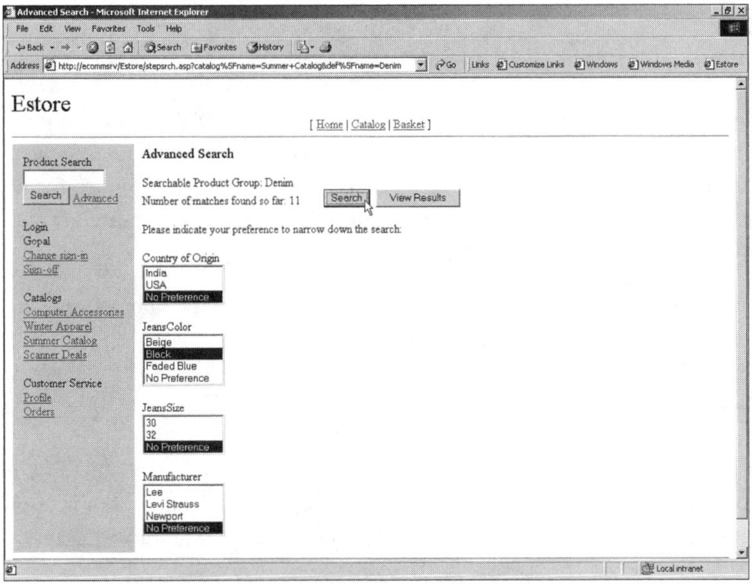

FIGURE 6.60

Displaying property values for refining a search.

The page lists the properties and values of all products in the Denim category. I can choose `Black` as the `JeansColor` and click the Search button again. The same process previously described happens, and if the returned recordset is greater than the threshold, this list page is shown, but without the `JeansColor` property (see Figure 6.61).

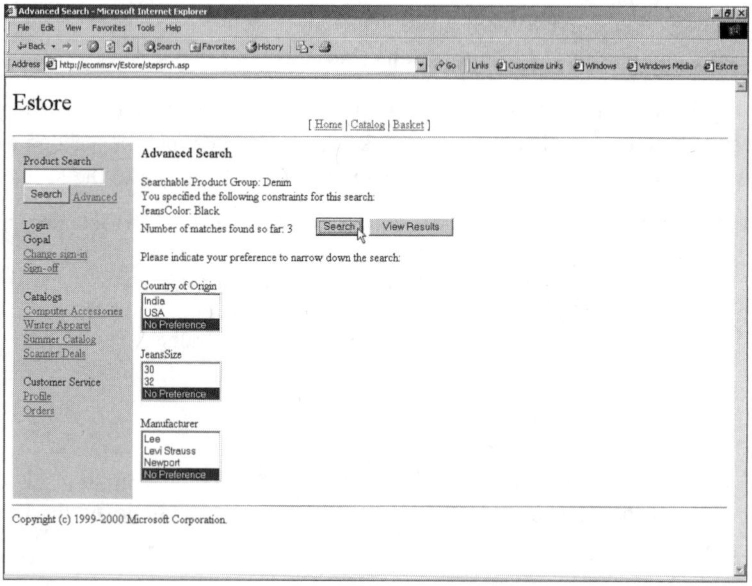

FIGURE 6.61
Properties are removed after successive iterations.

Thus this iterative process continues until the user clicks View Results at any point or the returned matches fall below the pre-set threshold. Also to work out the `Guaranteed SpecificationSearch` method, choose some combination of property values for which no product exists. Then click the Search button. The result page will say that your request didn't match any product and only the closest matches are displayed.

The ultimate results page displayed is the result of the routine `ShowSearchMatches`, which formats and produces the links necessary for display.

Summary

Catalogs are the core of an e-commerce site. They are the interactive agents of an online business. Therefore, it is necessary to understand how the catalog system works when implementing an e-commerce site with Commerce Server. In this chapter, you looked at the big picture of

6

the catalog system. Then you learned how a catalog is built with schema definitions for properties, categories, and products using the Catalog Designer Module. The Catalog Editor module was used to create catalogs, categories, and products.

You also learned how to import and export catalogs in XML and CSV formats. The concept of assigning catalogs to Catalog Sets and then enabling catalog sets for users was also discussed. You analyzed various COM objects that are used to interact programmatically with the catalog system. Several code examples were shown to help you understand these objects. Relationships between categories and products were analyzed and looked at through examples. Finally, I briefly discussed Search in Commerce Server. This chapter, when digested slowly and as a whole, will give you insight into the Commerce Server catalog system and some of the possibilities it provides.

User Management

IN THIS CHAPTER

- Fundamentals   188
- Profile Schemas   194
- Generating a Ticket   198
- Cookies-less Browsing   200
- User Registration   201
- A Little Personalization   206
- Managing Users from the Biz Desk   209
- Summary of the Profile System   212
- The Authentication Filter   212

An online business should always be aware of the fact that it is open for business 24 hours a day, 7 days a week, for 365 days a year. Contrast this against a physical store's operating hours, where we know that there will be real people to attend to customers during those hours. Therefore, serving users in a virtual shop is a challenge given the fact that anybody in the world might visit your site at any time. In order to serve them effectively, it is first necessary to know who the shoppers are, what part of the world they live in, their shopping interests, and other information that would help you satisfy customer needs. The collection of such information that describes a user is called the *user profile*. Once you have information about a user, the user profile, it is possible to deliver content, discounts, and other promotions based on such information. This creates lots of possibilities for personalization of the shopping experience that will ultimately make users delighted at shopping from your site.

Not only can the user profile be used for personalization but also for securing nonpublic content that your site offers. For example, your suppliers can log into a password-protected area of the site and will be able to download or upload catalogs. Also, in the public shopping area, you might require that users sign in before they can place an order. There is one more reason why user profiles are important for an online store. By knowing the shopping behavior of site visitors, business managers can analyze the site offerings and fine-tune the online business.

Therefore, user profiles are important for personalization, security, and site analysis. In this chapter, you are going to see how Commerce Server provides the basic infrastructure for managing users and ways to extend it.

Fundamentals

As always, Commerce Server provides you with sample application elements to show how to exploit its infrastructure. Therefore, we will again take the user-boat and explore what the Site Packager–generated site offers out of the box. This will help you in understanding the different concepts and code that are tied together.

Let's assume that a new shopper comes to the Estore site, which was built from the Retail package. Typically, the home page is the one that the user sees first (see Figure 7.1). You may or may not see catalogs for an anonymous user, depending on whether the Anonymous User Catalog Set contains any catalogs.

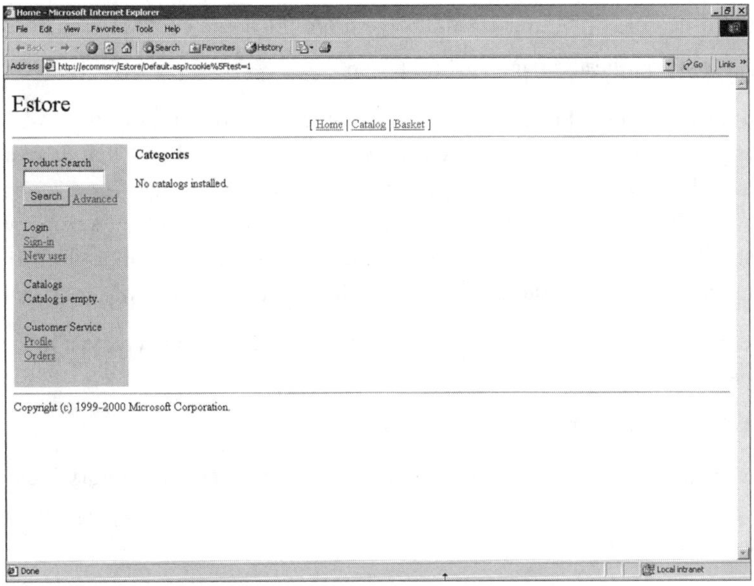

FIGURE 7.1

The home page for an anonymous user.

However, from a user-management perspective, quite a few things have happened in the system behind the scenes before this page was delivered to the client browser. Here are the key points to keep in mind after the Estore home page is accessed for the first time:

- Commerce Server puts a persistent cookie called MSCSProfile on the local machine.
- The UserObject table in the Estore_commerce database is populated with a row that was created for this anonymous user.

Here's a brief synopsis of the steps taken by the application pages:

1. Determine whether the user is authenticated.
2. Because the user was not authenticated already, treat the user as anonymous.
3. Check the login options set at the site level to see whether login is required upon entering the site.
4. Entry is free. Next, check whether the site privacy options allow profiling anonymous users.
5. Because the site allows anonymous profiling, create a unique ID for the user and populate a mostly blank profile in the database.
6. Find out whether the site supports cookies and whether the browser also allows cookies.

7. Send a profile ticket (the user ID and some more info) in a cookie to the browser.

8. Redirect to the requested page, `default.asp`.

Now we will discuss in detail how, where, and when these steps are executed. We will refer to these steps as part of our discussion in the following sections. We know that there are several server-side includes in the `default.asp` page as well as in other pages. The file `setupenv.asp` contains direct ASP code, so in whichever page it is included, the code in `setupenv.asp` gets executed first. After executing its own script, `setupenv.asp` makes a call to the `main()` subroutine of the main page (here, `default.asp`) in which `setupenv.asp` was included.

In our present context, code snippets in `setupenv.asp` instantiate and create a reference to the `MSCSAuthManager` object:

```
Set mscsAuthMgr = GetAuthManagerObject ()
```

Most of the standard subroutines, like this one, are defined in standard library includes. The `GetAuthManagerObject()` routine is defined in `std_access_lib.asp`. Ultimately, the reference to the object is obtained as this:

```
Set mscsAuthMgr = Server.CreateObject("Commerce.AuthManager")
```

The `MSCSAuthManager` COM object provides methods to authenticate and manage user information present in cookies or URL strings.

GetUserInfo()

After the object is instantiated, a call is made to the `GetUserInfo()` subroutine, which performs steps 1 and 2. This subroutine uses the `MSCSAuthManager` object to find out whether the current user is authenticated. This is done by invoking the following statement:

```
mscsAuthMgr.IsAuthenticated()
```

In our case, because at this stage the browser does not have a cookie or any URL string that says the user is authenticated, this method returns `FALSE`. Now local flags within the page are set to indicate that the user is anonymous and his or her visit is an anonymous visit. Also, the user does not have an ID yet. These flags are available in the variables:

```
m_userID
m_UserAccessType
m_UserType
```

After the user information is retrieved, `setupenv.asp` calls the `main()` routine in the `default.asp` page. In turn, `main()` makes a call to the `EnsureAccess()` routine to determine access privileges for the user. We know that every application page in the site has a `main()` method as the entry point for the page and that this routine first calls `EnsureAccess()` before doing anything else. This page-level access control is established in all pages; therefore, the EnsureAccess() routine should be called before any other statement.

EnsureAccess()

At this point, it has been established that the user type is anonymous. Now the site-level option for form login is checked. Remember that there are many properties set at the entire site level. There is site configuration information stored in an application-level dictionary variable called dictConfig in global.asa. You can see the properties and their values from Commerce Manager itself under the App Default Config Properties sheet, as shown in Figure 7.2.

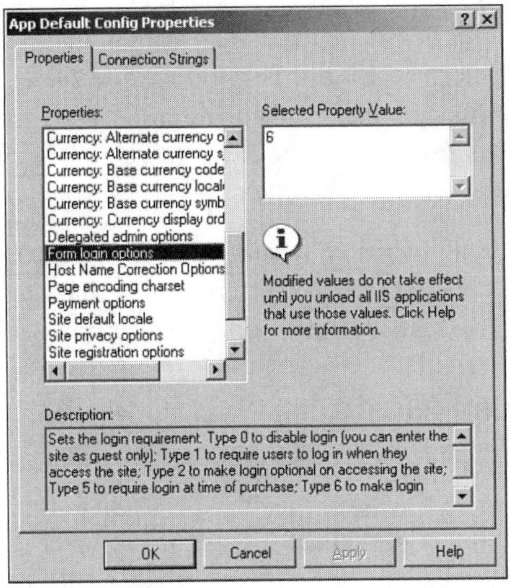

Figure 7.2

Form login options for a Commerce Server site.

From the Description box, you can see that one of many possible values can be given to the Form Login Options property. For instance, if you want users to sign in as soon as they enter the site, option 1 should be chosen. As already discussed, the values can be accessed from an instance of the AppConfig object. If form login were required, the user would have been redirected to the login/login.asp page for sign in. Because in Estore we don't have mandatory login, control still remains inside the EnsureAccess() routine. Therefore, step 3 in the list of steps discussed at the beginning of the "Fundamentals" section is accomplished here.

Tickets and Ticket Modes

A *ticket* is a combination of key/value pairs that Commerce Server generates for storing and accessing user information. Commerce Server generates two tickets: MSCSProfile and MSCSAuth. MSCSProfile is for an anonymous user, and MSCSAuth is for a signed-in user. These tickets contain user ID, time, and domain information. For instance, the MSCSAuth ticket might contain the following key/value pair combinations for a signed-in user:

```
User ID - {780858DB-08AB-11A3-B8D4-A1104B95EFEK}
Datetime- 12/31/2025
Domain-    Ecommsrv/estore
```

Here, User ID is the globally unique identifier for the user in the database. The Datetime value is the time until the ticket is valid. Domain information indicates whether other applications within the same domain can access this ticket to validate the user. Note that these values are encrypted, unlike those shown in the preceding example, and therefore can only be read by Commerce Server. The MSCSProfile ticket, however, has only User ID in it. You will see a real ticket in a moment.

Once Commerce Server generates a ticket, it can put the ticket into one of two modes: URL string or cookie. Therefore, the ticket mode is determined by the support for cookies both by the site and the browser. If cookies are not supported, tickets are placed in URL strings.

Determining Ticket Mode

Coming back to our workflow, EnsureAccess() determines the ticket mode. In Estore, the site property Site Ticket Options has a value of 2, which means that the site supports placing tickets in cookies. Now it is important to find out whether the browser supports cookies. This is done by sending a test cookie to the browser. If the test is successful, it means that both the site and the browser support cookies and hence the ticket mode is cookie (step 6).

It is not surprising to note that the MSCSProfile ticket is placed in the MSCSProfile cookie whereas the MSCSAuth ticket is placed in the MSCSAuth cookie. However, the difference between these cookies is that one is persistent and the other is nonpersistent. The MSCSProfile cookie is stored on the local hard disk of the browser whereas the MSCSAuth cookie is stored in the browser machine's temporary memory and is persistent only for the session. The reason for the difference is obvious: An authorization cookie should be valid only for the session whereas a general profile cookie can be persisted for purposes such as personalization.

Generating a Profile

As we've already discussed, a ticket is a combination of user information derived out of a user profile. Therefore, first it is necessary to generate a profile for the current user. The AppConfig property Site Privacy Options determines whether an anonymous user can be profiled. If the value is 1, profiling of anonymous users is allowed. In our case, it is allowed; therefore, anonymous profiling can be carried out (step 4).

The new profile is created by the following statement:

```
Set GetNewGuestUserProfile = MSCSProfileService.CreateProfile(MSCSGenID.
➥GenGUIDString, PROFILE_TYPE_USER)
```

This statement is found in the `GetNewGuestUserProfile` function, defined in the file `std_profile_lib.asp`. The `CreateProfile` method of the `MSCSProfileService` object is invoked with two parameters. The first one is a GUID, and the second is the type of profile to be generated. The constant `PROFILE_TYPE_USER` has a value of UserObject. We will talk about other profile types a little later. Note that constants such as `PROFILE_TYPE_USER` are defined conveniently in a single place either in `services/include/const.asp` or the AppConsts object included in `global.asa`. You could open the `<Microsoft Commerce Server>\SDK\Samples\ Solution Sites\appconsts.idl` file in a text editor to view the constant definitions in the AppConsts object. Also, as you can see, a GUID can be generated using the `MSCSGenID` object's `GenGUIDString` method, as in the preceding statement.

The `MSCSProfileService` object is used to create, update, delete, and retrieve `ProfileObject` objects. These two objects, `MSCSProfileService` and `ProfileObject`, are important to profile management in Commerce Server. An instance of a `ProfileObject` object points to an individual profile such as a user profile. The `MSCSProfileService` object is used to create and manage such profiles. Therefore, in the preceding statement, the `CreateProfile` method creates a profile of type UserObject with the primary key being the GUID. The `CreateProfile` object finally returns a reference to the `ProfileObject` object of type UserObject.

Each profile type is mapped to a physical data source table. The UserObject profile is mapped to a table called UserObject in the Estore_commerce database. A column in the table is typically mapped to a property of the profile. For instance, the `User_Type` attribute of the profile is mapped to the i_user_type column in the table. Each user has a row in the table; therefore, a UserObject profile gives access to a row in the UserObject table. The UserObject profile managed by the `ProfileService` object can point to different data sources, such as an Active Directory, SQL Server, and MS Access. A UserObject profile can be designed to map to one of these data sources in its entirety or can be split to have members from more than one data source. For example, in the solution site Estore, by default the UserObject is mapped in its entirety to the table UserObject in the SQL Server database Estore_commerce. It is also possible to have, say, user_id and user_security_password mapped to an Active Directory data source, whereas other information, such as first_name and last_name, can be mapped to a SQL Server database. The UserObject profile presents unified access to the underlying user information. The following section further discusses the profile schema. At this point, remember that we have just created a UserObject profile for the current anonymous user, in memory only.

We are yet to persist this to the underlying data store for the UserObject profile. We will do that once we come back from the profile schemas discussion.

Profile Schemas

A *profile* is a collection of information about an entity. The entity could be a user, a purchase order, a user address, and so on. Therefore, there can be many profile definitions, such as those provided by Commerce Server (UserObject, Organization, Addresses, BlanketPOs, and Targeting Context). Profiles are ultimately stored in a data source where physical storage takes place. The data source could be an OLEDB-compliant RDBMS such as SQL Server or an LDAP source. Each profile is mapped to a data object. With an RDBMS as a data source, each data object is a table in the database, and each data member is mapped to a column in that table. Figure 7.3 provides a diagram that illustrates these concepts.

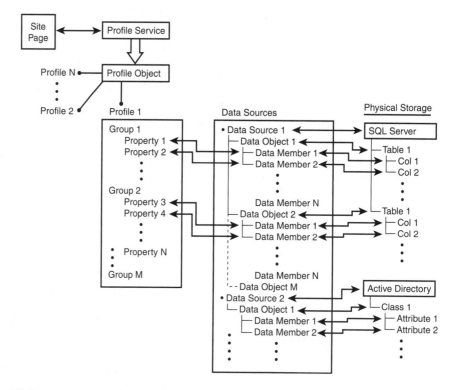

FIGURE 7.3

Example of the profile system architecture.

Programmatically, access to a profile goes like this:

```
'Get the instance of a specific profile
Set objProfile = objProfileService.GetProfile(Profile_Key,
➡strProfile_Name,bCreate)

'Set a values in the profile
ObjProfile.Fields("Group1.Property1").Value = "something"
ObjProfile.Fields("Group1.Property2").Value = "something"

'Persisit the profile to the underlying data storage
ObjProfile.Update()
```

To concretize the concepts, we will next discuss the UserObject profile.

The UserObject Profile

Commerce Server provides an out-of-the-box profile called UserObject. The profile User-Object models user information to be collected and used throughout the site. The UserObject profile provided by Commerce Server consists of the following underlying objects:

- A physical SQL Server database as the data source, the name of the data source being ProfileService_SQLSource.
- A database table called UserObject that has a back-end schema, as shown in Figure 7.4.

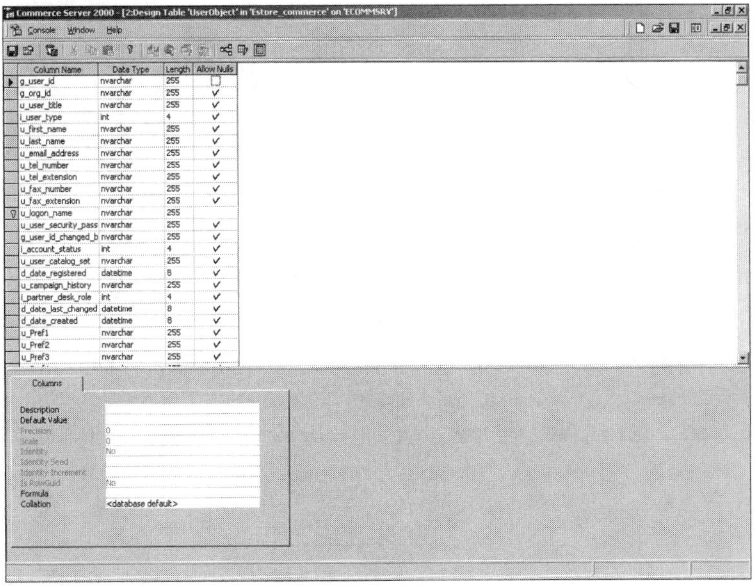

FIGURE 7.4

Schema of the UserObject table.

- A data object called User Object for the ProfileService_SQLSource data source. This data object is nothing but a representation of the back-end table with members representing the table columns (see Figure 7.5).

Notice that each of the data members on the right is simply a mapping to the columns of the table UserObject in the database.

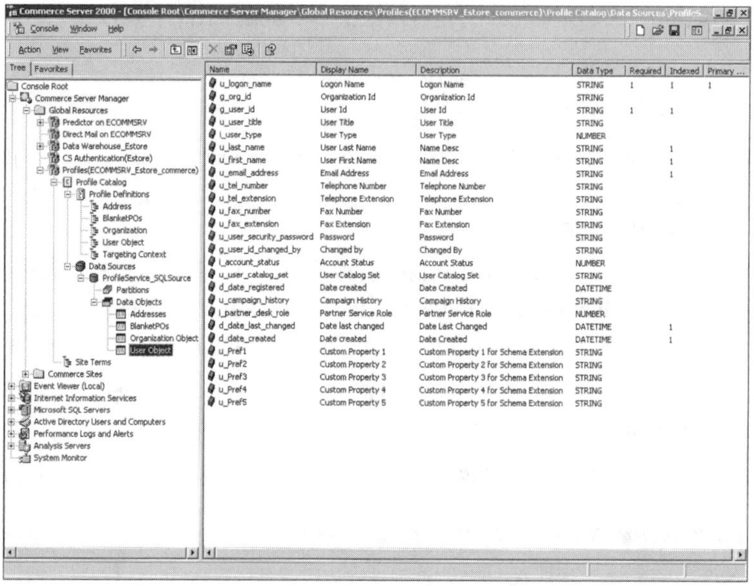

FIGURE 7.5

Data objects in a data source.

- A profile definition for the UserObject profile. This can be found under the Profile Definitions folder in the global Profiles resource for the Estore site (see Figure 7.6).

Here is an illustration of the UserObject profile to compare with the earlier discussion on the Commerce Server profiles architecture (see Figure 7.7).

When the UserObject profile under the Profile Definitions folder is clicked, the right pane displays the HTMLApplication provided for working with profiles. The same set of application pages can be accessed from the business desk from the Profile Designer module under Users.

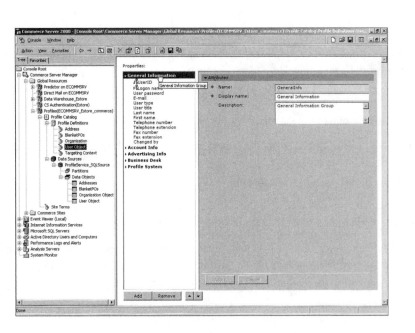

FIGURE 7.6

Definition of a profile.

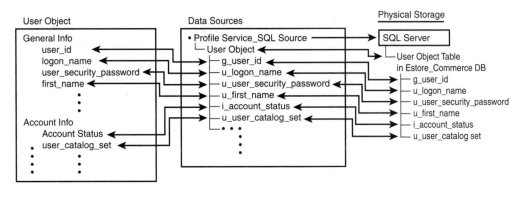

FIGURE 7.7

The CS2K-provided UserObject profile.

From Profile Editor, it can be seen that the profile UserObject is made up of individual properties grouped under common titles. For instance, profile properties such as UserID, Logon

Name, and Email are grouped under General Info. Groups are just for organizing data members so that accessing profile properties is convenient. We have already encountered examples of accessing profile properties. Here's an example:

```
sLoginName = mscsUser.Fields(GeneralInfo.logon_name).Value
```

In this case, `mscsUser` is an instance of the UserObject profile.

There are other profiles provided by the Retail package. The Address profile is used to collect address information of users. The Organization profile definition could be used to store and access profiles for organizations or groups of users.

Commerce Server provides you with the infrastructure to create many more such profiles based on unique requirements.

Using the reference to the user profile just created using the `GetNewGuestUserProfile` function, some of the profile properties of the current user are set to initial values (database columns and corresponding values are shown in parentheses):

```
user_type = GUEST_PROFILE ( in the table i_user_type=0)
account_status = ACCOUNT_ACTIVE (i_account_status=1)
date_created= Now()      (d_date_last_changed=current date)
```

Programmatically, a profile property is set using a statement like this:

```
GetNewGuestUserProfile.Fields("GeneralInfo.user_type").Value = GUEST_PROFILE
```

We have already discussed profile schemas and ways to access them using `ProfileObject` objects in the section "Profile Schemas." These values can be stored permanently in the database table using the following statement:

```
GetNewGuestUserProfile.Update()
```

Therefore, step 5 is accomplished using the COM objects associated with profiles. Also, the `date_last_changed` value is sent to the browser as a cookie called ProfileVersion.

Generating a Ticket

Note that the program flow control is still inside the `EnsureAccess()` routine defined in `std_access_lib.asp`. We have so far created a profile for the user and then persisted it to the database. At this point, we have already determined the ticket mode as well as generated a profile (user ID) for the anonymous user. The ticket to be generated is the MSCSProfile ticket because the user is anonymous and the ticket is to be placed in a cookie and sent to the browser. All this is done via a call to the `SetProfileTicket` method of the `MSCSAuthManager` object, inside the `EnsureAccess()` routine:

```
Call mscsAuthMgr.SetProfileTicket(sUserID, TRUE)
```

The second parameter to the method indicates ticket mode: TRUE for cookie, and FALSE for URL string. In our example, SetProfileTicket generates the persistent MSCSProfile cookie and sends it to the browser. Therefore, step 7 is accomplished. Finally, the page the browser requested—the generated contents of default.asp—is delivered (step 8).

Finally, here are our key observations illustrated. The MSCSProfile cookie on my hard disk is as shown:

```
MSCSProfile
95385A1F52DEA1A229D5B375420544645CA678B1C3151F07FE45F357D7A637B6AC9EBC3FD7B596
➡7CD819525236650EFB86EB47EC000AE63A85227AE92098BCEDFEFF63AB80131955E7B5
➡3342CA2B695BB3E7A5D315DAD2621F58A74D75604FDC7703F4E5909663CA9AC9FFB471
➡D6C28E5C34B9AD80C553C053E9869E289EC1AFAE855CE7B7340161
ecommsrv/Estore
0
4121806848
32111112
1084916688
29394947
*
```

Note that the cookie is encrypted and therefore can be read by Commerce Server only. The database table UserObject in the Estore_commerce database is populated with a row for the user with values as shown in Figure 7.8. Only a subset of columns is shown in this figure.

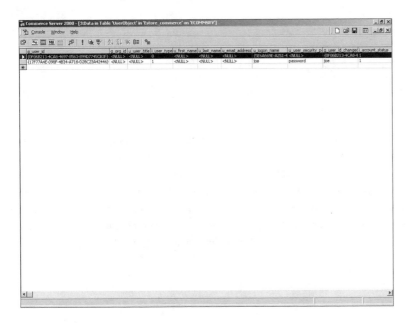

FIGURE 7.8

The data store for the UserObject profile.

Cookies-less Browsing

The example so far with Estore shows how different application pages, routines, and COM objects can interact for a specific instance of the workflow. As you might have guessed, there are a lot of combinations possible based on unique requirements—you might force login upon site entry, disable anonymous profiling, and so on. For example, if the browser is set to deny cookies, the MSCSProfile ticket would have been placed in a URL string (see Figure 7.9).

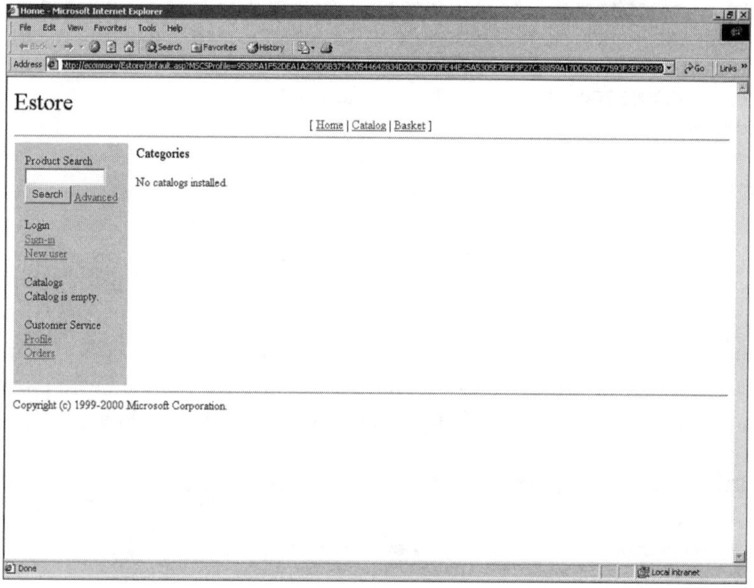

FIGURE 7.9

A ticket embedded in a URL string.

Estore does not force the user to sign in at any time. This means that anonymous users can browse catalogs available to them and place orders without having to register with the site. In real online life, stores such as Walmart.com allow this option as long as the anonymous user enters all the information required for processing the order. The advantage of signing in from the shoppers' point of view is that most sites fill out forms for them. Information such as shipping address, billing address, and credit card details is automatically filled in for the customer upon checking out the shopping cart. For the online store, it would be easy to personalize and target registered shoppers with appropriate merchandise. In terms of the back-end database, all shopping baskets, profiles, and orders will have the user ID as the key reference.

User Registration

The home page in Estore that the anonymous user sees displays no catalogs to the user (refer to Figure 7.1). This is because no catalogs were assigned to the Anonymous User Catalog Set. However, there might be other cases where users need to sign in. Therefore, let's see how a user registers and, after that, signs in. Click the New User link on the home page. Control goes to the login/newuser.asp page. As usual, setupenv.asp calls GetUserInfo() to find out the user type. The user type, if you remember, is guest, and the user ID is the GUID generated earlier. Once again, at the end of the GetUserInfo() routine, we have values in the following variables:

```
m_userID
m_UserAccessType
m_UserType
```

Next, inside the EnsureAccess() subroutine, the profile for the user is fetched using a call to the GetCurrentUserProfile function:

```
Set mscsUserProfile = GetCurrentUserProfile()
```

The GetCurrentUserProfile function, in turn, is defined in std_profile_lib.asp and executes the following statement to get the current user's profile object instance:

```
Set GetCurrentUserProfile = MSCSProfileService.GetProfileByKey(FIELD_USER_ID,
➡ m_UserID, PROFILE_TYPE_USER, RETURN_NOTHING_ON_NO_PROFILE)
```

The profile service fetches the user profile from the cache and returns a reference to the profile. The same sequence of GetUserInfo() and EnsureAccess() happens in most of the site pages to determine the user and get the user profile.

Once control returns to the main() subroutine in newuser.asp, the registration form is generated and displayed to the browser (see Figure 7.10).

Enter the values for user name and password and then click the Submit button. The form is posted to the same page (that is, newuser.asp). The IsFormSubmitted() routine in the included file form_lib.asp detects that the registration form is being submitted rather than the New User link being clicked from the home page. Then, the GetSubmittedFieldValues() routines fetch the form variables and the values. Note, again, that routines related to form operations are defined in form_lib.asp.

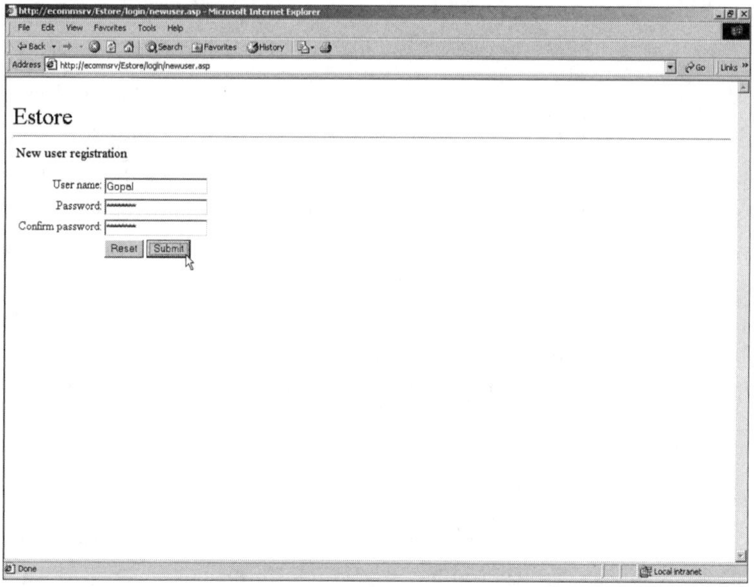

FIGURE 7.10

The registration form in the starter site.

After the values are retrieved from the form, the following validations are performed by the iValidateSubmittedRegistrationData() subroutine in newuser.asp:

- Check whether the password entered is between the maximum and minimum length.
- Check whether both passwords on the form match.
- Using the profile service cache or the database, check whether the user already exists.

If there is an error in any of these validations, the form will be displayed again with an appropriate error message.

The next step is to determine whether the user already has a guest profile. If so, it is necessary to move the user from the guest profile to the registered profile status. To find out whether the user has a guest profile, the following piece of code in newuser.asp is run:

```
If m_UserType = GUEST_USER Then
            Set mscsGuestUser = GetCurrentUserProfile()
                If Not mscsGuestUser Is Nothing Then
                        If mscsGuestUser.Fields(GetQualifiedName
                    ➥(GENERAL_INFO_GROUP, PROFILE_TYPE)).Value
                    ➥ = GUEST_PROFILE Then
                            bMustTransferProfile = True
                    End If
            End If
    End If
```

You can see from the preceding code that `bMustTransferProfile` is set to `True` if the user needs to be transferred from a guest status to the registered status. Because, in our example, the anonymous user has a guest profile, the user will be transferred by the `mscsTransferGuestUserProfile()` subroutine, which essentially achieves the transfer using the following statements:

```
mscsUser.Fields(GetQualifiedName(GENERAL_INFO_GROUP, LOGON_NAME)).Value =
➥sLoginName
          mscsUser.Fields(GetQualifiedName(GENERAL_INFO_GROUP,
          ➥LOGON_PASSWORD)).Value = sLoginPassword
          mscsUser.Fields(GetQualifiedName(GENERAL_INFO_GROUP, MODIFIED_BY))
          ➥.Value = sLoginName
          mscsUser.Fields(GetQualifiedName(GENERAL_INFO_GROUP,
          ➥PROFILE_TYPE)).Value = REGISTERED_PROFILE

          mscsUser.Fields(GetQualifiedName(ACCOUNT_INFO_GROUP,
          ➥ACCOUNT_STATUS)).Value = ACCOUNT_ACTIVE
          mscsUser.Fields(GetQualifiedName(ACCOUNT_INFO_GROUP,
          ➥DATE_REGISTERED)).Value = Now()
Call UpdateUserProfile(mscsUser)
```

The routine `UpdateUserProfile()` defined in `std_profile_lib.asp` ultimately calls the `Update()` method of the `ProfileObject` object to persist the profile changes to the database. You can see from the statements that the values updated in the UserObject table for the user are the logon name, modified_by, user_type, and date_registered columns. At this stage, if you look at the UserObject database table again, you can see that the row for the anonymous user is updated (see Figure 7.11).

Sending the MSCSAuth Ticket

The user was successfully registered; hence, the user is also automatically authenticated for this session. Therefore, the MSCSAuth ticket is sent as a cookie to the browser using the `SetAuthTicket` method of the `MSCSAuthManager` object, as shown here:

```
Call mscsAuthMgr.SetAuthTicket(sUserID, WRITE_TICKET_TO_COOKIE,
➥dictConfig.i_FormLoginTimeOut)
```

The third parameter to the `SetAuthTicket` method specifies the time that should be stamped on the MSCSAuth cookie. This is the time in minutes within which the login is valid. As shown in Figure 7.12, this time is specified at the site-level App Default Config Properties sheet as follows:

```
AuthManager AuthTicket Timeout = 60
```

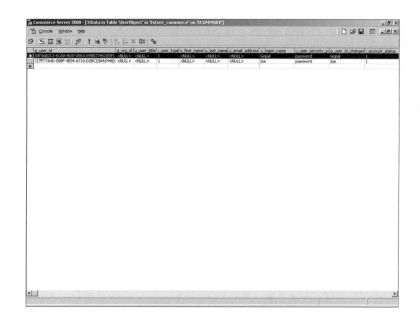

FIGURE 7.11

The user is moved from guest to registered status.

FIGURE 7.12

Time specified at the site-level App Default Config Properties sheet.

Note that the MSCSAuth cookie is nonpersistent and exists only as long as the browser session. Therefore, if the user closes all browsers and then hits the site, the user has to sign in again.

Finally, the browser is redirected to the `default.asp` page (see Figure 7.13).

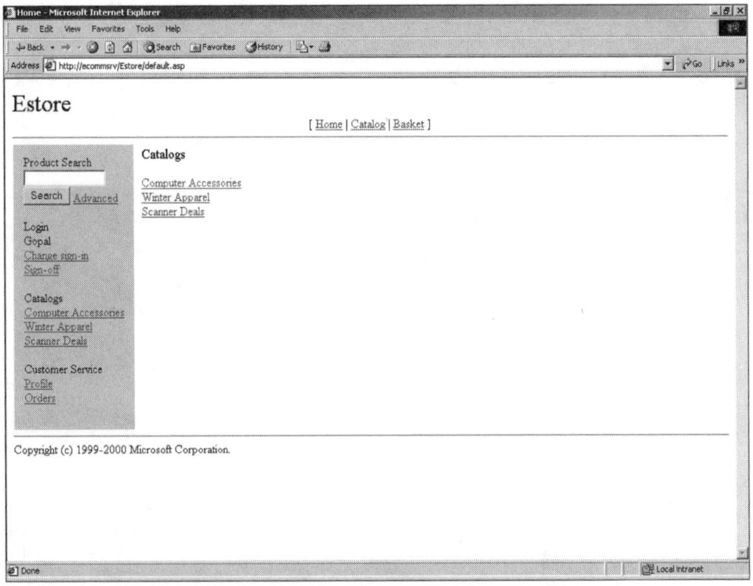

FIGURE 7.13

The home page for a registered user.

As you can see, the user now has a registered profile; therefore, catalogs available to the Registered Users Catalog Set are shown. Here's a summary of the steps taken in creating/ registering a new user:

1. Get the values from the registration form displayed in the `newuser.asp` page.
2. Do form validation and check for the existence of the user login.
3. If the current user has a profile and the type is guest profile, update the user profile as registered. Update other information such as logon name and password for the user.
4. If the user does not yet have a profile, create a new one with the registration form values.
5. Send the MSCSAuth ticket to the browser either as a cookie or URL string.

A Little Personalization

This section demonstrates a little of the personalization that our Estore already has. At this point, I have a registered login with the site. If I close all the open browser windows and hit the site again, the site recognizes me as a returning customer (see Figure 7.14).

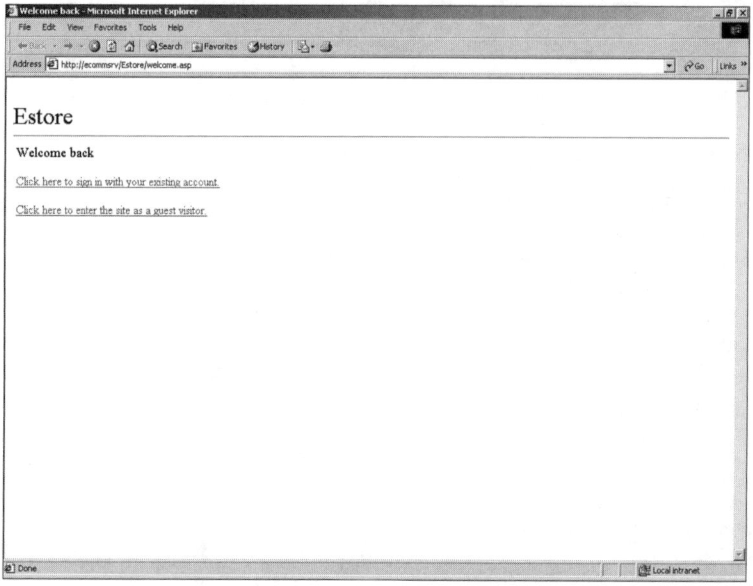

Figure 7.14

Detection of a returning customer.

Note that only the MSCSProfile ticket would have been there with my browser. The MSCSProfile has the user ID in encrypted form. The `GetUserInfo()` routines declares me as a guest user by finding the guest ticket(MSCSProfile):

```
mscsAuthMgr.GetUserID(GUEST_TICKET)
```

This user ID is used to get the profile of the user from the profile service cache or database from which the profile type of the user is determined. Because my profile is of type "registered," the system knows that I am a returning user. Therefore, my status now is a registered user with a guest status until I physically log in, after which I would be a registered and authenticated user. Hence, the welcome page is shown containing both the options of signing in as well as continuing as a guest visitor.

To recapitulate, at any point in time a visitor to the site will have guest status if the user has an anonymous profile with the status of "guest" and has not yet registered or has a registered profile with the status of "registered" and has not yet logged in. Only in the latter case is a welcome page shown.

Assume that we want to sign in with our existing account. Click the link shown in Figure 7.14. In the login form, shown in Figure 7.15, enter the user name and password but don't yet click the Submit button. We are going to actually see the MSCSAuth cookie being sent to the browser after authentication.

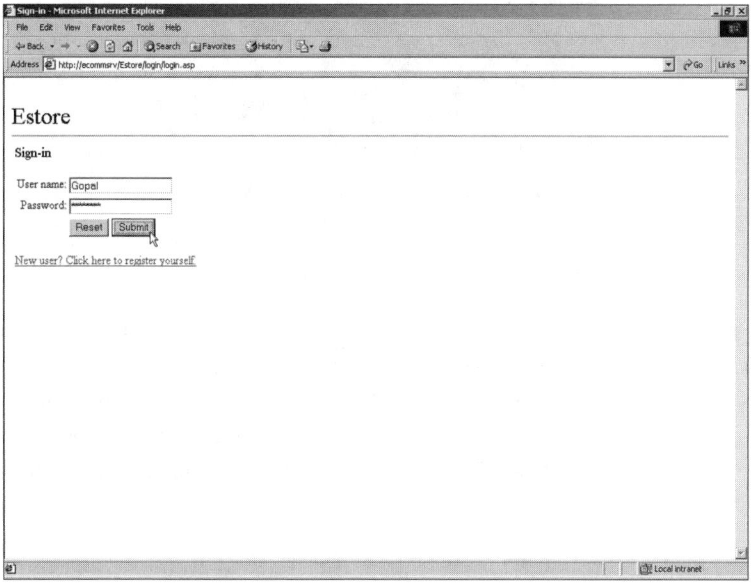

FIGURE 7.15
The login form for the starter store.

Before clicking the Submit button, change your browser option so that there will be a prompt before any type of cookie is accepted by the browser. For example, Internet Explorer (IE) 5.5 users would choose the Tool, Internet Options menu item, go to the Security tab, click the Custom Level button, and then change the Cookies settings for persistent and session cookies to Prompt. Now click the Submit button in the login form. If you, the user, are authenticated successfully, the browser is sent the MSCSAuth cookie with the information shown in Figure 7.16.

You would click the Yes button to accept the cookie. Something to observe in the Security Alert window is that the cookie expires at the end of session and therefore is not persisted to the hard disk. Also, the data in the cookie is encrypted.

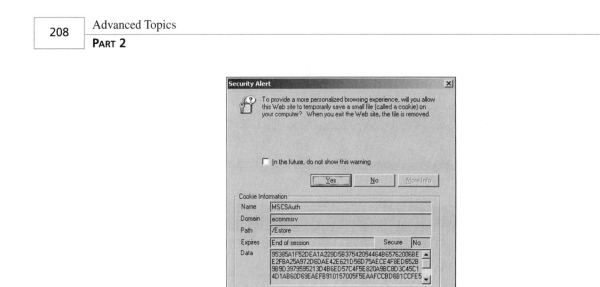

FIGURE 7.16

A browser receiving a Commerce Server cookie.

As soon as the Submit button is clicked in the login form, the program flow transfers to the `login/login.asp` page. The `login.asp` page works pretty much in a standard way. First, it collects the login form information and tries to fetch the user profile for the login name entered using the function `ValidateSubmittedLoginData`. After a couple more wrapper functions, a call is made to the `GetInfo()` method of the `ProfileObject` object for the current user:

```
Call rsProfile.GetInfo()
```

The `GetInfo()` method forces a database lookup. If there is no profile or some error occurs in the form, a corresponding error message is returned by this method. Upon a successful profile fetch, the `SetAuthTicket` method of `MSCSAuthManager` is called to send the MSCSAuth ticket to the browser, which you saw in the figure. At this point, you can change your browser settings again to automatically accept cookies.

You can use the `URLArgs()` method of the `AuthManager` object to generate custom cookie name/value strings to be attached to the ticket before it is sent. This way, you can put whatever personalization information you want in the cookie. Now let's take a look at the Biz Desk modules related to user management.

Managing Users from the Biz Desk

You already know that the `newuser.asp` page on the Web site can be used by site visitors to update their own profiles. It is also quite possible that an administrator has to attach a user to a company profile. In this exercise, we will see how to use the Biz Desk modules to create a company profile and link a user to the company. Launch the Biz Desk application for Estore. Click the Users menu in the navigation bar and then click the Organizations link to launch the module.

Let's say the name of the new company we want to create is Resellers Inc. This could be an upstream reseller organization. In the toolbar, click the New Organizations button or press the key combination ALT+N. The result is shown in Figure 7.17.

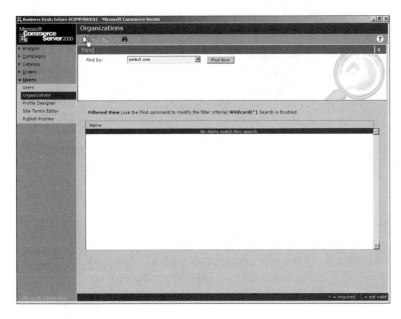

FIGURE 7.17

The Organizations profile.

Recall that the Organizations profile is provided by Commerce Server. You can look at the schema of the profile from either the Profile Designer module here in Biz Desk or from Commerce Server Manager under Profile Definitions in the global Profiles resource for the site.

In the New Organization edit page, shown in Figure 7.18, enter **Resellers Inc.** for the Name property and click the Save toolbar button.

Observe at this time that the select boxes for Administrative Contact, Receiver, and Purchasing Manager do not yet have any users. This is because we haven't attached any users to this organization. We will do it now. Click the leftmost arrow button on the toolbar to return to the organization's list page. Then click the link Users to access the Users module.

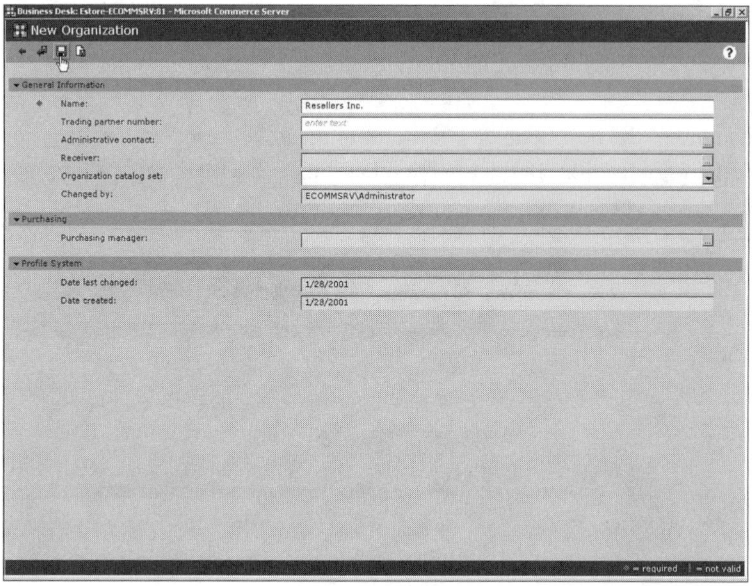

FIGURE 7.18

Creating and saving a new organization.

We will attach the user Gopal to the organization Resellers Inc. Therefore, in the Users module, do a search using any of the user profile properties to fetch the user and then click the user in the Filtered View results box (see Figure 7.19). Now click the Open User toolbar button or type ALT+O.

Browse available organizations by clicking the button next to the Organization ID field under the Account Info section. Then in the Select Organization dialog box, you may have to search for the organization we just added. Because wildcard searches are allowed, you can type **Res*** in the Name text box and click the Find Now button. Once "Resellers Inc." is found and displayed, choose it and click the OK button (see Figure 7.20).

Then click the Save User toolbar button or press the ALT+S key combination. Notice that it is possible to update other properties of the user profile from Biz Desk itself, such as First Name, Last Name, and so on. However, the user can update the profile by using one of the site pages (`services/customer/account.asp`) by clicking the Profiles link on the Estore site's navigation menu.

Now if you go back to the Organizations module and edit Resellers Inc., you should be able to see this user in the Select User dialog box, launched for properties such as Administrative Contact.

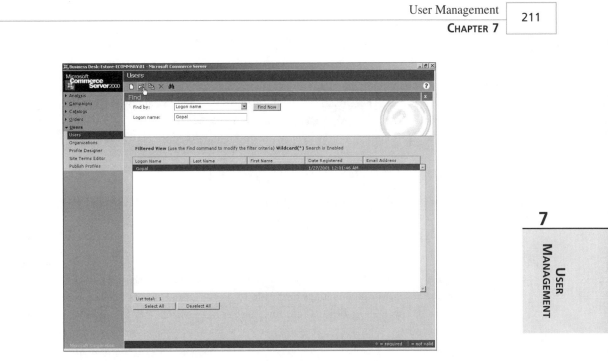

FIGURE 7.19

Searching for a user.

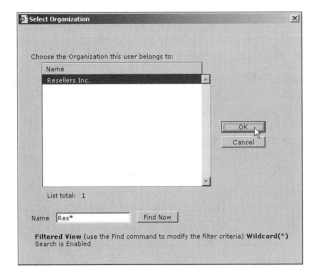

FIGURE 7.20

Linking an organization to a user.

Therefore, we can see how profiles can be linked and used for satisfying various requirements. For instance, if a company has many upstream reseller partners, there would be specialized catalogs for each partner. These catalogs would then be assigned in catalog sets to each organization. When a user of an organization logs in to the site, the site can display the catalog set assigned to the organization, overriding any assignments to the individual user profile.

Summary of the Profile System

Commerce Server provides a ready-made infrastructure to support creation and management of profiles. The solution sites are provided with prebuilt profiles, such as UserObject and Addresses. To be able to extend the profile system, one needs to understand its architecture and extensibility. Here are the important items in our discussions of the profile system so far:

- `ProfileService` *object*. This object is used to create, delete, and get access to individual profiles. Whenever any changes are made to profiles, the Profiles Service has to be synchronized with the database. Therefore, run Profile Service Refresh under Users in the business desk.

- `ProfileObject` *object*. This object is used to retrieve and update individual profiles. A profile is an address, user information, or an organization, as defined by the profile definitions. Therefore, a reference to a `ProfileObject` object of a particular profile type is obtained using the `ProfileService` object.

- *Profile definitions*. These are the schemas that define individual profiles. They map to corresponding back-end data sources. Use the Commerce Server Manager or the Biz Desk Profile Designer to edit profiles.

- *Data sources*. Each profile is mapped to a back-end data store, which can be an OLEDB database or an LDAP source. Typically, RDBMS tables map to profiles and table columns map to profile properties.

The Authentication Filter

You have seen so far that anonymous users are able to access `default.asp` and other site pages. Also, the `MSCSAuthManager` object is used in each of the pages to identify the type of user and then ensure that the user has access to the appropriate content. This type of access control is at the page level, coupled with the ability to use form login. There is another way that authentication can be applied—at the site level. This is accomplished by installing an Internet Server API (ISAPI) filter on the application site. The ISAPI filter will intercept all HTTP requests first and then redirect to the application. The filter provided by Commerce Server is called AuthFilter and is present in `<commerce_server_installation_dir>/SiteAuth.dll`.

The authentication filter can operate in one of two modes: authenticating against Active Directory or against a custom database. In Windows 2000, the system database is called the Active Directory, where information about various elements such as users, computers, and printers is stored. AuthFilter can be configured to authenticate users against the Active Directory or with another database, such as SQL Server.

Let's apply the authentication filter on Estore. In the Commerce Server Manager, expand the Applications folder for Estore. Right-click the <your_servername>/Estore node and choose the Properties menu item (see Figure 7.21).

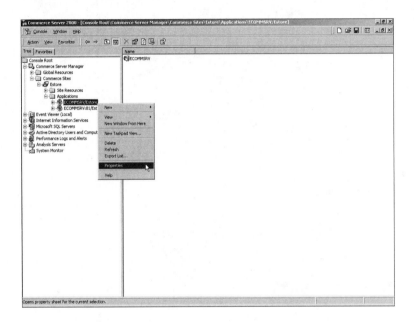

FIGURE 7.21
Launching the Properties dialog box of a CS application.

In the Properties dialog box, observe that initially the No Filter option is chosen for the authentication filter. Now change the filter to Windows Authentication and click the OK button (see Figure 7.22).

Now the filter is applied to the IIS application for Estore. We can verify this by right-clicking the Estore Web site (not the Estore virtual directory) and opening its Properties sheet using the Internet Information Services MMC snap-in. Click the ISAPI Filters tab (see Figure 7.23).

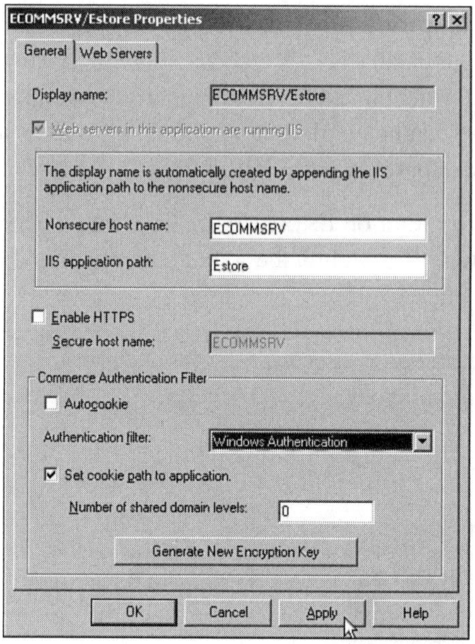

FIGURE 7.22

Modifying the authentication filter mode.

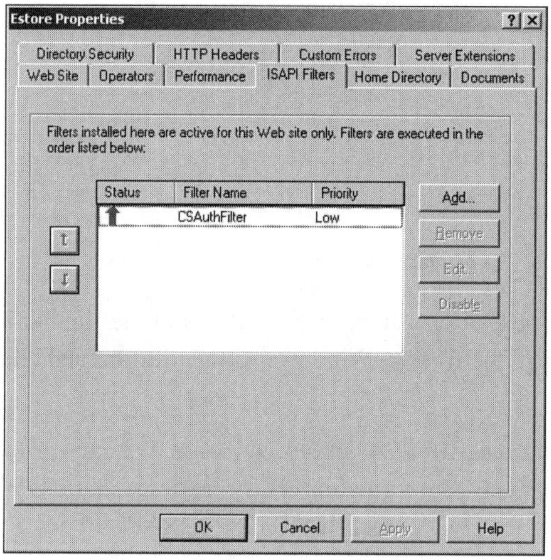

FIGURE 7.23

AuthFilter is applied to the IIS site.

Remember to unload the IIS application after making these changes. Now if a user hits the Estore web site, AuthFilter will intercept and automatically redirect to the Authfiles/login.asp page (see Figure 7.24).

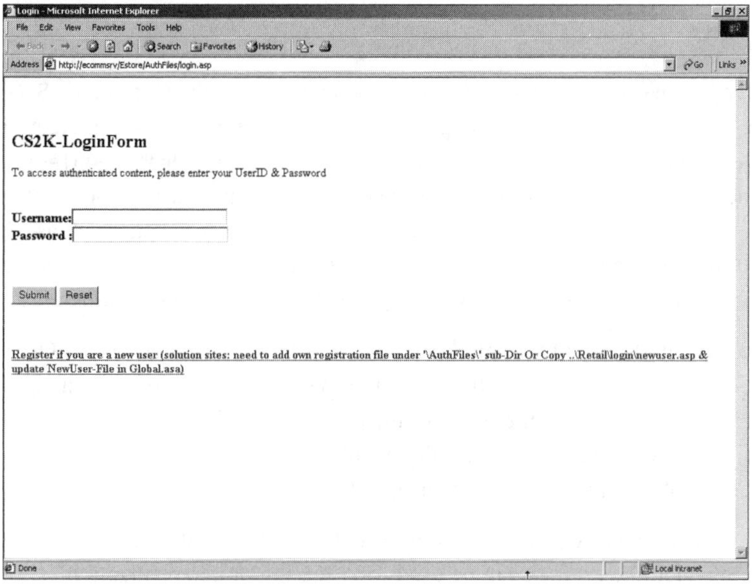

FIGURE 7.24
The login form for Windows or custom authentication.

You can choose to authenticate against Windows 2000 Active Directory or any Directory Service that is LDAP version 3 compliant. There are many commercial LDAP servers available in the market. To use a Windows Active Directory as the authentication database, remember that you should first create a data source for the Profiles Service global resource for the site. Before that, it is essential to have Active Directory installed on the machine that is a domain controller. Further, because Active Directory depends on DNS for name resolution, DNS also should be set up. Contact your system administrator to make sure the machine is configured to use Active Directory. Because implementing an Active Directory is a specialized topic in itself, you should refer to Microsoft documentation or to *Microsoft Active Directory Administration*, by Kevin Kocis (Sams Publishing, 2000).

Once a data source for Active Directory is created, the login.asp page can be customized to access the appropriate data source using the Profiles Service. Also, for a site authenticated against Active Directory, certain changes, such as removing anonymous access at the IIS site level and using LOGON_USER instead of AUTH_USER to retrieve the current user, are required to be performed. The PuP package SupplierActiveDirectory is a sample site that contains many of these changes preconfigured so that a company trying to build a partner Web site can use this package to start building the site.

Summary

In this chapter you learned how the starter site application uses the Commerce Server architecture to manage site users. We went through the steps involved in validating, creating, and retrieving users. The key COM objects, such as `ProfileService`, `ProfileObject`, and `MSCSAuthManager`, were utilized throughout the discussion. Specifically, the `MSCSAuthManager` object was used for page-level authentication and managing user tickets, such as MSCSProfile and MSCSAuth. The `ProfileService` and `ProfileObject` objects were used in the context of accessing specific instances of profile types, such as User Profile and Addresses.

We also went through the Biz Desk modules, such as Profile Designer, Users, Organizations, and Profile Service Refresh, that can be utilized in managing user profiles. The core of the Profile System was analyzed with regards to the profile definitions, data sources, and physical data stores. Finally, we discussed in brief the AuthFilter authentication filter, which can be installed to perform authentication using custom data sources.

This chapter provides a basic grounding in user authentication and profiling. The next chapter covers ways in which the profiles can be used for targeting or personalization.

Personalization and Targeting

IN THIS CHAPTER

- Methods of Profiling   218
- Methods of Targeting   219
- Catalog Sets   220
- Campaigns   223
- Applying a Site Wide Discount   224
- Targeting Discounts   233
- Catalog Expressions and
  Target Expressions   244
- Target Group   248

Given the option, my colleague always suggests that we go to a particular restaurant. Even though there are quite a few similar places around to eat, this restaurant seems to have something that keeps him going back frequently. Apart from the good food, the waiter probably knows what my friend likes best. You get special treatment instead of feeling like one in a thousand. Successful Web sites such as Amazon, Yahoo!, AOL, and MSN have found that making their online customers feel special makes the customers visit repeatedly. Even a recent study conducted by Nielsen/Netratings proves that personalization results in a manifold increase in customer loyalty.

Personalization of a Web site is yet to become a commonly accepted concept, let alone become an industry standard. Personalization means different things to different people, and is implemented in a variety of ways. *Portals* allow users to customize pages for stock, weather, news, and sports according to individual interest. E-Commerce sites welcome the user by name, fill out order form details such as address and credit card information automatically, and even help maintain wish lists. In recent times, several new approaches such as collaborative filtering and artificial intelligence techniques have begun to help sites provide meaningful content to browsers. Whatever the techniques or methods used, personalization means telling users that a site is designed for them. The content is targeted entirely to make the visit useful. This results in repeated visits and ultimately affects the bottom line.

Methods of Profiling

The first step in personalization is to know who the user is. To understand what the user wants, it is important to know who the user is and something about his usage behavior. The collection of such usage behavior could help predict a future user need. All user information is stored as a profile and is called the *user profile*. Commerce Server comes with a default profile called the *User Object*, which stores user information such as user ID, password, logon name, e-mail address, first name, last name, and so on. You can customize the object to store more or less of the user's information. When user information is available, it will be possible to deliver content based on certain algorithms. For example, based on the user's country of residence, MSN welcomes him with Hotmail news and articles specific to that country when signing off.

How does user information get into the system? User information gets profiled implicitly or explicitly. Asking a user to fill out a registration form is an example of *explicit profiling*. Automatically recording how frequently a user visits a site or page is known as *implicit profiling*. A good source for implicit profiling is the Web server logs. Both methods of profiling provide more information about the user and his behavior. Apart from serving pages based on user profile, the tendency to deliver content based on the context profile is also increasing. Both of these bases complement each other. A *context profile* is the information about content that the user is currently viewing or that is being delivered. For instance, it would make more sense to show an airline ad in a hotel reservation page instead of showing it in a book catalog.

Grouping pages by subject, such as sports pages, might help identify where to display sports ads. Commerce Server provides you with a default profile called *targeting context*. Thus, using the User Object and Targeting Context, one can target appropriate content to the right user in the right context.

Methods of Targeting

As I said earlier, algorithms are developed to serve the right content, given the user and context data as inputs. These algorithms could be relatively simple or exceedingly complex, depending on the need and sophistication desired by a site. While speaking about content delivery, these algorithms are generally referred to as *rules*. In Commerce Server, these rules are called *expressions*. For example the expression `userObject.purchases > 1000` might be true if the user has spent more than $1,000 on your site. The Expression Builder, provided with Commerce Server, can be a handy tool to create expressions. Once created, expressions can be used alone or combined with other expressions to determine the delivery rules. For instance, the following is a combination of expressions to form a group.

```
userObject.purchases > 1000 AND product.price < 100.0
```

Note that the data used in an expression can be anything such as user data, context data, and product data. The engine that applies the expressions to the user or context inputs is called the *Expression Evaluator* (see Figure 8.1). It is encapsulated in the COM object `ExpressionEval` provided with the installation.

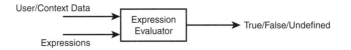

FIGURE 8.1

The Expression Evaluator.

The output of the Expression Evaluator will be `True` or `False`, depending on whether the user/ context data met the corresponding expression. Depending on the output, action will be taken to deliver specific content. As you can see, this method of targeting involves knowledge of

- User and/or context data
- Expressions
- Content to be delivered based on the expression.

Knowing all these elements provides an explicit framework for targeting content and hence can be called *explicit targeting*. The expression simply establishes a relationship between input (such as user data) and the output (such as specific content). This relationship is illustrated in Figure 8.2.

8

**PERSONALIZATION
AND TARGETING**

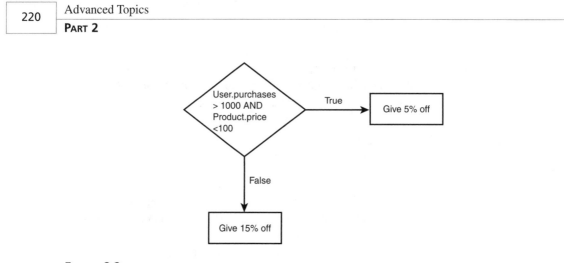

FIGURE 8.2

The explicit targeting rule.

A lot of times it might not be possible to know all the elements beforehand. For example, the user might not have entered information in an optional form field. Even if you have enough user or context information, it might be better to let other users or context dictate the delivery of content. A good example of this would be a section in Amazon.com suggesting what other customers of this book also bought. This technique of delivering content based on past user behavior is predictive in nature. The relationship between the various elements is derived out of vast amounts of user and transaction data collected in data warehouses. Then models are built based on this past data, establishing patterns between the elements of the model. Therefore, by supplying only a few attributes to the model, it is possible to predict the other attributes that form part of the model.

For instance, if it is known that a user is male, under 22, and is in college, your site can display products that were bought in the past by this segment of site visitors. This method of delivering content that will probably be liked by a site visitor is called *Prediction*. Prediction can be thought of as implicit targeting because we look at a few of the available parameters and then imply an output based on similarity. Commerce Server provides you with the necessary tools to build prediction models and ask for predictions using COM objects.

Catalog Sets

You have already seen a certain amount of personalization capability in Commerce Server. Remember the two default catalog sets? They are Anonymous User Default CatalogSet and

Registered User Default CatalogSet. The catalog pages, which deliver the catalog information to the browser, check whether any catalog sets are assigned in the user's profile. If found, catalogs in that particular catalog set are displayed. Otherwise, catalogs in one of the two default catalog sets are retrieved, depending on whether the user is anonymous or authenticated. Right now, if I visit the Estore Web site, the home page (see Figure 8.3) displays no catalogs because I am an anonymous user (guest user status).

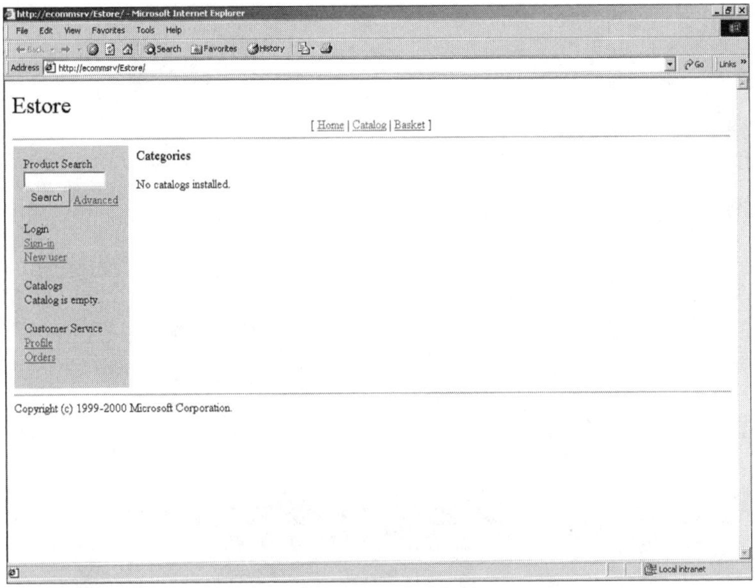

FIGURE 8.3
The home page for an anonymous user.

No catalogs are displayed because the Anonymous User Default CatalogSet has no catalogs assigned to it. This can be verified from the Catalog Sets module in Business Desk. Assign the Computer Accessories catalog to the Anonymous User Default CatalogSet. To do that, launch the Catalog Sets module from the Business Desk and then open the CatalogSet as shown in Figure 8.4.

Now choose Computer Accessories from the Available catalogs, and then click the Add button (see Figure 8.5). The catalog now becomes part of the Assigned catalogs list. Then save and exit this screen.

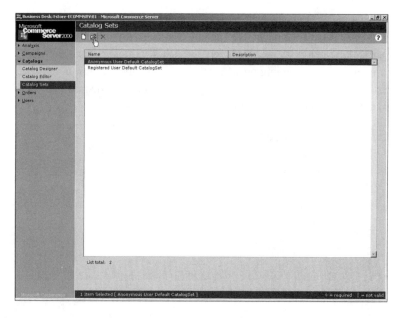

FIGURE 8.4

Editing a CatalogSet.

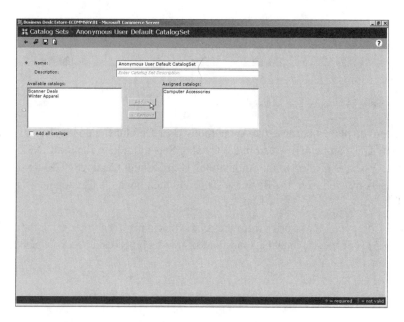

FIGURE 8.5

Editing the default CatalogSet for anonymous users.

Unload the Estore application from IIS. When I visit the site again, I find that as an anonymous user, I get access to the Computer Accessories catalog (see Figure 8.6).

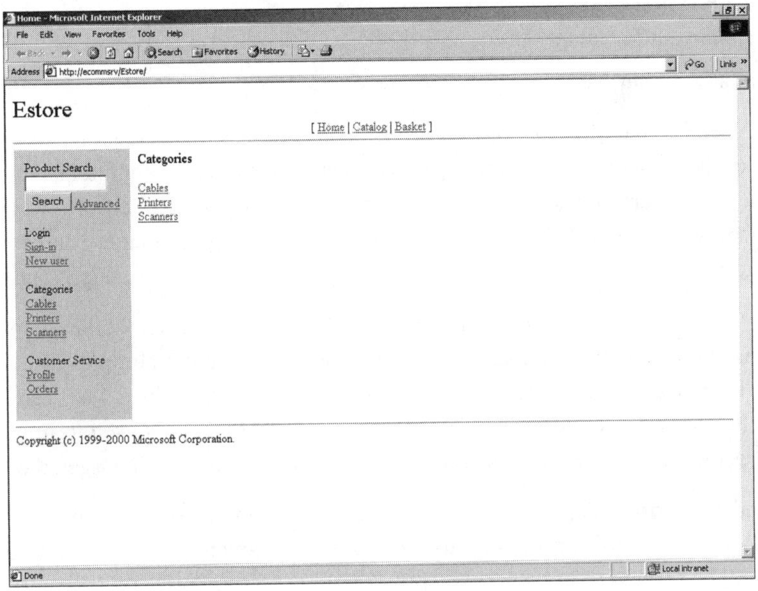

FIGURE 8.6

A catalog available to the anonymous user.

Observe that the categories of Computer Accessories are displayed directly at the first level. This is no surprise because if there is only one catalog to be displayed, the contents of the catalog are displayed directly.

The previous Catalog Sets example shows how catalogs can be served, depending on the user profile. It's possible to create multiple Catalog Sets and assign them to groups of users, thereby personalizing catalogs to individual users.

Campaigns

A company might have many marketing initiatives to increase sales. Programs such as seasonal discounts, promotional offers, and targeted advertisements are all part of those initiatives. In an online business too, these programs have a significant effect on site visits and sales. Commerce Server provides you with a facility called Campaigns to effectively address a variety of these marketing needs.

A *campaign* is thus a marketing program that uses various vehicles such as ads, discounts, and direct e-mails to achieve certain marketing goals. Typical marketing goals are to

- Promote a new product or service
- Increase the market share
- Sustain a customer base

The various vehicles that a campaign uses are called *campaign items*. Commerce Server offers ads, discounts and direct mails as campaign items. The ad campaign item helps you display ad banners targeted at users and context. These banners could be for yourself or for third-party advertisers who want to put their ads on your site. The Campaign Manager business desk module gives you the ability to store advertisers' information and create campaigns for them.

A discount is a standard way to attract shoppers and also increase cross-sell and up-sell opportunities. A discount campaign item can be created, indicating what amount of discount is offered on which products and under what conditions. Similarly, a Direct Mail campaign item can be launched to target users for sending mails. The List Manager is used to import e-mail IDs. The Direct Mailer is a service used to send customized e-mails to a targeted e-mail list.

To understand the various elements of the personalization and targeting engine of Commerce Server, I will use discounts throughout this chapter. Other campaign items such as ads and direct mail will be discussed in later chapters.

Applying a Site Wide Discount

The business desk modules under Campaigns are used widely to manage the campaigns on the site. I will start with a simple example of applying a site-wide discount. To break in to the world of e-commerce, Estore(the sample site) wants to offer a 25% discount on all products in its first month of launch. To implement this campaign, use the Business Desk module Campaign Manager. The essential steps to successfully create this discount campaign are as follows:

1. Creating the customer
2. Creating the campaign
3. Creating the discount
4. Publishing the campaign

Each of these steps will be discussed in the following sections.

Creating the Customer

Commerce Server requires that you first create a customer (advertiser) before you can add a campaign for him. In this case, Estore itself is the customer. Launch the Estore Business Desk and click the Campaign Manager module. To create a new customer (advertiser), click the toolbar button as shown in Figure 8.7.

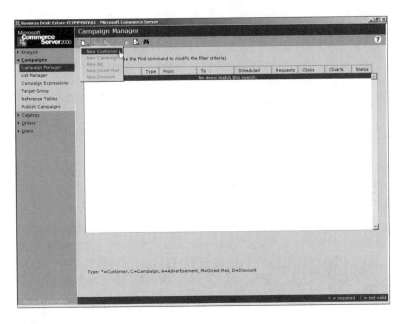

FIGURE 8.7
Creating a new customer.

In the Campaign Manager—New (Customer) page, give the Name of the customer as **Estore**. Choose Self as the Type. Note that the Type could be one of Self, Advertiser, or Agency. Because this campaign is a discount for your site, choose Self. The other values are to be used while creating advertising campaigns. Now click the Save and Back to Campaign Manager List toolbar button (or press ALT+K) to save the new customer to the database and return to the list page (see Figure 8.8).

Creating the Campaign

In the Filtered View list, you should see Estore as one of the customers. Click Estore, and from the file menu, choose New Campaign to create a campaign (see Figure 8.9).

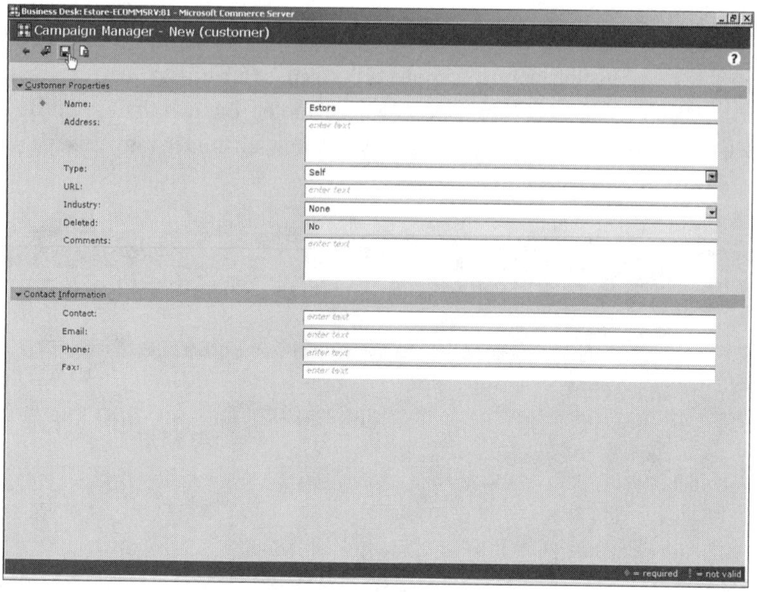

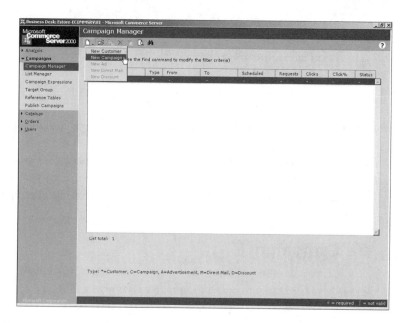

FIGURE 8.8

Saving a new customer to the database.

FIGURE 8.9

Creating a new campaign.

In the New Campaign page, enter the Campaign name as **Site Launch**. Set the Start and End dates for a one-month period in which the Status of this discount will be Active (see Figure 8.10).

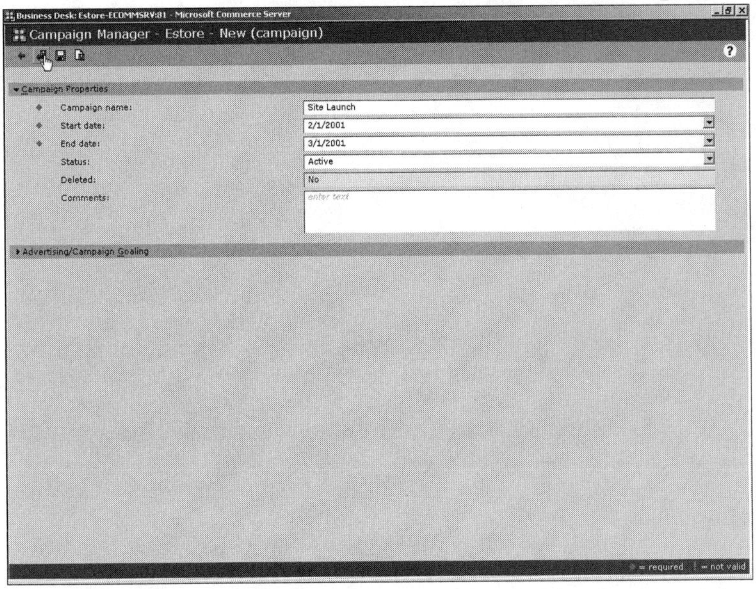

FIGURE 8.10
Creating and saving a new campaign.

Click the Save and Back to Campaign Manager List button, or press the ALT+K key combination on the keyboard. The Advertising/Campaign Goaling section will be covered in a later chapter.

Creating the Discount

Back in the Filtered view, expand Estore (customer) and click Site Launch (the campaign). From the File menu, choose New Discount as shown in Figure 8.11.

In the Discount Properties section (see Figure 8.12), enter the Discount Name as `Site-wide 25% off`. Also set the Start and End dates to cover the one-month of the campaign. The Status of the discount must be made Active.

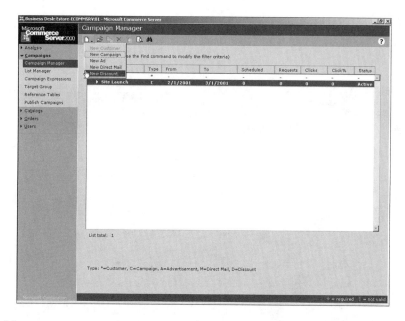

FIGURE 8.11

Menu for creating new discount.

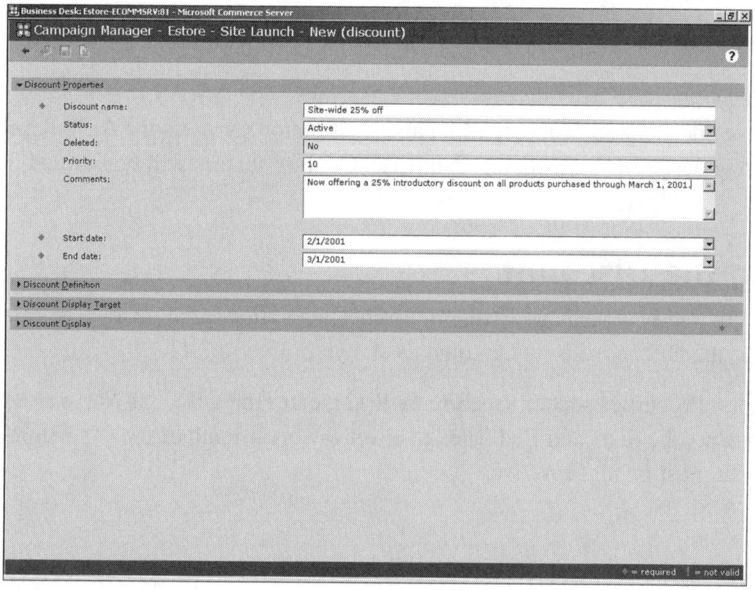

FIGURE 8.12

Discount Properties of a new discount.

The Priority field is used to assign a priority number to this discount. If more than one discount is applicable to a product, a discount with the highest priority is applied. The highest priority number is 10 and the lowest is defined as 200. Therefore, a discount with a priority of 20 will have more probability of being chosen instead of a discount with a priority of 60. I will talk more about the content selection framework in a later chapter.

Now expand the Discount Definition section, which is where you define all the rules involving discount, products, and expressions. Because you want to give a 25% discount on all products, check the Anything box in the Buy section. In the Get section, change the third box to Percent(%) and the fourth box to 25. Leave the Limit box as None (see Figure 8.13) because you aren't going to limit how many times in a session this discount is available to a user. After the selections are made, this row should read Unlimited of [any product] at Percent(%) 25 off. That is all you need in this section. The other elements can be used in various other discount scenarios.

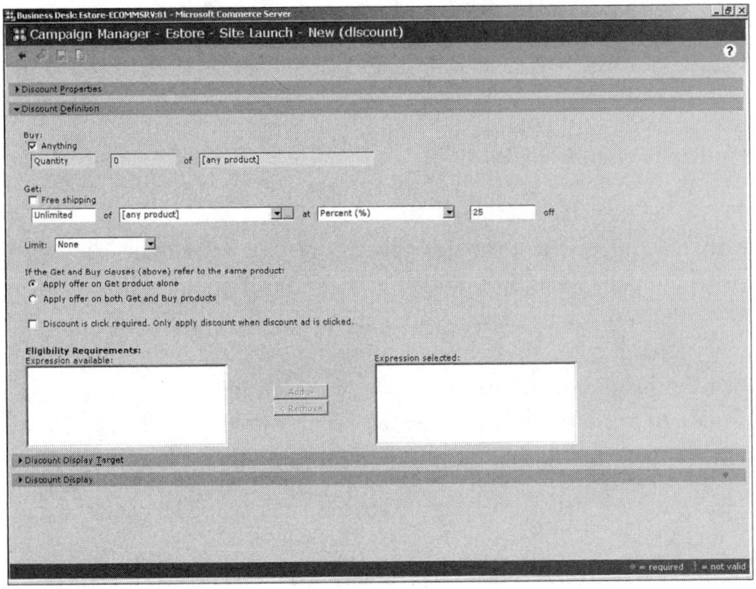

FIGURE 8.13
The discount definitions of the discount.

In the Discount Display Target, leave the Show On All Page Groups check box selected so that the discount is available to all the pages on the site (see Figure 8.14). Again, various options and values can be chosen here for a different discount scenario.

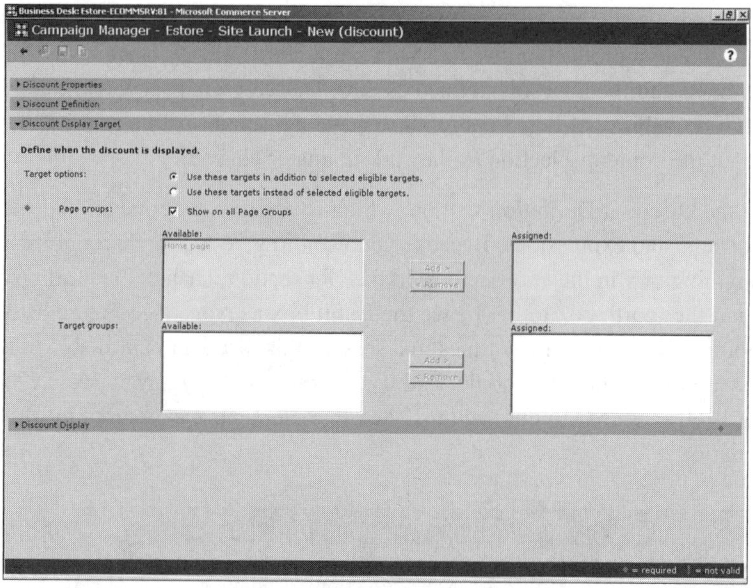

FIGURE 8.14

Defining where the discount should be displayed.

The last section on the new discount page is Discount Display (see Figure 8.15). This section is used to specify how the discount should appear to the user on the Web site. The Content to be displayed for a discount could be an image banner, HTML, plain text, and so on. These are normally used for delivering advertisements. There could also be scenarios in which a discount can be given only after the user clicks a banner. For this simple example, we will choose not to display a banner for this discount. Therefore, choose No Display as Content Type. You can give an explanation of this discount in the Basket Display field. This description will be displayed in the Basket page of the site.

At this point, the minimum necessary information has been entered for a discount item. Now press the Save and Return to Campaign Manager List button (or press ALT+K). Back in the Filtered view, you should now be able to see the customer, campaign, and the discount item created so far (see Figure 8.16).

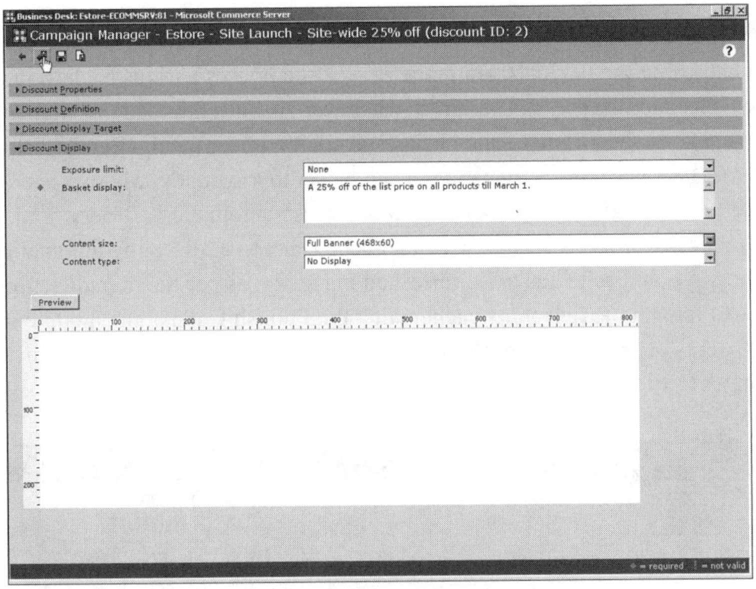

FIGURE 8.15

The Discount Display that will be seen in the Basket page.

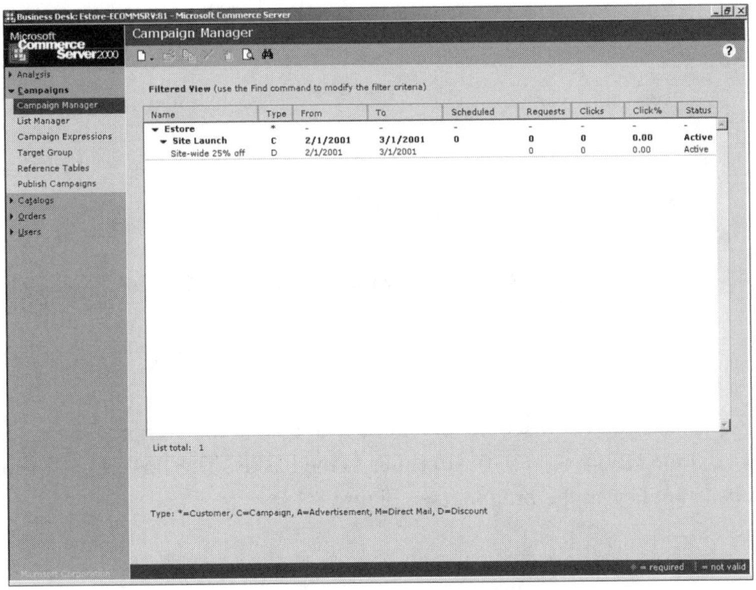

FIGURE 8.16

The site-wide 25% discount.

Publishing the Campaign

You already know that the default Commerce Server site houses various caches, including one for advertisements and discounts. Therefore, whenever changes are made to campaigns, these caches should be refreshed to make the changes available immediately. Recall that the RefreshInterval property of CacheManager can be set to N seconds, where N is the interval between refreshes. The advertising cache is set to refresh automatically every 5 minutes; but the RefreshInterval property of the discount cache is set to 0, disabling automatic refresh. Therefore, the discount cache has to be refreshed manually, as per the default settings in the solution site. To refresh the discounts cache, click the Publish Campaigns module link. In the Publish Campaigns page (see Figure 8.17), click the discounts cache, and then click the Publish Changes to Production and Refresh the Cache button (or press ALT+P).

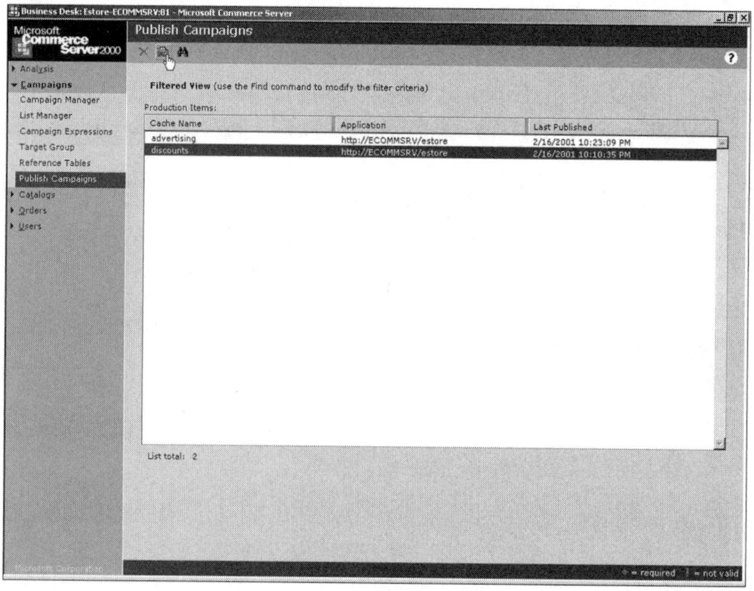

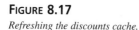

FIGURE 8.17

Refreshing the discounts cache.

The cache is refreshed and the discount should be available at the Web site. So visit the Estore site again and add the HP Deskjet 970cxi printer to the basket. The Basket page shows that the discount has been applied to the product (see Figure 8.18).

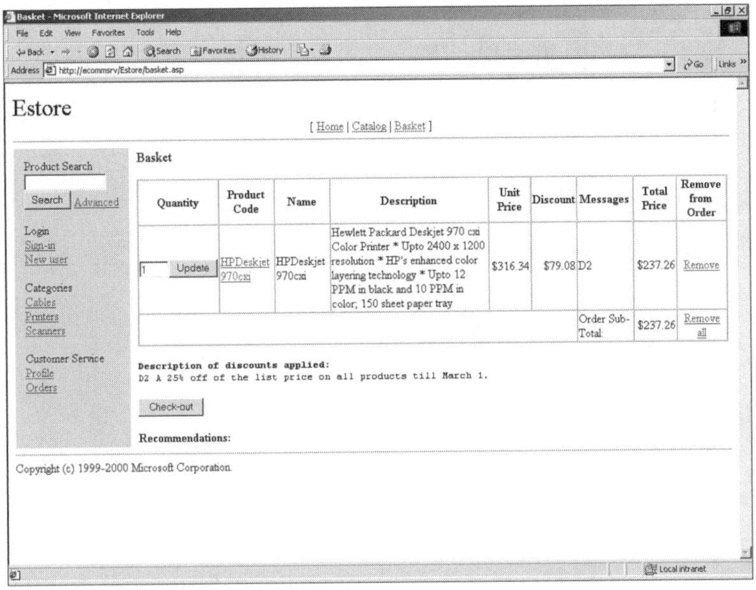

FIGURE 8.18
The discount shown in the basket.

Targeting Discounts

The previous scenario helped you understand some of the basics of the Commerce Server infrastructure such as customers, campaigns, campaign items, Campaign Manager, and Publish Campaigns. It is time to delve deeper into this system and explore the remaining elements. To do that, you will again work through a real-life scenario.

Assume that the marketing whiz kid of Estore comes out with a finding that customers over sixty years of age are proving to be early adopters of e-commerce. Therefore, he wants to offer a larger discount, 50% off list price, on all products to customers over sixty. The other customers would still continue getting the site-wide 25% off. Whatever the merit of the marketing finding, you feel that Commerce Server has everything ready to implement this custom discount idea.

Well, now comes the task of targeting a discount to specific users. The user profile does not contain age in its default schema. This can be seen from the profile page on the Estore site (see Figure 8.19) and from the schema for the back-end table UserObject.

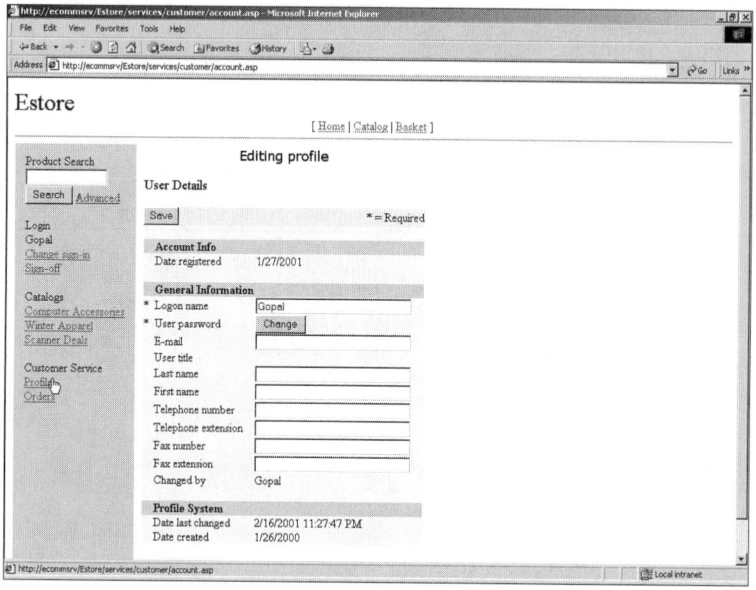

FIGURE 8.19
The profile page for a registered user.

Hence, the first step in implementing the discount will be to modify the user profile to capture the age of a customer. Next, an expression to evaluate that the age of a customer is greater than sixty should be built. Third, a discount will be created under the Site Launch campaign using the expression.

Modifying the User Profile

You have already seen the inter-relationship between data sources, profile definitions, and the database. Here you will add a property called Age to the user profile. The steps needed to achieve this are as follows:

1. Modify the database table schema.
2. Modify the data object in the data source.
3. Modify the profile definition.

Modify the Database Table Schema

In the MMC, navigate to the SQL Server Enterprise Manager snap-in. Expand the Estore_ commerce database and find the UserObject table. Right-click the table and choose Design Table (see Figure 8.20).

In the Design Table worksheet, create the following column and save the schema (see Figure 8.21).

```
u_age int NULL
```

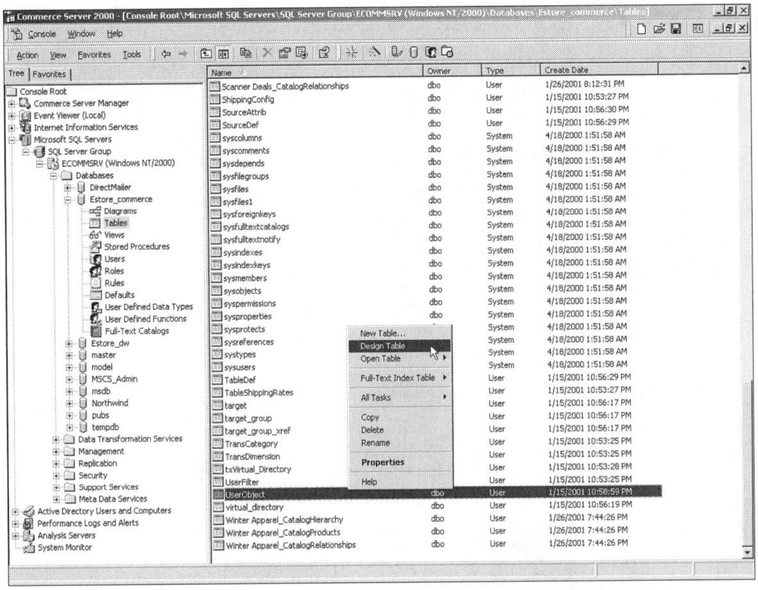

Figure 8.20

The schema of the UserObject table.

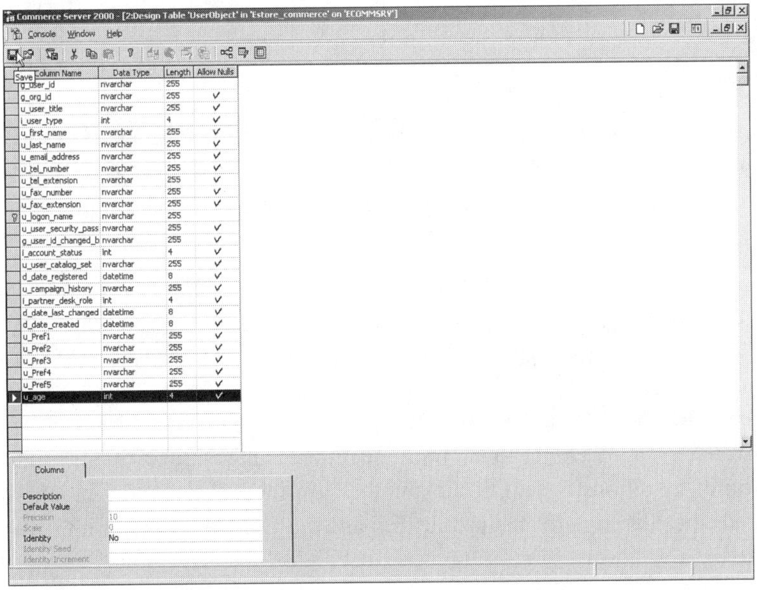

Figure 8.21

The column age being added to the UserObject table schema.

Modify the Data Object in the Data Source

After modifying the table schema, go to the Profiles resource and right-click the UserObject in the data source ProfileService_SQLService (see Figure 8.22).

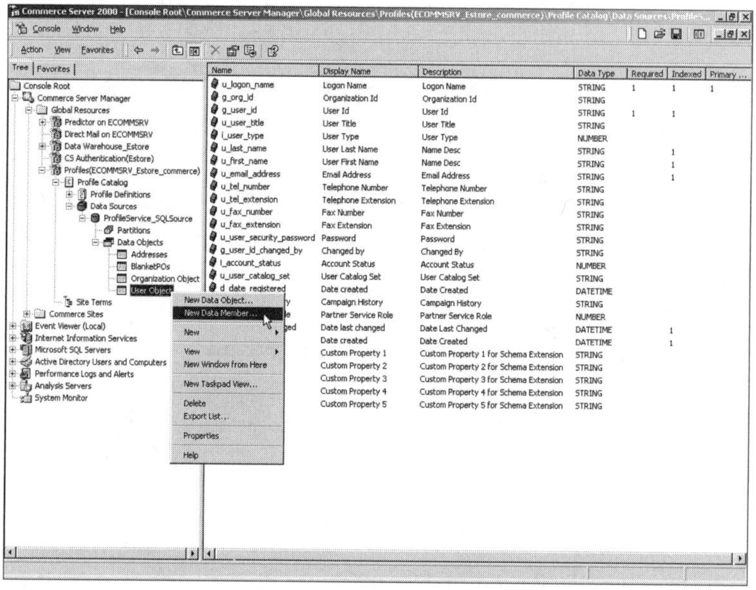

FIGURE 8.22

Adding a new member to the User Object data object.

Choose New Data Member to add the newly created database field as a part of this object. Basically User Object is a data object that is mapped to the physical database table UserObject. Therefore, in the New Data Member dialog box, scroll down to find the u_age column added to the table schema (see Figure 8.23).

You might want to modify the Display Name and Description fields to a suitable name and description as shown. Then click the Add button followed by the Finished button. You should be able to see that Age has been added to the data object.

Modifying the Profile Definition

To add this available data member to the profile definition, navigate to the User Object profile under the Profile Definitions node. On clicking the User Object profile definition, the right-hand pane loads the edit page for the profile. Expand the General Information section (see Figure 8.24).

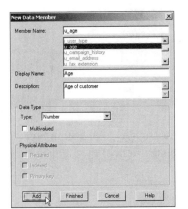

FIGURE **8.23**
FIGURE **8.23**
Creating the data object member.

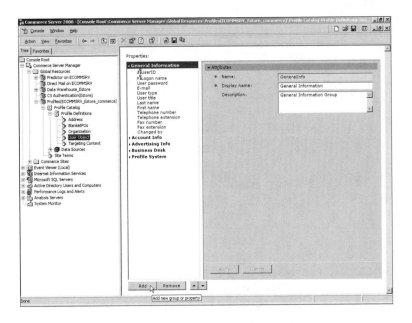

FIGURE **8.24**
The User Object profile definition.

Click the Add button. In the dialog box that pops up, choose the option that says Add a New Property. Then click the OK button (see Figure 8.25).

FIGURE 8.25

Creating a new property for the profile.

Fill in the Attributes section of the property as shown in Figure 8.26 and click the Apply button. Then click the Save button on the right of the toolbar.

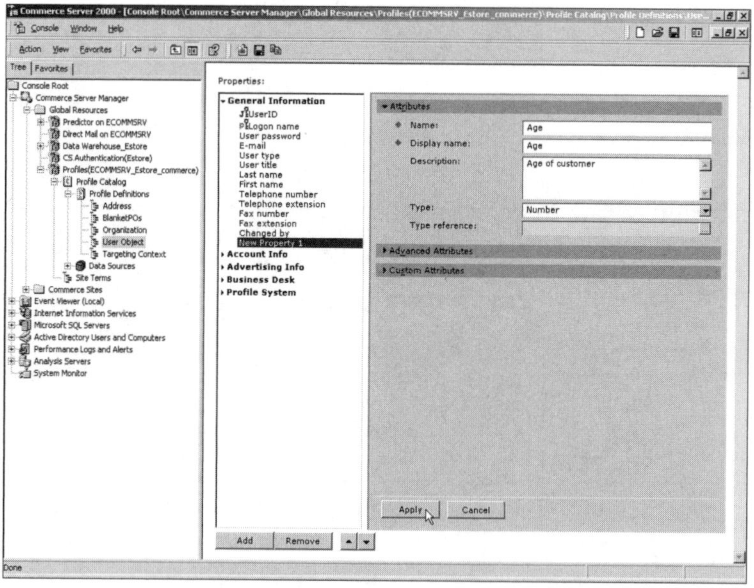

FIGURE 8.26

The attributes of the Age profile property.

Expand the Advanced Attributes section. Click the Browse button next to Map to Data. The Data Source Picker dialog box is launched. Go to the ProfileService_SQLService and then expand the User Object data source. Scroll down if needed and click the data member Age. Then press the OK button (see Figure 8.27).

Now Map to Data indicates that this property of the profile is mapped to the Age data member of the data source. Expand the custom attribute section and find the attribute sUserAccess. Edit the attribute and modify its value to 2. Custom attributes have three values. A value of 0 means that this attribute is hidden to the user, 1 means that it can be viewed, and 2 means that it can be viewed as well as edited by the user on the site (see Figure 8.28).

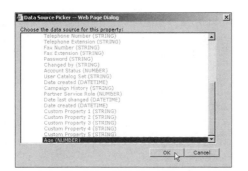

FIGURE 8.27

Mapping a profile property to a data source member.

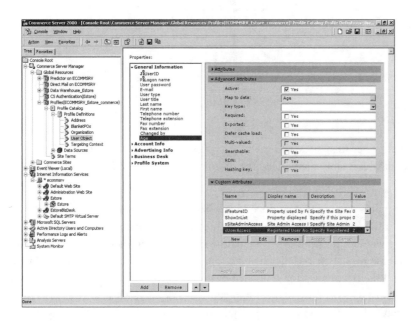

FIGURE 8.28

Setting the access level for the property for registered users.

Press the Apply button to save the Age property. Then click the Save button on the tool bar to save the User Object profile. Unload the application from the IIS snap-in and launch the Estore site again. Sign in and navigate to the Profile page (account.asp). You can see that Age is available as an editable item in the user's profile (see Figure 8.29).

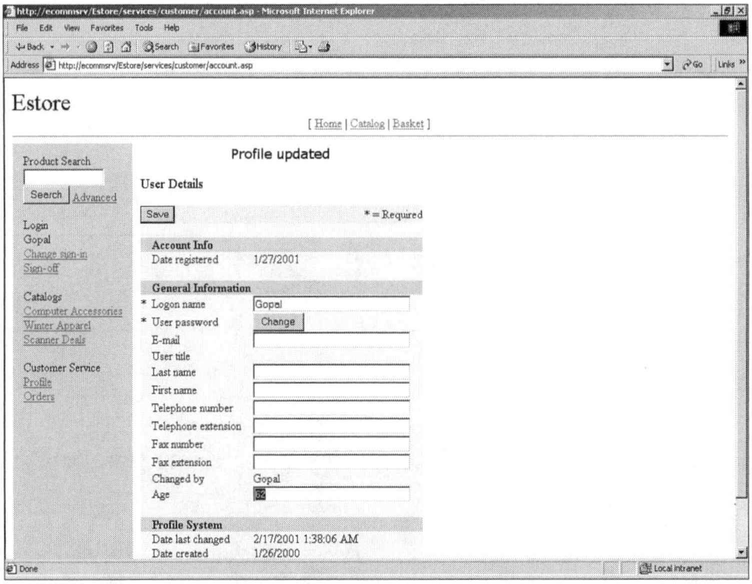

FIGURE 8.29

The profile property Age editable to the site user.

Enter an age greater than sixty and save the profile. You can check with the data in the UserObject database table that indeed the profile is updated with the age information for the user.

A couple of points need to be mentioned here. You could have created the Age attribute directly in Profile Definitions without going through the database table schema changes. The user attribute would have been available on the site. However, there wouldn't have been a permanent database persistence of the attribute. The value in the attribute only would have been available until the IIS application unloaded or the server itself restarted. This means that the value of the attribute was only in the computer's memory and wasn't saved to a database table column because there was no mapping. That's the reason we made table changes and then mapped the column to the UserProfile.

Unloading an IIS Application

From the knowledge of how the *Internet Information Server (IIS)* works, you know that an IIS site's objects and data are maintained in the server's memory pointed to by the Application name of the site. If changes are made to site configuration and to any other data that is held in the site's memory space, the changes wont be effective until the site's memory is refreshed. The way to do that is unload the application and load it again. To unload an IIS application, right-click the site or virtual directory, as the case might be, and click Properties . In the Home

Directory or Virtual Directory, click the Unload button next to Application Protection. IIS destroys the memory space occupied so far by the site.

After that, on the first request from a browser, IIS would load the object and data for the site in to memory, afresh. Therefore loading and unloading a site application is needed to make the site re-read changes to configuration or other important site data.

Building an Expression

Having added the required property to the user profile, you can now build an expression based on that property. Click the Campaign Expressions module in Business Desk. From the menu of the Module toolbar button, choose Target Expressions, as shown in Figure 8.30.

FIGURE 8.30

Target Expression menu in the Campaign Expressions module.

To create a new target expression, press ALT+N or the New Target Expression toolbar button. This launches the Expression Builder. Name the target expression **Over60** and fill in the description as **Age over 60**. Then click the New button. From the first drop-down box, choose User Object, General Information. Expand the General Information group and then choose Age. In the second box, choose the criteria Is Greater Than. In the third box, type a value of **60.0**. Click the Apply button and then the Save button (see Figure 8.31).

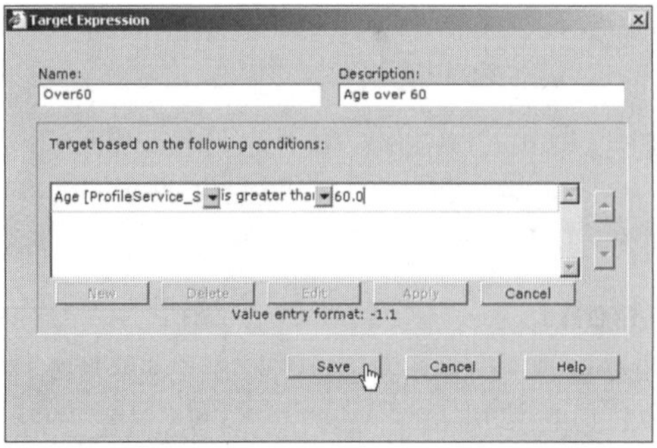

FIGURE 8.31

Creating an expression for Age > 60.

Creating the Targeted Discount

Before creating this discount for customers over sixty, it is a good idea to modify the priority number of the Site-wide 25% Off discount to something such as 60. Thus, you can give a higher priority number to the senior citizen discount you are going to create; for this example, use 30. Thus when a customer whose age is greater than 60 adds a product to the basket, both these discounts will be effectively applicable. But the senior citizen discount will be chosen because of its priority number relative to the other discount. Here is a summary of these two discounts in Estore:

Site-wide 25% Off	25% off	priority level 60
Senior Citizen	50% off	priority level 30

Now it's pretty straightforward to create the senior citizen discount. In the Campaign Manager module, expand Estore and click the Site Launch campaign. Then choose the New Discount menu item from the first toolbar button. In the new Discount Edit page, which you are now familiar with, under Discount Properties, enter the name of the discount as **Senior Citizen Discount** and change the Status to Active and Priority to 30 (see Figure 8.32).

In the Discount Definition section, check the Anything box under Buy. For the Get section, set the third drop-down box to Percent(%) and type **50** for the discount. Under Eligibility Requirements, choose the expression Over60 from the Expression Available box. Click the Add button to add the expression to the Expression Selected box. In the last two section on the page, repeat the same steps that you did for the Site-wide 25% Off discount. In the Discount Display section, you can give a description for Basket Display as Special discount for you.

Save and return to the Filtered view. Again go to the Publish Campaigns module and refresh the discounts cache.

Now to test that the discount is indeed targeted based on the user, visit the site as a guest user. After adding the HP Deskjet 970cxi to the basket, I find that the Site-wide 25% Off discount has been applied (as shown earlier in Figure 8.18). Now sign in as the user who is over 60 years of age. After adding the same product to the basket, the discount shows 50% off as well as the appropriate discount message (see Figure 8.33).

FIGURE 8.32

Introducing complex expressions for a discount.

8

FIGURE 8.33

The senior citizen discount applied to the site.

Catalog Expressions and Target Expressions

Suppose that the 50% off discount for senior citizens proved to be a success, and you find a wide variety of products being bought based on this. At this point, your hard-working accountant informs you that the marketing blitz is fine provided that, going forward, the following condition is met: 50% off can be given only on printers. This effectively results in the following algorithm, which addresses both marketing and costing needs:

> if ((UserObject.Age > 60) AND (Product.Category = "Printers"))
>
> then award 50% discount on product.

You already have the target expression related to age. You need to create a catalog expression checking the product category for printers. Both of these expressions then need to be combined in the Senior Citizen discount.

Creating a Catalog Expression

In the Business Desk, click the Campaign Expressions module. Using the first toolbar button, switch to the Catalog Expressions page (see Figure 8.34).

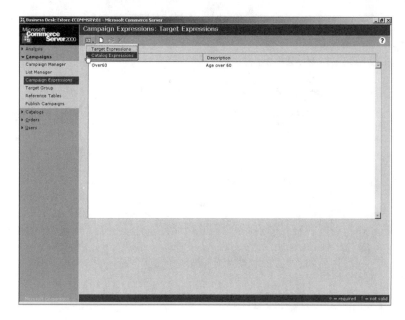

FIGURE 8.34
Menu for the Catalog Expressions page.

From the second toolbar button, choose the menu item New Catalog Expression (see Figure 8.35). Because you are going to create a generic expression to check whether the product belongs to the Printers category, use this menu item. If you were to build an expression based on a specific product, you would use the New from Product Picker option.

In the Catalog Expression dialog box (see Figure 8.36), choose Product, and then Categories in the first box. Choose the operator contains for the second box. For the third box, type **Printers**. Press the Apply button and then the Save button.

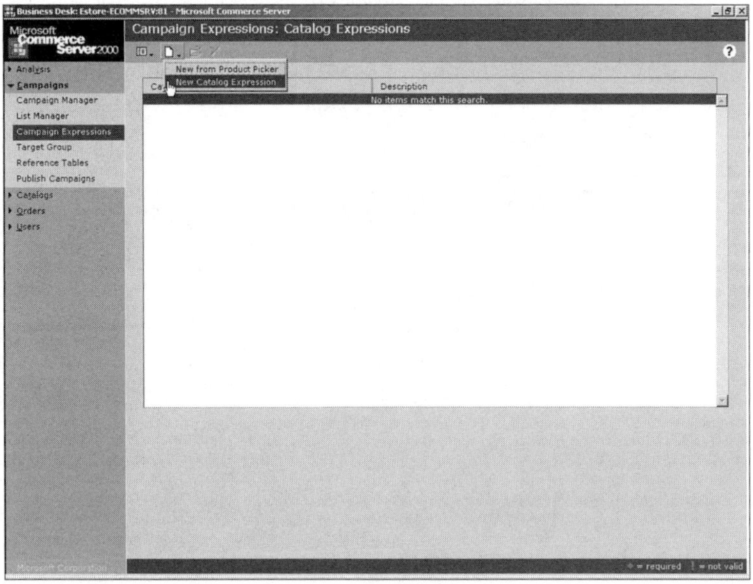

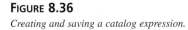

FIGURE 8.35
Menu to create a catalog expression.

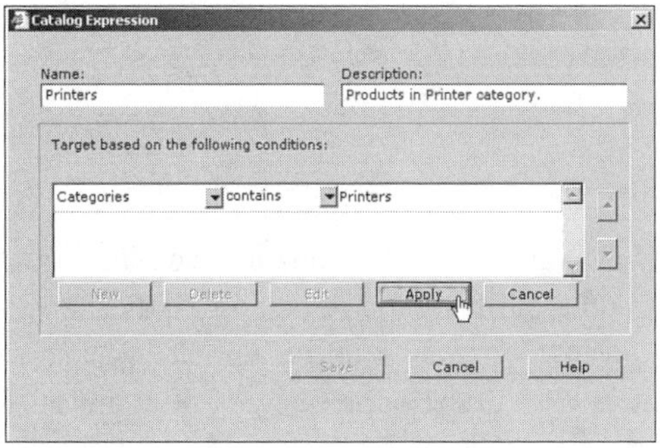

FIGURE 8.36
Creating and saving a catalog expression.

8

PERSONALIZATION
AND TARGETING

Adding the Catalog Expression

Now you have both the expressions we need. One checks the age of the user, whereas the other verifies whether the product category is Printers. When both expressions are combined in the discount, you achieve the goal of giving 50% off on printers to customers over 60.

To modify the Senior Citizen discount, go to the Campaign Manager module. Expand Estore and Site Launch. Click Senior Citizen Discount and then the open folder icon in the toolbar (or press ALT+O). In the edit page for the discount, expand the Discount Definition section. Under Buy, uncheck the Anything check box. Choose Quantity for the first box, 1 for the second box and Printers for the third box (see Figure 8.37). This means that the discount will apply to an item of type Printers in the basket.

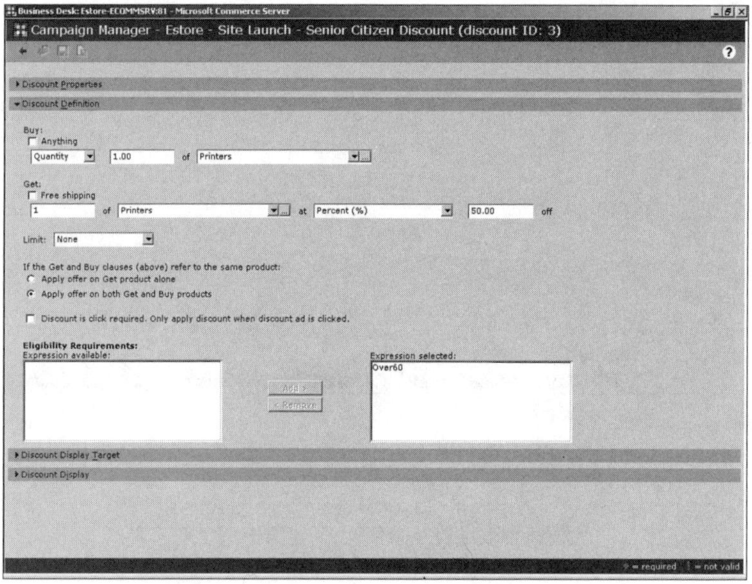

FIGURE 8.37
Modifying the discount definition.

In the Get section, modify the value of the first box to 1 and the second box to the catalog expression Printers. Leave the third and fourth boxes to indicate a discount of 50% (refer to Figure 8.37). Because you want to give 50% off on a printer when a user checks out a printer, both the Get and Buy clauses refer to the same category of products. Therefore, choose the second radio button option. Verify that the Eligibility Requirements is still Over60, the target expression that is selected. Save and return to the Filtered view. Then refresh the discounts cache using the Publish Campaigns module.

Remember that two discounts are active now for the site. One discount gives 25% Off on All Products with a priority of 60. The second discount awards 50% Off on Printers to Customers over 60, and the discount has a priority of 30. Table 8.1 provides an overview of these discounts.

TABLE 8.1 Combination of Awards, Expressions, and Eligibilities

Product Type	Customer Age	Discount Awarded
Printer	> 60	50%
Non-printer	> 60	25%
Printer	< 60	25%
Non-printer	< 60	25%

To test this, sign in as the user who is over 60. Then add the HPDeskjet 970cxi printer as well as a Hewlett Packard parallel printer cable to the basket (see Figure 8.38).

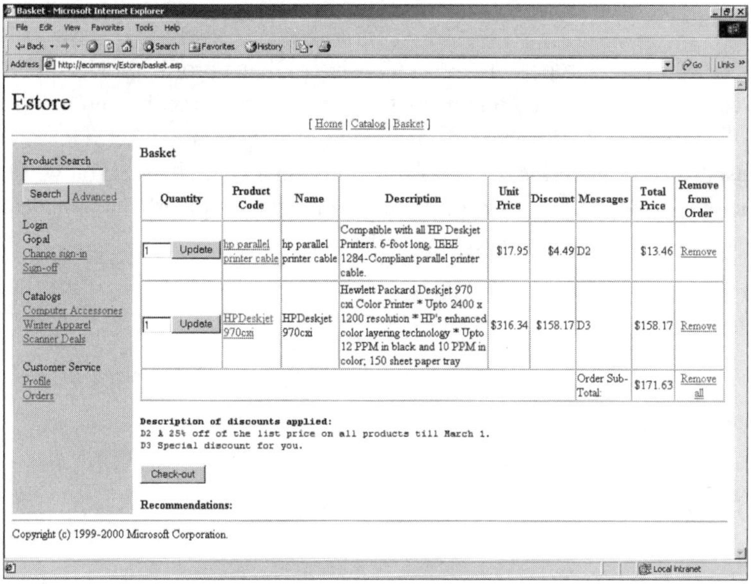

FIGURE 8.38

Targeted and general discounts at the basket.

You can see that the basket proves the truth table for a customer over 60. Similarly you can find that customers under 60 continue to get the 25% Site-wide Discount on All Products.

Target Group

You saw in the previous example how target and catalog expressions can be combined together to target the discount. Commerce Server offers a way to combine more than one target expression into target groups. For example, if you want to offer a discount for users who are over 60 and are male, you would combine the two target expressions together to form a target group.

Summary

This chapter should have helped you understand the possibilities for targeting and personalizing content using the Commerce Server infrastructure. I started out by discussing implicit and explicit profiling, targeting methods, expressions, and a simple example of targeting catalogs to anonymous users. Then I covered campaigns, campaign items, the default campaign vehicles such as ads and discounts, and the expression builder. You then created and published a Site-wide 25% Off discount campaign. Simultaneously, you ran a Senior Citizen discount targeted at customers over 60 who bought printers. In running through these cases, you had a chance to work with the Business Desk modules Campaign Manager, Campaign Expressions, and Publish Campaigns.

You also saw how to add a property to the default User Object profile provided by Commerce Server. I talked about implicit targeting using the Predictor resource, but did not discuss it further because the Predictor works on Analysis models, which in turn needs a lot of data in a data warehouse. I will be covering the data warehouse in a later chapter. You will learn how to use the Predictor service and the `PredictorClient` object to implicitly (automatically) target content such as is done in providing recommendations.

Commerce Server Pipelines

CHAPTER

9

IN THIS CHAPTER

- What Is a Pipeline?   250
- The Pipeline Editor   251
- Pipeline Stages and Components   251
- Modifying a Pipeline   257
- Standard Pipelines   259
- Pipelines in Brief   260
- High Precision in Currency   276

The age of industrialization introduced many new techniques to accomplish routine activities. Automation is one of the obvious changes that companies the world over have adopted. A good example is the automobile industry, which tries to automate the manufacturing process wherever possible. The process involves working on the car or part of a car in a sequence of operations. For instance, if unit A fits the chassis with the body, unit B paints the body, unit C applies wax, unit D polishes the car, and so on. Robots at each stage are designed to perform a specific task on the incoming material and pass it on to the next stage.

In the world of e-commerce, you would also expect robots to handle many aspects of the online store. Even more so because no human being welcomes the shopper, shows the products, suggests items, accepts the credit card, and finally generates an order receipt. Commerce Server provides the necessary infrastructure to accomplish all these activities in a streamlined manner. Similar to the assembly lines found in manufacturing plants, the pipelines provided by Commerce Server can calculate discounts, display order totals, calculate shipping and handling charges, apply taxes, and handle inventory.

What Is a Pipeline?

A Commerce Server pipeline is conceptually a software model of a business process and has stages that work sequentially. For example, in an Order Processing pipeline that processes a customer order, there are many stages such as validating the order details for required information, calculating the discount applicable for each item, arriving at the effective price for each item, calculating the order subtotal, and finally adding the shipping, handling, and taxes to generate the order total. Each stage performs some specialized type of action required by the process. Many different types of pipelines are related to processing orders, selecting content, and even to processing e-mail lists to send targeted e-mails. The central concepts in a pipeline are as follows:

- A pipelineis designed based on the business process it is to accomplish such as order processing, content selection and automated direct emails.
- A pipeline stage has one or more COM components that do the actual work.

How does a conceptual pipeline get translated into an implementation? A pipeline is essentially a *Pipeline Configuration File (.pcf)* that contains all the stages necessary for the business purpose of the pipeline. For example, Estore contains a pipeline that is used to calculate the order total. The pipeline is designed and stored as the total.pcf file under the pipeline directory of Estore. Open the .pcf file to understand more about a pipeline. Commerce Server provides you with a tool called Pipeline Editor to work with .pcf files.

The Pipeline Editor

To open the Pipeline Editor click Start, Programs, Microsoft Commerce Server, Pipeline Editor. You can also launch the Pipeline Editor by double-clicking a .pcf file. On my server, the total.pcf file for Estore is located under the following:

```
E:\Estore\Estore\pipeline\total.pcf.
```

On double-clicking the file, the Pipeline Editor is launched with the total.pcf file loaded (see Figure 9.1).

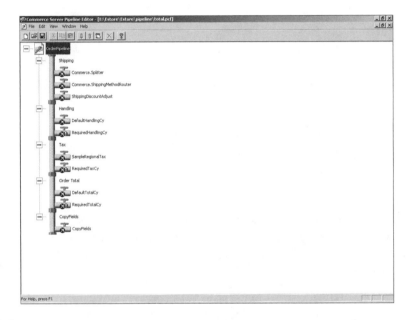

FIGURE 9.1

A Commerce Server pipeline.

Pipeline Stages and Components

As you can see, the Pipeline Editor depicts the pipeline configuration file as a pipe, with the space between two bolts forming a stage and individual valves inside a stage representing a COM component. To understand what I am talking about, collapse the nodes by clicking the - sign. Now you can see clearly the different stages in this pipeline (see Figure 9.2).

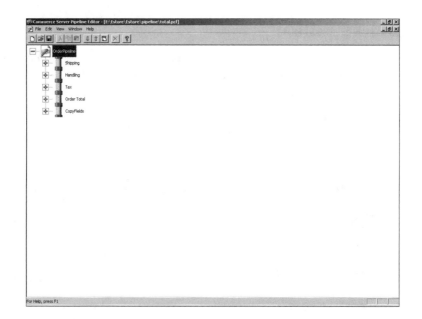

FIGURE 9.2

Stages in a pipeline.

This pipeline has five stages: Shipping, Handling, Tax, Order Total, and Copy Fields. The name of each stage makes it obvious about what function that stage performs. For instance, the Shipping stage calculates shipping charges, the Tax stage calculates applicable taxes, and so on. By now you might have a few questions: Does a stage execute by itself? If so, what do the valves in the pipe mean?

The actual execution of the business functionality of a stage is carried out by the COM components, which are represented as valves. The concept of a stage is simply a convenient way to group these components. For example, in the total.pcf pipe, you know what the Tax stage does. The actual execution is done by the components in that stage (see Figure 9.3). Expand the Tax stage node to see what components work at that stage.

The `SampleRegionalTax` component calculates taxes based on the items in the order and place where the shipments are made. The `RequiredTaxCy` component checks to see whether the order form now has taxes calculated. If not, it writes an error to the order form, which will be discussed in detail later.

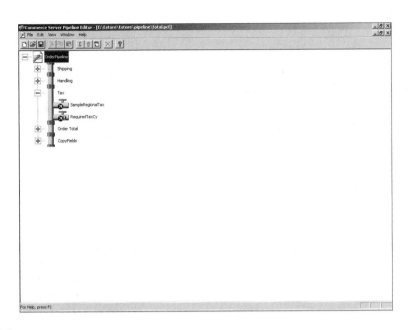

FIGURE 9.3
Components in Tax stages.

A pipeline consists of a number of stages, and each stage has a number of components that actually do the work. The stages are executed sequentially from top to bottom. The input to a pipeline is typically a *dictionary* type object, whose values are read and written by components at each stage. Each component in each stage works on the object, much like each stage in a car assembly line works on the incoming part. After the last component in the last stage has finished, the pipe ends its execution, and we have the object that has been completely worked on. In an e-commerce store such as Estore, an ASP page calls a pipeline passing on the object to be worked on with certain other inputs. The object passes through the pipe and at the end, the calling ASP page gets back the object and continues with its own function. Figure 9.4 reflects this idea.

The illustration also throws some light on how a specific pipeline (.pcf) is loaded and executed. A special pipeline object provided by Commerce Server loads the .pcf file. Imagine the pipeline object as the hardware that is used to load and execute software. You would have many pipeline files (.pcfs) depending on the business processes, such as one for order total calculation, one for applying discounts, one for processing the order, and so on. Therefore, a pipeline object will load different .pcfs in different circumstances throughout the site pages. Again, an illustration is useful (see Figure 9.5).

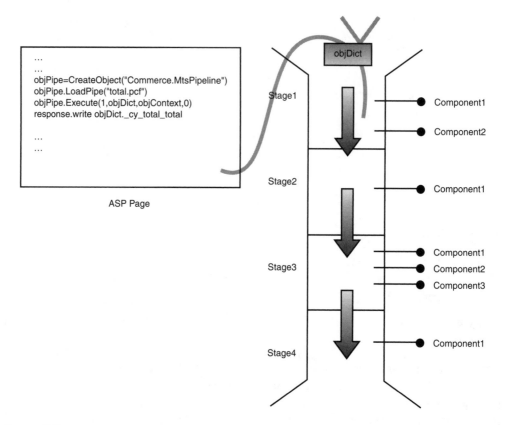

FIGURE 9.4

Interaction between a site page and a pipeline.

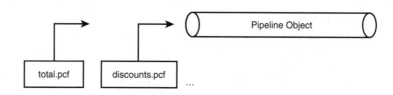

FIGURE 9.5

Pipeline objects and pipelines.

To complete the picture, Commerce Server has more than one pipeline object used to load pipes. In fact, six pipeline objects can be used to load pipes. They are as follows:

- `MtsPipeline`—Use this pipeline object to load pipes (.pcf files) that do not require transactional ability. The `MtsPipeline` object is registered with COM+ Applications as `"transactions not supported"`.

- `MtsTxPipeline`—Use this pipeline object to load pipes (.pcf files) that require transactions. The `MtsTxPipeline` object is registered with COM+ Applications as `"transactions required"`.

- `PooledPipeline`—Use this pipeline object to take advantage of COM+ object pooling that could result in improved performance. This is similar to `MtsPipeline` in that it is non-transactional and is registered with COM+ Applications as `"transactions not supported"`.

- `PooledTxPipeline`—Use this pipeline object to take advantage of COM+ object pooling that could result in improved performance. This is similar to `MtsTxPipeline` in that it is a transacted pipeline and is registered with COM+ Applications as `"transactions required"`.

- `OrderGroup`—Use this object when working with multiple orders aggregated into an order group. `OrderGroup` is actually an object that has the capability to invoke any of the preceding four pipeline objects once for each of its orders.

- `OrderPipeline`—Use this to load content selection pipes. This object is not registered with COM+ Applications.

Using Component Services in Administrative Tools, you can verify that these components are registered with COM+ Applications under CommercePipeline applications. In the property page of each component, the Transactions and Activation tabs are used to set the transactional and pooling capability, respectively.

Where can you indicate whether a specific pipeline (.pcf) needs to be run in a transactional mode? Right-click the name of the pipe and click Properties (see Figure 9.6).

In the Properties page (see Figure 9.7), you specify whether this pipe requires transaction, doesn't require transaction, or doesn't care.

Poolable components in a pipeline take advantage of COM+ pooling when run by a pooled pipeline object because they are held in the object pool. On the other hand, non-poolable components are created each time the pipe is executed.

FIGURE 9.6

Properties of a pipeline.

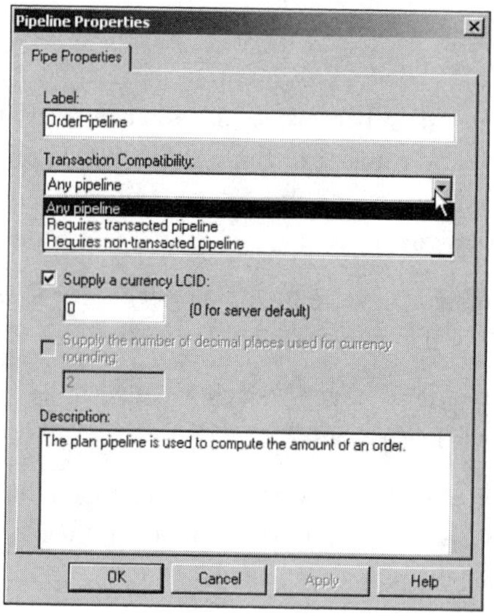

FIGURE 9.7

Setting properties for a pipeline.

In Commerce Server, the term pipeline refers to a pipeline configuration (such as total.pcf) rather than the pipeline object (such as MtsPipeline).

Modifying a Pipeline

Using the Pipeline Editor, you can modify a .pcf file to add or delete stages and components. In case you want to add or delete functionality present in a pipe, you would add or delete stages and components. For example, if your site caters to shoppers from Japan, you can add a component that would calculate taxes for that country. In the Pipeline Editor, right-click on an existing component, click Insert Component, and choose either Before or After (see Figure 9.8).

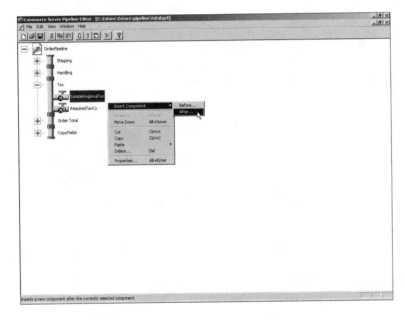

FIGURE 9.8

Inserting a component in a stage.

The Before or After option is important because of the sequential nature of the pipeline. A component works on values written by a previous component. Therefore, each component has the responsibility to modify only what is required without overwriting the work of earlier components.

In the Choose a Component dialog box, choose SimpleJapanTax and click the OK button (see Figure 9.9).

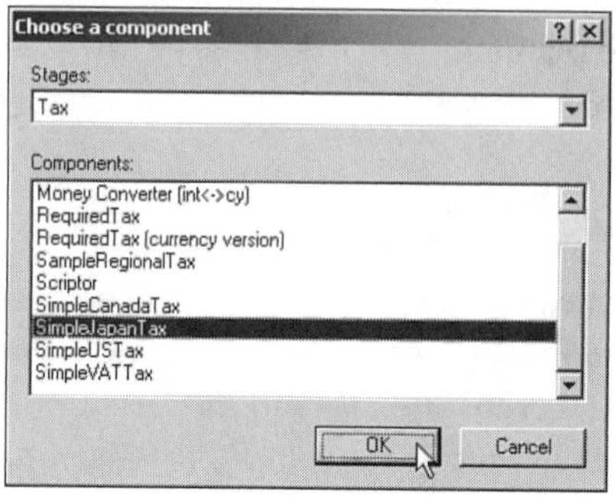

FIGURE 9.9

Choosing from pipeline components to plug in.

You can reorder the components by right-clicking on a component and choosing either Move Up or Move Down. Also it is possible to reorder stages as well as completely remove stages and components conveniently using the Pipeline Editor.

We have already seen that business components such as SampleRegionalTax are COM components. Commerce Server provides you with a variety of ready-made components for various purposes. Depending on the specific requirements of a site, these components can be plugged in to the pipes. It is also possible to write custom pipeline COM components for use in Commerce Server pipelines. A number of Commerce Server pipeline compatible COM components are also available from independent vendors catering to different functionality such as tax, shipping, credit card processing, and so on.

NOTE

Another concept you must have noted while working on Figure 9.9 is that a component has an affinity with certain stages. When you choose Tax from the Stages drop-down list, the components listed are those that have something to do with calculating taxes. If you had chosen the All option for Stages, all Commerce Server pipeline components would have been listed. Apart from an affinity with a stage, components might have a connection to specific pipelines too.

Standard Pipelines

Because pipelines are basically .pcf files designed to model business processes, the pipelines used in a site would vary depending on unique requirements. However Commerce Server comes with standard templates on which you can base your pipeline. These templates are available as .pct (pipeline configuration template) files and cover a broad range of business functionality. These templates include

- Content Selection Pipeline (ContentSelection.pct)—This pipeline would help in determining content like advertisements and discounts that should be delivered to a user, depending on user profile and context profile.

- Event Processing Pipeline (EventProcessing.pct)—This pipeline is used to record events like clicking on an ad or discount. The recorded information would then be used for analysis purposes.

- Direct Mailer Pipeline(DMLPipe.pcf)—There is no template for this, but a pcf file is provided. This pipeline is used to send personalized e-mails to users based on static or dynamic content.

- Order Processing Pipelines—This is a common name for a set of three pipelines described as follows:

  Product Pipeline (Product.pct)—This Product pipeline fetches the price for items and writes shopper information to the order, if the information exists.

  Plan Pipeline (Plan.pct)—This Plan pipeline has fourteen stages and performs various functions such as checking the order for valid entries, computing shipping, handling, and tax. It gives the order total.

  Purchase Pipeline (Purchase.pct)—The This structure of the Purchase pipeline helps in accepting an order, processing the payment, and generating a receipt. Optionally, you could update inventory too.

The preceding pipelines are the key ones provided by Commerce Server. Two more pipeline templates are called Empty.pct and Test.pct. Empty.pct is used as a blank template from which any type of custom pipe can be designed from scratch. Test.pct is a single stage pipeline to be used to test components before plugging into other pipelines.

All these template files should be available in the *templates* directory of the Commerce Server installation directory. In my server, these .pct files are found under `E:\Microsoft Commerce Server\Templates`. In order to create a new pipe, you would open one of these templates. Then make the necessary modification to the pipeline by removing or adding stages and components. Finally, when you save the changes, the configuration would be saved as a .pcf file.

Pipelines in Brief

Because most variations of implemented Commerce Server pipelines are derived from the provided templates, it would be useful to take a brief look at these standard pipelines. This will give you a better idea of the inputs to the pipelines, stages, and components, and their overall behavior.

Content Selection Pipeline

The *Content Selection Pipeline (CSP)* is a part of the *Content Selection Framework (CSF)* because it uses components that make up the CSF. Another pipeline that is also part of the CSF is the Events Processing pipeline.

The CSF involves various components that can be used to score content, evaluate target expressions, select matching content, format content for delivery, and record the delivery of such content. Commerce Server already has the required infrastructure to target and deliver advertisements, discounts, and direct e-mails. It is possible to extend the CSF to be able to target custom content.

Coming back to the CSP, the ContentSelection.pct has the following seven stages as the base (see Figure 9.10).

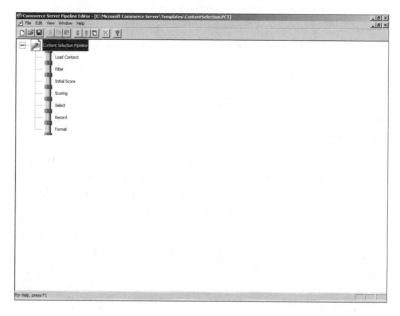

FIGURE 9.10

Stages of a Content Selection pipeline.

Table 9.1 can be used as a quick reference to the CSP.

TABLE 9.1   Components in a Content Selection Pipeline

Stage	Purpose	Component Example	Purpose of Component
Load Context	Prepare pipeline for execution.	InitCSFPipeline	Creates dictionaries and initializes values for use throughout the pipeline.
		LoadHistory	Retrieves a history string from one of the following sources: User profile, cookie or a Session object.
Filter	Filters the content list.	FilterContent	Applies filters to the list of content in order to eliminate content at an early stage itself.
Initial Score	Assigns initial scores to the content items in the content list.	AdvertisingNeed OfDelivery	Sets the NOD of each content item. An item with an NOD greater than 1 indicates lagging delivery, while an NOD less than 1 indicates that the goals for the item delivery have been exceeded.
Scoring	Adjusts the scores generated in the previous stage.	EvalTargetGroups	Applies a multiplier to each content item based on target expressions.
		HistoryPenalty	Applies a penalty score to reduce the likelihood of recently delivered content items.
		Score Discounts	In the context of discounts, this component applies a multiplier to each item depending on discount rules.
Select	Selects the content items to be delivered.	SelectWinners	Selects and returns winning content items up to the requested number.

9

COMMERCE SERVER PIPELINES

TABLE 9.1   Continued

Stage	Purpose	Component Example	Purpose of Component
Record	This stage records the content selection.	IISAppendToLog	Using this component at this stage would record the selected items as a QueryString in the IIS log.
		RecordEvent	The winning items are recorded in a dictionary for future CSF use.
		RecordHistory	The winning items are recorded in a history string for future CSF use.
		SaveHistory	The winning items are recorded in one of the three places: User Profile object, an ASP session object or the HTTP Cookie.
Format	Format the content items to a displayable form.	FormatTemplate	Return the content items as HTML or XML strings.

NOTE

Table 9.1 is a representation of the basic CSP pipe. A specific CSP pipeline would have more or fewer stages and more or fewer components at each stage. For instance, in the Record stage you might decide not to append the information about selected items to the IIS logs or save history to a permanent object.

I already discussed how the CSP and *Event Processing pipelines (EPP)* use the same infrastructure of the CSF. Therefore, it is not surprising to find that the EPP is a subset of the CSP and basically has Load Context, Record, and Format stages (see Figure 9.11).

Both Content Selection and Event Processing pipelines commonly use the components designed for the *Content Selection Framework (CSF)*. I will discuss CSF and its components in detail in Chapter 11, "Direct Mailer and Content Selection Framework Pipelines."

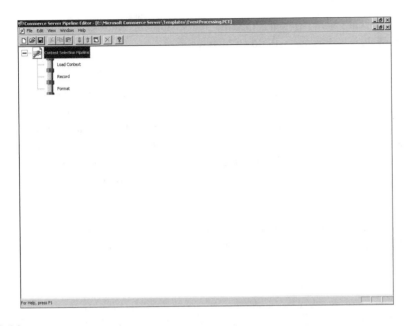

FIGURE 9.11

Stages of an Event Processing pipeline.

Order Processing Pipelines

Order Processing Pipelines (OPP) refer to a set of three pipelines that deal with processing orders in a retail scenario: the Product, Plan, and Purchase pipelines. But before we look at those, you need to understand some of the other important objects and components involved in order processing.

The input dictionary object passed to these pipelines from the calling ASP page is OrderForm. OrderForm is a dictionary object that represents a purchase order. The components in these pipelines read from and write to the OrderForm. Other important objects and components include the Context Dictionary, Error Collections, and the default and required components of a pipeline. I will cover these elements first before actually looking at a pipeline.

The OrderForm Object

The OrderForm object is a key COM object used by Commerce Server to model a purchase order in an online store. A purchase order typically contains details such as customer information, item quantity, item price, discounts, shipping, handling, taxes, order total, and so on. The OrderForm object is basically a *dictionary* object that contains key/value pairs for individual information in a purchase order. For example the OrderForm object has a key called ship_to_state that's value indicates the state in the shipping address. The components that read or write values to this key will do so by referring to

order.ship_to_state

where order is an instance of the OrderForm object. Here the key is ship_to_state and the value would be the value stored in the key. Because an order can contain multiple items, the OrderForm object also internally has a SimpleList object used to handle items in the order. This SimpleList object is referred to as the *items* collection. You would loop through the items collection to work with individual items in an order. Properties of an individual item are accessed the same way. For example, to read or write list price of an item, you would use

item1.list_price

Thus, an OrderForm object is a complex structure designed to hold various types of elements in a purchase order. Here is a visual illustration of an OrderForm object and its contents (see Figure 9.12):

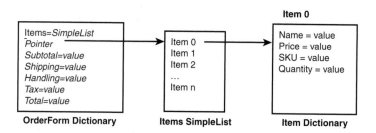

FIGURE 9.12

An OrderForm object.

The order is persisted to as well as retrieved from the database by using the DBStorage object. Some of the keys of the OrderForm object start with an underscore (_)symbol. It means that these values are not persisted in the OrderForm storage, but they are finally saved in a receipt table in the database instead.

The Context Dictionary

While executing an OPP, an object other than the OrderForm is passed to the pipeline from an ASP page. The Context is a dictionary object that contains references to the user profile, default language, the CatalogManager object, the Profile Service, the Cache Manager object, the MessageManager object, and so on. Imagine the OrderForm object as the business object that contains the purchase order information, whereas the Context dictionary is an object that helps the processing by giving the pipeline ready access to the site's application objects such as Profile Service and MessageManager objects. Therefore, if you are developing a custom pipeline object that expects peripheral information for processing the order, that information is passed in this Context dictionary.

Error Collections

The `OrderForm` contains error collections to store errors detected by components. The two most important error collections are _Basket_Errors and _Purchase_Errors. Error messages are retrieved using the `MessageManager` object present in the Context and stored in these collections. On encountering an error while processing the order, components set the error level to 2 and also write error strings to the error collections. After the pipeline returns, the calling ASP page checks for the error level. If there was an error, it prints out the error strings to the browser.

A pipeline component returns error level 1 if the execution was a success, returns 2 if there was a warning, and 3 if execution failed. In case of error level 2, the pipeline component writes error messages to one of the error collections. This error level means that there was some logical error that can be possibly corrected, such as when displaying a message for a bad credit card number. The user would then correct the error and process the order again.

Errors occuring while processing a basket are written to the _Basket_Errors collection. For example, suppose that a user comes back to browse his basket after a few days. If the prices or discounts are changed now, messages are written to the basket errors collection and finally displayed on the basket page. Similarly, while checking out the basket using a credit card, if an invalid credit card number is specified, an error is written to the _Purchase_Errors collection.

These error messages are maintained in the rc.xml file and are loaded into memory by the `MessageManager` object. That's the reason you pass a reference to the `MessageManager` object in the Context dictionary.

Default and Required Components

Commerce Server provides certain components that serve to initialize values in the stage they operate. These components can be left as such or replaced by custom initialization components. Components that are marked Required using the property page in the Pipeline Editor are used to verify that the stage has set the proper values to the order form that it is supposed to. If those values are not found, it raises an error and writes to one of the error collections. Typically the name of the components begin with Default and Required for the default and required components, respectively.

The Product Pipeline

The components in the Product pipeline calculate the discounts and prices applicable to each item in the order. Typically, the Product pipeline is used by the product.asp site page to display product information to the shopper. A Product pipeline is built using the product.pct template, which has the stages shown in Figure 9.13 in its default configuration.

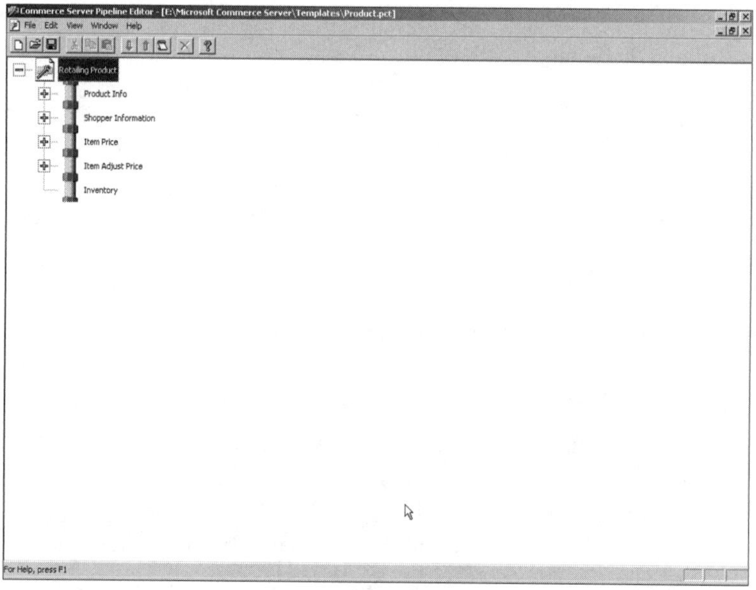

FIGURE 9.13

Stages of a Product pipeline.

Table 9.2 is a quick reference table for the Product pipeline. These are just a few of the commonly used components available at each stage, but there might be more components.

TABLE 9.2   Components of a Product Pipeline

Stage	Purpose	Component Example	Purpose of Component
Product Info	Retrieves information about the order items from the product catalog.	QueryCatalogInfo	Queries the database to retrieve information about each item in the order. If an item is not found in the product catalog, it marks the item as deleted in the OrderForm.
		RequiredProdInfo	Deletes the items that are marked as deleted by the previous component.

TABLE 9.2 Continued

Stage	Purpose	Component Example	Purpose of Component
Shopper Information	Writes information about the shopper to the order form.	DefaultShopperInfo	Copies the shopper profile from the context dictionary to the order form.
Item Price	Sets the item price for each item from the prices retrieved by the Product Info stage.	DefaultItemPrice	Sets the _iadjustregularprice key to the value retrieved by the product info stage. This component is for backward compatibility only, since many components look at this key.
		RequiredItemPrice	Verifies that the key _iadjustregularprice is indeed initialized with a value.
Item Adjust Price	Sets the current price for each item taking into account sales or promotions.	RequiredItem AdjustPrice	Verifies that the item price is current and has not changed.
Inventory	Components in this stage can be used to verify availability of items in stock.	FlagInventory	Verifies that items are in stock and generates error if not.

The Plan Pipeline

The Plan pipeline is also an OPP and has similar stages and components as the Product pipeline. Additionally, the Plan pipeline has stages and components to compute shipping, handling, and taxes as well as to arrive at the order total. Figure 9.14 shows the default stages of the Plan pipeline.

A Plan pipeline is usually used from basket.asp or order.asp when it is required to find out the order subtotal or order total. The plan.pct file acts as a template to the Plan pipelines. The first few stages and components in a Plan pipeline are the same as in a Product pipeline. However, in a Plan pipeline, we start calculating the order subtotal, apply shipping, handling, and taxes to arrive at the order total. Therefore, Table 9.3 presents only the stages and components unique to a plan pipeline.

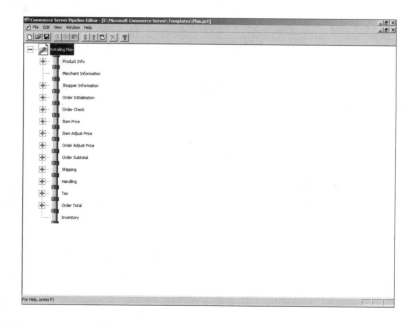

FIGURE 9.14

Stages of a Plan pipeline.

TABLE 9.3   Components of a Plan Pipeline

Stage	Purpose	Component Example	Purpose of Component
Order Initialization	Generates an Order ID and initializes values at the Order level.	RequiredOrderInit	Creates an Order Id and writes to the order form. Also initializes values such as order subtotal, total, shipping total and tax total to null values.
OrderCheck	Confirms that the order can be processed further.	RequiredOrder Check	Verifies that the order contains at least one item.
Order Adjust Price	Finalizes the price for each item in the order.	RequiredOrder AdjustPrice	Computes the effective price of each item taking into account discounted and non-discounted quantities.

TABLE 9.3 Continued

Stage	Purpose	Component Example	Purpose of Component
Order Subtotal	Calculates the subtotal for the order.	DefaultOrder Subtotal	Sums up the total cost of each item and arrives at the order subtotal.
		RequiredOrder Subtotal	Verifies that the order sub-total is set and has a value other than the initial value of null.
Shipping	Calculates the total shipping cost for the order.	DefaultShipping	Initializes the shipping total for the order to zero.
		FixedShipping	Applies a fixed cost to the shipping total as specified in the component's property page.
		RequiredShipping	Checks if the shipping total has been set for the order.
Handling	Sets the handling charges for the order.	FixedHandling	Applies a fixed cost to the handling total as specified in the component's property page.
		RequiredHandling	Checks if the handling total has been set for the order.
Tax	Computes the tax for each item and the order tax total.	DefaultTax	Initializes the tax total to zero.
		SampleRegional Tax	Calculates tax for multiple-shipment orders.
		RequiredTax	Verifies that the tax compu-tations have been completed for the order.
Order Total	Calculates the order total.	DefaultTotal	Computes the order total from the subtotal, shipping, handling and tax totals. If one of the four values are missing, generates an error.
		RequiredTotal	Makes a final check to see if the values in the form are not tampered with by mali-cious entities.

9

COMMERCE SERVER PIPELINES

At this point, I must stress that the components described in each of the stages are not exhaustive. More components are available, and a specific site's pipeline might not contain one of the components listed in Table 9.3. For example, a localized Japanese Web site would have a `SimpleJapanTax` component at the Tax stage instead of another component. Similarly, at the Shipping stage, you might not have the Fixed Shipping component; instead you could have the `LinearShipping` component that computes the shipping costs in a different way.

Appendix B, "Pipeline Components: A Quick Reference," should be handy for a quick reference to the various components and their functionality. A detailed reference can be found in the product documentation too.

The Purchase Pipeline

After the Plan pipeline has been run to prepare a good purchase order, you would get the confirmation of the customer to complete the purchase. After getting the confirmation, the Purchase pipeline is run on the prepared order to finalize the order, store the order, and generate any receipts if needed. Purchase pipelines are usually built using the purhcase.pct template file and contain three stages by default (see Figure 9.15).

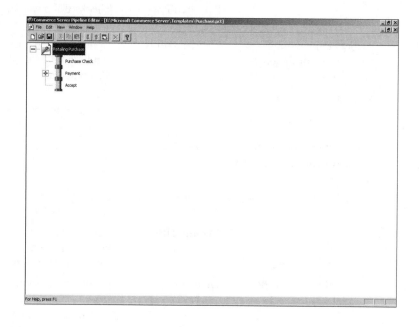

FIGURE 9.15

Stages of a Purchase pipeline.

Table 9.4 contains a high-level summary of a Purchase pipeline.

TABLE 9.4 Components of a Purchase Pipeline

Stage	Purpose	Component Example	Purpose of Component
Purchase Check	Check to verify the information provided by customer.	ValidateCCNumber	Checks that the entered credit card number has a valid date and number format. Does not check if the card account exists.
Payment	Processes the payment information provided by customer.	DefaultPayment	Initializes the payment authorization key to a value of FAITH, a simple string.
		RequiredPayment	Ensures that the payment authorization key is not null.
Accept	Components here execute custom functionality such as persisting order and receipt, sending confirmation e-mail, and updating inventory.	SaveReceipt	Saves the order to the database using the DBStorage object.

The Direct Mailer Pipeline

There is one more special purpose pipeline configuration that Commerce Server provides called the *Direct Mailer pipeline (DMP)*. This pipeline usually isn't called from any of the site pages and hence does not have a configuration template file (.pct). Commerce Server comes with a .pcf file called DMLPipe.pcf that is present under the installation root directory. The Direct Mailer global resource uses the Windows 2000 service DMLRun.exe to process personalized e-mail delivery to site visitors. The *Direct Mailer (DML)* sends e-mails using the standard *Simple Mail Transfer Protocol (SMTP)* server.

It is the Direct Mailer global resource that runs the DMP to process recipient lists, build dynamic content, add attachments, and send e-mails to recipients. The DMP has seven stages by default as shown in Figure 9.16.

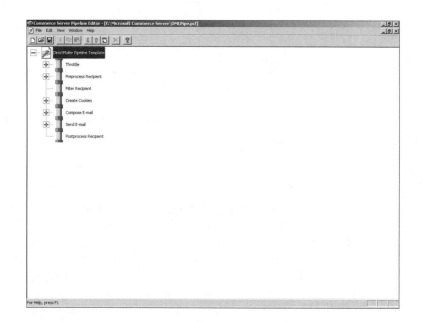

FIGURE 9.16

Stages of a Direct Mailer pipeline.

Table 9.5 shows a summary table for the DMP.

TABLE 9.5   Components in a Direct Mailer Pipeline

Stage	Purpose	Component Example	Purpose of Component
Throttle	Adjusts the speed of message processing to optimize the SMTP server.	ThrottleDML Performance	This component simply generates a delay between messages. The delay is set by the DML service.
Preprocess Recipient	Makes sure that the e-mail message can be processed further.	VerifyRecipient Data	Checks for valid e-mail address. Determines formatting of the message body.
Filter	Custom components to filter the e-mail list.	None	Could build custom components to implement say opt-out and so on.
Create Cookies	Generate cookies to be used by an ASP page that personalizes content.	CreateUPMCookie	Using the context and order dictionary inputs, creates cookies and is stored in a dictionary.

TABLE 9.5   Continued

Stage	Purpose	Component Example	Purpose of Component
Compose E-mail	Builds the body of the message to be sent.	ComposeDML Message	Creates the message body and uses the cookie string if it is a personalized e-mail message.
		AddAttachments	Adds attachments to the message body using the Collaborative Data Objects(CDO).
Send E-mail	Verifies the message body and sends the e-mail.	VerifyMessage Body	Verifies that the message body is not blank and that the correct number of attachments are present.
		SendPrecomposed Message	Sends an e-mail using the CDO of Windows and writes the e-mail count back to the pipeline.
PostProcess Recipient	Custom components for additional functionality.	None	Custom components.

We have seen the structure of the important Commerce Server pipelines and a few components used in them. Table 9.6 is the final quick reference table that lists out all the pipeline components provided by Commerce Server and their stage-pipeline affinities.

TABLE 9.6   Readily Available Pipeline Components

Pipeline Component	Used in Pipeline...	Stage Affinity
AddAttachments	Direct Mailer	Compose E-mail
AdvertisingNeedOfDelivery	Content Selection	Initial Score
ComposeDMLMessage	Direct Mailer	Compose E-mail
CreateUPMCookie	Direct Mailer	Create Cookies
DBOrderPromoADO	Order Processing	Order Adjust
DefaultHandlingCy	Order Processing	Handling
DefaultItemPriceCy	Order Processing	Item Price
DefaultOrderSubTotalCy	Order Processing	Order Subtotal

9

COMMERCE
SERVER PIPELINES

TABLE 9.6 Continued

Pipeline Component	Used in Pipeline...	Stage Affinity
DefaultPayment	Order Processing	Payment
DefaultShippingCy	Order Processing	Shipping
DefaultShopperInfo	Order Processing	Shopper Information
DefaultTaxCy	Order Processing	Tax
DefaultTotalCy	Order Processing	Order Total
EvalTargetGroups	Content Selection	Score
ExecuteProcess	Any	Any
FilterContent	Content Selection	Filter
FixedHandling	Order Processing	Handling
FixedShipping	Order Processing	Shipping
FlagInventory	Order Processing	Inventory
FormatTemplate	Content Selection	Format
HistoryPenalty	Content Selection	Score
IISAppendToLog	Event Processing	Record
InitCSFPipeline	Content Selection	Load Context
ItemPromo	Order Processing	Adjust Price
LinearHandling	Order Processing	Handling
LinearShipping	Order Processing	Shipping
LoadHistory	Content Selection	Load Context
LocalInventory	Order Processing	Inventory
MakePO	Order Processing	Accept
MoneyConverter	Order Processing	Any
OrderDiscount	Order Processing	Order Adjust Price
POtoFile	Order Processing	Accept
QueryCatalogInfo	Order Processing	Product Info
QueryProdInfoADO	Order Processing	Product Info
RecordEvent	Event Processing, Content Selection, Order Processing	Record in CSP,EPP Receipt in OPP
RecordHistory	Content Selection	Record
RequiredHandlingCy	Order Processing	Handling
RequiredItemAdjustPriceCy	Order Processing	Item Adjust Price
RequiredItemPriceCy	Order Processing	Item Price

Table 9.6   Continued

Pipeline Component	Used in Pipeline...	Stage Affinity
RequiredOrderAdjustPriceCy	Order Processing	Item Adjust Price
RequiredOrderCheck	Order Processing	Order Check
RequiredOrderInitCy	Order Processing	Order Initialization
RequiredOrderSubtotalCy	Order Processing	Order Subtotal
RequiredPayment	Order Processing	Payment
RequiredProdInfo	Order Processing	Product Info
RequiredShippingCy	Order Processing	Shipping
RequiredTaxCy	Order Processing	Tax
RequiredTotalCy	Order Processing	Order Total
SaleAdjust	Order Processing	Item Adjust Price
SampleRegionalTax	Order Processing	Tax
SaveHistory	Content Selection	Record
SaveReceipt	Order Processing	Accept
ScoreDiscounts	Content Selection	Scoring
Scriptor	Any	Any
SelectWinners	Content Selection	Select
SendPrecomposedMessage	Direct Mail	Send E-mail
SendSMTP	Any	Any
ShippingDiscountAdjust	Order Processing	Shipping
ShippingMethodRouter	Order Processing	Shipping
SimpleCanadaTax	Order Processing	Tax
SimpleJapanTax	Order Processing	Tax
SimpleUSTax	Order Processing	Tax
SimpleVATTax	Order Processing	Tax
Splitter	Order Processing	Any
SQLItemADO	Order Processing	Accept
SQLOrderADO	Order Processing	Accept
TableHandlingADO	Order Processing	Handling
TableShippingADO	Order Processing	Shipping
ThrottleDMLPerformance	Direct Mailer	Throttle
ValidateCCNumber	Order Processing	Payment
VerifyMessageBody	Direct Mailer	Send E-mail
VerifyRecipientData	Direct Mailer	Preprocess Recipient

9

COMMERCE SERVER PIPELINES

High Precision in Currency

Quite a few components have a cy at the end of their name. An example is `DefaultTaxCy`. The cy components have a low precision counterpart named without the cy. Thus there is a component called `DefaultTax`, which has a lower precision compared to `DefaultTaxCy`. Commerce Server introduces high precision in money values compared to Site Server 3.0 Commerce Edition (SSCE). If you have worked with SSCE, you probably remember that you had to type 500 for 5.00 dollars. Now the money value can be entered directly as a decimal. To maintain backward compatibility with SSCE pipelines and components, there are identical components that differ only in how they handle the money value. As a corollary, the `DefaultTax` component would write the tax value to the `_tax_total` key in the `OrderForm`, whereas the `DefaultTaxCy` would write to the `_cytax_total` key.

Summary

Pipelines are a good representation of the philosophy of Commerce Server; they offer the necessary infrastructure and pre-built components to implement business processes quickly and easily on your e-commerce site. Pipelines also offer great flexibility in terms of customization to meet unique site requirements.

This chapter is intended to give a thorough introduction to Commerce Server pipelines. At the end, you should be able to answer typical queries on

- The concepts of pipelines, stages, and components.
- Technical implementation of pipelines—.pcf and .pct files, pipeline objects, and ASP pages.
- Different types of pipeline objects such as `MtsPipeline` and `MtsTxPipeline`.
- Modifying pipelines by adding, removing or reordering stages and components.
- Editing pipeline configuration files using the Pipeline Editor.
- The default pipelines provided by Commerce Server.
- An overview of stages and components and their purpose in each of the standard pipelines such as Content Selection, Product, Plan, Purchase, Event Processing, and Direct Mailer pipelines.
- Operation details about Order Processing Pipelines—`OrderForm` object, Context dictionary, Error collections, Default and Required components, and so on.

After digesting most of this chapter, you should be raring to plumb one of the pipes in Estore. That is what you are going to do in Chapter 10, "Order Processing Pipelines"—bare the connection between a site and the pipelines.

Order-Processing Pipelines

IN THIS CHAPTER

- Global Initialization   278
- The Product Page   279
- The Basket Page   286
- Checkout Processing   312

The last chapter introduced the Commerce Server pipelines, including the Order-Processing Pipelines (OPPs). You learned that Commerce Server provides the Product, Plan, and Purchase pipelines as part of the OPP. Further, there was a brief overview of the OPP pipeline components used in each of the OPP pipelines.

In this chapter, you will see when and where these OPPs are used and how they accomplish their tasks. We are going to make use of the Estore site for all our discussions.

Global Initialization

The Application_OnStart event handler defined in global.asa creates and stores references to various Commerce Server objects to be used throughout the site pages. These references are stored in application scope. The file setup_env.asp is included in all the site pages and is responsible for getting the references in application variables to local page variables for use. The references to all the pipelines used in Estore are created in global_siteconfig_lib.asp using the function InitSitePipelines (), which is listed here:

```
Function InitSitePipelines ()
    Dim objPage, dictPipeline
    Dim MSCSEnv

    Set dictPipeline = GetDictionary()

    dictPipeline.Folder      = GetRootPath() & "pipeline\"

    ' You must grant Internet Guest Account (IUSER_machinename)
    ' write permission on the following directory to enable logging
    dictPipeline.LogFolder = GetRootPath() & "pipeline\logfiles\"

    If MSCSEnv = DEVELOPMENT Then
        dictPipeline.LoggingEnabled  = False
        dictPipeline.LogsCycled      = False
    ElseIf MSCSEnv = PRODUCTION Then
        dictPipeline.LoggingEnabled  = False
        dictPipeline.LogsCycled      = False
    End If

    dictPipeline.Product  = dictPipeline.Folder & "product.pcf"
    dictPipeline.Basket   = dictPipeline.Folder & "basket.pcf"
    dictPipeline.Total    = dictPipeline.Folder & "total.pcf"
    dictPipeline.Checkout = dictPipeline.Folder & "checkout.pcf"
    dictPipeline.Fragment = dictPipeline.Folder & "fragment.pcf"
    dictPipeline.ReceivePO = dictPipeline.Folder & "recvpo.pcf"
    dictPipeline.Advertising = dictPipeline.Folder & "advertising.pcf"
    dictPipeline.Discounts  = dictPipeline.Folder & "discounts.pcf"
```

```
    dictPipeline.RecordEvent = dictPipeline.Folder & "RecordEvent.pcf"

    Set InitSitePipelines = dictPipeline
End Function
```

As shown in the code in `InitSitePipelines`, references to the pipeline configuration file (PCF) paths are stored in a dictionary with convenient key names. These PCF files can be found under the `pipeline` directory of Estore.

Therefore, to access `discounts.pcf`, you only need to access the following key:

`dictPipeline.Discounts`

This key contains the reference to the discounts pipeline configuration file.

This dictionary of *pipeline-name/path-value* mappings is stored in application scope by `global_main_lib.asp` using the following statements:

```
Set MSCSPipelines = InitSitePipelines()
Set Application("MSCSPipelines") = MSCSPipelines
```

Because the references to pipelines are stored at application scope, they are readily accessible from any ASP page on the site.

The Product Page

We are going to follow the normal process flow in Estore. Because we have already seen this flow at a higher level in Chapter 5, "Understanding the Site Architecture," we will concentrate on the OPP components, such as `OrderForm`, `OrderGroup`, pipelines, and baskets, which we discussed in the last chapter. Therefore, the place to start would be the product page, where the site displays built-in as well as user-defined properties of the product. In our Estore site, I navigated to the Cables category under the Computer Accessories catalog and then drilled down to the detailed page of the product "hp parallel printer cable" (see Figure 10.1). If your product page doesn't have as a good picture as mine, feel free to "borrow" for temporary use from the HP site!

We know that Commerce Server objects such as `MSCSCatalogManager` and `MSCSProduct` are used to access catalog and product information. The `product.asp` page uses these objects to display built-in properties such as name, price, and description as well as user-defined properties such as SKU, PPM, and so on. Finally on this page, a small form is displayed to enable the user to add a specific quantity of this product to the basket. The action element of this form points to an intermediate ASP file called `_additem.asp`. Therefore, when the user enters a quantity and clicks the Add to Basket button, control transfers to the `_additem.asp` script. Pages such as `_additem.asp` and `_delitem.asp` are intermediate pages that are meant to do some processing before transferring control to a user interface–generating ASP page.

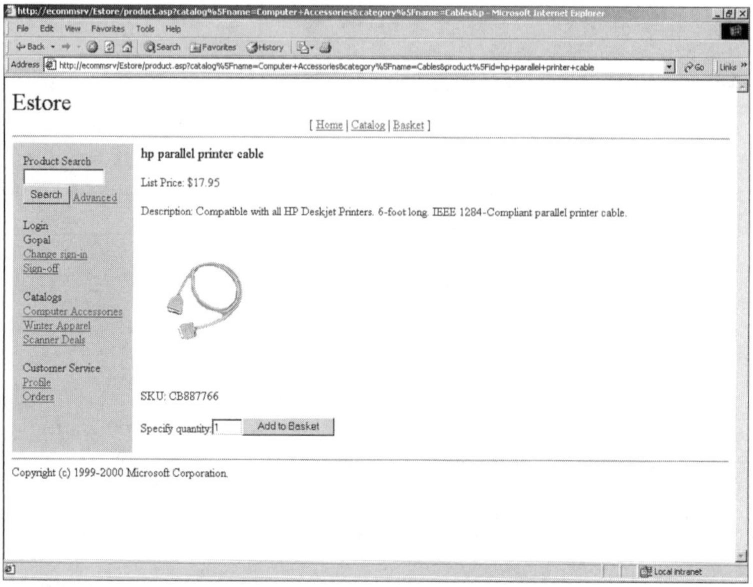

FIGURE 10.1

A product details page.

Add Item Script

The _additem.asp page is the first page in Estore that creates OrderGroup and OrderForm objects and persists information in the basket. Here is a snippet from _additem.asp that contains important code to accomplish these tasks:

```
    ....
    ....
Set mscsOrderGrp = LoadBasket(m_UserID)

    Set dictItem = Server.CreateObject("Commerce.Dictionary")
    dictItem.product_catalog = sCatalogName
    dictItem.product_catalog_base = mscsCatalog.BaseCatalogName
    dictItem.product_id = sProductID
    dictItem.Quantity = iProductQty
    dictItem.product_category = sCategoryName

    If Not IsNull(sVariantID) Then
        dictItem.product_variant_id = sVariantID
    End If
```

```
' Add the item to the appropriate OrderForm
ApplyVendorInfo dictItem, sCatalogName
Call mscsOrderGrp.AddItem(dictItem)

' Note: you may want to run pipeline here if the site is structured not to
➡ redirect to basket,
' for example if you need to keep a total up-to-date, or if you want to
➡notify users
' of basket warnings (e.g. product or discount no longer available)
➡immediately

Call mscsOrderGrp.SaveAsBasket()

Call Analysis_LogAddToBasket( _
                              sCatalogName, _
                              sCategoryName, _
                              sProductID, _
                              sVariantID _
                  )
....
....
```

`OrderGroup` and `OrderForm` Objects

Recall that `OrderForm` is a Commerce Server object that encapsulates the real-world order placed in a typical retail shop. It contains information such as line items, shipping address, taxes, user information, and subtotal. The `OrderGroup` object is a container for `OrderForm` objects and contains aggregate-level information. `OrderForm` objects are accessed using the `OrderGroup` object, and typically one `OrderGroup` object will contain a single `OrderForm` object. In some instances where items in an order are supplied by different vendors, an order group helps in presenting a "single point of purchase" experience by generating multiple order forms corresponding to items. In short, the main object we will be dealing with is the `OrderGroup` object, which is used to manipulate `OrderForm` objects.

Coming back to _additem.asp, the statement

```
Set mscsOrderGrp = LoadBasket(m_UserID)
```

helps in loading the basket of a shopper.

The subroutine `LoadBasket` is defined in `std_ordergrp_lib.asp`, which is defined as:

```
Function LoadBasket(ByVal sUserID)

    Dim mscsOrderGrp
```

10

```
      Set mscsOrderGrp = GetOrderGroup(sUserID)
      Call mscsOrderGrp.LoadBasket()
      Set LoadBasket = mscsOrderGrp
End Function
```

The GetOrderGroup routine, in turn, is defined in the same file, as shown here:

```
Function GetOrderGroup(ByVal sOrderID)

    Dim mscsOrderGrp

    Set mscsOrderGrp = Server.CreateObject("Commerce.OrderGroup")
    Call mscsOrderGrp.Initialize(dictConfig.s_TransactionsConnectionString,
    ➥ sOrderID)
    Set GetOrderGroup = mscsOrderGrp
End Function
```

In the GetOrderGroup routine, first a new OrderGroup object is instantiated by using the prog ID "Commerce.OrderGroup".

The Initialize method uses the passed user ID and database connection string to initialize an OrderGroup object in memory. This initialized OrderGroup object is returned to the LoadBasket routine, which calls the LoadBasket() method of the OrderGroup object, as shown here:

```
Call mscsOrderGrp.LoadBasket()
```

The LoadBasket() method loads a basket if the basket exists for a shopper in the database table BasketGroup. In case of a new shopper (like us at this moment in Estore), the method creates an empty basket in memory for the user. Note that the user corresponds to the user ID passed to the Initialize method of the OrderGroup object.

The empty basket created is returned to the calling _additem.asp page in mscsOrderGrp. Now a dictionary is created for query string values that were passed on to this page, such as catalog name, product ID, category, quantity, and any variant chosen:

```
Set dictItem = Server.CreateObject("Commerce.Dictionary")

    dictItem.product_catalog = sCatalogName
    dictItem.product_catalog_base = mscsCatalog.BaseCatalogName
    dictItem.product_id = sProductID
    dictItem.Quantity = iProductQty
    dictItem.product_category = sCategoryName

    If Not IsNull(sVariantID) Then
        dictItem.product_variant_id = sVariantID
    End If
```

These are the product details chosen by the user to add to his basket; therefore, they will form the line item of an `OrderForm` object. The following statement creates the `OrderForm` object for this new shopper:

```
Call mscsOrderGrp.AddItem(dictItem)
```

The `AddItem` method of the `OrderGroup` object adds a line item to a specified order form. If there are no order forms specified, as in our case, the method will create a new order form called "default" and add the items in the dictionary `dictItem` to this order form.

At this point, the `OrderGroup` object in memory holds a single `OrderForm` object that, in turn, contains a dictionary that holds information about the item chosen. Figure 10.2 provides an illustration of this to make things clearer.

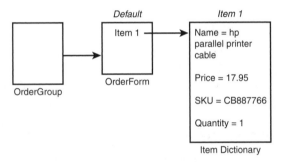

FIGURE 10.2
The `OrderGroup` *object contains an* `OrderForm` *object that contains an Item dictionary.*

Now the basket for the user is ready, but only in memory. It needs to be persisted to the database. Here's the statement in `_additem.asp` that does this:

```
Call mscsOrderGrp.SaveAsBasket()
```

The `SaveAsBasket()` method persists the order group to the database. Recall that the database was specified by the connection string parameter passed to the `Initialize` method of the `OrderGroup` object. The order group is persisted to the BasketGroup database table with order_status_code as 1. An order with a status of 1 means it is still in the basket and yet to be confirmed for purchase. This means that our order is still in basket status. Note that order-group_id, the primary key of a record in BasketGroup, will be the same as the user GUID.

After the order is saved to the basket, the next call in `_additem.asp` logs this activity to the IIS log:

```
Call Analysis_LogAddToBasket( _

                            sCatalogName, _
                            sCategoryName, _
                            sProductID, _
                            sVariantID _
                   )
```

This routine is implemented in the `analysis.asp` file. This routine just builds a string containing certain *name=value* pairs, with the event parameters as CEVT (Commerce Event). This string is appended to the IIS log by calling the `AppendToLog` method of the `Response` object. Log files may be used for analysis. We will look at the log in a moment.

Finally, the next set of statements checks the redirect options set at the site-configuration level using the following line of code:

```
dictConfig.i_AddItemRedirectOptions
```

If the option was to redirect to the basket page after adding an item, the user is redirected to the `basket.asp` page. In my Estore configuration, the redirection is to the product page. Therefore, after adding the item to the basket, I am shown the product page again, with a text display at the bottom stating "Item added to the order" (see Figure 10.3).

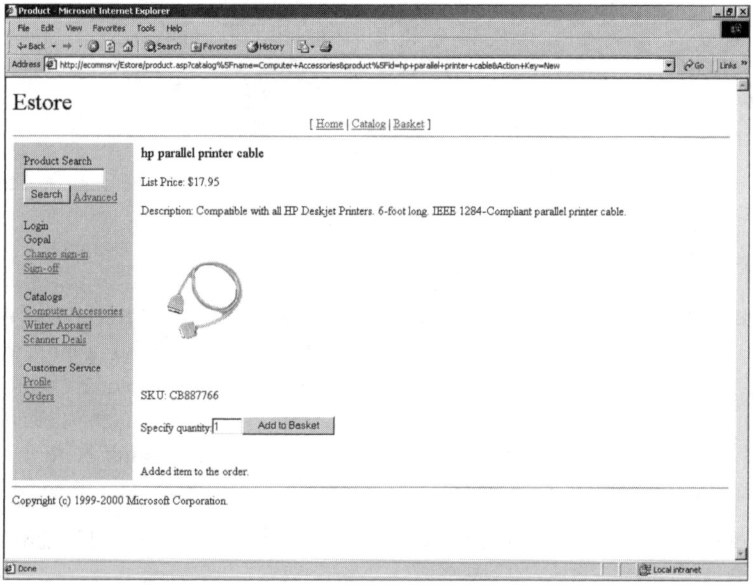

FIGURE 10.3

The product details page after the item is added to basket.

Now let's take a look at expected changes. First, let's examine the database table `BasketGroup`. It shows that an `OrderGroup` object has been added with an ordergroup_id value of user id, an order_status_code value of 1, and a total_lineitems value of 1 (see Figure 10.4). For the sake of convenience, I have shown only some of the important columns in the table.

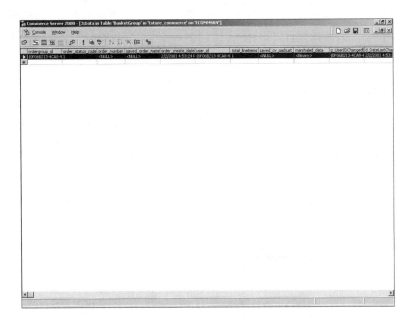

FIGURE 10.4
The BasketGroup table.

There are quite a few columns in the BasketGroup table schema. One of the important ones is the marshaled_data column. The `SaveBasket` method saves the `OrderGroup` object as binary data under the marshaled_data column. This speeds up the fetching of baskets. The order keys that don't have matching database column names are saved to the marshaled_data column. Also, remember that order keys with a leading underscore(_) are not persisted to the database.

Now let's look at the IIS log file. It shows that _additem.asp has indeed appended entries to the log, as shown here:

```
2001-02-02 21:53:24 127.0.0.1 - 127.0.0.1 80 POST /Estore/_additem.asp
➥&CEVT={T=BSK,EVT=AIBSK,PRID="Computer+Accessories%3Bhp+parallel+
➥printer+cable"} 302 89 1249 Mozilla/4.0+(compatible;+MSIE+5.5;+Windows
➥+NT+5.0)
➥MSCSProfile=95385A1F52DEA1A229D5B37542054464B65762006BEE2FBA25A972D6DA
➥E42E621D56D75AECE4F8ED652B9B9D3979595213D4B6ED57C4F5E820A9BC8D3C45C14D
➥1AB60D69EAEFB910157005F5EAAFCCBD6B1CCFE5ACEA193A504FB28A34C47EF625A27A
```

➡A845F365623C91079576C4EB0A0CAA19064ABEF28F42F662BEC20359EF9BAE203E4DA9
➡FCAA;+CampaignHistory=2;+MSCSAuth=95385A1F52DEA1A229D5B37542054464B657
➡62006BEE2FBA25A972D6DAE42E621D56D75AECE4F8ED652B9B9D3979595213D4B6ED57
➡C4F5E820A9BC8D3C45C14D1AB60D69EAEFB910157005F5EAAFCCBD6B1CCFE5ACEA193A
➡504FB28A34C47EF625A27AA845F365623C91079576C4EB0A0CAA19064ABEF28F42F662
➡BEC20359EF9BAE203E4DA9FCAA;+ASPSESSIONIDGQGQQOXO=IEMLPFJBKCPLFAMCBAABBOHO

Now that a product has been added to the basket, its time to take a look at the page that displays a shopper's basket.

The Basket Page

If your site configuration had the redirect option to the basket, you would have been automatically taken to the basket page. Note that this site-configuration option is called Add Item Redirect Options and can be set from the Commerce Server Manager by right-clicking the AppDefault Config site resource for Estore (see Figure 10.5).

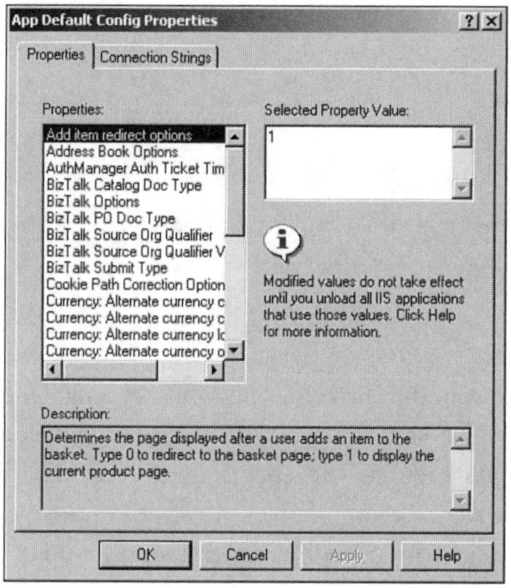

FIGURE 10.5

The Add Item Redirect Options property for a site.

Otherwise, you can click the Basket link on the navigation bar to go to the basket page. Regardless of the method of redirection, `basket.asp` is the script responsible for displaying the basket to the user.

Inside `basket.asp`

When control goes to `basket.asp`, it starts its main work with the following call:

```
Call InitializeBasketPage(mscsOrderGrp, bBasketIsEmpty, bMustSaveBasket,
➥oOrderFormDisplayOrder)
```

The routine `InitializeBasketPage` is defined within the `basket.asp` page itself as follows:

```
Sub InitializeBasketPage(ByRef objOrderGroup, ByRef bBasketIsEmpty, ByRef
➥bMustSaveBasket, ByRef oOrderFormDisplayOrder)
    bBasketIsEmpty = True

    Set objOrderGroup = LoadBasket(m_UserID)

    If objOrderGroup.Value(TOTAL_LINEITEMS) > 0 Then
        bBasketIsEmpty = False
    End If
    bMustSaveBasket = False 'Assume that view basket operations don't require
➥a SaveBasket.
                            'This may be an invalid assumption for certain
                            ➥pipelines.
                            'If this applies to your pcf, initialize this
                            ➥variable
                            'to "Not bBasketEmpty"
    Set oOrderFormDisplayOrder = Nothing
End Sub
```

Again, the order group for the user, which is the basket, is loaded into memory with the following statement:

```
Set objOrderGroup = LoadBasket(m_UserID)
```

At this moment, the user has a basket. Therefore, the basket for the user is loaded from the database and loaded into memory for further manipulation. It is then easy to check the total_lineitems column of the order group. If it is 0, the flag `bBasketIsEmpty` is set to `True`, meaning that the basket is empty.

Once the basket is found not to be empty, the routine `CheckBasket` is called:

```
Call CheckBasket(mscsOrderGrp, bBasketIsEmpty, iErrorCount, bMustSaveBasket,
➥ oOrderFormDisplayOrder)
```

The `CheckBasket` routine, which is defined within the same `basket.asp` script, runs an OPP pipeline and checks the validity of the basket. Here's the statement that attempts to run the pipeline:

```
iErrorLevel = RunMtsPipeline(MSCSPipelines.Basket, GetPipelineLogFile
➥("Basket"), mscsOrderGrp)
```

The routine RunMtsPipeline is defined in std_pipeline_lib.asp. Observe that the pipe to be run (basket.pcf) is passed as the first parameter. We already know that the dictionary MSCSPipelines is available to all site pages. MSCSPipelines.Basket points to the path of basket.pcf for Estore. The second parameter in this code statement is the log file for the pipeline, which is usually the path *pipeline/logfiles/filename* for the site. The third parameter is the OrderGroup object of the user, which may or may not contain more than one OrderForm objects.

The RunMtsPipeline routine builds the context dictionary (dictContext) needed to run a pipeline. This dictionary contains references mainly to the following items:

- MSCSMessageManager
- MSCSDataFunctions
- MSCSCatalogManager
- MSCSCacheManager
- MSCSProfileService

Specifically, to run the basket pipe, references to language, MSCSExpressionEvaluator, discounts cache, and user profile are also included to the context dictionary. Then this statement runs the basket.pcf pipe:

```
iErrorLevel = mscsOrderGrp.RunPipe(sPipeName, g_sPipelineProgID, dictContext)
```

The RunPipe method of the OrderGroup object is used to run a pipeline on each of the order forms that the order group contains. The object that the basket.pcf pipeline works with is OrderForm. Therefore, the pipe is invoked for each order form the order group contains and is executed as if the pipeline were invoked separately for each order form.

The RunPipe method's first parameter is the path of the PCF file to be run; in our example, it is the basket.pcf file path. The second parameter is the prog ID of the pipeline object used to run this pipe, which is, by default, PooledPipeline for Estore, as defined in the include file header.asp:

```
dim g_sPipelineProgID
g_sPipelineProgID = "Commerce.PooledPipeline"
```

If you need to run a transacted pipeline, you simply need to include txheader.asp instead of header.asp.

The third parameter to the RunPipe method is the context dictionary.

Now the basket pipeline (basket.pcf) is loaded and run by the pipeline object. Figure 10.6 shows the basket.pcf pipeline file for Estore, as displayed in the Pipeline Editor.

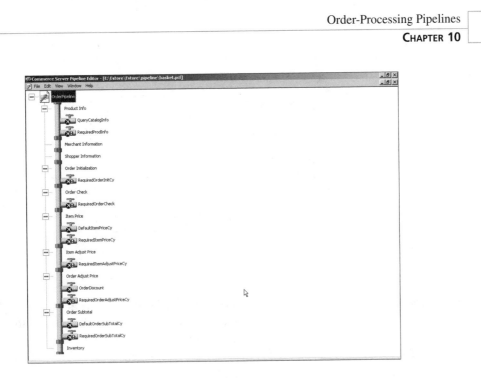

FIGURE 10.6

The basket pipeline for Estore.

The Basket Pipe

Shown in Figure 10.6 are the stages and components in the basket pipeline used by Estore. We have already seen at a higher level in the last chapter what these stages and components accomplish. Here, we will dig down a little more to see what these components actually do. Again, remember that for an instance of a pipeline execution, the input is a single OrderForm object that represents a single order.

Product Info Stage

In the Product Info stage, the component QueryCatalogInfo retrieves catalog information for each item in the order form and writes to the item dictionary. To find out what a component reads and writes, right-click the component in the Pipeline Editor and go to the Component Properties page. Then click the Values Read and Written tab. Figure 10.7 shows the values read and written by QueryCatalogInfo.

The Values Read box shows the properties read from the OrderForm object that was passed to the pipe. The Context Values Read box indicates what properties are read from the context dictionary passed on to the pipe. As seen from the property page, QueryCatalogInfo uses the CacheManager and CatalogManager objects as well as item information such as product_catalog, product_id, and product_variant_id. The Values Written box shows the properties that are written by the component to the order form.

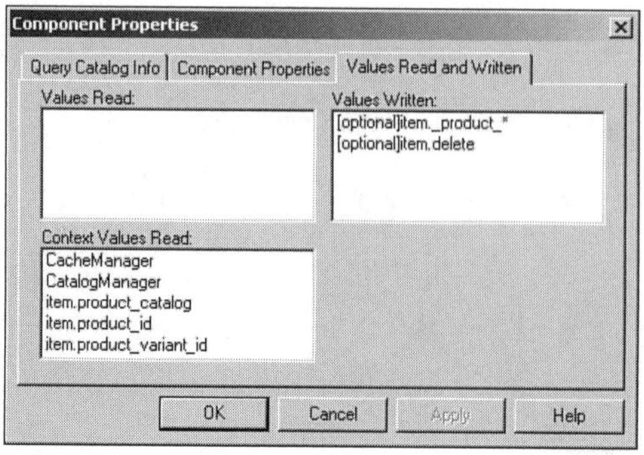

Component Properties

Query Catalog Info | Component Properties | Values Read and Written |

Values Read:

Values Written:
[optional]item._product_*
[optional]item.delete

Context Values Read:
CacheManager
CatalogManager
item.product_catalog
item.product_id
item.product_variant_id

OK   Cancel   Apply   Help

FIGURE 10.7

Values read and written by a pipeline component.

QueryCatalogInfo queries the Commerce Server catalog database for the given product ID, catalog name, and variant ID combination. If the component does not find any details for this combination, it sets the value of the key `item.delete` to 1, meaning that the item no longer exists in the catalog and can be deleted from the basket. If details exist for the item, the information is written to the order in the following format:

`item._product_<column_name>=<column_value>.`

For example, if the SKU of the item is CB887766, the value written to the item dictionary is this:

`item._product_SKU="CB887766"`

It is also possible to specify the columns to retrieve from the database using the property page for QueryCatalogInfo (see Figure 10.8).

The columns to be retrieved can be entered, separated by commas, in the Columns box. Note that many pipeline components have their own tabs in the property page for setting conditions or for further input. The QueryCatalogInfo tab is one good example of this. If there is nothing specified in the Columns box, QueryCatalogInfo fetches all columns for the product.

The next component in the stage is RequiredProdInfo. This component checks the `item.delete` key for each item set by the earlier component. If an item had its `delete` value set to 1, RequiredProdInfo deletes that item from the items collection and writes an error message to the simple list *_Basket_*Errors.

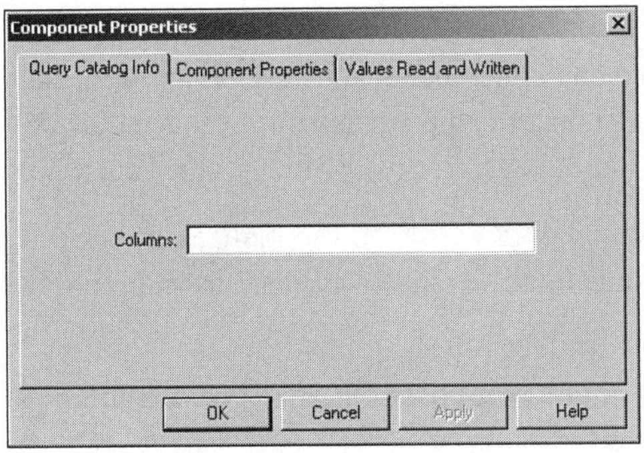

FIGURE 10.8
Product attributes to be retrieved by QueryCatalogInfo.

Assume that a user adds an item to his basket and returns a week later to finalize the order. It may be possible that the item is no longer in the catalog. When the user goes to the basket page, basket.pcf is run on the user's persisted basket. QueryCatalogInfo attempts to retrieve the item details from the catalog but finds no information about the item. Therefore, it sets the item.delete value to 1. The next component in the stage, RequiredProdInfo, finds that the item should be deleted and hence deletes the item from the items collection. RequiredProdInfo then retrieves a message using the MSCSMessageManager object corresponding to a constant value, pur_badsku.

Recall that the error messages for the site are stored in an XML file called rc.xml at the root folder for the site. Global.asa uses the GetMessageManagerObject() routine defined in global_messagemanager_lib.asp to read the error messages from rc.xml and adds them to the MessageManager object dictionary. The MessageManager object is always in memory in application scope so that any page can access error messages. Basket.asp passes a reference to this object in the context dictionary to the pipeline; therefore, error message strings are available to the components in the pipe.

After deleting an item, RequiredProdInfo retrieves the error string corresponding to the key pur_badsku and writes to the *_Basket_*Errors simple list on the order form. The error string corresponding to pur_badsku is "Please note that one or more items were removed from your order because the product is no longer sold." You can add or modify messages by editing the rc.xml file.

Order Initialization

In our pipe, we don't have any components at the Merchant Information and Shopper Information stages. You can insert components in these stages to add vendor and shopper information to the order form for easy reference or for any other unique purpose, if required.

The next component is RequiredOrderInitCy. It initializes certain values at the order level to NULL. These values include totals for the order, such as shipping, handling, tax, and subtotal. The name of the keys starts with _cy.

The subtotal of the order (that is, the cost of all items before adding shipping, handling, and taxes for the order) is stored in the key _cy_oadjust_subtotal.

The key _cy_shipping_total stores the total cost of shipping the items in the order. Similarly, the other keys that are set to NULL are _cy_tax_total and _cy_handling_total. The key _cy_total_total stores the total cost of the order after shipping, handling, and taxes are added to the order subtotal.

The component also initializes keys for the calculation of discounts by later components. The component initializes the key item._n_unadjusted to the quantity of items ordered. Then each item's _oadjust_adjustedprice key is set to a value of zero (0). The key _payment_auth_code is also initialized to NULL. This key will be used by purchase pipeline components.

Order Check

A simple verification component called RequiredOrderCheck checks whether there is at least one item in the order form. It does this by checking whether there is at least one entry in the items collection of the OrderForm object. If there are no items, it retrieves the error string from the MessageManager object corresponding to the constant pur_noitems and writes the message to the error collection _Purchase_Errors.

Item Price

Remember that the QueryCatalogInfo component in the Product Info stage retrieves the details of each item in the order form from the database catalog. For instance, it sets the price of an item by using the cy_list_price column value in the database for the item to the key item._product_cy_list_price.

Now, the DefaultItemPriceCy component just copies the value in the key _product_cy_list_price to the key item._cy_iadjust_regularprice, which is the regular price (before any discounts) of the item. Here's an example:

```
Item._cy_iadjust_regularprice = item._product_cy_list_price
```

The components down the line depend on the _cy_iadjust_regularprice key of an item to get the price. Therefore, the next component in the Item Price stage, RequiredItemPriceCy, ensures that there is some value in the _iadjust_regularprice key for each item. If there is no value in this key, the component raises an error to the pipeline. We will further discuss errors raised by components in a pipeline a little later.

Item Adjust Price

Our basket pipeline has a single component called RequiredItemAdjustPriceCy at this stage. This component deals with three keys of an item in the order form. It checks whether the key _cy_iadjust_currentprice exists for the item. For a new basket access, as in our case, the pipe won't find this key. In that case, the component creates the key _cy_iadjust_current price and initializes to the regular price stored in the _iadjust_regularprice key. Also, the component checks for another key, cy_placed_price; if the key doesn't exist, it is created and initialized to the current price in _cy_iadjust_currentprice. If cy_placed_price already exists but its value is different from the current price, _cy_iadjust_currentprice, the component retrieves the error string corresponding to pur_badplacedprice from the MessageManager object and writes to the _Basket_Errors collection.

Note that there are other components available at this stage, such as ItemPromo and SalesAdjust, to adjust the current price for sales promotions. Our pipe doesn't contain these components because it is better to use the OrderDiscount component in a later stage. OrderDiscount has access to the Commerce Server targeting and personalization information and therefore is better than the other components used to adjust price.

Order Adjust Price

The OrderDiscount component uses the Commerce Server advanced targeting system to apply discounts to the items in the order form. Discounts are usually scheduled as campaigns using the Business Desk. The component reads and writes several keys in the order form. Important among them is the key order._cy_oadjust_adjustedprice, which contains the price of an item after discounts have been applied. The _winners key contains the discount campaign IDs of all discounts applied to all items in the basket. The _n_unadjusted key stores the quantity of items that have not been included for discounts. For example, in a discount such as "buy one get the second 50 percent off," only one quantity of the item will receive 50-percent discount whereas the other is not discounted. We will discuss in detail the targeting system and how discounts are awarded in Chapter 11, "Direct Mailer and Content Selection Framework Pipelines."

The RequiredOrderAdjustPriceCy component takes the discounted and nondiscounted quantities and calculates the price for them. Finally, it arrives at the total cost for the item and stores it in the _cy_oadjust_adjustedprice key of the item. The discount for the item is stored in _cy_oadjust_discount.

Order Subtotal

The component DefaultOrderSubtotalCy calculates the sum of all adjusted prices of each item in the order form to arrive at the subtotal of the order. Simply, it adds up the values in the _cy_oadjust_adjustedprice key of each item and stores the sum in the _cy_oadjust_subtotal key of the order form.

The RequiredOrderSubtotalCy component in this stage checks to see whether the order has a subtotal (that is, the value of the key _cy_oadjust_subtotal is not NULL). If it is NULL, the component raises an error.

Error Handling in Pipelines

What happens if a component does not find a key that was supposed to be set by an earlier component? What happens, say, if the current price is different from the placed price of an item?

Error handling in pipelines is broadly divided into two activities carried out by the pipeline components:

- Return an error level to the pipeline
- Write an error string to an error collection in the order

Every pipeline component returns an error level to the pipeline object. The error level is a long integer, which can be one of the following:

- 1 for success
- 2 for warning
- 3 for failure

The pipeline object keeps in memory the error level returned by each of the components in the pipe. It is up to a stage to decide whether to continue its processing or exit from the pipeline, depending on its tolerance level for errors generated by components. This tolerance level of a stage can be modified using the Pipeline Editor. Right-click a stage (say, OrderCheck) and choose Properties (see Figure 10.9).

In the Stage Properties dialog box, you can see the value set for the stage in the Error Level edit box (see Figure 10.10).

The stage will continue execution while components in the stage generate error levels less than the one set in the Error Level box for the stage. For example, in the case of OrderCheck, shown in Figure 10.10, if any component generates either 2 or 3, the stage will not proceed with the next component but will stop execution and generate an error. Therefore, this stage accepts only 1 (success) to continue execution.

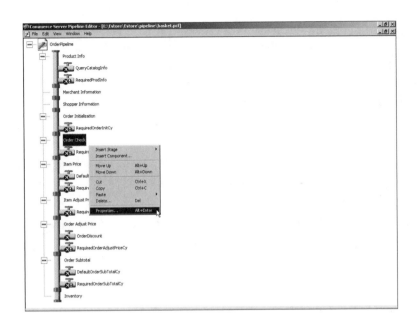

FIGURE 10.9

Viewing the property page of a pipeline stage.

FIGURE 10.10

Error tolerance setting of a pipeline stage.

Apart from generating an error level, a pipeline component retrieves error messages using the `MessageManager` object and writes to either the Basket or Purchase errors collection, in case of a warning. Typically, here is what a pipeline component does:

- *Returns error level 1.* Returned when processing was successful.

- *Returns error level 2.* Component found some order form problems such as bad SKU or changed prices. In this case, the component returns 2 to the pipeline and also retrieves a corresponding error message and writes to the *_Basket_*Error or *_Purchase_*Error collection, depending on the nature of component.

- *Returns error level 3.* Returned if something was fatally wrong, such as trying to access a key that should have been there but is missing in the order form.

Therefore, when a pipeline completes its execution, either successfully or unsuccessfully, the error level is returned from the pipeline. The calling ASP page then checks this error level for 1 (success). If the error level is greater than 1, there could be an error message written by a component that can be displayed to the user on the site page.

Figure 10.11 provides an illustration of how components interact with the pipeline object when a pipe is run.

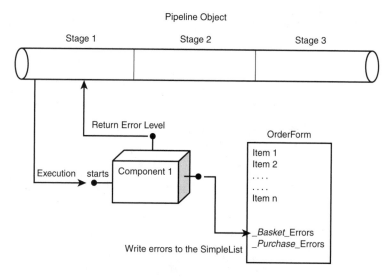

FIGURE 10.11
Component interaction with a pipeline.

The Basket Pipe Returns

Recall that the pipeline was loaded and executed by the RunMtsPipeline() routine, which was called by the CheckBasket routine in basket.asp. The return value from the pipeline execution, as we know, is a long value, which is the error level returned by the pipeline. If the error level is greater than 1, meaning either 2 or 3, the _Basket_Error collection is checked for any entries. If there were any entries found in this errors collection, it means that some component has discovered some changes in product information, such as price. Therefore, the bMustSave

`Basket` flag is set to `True`. If you don't want to save a basket automatically if there is any information change, you would set this flag to `False` and inform the user of the changes before saving the basket with the modified information.

After the `CheckBasket` routine is complete, control once again returns to the `Main()` routine of `basket.asp`. Now the procedure `AddDiscountMessages()` is called to add the name of the discounts that were applied to the basket. Remember that the OrderDiscount component writes the campaign IDs of all discounts that were applied to items in the `discount_applied` key of each item. The `AddDiscountMessages` procedure iterates through each item in the order form and prints out the discount information to the HTML stream in the following format:

`D<campaign id>-<discount description entered in Campaign Manager module>`

An example would be something like the following:

`D2- Discount for printers`

After these discount messages are generated, the basket is saved using the `SaveAsBasket()` method of the `OrderGroup` object. Finally, the basket (the contents of the order form in the `OrderGroup` object) and discounts applied to the basket are displayed on the Web site page using the routine `RenderBasketPage()`, defined in `basket.asp` itself.

Figure 10.12 shows my page after the pipeline is run and the basket is checked.

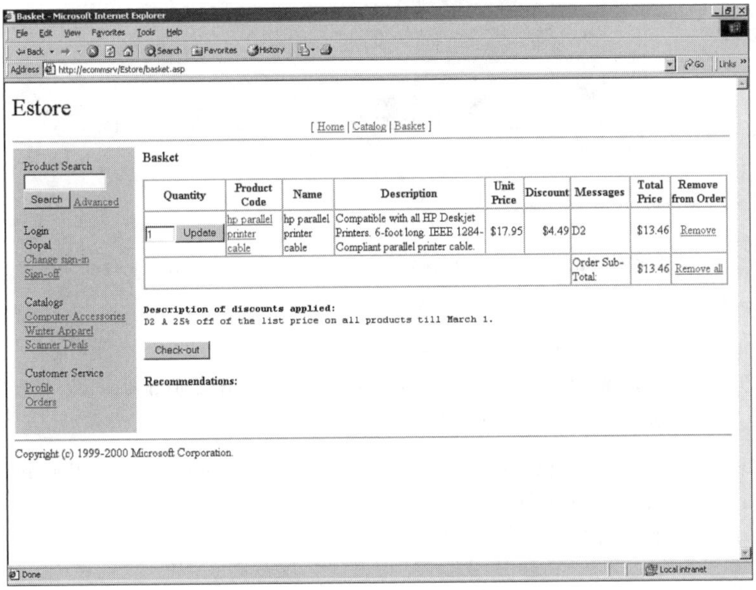

Figure 10.12

The basket page for a user.

The Check-out Button

The basket page contains the Check-out button, which when clicked will submit the form to another page to handle addresses for the order. There are basically two ways in which a user can specify an address for the order. One is to choose an address from an address book (addrbook.asp); the other is to specify an address directly for this order (addrform.asp). The Check-out button in the basket page submits the form to the address book for the user if the site configuration option Address Book Options is set to allow access to the address book (see Figure 10.13). Otherwise, the user is redirected to a standard address form.

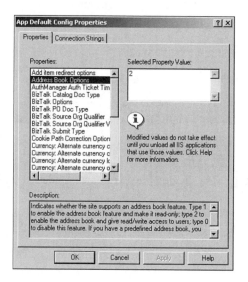

FIGURE 10.13

Enabling Address Book Options for the site.

For a first-time shopper, the address book is probably going to be empty (see Figure 10.14). Therefore, the user has to click the link to add an address.

All the routines needed to access the Address profile object are contained in the include/addr_lib.asp file. The user enters the address information and clicks the Submit button (see Figure 10.15).

The entered address is updated in the Addresses table of the Estore database through the Addresses profile service object. Once addresses are found in a user's address book, they are retrieved for the user to choose for the order (see Figure 10.16).

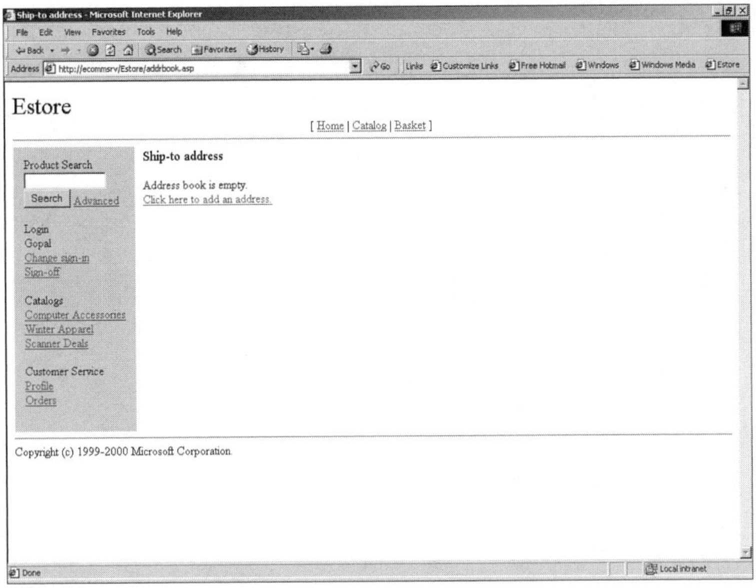

Figure 10.14

An empty address book for a user.

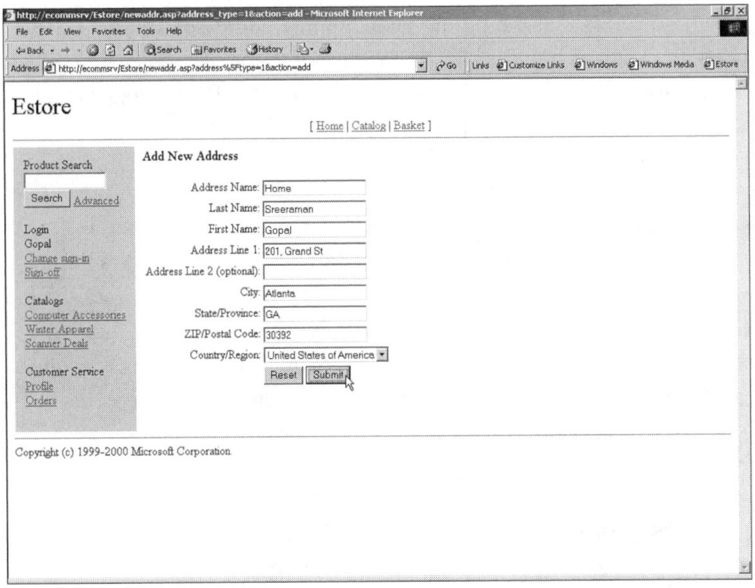

Figure 10.15

User interface for adding addresses to the address book.

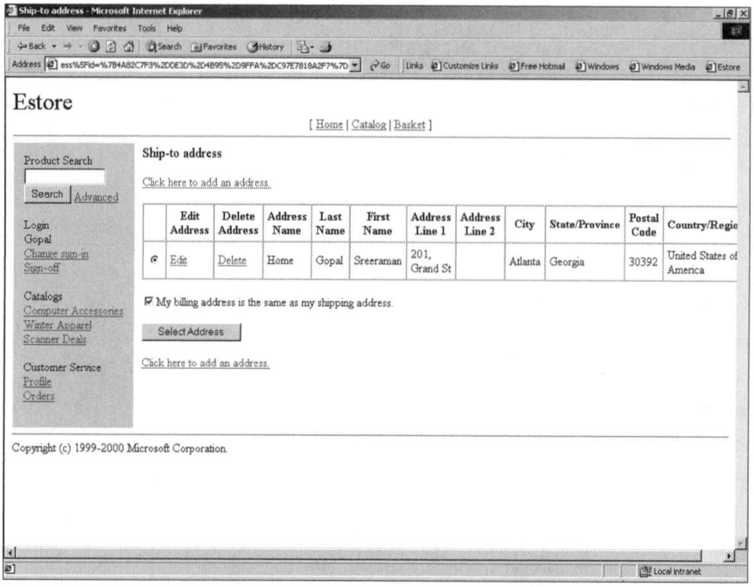

Figure 10.16

Choosing a shipping address for the order.

Note that the first address asked for is the ship-to address and the check box on the page is checked by default, meaning that the billing and shipping addresses are the same. If this check box is unchecked, the address book is shown once more to the user so he can pick a billing address. In our example, let's say shipping and billing addresses are going to be the same.

Setting Addresses for the Order

Now if the user proceeds and clicks the Select Address button, the action flows to the interme-diate page _setadrs.asp, whose responsibility it is to set the shipping and billing addresses on the order form. In _setadrs.asp, the routine FetchData() loads the user's basket from the database and also gets a reference to the user's Address profile object. Using the user's Address profile object, the General Info section of the profile is copied to a local dictionary. Remember that the General Info section of the Address profile contains address information such as Address Line1, Address Line2, City, State, Country Code, and so on. Here's the statement that accomplishes this task in _setadrs.asp:

```
Set dictAddr = RsToDict(rsAddr("GeneralInfo").Value)
```

Here, rsAddr is the user's address profile object and RSToDict is a helper routine (defined in std_util_lib.asp) that copies the record set to the temporary dictionary dictAddr.

Once the address of the user is available, it is added to the order form using the SetAddress() method of the OrderGroup object:

```
Call mscsOrderGrp.SetAddress(sAddrID, dictAddr)
```

Here, sAddrID is the Address profile ID of the user.

This adds the address to the Addresses collection of the OrderForm object. The Addresses collection is a SimpleList object in the order that stores the IDs of addresses. Once this collection is populated with addresses, the shipping_address_id or billing_address_id key has to be set just to refer to the address ID in the Addresses collection.

The shipping address for each line item is set by using the SetShippingAddress() method of the OrderGroup object:

```
Call mscsOrderGrp.SetShippingAddress(sAddrID, True)
```

This statement sets the value of the shipping_address_id key on the order form to the address ID of the user.

Because the check box was selected, indicating the billing address is the same as the shipping address, the billing_address_id key of each line item on the order form is also set to the same address ID in the Addresses collection by calling the following routine:

```
Call SetKeyOnOrderForms(mscsOrderGrp, BILLING_ADDRESS_ID, sAddrID)
```

The routine SetKeyOnOrderForms, defined in std_ordergroup_lib.asp, instead calls the PutOrderFormValue method of the OrderGroup object to set the shipping_address_id key and its value on the order:

```
Call mscsOrderGrp.PutOrderFormValue(sKey, sValue, sOrderFormName)
```

Note that the PutOrderFormValue() routine is defined in std_ordergrp_lib.asp. The input parameter sKey is going to be billing_address_id, and sValue is going to be the address ID in sAddrID.

Therefore, the shipping ID of an item can be accessed as Item.shipping_method_id, and so on. After populating the addresses in the Address collection and setting billing_address_id and shopping_address_id to an address in this collection, the order form is saved to the basket again. Then the user is redirected to pickship.asp in order to choose a method of shipping (see Figure 10.17). If you don't yet have any shipping method defined, use the Shipping Methods module in EstoreBizDesk to create any shipping method you require.

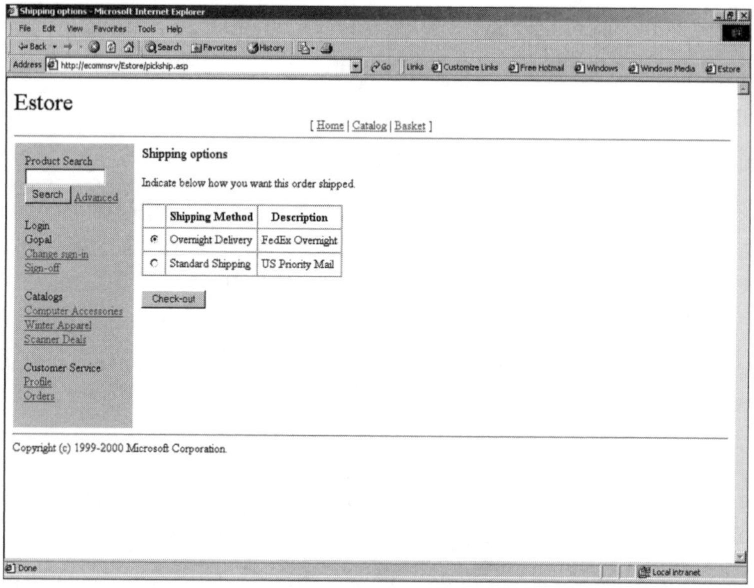

FIGURE 10.17

Choosing a shipping method.

Shipping Method

`Pickship.asp` first tries to look at the cache `ShippingMethods` to retrieve the shipping methods available for the site. If it is not found in the cache, a database lookup is done using the `ShippingMethodManager` object in the routine `rsGetShippingMethods()`, defined in `pick ship.asp`. The returned record set is iterated through to render the shipping methods. The first method is selected by default. The Check-out button transfers control to another intermediate page, `_setship.asp`, passing on the ID of the shipping method chosen by the user.

The name of the shipping method corresponds to the shipping ID retrieved from the cache. Then the keys `shipping_method_id` and `shipping_method_name` on the order form are set using the following statements:

```
Call mscsOrderGrp.PutItemValue(SHIPPING_METHOD_KEY, sSelectedMethodID, True)
    Call mscsOrderGrp.PutItemValue(SHIPPING_METHOD_NAME, sSelectedMethodName,
    ➥ True)
```

Note that the `PutItemValue` method of the `OrderGroup` objects is a versatile one that can be used to set just about any key/value pair on the order form and line items. It has a few optional parameters. For example, in the call to the method in the preceding code snippet, only three parameters are specified. The fourth parameter indicates on which specific item this key should be set. Because nothing is passed for this parameter, the method sets the key of all line items to the value specified. Therefore, the key shipping_method_name for all items will be set as Overnight Delivery, if that method was chosen.

After the keys on items are saved, the order is again saved to the basket. Then the user is redirected to summary.asp.

Order Summary

The routine InitializeSummaryPage in summary.asp is used to run the order form through various payment and pipeline checks. Inside InitializeSummaryPage, the routine GetPayment MethodsForUser() (defined in payment.asp) is used to retrieve the valid payment methods for the user. This option is set at the Estore application level, as shown in Figure 10.18.

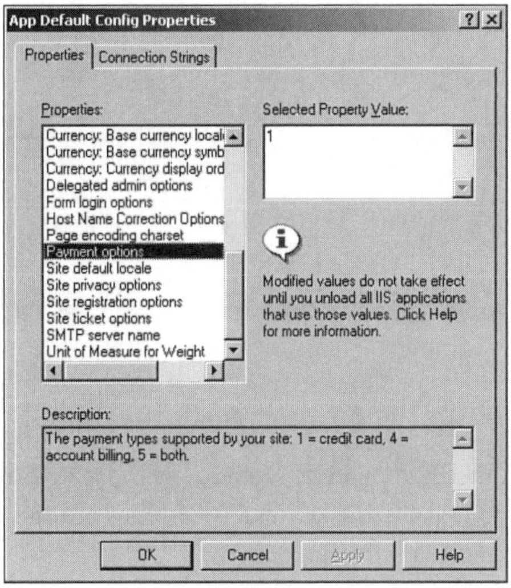

FIGURE 10.18

Setting payment options available on the site.

After the list of payment methods is retrieved, the CatchError routine helps in verifying whether there is at least one payment method and that each line item already has shipping addresses and methods defined for it. Now the basket pipe is run again on this order using the RunMtsPipeline subroutine to apply any changes in prices or discounts since the last time the basket was saved by the user. Then the Total pipe (total.pcf) is run on the basket, again using the RunMtsPipeline routine. In the next section, we will discuss the stages and components in the Total.pcf pipeline.

The `total.pcf` Pipe

Figure 10.19 shows the `total.pcf` pipeline in the editor.

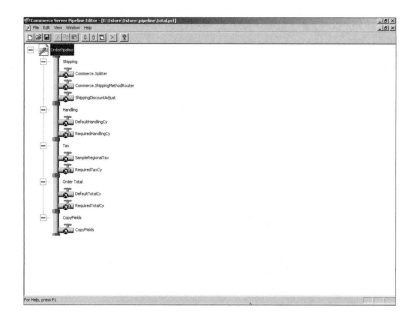

FIGURE 10.19
The total.pcf pipe of Estore.

This is a derived version of the Plan pipeline, containing only the Shipping, Handling, Tax, and Order Total stages. Also note that the Basket and Total pipes are run one after the other, rather than a single long pipe like the Plan pipeline template.

The next several sections present a summary of the stages and components of the Total pipe.

Shipping

The first component in the stage is Splitter. The Splitter component is one of the components used in the multiple-shipment architecture supported by Commerce Server. Commerce Server allows an order to be split for the purpose of different shipments. Splitting an order could be due to different shipping addresses, different shipping methods, different vendors, and so on. The basis for splitting an order can be set by using the Order Splitter tab of Component Properties (see Figure 10.20).

The Input Distinguishers box is used to specify the keys the Splitter should use to split the order. By default, the keys `shipping_method_id` and `shipping_address_id` are used. The Output Structure box is used to indicate the name of the simple list structure used to store the split records (dictionaries). The default name is Shipments.

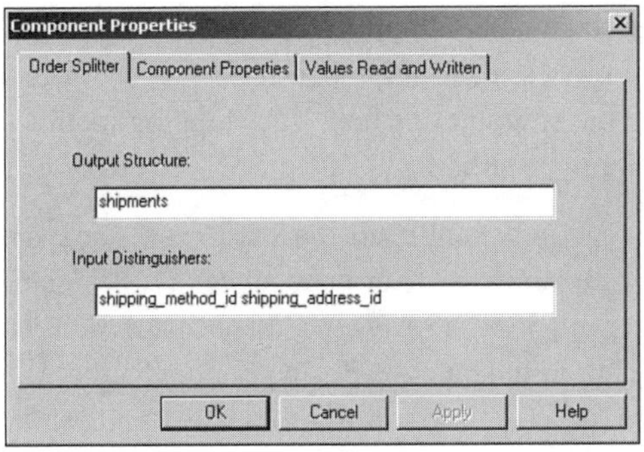

FIGURE 10.20

Configuring the basis for splitting orders.

For example, assume that the order form contains the items identified in Table 10.1 in its items collection.

Table 10.1 A Sample Items Dictionary in an Order

Item . No	Shipping_ method_id	Shipping_ address_id	Catalog	Product
0	OverNight	MyHome	Computer Accessories	HPDeskjet 970cxi
1	Standard	MomsHome	Computer Accessories	HP parallel printer cable
2	OverNight	MomsHome	Winter Apparel	Sorrel Blizzard Winter Boots
3	OverNight	MyHome	Scanner Deals	Astra 2000U Scanner

The Splitter component splits the order based on the input distinguishers and creates a record (dictionary) for each unique item. It stores a reference to each dictionary in the Shipments simple list. For the sample order information in Table 10.1, the Splitter would create the dictionaries shown in Table 10.2.

Table 10.2 The Shipments List After Splitting the Order

Shipping_method_id	Shipping_address_id	Item Indexes
OverNight	MyHome	0, 3
Standard	MomsHome	1
OverNight	MomsHome	2

The next component in the stage is the ShippingMethodRouter component, whose job is to take the Shipments list and process each shipment. It does so by instantiating different shipping components, depending on the shipping method. The shipping methods are set using the Business Desk module Shipping Methods.

The ShippingDiscountAdjust component reads the key `order._shipping_discount_type` to find whether the discount is by amount (1) or percentage (2). The value of the discount is given in the key `order._cy_shipping_discount_value`. Note that these keys were originally set by the OrderDiscount component in the `basket.pcf` pipe. Finally, the value of the `order._cy_shipping_total` key is set to the adjusted shipping cost, taking the discount into account.

Handling Stage

The DefaultHandlingCy component sets the key `order._cy_handling_total` to a value of zero (0). The required component RequiredHandlingCy checks whether the key `order._cy_handling_total` is present in the order. If the key doesn't exist, the component retrieves the error string corresponding to the `pur_badhandling` key from the `MessageManager` object and writes to the `_Purchase_Errors` collection.

As you already know, there are a few more MSCS-provided pipeline components to be used at the handling stage, such as LinearHandling, FixedHandling, and TableHandlingADO. For a comprehensive list of available components for each of the pipeline stages, refer to Appendix B, "Pipeline Components: A Quick Reference."

Tax Stage

The SampleRegionalTax component reads each shipment from the Shipments simple list of the order. Recall that Commerce Server supports multiple shipments of an order, and these individual shipments are sorted in the Shipments list. The SampleRegionalTax component retrieves the tax rate from the RegionalTax database table based on the country and region code from the shipping address for an item. Therefore, the component calculates and accumulates applicable taxes for the shipments and each item in the order. The key `item._cy_tax_total` gives the tax total for an item, whereas the key `shipment._cy_tax_total` gives the total tax for the shipment.

All these tax totals are summed up to arrive at the tax total for the order, stored in `order._cy_tax_total`. The RequiredTaxCy component is a typical verification component; it checks whether the tax total is calculated for the order. Otherwise, an error string corresponding to the error `pur_badtax` is retrieved from the `MessageManager` object and written to the `_Purchase_Errors` collection.

Order Total

The DefaultTotalCy component adds the values present in the four keys:

- `_cy_oadjust_subtotal`
- `_cy_shipping_total`
- `_cy_tax_total`
- `_cy_handling_total`

The sum of these values of the order is stored in the key `order._cy_total_total`, which indicates the total cost of the order to the user. The next component, RequiredTotalCy, seems to be yet another component that checks for some required keys. But it has some interesting functions to perform. The RequiredTotalCy component compares the page values with a dictionary on the order form and verifies that the key/value pairs are not tampered with while the page is being sent. The dictionary that holds the key/value pairs to be verified is `order._Verify_With`. The component checks that each of these keys is present on the page and has the same value. For example, in the confirmation page, the order total might be, say, $550.00. Then, in the order form, the `order._total_total` key would be set to 550.00. When the user confirms the purchase and sends the order, the component verifies that the order total in `order._total_total` is indeed equal to the value in `order._Verify_With._total_total`.

CopyFields

CopyFields is a custom stage provided in the Estore solution site's `total.pcf` pipeline. This stage has a single Scriptor component inserted for the purpose of copying the keys that start with an underscore to keys that start with the prefix "`saved_`". Remember that order keys with a leading underscore are not persisted to the database. To take a snapshot of these values, corresponding keys are created with a "`saved_`" prefix. These keys have corresponding database columns, such as saved_cy_total_total and saved_cy_oadjust_subtotal. These columns help in performing database searches on these order form values without having to load the order form or run through a pipeline. Here is a code snippet from the source of the Scriptor component:

```
Option Explicit

...

...

Function MSCSExecute(config, orderform, context, flags)
    Dim objProfileService, user_id, objUserProfile, org_id, objOrgProfile

    MSCSExecute = 1
```

```
'Copy some lineitem-level fields
Dim item
For Each item In orderform.value("items")
    item.value("cy_unit_price") = item.value("_cy_iadjust_regularprice")
    item.value("cy_lineitem_total") = item.value("_cy_oadjust_
    ➥adjustedprice")
    item.value("description") = Mid(item.value("_product_description"), 1,
    ➥ 127)
    item.value("saved_product_name") = item.value("_product_name")
Next

'Copy some orderform-level fields
orderform.value("saved_cy_oadjust_subtotal") = orderform.value("_cy_
➥oadjust_subtotal")
orderform.value("saved_cy_total_total") = orderform.value("_cy_total_
➥total")
orderform.value("saved_shipping_discount_description") = orderform.value("
➥_shipping_discount_description")

' **************************************************
' Copy some fields from the user profile
' **************************************************
' Get the ProfileService from the context
If Not IsObject(context.ProfileService) Then Exit Function
Set objProfileService = context.ProfileService
If objProfileService Is Nothing Then Exit Function

' Get the user's profile
user_id = orderform.user_id
If IsNull(user_id) Then Exit Function
Set objUserProfile = objProfileService.GetProfileByKey("user_id", user_id,
➥ "UserObject", False)
If objUserProfile Is Nothing Then Exit Function

' Copy some user fields
orderform.Value("user_first_name") = objUserProfile.Fields.Item(
➥"GeneralInfo.first_name")
orderform.Value("user_last_name") = objUserProfile.Fields.Item(
➥"GeneralInfo.last_name")
orderform.Value("user_email_address") = objUserProfile.Fields.Item(
➥"GeneralInfo.email_address")
orderform.Value("user_tel_number") = objUserProfile.Fields.Item(
➥"GeneralInfo.tel_number")
orderform.Value("user_fax_number") = objUserProfile.Fields.Item(
➥"GeneralInfo.fax_number")
```

```
' Get the user's org profile, if avail
org_id = objUserProfile.Fields.Item("AccountInfo.org_id")
If IsNull(org_id) Then Exit Function
Set objOrgProfile = objProfileService.GetProfileByKey("org_id", org_id,
➥"Organization", False)
If objOrgProfile Is Nothing Then Exit Function

' Copy some org fields
orderform.Value("user_org_id") = org_id
orderform.Value("user_org_name") = objOrgProfile.Fields.Item(
➥"GeneralInfo.name")

End Function
```

As you can see from this script, many of the keys with a leading underscore are copied to keys starting with "saved_". For example, the order total in the key _cy_total_total is copied to saved_cy_total_total. Because there is a corresponding database column in the BasketGroup table with the same name as saved_cy_total_total, the order total is saved in that column when the order is saved in the "basket" status. Similarly, when the order is confirmed for purchase, the key saved_cy_total_total will be persisted in a similar column in the OrderGroup table.

From the preceding script, note that some of the user profile–related values are also stored in keys starting with "user_", such as user_first_name and user_last_name. These keys have similarly named columns in the tables BasketGroup and OrderGroup so that key values will be persisted for easy lookup.

Inventory

This stage is not present in the total.pcf pipeline. However, you could add the stage and the CS-provided components here to integrate the site with your inventory information. The two components provided by default for this stage are FlagInventory and LocalInventory.

Recall that the component QueryCatalogInfo in the basket pipeline retrieves all columns in the database for the products and stores them in "_product_" keys. For example, item._product_name will have the name of the product, whereas item._product_manufacturer will have the manufacturer of the product, and so on. If you had a column called in_stock for the product in the database, it would be stored in the key item._product_in_stock for the item in the order form. Even if you don't have a database column called in_stock but store inventory in a different column, you could use a Scriptor component to copy the stock column key to the item._product_in_stock key. Here's an example:

```
item.value("_product_in_stock")= item.value("_product_<column_name_in_the_
➥database>"
```

The copying is required because the FlagInventory column always deals with the key item._product_in_stock.

The FlagInventory component checks the item key _product_in_stock. If that key has a value of zero (0), the component sets the item key item._inventory_backorder to the shortage quantity, the quantity in the key item.quantity. Furthermore, if Disallow Backorder is selected in FlagInventory's configuration, the component generates an error and writes to the _Purchase_Errors collection. The message written corresponds to pur_out_of_stock, retrieved using the MessageManager object. The Disallow Backorder check box on the Component Properties page of the FlagInventory component can be used to allow or disallow backordering. If backordering is not allowed, in case of shortages, the order will not be further processed but rather error messages will be shown to the user.

Very much similar to the FlagInventory component, the LocalInventory component writes to the item key _inventory_backorder and generates a purchase error, depending on the Disallow Backorder configuration. But this component is different in that the values in item._inventory_backorder are set to the difference between the values in item.quantity and item._product_local_inventory. Once again, the key item._product_local_inventory is fetched from the product database table or written by a pipeline component such as Scriptor.

Display of Summary Page

Essentially, after the total pipe is run on the order form, the order summary is rendered (see Figure 10.21).

The Check-out button submits the form to either crdtcard.asp or po.asp, depending on whether credit card or account billing is set as the value for the Payment_Method key in the order. The routine that checks this key and determines the action URL is GetPaymentPageFromPaymentMethod(), defined in payment.asp.

In our example, the user has the credit card option enabled; therefore, clicking the Check-out button will take him to the crdtcard.asp page. Also, at this point, note that there is a hidden value in the form for the order total passed in the name verify_with_total.

As soon as the user clicks the Check-out button, the crdtcard.asp page renders a simple credit card form (see Figure 10.22).

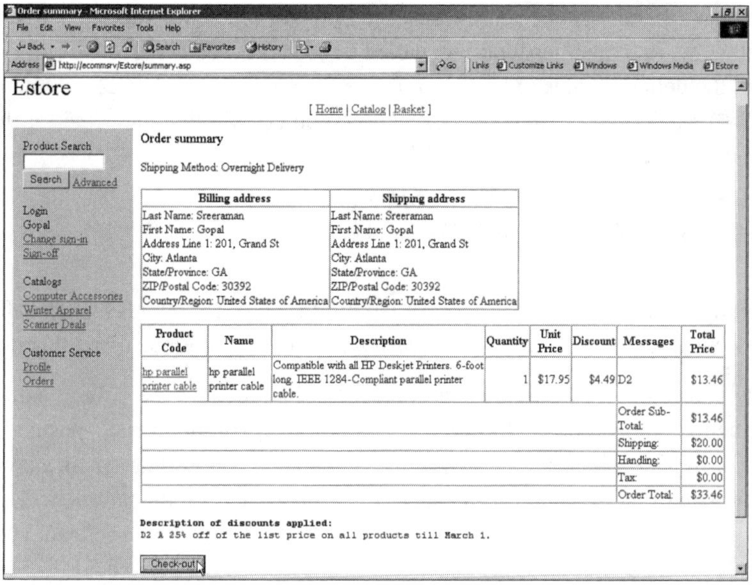

FIGURE 10.21

The summary page after the total pipe is run.

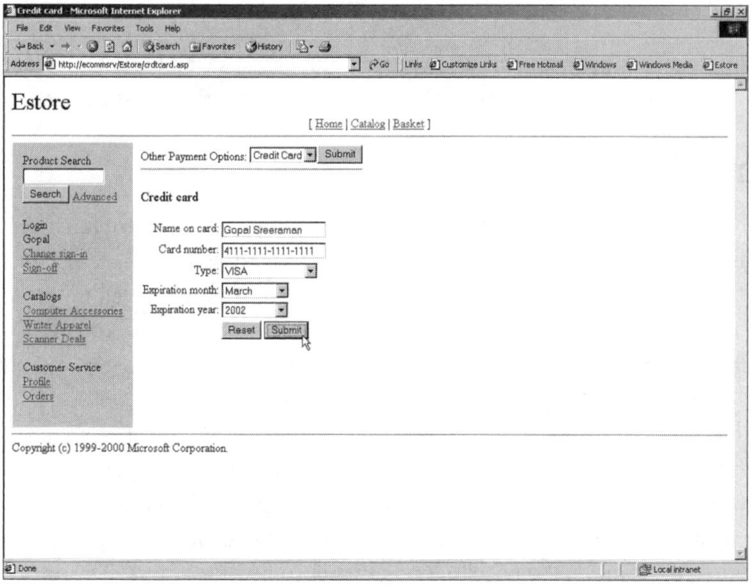

FIGURE 10.22

The credit card capture form.

The `InitializeCreditcardPage` routine is where most of the action takes place. Inside this routine, a call is made to another function, called `GetDefaultValuesForCreditCardFields`, which returns the default values to be shown in the form (see Figure 10.22). Inside the `GetDefaultValuesForCreditCardFields` function, you can see that the value for the credit card number is set as follows:

```
If Application("MSCSEnv") = DEVELOPMENT Then
      dictFldVals.Value(CC_NUMBER) = "4111-1111-1111-1111"
   End If
```

This is a dummy number for a VISA card, satisfying the rules for the checksum calculated by a pipeline component later. For development purposes, you can continue using this number.

The user enters the values for the fields in the form and then clicks the Submit button. The URL for the action element of the form is `crdtcard.asp` again; the form is posted to the same page. However, the `IsFormSubmitted()` routine in the page detects that this is a credit card submission instead of a credit card form-rendering request. The credit card details are now passed through some elementary validations using the `ValidateSubmittedCreditCardData()` routine defined on the same ASP script (`crdtcard.asp`). Then the `SetCreditCardInfo()` routine sets the credit card information on the order form. The key set is `payment_method`, with the value `"credit_card"`. After the credit card information on the order is set, the statement

```
iPipeErrorLevel = CheckOut(mscsOrderGrp, sVerifyWithTotal)
```

calls the routine `CheckOut()`, defined in `crdtcard.asp`.

In the preceding statement, `mscsOrderGrp` refers to the user's saved basket (order object) and `sVerifyWithTotal` indicates the order total generated by the `summary.asp` page.

Checkout Processing

The function `Checkout()` is defined in `payment.asp`. Inside the `Checkout` function, the basket and total pipelines are run again on the order form using—guess what—the `RunMtsPipeline` function. If there are any errors from the basket pipe, the user is redirected to the basket page. If any errors occur during the total pipeline run, the user is redirected to the order summary page. The `sVerifyWithTotal` value retrieved from the form posting is compared with the order form key `saved_cy_total_total`. Remember that the CopyFields Scriptor component in the last stage of the `total.pcf` pipe copies `order._cy_total_total` to `order.saved_cy_total_total`. If the `sVerifyWithTotal` value is not equal to `order.saved_cy_total_total`, the order total is set to `sVerifyWithTotal` and the basket is saved again. Then the user is redirected to the order summary page to verify the order total. Finally, the `checkout.pcf` pipeline is run on the order. Figure 10.23 shows the checkout pipeline designed for Estore. This pipe resembles a pipeline that is created using a `Purchase.pct` Commerce Server pipeline template.

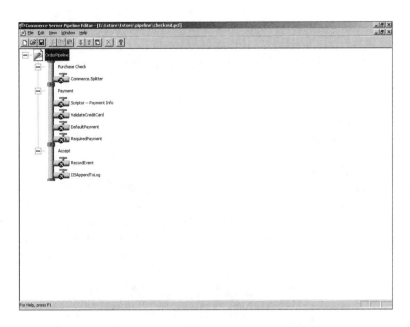

FIGURE 10.23

The checkout.pcf *pipe used at checkout.*

Purchase Check Stage

The Splitter component is once again used in this pipeline at this stage. It essentially is used here to split the shipments based on vendors, as shown in the Component Properties page of the component (see Figure 10.24).

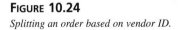

FIGURE 10.24

Splitting an order based on vendor ID.

Note that the _vendors simple list item in the order will point to dictionaries that contain the shipments sorted based on vendor ID. If there is no vendor ID assignment to any of the items, this simple list contains nothing. This is the case in our current example.

Payment Stage

The first component in this stage is a Scriptor component. This is a special type of pipeline component that Commerce Server provides.

Scriptor Component

A Scriptor component is used to write code directly into the pipeline without the need to build a pipeline component using, say, Visual C++ or Visual Basic. In a sense, a Scriptor is a readily available blank pipeline component that can be filled by your custom script. To see what a Scriptor component can contain, right-click the Scriptor component in the Payment stage and choose Properties to view the Component Properties dialog box (see Figure 10.25).

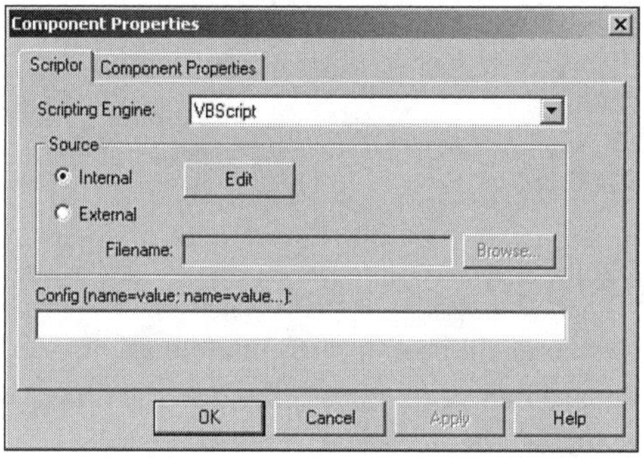

FIGURE 10.25
The property page of a Scriptor component.

The Scriptor component basically executes a script written in VBScript or JScript. The engine to execute your script can be chosen from the Scripting Engine drop-down box. The actual code itself can be written and saved as part of the pipe using the Internal option in the Source section. If the script is stored internally in the pipe itself, the Edit button should be clicked to create or modify the script. In case you want to store the script as a separate file outside the pipe and want Scriptor to load the script, use the External option along with the Browse button to get the path to the file. Regardless of the way you choose to save the script, the structure of the script is the same, which you will see in a moment.

By default, this Scriptor component in the Payment stage stores the script internally. Therefore, click the Edit button to open the Source Code Edit dialog box (see Figure 10.26).

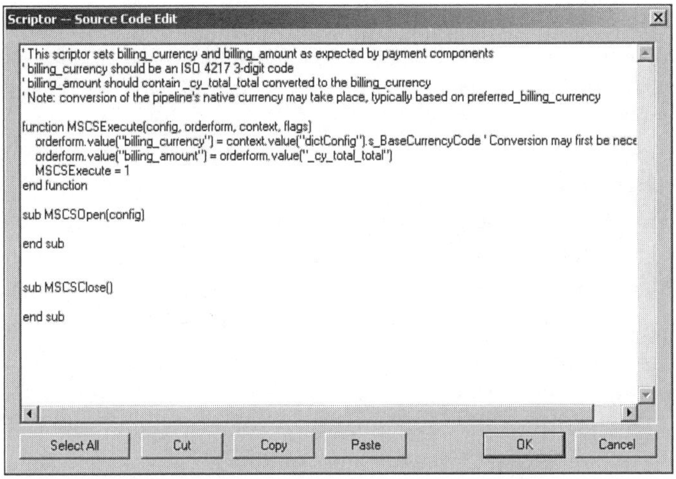

FIGURE 10.26

Editing a script inside a Scriptor component.

As shown in this script, the source code of a Scriptor has three procedures:

- MSCSOpen
- MSCSExecute
- MSCSClose

MSCSOpen is called first by the Scriptor, and the input parameter to this routine is the Configuration dictionary. This is a dictionary with the name/value pairs entered using the Component Properties dialog box (refer to Figure 10.25). If the developer enters any information in the Config(name=value) box, the pairs are available in the config dictionary. In checkout.pcf, the Scriptor at the Payment stage does not have anything to do in the MSCSOpen procedure. It is perfectly OK to do nothing in this routine.

The next procedure called is the routine MSCSExecute, where processing the order form information takes place. The main inputs to this procedure are the configuration dictionary, the order form, and the context dictionary. This is the procedure in which you place the code required to carry out the purpose of the Scriptor. In our case, this procedure sets two keys on the order form. The key billing_currency is set to the base currency code stored in the site configuration, whereas the key billing_amount is set to the grand total of the order stored in the key _cy_total_total. This is required because components in the Payment stage depend on the key billing_amount. After setting the keys, the routine exits by returning a value of 1. A value of 1 indicates successful operation by the component; 2 indicates a warning, and 3 denotes there was a failure.

Finally the MSCSClose routine is invoked after MSCSExecute completes. Similar to the MSCSOpen procedure, the MSCSClose may or may not contain any code. Note that MSCSExecute is in fact implemented as a function when writing in VBScript, whereas other procedures are subroutines.

ValidateCreditCard

The next component in the Payment stage is ValidateCCNumber. Observe that the name of the component in the pipe is seen as ValidateCreditCard. This is just a friendly name you can give whenever you insert components into a pipeline. You will find the actual name of the component from the program ID when you navigate to the Component Properties dialog box for a component. This component has its own configuration parameters that can be set from the Component Properties dialog box (see Figure 10.27).

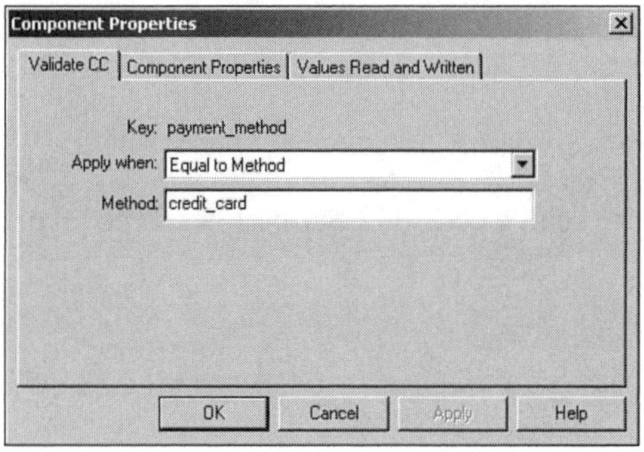

FIGURE 10.27
Configuring when to execute ValidateCCNumber.

The pipeline designer can choose when the component should check the credit card details using the preceding dialog box. The component reads the key payment_method of the order. If you set the Apply When option as Equal to Method, the component will apply its validations only when the payment_method key of the order has a value specified in Method. For instance, in Estore, the validation is to be done when payment_method is equal to credit_card. Recall that the crdtcard.asp page sets this key in the order when a user chooses a payment option.

The other options under the Apply When drop-down box are Has Any Value and Always, which can be used depending on the requirements. Apart from the payment_method key, the ValidateCCNumber component reads other keys on the order form relevant to credit card details. The credit card details are card type, expiry month, expiry year, and card number stored, respectively, in

- Order.cc_type
- Order._cc_expmonth
- Order._cc_expyear
- Order._cc_number

The component first checks to see whether cc_type is one of VISA, MasterCard, American Express, or Discover. Then _cc_expmonth and _cc_expyear are checked to see whether the card has expired. Finally, the component performs an algorithm to find whether the credit card number (_cc_number) entered is valid for the card type. For instance, all VISA cards start with the digit 4 and have a total of 16 characters.

Remember that keys with a leading underscore are not persisted to the database. Therefore, credit card keys _cc_number, _cc_expyear, and _cc_expmonth are not saved to the database. If you want to persist them, you need to insert a component in the checkout.pcf pipeline and copy these keys into different keys that can be persisted. For example, the following statement in a Scriptor that is inserted in, say, the Accept stage would help save the credit card number to the saved_cc_number column in the OrderFormHeader table:

```
orderform.value("saved_cc_number") = orderform.value("_cc_number")
```

If there are any errors found in the checking process, the error string corresponding to the key pur_badcc is retrieved using the MessageManager object and written to the _Purchase_Errors collection on the order form.

DefaultPayment

The component DefaultPayment sets the order key _payment_auth_code to the string value FAITH. Note that here is where custom payment processing components are used that would finally set the auth code depending on whether the payment was successfully authorized. The next and last component in the Payment stage is RequiredPayment, which just checks the key _payment_auth_code. If the key has a NULL value, the component retrieves the error string corresponding to the key pur_badpayment using the MessageManager object and writes the string to the _Purchase_Errors collection.

Accept Stage

The Payment stage is where the site validates the payment information supplied by a shopper. The components in that stage are used to perform tasks such as verifying the credit card number, getting authorization from a credit card processor, and so on. When these components are executed successfully without errors, it means that the payment information supplied by the shopper can be accepted, and based on that, the site can start shipping the products. Therefore, the Accept stage is ideally used to integrate any accounting system with the payment information supplied by the user, record the purchase for future analysis with the data warehouse, and so on. Here is where you would add a custom component, say, a Scriptor, to copy credit card information keys to keys starting with "saved_" to persist credit card information. Let's quickly look at the default components provided at this stage.

The pipeline component CSFRecordEvent is used to record events such as Request, Click, and Sold that happen on the site. These events are defined in the database table event_type, where custom events can be added. This component writes to a dictionary called _performance the incremental count of winners in the order form. Recall that _winners is the collection that stores what content items, such as discounts, are selected. Therefore, the occurrence of these content items is incremented in the running total in the database table performance_ total. The final component in the checkout pipe is IISAppendToLog. It appends a QueryString object to the URL requests in the IIS log in the following format:

```
&CVET={T=class, property=value, property=value1+value2}
```

Here, CVET{ denotes the beginning of a Commerce Server event entry in the log, and the closing "}" is the end of the entry. T is a class defined in the data warehouse, which is by default CLASS. The other parameters in the query are name/value pairs such as CI=2 and EVT=REQUEST. The name property is CI for Campaign Item, EVT for an event, CNT for count, PG for page group, and so on. All this log information can be imported to a data warehouse for further analysis.

The Content Selected Framework (CSF) is discussed in detail in Chapter 11. There you will find that the CSF components filter, score, and finalize the winners among various content (ads or discounts) available for delivery. The winning items are written to the order form in keys such as _event, _winners, and _winnerindexes.

The pipeline completes execution and returns to the CheckOut() routine in payment.asp from where it was invoked. If there are no errors, CheckOut returns successfully to its calling procedure, ValidateSubmittedCreditCardData. Finally, the return status of the checkout pipeline is verified. If there are no errors, the following statement is executed to save the basket as an order:

```
SaveBasketAsOrder(mscsOrderGrp)
```

Here, mscsOrderGrp is the OrderGroup object of the user. The procedure SaveBasketAsOrder is defined in payment.asp, which essentially saves the basket with an order status and finally deletes the order group basket. The basket is saved as an order using the following statement:

```
Call mscsOrderGrp.SaveAsOrder()
```

The `SaveAsOrder` method of the `OrderGroup` object saves the basket with the status as Order. In terms of database operation, this means that a new order group ID is generated and a database insert is done to the OrderGroup table. This row in the OrderGroup table represents a confirmed order, and the column order_status_code has a value of 4. Also, the order form, addresses, and items are persisted in the tables OrderFormHeader, OrderGroupAddresses, and OrderFormLineItems, respectively, for easy reference.

To delete the order that had a basket status in the BasketGroup table that used the user GUID as the ordergroup_id, a call is immediately made, as shown here:

```
Call mscsOrderGrpMgr.DeleteOrderGroupFromDisk(m_UserID)
```

Here, `mscsOrderGrpMgr` is the `OrderGroupManager` object and `DeleteOrderGroupFromDisk` is the method that will delete the order in the BasketGroup table that has the ordergroup_id equal to `m_UserID`. The newly generated order group ID is stored in the global variable `iOrderGroupID` on the page. Ultimately, control returns to the `htmRenderCreditCardPage()` routine in the `crdtcard.asp` script, which checks for the global flag `bSuccess`. The flag `bSuccess` is set after the checkout pipeline is executed. If `bSuccess` is `True`, there is a redirect to `confirm.asp`, with the order ID passed in the query string. Figure 10.28 shows how my order confirmation page looks.

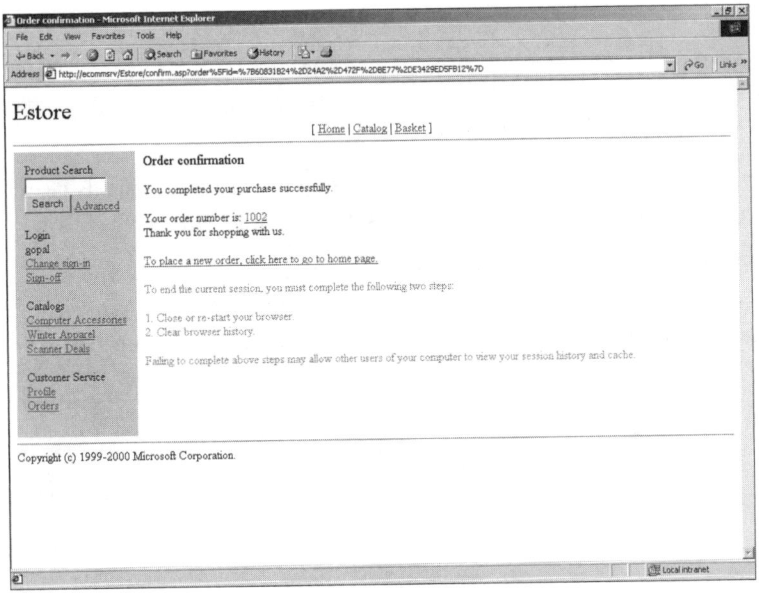

FIGURE 10.28

Confirmation of an order.

Now when I look at the database modifications, I find that the row corresponding to the user's order group has been deleted from the BasketGroup table, whereas a row has been inserted for the new order with ordergroup_id and order_group_status (4) as shown in Figure 10.29.

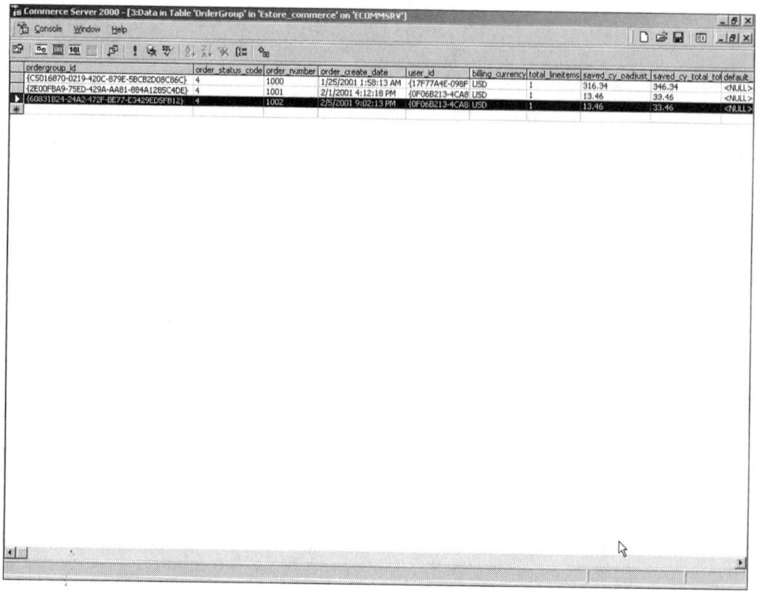

FIGURE 10.29

The database changes after committing the order.

You can also verify that information corresponding to this ordergroup_id has been inserted in the tables OrderFormHeader, OrderGroupAddresses, and OrderLineItems.

Note the order number generated and shown on the confirm page is user friendly compared to the GUID of ordergroup_id. This is a numbering system that simply increments the order numbers based on a tracking table called Counters in the database (see Figure 10.30).

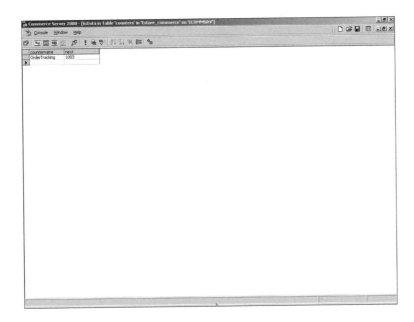

FIGURE 10.30
The friendly order number.

Summary

In this chapter, we used the familiar user behavior as our guide to getting under the hood of Commerce Server. We started from product details, added an item to the basket, and checked out the basket, specifying the shipping and billing addresses, shipping method, and credit card details. Throughout this process, we found when and how pipelines are used. The `basket.pcf` pipe was used to validate the order in basket status. The `total.pcf` pipe helped in streamlining the calculation of shipping, handling, taxes, and total information for the order. The `checkout.pcf` pipe was instrumental in processing the order for payment and logging in the events for later analysis.

All these pipes are basically derived out of and hence variations of the generic OPP pipe templates we analyzed in the previous chapter. Therefore, the discussions in this chapter have thrown light on how customized pipes are designed and when they are used at appropriate places in the shopping process. We had a chance to observe the database access and modifications as the process takes place. Also, a different site-level configuration in App Default Config was used at various moments. By now, you must have a clear picture of pipeline objects, pipes, stages, components, and the order processing. In Chapter 13, "Building and Customizing Pipelines," we will discuss building and customizing pipelines to satisfy the unique requirements of a site.

10

ORDER-
PROCESSING
PIPELINES

Direct Mailer and Content Selection Framework Pipelines

IN THIS CHAPTER

- **The Direct Mailer** 324
- **Content Selection Framework** 344

For those of us who believe business is marketing, Commerce Server provides the necessary infrastructure to indulge in applying the philosophy of marketing to an online business. The targeting and delivery mechanisms built around this infrastructure will enable e-commerce sites to effectively maintain a loyal customer base forever by somehow knowing what the customer "wants." The Direct Mailer service and its associated elements give a site the power to send personalized e-mails to highly targeted users automatically at frequent intervals. On the other hand, the Content Selection Framework encapsulates the components, pipelines, and related services that help the site to make quick decisions while delivering content to the target audience. Without much further ado, let's get to know these Commerce Server resources in order to understand what they are and how to use them.

The Direct Mailer

Direct Mailer (DM) is a service provided with the installation of Commerce Server. This service is implemented in `DMLService.exe`, which should be present under your Commerce Server installation directory. `DMLService.exe` runs as a Windows 2000 service and is automatically started by Commerce Server, which you can verify from the Processes tab of the server's Windows Task Manager.

Global Resource

The Direct Mailer is available to the Commerce Server infrastructure as a global resource. While creating the first site on the server using the Site Packager, we created several resources at the site as well as at the global level. One such global-level resource is the Direct Mailer. To be able to use the DM service, the site needs to have a site-level direct mail resource, which is nothing but a pointer to the global direct mail resource (see Figure 11.1). Commerce sites created subsequently by unpacking PuP packages would just need to create a new site-level direct mail resource mapping to the already created global-level direct mail resource. Note that there can only be one instance of `DMLService.exe` running on the server; this in no way stops us from creating multiple direct mail resources at the global level. Having more than one global-level direct mail resource will make sense only if the sites need to access the Direct Mailer service running on another server. Otherwise, there just needs to be one global-level resource that services many commerce sites.

Direct Mailer and Content Selection Framework Pipelines

CHAPTER 11

325

11

DIRECT MAILER
AND CONTENT
SELECTION

FIGURE 11.1
The Direct Mail global resource.

Direct Mailer Database

Direct Mailer has a database of its own that it uses to manage mailing lists, to maintain job history, and to schedule recurring jobs. This database is called *DirectMailer*. The important tables used are dml_jobs, dml_job_errors, and dml_attachments. Direct Mailer uses either SQL Server 7.0 or SQL Server 2000 for its database. Direct Mailer and its associated database has to reside on the same machine. Because DM uses SQL Server, it needs ActiveX Data Objects (ADO) to access its database. The connection string to this database is set in the global resource (see Figure 11.2).

To schedule and run recurring jobs, Direct Mailer uses SQL Server Agent. Therefore, SQL Server Agent should be installed and running if recurring e-mails are planned.

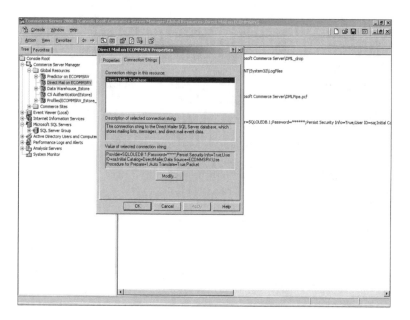

FIGURE 11.2
Database connection string for the Direct Mail global resource.

What Can It Do?

So what can the Direct Mailer do apart from being a global resource for Commerce Server sites, having its own database, and running as a Windows service? Here is a brief list of what Direct Mailer is designed to do:

- Quickly process a large list of e-mail recipients to whom you want to send e-mail
- Prepare a nonpersonalized e-mail message from a standard flat text file
- Generate a personalized e-mail message from an ASP file
- Format the message body to send content as Text, Multipurpose Internet Mail Extensions (MIME), or MIME Encapsulation of Aggregate HTML Documents (MHTML)
- Make file attachments possible
- Send the e-mail message using SMTP servers
- Schedule recurring e-mails as Direct Mailer jobs

Figure 11.3 shows you a "big picture" of Direct Mailer and its interaction with the various system elements.

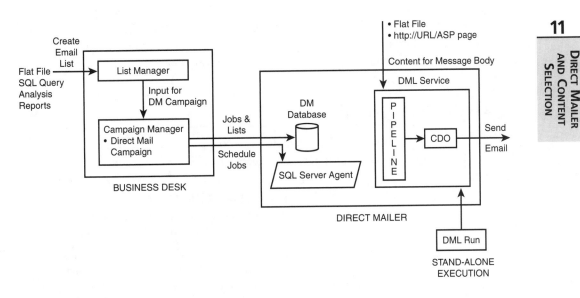

FIGURE 11.3

The Direct Mailer system.

There seems to be too much detail in this big picture, so let's apply the "divide and conquer" method. I will frequently refer to this figure as we cover the various aspects.

Fundamentally, you can see that there are two ways to access the Direct Mailer. One is through the graphical user interface (GUI) generated by Business Desk; the other is by invoking Direct Mailer in an external or standalone mode using the DMLRun.exe runtime executable. We will talk about standalone execution a little later. Let's start by discussing how Direct Mailer works when used from the interfaces in Business Desk. The e-mail to be sent is to be created as a Direct Mail campaign.

List Manager

The first requirement in the process of sending an e-mail is to get the list of e-mail addresses. Therefore, before we create a Direct Mail campaign using the Campaign Manager module, a valid e-mail list should be created using the List Manager module.

An e-mail list is created in List Manager by importing from one of the following sources:

- A flat text file with comma-separated values (CSV)
- A SQL query used to fetch the list
- An exported list from running an analysis report
- An exported list from the Segment Viewer module

What should this list contain or what should be the format of this list to be a valid e-mail list accepted by List Manager? The list will contain as many rows as there are e-mails to be sent, where each row corresponds to a single e-mail/user. Each row should have the structure shown in Table 11.1.

Table 11.1   List Manager E-mail List Format

Parameter	Description
E-mail address	Example: gopal@somedomain.com. This is a required field.
GUID	The user ID of the user, required for generating personalized messages from ASP pages. This field is optional.
Format	The format in which the message will be sent. Valid values are Text, MHTML, and MIME. This field is optional.
Language	The code-page value that should be sent along with the message. Used for sending multilingual e-mails. This field is optional.
URL	This field can be used to send unique URL links to each user. This field is optional.

Importing a Mailing List from a CSV File

If, for example, you are importing from a flat text file, the following entries in the file will result in the successful creation of a list:

```
"gopal@somedomain.com","",,"",""
"becky@somedomain.com","",,"",""
```

Create a text file called maillist.txt that contains data similar to the preceding file entries. Note that newline characters appear at the end of each line, including the last line in the file (newline characters are entered using the Enter key). Also, you can see that each row is in the required format, with successive commas separating parameters that are skipped.

In the List Manager, click the Import List task icon (or use the Alt+I key combination). In the Import a List dialog box, shown in Figure 11.4, choose Static as the List Type setting and enter the name of list as **testlist**. In the List Source box, choose From File, and in the File Name box, enter the file path to the text file you just created. Click OK to start the import process.

The status bar should say Importing List. In the list page, you should see the list with the status as Pending. After the list has been successfully imported and created, the status should change to Idle and the number of e-mails and recipients in the list will be visible (see Figure 11.5).

Direct Mailer and Content Selection Framework Pipelines

CHAPTER 11

329

11

DIRECT MAILER
AND CONTENT
SELECTION

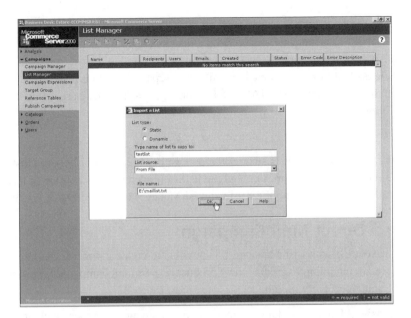

FIGURE 11.4
Importing a list from a flat file.

FIGURE 11.5
An e-mail list in List Manager.

Observe that the list does not have any user ID information and hence cannot be used to send personalized e-mails. List Manager stores and maintains lists in the commerce database, (Estore_commerce, in the case of Estore). The main tables used are lm_master and lm_master_operations. Additionally, for each e-mail list, a separate table corresponding to the list is created with the table name LM_MAILLIST_<some guid>. The structure of that table is expected as follows:

```
rcp_email,rcp_guid,rcp_fmt,rcp_locale,rcp_url
```

This is true in the case of static lists such as the one we just created. For dynamic lists, only the list definition is stored in lm_master, and the list itself is created at the time of running a Direct Mail campaign or exporting the list from List Manager to an external file or database.

Creating a Direct Mail Campaign

Now that we have a list with List Manager, it is possible to create a direct mail campaign. Assume that we are intending to create a new product release mail campaign for Estore. The e-mail will be sent once every month.

Click the Campaign Manager module and make sure a campaign is chosen, such as the SiteLaunch campaign of Estore. Then click the New Campaign Item (Alt+N) menu icon and choose New Direct Mail. In the Direct Mailer Properties section, enter the values as shown in Figure 11.6.

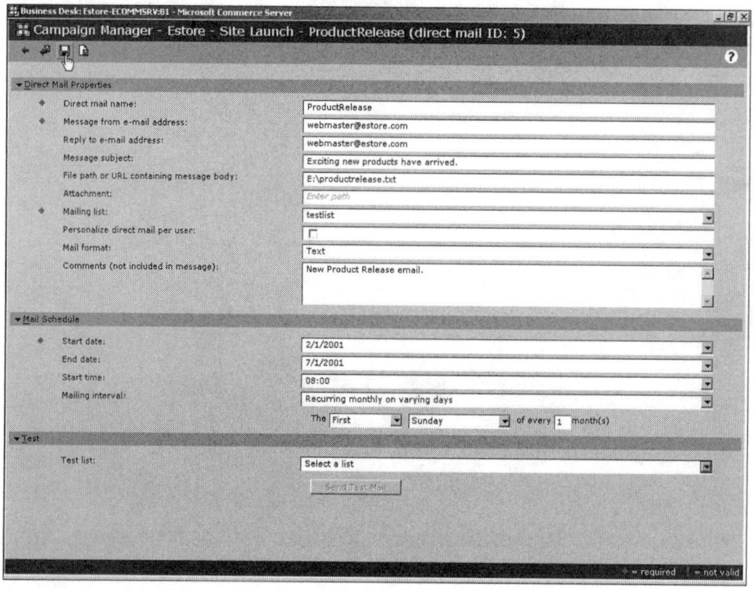

FIGURE 11.6

Creating a new direct mail campaign.

The message for the e-mail is coming from a flat file called `E:\productrelease.txt`. First, create such a file to be used for the example. If the file is not found, the Direct Mailer job will fail. My `productrelease.txt` file has the following simple content:

Dear Site Visitor,

We have added some exciting new products to our Web site. Come visit our site today!

Next, set Mail Format to Text. In the Mail Schedule section, note how by varying the Mailing Interval setting, one can schedule the mail to be sent as required by the site. In this example, we plan to send it the first Sunday of every month for six months. In effect, this e-mail has flat content (nonpersonalized) going to everyone in the list specified. Save the campaign item by clicking the Save Direct Mail task icon (Alt+S). The job is now scheduled with the SQL Server Agent running on the server (see Figure 11.7). Until the time the job is actually executed once, you won't see the job information in the Direct Mailer database.

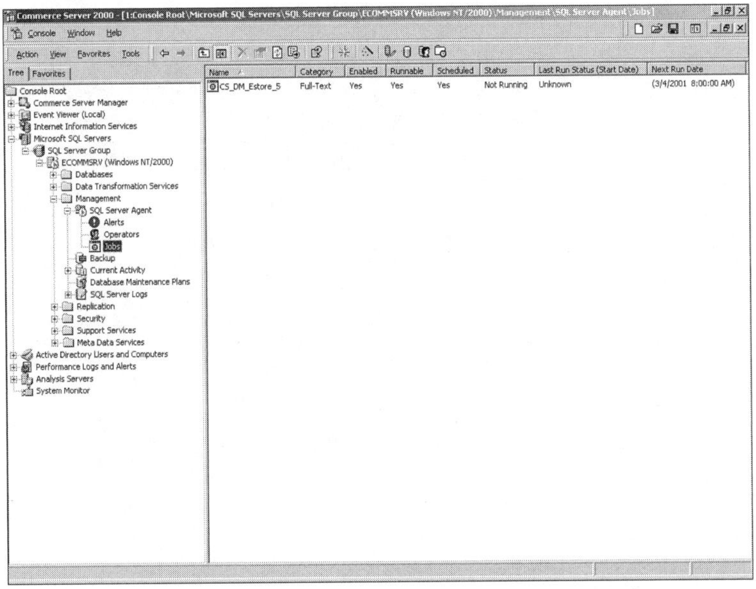

FIGURE 11.7
The recurring Direct Mail job with SQL Server Agent.

Sending a Test Mail

This job will run as scheduled; also, it can be run at any time by right-clicking the job and clicking Start Job. To test whether the mail campaign is working with the required message being sent to the identified list, you can use the Test section (refer to Figure 11.6). A test list has to be chosen. Then simply click the Send Test Mail button to send the mail to the test list. This can be done before actually scheduling the mail for an actual mailing list. Clicking the button sends the mail to the test list, and a message box will indicate that a test job was executed. When I did it, I got the message "Job 'TEST_CS_DM_Estore_5.0.401411' started successfully."

Now the job and the associated list are stored in the Direct Mailer database (refer to Figure 11.3) in dml_jobs. Also, the e-mail list is stored in a newly created table called ML__<some guid for the DM job>. This table holds a structure similar to that of the List Manager table for a list we discussed earlier.

The Mail Drop

So where does the test mail go? To the recipients in the list? Well, it depends on two configuration properties set at the Direct Mailer global resource: Delivery Location and Delivery Method (see Figure 11.8).

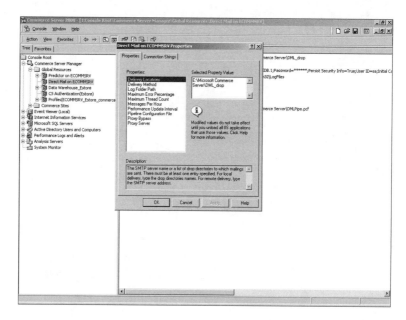

FIGURE 11.8

The mail drop configuration.

Delivery Location specifies the path at which the generated e-mails will be dropped. Delivery Method indicates whether the drop is a local directory or an SMTP server address. In the development phase, it might be enough to have these e-mails dropped to the local directory for the purpose of testing and development. Once they have been tested here, the location and method can be changed to use an SMTP server to push the e-mail out.

As a result of my configuration, I found two e-mails in the `<CSInstallation Directory>/` `DML_Drop` folder corresponding to two recipients in the list. Opening one of the e-mails with a mail client such as Microsoft Outlook will help test the e-mails sent (see Figure 11.9).

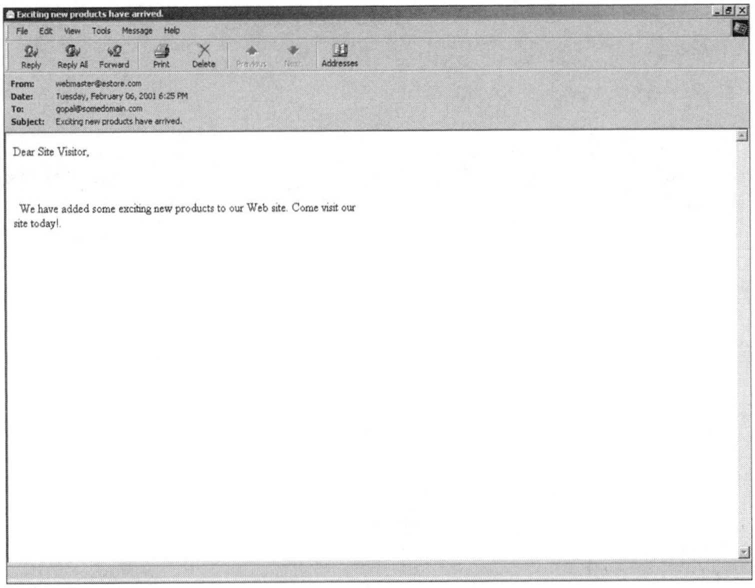

FIGURE 11.9
The e-mail from Direct Mailer.

Sending a Personalized Page

It is a proven fact that personalized mail elicits more interest from a shopper than something that looks like it was done for mass consumption. For instance, I would find an e-mail personally interesting if it starts with "Dear Gopal" instead of "Dear Site Visitor." Even without going through it, I would decide that the latter is a run-of-the-mill e-mail sent to everyone in the world. The strength of Direct Mailer is its ability to send personalized e-mail to a targeted audience to increase the probability of a successful mail campaign.

Let's take the ProductRelease mail campaign and modify it so that we have a personalized and targeted mail campaign. To have a highly targeted campaign, the first requirement is to have the target e-mail list. In our previous example, we just used an arbitrary flat file to import and create a static list with List Manager. This time, let's create a dynamic list using a SQL query.

Creating a Dynamic E-mail List

In the List Manager module, click the task icon Import List (Alt+I). In the Import a List dialog box, set List Type to Dynamic and type **RegisteredUsers** as the name of the list. In the List Source box, choose From SQL Database. Now we need to provide the database connection string and the SQL query to be executed. For this example, you could create a system data source name (DSN) using the Data Sources (ODBC) Manager on your server, pointing to the commerce database where the UserObject table exists. My DSN is called *LocalServer*, and it points to the Estore_ecommerce database on the server. Enter the following connection string, as shown in Figure 11.10:

```
DSN=LocalServer;UID=sa;PWD=;
```

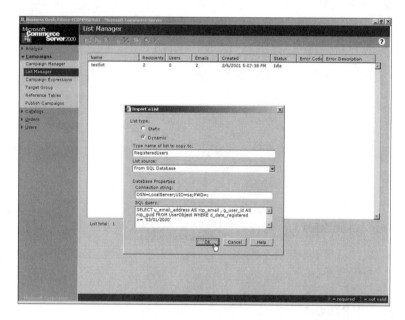

FIGURE 11.10

Creating a dynamic e-mail list from a SQL query.

In the SQL Query dialog box, enter the following query to fetch the e-mail address and user GUID of all users registered after March 2000 (note that for a personalized e-mail, we need the user GUID in the list):

```
SELECT u_email_address AS rcp_email , g_user_id AS rcp_guid FROM UserObject
➥ WHERE d_date_registered >= '03/01/2000'
```

Direct Mailer and Content Selection Framework Pipelines

CHAPTER 11

335

11

DIRECT MAILER
AND CONTENT
SELECTION

After entering the query, click the OK button. You may observe that nothing happens, except the definition of the list is created. In the List Manager, the Recipients column states that this is a dynamic list. If we had created this as a static list, the SQL query would have been executed and the list populated with rows of recipients. However, the populated list would always remain the same—this is the disadvantage of a static list. Therefore, if new users register after the list is created, they won't get this ProductRelease e-mail if we schedule the campaign for a static list. On the other hand, the dynamic list is executed at the time the mail job is scheduled to run, so the list of users is always current.

You can test a dynamic list by exporting the list to a file using the Export List task icon (Alt+E). This executes the SQL query and fetches the records to be saved in a specified file. This should satisfy the requirement that the dynamic list, when it is generated, must be valid. As you already know, the user profile should have a valid e-mail address so that a list can be a valid mailable list. You can use the Users module to update your users with valid e-mail addresses before running these examples.

The Personalized Mail Campaign

Now that we have a targeted user list, we need a page that can be used to send content in a personalized way. This is a job for an ASP page! How does Direct Mailer personalize the page given the URL to an ASP file? For each of the recipients in the list, Direct Mailer generates a User Profile Manager (UPM) cookie based on the GUID of the user. Now, with the cookie in hand, Direct Mailer impersonates the user and requests the ASP page, behaving pretty much like a Web browser. Therefore, the ASP page can be developed to retrieve user profile information with the cookie information. The solution sites already contain a sample ASP page called ServiceReminder.asp that has basic code to do this. Let's use this as our personalized content page for our example.

To modify the previously created plain-text ProductRelease campaign, click the campaign in Campaign Manager. Then open the campaign by clicking the Open task icon (Alt+O). In the File Path text box, change the path to the URL of the ServiceReminder.asp page (see Figure 11.11). Change the mailing list to RegisteredUsers. Also, check the Personalize Direct Mail Per User check box. Furthermore, we can now change the mail format to MHTML because the generated page will contain HTML content. Once again, let's test the personalized e-mail using the Test section, but now choosing the RegisteredUsers list.

When you click the Send Test Mail button, the same message box pops up telling you about the test job that was started successfully.

Next, check the DML_Drop folder, where you will find e-mails generated due to this job. Figure 11.12 shows how the e-mail looks.

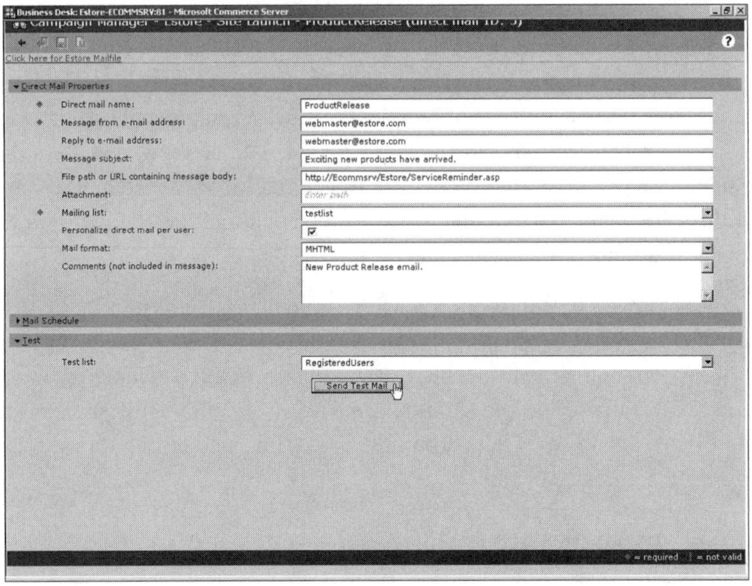

FIGURE 11.11

Testing a personalized e-mail.

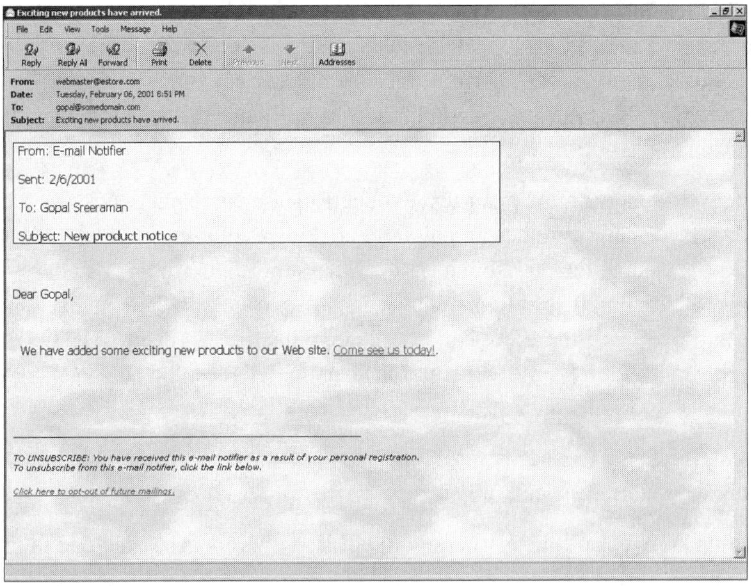

FIGURE 11.12

The personalized e-mail sent using Direct Mailer.

This is what the `ServiceReminder.asp` page generates by default. Here we have the e-mail addressing the user by name. Also, there is a link on the sentence "Come see us today!" that will take the user directly to the site, passing on the user cookie (MSCSProfile) generated by Direct Mailer. Therefore, the user will see the welcome page on the site by clicking the link.

The content could be more personalized, and the look and feel can be made to include your ad images and so on. If you open `servicereminder.asp` in Visual InterDev, you will find that the file itself is simple. The highlights are presented in the following section.

ASP Page for Personalization

In `servicereminder.asp`, the user ID of the recipient is retrieved from AuthManager as this:

```
strUserID = objAuthManager.GetUserID(1)
```

Remember that Direct Mailer has already received the authentication cookie while accessing `servicereminder.asp`, thus effectively impersonating the user. Then the profile of the recipient is obtained as follows:

```
....
Set objUPM = Application("MSCSProfileService")
....
Set objProfile = objUPM.GetProfileByKey("User_ID", strUserID, "UserObject")
....
```

`objProfile` is the profile instance of the specific recipient (user) for whom the page was requested. Therefore, in the HTML portion, content is generated by accessing `objProfile` to write out the first name and last name of the user.

Opt-out List

Finally, there is a link at the very bottom of the e-mail enabling the user to opt out of future e-mails (refer to Figure 11.12). This is the standard method of giving an option to the e-mail recipient to opt out of receiving future e-mails. The opt-out in this example is implemented by the `opt-out.asp` page, provided by default with the initial solution site. The URL on the opt-out has the following query strings:

```
opt-out.asp?rcp_email=gopal@somedomain.com&campitem_id=5&campitem_
➥name=ProductRelease&MSCSProfile=<the GUID>
```

If the campaign item ID was passed, the user is placed in an opt-out list for the campaign. Otherwise, the user is placed in a global opt-out list. Therefore, generate the campitem_id according to what you want the link to do. This ASP file accesses the dm_item database table to find whether there is already an opt-out list for this list. If there is one, the user is added to that list. If no opt-out list is found, a new opt-out list is created for the list using the following statement:

```
CreateOptOutList = listmanager.CreateEmpty(sListName, sListDescription,
➥lFlags, 0)
```

The name of the list is generated as follows:

```
Opt Out(<campitem_id>)
```

This opt-out list is set for the campaign item in the g_dmitem_optout column of the dm_item table. Finally, the user is added to this opt-out list using the following statement:

```
listmanager.AddUserToMailingList CStr(list_id), rcp_email
```

Here, list_id is the ID of the opt-out list for the campaign item.

Once the user is successfully added to the opt-out list for the campaign item, an appropriate descriptive message is written out to the generated HTML page. After I click the opt-out link on the e-mail, the list appears in the List Manager as shown in Figure 11.13.

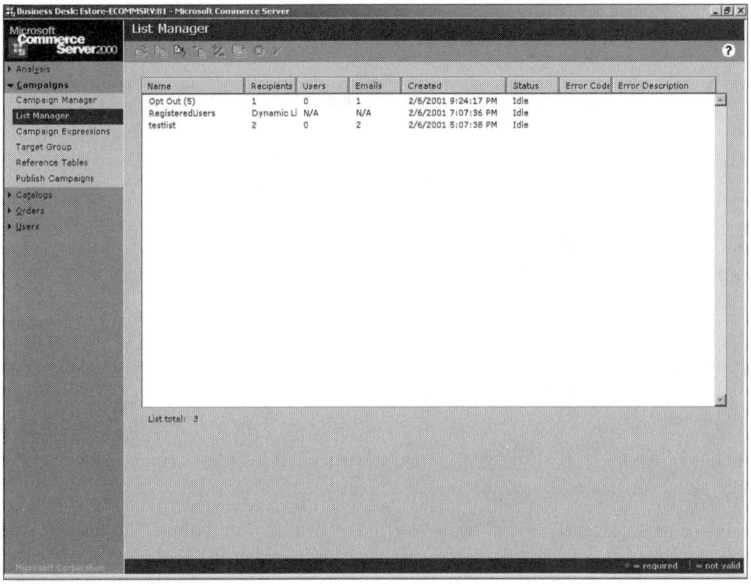

FIGURE 11.13
The opt-out list for a Direct Mail campaign.

As you can see, one recipient is added to the opt-out list for the campaign item ProductRelease that has a campaign ID of 5. Therefore, in the future, whenever the job for mail campaign item 5 is executed, the opt-out list can be subtracted from the mailing list specified in the job and the resulting list may be used to send e-mails.

Direct Mailer and Content Selection Framework Pipelines

CHAPTER 11

339

11

DIRECT MAILER
AND CONTENT
SELECTION

Direct Mailer Pipeline

You already know that the DMLService is actually responsible for processing lists and sending mails. But how does it do it? The DMLService makes use of a pipeline to process direct mail jobs. The pipeline configuration file used is set at the Direct Mail global resource level. It is set as the Pipeline Configuration File property (refer to Figure 11.8). For a Site Packager–generated site, this is usually the DMLPipe.pcf file located under the Commerce Server installation directory. Figure 11.14 shows the DMLPipe.pcf file used by Estore.

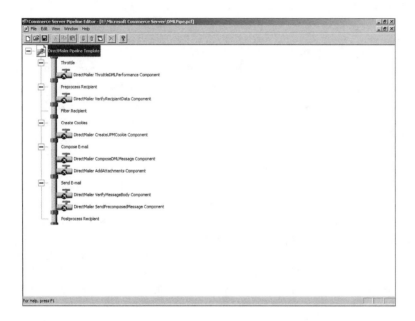

FIGURE 11.14
The Direct Mail global resource.

For each of the recipients in the mailing list for a job, the DMLService invokes the pipeline. Like other pipelines, the Direct Mailer pipe also has the Order and Context dictionaries as its input. You can use the option Save Values Read and Written in the File menu of the Pipeline Editor to find out the various properties that are read and written in the pipe.

Throttle Stage

The first stage in the pipe is called *Throttle*, and it is appropriately named to manage the speed of processing messages. This stage ultimately reduces the load on the SMTP server. The only component at this stage is ThrottleDMLPerformance. This component reads the following key:

```
Context.delay_msec
```

Then it simply produces a delay for the milliseconds specified in the key. This key is originally set by the DMLService.

Preprocess Recipient Stage

The component VerifyRecipientData at this stage verifies certain values in the Order dictionary, including the following:

- rcp_bypass
- rcp_email
- rcp_formatting

The component skips processing if rcp_bypass is set to True. It then checks rcp_email to find out whether it has a valid e-mail address. It also verifies that rcp_formatting has some valid format (Text, DHTML, and so on). If not, it uses the format specified in Context.default_ formatting. If any of the checks fail, the component simply sets the rcp_bypass key to True.

FilterRecipient Stage

Commerce Server does not provide any component for this stage. Therefore, this is a good place to implement a custom component to filter recipients. For example, just a few pages back you saw how to create an opt-out list. But creating an opt-out list alone does not eliminate the opted-out recipients from the mailing list to be sent. At this stage, we could build a custom component that compares the recipient's e-mail address with those present in the opt-out list for the campaign item. If the recipient's e-mail address is in the opt-out list, this component will set the rcp_bypass key to True, making other components skip processing and thereby not sending mail for the recipient. However, the flipside to this kind of filtering is that the opt-out list has to be read and compared against each of the recipients in the mailing list, because the pipe is called for each of the recipients. Of course, we could use some more caching here.

As an aside, a better way to implement the opt-out filtering would be to create the final list by subtracting the opt-out list from the initial mailing list. In our example for the ProductRelease campaign item, the final list would be as follows:

```
RegUsersForProductRel = RegisteredUsers - Opt Out(5)
```

In the List Manager module, click the opt-out list and then click the Add/Subtract List (Alt+S) task icon (the one with the +/- signs). In the Add/Subtract Lists dialog box, choose Subtract From as the operation. The target list is RegisteredUsers. Enter **RegUsersForProductRel** as the name for the new list (see Figure 11.15).

Once the final list is defined, the campaign item can be modified to refer to this list as the mailing list. New users can register, and at the same time, some of the existing users can opt out of receiving future e-mails. However, now the final list that's used is the net of these effects every time the mail job is run.

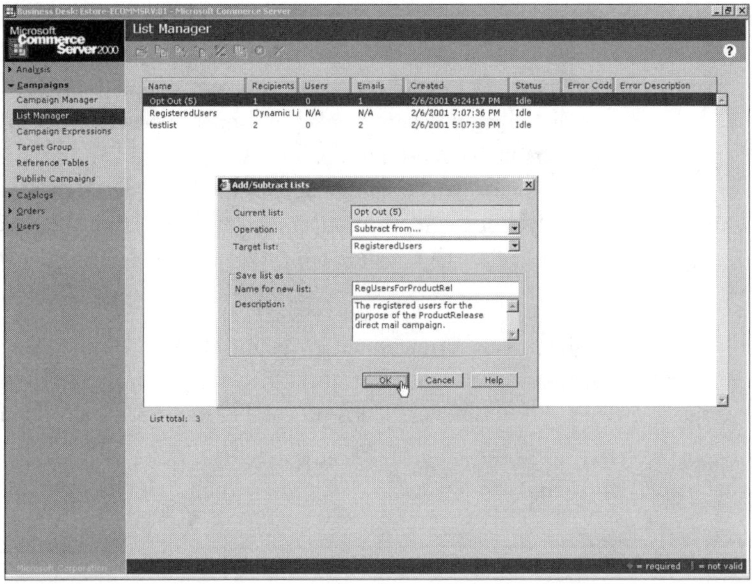

Direct Mailer and Content Selection Framework Pipelines

CHAPTER 11

341

11

DIRECT MAILER
AND CONTENT
SELECTION

FIGURE 11.15
Subtracting the opt-out list from the main list.

Create Cookies Stage

In this stage, the component CreateUPMCookie is used to generate cookie information that can be later used to create a cookie. The cookie would then be passed on to the ASP file to personalize the page for the user. Note that this component does nothing if the following keys have the specified values:

```
order.rcp_bypass = true      'Set by previous components
order.rcp_personalize = 0     'No personalization required
context.default_url_isfile= true    ' If the URL is a file and not a
➥HTTP:// path
```

After these checks, the CreateUPMCookie component generates a dictionary and stores it in the key Order.cookie.

Note that the cookie itself is generated by the ComposeDMLMessage component, whereas the information to generate the cookie is stored in the aforementioned dictionary. The content of the dictionary has key/value pairs of the following form:

```
MSCSProfile    = <encrypted GUID string>

CampaignItemID    = <string value>

CampaignItemName    = <string value>

UserEmail    = <string value>
```

Compose E-mail Stage

The first component in this stage is ComposeDMLMessage, which loads the message from a flat file or a personalized ASP page. In case of a flat file, the contents are preloaded into the rcp_url_content key or the default_url_content key to improve performance. While a message is being composed for a personalized e-mail job, a cookie is created from the information stored in the Order.cookie dictionary. This component uses the Windows 2000 CDO to create the e-mail message. It uses the CDO.Message and CDO.Configuration objects, whose references are stored by the DMLService in the keys Context.cdo_message and Context.cdo_config, respectively.

The next component in this stage is AddAttachments, which simply adds file attachments specified in the simple list Orders.attachments using the CDO.Message object available in context.cdo_message. However, this component skips processing in any of the following cases:

```
order.rcp_bypass = true     'set by earlier components
order.cdo_result is not equal to S_OK     ' error in most recent CDO operation
```

Send E-mail Stage

The VerifyMessageBody component checks the message body, depending on the value in Order.user_flags. If this flag is set, the component ensures that the body is not blank. Also, the number of attachments in the message is verified to be correct. If any of these conditions (nonblank message or correct number of attachments) are not met, the rcp_bypass flag is set to True and the component skips processing.

The final component in this stage is SendPrecomposedMessage, which sends the composed message using the CDO object.

Postprocess Recipient Stage

This stage does not have any default components. However, custom components can be built for this stage. For example, the direct mail could be logged as a campaign event in the log files and analyzed later for request and click counts.

Direct Mailer as Standalone

From the illustration shown earlier in Figure 11.3, you know that direct mail jobs can be executed using the Business Desk. However, another way to run direct mail is to use the runtime executable DMLRun.exe, provided in the Commerce Server installation folder. This application can be invoked from a command line with appropriate input parameters. In a Win32 console (the command-line window), type **DMLRun** and press the Enter button. You will see a list of options and switches to be used with the command.

For example, to list all Direct Mailer jobs on the server, use this:

```
dmlrun  /list
```

Here's an example of the information produced about jobs in the database:

```
Job ID  Job status  Job description  Site Name  CampItem ID  CampItem Name
```

If you want to run a specific job, use the following switch:

```
/run:<Job ID>
```

Similarly, to stop a job, use this switch:

```
/term:<Job ID>
```

Using the /create switch, you can create a job out of a Direct Mailer job specification file. The switch /execute can be used along with the /create switch to simultaneously create and execute a job.

Whether a direct mail job is created and executed using Business Desk or DMLRun, the recipients are always passed through the Direct Mailer pipeline.

Troubleshooting Tips

If the direct mail job does not succeed at first, you can perform a couple of checks. First, check the Application Log in Windows 2000 Event Viewer to find out which part of the job is failing: a SQL query access to obtain a list, an access failure to an ASP, or whatever. Most unexplained errors occur due to access failure to the URL specified in File Path setting of the Direct Mail campaign. Make sure you use forward slashes as in http://. Also, the URL should be accessible to at least IUSR_ECOMMSRV, which is the anonymous access account used by Direct Mailer. Therefore, check the file-level Access Control List (ACL) and IIS security settings on the ASP page.

Another way to find access problems is to analyze the logs generated by the site delivering the ASP page. For example, a GET command for the file followed by a 404 status indicates "file not found." Also, use the command-line executable dmlrun /list to list all jobs and their statuses.

Other Sources of E-mail Lists

Because targeting is an important part of closing the loop with customers, we need to find the best e-mail list to send appropriate messages. For example, what if the marketing manager wants to send a message to female users over 30 living in the East region of the U.S. who have bought a printer from the site? This is definitely a query for the data warehouse to answer! Sure, we could use a SQL query to create a dynamic user list, but imagine having to run this multirelational query on a live transaction database. That's specifically the reason why data warehouses are built and answers are sought from the aggregated values in them. Therefore, we can run a data warehouse analysis report from the Business Desk that would answer queries such as this one and generate a report. The list of users in such a report can be exported to the List Manager. You will learn more about data warehouse and analysis in Chapter 15, "Data Warehouse, Reports, and Prediction."

Content Selection Framework

In an earlier chapter, while discussing Order Processing Pipelines (OPP), we saw how discounts can be created and applied to orders. To demonstrate the concepts, we created two discounts. One was called "Site-wide 25% Off Discount," which gives 25 percent off on all products to all users. The other discount was called "Senior Citizen Discount," and it awards a 50-percent discount specially to users over 60 on the purchase of a printer. So what if a 60-year old user checks out a printer? Will the site-wide 25 percent off discount apply or the special 50-percent discount? The special discount is applied because it was created with a priority of 30, whereas the site-wide discount has a lower priority, 60. Therefore, when more than one discount is applicable, the one with the higher priority is applied. In the case of Priority for Discounts, the lower the number, the higher is the priority for a discount.

Now the question is, when in the OPP is this discount selected and applied? The discounts are applied to the basket by the OrderDiscount component in the OPP. OrderDiscount components use the Discounts cache to retrieve a simple list of discounts that are selected and already scored. So then how were these discounts scored? They were scored by the ScoreDiscounts component in `discounts.pcf`, which is a Content Selection Pipeline.

Commerce Server provides you with components that can be used to build a framework to select and deliver targeted content. This framework can be found already in the retail solution site Estore. By default, the Content Selection Framework (CSF) is utilized to select advertisements and discounts for the site. However, the framework can be extended to select any custom classification of content.

Components of the Content Selection Framework

At a very simplistic level, the CSF can be illustrated as shown in Figure 11.16.

The ASP page asks for content using the `ContentSelector` object. The `ContentSelector` object then runs a CS pipeline, passing on the content cache and the content context dictionaries. The content cache consists of a list of available content, among other things. The pipeline runs through the content list with the following stages:

- *Filter*. Uses prebuilt filters to eliminate content items
- *Initial Score*. Initializes the scores for content items, depending on need for delivery
- *Score*. Assigns number scores to content items and adjusts scores based on targeting criteria and exposure limits of items

Direct Mailer and Content Selection Framework Pipelines

CHAPTER 11

345

11

DIRECT MAILER
AND CONTENT
SELECTION

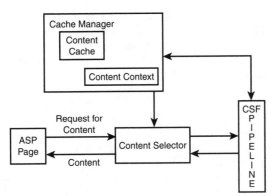

FIGURE 11.16

An overview of the Content Selection Framework.

- *Select*. Selects a content item as the winner based on the scores of content items
- *Record*. Records the selection of the item to the persist history and saves the selection for the user history
- *Format*. Formats the selected content based on a template and returns the generated end-use content

When the pipe returns after execution, the `ContentSelector` object has the generated content, which is written to the ASP page. There are several pipeline components at each of the stages that help complete the stages of the pipeline.

Now let's look at the various CSF elements in the retail solution site Estore.

Content Cache

Remember that we have many caches for the site maintained by the CacheManager, such as caches for the product list, shipping charges, and even the menu section of the `default.asp` page. Among these caches are two caches used by the CSF—one each for Advertising and Discounts. The `InitCacheManager` routine, defined in `global_cache_lib.asp`, initializes all the caches. Here is a snippet of the routine that prepares the Advertising cache:

```
....

' Create CacheManager object
    Set oCacheManager = Server.CreateObject("Commerce.CacheManager")

....
```

```
Set dictCampaignConfig = GetDictionary()
    dictCampaignConfig("ConnectionString") = dictConfig.s_
    ➡CampaignsConnectionString 'connection string to the database
    Set dictCampaignConfig("Evaluator") = oEvaluator 'reference to the
    ➡ExpressionEvaluator object

....


oCacheManager.RefreshInterval("advertising") = 5*60
    oCacheManager.RetryInterval("advertising") = 60
    oCacheManager.LoaderProgId("advertising") =
    ➡"Commerce.CSFLoadAdvertisements"
    oCacheManager.WriterProgId("advertising") = "Commerce.CSFWriteEvents"
    Set oCacheManager.LoaderConfig("advertising") = dictCampaignConfig
    Set oCacheManager.WriterConfig("advertising") = dictCampaignConfig

...
```

You know that caches are maintained by the `CacheManager` object, which is created using the Prog ID `Commerce.CacheManager`. The properties of the `CacheManager` object are accessed as follows:

`oCacheManager.<property_name>("<cache name>")`

Here, `<cache name>` is the name of the cache, such as Advertising. Each cache managed by the CacheManager can be implemented as a dictionary or an LRUCache. The data type of the cache is specified using the property `CacheObjectProgId` of the `CacheManager` object. By default, this property has a value of `Dictionary`. This property is not specifically set for the Advertising cache because it uses a dictionary. The `RefreshInterval` property of the CacheManager is set for the time between automatic refreshes of the cache. For the Advertising cache, automatic refresh is set as 5 minutes (5 * 60 seconds). `RetryInterval` specifies the time between retries if the refresh fails. The `LoaderProgId` property is to specify the Prog ID of a loader component used to populate the cache. In the case of the Advertising cache, the loader component is CSFLoadAdvertisements.

CSFLoadAdvertisements connects to the database and retrieves the ad items in a `ContentList` object. To do this, the component uses the service of the `ContentFactory` object. The `ContentList` object is the one that contains the content items (ads, in this case) and the methods to filter, score, and select content. The `ContentList` object returned by the execution of CSFLoadAdvertisements typically has a schema for ad information that includes ad_type, campaign_id, customer_id, start_date, end_date, size, width, and so on. Therefore, `ContentList` is the central repository of the list of contents returned by a loader component. Note that `ContentList` is returned upon execution of the loader component (in this case, CSFLoad-Advertisements), and we are just looking at the simple configuration of a loader component for

Direct Mailer and Content Selection Framework Pipelines

CHAPTER 11

347

11

DIRECT MAILER
AND CONTENT
SELECTION

the cache and not the execution. Regardless, the loader component needs the database connection and other configuration information when it executes. This is specified using the LoaderConfig property. In the case of the Advertising cache, the loader config is set to dictCampaignConfig, which contains references to the database connection string and an ExpressionEvaluator object.

Similar to the loader component, there could be a writer component for a cache that is used to write event information to the database so that adjustments can be made to the content delivery schedules. In the case of the content cache Advertising, the component CSFWriteEvents is used as the write component. This component needs the Order and Context dictionaries to work. It reads the key order._dictionary, which is a dictionary that stores the delta count of ad items chosen so far. This dictionary is written to the database by the CSFWriteEvents component. The CSFWriteEvents component is executed either by calling the RefreshCache() method of the CacheManager or when the cache automatically refreshes at the set RefreshInterval value. The Prog ID of the writer component is set using the WriterProgID property of CacheManager, and the configuration for the writer is set using the WriterConfig property.

Refresh again so that the code snippet we are discussing is just used to set the various types of configuration information for the Advertising cache. The loader and writer components are not yet created, nor are they executed.

Similar to the Advertising cache, the Discounts cache is also created in the global file routine:

. . . .

```
oCacheManager.RefreshInterval("discounts") = 0
    oCacheManager.RetryInterval("discounts") = 60
    oCacheManager.LoaderProgId("discounts") = "Commerce.CSFLoadDiscounts"
    oCacheManager.WriterProgId("discounts") = "Commerce.CSFWriteEvents"
    Set oCacheManager.LoaderConfig("discounts") = dictCampaignConfig
    Set oCacheManager.WriterConfig("discounts") = dictCampaignConfig
```

. . . .

There are two differences between the caches. In the Discounts cache, automatic refresh is disabled by setting RefreshInterval to 0. The second difference is that the loader component that loads the discounts from the database is CSFLoadDiscounts.

Content Context

After the content caches are set, the global file global_mail_lib.asp makes a call to the routine InitCSF(), which is defined in global_csf_lib.asp. InitCSF initializes two context dictionaries, corresponding to advertisements and discounts. The advertisement context is set as follows:

```
sRedirectUrl = GetBaseUrl() & "/redir.asp"
...

Set CSFAdvertisingContext = CreateObject("Commerce.Dictionary")
    Set CSFAdvertisingContext("CacheManager") = oCacheManager
    CSFAdvertisingContext("CacheName") = "Advertising"
    Set CSFAdvertisingContext("Evaluator") = oExpressionEvaluator
    CSFAdvertisingContext("RedirectUrl") = sRedirectUrl
    Set oPipe = Server.CreateObject("Commerce.OrderPipeline")
    oPipe.LoadPipe(oPipelineMap.Advertising)
    Set CSFAdvertisingContext("Pipeline") = oPipe
    Set Application("CSFAdvertisingContext") = CSFAdvertisingContext

...
```

As you can see, the context CSFAdvertisingContext has important information, such as the name of the advertising cache and the pipe to be executed for this content context. Other information includes references to the CacheManager, ExpressionEvaluator, and pipeline objects. Note that the pipeline object used to execute a pipe is OrderPipeline, as opposed to MtsPipeline, PooledPipeline, and so on, which are used by OPPs. Next, the pipe for advertisements, advertising.pcf, is loaded for this content context. Finally, a reference to this ad context is set at application scope so that ASP pages can get the context and request for ads using the ContentSelector object.

As is the case with the context for ads, we need a context for discounts, too. This is created in the same routine:

```
....

Set CSFDiscountContext = CreateObject("Commerce.Dictionary")
    Set CSFDiscountContext("CacheManager") = oCacheManager
    CSFDiscountContext("CacheName") = "Discounts"
    Set CSFDiscountContext("Evaluator") = oExpressionEvaluator
    CSFDiscountContext("RedirectUrl") = sRedirectUrl
    Set oPipe = Server.CreateObject("Commerce.OrderPipeline")
    oPipe.LoadPipe(oPipelineMap.Discounts)
    Set CSFDiscountContext("Pipeline") = oPipe
    Set Application("CSFDiscountContext") = CSFDiscountContext

...
```

You can see that this context is for discounts. This is indicated by the cache name and the discounts.pcf pipeline file.

Content Selector

From the framework illustrated earlier in Figure 11.16, we now have the content caches, context dictionaries, and the pipelines (`advertising.pcf` and `discounts.pcf`) for content (ads and discounts). So, any ASP page needing to display content such as ads needs to use the `ContentSelector` object and get the ads as shown in the following code (see the comments)

```
'First create the ContentSelector object
Set oCSO = Server.CreateObject("Commerce.ContentSelector")

'Set some properties on the CSO
oCSO.Border = 1
oCSO.TargetFrame = "_top"
oCSO.NumRequested = 1
oCSO.Trace = False


'Use the GetContent method to get content. The ad context dictionary is got
➥from the application scoped variable.
Set oAdContent = oCSO.GetContent(Application("CSFAdvertisingContext"))

' oAdContent is a SimpleList containing the selected content.
' Iterate through the list and write the content to the page.
For Each Ad in oAdContent
 Response.Write(Ad)
Next
```

Don't worry if this code doesn't work on its own; we will have a chance to see this code in the `banner.inc` include file while we try to actually deliver an advertisement in Chapter 12, "Running Ads and Auctions."

That's is all there is to using the CSF and getting content—whether it's an ad, a discount, or some other custom classification of content—except for that gigantic software assembly line called the *pipe*, which does the brunt of the filtering, scoring, selection, and formatting work required to deliver the content in the `SimpleList` object.

For starters, the `GetContent()` method of the `ContentSelector` object (CSO) executes the loaded pipeline stored in the `pipeline` key of the content context passed to it. For example, the loaded pipeline is `advertising.pcf` for the ad context CSFAdvertisingContext. The `GetContent()` method creates and passes two dictionaries to the pipe: Order and Context. The Order dictionary is sent empty, whereas the Context dictionary is set with a reference to the following CSO:

```
Context.ContextProfile = oCSO.
```

Ultimately, when the pipe completes execution, it returns the content in a `SimpleList` object in the key `order._formatted`, which is accessible to the calling CSO. Finally, the circular reference to the CSO is also removed.

Now that you know the CSP is invoked with the Order and Context dictionaries, let's dig deep into those pipes to understand how the content-selection process works.

Content Selection Pipelines

The Content Selection Pipelines (CSPs) for selecting content are provided by Commerce Server in the template `ContentSelection.pct`. The PCF files `advertising.pcf` and `discounts.pcf` are created using this template. Figures 11.17 and 11.18 show these pipes for quick reference.

FIGURE 11.17
The Content Selection Pipeline for advertising.

As you can see, the pipes used in Estore have similar components and stages, with just a few differences. Therefore, will look at all the available CSP components and stages, noting where they differ for the ad and discount pipes.

FIGURE 11.18
The Content Selection Pipeline for discounts.

Stages and Components

Keeping in mind that the Order and Context dictionaries are passed to the pipeline, let's look at what the pipe does. As with other pipes, you can find out the exact keys/values read and written by the CSP by using the Pipeline Editor's File, Save Values Read and Written menu option.

Load Context Stage

The first stage in the pipe initializes and sets values that will be needed by the rest of the pipeline components. The InitCSFPipeline component sets up a number of values in the Order and Context dictionaries to be used later. The component reads much of the values from the ContentSelector object (CSO) passed in the key `Context.ContextProfile`. The CSO has many properties, such as `NumRequested` (indicating number of content items requested) and `Trace` (enabling tracing of the scoring process). There are other properties of the CSO read by the InitCSFPipeline component to prepare the Order and Context dictionary values. The most important initialization done by this component is creating and initializing a new `ContentList` object in the following key:

```
order._content = oContentList
```

This content list is created with the knowledge of the cache name and the ContentListFactory object of the cache using the following method:

ContentListFactory.CreateNewContentList()

Once the content list is created, you will see that the methods of the ContentList object are used to do most of the operations, such as filtering and scoring.

The InitCSFPipeline component also creates a reference to the performance dictionary in the content cache, storing it in the order key order.performance.

If the cache does not have a performance dictionary, one is created. This dictionary will be used later by the RecordEvent component to write the winning items. Also, this dictionary is used by the AdvertisingNeedOfDelivery component later to adjust the score of items.

The values that are copied from the CSO object are as follows:

- order.NumRequested = ContextProfile.NumRequested
- order.FilterRequire = ContextProfile.FilterRequire
- order.FilterExclude = ContextProfile.FilterExclude
- Context.Trace = ContextProfile.Trace
- Context.Evaluator = ContextProfile.Evaluator
- Context.PageHistory = ContextProfile.PageHistory

The FilterRequire and FilterExclude dictionaries, if existing in Order, will make the later pipe component FilterContent filter the items using the Filter method of the ContentList object.

After these initializations, the next component in the stage, LoadHistory, retrieves a string that stores the history of content items selected so far for the user. The source of the history string could be one of the following:

- A property in the user profile object
- A session variable
- An HTTP cookie

The source for the history string can be set using the property page of the LoadHistory component (see Figure 11.19).

The retrieved history string is copied to the key order._history.

Direct Mailer and Content Selection Framework Pipelines

CHAPTER 11

353

11

DIRECT MAILER
AND CONTENT
SELECTION

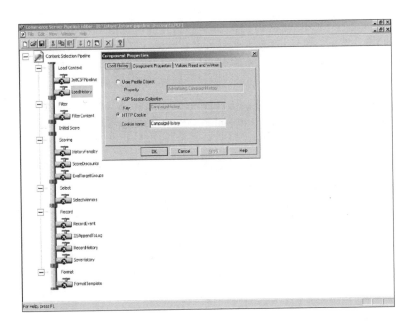

FIGURE 11.19
The source for a history string.

Filter Stage

The Filter stage is where the content list can be trimmed using the filter criteria specified in the Order keys `FilterRequire` and `FilterExclude`. A criterion in the `FilterRequire` dictionary means an item should match the criterion; otherwise, the score for the item will be set to 0 (not considered for selection). On the other hand, an item should not match any criterion in `FilterExclude`; otherwise, its score is set to 0.

Both of these dictionaries have keys corresponding to the values required to be used as filters. For example, the `FilterInclude` dictionary might have a key/value pair as

```
date_end = "03/01/2001"
```

to filter only items whose schedule is going by March 1, 2001. Note that a filter key such as `date_end` should exist as a column in the `ContentList` records. The FilterContent component at this stage uses a filter method such as

```
order_content.Filter("Score",2,FILTER_INCLUDE)
```

because `_content` is the reference to the `ContentList` object.

The `Filter` method is called for each key in both the filter dictionaries. If the item's column value does not match the value in the corresponding filter key, the Score column for that item in the list is set to 0, in case of a `FilterInclude` dictionary key. The reverse is true for `FilterExclude`.

Therefore, after this stage is run, the Score column of each item will indicate whether to include this item in the selection (nonzero value) or not (a value of 0).

Initial Score Stage

This stage is used in an advertising pipe to initialize the "score" of items based on Need of Delivery (NOD). Need of Delivery of an ad campaign is calculated as follows:

$$NOD = \frac{(Events\ scheduled\ /\ Total\ campaign\ time)}{(Events\ served\ /\ Time\ elapsed\ since\ campaign\ start\ time)}$$

For ads that are on schedule, obviously the NOD will be closer to 1.0, whereas for lagging ads, the NOD is greater than 1.0.

The AdvertisingNeedOfDelivery component at this stage calculates the NOD if the invalid_nod column of an item in the list is set to `True` or depending on the last time NOD is calculated, which is set in _cache._LastNODRecalc.

The component sets the following values on each item (the example assumes item 0 in the list):

- `_content(0).need_of_delivery = NOD`
- `_content(0).invalid_nod = false`
- `_content(0).score = NOD`

The score of the item is initialized with the NOD. Also, the component updates the time of NOD calculation in _cache._LastNODRecalc.

This component is not present in a discount pipe.

Scoring Stage

The Scoring stage is where components adjust the score of each content item in the content list. The first component is EvalTargetGroups, which adjusts the score of an item based on an extensive evaluation of target expressions. The target expressions to evaluate are in the `Context.TargetGroups` key. `TargetGroups` is a dictionary of `SimpleList` objects, the keys in the dictionary being target group identifiers. Therefore, there is a simple list for a each target group. The simple list contains two entries for each expression. The first entry is for the expression name, and the second is for the action needed. For example, in the `SimpleList` object for target group 1, the first entry would be the name of the first expression, followed by

Direct Mailer and Content Selection Framework Pipelines

CHAPTER 11

355

11

DIRECT MAILER
AND CONTENT
SELECTION

the action of the first expression. The third entry would be the name of the second expression, followed by the fourth entry, which is the action of the second expression. This continues for all expressions in that target group. The action entry for an expression determines the evaluation of that expression and can be one of the following:

- Target
- Require
- Exclude

If an expression evaluates to True for an item, a multiplier called *Match multiplier* is applied to the score of the item (score * Match multiplier). If the expression evaluates to False, the Mismatch multiplier is applied to the score. The value of these multipliers can be configured using the property page of the EvalTargetGroups component (see Figure 11.20). If more than one expression evaluates to True for an item, the expression with the highest multiplier is considered.

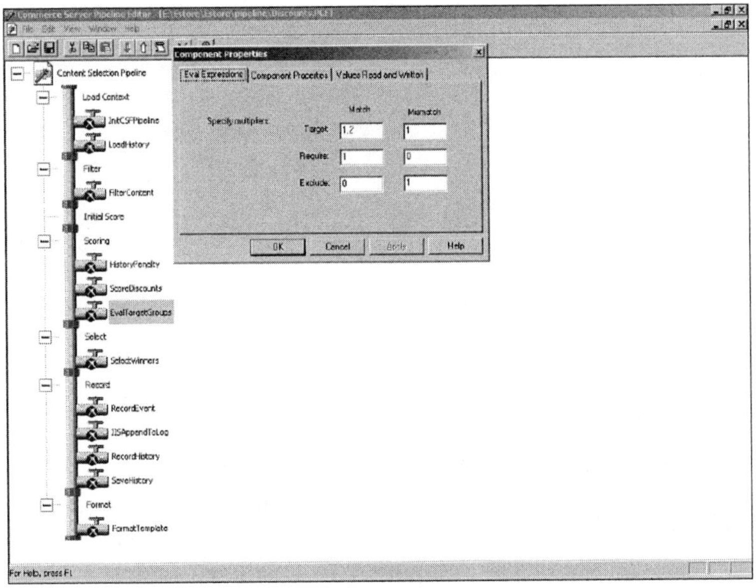

FIGURE 11.20
The multipliers for the EvalTargetGroups component.

The EvalTargetGroup components evaluate expressions with the aid of the ExpressionEval object. Even though both the components cache a lot of items to help with performance, it is better to move, if possible, the target expressions to filter criteria in the Filter stage.

Another component used in the Scoring stage is HistoryPenalty. This component applies a penalty multiplier to the score, depending on how recently items were shown to the user, the information about which is available in the history string _history. The penalty multiplier can be configured using the property sheet of the component (see Figure 11.21).

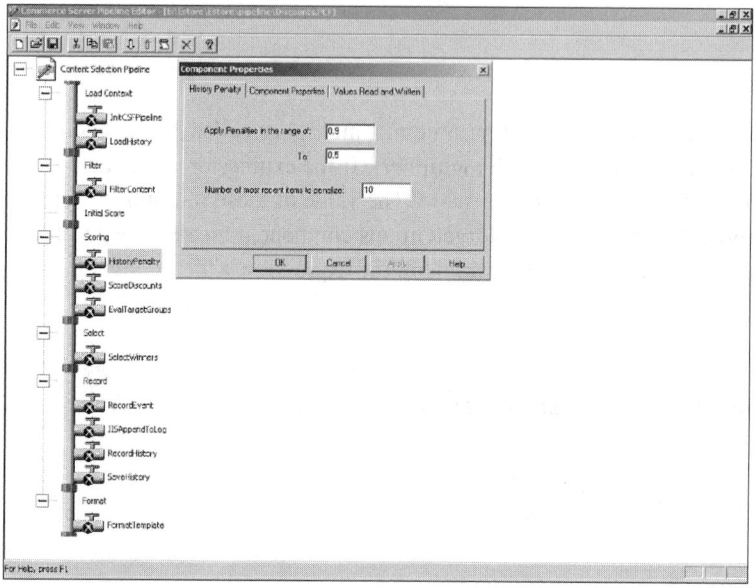

FIGURE 11.21

The penalty multiplier configuration for HistoryPenalty.

A penalty range of, say, 0.5 to 0.9, for the most recent 10 items will result in applying a multiplier of 0.5 to the most-recent item and 0.9 to the least-recent item of the 10 items. The other items in the list will be penalized by their order of recency in increments of 0.04 [(0.9 - 0.5) / 10]. The second-most-recent item will have a multiplier of 0.54, whereas the second-least-recent item will have multiplier of 0.86, and so on. A multiplier between 0 and 1 always reduces the score of an item. Therefore, ultimately an item with a higher score has more chance of being selected than an item with a comparatively lower score.

Also, the exposure_limit key of an item tells how many times the user can get the content item. If that limit is reached, the score for the item is set to 0.

There is one more component at this stage that's used in the case of a discount pipe. This component, called ScoreDiscount, is the alter-ego of AdvertisementNeedOfDelivery, used in an advertising pipe. The ScoreDiscount component is much more complicated because it evaluates conditions as well as the history if the condition was met previously. Here are the main values this component reads:

Direct Mailer and Content Selection Framework Pipelines

CHAPTER 11

357

11

DIRECT MAILER
AND CONTENT
SELECTION

- `context.contextprofile.products`

- `context.contextprofile.items`

Here, the `products` key is a list of products the user is currently browsing. The `items` key holds the Items collection of the `OrderForm` object. The expressions to be met for the discount item are found in the following keys:

- `_content.condition_expr`

- `_content.award_expr`

- `_content.date_start`

- `_content.date_end`

The component then has an internal algorithm that considers factors such as the discount's start and end dates, whether the discount is already applied to the basket, and so on. Depending on a combination of these outcomes, multipliers usually range from 0.5 to 1.0. Although it is possible to make multipliers greater than 1.0, it's really up to you because item scores are considered relative to each other.

Select Stage

In the Select stage, the SelectWinners component is used to select the content item to be delivered based on the final scores of the items. In the case of discounts, the discount items with the highest scores are returned up to the NumRequired quantity. For an advertising item, more options are available, such as avoiding two ads from the same industry, avoiding showing already selected ads for the same page, as per the `context.PageHistory` key, and so on. Finally, the content item indexes of winners are written to the newly created `SimpleList` object `order._winnerindexes`. The `order._event` key is set to the string `REQUEST` to enable components in next stage to record the delivery event of a content item.

Record Stage

This stage has components that record the winners to the IIS log file, write to the history string, and save the string. The IISAppendToLog component appends a query string to the IIS log file in the following format:

```
&CEVT={T=CAMP,CI=3,CNT=2,EVT=REQUEST,PG=2}
```

Here, `CEVT` is the string that identifies a Commerce Server event in the log file. `T=CAMP` is the class definition for an event class in the data warehouse. `EVT` is the event type, `CI` is the campaign ID, `CNT` is the event count, `PG` is the page group, and so on. This component uses `order._eventcount`, which has the count for each item in the `_winners` list. The event type can be one of four predetermined types: `REQUEST`, `CLICK`, `DOWNLOAD`, or `SOLD`. The RecordEvent component modifies the `order.performance` dictionary to include the winning items and their event counts. Frequently, when the content cache is refreshed, the WriteEvent write component updates the running total in the database with the new count for the content items found in the _performance delta dictionary.

The RecordHistory component updates the history string in order._history with the winning item IDs. You can set the maximum number of items to be saved in the history string of a user, using the property page of the RecordHistory component. Next, the SaveHistory component saves this history string to one of three locations, which are identical to the choices for the LoadHistory component: as a property of the user profile, in a session variable, or in the HTTP cookie CampaignHistory.

Format Stage

This is the final stage, where the winners are converted to a displayable format for use in the ASP page. The FormatTemplate component looks at the values column of an item. The values dictionary is created using the creative_property and creative_property_values tables to accommodate content items that don't conform to the rigid schema of a ContentList object. The template key of an item provides maps to the Format Template dictionary, which is used to merge content with the template. The template dictionary contains the text string that contains placeholder substitution variables such as {%item_name%}. The source of the data for substituting variables is given in the format <variable name>_source, such as item_name_1. The source value of 1 means the column with the same variable name will be searched for first in the values dictionary and then the columns of the content list. Another key in the Format Template dictionary, <variable name>_default, specifies a default value for the variable if it can't be found.

Therefore, after values from different sources are merged with the template string, the resulting string is written to the SimpleList object stored in the order._formatted key. Note that the context.RedirectURL key is used by <variable name>_encoding to format a proper URL value that should be used when the user clicks the content (say, an ad). This URL happens to be the redir.asp file for our ad context.

Now the ASP page that called the CSO's GetContent() gets the content in a simple list, which it must iterate to write out the strings for each item selected.

Tips

While running the CSP, we can switch on the Trace flag of many of the components to debug the pipe. This is done by switching on the Trace flag of the CSO before the call to the GetContent() method. Components would then check for this flag in the context dictionary and produce trace strings for their operations. Also, the SetLogFile method of the OrderPipeline can be used so that the entire pipeline processing is logged.

Direct Mailer and Content Selection Framework Pipelines

CHAPTER 11

359

11

DIRECT MAILER
AND CONTENT
SELECTION

Event Processing Pipeline

The CSP selects the content and records the selection as the event REQUEST, using the RecordEvent component. When the user actually clicks the content of, say, an ad banner, the CLICK event of the ad item should be recorded. This could be mandated by customer agreements for required delivery of an ad. This is accomplished by an Event Processing Pipeline (EPP), which is essentially a subset of the CSP as we saw earlier. The Estore has a pipe for the EPP called RecordEvents.pcf (see Figure 11.22).

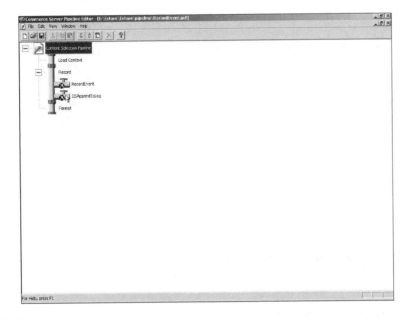

FIGURE 11.22
An Event Processing Pipeline for recording events.

Once a user clicks a clickURL content, such as an ad banner, the control is redirected to the redir.asp file. The redir.asp file executes the EPP RecordEvents.pcf pipe. The pipe is configured in the same InitCSF() routine in the global_csf_lib.asp file where the other CSF pipes are also loaded:

....

```
' Create an event processing pipeline which we call directly from redir.asp
    Set oPipe = Server.CreateObject("Commerce.OrderPipeline")
    oPipe.LoadPipe(oPipelineMap.RecordEvent)
    Set Application("CampaignsCSFEventPipe") = oPipe
```

....

The pipe reference is retrieved in `redir.asp` as follows:

```
Set oPipe = Application("CampaignsCSFEventPipe")
```

The `redir.asp` file can get many query strings, such as the cache name of the content item, the item ID (`CI=`), the event type (`EVT=CLICK`), and the event count (`CNT`). You already know that the EPP (similar to the CSP) needs all those dictionaries and keys, such as Order, Context, _event, _winners, and so on. The Order and Context dictionaries are created. Then, the _winners key of the Order dictionary is set as the item ID received from the query string:

```
....

dictOrder("_winners") = ciid

....
```

Similarly, the event and event counts to be recorded are created as follows:

```
....

dictOrder("_event") = sEvt
....

Set dictorder("_eventcount") = listCount

....

Then the ContentList is created using

....

Set oFactory = dictCache("Factory")
Set oContentList = oFactory.CreateNewContentList
Set dictOrder("_content") = oContentList

....
```

Finally, the EPP is executed to record the event:

```
oPipe.orderExecute 1, dictOrder, dictContext, Errlvl
```

This is the essence of `redir.asp` and how it uses the EPP.

Summary

In this chapter, we started with the theme of personalization and targeting. The Direct Mailer provides you with an effective way to send nonpersonalized as well as personalized e-mails to targeted user lists. The List Manager is used to create mailing lists using a source such as a flat file, a SQL database, or an analysis report. The Campaign Manager module is used to create Direct Mail campaigns to test as well as schedule these mailings. The DMLService, the core of the Direct Mailer system, uses the Direct Mailer pipeline to process the recipients, format messages, and send e-mails using the Windows CDO. You also saw, in brief, how the Direct Mailer can be used in a standalone mode.

Then we moved on to the Content Selection Framework provided by Commerce Server. You learned how a combination of pipelines elements, such as a content cache, a content context, the ContentSelector object, and a CSP pipeline, form the CSF. The Advertising and Discounts pipeline are CSPs that have various pipeline components to filter, score, select, record, and format content items such as ads, discounts, or other custom classifications of content. The EPP pipeline is a subset of the CSP, used only to record events arising out of the delivered content. In the next chapter, you will learn more about scheduling and running advertisements using the CSF. You will see how the Content Selection Framework filters, scores, selects, records, and formats advertisements, as we run an ad campaign for one of the leading travel companies in the universe!

Running Ads and Auctions

IN THIS CHAPTER

- The Advertising Infrastructure 364
- Enabling Auctions 385

Advertising is one of the most important tools in the marketing arsenal of an enterprise. Almost every business, both private and public, has its own advertising strategy, with the amount of money spent varying with the size and goals of the company. With the wide reach that the Web has made possible today, advertisers have never had a better time. It's almost like a worldwide telecast of a single TV show in which your ad appears! With the Web catching up with traditional ad media, a recent study by the Internet Advertising Bureau (IAB) confirms the effectiveness and impact of online advertising. The report (`http://www.mbinteractive.com/site/iab/exec.html`) states that a single exposure to an ad banner can generate increases in the following areas:

- Ad awareness
- Brand awareness
- Product attribute communication
- Purchase intent

The report also claims that the Web can generate these increases at levels greater than or comparable to other media, such as television, print, and radio. Further, advertisers feel that the engaging nature of the Web results in greater retention of ads. The proof is in the continuing increase in the money spent on online advertising every year. The Internet advertising revenues for the third quarter of 2000 reached $2 billion according to a release by the New Media Group of PricewaterhouseCoopers.

Even with a slack in the "New Economy," Web sites continue to earn a lot of revenue by selling advertisements. Therefore, chances are the more popular your commerce site becomes, the more revenue you can earn from selling cyberspace on your site. Commerce Server provides you with the required advertising infrastructure using the Content Selection Framework (CSF), which we discussed in the last chapter. The CSF, as you know, uses the Content Selection Pipeline components to filter, score, select, record, and format ads for delivering to a highly targeted audience. There is no more need to blindly mass-advertise when CSF can help in delivering the right content to the appropriate user in the correct context. In this chapter, you will see how to create and schedule ads as well as record their effectiveness.

In the final sections of this chapter, we will talk about how to enable the Auction capabilities of your commerce site. Even though auction sites such as eBay and AutoExchange have specialized in that domain, more and more successful Web companies, such as Yahoo!, have expanded their selling capabilities by providing auctions on their sites.

The Advertising Infrastructure

Commerce Server provides you with the necessary infrastructure to maintain customer information, schedule campaigns and ads for them, target ads based on the objectives required by the customers, and record ad delivery. Here are a few fundamental applications of this infrastructure that you can use on a site:

- Enable customers to deliver ads based on objectives set either at the ad level or at the entire campaign level, assigning weights to ads correspondingly
- Schedule ads to be run specifying different combinations of date and time filters
- Target ads based on the user profile of the site user
- Target ads based on the context of a site page
- Rotate ads by setting exposure limits on individual ads
- Deliver ads to be displayed in any one of several standard formats, such as banner, text, html, buy now, vignette, and so on
- Avoid competitors' ads appearing on the same page
- Show multiple but unique ads on the same page
- Record the delivery of an ad either as a Request or a Click, depending on the ad objective

Figure 12.1 is an attempt to illustrate the many elements that are part of the ad infrastructure.

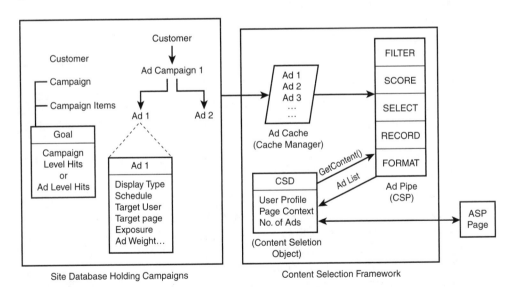

FIGURE 12.1

Commerce Server elements for advertising.

As you can see, the database that holds campaigns has the required information about customers, campaigns, campaign items, schedules, targeting, and so on. The different types of information pertaining to an ad campaign are created using the Business Desk. The campaigns database may contain information for multiple ads. The CacheManager is used to maintain a cache of all these ads. You know from the last chapter that the Loader component loads all these ads, whereas the Writer component writes events such as `Request` and `Click` events back to the database for maintaining delivery records.

But not all the ads in the cache are to be displayed on a page, right? The Content Selection Pipeline (CSP) for advertising filters and scores these ads before selecting ads for delivery. For each of these stages, it uses information from the ad itself and the requesting `ContentSelector` object (CSO). Information from an ad, such as target audience and target context, are matched with the CSO's information on user profile and page context to filter ads. After the list of available ads is filtered, the filtered ads are given scores based on information such as delivery goals, delivery history for an ad, and exposure limits. The ads with the highest scores are selected—the quantity based on the number of ads requested by the CSO. The selected ads are formatted for delivery before being returned to the CSO. The delivery of an ad is recorded as a `Request` event for the ad. The CSO gets the ad and writes it to a site ASP page.

Concepts to Know

Before looking at an ad campaign in action, let's briefly walk through some of the important concepts illustrated in Figure 12.1:

- *Customer*. This is the basic element in a Commerce Server ad. A customer is first created in the database before ads are scheduled for the customer. A customer is an entity such as an ad agency or a company wishing to put an ad on your site.

- *Campaign*. A campaign is a holder for all campaign items. The campaign could be for any marketing objective, such as to introduce a product, improve customer loyalty, or increase brand awareness.

- *Campaign item*. An advertisement is a campaign item much like discounts and direct mails.

- *Campaign goals*. Customers pay for their campaigns based on the hits they want their ads to receive on your site. Therefore, the goal of the campaign is quantified as the desired number of hits. This "goaling" can be done either at the campaign level or at the individual ad item level. For example, if AdCampaign1 has a goal of 5,000 hits, then the ads Ad1 and Ad2 will need to be configured with their individual weights—say, 40 and 60. Therefore 40 percent of the 5,000 hits for the campaign will be delivered by Ad1 and 60 percent by Ad2. If the goal is at the ad level, each ad has a specified quantity to be delivered. You can change from one goaling type to another.

- *Ad properties*. When an ad is being created, several pieces of information for the ad are entered. The display type provides the form of the ad at the displayed Web page, such as a clickable image, banner, plain text, HTML, and so on, along with the size and redirect URL, if any. The ad schedule contains the date and time ranges in which the ad should be considered. The weight of an ad is entered to assign a weight relative to other ads in the campaign. Exposure limit is a hard number that indicates how many times in a session a user can get the ad. Different types of targeting information, such as target groups and page groups, are used to target the ad for specific user profiles and page contexts, respectively. All these properties are used by the CSP to determine the suitability of the delivery of the ad.

- *House ads versus paid ads.* Another property of an ad indicates whether it's a house ad or a paid ad. House ads are used to fill in when paid ads are ahead of their schedules.

- *Ad cache.* The CacheManager is used to maintain a cache called "advertising" that includes all ads in the database. This cache is periodically refreshed for loading ads as well as writing the ad performance to the database.

- *Content Selection Pipeline (CSP).* The CSP advertising.pcf file is used to process ad requests from the CSO. The CSP processes the ads in the cache with information obtained from the ad properties as well as the CSO. The ads are filtered, scored, selected, recorded, and formatted for delivery to the CSO. In scoring ads, the CSP uses the Need of Delivery (NOD) formula. We discussed this in Chapter 11, "Direct Mailer and Content Selection Framework Pipelines," but as reminder, here it is again:

$$NOD = \frac{(\text{Events scheduled / Total campaign time})}{(\text{Events served / Time elapsed since campaign start time})}$$

For ads that are on schedule, obviously the NOD will be closer to 1.0, whereas for lagging ads, the NOD is greater than 1.0. The NOD is applied as a multiplier to the score of an ad, effectively increasing or decreasing the probability of the ad getting selected for delivery.

- ContentSelector *object.* The ContentSelector object is the client-side interface on the ASP page that requests an ad using the GetContent method by passing on the ad context. The CSO supplies information to the CSP, such as user profile, page context, number of ads requested, trace flag, and so on.

The Case of StarTrek Travels

The advertising infrastructure has numerous elements, so what better way to understand it than to actually use the elements to create and deliver ads? We will use the case of StarTrek Travels, which is a leading travel agency (in my imagination!) headquartered on Vulcan. StarTrek Travels arranges for travel anywhere in the universe. It has found that your site (say, Estore) has become very popular with the folks on Earth and, with the growing reach of the Web, has decided to place ads on your site to promote its brand awareness. StarTrek has also decided to participate in the World Travel Expo, to be conducted here. Therefore, it would like to place an ad to promote its presence at that convention. Further, to infuse confidence in us earthlings, StarTrek wants to show it can easily take a customer to the top of the Himalayas in a moment, so it wants to run an ad for this service.

Considering that the expeditions are expensive, the marketing manager of StarTrek Travels thinks that its ads should be displayed when customers are in a paying mood—that is, when they are in pages such as credit card details, specifying shipping address and order confirmation. Also, he would initially like to target customers enjoying a retired life—those over age 60.

Along with some more information, the basic design sheet looks like this:

Customer	StarTrek Travels
Campaign	Brand Awareness
Campaign goaling	Campaign Level
Goals	5,000 deliveries
Ad 1	World Travel Expo
Ad 1 properties	
Weight	40
Exposure limit	10
Schedule	All days between 2/1/2001 and 2/20/2001. Time between 10 A.M. and 10 P.M.
Target pages	Purchase pages
Target users	Users over 60
Display	
Size	468×60
Type	Non-clickable image
Image source	Some URL
Ad 2	Himalayas
Ad 2 properties	
Weight	60
Exposure Limit	None

Schedule	All days between 2/1/2001 and 2/20/2001. Time between 10 A.M. and 10 P.M.
Target Pages	Purchase pages
Target Users	Users over 60
Display	
Size	468×60
Type	Clickable image
Image Source	Some URL
Click URL	Some URL

Using this information, we will create the campaign for StarTrek Travels on the Estore site. During the process, we will discuss many of the other details that developers and managers need to know to successfully create and manage ads.

Define Ad Metadata

The Reference Tables module in Business Desk is used to set some site-level metadata that can be used by the ad infrastructure to validate ad display sizes, check for industry affiliation of ads, and maintain page groups. The Reference Tables module provides a list-cum-edit page where content sizes, industry codes, and page sizes can be maintained (see Figure 12.2).

Content Sizes

Check under the section Content Sizes to verify whether there is a tag defined for a size of 468 (width) by 60 (height). The default installation of the site comes with standard sizes approved by the IAB. These sizes will be available to a manager while creating an ad. You can see that the size the customer wants is already available as the tag Full Banner. The content sizes are stored in the database table creative_size.

Industry Codes

Under the section Industry Codes, some standard classifications of industries are listed. While creating a customer as well as an ad, you could choose an industry affiliation for the ad. The industry connection on an ad helps the CSF to prevent showing two ads belonging to competitors on the same page. For example, it would not be appropriate to show an ad from StarTrek Travels along with an ad for XYZ Travels. You can configure the depth of competitiveness as you wish, such as showing all travel-related ads on a page but distinguishing between companies specializing in travel by air or sea. The industry codes are maintained in the database table industry_code.

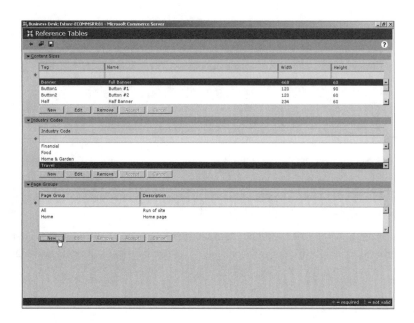

FIGURE 12.2

Reference Tables module.

Page Groups

The last section in the Reference Tables module is for maintaining logical groupings of your site pages. One or more pages can be combined to form a group. A page group is used to specify targeting of an ad to only pages in that group. Remember that the CSO is instantiated from an ASP page to request for an ad. The CSO finds the group the page belongs to and passes that information to the CSP. The CSP compares that against the Page Group property of the ad to include or eliminate the ad in the probable list of deliverable ads.

Because StarTrek Travels wants to target its ads on purchase pages, we need to create a new group. Click the New button (refer to Figure 12.2) to enter the Page Group as **Purchase**. Enter the description as **Purchase pages** and then click the Accept button. Finally, save the data by clicking the appropriate task bar icon in the module. The page groups are stored in the database table page_group.

Creating Target Groups

Because the ads need to be targeted at users over 60, we need to create a target group including such users. Click the Target Group module and then choose New Target Group from the menu icon. In the edit page for a new group, enter the required information (see Figure 12.3).

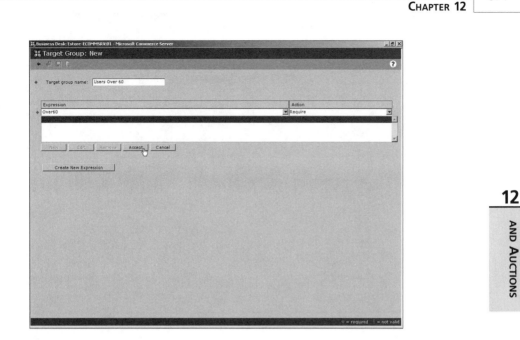

FIGURE 12.3

Creating a target group.

For the target group name, enter **Users Over 60**. To add an expression to the group, click the New button. The field for Expression should provide a drop-down list of available expressions. We created an expression for users over 60 in Chapter 4, "From the Business Desk." Choose that expression. In the Action box, choose Require from the drop-down box. This is one of four options we discussed in the CSP where we assign multiplier numbers to the outcome of each action. Here is the pipe produced for reference (see Figure 12.4).

The EvalTargetGroups components, while scoring an ad from a list of ads, will multiply the score of the ad with the multiplier specified, as shown in Figure 12.4. For example, the expression "Users Over 60" will evaluate to True if the user is above 60 years of age and evaluate to False if the user is not. Because the action for the expression in the target group is Require, 1 would be multiplied with the score of the ad in case of True, whereas 0 would be multiplied in case of False, thus removing the ad from consideration.

The Exclude action acts in the opposite way; it applies a 0 if the expression evaluates to True and multiplies by 1 if the expression evaluates to False. The action of Target is a middle way of targeting, improving the score when the expression matches but not removing the ad when the expression evaluates to False.

FIGURE 12.4

Target expression multipliers.

You could create a new expression using the New Catalog Expression button or the Campaign Expressions module. More than one expression (with various actions) can be combined in a group. For our case, having created the group Users Over 60, we will save the group by clicking the Accept button for expressions.

Creating a Customer

Now that we are sure about the reference tables, the next step is to create a customer account for StarTrek Travels. This can be done by using the menu icon New Customer in the Campaign Manager module. In the New Customer edit page, enter the details of the customer. Only Name is a required field. The Type field can be switched between Advertiser, Agency, and Self. You would typically use Self if you were floating ads for your own site (house ads). Next, the Industry code could be set as Travel for this company. After entering all the information, save the customer by clicking the task icon (see Figure 12.5).

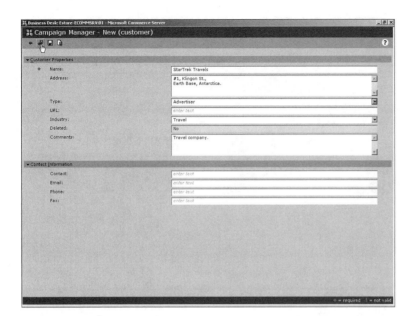

FIGURE 12.5

New customer.

Creating the Ad Campaign

The next step is to create a campaign for the customer. From the Campaign Manager list page, choose StarTrek Travels. Then choose New Campaign from the task menu icon. In the New Campaign edit page, enter the required data, as shown in Figure 12.6. Name the campaign "Brand Awareness." According to the requirements, the campaign should run between a start date of 02/01/2001 and an end date of 02/20/2001. Because the goal is at the campaign level, choose Campaign in the Set Goals By box in the Advertising/Campaign Goaling section. The Quantity Ordered setting should be 5000, as per the requirement. Also, let's assume that the requirement for a hit is a successful delivery of an ad to a page and not necessarily the clicking of an ad. Therefore, choose Requests as the value for the Scheduled By field. Choose the Save icon from the task bar to save the campaign.

As an aside, the IAB report we discussed at the beginning of the chapter has found that banner exposure (requests) contributes 96 percent toward brand enhancement versus the 4 percent provided by click-through ads.

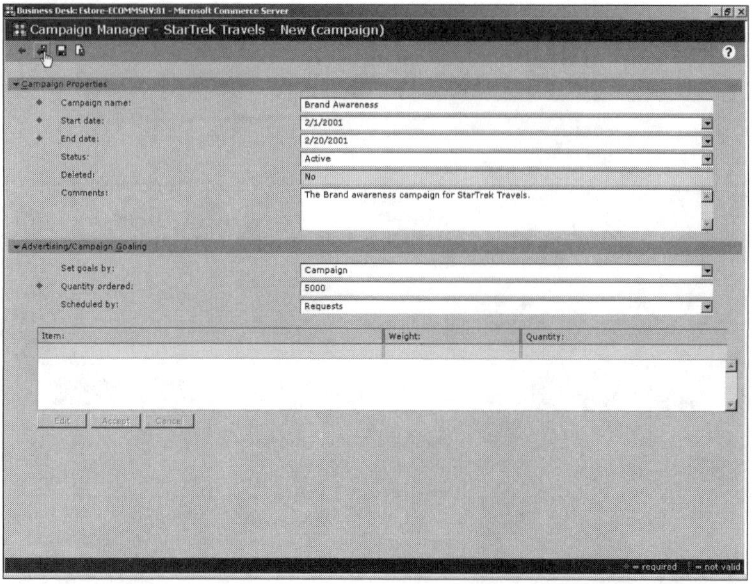

FIGURE 12.6

Creating and saving a new campaign.

Creating an Ad

Let's now see what information goes into creating an ad item. Choose the Brand Awareness campaign we just created in the list page and click the menu icon for New Ad. In the edit page, shown in Figure 12.7, enter the required information for all four sections. Beginning with the Ad Properties section, enter the ad name as World Travel Expo. Change the Status setting to Active if the ad should be available on the site. In the Type field, choose Paid Ad. Assign a weight of 40 to this ad, as required. Note that you could just as well assign 2 here and 3 to the next ad because the weights are relative to the total weight. That is to say, 40:60 is the same as 2:3 for a combination of two ads. Set the Exposure Limit field to 10 and the Industry field to Travel.

Scheduling the Ad

In the Ad Schedule section, set the Start Date and End Date defaults to that of the campaign dates. Choose all the days for the ad. Then set Start Time and End Time to 10 A.M. (10:00) and 10 P.M. (22:00), respectively, as per the requirement.

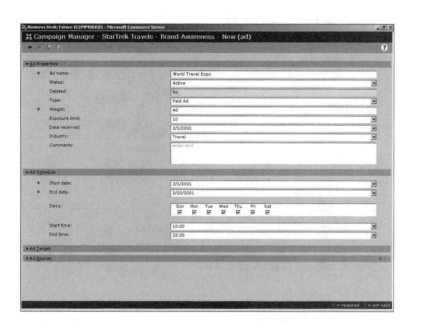

FIGURE 12.7

Ad properties and schedule.

Targeting the Ad

In the Ad Target section, unselect the Show on All Page Groups check box because the ad is to be targeted toward a specific group only. From the Available box, choose Purchase Pages and then click the Add button to add the group to the Assigned box. Now the ad is targeted on the purchase pages of the site.

To target the ad based on the user profile, choose the Users Over 60 target group from the Available Target groups box. Click the Add button (see Figure 12.8). By default, the solution site contains the page group Home Page only and no target groups. Therefore, in the figure you can see that I have created more page and target groups, which we needn't bother about for our example.

Configuring Ad Display

In the Ad Display section, choose Full Banner as the Size setting. Here you can see that all content sizes from the references table are listed. In the Type box, choose ad type Non-Clickable Image. This will enable display of a standard banner that is not a click-through banner. Also, in the Type box, you can see many other types supported, such as Buy Now, HTML, Text, and even multimedia formats such as Windows Media Services. As you choose each of these supported types, a small box just below it is modified to capture details about the source file of the type chosen. For example, because we chose Non-Clickable Image, the section asks for an image URL and alternate text.

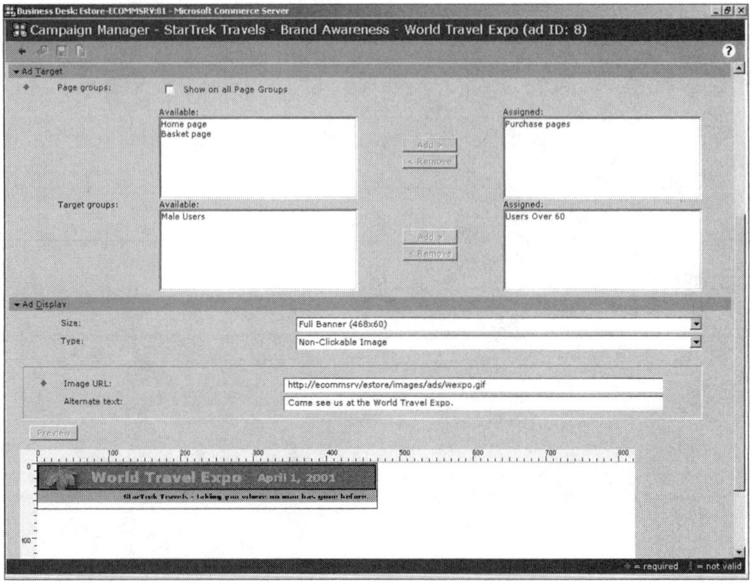

FIGURE 12.8

Targeting and display details of an ad.

Now enter the URL of the ad banner for this ad in the Image URL box. You may also type text in the Alternate Text box. You can click the Preview button to see how the image will appear on the Web site (refer to Figure 12.8). The figure displays one of the images I put together for StarTrek Travels. Click one of the save icons on the task bar to save the ad.

Go ahead and create the second ad for the Himalayas, much the same way we did for World Travel Expo. Note the differences from the design sheet for the Himalayas ad:

Exposure limit:	None
Weight:	60
Image type:	Image (resulting in a clickable image)
Click URL:	`http://startrektravels.com.earth`

Figure 12.9 shows a snapshot of the ad details on my server.

After saving both the ads for the campaign, you should see in the list page for the Campaign Manager that the campaign level goal has indeed been split for both the ads based on the Weight setting (see Figure 12.10).

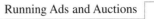

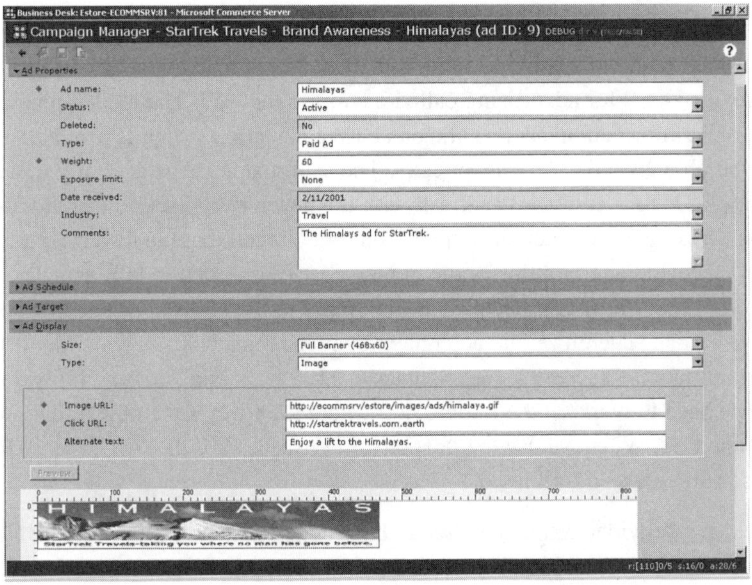

FIGURE 12.9

Details of the Himalayas ad.

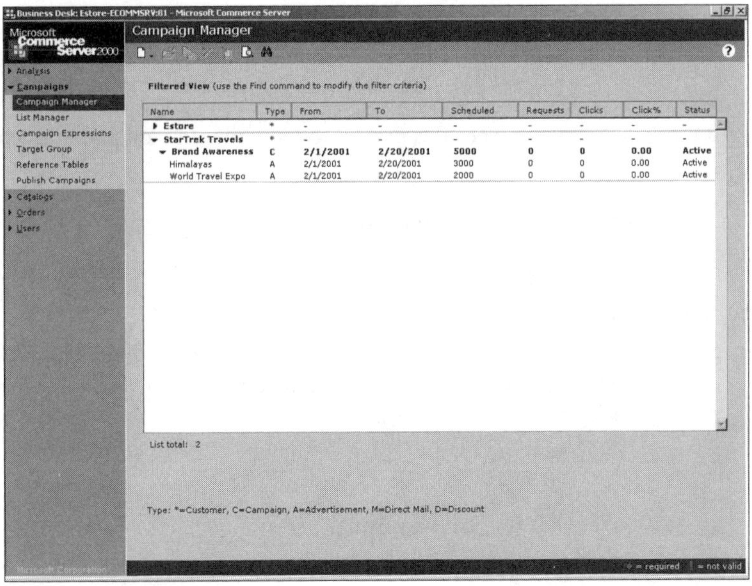

FIGURE 12.10

Campaign goal is split among ad items.

Using the `ContentSelector` Object

We just completed building ads in the campaign database. Already we have a Site Packager–provided CSP for advertising called `advertising.pcf`. The loaded pipe as well as ad-related context information, such as the database connection string, is available in the application-level variable `CSFAdvertisingContext`. The advertising cache is configured to refresh every 5 minutes. Therefore, it would refresh with the new ads by itself; we could also manually refresh the advertising cache later. As a quick reminder, recall that the advertising cache is set up in the `InitCacheManager` routine in the global file `global_cache_lib.asp`. This advertising cache is set on the `CSFAdvertisingContext` dictionary in the `InitCSF` routine in `global_csf_lib.asp`. Therefore, the ad context contains the ad cache, which in turn has connection information to access the ads database. The "back end" of the ad infrastructure is ready. Now we have to work on the middle tier, where the CSO is the object that provides the execution of the CSP. When we use the `GetContent()` method of the CSO, the CSP is run and any chosen ads are returned formatted.

The Site Packager–provided retail site already has code to instantiate and use the CSO. It is found in `banner.inc` file, which is included in `layout1.asp`. We already know that `layout1.asp` is the main page that acts as a framework for content in a site page—for the main, navigation, menu, and footer areas, for example. Therefore, `banner.inc` is included in `layout1.asp` and is responsible for displaying ad banners:

```
...

<CENTER><!— #INCLUDE FILE="banner.inc" —></CENTER>
...
```

Both the `layout1.asp` and `banner.inc` files can be found under the template directory of the site.

Now `banner.inc` needs to be modified so that we can pass the page group, user profile, and quantity of ads requested using the CSO.

Modifying the Banner File

Open `banner.inc` for editing. Declare a variable called `strPageSet`, initialize it, and assign it the value `"Purchase"`, depending on whether the current page (that includes `banner.inc`) belongs to the PurchasePageSet:

```
.....

Dim oCSO, Ads, Ad, oUserProfile,strPageSet

strPageSet=""
```

```
If IsEntityInSet(sThisPage, MSCSPageSets.PurchasePageSet) Then
    strPageSet="Purchase"
End If
```

....

This string value is the name of the page group we targeted while creating the ads. The various page sets of the site are generated in the routine `InitPageSets` in the global initialization file `global_siteconfig_lib.asp`. This is a dictionary that points a page set to a list of pages defined in `MSCSSitePages`, as shown here:

....

```
Set dictSets = Server.CreateObject("Commerce.Dictionary")

    dictSets.PurchasePageSet = CreateSet( _
                        Array( _
            MSCSSitePages.Dispatch, _
            MSCSSitePages.CreditCard, _
            MSCSSitePages.PurchaseOrder, _
            MSCSSitePages.ShippingMethods, _
            MSCSSitePages.SetShippingMethod, _
            MSCSSitePages.AddressForm, _
            MSCSSitePages.AddressBook, _
            MSCSSitePages.AddAddressToAddressBook, _
            MSCSSitePages.SetAddress, _
            MSCSSitePages.OrderSummary, _
            MSCSSitePages.Confirm _
                        ) _
                        )
```

....

Returning to `banner.inc`, we see that the helper routine `IsEntityInSet` is used to find whether the current page is found in the `PurchasePageSet`. Note that because `layout1.asp` is the template for all site pages, `banner.inc` is executed in all site pages, including the login page. Hence, you need to check the current page against all possible page sets and assign a value to the `strPageSet` variable. Therefore, if a page such as `login.asp` is not part of any page sets, `strPageSet` should have no value and hence we wouldn't do anything related to ads on that page:

....

```
if(strPageSet<>"") then
Set oCSO = Server.CreateObject("Commerce.ContentSelector")
```
....

```
oCSO.NumRequested = 1
oCSO.PageGroup = strPageSet
....
```

In the preceding snippet, the `NumRequested` property of the CSO is set to 1 because we are requesting only one ad for a page. Then the `PageGroup` property is set to the page group this page belongs to. Next, we set the `UserProfile` property of the CSO to the current user's profile:

```
Set oCSO.UserProfile = oUserProfile
```

This is needed because we are targeting ads based on user profiles, too, such as age over 60. After the properties of the CSO are set, the `GetContent()` method is called with the advertising context dictionary passed as the reference:

```
Set Ads = oCSO.GetContent( Application("CSFAdvertisingContext")
```

The `GetContent()` method invokes the loaded pipe `advertising.pcf` (CSP), specified in the context dictionary `CSFAdvertisingContext`. The ad pipe gets a list of ads from the advertising cache. Then, for each ad in the list, it filters and assigns a score matching the information passed with the CSO and the properties of the ad. We have already discussed in detail the various stages and components of the CSP in the last chapter.

Finally, the Format stage of the pipe creates a `SimpleList` object and returns the list with the HTML source code for the number of ads requested. This HTML code contains the chosen ads. In the ASP page, this list is iterated to write all the ads to the page. In our example, because we requested only one ad, a maximum of one ad will be written to the ASP page:

```
.....

For Each Ad In Ads
        Response.Write(Ad)
    Next

....
```

Listing 12.1 provides a complete listing of `banner.inc`.

Listing 12.1   The Code for `banner.inc`

```
<%

Dim oCSO, Ads, Ad, oUserProfile,strPageSet

strPageSet=""
If IsEntityInSet(sThisPage, MSCSPageSets.PurchasePageSet) Then
    strPageSet="Purchase"
```

Listing 12.1 continued

```
End If
if(strPageSet<>"") then

    Set oCSO = Server.CreateObject("Commerce.ContentSelector")
    oCSO.Border = 1
    oCSO.TargetFrame = "_top"
    oCSO.NumRequested = 1
    oCSO.PageGroup = strPageSet

    Set oUserProfile = GetCurrentUserProfile()
    If Not oUserProfile Is Nothing Then
        Set oCSO.UserProfile = oUserProfile
    End If
    Set Ads = oCSO.GetContent( Application("CSFAdvertisingContext") )

    For Each Ad In Ads
        Response.Write(Ad)
    Next

end if

%>
```

After modifying and saving banner.inc, you may refresh the advertising cache with the new ads using the Publish Campaigns module. Now the site is ready to display the ads to the user.

Troubleshooting Ad Campaigns

Having set up everything to deliver targeted ads, I enter Estore again and browse to my basket. The two ads we created and scheduled in this chapter won't show until I click the Check-out button in the basket. This is because the PurchasePageSet such as address book, credit card form, and order summary come after the catalog, product selection and basket pages. When I click the Check-out button, I can't find the ads on the addrbook.asp page.

In order to debug the delivery of ads, Commerce Server provides you with two files: TraceScores.asp and DumpContentList.asp. Both these files can be found in the following folder:

<MSCS Installation folder>SDK/Samples/Marketing/Debug

TraceScores.asp helps in debugging the filtering, scoring, and selection process of the CSP. DumpContentList.asp dumps the content list available in the memory cache for advertising, with details about each ad and its properties.

Let's use `TraceScores.asp` to debug what's happening with all the ads that seem to be stuck in the ad pipe. Copy the file to the template directory of the site. Include the file in `layout1.asp` as the first line; we will use a routine defined in the file:

```
<!—#include file="tracescores.asp"—>
```

In `banner.inc`, insert the following code, shown in bold, to enable tracing:

```
....

Set oCSO = Server.CreateObject("Commerce.ContentSelector")
oCSO.Trace = true
oCSO.Border = 1

....
```

Then make a call to the `TraceScores` routine defined in `TraceScores.asp`:

```
....

For Each Ad In Ads
        Response.Write(Ad)
    Next
    Response.Write("<P>")
    Call TraceScores(oCSO)

....
```

Save the `banner.inc` file after the changes. Now browsing to a page belonging to the `PurchasePageSet` will give me detailed messages about the filter and scoring results (see Figure 12.11). Again the picture shows a couple of test ads that I have got apart from StarTrek Travel's ads. Feel free to add as many ads as you want so that you can see vividly how scores are assigned and selections are made.

The banner portion of the page lists all available ads with important information about how they were processed. For instance, all ads have a score of 0, which means they were not eligible for delivery and hence didn't show up on the page. For each ad, the debug information shows at which component in the pipe it got its scores. For example, the score of testad1 and testad2 became 0 at the filtering stage, where the `CSFFilterContent` component adjusted their scores because both ads were targeted toward the basket page group. On the other hand, our StarTrek ads got a score of 0 at the `CSFAdvertisingNeedOfDelivery` component because their NOD turned out to be zero. This could be due to any number of reasons, such as the user profile not matching the ads' profile target (users over 60) or the time of day not being between the start and end time for the day (10 A.M. to 10 P.M.). You can drill down to find out the reasons by using the `DumpContentList()` routine defined in `DumpContentList.asp`. This file has to be included and the routine used in much the same way we did for trace scores.

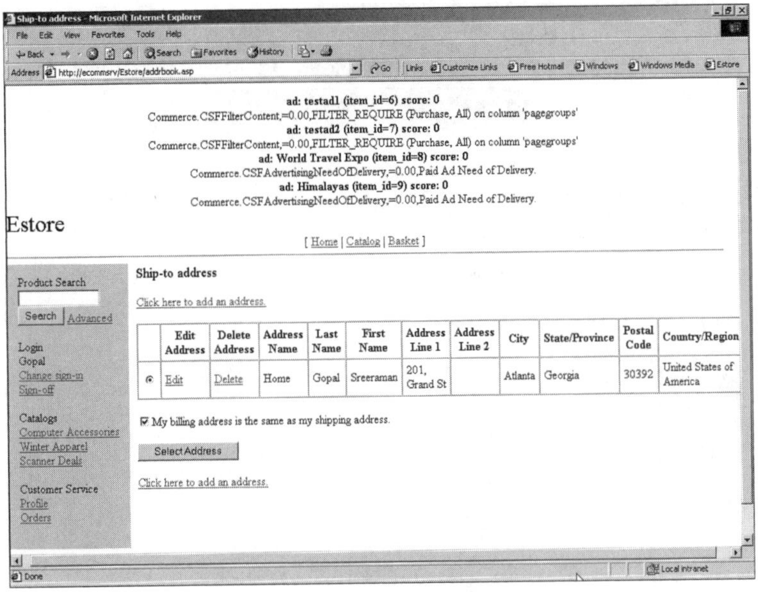

FIGURE 12.11
Debugging the CSP ad delivery.

I analyzed the ad properties to find that the ads will not be delivered until the current system date becomes the Date Received property of the ads. Once my system date crossed that date, the NOD of my ads became nonzero and were then eligible for delivery. Apart from that, I verified that various targeting and filtering criteria were satisfied for at least one ad. Once I start receiving the ads, I can remove the debugging code because it degrades performance while in production. Only the ad appears now on the purchase pages of the site (see Figure 12.12). The World Travel Expo ad appears as a banner that has no clickable link on it.

The Himalayas ad appears as a click-through ad with the URL pointing to

```
http://ecommsrv/estore/redir.asp?ciid=9&cachename=Advertising&PageGroupId=4&
➥url=http://startrektravels.com.earth
```

where `ciid` is the campaign ID, `cachename` gives the name of the cache that holds the ads, `PageGroupId` is the page group ID, and `url` points to the target URL to which the user will be taken upon clicking the ad banner.

Recording Ad Delivery

The CSP records the delivery of each ad as an event of type REQUEST, along with incrementing the count of this event while ads are selected for delivery. This event count is written to the advertising cache and flushed to the database frequently. You can see the number of requests made so far in the list page of the Campaign Manager module for each ad and campaign.

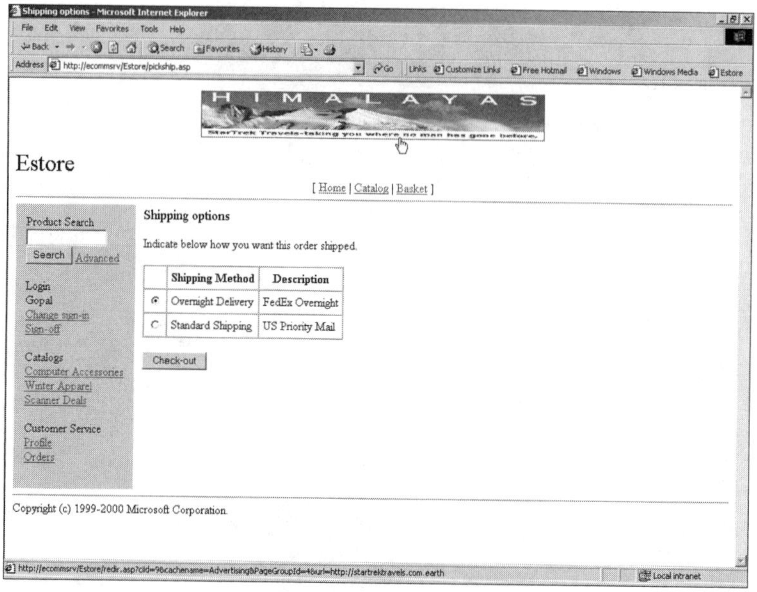

FIGURE 12.12

Ads rotated on targeted pages.

When a user clicks a click-enabled ad, such as the Himalayas ad, an event of type CLICK is recorded for the ad, along with the incremented count for the ad. The keys _event and _eventcount are set on the dictionary passed to the pipeline. This work is accomplished by an intermediate page, redir.asp, that records the event and ultimately redirects the users to the click-URL.

The code in redir.asp basically executes the Event Processing Pipeline (EPP) called RecordEvents.pcf in the Estore site. Redir.asp creates the Order and Context dictionaries. It sets ciid, event, and eventcount on the Order keys _winners, _event, and _eventcount, respectively. The EPP writes this information to the _performance dictionary in the advertising cache, which would later update the running total for ad requests and clicks.

The event is also recorded in the IIS log in a query string such as the following:

```
&CEVT={T=CAMP,CI=9,CNT=1,EVT=CLICK,PG=4}
```

Then the user is redirected using the standard statement:

```
Response.redirect(sUrl)
```

This example should have given you a thorough picture of the advertising infrastructure that Commerce Server provides and the various options in scheduling and delivering ads.

Enabling Auctions

The needs of human beings go beyond food and water. These numerous needs change so frequently that what we needed yesterday is no longer wanted today, and the opposite is also true in this complex world. Fortunately, what we no longer want today is often wanted by others. Therefore, there exists a market for auctioning items that people have, either new or used. Web companies such as eBay and Mercata have successfully used the auction model as their business. Your site might decide to auction off old products, slightly defective stock, and so on. Commerce Server provides sitelet resources in the SDK to manage and deliver auctions on a site. These resources are just very fundamental and might require a lot of customization to suit current-day auction sites. I am sure the next version of Commerce Server will have better facilities to develop online auctions. However, these resources can provide you with a basic auction service, so let's look at them.

Basically, the data store for an auction is comprised of two tables: Catalogproducts_ AuctionItem and Catalogproducts_AuctionBid. The auction sitelet SDK provides Business Desk files for the category Auction and the modules Auction Manager and Bids Manager. Using these Business Desk modules, you can create an auction and manage bids. The SDK also provides sample site pages that can be integrated with an existing site. For dealing with auctions, the `Auction` object is instantiated as follows:

```
Set oAuction = Server.CreateObject("Commerce.Auction")
```

The `Auction` object's properties and methods are used to process auctions and bids on the site. Next, we will discuss the steps needed to "auction-enable" the retail site Estore.

Adding Message Strings

The `Auction` object uses the `MessageManager` object to access error strings and messages needed for its processing. Therefore, messages corresponding to auctions should be added to the site's message file `rc.xml`. Remember to back up files whenever you are beginning to make new changes. Now open the file `rc.xml` from the following folder:

```
<MSCS Installation Folder>\SDK\Samples\Sitelets\Auction\ \source
```

Copy only the message strings formatted and enclosed by the `<Entry>..</Entry>` tags. Open the `rc.xml` file from the Estore root directory. Paste the copied `<Entry>` tags just before the ending `</MessageManager>` tag. Note that the globally initialized `MessageManager` object has to be refreshed so that it reads the new error strings. Save and close the `rc.xml` file for Estore.

Preparing the Biz Desk

Because auctions have to be created first using the Biz Desk before they appear on the site, let's enable Biz Desk to manage auctions.

Adding the Auction Module

The tasks and actions for the auction modules Auction Manager and Bids Manager are defined in the file `auction.xml`, present under the following folder:

```
<MSCS Installation Folder>\SDK\Samples\Sitelets\Auction\bizdesk\config
```

Copy the file to the `config` directory of the `EstoreBizDesk` folder:

```
E:\EstoreBizDesk\EstoreBizDesk\config
```

Modifying Biz Desk Master Configuration

To make available the auction modules in the Biz Desk under the new category Auction, the master configuration file `bizdesk.xml` has to be modified. Edit the `bizdesk.xml` file from the following folder:

```
<
E:\EstoreBizDesk\ EstoreBizDesk\config
```

Add the following section (needed to create a new category) to the `<categories>` section:

```
<category id="auction">
    <name>&lt;U&gt;A&lt;/U&gt;uction</name>
    <key>A</key>
    <tooltip>Manage Auctions</tooltip>
</category>
```

In the `<moduleconfigs>` section, insert the following tag to include the auction modules under the category `auction`:

```
<moduleconfig id="auction.xml" category="auction"/>
```

Save `bizdesk.xml`. Restart the Biz Desk IIS application for the changes to take effect.

Developing Action Pages

To create the action pages specified in the module configuration file `auction.xml`, first create a folder called `auction` under the root folder of the Biz Desk application. Then copy to that folder all the ASP files from the `bizdesk` folder for the auction sitelet SDK:

```
<MSCS Installation Folder>\SDK\Samples\Sitelets\Auction\bizdesk
```

Also, from the same path, copy the entire `include` directory to the `auction` folder under the Estore Biz Desk application.

Creating an Auction

With the Biz Desk enabled to manage auctions, we can start creating auctions using the Auction Manager module. After the Biz Desk application has been restarted, the category Auction and the two auction modules should appear in the navigation pane (see Figure 12.13).

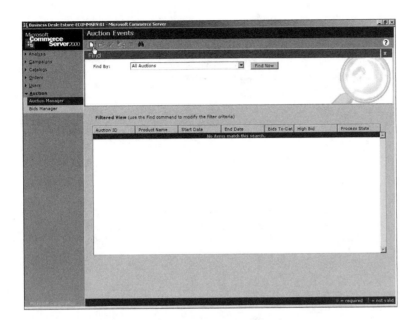

FIGURE 12.13

Creating a new auction.

Click the Auction Manager module. From the auction list page, choose the New Auction (Alt+N) menu icon in the task bar to create a new auction. The New Auction Item edit page displays a form to be filled to create the auction (see Figure 12.13). In the Product Identifier box, choose the product picker button and select a product you want to auction. Next enter the reserve price for the auction, which is an amount that should be reached for a bid to win. In the Number Available box, enter the quantity of the product available in the auction. In the Bid Increment box, enter the minimum amount by which a user should increase his bid from a previous bid.

The Auction Type field is set to Winning Bid by default because this is the only type supported right now. This means that the Auction object will flag that the auction has ended when a bid is received with an amount greater than the reserve price, satisfying all other conditions, too. Then that bid becomes the winning bid.

Next, enter the starting amount for the bid in the Minimum Bid box. Mark the auction as Active by choosing Yes. Then choose a start and end date for the auction. The auction will be made available only within these dates. Check the dates once again because the calendar sometimes defaults to a previous year. Finally, enter the number of seconds after the end date that the auction should close automatically. For example, enter **300** for 5 minutes. Use the task bar icon to save and go back to the auction list page. In the result pane, the new auction with an auction ID should be shown. The status of the auction is Pending Processing. Click the auction and then choose the Process Auction (Alt+P) task bar icon to set the processed state of the auction to 1 (Processed). Now save the auction using a task bar icon (see Figure 12.14). Note that Number of Bids and Created Date will be blank until you save the auction.

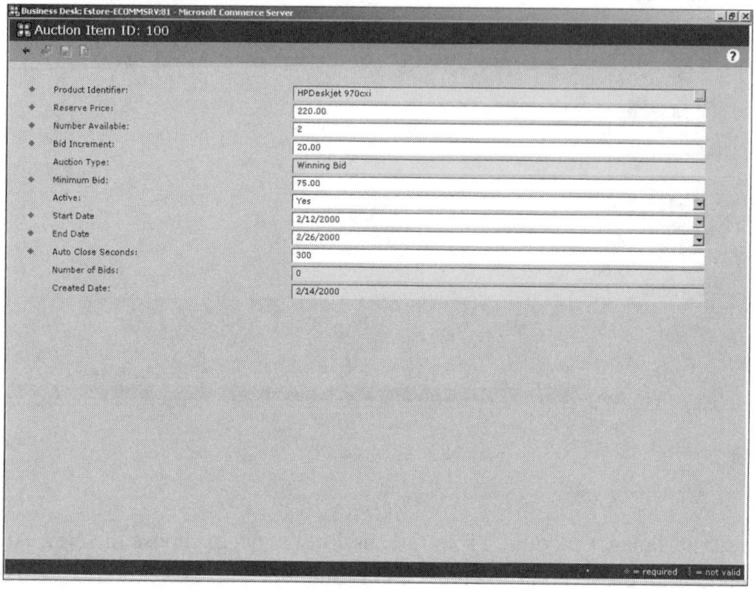

FIGURE 12.14
Saving auction details.

Go back to the auction list page. To make the auction available to the site, choose the auction and click the Process Action (Alt+P) task icon. This will change the status of the auction to Processed.

Preparing the Site

The auction is now available to the site. But in order for the auction to appear on the site, various ASP pages have to be created for retrieving auctions and placing bids. Fortunately, these samples are also found in the auction sitelet SDK. However, they are present in the form of a package and need work to become integrated with an existing site. In this example, we are going to use the same sample files with a few modifications to get the auctions running.

From the SDK folder (<MSCS Installation Folder>\SDK\Samples\Sitelets\Auction\ source), copy only the following files to the root of the site Estore:

- `Auctions.asp`
- `Auctiondetail.asp`
- `Auctionbid.asp`

Then from the `include` directory, under the previously mentioned source directory, copy all the files to the `include` directory of Estore. Edit each of the ASP pages we copied a moment back and correct the file path for the include files. For example, change

```
<!— #INCLUDE FILE="./include/helper.asp" —>
```

to

```
<!— #INCLUDE FILE="include/helper.asp" —>
```

and so on.

Then in the include file `auctionlib.asp`, make the SQL query workable by inserting the changes for the `datediff` function:

```
Function GetActiveAuctionList()

....

strAuctionQry = "SELECT auction_id,product_id," _
                & "product_name,catalog_name,auto_close_date " _
                & "FROM CatalogProducts_AuctionItem " _
                & "WHERE active = 1 and (datediff(ss,'" & dteNow & "',end
                [ic:ccc]_date)>0)" _
                & "AND (datediff(ss,'" & dteNow & "',auto_close_date)>0)"

....

....
```

In `Auctiondetail.asp`, replace `Application ("MSCSSiteName")` with `Application("MSCSCommerceSiteName")`, which will give the correct site name from the config. Make the modification in the following statement:

```
Set oAuthMgr = InitAuthMgr(Application("MSCSSiteName"))
```

The same change has to be made in `Auctionbid.asp`, too.

The remaining task is to get a link on the home page to the `Auctions.asp` page. This can be done in the file `menu.asp`, found in the `template` directory of Estore. In the `htmRenderMenu` function, insert the following segment of code (the block within the `'***added***` comments) to produce the link text on the menu section:

```
....
....

'***added***
dim urlLink,htmLinkText
    urlLink = GenerateURL("auctions.asp", Array(), Array())
    htmLinkText = RenderText("Auctions", MSCSSiteStyle.Body)
htmRenderMenu = htmRenderMenu &  RenderLink(urlLink, htmLinkText, MSCSSite
[ic:ccc]Style.Link) & CRLF

'***added****

    htmRow = "<TR><TD NOWRAP>" & htmRenderMenu & "</TD></TR>"
    htmRenderMenu = RenderTable(htmRow, MSCSSiteStyle.MenuTable)

....
....
```

Of course, in this example, we have hard-coded the values for the purpose of demonstration. To maintain consistency, the file `Auctions.asp` should be stored in the application-level dictionary `MSCSSitePages` as this:

```
MSCSSitePages.Auction = "auctions.asp"
```

The string "Auctions" that appears on the menu section of the Web site could also be made part of the `rc.xml` file. Furthermore, you may want to build more validations, such as registration requirements, before showing the auction's link to the user.

The Sample Auction Page

When the user clicks the Auction link from the menu bar, the auction listing page (`Auctions.asp`) displays the auctions running at that time (see Figure 12.15). Because we are integrating a mostly standalone sitelet to the Estore site, some of the constant declarations might be redefined and you may get errors. Therefore, you might need to comment out constants such as `PROFILE_TYPE_USER`, `USER_ID`, and `USER_PASSWORD`, depending on the errors you get.

`Auctions.asp` uses the routine `GetActiveAuctionList` to get a list of all active auctions. This routine is defined in the include file `auctionlib.asp`. This is the routine that fetches auctions from the CatalogProduct_AuctionItem table. The recordset is iterated and written to the page.

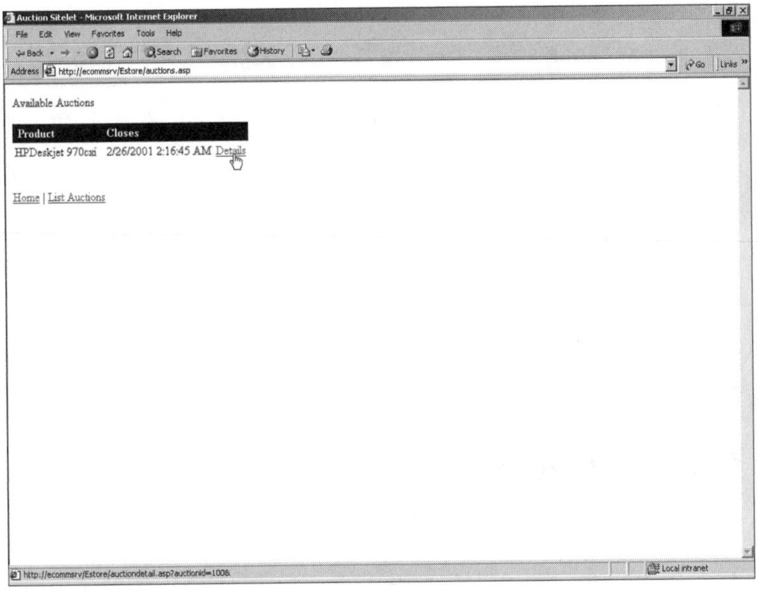

FIGURE 12.15

The Auction page.

The Bid Page

The detail page or the page for bidding for an auction is generated by `Auctiondetail.asp`.
Upon clicking Details (refer to Figure 12.15), the details for that auction are shown. The
details show the product information and auction information, such as quantity of items available, reserve (minimum) price, current bid, and minimum bid. The minimum bid is always calculated as the current bid plus the bid increment. Note that most sites don't reveal the reserve
price of an auction. In the Bid Now section, the user can enter the quantity required and then
bid an amount. Also, there is a check box to accept a lesser quantity than the requested quantity if the auction is awarded. There is also a section that lists the bid history on the product
(see Figure 12.16). Because e-mail addresses are usually used, it may be important to enable
auctions only for registered users.

Once the OK button is clicked, the bid is processed by the `Auctionbid.asp` page. A "success"
message is generated if the bid is placed successfully. Otherwise, error messages are written to
the page. Errors could happen for various reasons, such as when the user enters an amount not
greater than the minimum bid or chooses a larger quantity than available but does not check
the Take Less box. All these error messages provided by the `Auction` object are a result of its
`AuctionAddBid()` method being called to add the bid to the auction item.

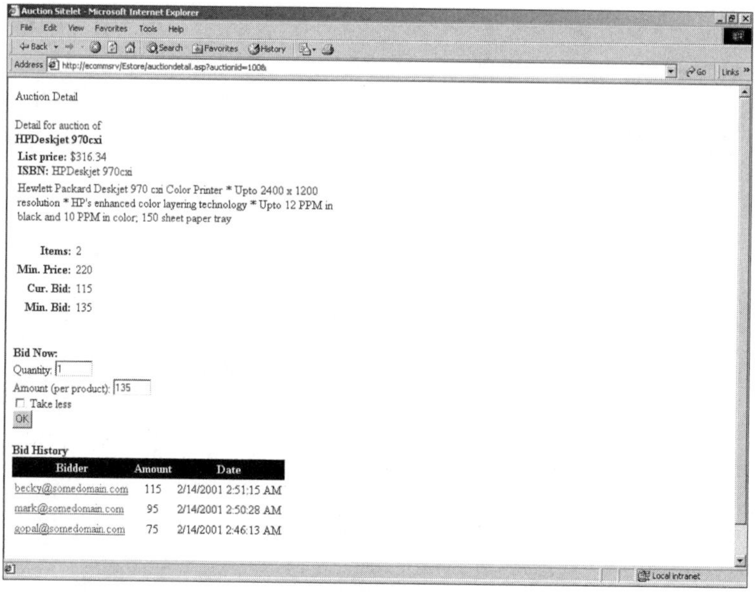

FIGURE 12.16
Details of an auctioned product.

The bidding goes on until the auction closes at the end date or is made inactive, or until a winning bid emerges that is above the reserve price. The Bids Manager module is used to find and view all the bids on various auctions created at the site (see Figure 12.17).

The auction sitelet and the `Auction` object present a basic framework for you to build upon. As mentioned earlier, you might need more customization to build a full-fledged auction site out of this sitelet—basically, you might need to integrate the CatalogProducts_AuctionItem table with the different catalog tables.

Summary

Continuing from the last chapter on the Content Selection Framework, you saw in this chapter various aspects of creating an ad campaign and scheduling it for a customer. Ads an be goaled at the campaign level or the individual ad level. Weights are assigned to ads that participate in campaign-level goaling, whereas exact numbers are assigned to ads that participate in an ad-level goaling campaign. The Commerce Server infrastructure provides effective ways to target ads to a user profile and/or a page context. It is possible to build complex target groups to highly target ads. Ads can be scheduled for any date and time ranges. More granular control of ads, such as setting exposure limits and types of display, are possible using the Campaign Manager module. Ultimately, ads are requested by the Content Selector Object from an ASP page. The GetContent() method of the CSO runs the CSP for advertising that filters, scores, selects, records, and formats ads for delivery. The CSP uses the ad cache and CSO information to do its job. Ultimately, ad requests and clicks are recorded for account-keeping purposes.

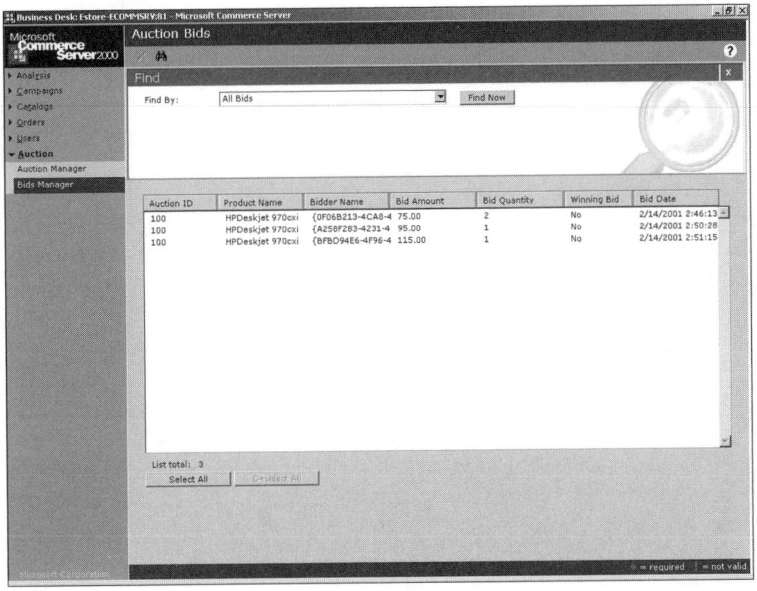

FIGURE 12.17
Bids for an auction.

In the final pages of the chapter, we discussed enabling auctions for the site. Auctioning is a highly specialized business; however, Commerce Server provides the fundamental framework that can be used to further customize auctions. For instance, you could build a cache to hold auction items. We enabled the auction modules Auction Manager and Bids Manager to be shown on the Biz Desk category Auction. Using the list and edit pages, we created an auction, specifying typical details such as minimum price, bid increment, and auction closing date. The site pages were also prepared to display the auctions and accept bids from the users.

Both advertisements and auctions, when designed and developed effectively, have the potential to boost any site's revenue-generating ability.

Building and Customizing Pipelines

IN THIS CHAPTER

- Customizing a Pipeline: E-mail on Order Confirmation   396

- The Component Object Model (COM)   401

- Building a Pipeline Component Using VB   403

- Debugging Pipelines   416

- Ready for Production?   422

- Building Pipeline Components with Visual C++   422

Pipelines in Commerce Server provide a linear and systematic way of processing business information, such as a purchase order or a list of ads scheduled for delivery. The two types of pipes provided by Commerce Server are Order Processing Pipelines (OPPs) and Content Selection Pipelines (CSPs). These pipelines receive the business information of the site in the form of an OrderForm or Dictionary object. The components in the pipeline are executed sequentially as each component does its work by reading or writing information on the business object. At the end of the pipe execution, the processed business object may be persisted in the database or used to display information to the site visitor.

Even though Commerce Server provides prebuilt pipes and pipeline components, unique requirements of a site may necessitate customizing an existing pipe or building new pipeline components. A pipeline can be customized by inserting and removing prebuilt or custom components. Although a custom component can be prototyped as a Scriptor component, the final component for production is one that is built using Visual Basic or Visual C++. There are differences even between components built using these two well-known software packages. In this chapter, the discussions will focus on customizing existing pipes and building custom components using Visual Basic and the Active Template Library (ATL) in Visual C++.

First, you will see an example of customizing an Order Processing Pipeline to send e-mail to the user, confirming an order placed on the site.

Customizing a Pipeline: E-mail on Order Confirmation

Let's suppose customers on Estore need to get an e-mail after they have confirmed an order. The pipe that is run at the end of the purchase process, as you know, is checkout.pcf (see Figure 13.1).

Once the user confirms the order and the order is successfully processed, we can use the SendSMTP component in the Accept stage to send an e-mail. Let's assume the requirements of an e-mail are as follows:

A valid To e-mail address: user@somedomain.com

E-mail Subject: Order Confirmation

E-mail Body:

Thank you for your recent order with tracking number : AB34CDE4FGHIJ0923891

Purchase Total : $298.50

Please don't forget to include the tracking number in all future email enquiries.

Thanks,

Marketing Manager

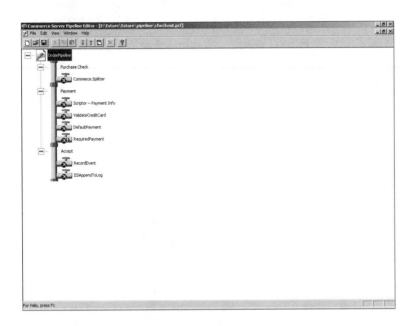

FIGURE 13.1

The Purchase pipe checkout.pcf.

The To, Subject, and Body elements of the e-mail should be generated and inserted into the appropriate keys of the OrderForm object. This will enable SendSMTP to access the corresponding OrderForm keys to retrieve the subject and body for the e-mail.

Preparing the E-mail with a Scriptor Component

We will insert a Scriptor component at the end of the Accept stage. This Scriptor component will generate the e-mail subject and body. The e-mail subject will be added to the Order key:

Order.[_email_subject]

The e-mail body will be stored in this key:

Order.[_email_body]

Note that Order already has the e-mail address of the shopper in the key:

Order.[user_email_address]

Because we require an e-mail address, the site should make sure the user profile contains the e-mail address of the user. However, if the profile does not have an e-mail address, it is necessary to set the value of the preceding key to the string "None". Doing this will make SendSMTP avoid any attempt to send e-mail. This will take care of the scenario where an anonymous user can order items without supplying profile information to the site.

The composition of the e-mail body itself will require values in Order keys:

```
Order.[order_id] and
Order.[_total_total]
```

Here is what the pipeline script will look like:

```
Function mscsexecute(config, orderform, context, flags)
    Dim  oDataFunctions
    Set oDataFunctions = context.DataFunctions
    if(orderform.[user_email_address])="" then
        orderform.[user_email_address] = "None"
    end if
    orderform.[_email_subject] = "Order Confirmation"
    orderform.[_email_body] = "Thank you for your recent order with tracking
    ➥ number :"_
                & orderform.[order_id] & "." _
                & chr(10) & chr(13) _
                & chr(10) & chr(13) _
                & "Purchase Total: " _
                & oDataFunctions.Money(CLng(orderform.[_total_total])) _
                & chr(10) & chr(13) _
                & chr(10) & chr(13) _
                & "Please don't forget to include the tracking number in all
                ➥future email enquiries." _
                & chr(10) & chr(13) _
                & chr(10) & chr(13) _
                & "Thanks," _
                & chr(10) & chr(13) _
                & "Marketing Manager"
    mscsexecute = 1
End Function
```

As you can see, the script checks for the presence of the user's e-mail address. Then the e-mail subject is written to the order form. The e-mail body is generated, as required, using the order-tracking number and the order total values. Note that the chr(10) and chr(13) functions correspond to inserting a carriage return and line feed in the text of the e-mail. Save the preceding script in a file called emailformat.vbs under the template directory of your site. Here's an example:

```
E:\Estore\Estore\template\emailformat.vbs.
```

We will use this file as the script for a Scriptor component.

Next, in the `checkout.pcf` pipe, insert a Scriptor component at the end of the Accept stage, probably after the IISAppendToLog component. In the Component Properties page, choose VBScript as the scripting engine. Specify "External" as the source for the script. Click the No button when the message "Do you wish to export the internal source code?" pops up. In the Filename field, browse for the `emailformat.vbs` file we created a moment ago. Then click the OK button (see Figure 13.2). You may rename the Scriptor to something more meaningful, such as "Prepare Email," using the Component Properties tab and the Label box.

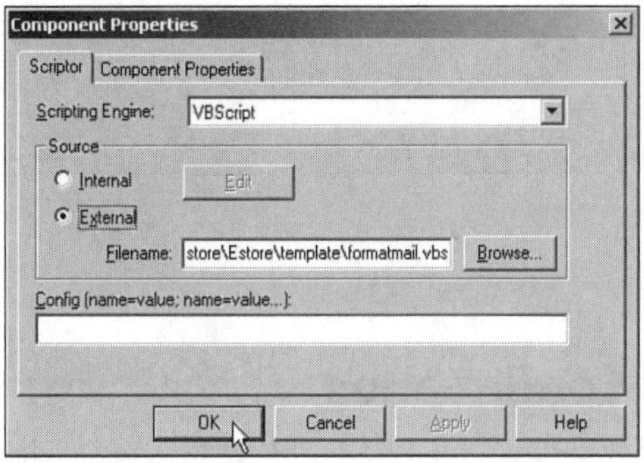

Figure 13.2

An external source for a Scriptor component.

Inserting the SendSMTP Component

Having made sure the OrderForm object has the e-mail address, subject, and body, we then proceed to insert the SendSMTP component. Insert this component right after the Scriptor component at the end of the Accept stage. Then right-click the SendSMTP component and open the Component Properties page (see Figure 13.3).

In the SendSMTP tab, enter an actual e-mail address in the From box. This is typically an address where the user can reply to. In the SMTP Host box, give the name of the SMTP server that will process and send the e-mail messages.

In the To field, type the name of the order key that has the value of the shopper's e-mail address. In this case, it is *user_email_address*. Similarly, type the order key *_email_subject* in the Subject box and *_email_body* in the Message Body box. These keys will be read by the component from the order form. Because our message contains plain text, choose Text Body as the Message Body option. Click the Apply button to save the configuration for SendSMTP. You can navigate to the Test SendSMTP tab and click the Send Test Email button just to make sure the SMTP server is working.

Finally, save the pipe and unload the Estore IIS application before testing the e-mail upon order confirmation.

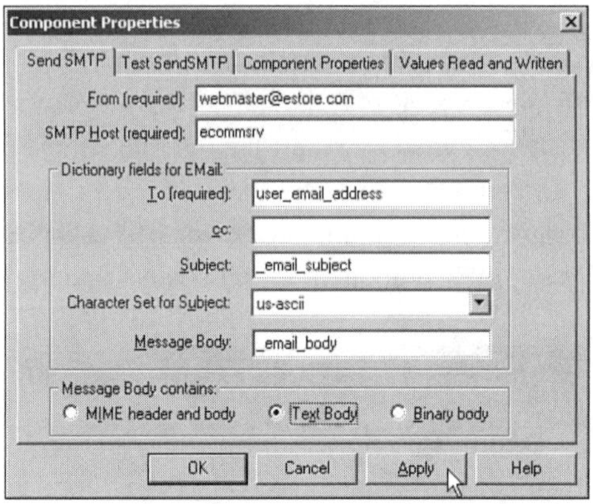

FIGURE 13.3

Configuring the SendSMTP pipeline component.

Verifying Order Confirmation

After the user clicks the Submit button in the credit card page, the checkout pipe is executed and an e-mail is sent to the user upon successful order confirmation (see Figure 13.4). Note that because SendSMTP is the last component in the pipe it would be executed only if all other components in the pipe have completed successful execution. This guarantees that e-mail is sent out only for a successful order.

The strings for e-mail subject and body could be stored in the `rc.xml` file, along with other strings. This would enable fetching multilanguage strings using the `MessageManager` object. Also, you can customize the e-mail by providing links and other information, as needed.

How do we know whether a value existed for the `user_email_address` key? In any pipe, how do we debug to find out the cause for pipeline errors? The section "Debugging Pipelines," later in this chapter, will throw light on ways to look at the business objects in a pipe as well as the state of components as they sequentially execute one after the other.

Having seen how to customize an existing pipeline, you now know that components can be inserted or removed for customizing stages in a pipeline. Also, it must be clear now that Commerce Server provides quite a few pipeline components to be used for specific purposes. More often than not, your site will need a pipeline component to accomplish some custom functionality not available with CS2K-provided components. In such a case, you will need to build a pipeline component yourself and plug it into a pipeline. In order to successfully build a custom pipeline component, you need to understand the COM interfaces the component needs to implement, the methods that need to be implemented, and other requirements, such as registering the component. In the next section, we will begin with a quick refresher on Component Object Model (COM) and then move on to discuss the requirements for a pipeline component.

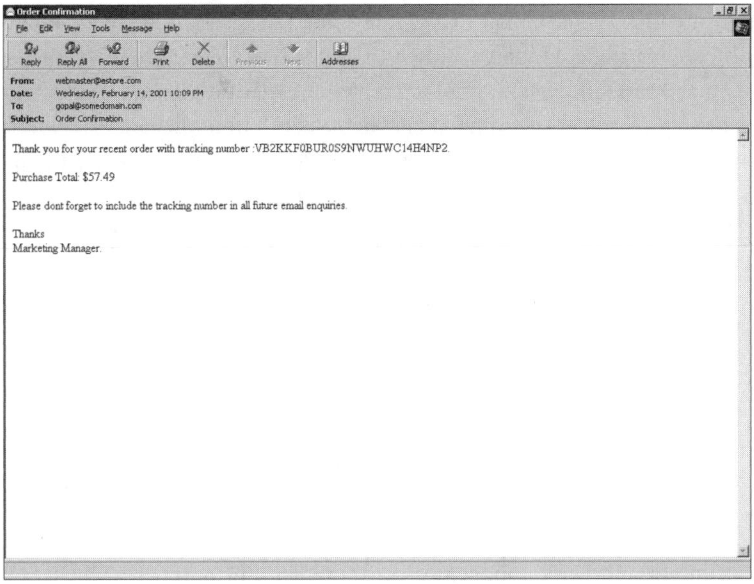

FIGURE 13.4

The order confirmation e-mail.

The Component Object Model (COM)

Software systems are becoming large and complex due to the increase in size and complexity of applications—and so are their interactions within a process boundary or even across remote machines. There are a variety of operating systems, networking software systems, and different versions of software components from different vendors trying to work together in modern-day enterprises. All this adds to the complexity of developing and maintaining cost-effective systems. Here is where COM provides an implementable model; when followed, it enables software components to communicate regardless of whether they are in the same process on the local machine or interacting across a network.

Objects built based on COM expose their functionality through *interfaces*. Interfaces are like immutable contracts between components that guarantee that they always behave in an expected way. Interfaces are implemented by objects that expose a group of related methods that do the actual work. When a component desires to seek the services of another component, it asks the COM library for a pointer to an interface provided by the server component. The interface pointer is the only method to access and navigate through the different functionality offered by a COM component.

COM is a model that defines a binary standard. Hence, a COM-compliant component can be written and built using any language that supports pointers to functions. The only requirement is that after they are compiled to binary form, their interfaces should be made known to the COM library by registering components. Most tools, such as Visual C++ (VC++), Visual Basic (VB), Java, C, and SmallTalk, can be used to create perfectly COM-compliant components. However, at a minimum, all COM components are required to implement the interface IUnKnown. Usually, interfaces are named starting with *I*. IUnKnown is supposed to provide three methods—QueryInterface, AddRef, and Release—to provide navigation and reference-count mechanisms of a component. A COM component can implement other interfaces, as is required by the functionality of that component (see Figure 13.5). Interfaces are marked by using the Interface Definition Language (IDL).

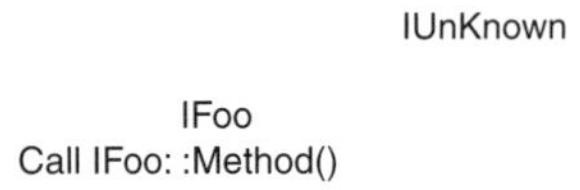

IUnKnown

IFoo
Call IFoo: :Method()

FIGURE 13.5
A COM object representation.

A client connecting to a server component specifies either a Prog ID or a CLSID to the COM system before requesting an interface pointer. The COM library checks whether the object is already in memory; otherwise, it creates the object and hands over the IUnKnown pointer to the client. A client passes the required interfaces identifier (IID) to the method IUKnown: :QueryInterface and gets a pointer to the required interface, such as IFoo. Then the client may call any of the methods supported, using IFoo: :*Method*(), to get its work done. All this happens with complete location transparency, and COM manages many aspects of memory allocation, with some responsibility taken on by the components.

To get more information about COM and related technologies, start with www.microsoft.com/COM.

A Pipeline Component

If a COM component has to be used by any of the Commerce Server pipeline objects, such as MtxPipeline, the component has to implement, at a minimum, the interface IPipeline Component. In other words, in order to show up within Pipeline Editor, a component has to implement the required interface IPipelineComponent. The definition of what actually should be coded for this interface is present in the file Pipecomp.idl, found under the path <MSCS Installation folder>/SDK/Include. If you open the file, you can see that various other interfaces can also be implemented by a component to take advantage of advanced features.

Here is a brief description of the important interfaces a pipeline component would implement:

- `IPipelineComponent`. This is the only required interface that needs to be implemented by a component for it to become a "pipeline component." This interface has the `Execute` method, which takes as input, among other things, pointers to the Order and Context dictionaries. The output parameter of this method is `Error Level`. Custom code to process the order is built in to this method.

- `IPipelineComponentAdmin`. Implement this interface if you want to set configuration values at design time. Remember that many of the prebuilt components have this ability. The `SetConfigDat` and `GetConfigData` methods in this interface work on a `Dictionary` object passed from the configuration. This interface uses the `IPipelineComponentUI` and `IpipelineComponentSpecifyUI` interfaces to provide a launchable user interface, and it's an alternative to using the Win32 OLE interface, typically loaded by `ISpecify PropertiesPages`.

- `IPipelineComponentDescription`. This interface is used to tell the pipeline component what `Order` and `Context` keys to display when the Values Read and Written tab is chosen from the Pipeline Editor.

- `IPersistStreamInit`. When a component exposes property pages for configuration, the set values must be stored and retrieved in the pipeline configuration. The `IPersistStreamInit` interface provides methods such as `InitNew`, `Load`, and `Save` to load and save configuration data from a persisted stream.

- `IDispatch`. If the component needs to be accessed by ActiveX-enabled scripting languages that bind late, such as VBScript, you should implement this interface. An example would be instantiating the object directly from an ASP page, about which we will talk later.

Note that the preceding list of components is not comprehensive but rather indicatory only. We will see more of the optional interfaces while actually building the components in the sections that follow.

One could manually construct all the files necessary to code the classes and methods needed to implement the interfaces. However, Commerce Server provides wizards for use in both VB and VC++ that generate all the necessary files with skeleton code. This makes it much easier for developers to concentrate on the component functionality instead of setting up the COM-required syntax and semantics.

Building a Pipeline Component Using VB

Visual Basic 6.0 is required to develop pipeline components using the Commerce Server–provided VB Pipeline Wizard. The wizard makes life easy for pipeline component developers by providing the code structure needed to implement the necessary interfaces as well as the supporting data structures. The wizard asks a series of questions to generate the required framework. To start using the wizard from VB, you need to first register the wizard and make it available to VB.

Installing the VB Pipeline Component Wizard

The wizard is available through the file `PipelineCompWizard.dll` found under the SDK directory:

```
<MSCS Installation Folder>\SDK\Tools\VB Pipe Wizard
```

To register the wizard, click the Start button and then choose Run. Use the `Regsvr32` command followed by the full path to the DLL in order to register the wizard. For example, type the following command in the Run box and click the OK button:

```
Regsvr32 "<MSCS Installation Folder>\SDK\Tools\VB Pipe Wizard\Pipeline
➥CompWizard.dll"
```

You should see a success message. Now the wizard is available in the New Project dialog box of VB.

Building an Order-level Discount for Visa Corp

You already knowthat discounts can be applied either at the item level or at the entire order level. Commerce Server provides only one order-level discount, free shipping, that can be configured using the New Discount menu in the Campaigns Manager Biz Desk module. Any other order-level discount has to be custom built.

Let's suppose that Visa Corporation wants to sponsor a discount on Estore to customers if they use a Visa card for their purchases and their total order exceeds a certain amount. The discount will be a certain percentage off the total order amount. To implement this special discount on the site, we will build a pipeline component for the Payment stage of the Purchase pipeline of the site.

The discount percentage and the minimum order amount to qualify for the discount should be configurable using the property page of the component at design time. That is, the component should be configurable for these values from the Pipeline Editor.

Note that the wizard will build the framework for an active dynamic link library (DLL) in which the interfaces will be implemented.

Using the VB Pipeline Wizard

Open the Visual Basic 6.0 program. If the New Project dialog box doesn't open automatically, choose File, New Project. In the New Project dialog box, choose Commerce Server Order Pipeline Component and then click the Open or the OK button to start the wizard (see Figure 13.6).

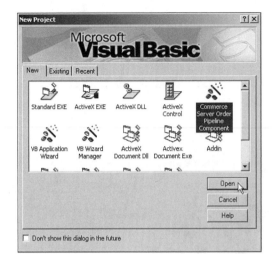

FIGURE 13.6

The Pipeline Component Wizard for a new project.

The wizard has, in all, seven screens to collect information from you. In the first screen (Step 1 of 7), click the Next button. Step 2 asks whether you want this component to be used from a transaction-enabled pipeline, such as MtsTxPipeline or PooledTxPipeline. Choose Yes and then click the Next button. Step 3 enquires about having code automatically generated to handle the multiple-shipment capability provided by Commerce Server. If you are building a custom shipping component, you might use this in the future. Now choose No and then click the Next button.

The screen for Step 4 collects information about the property page interface's data structure. For example, because we are configuring discount percentage and the minimum required order amount from a property page interface, we need to specify corresponding variables in this wizard. This will enable the wizard to declare these variables and generate code needed to get or set values from the interface.

Let's keep the property name for discount percentage as Disc_Percent. The data type will be Double. Click the Add button on this screen. Then type the property name and choose the appropriate data type (see Figure 13.7).

Now click the OK button. Repeat the same steps to add the parameter Min_Amt, with data type Double, to store the minimum required amount value. Click the Next button.

In the screen for Step 5, give appropriate names for the project, the component, the UI component, and the property form (see Figure 13.8).

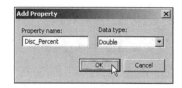

FIGURE 13.7

Adding a property for the property page.

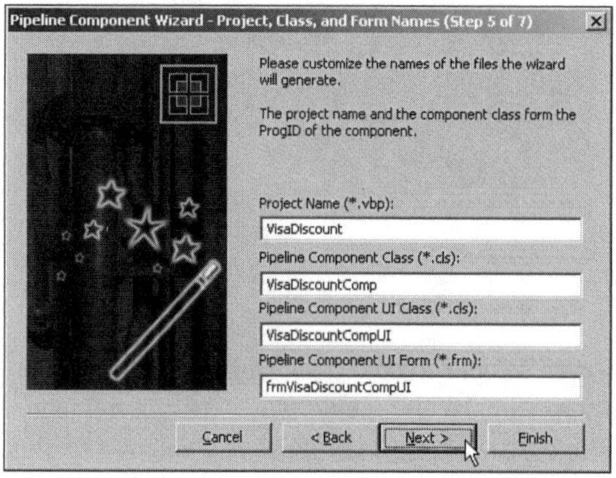

FIGURE 13.8

Naming the project, classes, and the UI form.

In Step 6, you need to choose a directory where the project files will be saved. Then click the Next button. Finally, if you have provided all the information, click the Finish button in the Step 7 screen. In a flash, the wizard generates all the skeleton code needed to implement the required and other interfaces for the component.

Checking the Generated Code

In order to check whether the code generated contains all the interfaces and data structures we need, press the Ctrl+R key combination to bring up the Project Explorer. We can see in a moment that VisaDiscountComp.cls is the main class module that will implement the necessary interfaces. The other module, VisaDiscountCompUI.cls, along with the form frmVisaDiscountCompUI, will be the elements required for the Configuration tab interface on the component at design time.

Now let's check some of the key code elements in the file VisaDiscountComp.cls. At the beginning of the file, it is clear what interfaces this module implements:

```
Implements IPersistDictionary
Implements IPipelineComponent
```

```
Implements ISpecifyPipelineComponentUI
Implements IPipelineComponentDescription
Implements IPipelineComponentAdmin
```

We make sure that the only required interface, `IPipelineComponent`, is implemented. Also, the `IPersistDictionary` interface is used mainly to save and load the dictionary values (entered as Configuration tab values) from the pipeline file. The values entered using a pipeline component's configuration interface are saved and loaded from the pipeline configuration file (PCF) where the component is plugged into.

The interface `IPipelineComponentDescription` will be responsible for the display strings when a user invokes the Values Read and Written tab on the component's property page.

The next code to observe is the declaration of variables that we defined as property names using the wizard:

```
Private m_dblDisc_Percent As Double
Private m_dblMin_Amt As Double
```

The wizard has prefixed its own naming convention to the property named we specified. Next, we come to the most important method of the `IPipelineComponent` interface—the `Execute` method.

You already know the inputs, the output, and that this method is called by the pipeline object (such as `MtsPipeline`). The signature of this method is as follows:

```
Private Function IPipelineComponent_Execute(ByVal objOrderForm As Object,
➡ByVal objContext As Object, ByVal lFlags As Long) As Long
```

Note that `objOrderForm` is the reference to the `OrderForm` dictionary rather than a copy of it. This might be confusing because of `ByVal`. Actually, the address of the `OrderForm` object is passed as a value in the parameter. The same idea applies to the Context dictionary, `objContext`. The parameter `lFlags` is reserved and has no meaning currently. The return value of the `Execute` function is defined as a Long pointer in the `pipecomp.idl` file. That's what the return value, Long, of the function `MSCSExecute` signifies, as well as the statement that sets the return value of the function, as can be seen from the following code snippet:

```
' Return 1 for Success
   IPipelineComponent_Execute = 1
```

Variables are defined first, conveniently, to refer to objects such as the pipe context dictionary, the Items dictionary, and the `MessageManager` object:

```
Dim objPipeCtx  As CDictionary 'Pipe Context
Dim objItems As CSimpleList 'Items
Dim objMsgMgr As Object 'Message Manager
```

13

For example, CDictionary refers to the data type of Commerce.Dictionary and is defined in the included type library. You can verify using the menu item Project, References that the Microsoft Commerce Core 2000 Components Type Library is automatically added as a reference in the project by the wizard.

Next, inside the Execute routine, the previously declared variables are initialized to refer to their corresponding objects, such as OrderForm, the Context dictionary, the Items dictionary, and MessageManager.

Apart from these, there is not much code here; essentially, this is a to-do section for us.

By browsing through the rest of the code we can see how the method

```
IPipelineComponentAdmin_GetConfigData()
```

creates a dictionary and stores the configuration interface key/value pairs.

Modifying the Configuration Interface

From the Project Explorer, launch the form frmVisaDiscountCompUI, which is the user interface for the configuration page of the component. Click once on the form and press the F4 key to bring up the Properties window for this form. Here, you can modify the caption of the form, change the initial display text in the boxes, include some label text if you want, and make any other additions or changes (see Figure 13.9).

Save the modified form. Next, we will add code to the class module to process the order and to set the appropriate discount.

Modifying IPipelineComponent_Execute

Now let's come back to the Execute method, where we are going to build the code needed for the discount. First, we will declare a set of variables used for purposes described later:

```
Dim dblOrderTotal As Double 'Order Total
Dim dblDiscAmount As Double 'Discount Amount calculated
```

Next, we need to get the order total:

```
dblOrderTotal = CDbl(objOrderForm.Value("_cy_total_total"))
```

Note how easy it is to access a key from the order form. Now we need to compare the order total with the minimum required amount:

```
If ((objOrderForm.Value("cc_type") = "VISA") And (dblOrderTotal >= m_dblMin_
➡Amt)) Then
....
```

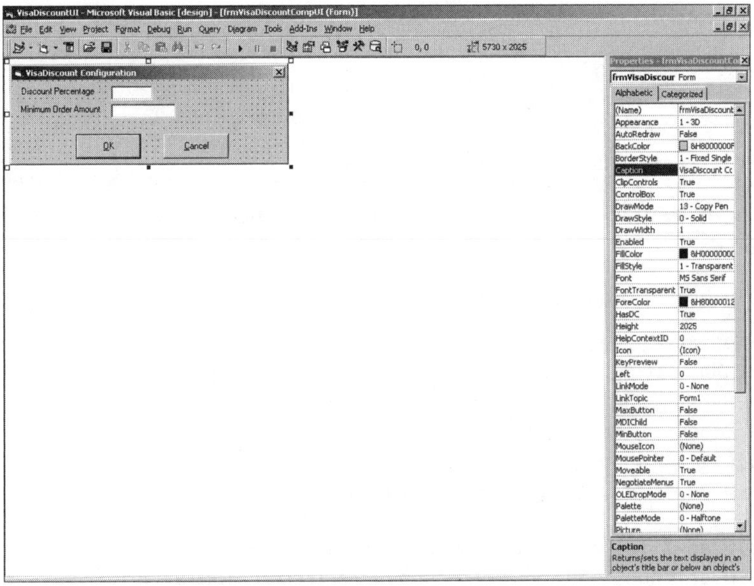

FIGURE 13.9

The Configuration tab interface after modifications.

The preceding expression checks whether the credit card used is VISA and whether the order total meets the minimum required amount for the discount.

If the preceding expression evaluates to True, we do the following:

1. Calculate the discount amount on the total:

   ```
   dblDiscAmount = dblOrderTotal * (m_dblDisc_Percent / 100)
   ```

2. Set the order total stored in the key _cy_total_total to the amount after the discount is subtracted from the order total:

   ```
   objOrderForm.Value("_cy_total_total") = dblOrderTotal - dblDiscAmount
   ```

3. Set a key called disc_pc on the order to store the discount percent:

   ```
   objOrderForm.Value("disc_pc") = m_dblDisc_Percent
   ```

4. Set a key called ord_disc on the order to store the discount amount and then close the If statement:

   ```
   objOrderForm.Value("ord_disc") = dblDiscAmount
   End If

   ....
   ```

13

Now you can move the return assignment to just before the End Function statement for Execute:

```
' Return 1 for Success
   IPipelineComponent_Execute = 1
```

This is a standard practice—that is, to enable returning other values earlier if the component finds errors with the order. Now you could clean up unwanted code in the wizard-generated Execute function.

Here is the final code for the Execute function:

```
Private Function IPipelineComponent_Execute(ByVal objOrderForm As Object,
➡ ByVal objContext As Object, ByVal lFlags As Long) As Long

    Dim objPipeCtx  As CDictionary 'Pipe Context
    Dim objItems As CSimpleList 'Items
    Dim objMsgMgr As Object 'Message Manager

    Dim dblOrderTotal As Double 'Order Total
    Dim dblDiscAmount As Double 'Discount Amount calculated

    ' Initialize the Pipe Context and Order Form

    Set objPipeCtx = objContext
    Set objOrderForm = objOrderForm

    ' Initialize the Message Manager and get the Items from the Order Form
    Set objMsgMgr = objPipeCtx.Value("MessageManager")
    Set objItems = objOrderForm.Value("Items")


    dblOrderTotal = CDbl(objOrderForm.Value("_cy_total_total"))

    If ((objOrderForm.Value("cc_type") = "VISA") And (dblOrderTotal >= m_db
➡lMin_Amt)) Then
        dblDiscAmount = dblOrderTotal * (m_dblDisc_Percent / 100)
        objOrderForm.Value("_cy_total_total") = dblOrderTotal - dblDiscAmount
        objOrderForm.Value("disc_pc") = m_dblDisc_Percent
        objOrderForm.Value("ord_disc") = dblDiscAmount
    End If

    ' Return 1 for Success
    IPipelineComponent_Execute = 1
End Function
```

Recall that for a pipeline component, an error level of 1 means success, 2 means user errors (basket or purchase) occurred, and 3 means a fatal component-related error had occurred. The pipeline stages check this error level before continuing with another component.

Setting Values Read and Written

Let's now set the string values that will be displayed in the Values Read and Written property page of the component. The component is reading from and writing to the order key _cy_ total_total. Therefore, modify the IPipelineComponentDescription methods as follows:

```
Private Function IPipelineComponentDescription_ValuesRead() As Variant

    IPipelineComponentDescription_ValuesRead = Array("Order._cy_total_total")

End Function

Private Function IPipelineComponentDescription_ValuesWritten() As Variant

    IPipelineComponentDescription_ValuesWritten = Array("Order._cy_total_
    ➡total ")

End Function
    ....
```

If you have more than one key to read and write, you would build an array with the strings and pass the array.

Compiling and Building the Component

After you have made all these changes, save the VisaDiscountComp.cls file.

From the File menu, choose Make VisaDiscount.dll to build the ActiveX DLL that implements IPipelineComponent and the other interfaces. In the Make Project dialog box, specify a place to save the DLL.

Switch to the VisaDiscountCompUI module from the Project Explorer. Using the File, Make menu item, build the VisaDiscountUI.dll module. Save it in a directory.

Registering Pipeline Components

Commerce Server provides an easy way to register the pipeline components as well as set their affinity to a pipeline stage. Yes, yet another wizard is available to help save you time! The SDK tool pipereg.exe, also called the Pipeline Component Registration Wizard, is found under the following folder:

```
<MSCS Installation Folder>\ SDK\Tools\Registration Tool
```

Double-click the executable `pipereg.exe`.

In the first screen of the Pipeline Component Registration Wizard, you can choose the Select Component by Prog ID radio button and specify the Prog ID of our component, which is `VisaDiscount.VisaDiscountComp`. Otherwise, you can select the second option, Select Component Type Library, and browse to choose the path of the `VisaDiscount.dll` file (see Figure 13.10).

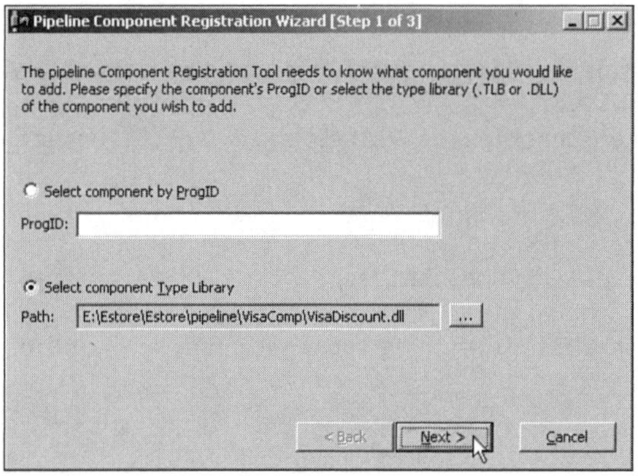

FIGURE 13.10

Selecting a type library.

Click the Next button. In the next screen, choose the stage this component should have. Select "Payment" from the Available Categories list and add it to the Selected Categories box (see Figure 13.11). We have chosen this stage because the component will be inserted at the Payment stage in the Purchase pipe (`checkout.pcf`) of Estore. Other components in the Payment stage validate the credit card information supplied by the user.

Click the Next button. The final screen helps in registering the component as well as adding appropriate Registry entries to affiliate the component with the stage. Therefore, choose Register and Export Data and click the Next button. The saved Registry file can be used on distributed machines while installing the component.

Finally, the wizard does its job and comes up with a confirmation box. Close the wizard.

The wizard will register the component and include the GUIDs of affiliated stages under the `Implemented Categories` Registry key:

`\HKEY_CLASSES_ROOT\CLSID\<Component CLSID>\Implemented Categories`

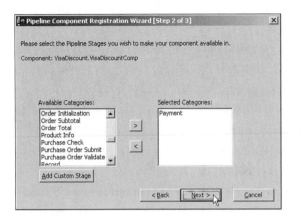

FIGURE 13.11
Choosing the Pipeline stage for a component.

Therefore, the component is now available to the pipeline object and the Pipeline Editor.

Inserting the Component in the Pipeline

We can now insert the component in the Payment stage of the `checkout.pcf` pipe in Estore.

Open `checkout.pcf` in the Pipeline Editor. Right-click the last component, such as RequiredPayment, in the Payment stage. Then choose to insert the component after RequiredPayment. Now the component we built should appear in the list. Choose the component and click the OK button.

Setting Configuration Values

Because we need to set the discount percentage and minimum amount, right-click the component to open the property page. You may want to modify the label to a shorter name. More importantly, click the Custom Properties tab. You will see a button called Custom User Interface. Remember that we implemented the `IPipelineComponentAdmin` interface instead of the `ISpecifyPropertyPages` interface.

Click the button to launch the user interface. In the dialog box, enter the discount percentage and the minimum amount of the order required to apply the discount (see Figure 13.12).

Click the OK button; then click the OK button of Component Properties page. Save the pipeline configuration file. You need to restart the IIS site application so that the modified PCF can be read again by the application.

13

BUILDING AND
CUSTOMIZING
PIPELINES

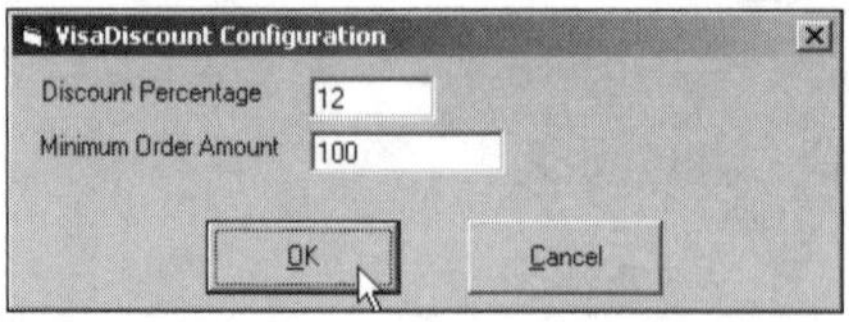

FIGURE 13.12

The user interface in a property page of a component.

Reporting the Discount

As you have seen, the user enters his credit card information for the site in the `crdtcard.asp` page. Only after the user clicks the Check-out button in that page do we know what type of credit card was used. Immediately, `checkout.pcf` processes the payment, and the `confirm.asp` page is shown to the user confirming the order. Therefore, there is really no place the information about this order-level discount can appear on the site to be made known to the user. Of course, he would know from the credit card statement. But it is always better to avoid this kind of a surprise, even if it is beneficial!

We could pop an intermediate page between the credit card form and the confirmation page, showing the summary of the order again with the order-level discount. But on our site, let's assume that we run ads for Visa that talk about this discount. We would put these ads on pages such as `crdtcard.asp` and basket pages so that the user can decide which card to use before checkout.

Let's suppose that we will show the adjusted order in the user's order history. To be able to do that, we need to make some modifications in the report generated by the `view_orders.asp` file. After some analysis, it's easy to find that the include file `render_orders.asp` generates the Order Details section of the report, using the routine `tblRenderOrderDetailsContents`. We will add code to this routine so that it displays the discount.

You can find `render_orders.asp` under the `services\include` folder at the root of Estore. Open `render_orders.asp` in a text editor or Visual InterDev. Go to the function `tblRender OrderDetailsContents`. Include the following snippet of code, just after the `render` statement for the *saved_cy_tax_total* key:

```
'***Begin custom code
    Dim nOrdDisc,strMsg,nDiscPc
    nDiscPc = mscsOrderGrp.Value("OrderForms").Value("default").Value("disc_
    ➡pc")
```

```
nOrdDisc = mscsOrderGrp.Value("OrderForms").Value("default").Value("ord_
➥disc")
strMsg = "<b><font color='#0000FF'>" & nDiscPc & " % Extra discount
➥courtesy of VISA. — — — — — — — —></font></b>"
if(nOrdDisc > 0) then
htmRow = htmRow  & _
         cellRenderReadOnlyProperty( _
                                "ord_disc", _
                                strMsg, _
                                nOrdDisc, _
                                "-" & htmRenderCurrency(nOrdDisc) _
)
    end if
'***End custom code
```

This is a simple piece of code that fetches the discount percentage and discount amount on the order and stores them in the variables nDiscPc and nOrdDisc, respectively. Then we build the string to be displayed—in this case, "15 % Extra discount courtesy of Visa. ——>"—next to the discount amount column. Probably, as you build more custom code, it would be wise to use the rc.xml file and the MessageManager object to retrieve string messages. Next, we check whether an order-level discount was applied (that is, whether the discount amount is greater than 0). Then the message and the discount amount are added as a row to the table being generated for display. Save the file.

Testing the VisaDiscount Component

We need to restart the IIS application for the site. Once you have done that, browse all the way to specifying a credit card for an order. After specifying Visa as the credit card and supplying all the other details, click the Check-out button. The order is processed, and the confirmation page is shown with the order number. Click the order number link or the Orders menu link anytime. The Order Details section of the report for the specified order will now show the special discount (see Figure 13.13).

Of course, we would test for a variety of scenarios, such as a card other than Visa being used, the order total being less than the required amount, and so on.

More often than not, at least initially, it will be necessary to debug the pipe when a component fails. It is also true that even with standard pipes, we will want to know what has happened when something has failed or produced unexpected values. Don't worry if your component fails the first time. You will learn methods of debugging the pipeline in the next section.

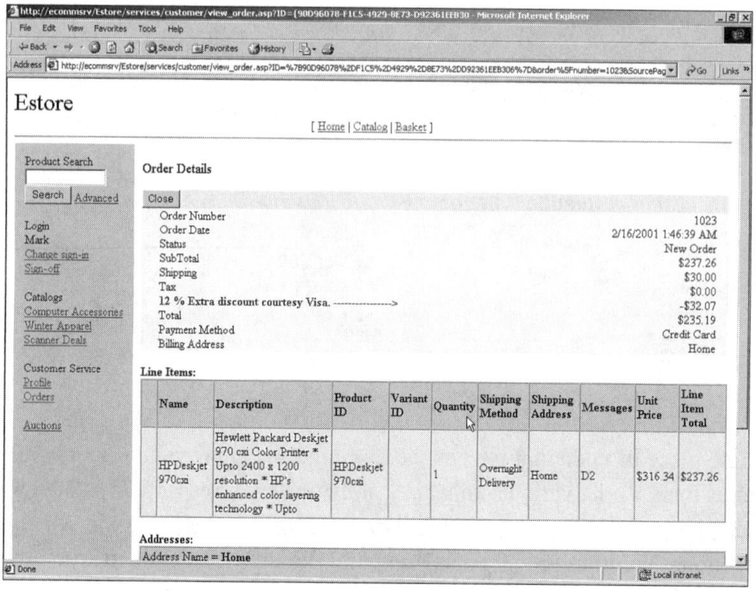

FIGURE 13.13

Reporting the Visa discount after user confirmation.

Debugging Pipelines

Pipelines are used extensively for order processing and content selection in Commerce Server sites. Custom components are plugged into the pipelines to satisfy unique requirements of a site. In the course of pipeline execution, there could be different types of errors occurring due to the pipeline components. To determine whether a system error is because of a component's behavior, network problems, or database access issues, for example, we need more information from the pipeline object. Also, even if there were no execution problems, logical errors could creep in when complex calculations are performed on the Order dictionary.

To understand problems with a pipeline, we could dump the OrderForm contents, log the pipeline object's activity, or run the custom component in an isolated pipe. We will discuss these methods specifically now.

Dumping the Order Form

Commerce Server provides a script called DumpOrder.vbs in the SDK directory:

```
<MSCS Installation Directory>\SDK\Samples\Sitelets\Order\source\pipeline
```

We can use this file as the source for a Scriptor component that would be inserted into a problematic pipe. Open the pipe with which you are having issues. Identify the stage at which you want to dump the contents of the OrderFrom object. The Scriptor will not stop the pipeline; instead, after dumping the order, the pipe continues with the next component. Therefore, an order dump is a snapshot at the point in the pipeline where the Scriptor is inserted. Hence, if you feel there is a problem with a particular component, you could dump the order form contents before and after the problematic component.

In the pipe, right-click the stage or component and insert the Scriptor component. Right-click the Scriptor component to open the property page. In the Scriptor tab, choose External as the source. Then answer no to the question "Do you wish to export the internal source code?" For the Filename box, use the Browse button to locate and choose dumporder.vbs (see Figure 13.14).

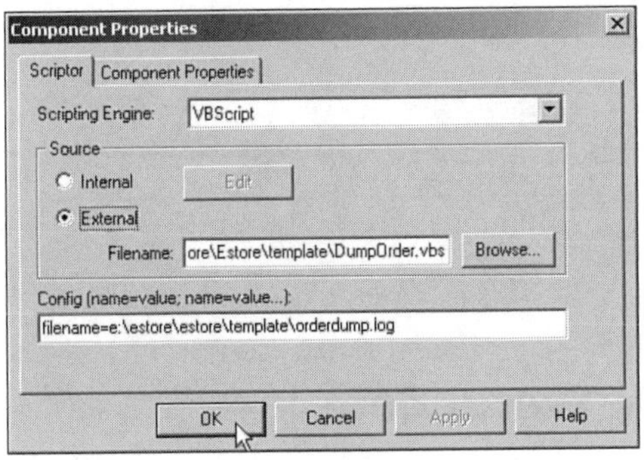

FIGURE 13.14
Scriptor for dumping the order form.

13

BUILDING AND
CUSTOMIZING
PIPELINES

In the Config box, type the path to the dump file. Here's an example:

```
filename=c:\orderdump.log
```

Note that the file path must exist, the file must exist, and the dump file should be accessible for writing to at least the IUSR_<machine_name> account. This will make sure that the pipeline is able to log its actions.

Click the OK button. You may want to give a unique name to the Scriptor to differentiate it from other Scriptor components in the pipeline. Save the pipeline configuration file. The IIS application must be restarted for the PCF changes to take affect.

The next time the pipe is run (checkout.pcf, for example), the order form is dumped. The dump can be used to analyze problems such as discounts not applied, wrong order total, and so on. Figure 13.15 shows an example of an order dump.

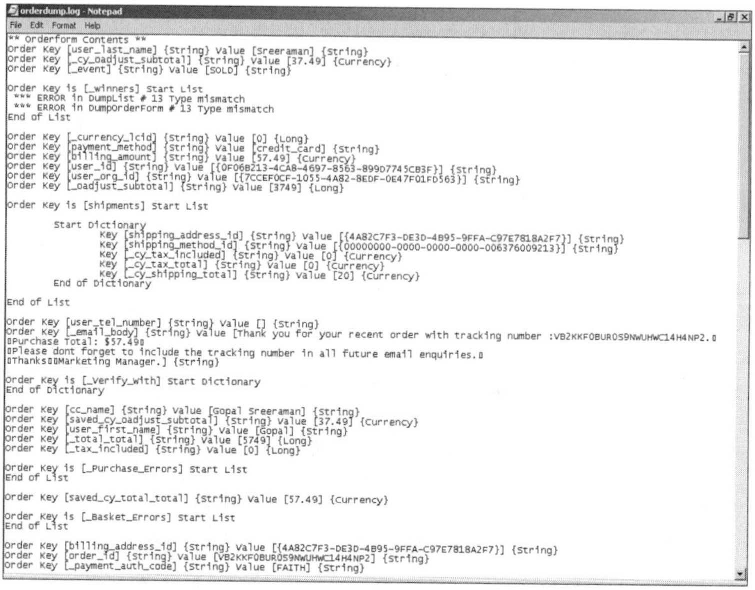

FIGURE 13.15
The order form contents.

Logging Pipeline Execution

Another way of knowing what happens when a pipeline is loaded and executed is to log all the actions of the pipe. Logging has to be enabled for a pipeline object just before the pipe is executed. For example, the `SetLogFile` method should be used for an `MtsTxPipeline` object just before the `Execute` method to enable logging.

In a Commerce Server site, the log folder is specified and logging is enabled in the `InitSitePipelines` routine of the global initialization file `global_siteconfig_lib.asp`:

```
....

dictPipeline.LogFolder = GetRootPath() & "pipeline\logfiles\"

....

If MSCSEnv = DEVELOPMENT Then
        dictPipeline.LoggingEnabled    = TRUE
        dictPipeline.LogsCycled        = False
```

```
ElseIf MSCSEnv = PRODUCTION Then
        dictPipeline.LoggingEnabled   = False
        dictPipeline.LogsCycled       = False
End If
```

. . . .

Most of the OPP pipes are executed from the `RunMtsPipeline` routine defined in `std_pipeline_lib.asp`. There, the following code snippet checks for logging and enables logging before the `OrderGroup` object's `RunPipe` method is called:

```
If MSCSPipelines.LoggingEnabled Then
```

. . . .

```
mscsOrderGrp.LogFile = sPipeLogName
```

. . .

```
End if
```

. . . .

```
iErrorLevel = mscsOrderGrp.RunPipe(sPipeName, g_sPipelineProgID, dictContext)
```

. . . .

Each pipe generates a different log file. A pipeline log file answers a lot of questions, such as when the pipeline started execution, what components were executed, when a component started and ended, the key/value pairs read and written, return values of components, and so on. Figure 13.16 shows part of a log file.

The information in a pipeline log file can sometimes be overwhelming. To help make good sense of it, you could import it into a spreadsheet application such as Microsoft Excel. Then you could remove, modify, and manipulate data according to your analysis needs.

The Micropipe

If we consider pipelines as being gigantic pieces of an assembly-line infrastructure in Commerce Server, there is also a pipeline that is a miniature version. The Micropipe object provided by Commerce Server helps run a single pipeline component from an ASP page, thus avoiding the need to plug in the component and run an entire pipeline.

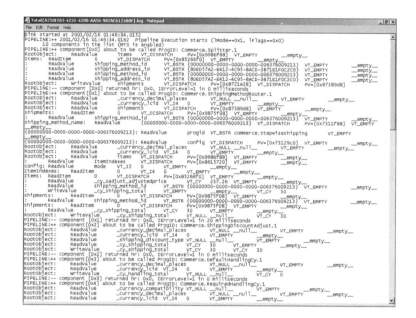

FIGURE 13.16

A pipeline log file.

The Micropipe is instantiated using the Prog ID `Commerce.MicroPipe` in an ASP page. The Order and Context dictionaries are created on the page. The pipeline component to be tested might require values to be configured using its property page. For instance, the VisaDiscount component we developed in this chapter expects a discount percentage and an amount from the property page setting. Because we are not going to use a pipe, and therefore the Pipeline Editor, at all, how do we set the configuration values of the component? This is where the `IPipelineComponentAdmin` interface is needed because it enables setting values from an Active X environment such as ASP. Any pipeline component that implements this interface can be passed values from an ASP page. The `SetConfigData` method of the interface is called on the page.

It is also possible to pass the value to the property directly, which will be demonstrated now.

Here is a sample code listing that shows how the VisaDiscount pipeline component can be tested using the Micropipe:

```
<%

' Create to simulate the necessary Order and Context 'dictionaries.
Set oOrder = Server.CreateObject("Commerce.Dictionary") 'Order
Set oContext = Server.CreateObject("Commerce.Dictionary") 'Context
```

```
' Create an instance of the VISADiscount pipeline component.
Set oVISADiscount = Server.CreateObject("VISADiscount.VISADiscountComp")

'Configure the component with config dictionary

'***You can use SetConfigData...
' Create a dictionary for the configuration parameters
'Set oConfig = Server.CreateObject("Commerce.Dictionary") 'Config
'oConfig("Disc_Percent")=12
'oConfig("Min_Amt")=100
'oVISADiscount.SetConfigData oConfig
'***You can use SetConfigData...

'***OR Set the properties directly AS
oVISADiscount.Disc_Percent = 12
oVISADiscount.Min_Amt = 100

'*** Simulate the order form value
oOrder.Value("_cy_total_total")= 150
' Create an instance of the MicroPipe object.
Set oMicropipe = Server.CreateObject("Commerce.MicroPipe")

' Tell MicroPipe to run the specific component.
oMicropipe.SetComponent oVISADiscount
oMicropipe.SetLogFile("E:\estore\estore\pipeline\visacomp\micropipe.log")
errVal = oMicropipe.Execute(oOrder,oContext,0)

' Check for pipeline errors
If(errVal > 1) Then
    Response.Write "Errors occurred in the pipe. Look at the log file."
Else
    Response.Write "Component executed successfully. Anyway check log file
    ➥for modified values."
End If

' Do clean up here.
Set oOrder = Nothing
Set oContext = Nothing
Set oConfig = Nothing
Set oVISADiscount = Nothing
Set oMicropipe = Nothing

%>
```

Save the preceding code as, say, `micropipe.asp` under the site folder. Run it from a browser to test the component.

13

Ready for Production?

Having developed a pipeline component using VB and tested it using many methods, we are now satisfied with its functionality. It is time to move this pipeline component to production, right? Not so soon—we don't want to move a component developed in VB to a site where millions of users hit the site all at the same time. There are many reasons for this—the main one being the threading capabilities. VB can support, at best, an apartment model, which offers less performance than free-threaded model–based components. In short, an apartment model component waits on a single thread for the COM system to route messages back and forth and synchronize events, whereas free-threaded components can execute on multiple threads at the same time and need not depend on COM to help them with message synchronization.

So is there an alternative?. Yes, Visual C++ can be used to develop free-threaded, small, performance-tuned components that can hold their own in a production environment. What's more, Commerce Server provides you with a wizard to be used with the Active Template Library (ATL) in VC++. This wizard can be used to develop pipeline components that are built for scalability.

Therefore, VB pipeline component using VB and tested it using many should be used to prototype components and test functionality. Ideally, the component should be built with VC++ and moved to production.

Building Pipeline Components with Visual C++

Using Visual C++ to build pipeline components involves much more work compared to building components in VB. The language structure and constructs in VC++ are pretty complex, particularly when working with items such as pointers, variants, COM classes, and so on. Therefore, to start building components for the pipeline using VC++, you need at least a basic understanding of VC++ and COM. Fortunately, the Active Template Library (ATL) has already reduced much of the burden that developers used to undergo.

In spite of the magnitude of the work involved, the ATL Pipeline Component Wizard provided by Commerce Server makes it much easier to build pipeline components. In this section, we will go through, step by step, how to build the VisaDiscount component that we prototyped with Visual Basic.

You need Visual C++ 6.0 in order to use the ATL Pipeline Component Wizard. Make sure you have the latest service pack and any hot fixes, as required for VC++ 6.0.

Similar to the wizard for VB, the ATL Pipeline Component Wizard first has to be registered before it can be used. Use the `regsvr32` command with the path to the `CommerceDLG.dll` file:

```
Regsvr32 "<MSCS Installation Folder>\SDK\Tools\ATL Pipe Wizard\commercedlg.
➥dll"
```

A success message appears, indicating that the DLL is now registered and is available in VC++ (see Figure 13.17).

FIGURE 13.17
Registering the ATL Pipeline Component Wizard.

Creating the Project

The ATL COM AppWizard generates headers, source files, and other resources for the project. First, let's start with creating a new project for the pipeline component. Click File, New from the menu bar in VC++. In the New dialog box, choose ATL COM AppWizard. Name the project OrdLevelDiscount, which stands for the order-level discount the component will provide. Choose a location for the project files to be stored. Keep the box for Win32 platform checked.

The ATL COM AppWizard has only one screen that asks questions! Set the Server Type field to DLL. Choose all the check boxes for supporting MFC and MTS and merging proxy/stubs. Then click the Finish button. The New Project Information box shows you the key files, among others, that will be generated. Click the OK button.

The ATL COM AppWizard takes a few seconds to generate all the files required for the project.

Using the ATL Pipeline Wizard

Now we will generate the files necessary to implement IPipelineComponent and the other interfaces of a pipeline component. From the Insert menu, choose New ATL Object. In the ATL Object Wizard, choose Objects in the Category list. Then select Pipeline Component Object and click the Next button. In the Names tab, type the short name **VisaDisc**. The names for the other files are automatically derived from the short name (see Figure 13.18). Accept those values and go to the Pipeline Component tab in the same dialog box.

In the Pipeline Component tab, choose all the interfaces, such as IPipelineComponent, IPersistStreamInit, and so on. Then click the OK button. The ATL Object Wizard generates the necessary files and skeleton code for implementing these interfaces.

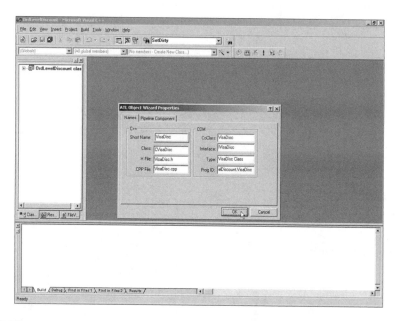

FIGURE 13.18

Generating the files needed for the component.

Inserting the Property Page UI

Next let's insert the configuration property page we need for the VisaDiscount component. We need two edit boxes for capturing discount percentage and minimum order amount, which are required to qualify for the discount. From the Insert menu, choose New ATL Object. Choose Controls in the Category box and then select Property Page from the list of objects. In the ATL Object Wizard properties, enter the short name as **VisaDiscUI**. The *UI* stands for the user interface displayed in the property page. Accept all other values for the names of various files, interfaces, and Prog IDs (see Figure 13.19).

In the Attributes tab, you specify the type of component, such as apartment or free-threaded model, and other COM-related information. Set the Threading Model field to Free Threaded. Leave the other configuration at the default values. Next, navigate to the Strings tab and enter the title as **VisaDiscount Configuration** or something similar. This is the string that will be displayed in the title of the tab in the property page. Now click the OK button.

The wizard inserts an empty dialog box and related files for this interface. Modify the UI to capture the required information, as shown in Figure 13.20.

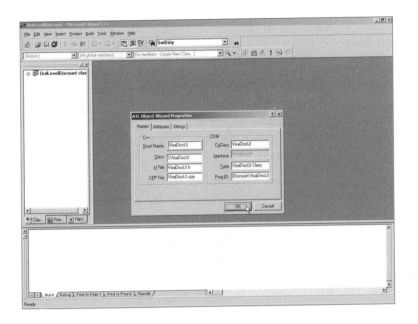

FIGURE 13.19

Generating files to implement the property page.

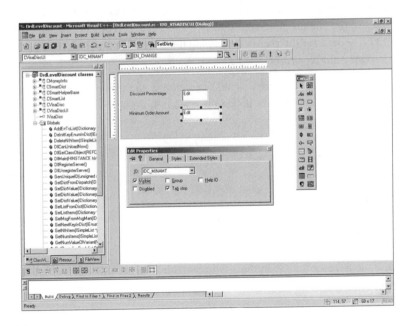

FIGURE 13.20

The property page dialog box resource.

Remember to name the IDs of the edit boxes as IDC_PERCENT and IDC_MINAMT, respectively. Save the changes.

You may now want to take a look at the files generated by the wizards so far. You need to choose View Workspace. In the Class View of the workspace, you can see that two classes, CVisaDisc and CVisaDiscUI, have been created. These classes will implement the interfaces for the component and its property page user interface, respectively. Also note that the custom interface IVisaDisc is the main interface used by a client (in this case, the pipeline object) to access Execute and the other methods.

You can also see from the Globals hierarchy that the wizard has generated methods such as GetDictValue, PutDictValue, and GetMsgFromMsgMan. These functions will be utilized to manipulate the Order and Context dictionaries that we are dealing with in the component.

In the File View, the files in the project are listed. VisaDisc.h and VisaDisc.cpp are the files that contain the definition and implementation code for the component. Similarly, Visa DiscUI.h and VisaDiscUI.cpp are generated for the property page UI of the component. The Resource View will show the dialog box for the property page and the resources for the project.

Writing the Code

We will begin writing code by starting with the Execute function of the IPipelineComponent interface. In most of the wizard-generated code, you will see //TODO comments, indicating that something is to be written for the required functionality. Therefore, it isn't difficult to locate places where code should be written.

First, we need two variables that store discount percentage and minimum amount, respectively. In VisaDisc.h, declare these variables inside the class definition for CVisaDisc:

```
class ATL_NO_VTABLE CVDisc :
    .....
    ......
{
public:
    float fltDiscPercent;
    float fltMinAmt;
.....
....
```

Next, let's write the necessary code in the Execute method to accomplish the functionality of the component.

Fleshing Out IPipelineComponent::Execute

The Execute method is where the order total _cy_total_total should be fetched and compared with fltMinAmt. You are now familiar with the functionality because we have already built the component using VB earlier. If the order total is greater than or equal to the minimum amount, and the user specifies a Visa card for purchase, we calculate the discount applicable and adjust the discount with the order total. The following code shows the Execute method implemented in the VisaDisc.cpp file:

```cpp
STDMETHODIMP CVISADisc::Execute (
                IDispatch*   pdispOrder,
                IDispatch*   pdispContext,
                LONG         lFlags,
                LONG*        plErrorLevel)
{
    LONG lErrorLevel = OPPERRORLEV_SUCCESS; //Start with a feeling of
    ➥success !
    IDictionary *lpdictOrder;                //Pointer to a dictionary
    VARIANT varCyTotalTotal;                 //The store the value in order._
    ➥cy_total_total
    VARIANT varCCType;               //The store the value in order.
    ➥cc_type
    VARIANT varTemp;                         // For conversions between data
    ➥types
    bool    bVISA;                           // VISA card or not

    //For calculating discount amount and adjusted order total.

    double dblOrdTotal=0;
    double dblDiscAmt=0;
    double dblAdjustTotal;

    //Get a pointer to the Order dictionary in lpdictOrder

    if(GetDictFromDispatch(pdispOrder,&lpdictOrder) != S_OK)
            goto cleanUp;

    //Get the value of cc_type

    if(GetDictValue(lpdictOrder,L"cc_type",&varCCType)  != S_OK)
            goto cleanUp;

    //Get the value of _cy_total_total
```

```
    if(GetDictValue(lpdictOrder,L"_cy_total_total",&varCyTotalTotal)  != S_OK)
        goto cleanUp;

    //Change the type of _cy_total_total to double to enable calculations

    if( VariantChangeType(&varCyTotalTotal,&varCyTotalTotal,0,VT_R8) != S_OK)
        goto cleanUp;

    //Change the type of cc_type to bstr to enable comparison

    if( VariantChangeType(&varCCType,&varCCType,0,VT_BSTR) != S_OK)
        goto cleanUp;

    //String in cc_type will be VISA for a VISA card

    BSTR bstrVISA ;
    bstrVISA = SysAllocString(L"VISA");
    if ( !bstrVISA )
        return E_OUTOFMEMORY;

    //Find out if the user specified a VISA card
    bVISA = false;
    int nTemp;
    nTemp=1;

    nTemp = _wcsicmp((const unsigned short*) (bstrVISA),(const unsigned
    ➥short*)(varCCType.bstrVal ));
    if(nTemp == 0 )
    {
        bVISA = true; //The user has given a VISA card to make the purchase
    }
    SysFreeString(bstrVISA);


    //Get the order total as double

    dblOrdTotal = varCyTotalTotal.dblVal ;

    //Check the order total with MinAmt

    if((bVISA) && (dblOrdTotal >= fltMinAmt))
    {
        //Do the calculations

        dblDiscAmt = dblOrdTotal * (fltDiscPercent / 100);
        dblAdjustTotal = dblOrdTotal - dblDiscAmt;
```

```
    //Write the  adjusted order total back to Order._cy_total_total

    varTemp.dblVal  = dblAdjustTotal;
    varTemp.vt = VT_R8;
    if(VariantChangeType(&varTemp,&varTemp,0,VT_CY) != S_OK)
        goto cleanUp;
    if(PutDictValue(lpdictOrder,L"_cy_total_total", varTemp)!= S_OK)
        goto cleanUp;

    //Write the applied Discount Percentage  to Order.disc_pc to be later
➥ used by the reporting ASP page

    varTemp.fltVal  = fltDiscPercent;
    varTemp.vt = VT_R4;
    if(VariantChangeType(&varTemp,&varTemp,0,VT_R4) != S_OK)
        goto cleanUp;
    if(PutDictValue(lpdictOrder,L"disc_pc", varTemp)!= S_OK)
        goto cleanUp;

    //Write the calculated Discount amount to Order.disc_pc to be later
➥used by the reporting ASP page

    varTemp.dblVal  = dblDiscAmt;
    varTemp.vt = VT_R8;
    if(VariantChangeType(&varTemp,&varTemp,0,VT_CY) != S_OK)
        goto cleanUp;
    if(PutDictValue(lpdictOrder,L"ord_disc", varTemp)!= S_OK)
        goto cleanUp;

    }


//Having reached here, we are successful, now do clean up.

    lpdictOrder->Release();
    lpdictOrder = NULL;
    return S_OK;

//Unsuccessful jump here, do cleanup and return the failure code.
cleanUp:
    if(lpdictOrder)
    {
        lpdictOrder->Release();
        lpdictOrder = NULL;
    }
    *plErrorLevel = OPPERRORLEV_FAIL;


}
```

Working with the Property Page

The property page captures the discount percent and minimum amount values. We have already declared the variables fltDiscPercent and fltMinAmt to store these values. However, we need the "get" and "put" methods to work between the property page and the variables. Remember that the property page has values in a Unicode Variant format, but the variables are declared as Float. Therefore, we need to perform conversion before storing or retrieving the values.

To generate the skeleton for the put and get methods, all we need to do is add the properties to the interface IVisaDisc. Right-click IVisaDisc from the Class View and choose Add Property. Set the Property Type field to VARIANT and enter **Disc_Percent** as the name. Then click the OK button to generate the put and get methods (see Figure 13.21).

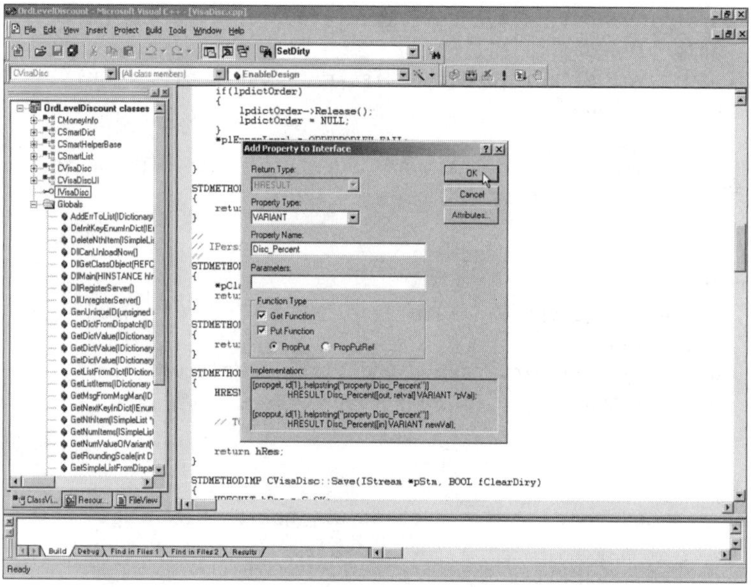

FIGURE 13.21

Creating a property for the interface.

Similarly, add a property for Min_Amt. In VisaDisc.cpp, you should now see the skeleton generated for the put and get methods for both these properties. Flesh them out as follows:

```
STDMETHODIMP CVISADisc::get_Disc_Percent(VARIANT *pVal)
{
    pVal->fltVal = fltDiscPercent;
    pVal->vt = VT_R4;

    return S_OK;
}
```

```
STDMETHODIMP CVISADisc::put_Disc_Percent(VARIANT newVal)
{
    HRESULT hr;
    hr = VariantChangeType(&newVal,&newVal,0,VT_R4);
    if(hr == S_OK)
        fltDiscPercent = newVal.fltVal ;


    return hr;
}

STDMETHODIMP CVISADisc::get_Min_Amt(VARIANT *pVal)
{
    // TODO: Add your implementation code here

    pVal->fltVal = fltMinAmt;
    pVal->vt = VT_R4;

    return S_OK;
}

STDMETHODIMP CVISADisc::put_Min_Amt(VARIANT newVal)
{
    HRESULT hr;
    hr = VariantChangeType(&newVal,&newVal,0,VT_R4);
    if(hr == S_OK)
        fltMinAmt = newVal.fltVal;

    return S_OK;
}
```

You will see in a moment that these are the methods called from the property page to retrieve or save values in the variables. Therefore, conversion of data types between Float and Variant is necessary. `VariantChangeType` is a convenient function for manipulating variants.

The `Activate` Method

When the property page is displayed, its `Activate` method is called by the pipe. You can think of it as similar to an `OnLoad` event handler for a DHTML element. Therefore, we will use the `Activate` method to load the property values using their corresponding "get" methods. The wizard does not generate the skeleton for the `Activate` method. Therefore, we need to insert the prototype in the `VisaDiscUI.h` header file and implementation in the `VisaDiscUI.cpp` file.

In the `VisaDiscUI.h` file, add the following declaration just after the `END_MSG_MAP()` marker in the `CVisaDiscUI` class definition:

```
STDMETHOD (Activate)(HWND hWndParent, LPCRECT pRect, BOOL fModal);
```

In CVisaDiscUI.cpp, implement the Activate method as follows:

```
STDMETHODIMP CVISADiscUI::Activate(HWND hWndParent, LPCRECT pRect, BOOL
➥fModal)
{

        VARIANT varPropVal;

        IPropertyPageImpl<CVDiscUI>::Activate(hWndParent,pRect,fModal);

        //Get a pointer to the component

        CComQIPtr<IVISADisc,&IID_IVISADisc>pVISADisc(m_ppUnk[0]);

        //Retrieve the Discount Percent and load it in the edit box in the
        ➥property page

        pVISADisc->get_Disc_Percent(&varPropVal);
        VariantChangeType(&varPropVal,&varPropVal,0,VT_BSTR);
        SetDlgItemText(IDC_PERCENT,varPropVal.bstrVal);

        //Retrieve the Minimum Amount and load it in the edit box in the
        ➥property page

        pVISADisc->get_Min_Amt(&varPropVal);
        VariantChangeType(&varPropVal,&varPropVal,0,VT_BSTR);
        SetDlgItemText(IDC_MINAMT,varPropVal.bstrVal);

        SetDirty(FALSE);

        return S_OK;
}
```

This is a pretty simple method that fetches the values from the variables using the get_
<variable name> method of the component and loads the edit boxes with these stored values.

So what should be done when values are entered by the user in the edit boxes in the
VISADiscUI property page? The Apply method is called when the OK button is clicked in the
property page for the component. Therefore, we need to write code in the Apply method that
uses—you guessed it!—the put_<variable_name> methods to transfer the values from the UI
to the variables.

The Apply Method

The wizard has already generated a skeleton for this method in the header file VisaDiscUI.h.
Leave only the signature in the header file as

```
STDMETHOD(Apply)(void);
```

Here's the implementation in VisaDiscUI.cpp:

```
STDMETHODIMP CVISADiscUI::Apply(void)
    {
        HRESULT hRes = S_OK;
        VARIANT varDiscPercent;
        VARIANT varMinAmt;
        CComBSTR bstrEditboxVal;

        //Get a pointer to the component

        CComQIPtr<IVISADisc, &IID_IVISADisc>pVISADisc(m_ppUnk[0]);

        //Get the Discount Percent from the dialog box
        GetDlgItemText(IDC_PERCENT,bstrEditboxVal.m_str);
        varDiscPercent.bstrVal = SysAllocString(bstrEditboxVal);
        varDiscPercent.vt = VT_BSTR;

        //Convert the variant to double for storage

        if(VariantChangeType(&varDiscPercent,&varDiscPercent,0,VT_R4) != S_OK)
        {
            MessageBox(L"Discount Percentage must be a valid number",L"Error"
            ➡,MB_OK);
            return E_UNEXPECTED;
        }

        //Get the Minimum Amount from the dialog box

        GetDlgItemText(IDC_MINAMT,bstrEditboxVal.m_str);
        varMinAmt.bstrVal = SysAllocString(bstrEditboxVal);
        varMinAmt.vt = VT_BSTR;

        //Convert the variant to double for storage

        if(VariantChangeType(&varMinAmt,&varMinAmt,0,VT_R4) != S_OK)
        {
            MessageBox(L"Minimum amount must be a valid number.",L"Error",
            ➡MB_OK);
            return E_UNEXPECTED;
        }

        //Call the put functions to store the values in fltDiscPercent and
        ➡fltMinAmt
```

13

BUILDING AND
CUSTOMIZING
PIPELINES

```
pVISADisc->put_Disc_Percent(varDiscPercent);
pVISADisc->put_Min_Amt(varMinAmt);

SetDirty(TRUE);
return S_OK;
}
```

Persisting Values Using `IPersistStreamInit`

You already know that the configuration values entered through the component's property pages are stored along with the pipeline configuration. Therefore, our component could implement the `IPersistStreamInit` methods in order to load and save from a medium. The methods for this interface, such as `InitNew`, `Load`, and `Save`, are already generated in the skeleton. A pointer to `IStream` is passed to these methods for reading and writing to the stream. All we have to do is use the `Read` and `Write` methods of the `IStream` interface to get the job done. Here are the methods in `VisaDisc.cpp`:

```
// IPersistStreamInit Methods
//
STDMETHODIMP CVISADisc::GetClassID(CLSID *pClassID)
{
    *pClassID = GetObjectCLSID();
    return S_OK;
}


STDMETHODIMP CVISADisc::IsDirty(void)
{
    return S_OK;
}


STDMETHODIMP CVISADisc::Load(IStream *pStm)
{
    HRESULT hRes = S_OK;

    pStm->Read(&fltDiscPercent,sizeof(float), NULL);
    pStm->Read(&fltMinAmt,sizeof(float), NULL);
    return hRes;

}


STDMETHODIMP CVISADisc::Save(IStream *pStm, BOOL fClearDiry)
{
    HRESULT hRes = S_OK;

    pStm->Write(&fltDiscPercent,sizeof(float), NULL);
    pStm->Write(&fltMinAmt,sizeof(float), NULL);

    return hRes;
}
```

```
STDMETHODIMP CVISADisc::GetSizeMax(ULARGE_INTEGER *pcbSize)
{

    pcbSize->LowPart  = sizeof(fltMinAmt) + sizeof(fltDiscPercent);
    pcbSize->HighPart = 0;

    return S_OK;
}

STDMETHODIMP CVISADisc::InitNew(void)
{
    // TODO: Add any component initialization

    fltMinAmt = 0;
    fltDiscPercent=0;
    return S_OK;
}
```

The GetSizeMax method is used to set the buffer limit for the object stream.

Supporting IPipelineComponentAdmin

We need to support the IPipelineComponentAdmin interface for accessing values from the dictionary directly from, say, an ASP page, in which case the property page is not used to set or retrieve values. Instead, as you saw in the section "The MicroPipe," earlier, we use the SetConfigData and GetConfigData methods of the component to access the configuration dictionary directly. Here are the two implementations in VisaDisc.cpp:

```
STDMETHODIMP CVISADisc::GetConfigData(IDispatch * * ppDict)
{
if (ppDict == NULL)
        return E_POINTER;

    HRESULT                   hr;
    CComQIPtr<IDictionary>    pdictPtr;

    //Dictionary Keys

    CComBSTR                  bstrDiscPercent = L"DiscPercent";
    CComBSTR                  bstrMinAmt = L"MinAmt";

    //Dictionary Values

    CComVariant               varDiscPercent = fltDiscPercent;
    CComVariant               varMinAmt = fltMinAmt;
```

```
        // Get a pointer to the dictionary
        pdictPtr.CoCreateInstance(L"Commerce.Dictionary");

        //Put values in the dictionary corresponding to key/value pairs
        hr = pdictPtr->put_Value(bstrDiscPercent,varDiscPercent.fltVal);
        if(FAILED(hr))
        {
            return Error(L"An unknown error occurred writing DiscPercent to the
            ➥Dictionary.",GUID_NULL,hr);
        }
        hr = pdictPtr->put_Value(bstrMinAmt,varMinAmt.fltVal);
        if(FAILED(hr))
        {
            return Error(L"An unknown error occurred writing MinAmt to the
            ➥Dictionary.",GUID_NULL,hr);
        }

        return pdictPtr->QueryInterface(IID_IDispatch, reinterpret_cast<void**>
        ➥(ppDict));
}
```

We have modified the skeleton code in VisaDisc.cpp to get the configuration values in the dictionary. Next, the SetConfigData method will set the configuration values from a dictionary passed to it:

```
STDMETHODIMP CVISADisc::SetConfigData(IDispatch * pDict)
{

    CComQIPtr<IDictionary>      pdictPtr;
    //Dictionary Keys

    CComBSTR                    bstrDiscPercent = L"DiscPercent";
    CComBSTR                    bstrMinAmt = L"MinAmt";

    //Dictionary Values

    CComVariant                 varDiscPercent ;
    CComVariant                 varMinAmt ;

    HRESULT                     hr;

    // Performs implicit QI for the proper interface.
    pdictPtr = pDict;

    //Get DiscPercent and store it in fltDiscPercent
    hr = pdictPtr->get_Value(bstrDiscPercent,&varDiscPercent);
```

```
    if(FAILED(hr))
    {
        return Error(L"An unknown error occurred reading 'ConnectionString'
        ➥from the provided Dictionary.",GUID_NULL,hr);
    }

    if (VT_BSTR != varDiscPercent.vt)
    {
        return Error(L"Invalid data type in 'DiscPercent'.", GUID_NULL,E_
        ➥INVALIDARG);
    }

    fltDiscPercent = varDiscPercent.fltVal ;


    //Get MinAmt and store it in fltMinAmt
    hr = pdictPtr->get_Value(bstrMinAmt,&varMinAmt);
    if(FAILED(hr))
    {
        return Error(L"An unknown error occurred reading 'ConnectionString'
        ➥from the provided Dictionary.",GUID_NULL,hr);
    }

    if (VT_BSTR != varMinAmt.vt)
    {
        return Error(L"Invalid data type in 'MinAmt'.",
GUID_NULL,E_INVALIDARG);
    }

    fltMinAmt = varMinAmt.fltVal ;

    return S_OK;


}
```

Implementing `IPipelineComponentDescription`

As a useful embellishment to the component, consider describing what values are read or written by the component. The methods to be implemented for this are `ContextValuesRead` for the
Context dictionary and `ValuesRead` and `ValuesWritten` for the values from the Order dictionary. These values are returned in `SafeArray` pointers. All we need to do in the skeleton code
is modify the input to the `SysAllocString` function to the string we want to be displayed in
the Values Read and Written page for the component.

For example, in the `ContextValuesRead` method, change the string value to this:

```
V_BSTR(pvarT) = SysAllocString(L"<None>");
```

Similarly, for the `ValuesRead` and `ValuesWritten` methods, change the value to this:

```
V_BSTR(pvarT) = SysAllocString(L" _cy_total_total ");
```

Making the Property Page Available

In an earlier section (while building with VB), you saw how `IPipelineComponentAdmin` can be used to launch a separate interface screen for the property page as an alternative to the standard Win32 OLE property page. Here, we will implement the standard Win32 property page using `ISpecifyPropertyPages` to enable the pipeline to show the property page. The method `GetPages` is called to get a pointer to the dialog box, which should be shown as the property page. This method is already implemented by the wizard with enough code; we just need to make minor modifications:

```
STDMETHODIMP CVISADisc::GetPages(CAUUID *pPages)
{
    if (NULL == pPages)
        return E_INVALIDARG;

    pPages->cElems = 1;
    pPages->pElems = (GUID*)CoTaskMemAlloc(1*sizeof(GUID));
    if(!pPages->pElems){
        pPages->cElems = 0;     return E_OUTOFMEMORY;
    }
    memcpy(pPages->pElems, &CLSID_VISADiscUI, sizeof(GUID));

    return S_OK;


}
```

Just uncomment, as per the wizard-generated instructions. Make sure the CLSID is for `VisaDiscUI` in the `memcpy` function.

Code for Registering the Component

Last but not least, we need to register the component and also choose a stage with which the component has affinity. A convenient method with which to do this `UpdateRegistry`. This method already has a good skeleton in `VisaDisc.h`. As is the case in the VB example, the Registry key `Implemented Categories` should contain a reference to the stage with which this component is affiliated. We do this using the method `RegisterCATID` defined in `computil.h`:

```
static HRESULT WINAPI UpdateRegistry(BOOL bRegister)
    {
        HRESULT hr = _Module.UpdateRegistryFromResource(IDR_VISADISC,
        ➥bRegister);
        if (SUCCEEDED(hr))
        {

            // TODO: Add stage affinities here
            hr = RegisterCATID(GetObjectCLSID(), CATID_MSCSPIPELINE_
            ➥COMPONENT);
            hr = RegisterCATID(GetObjectCLSID(), CATID_MSCSPIPELINE_PAYMENT);
        }
        return hr;
    };
```

The IDs of the pipeline stages are defined in the pipe_stages.h file.

Tips on Building the Component

That's it! We now just need to build OrdLevelDiscount.dll using the Build menu. But before you beginning to build the project, make sure the following files are in a directory accessible to the project files (otherwise, it may result in compilation errors):

- commerce.h
- computil.cpp
- Mspu_guids.h
- pipeline.h
- pipecomp.h

These files can be found under the SDK directory:

<MSCS Installation Folder>\SDK

This project may not produce zero errors and zero warnings the very first time you build it, but then that's the case with any complex VC++ project. Patience and perseverance are the other important tools while beginning to work with VC++.

Another SDK resource that's helpful in analyzing the various code elements in an ATL-generated pipeline project is the MinMaxShip component, provided in the SDK directory:

<MSCS Installation Folder>\SDK\Samples\Order Processing

It contains complete project files for use with both VC++ and VB to build the MinMaxShip component. It would be a good exercise to build this component using both tools. Once you

13

BUILDING AND CUSTOMIZING PIPELINES

have successfully built a couple of components, it would then be relatively simple to build new components and functionality.

Summary

Pipelines are a part of the core infrastructure of a Commerce Server site. The unique requirements of a site may often necessitate building or customizing pipeline components. We started this chapter by customizing the Purchase pipeline of Estore to send an e-mail confirmation upon a successful order using the SendSMTP component.

One quick way to insert functionality in a pipeline is to use the Scriptor component. But beyond that, we need a full-fledged component to handle the requirements of performance and complex functionality. Visual Basic is an ideal tool to quickly prototype complex components and test for functionality. Commerce Server provides the VB Pipeline Component Wizard to help implement the required interfaces. After a VB component is tested for functionality, you can port the component to VC++ using the ATL Pipeline Component Wizard. Working with VC++ sometimes requires a lot of effort when you're developing COM objects using ATL, as compared to the effort needed when you're developing in VB.

Regardless of the tool used to develop a component, you may need to debug the component to identify errors and finally certify it for use in production. To analyze execution errors, you need to enable the logging of pipeline execution. This is done using the `SetLogFile` method of a typical pipeline object.

In cases of logical errors, one way to find what the component has done is to dump the Order dictionary using the `dumporder.vbs` script inserted in a Scriptor. Also, to isolate the component and enable quick testing, use the Micropipe object—it can be called from an ASP page, too.

Ultimately, you should see that the custom component does not step on the work of previous components in a pipe and achieves its implementation objectives.

Extending the Business Desk

IN THIS CHAPTER

- **Understanding the Architecture**   442
- **Building a Module**   464

As mentioned earlier in this book, Commerce Server provides business managers with a Web-based site management tool called the Business Desk. Business Desk enables managers to update, analyze, and manage the site from a business point of view. For instance, a discount can be configured quickly and published to the site immediately. Later, an analysis of the impact of the discount on sales or site visits could be determined. All this can be done from the very nontechnical, user-friendly environment of the Business Desk.

Managers most often need to respond to the dynamics of the business environment and have to effect changes quickly. Traditionally, business analysts and managers have depended on the technical members of the team to generate analysis reports or to update business data in the databases. This usually involved having to write SQL queries or custom front-end applications. The people responsible for updating business data had to wait for a long time before attempting to "close the loop" between the customer and the business. With Site Server Commerce Edition 3.0, Microsoft introduced the concept of a separate Web application that would be used by managers to update the site's database. One could securely connect to this IIS application over the Internet using almost any browser and update the database with simple forms designed for a specific purpose. Standard reports were also part of this Web application.

In Commerce Server, this concept has been extended in the form of Business Desk, which is nothing but a Web application on the server that has been designed to be accessed within a specific browser and requires the installation of the Business Desk client. Throughout the previous chapters, we have used the Business Desk to create, modify, and delete various aspects of the site, such as catalogs, campaigns, and users. In this chapter, we will look under the veneer of the Business Desk to understand its architecture and build extensions to the framework.

Understanding the Architecture

When we use the Site Packager to unpack and create an initial site, there is also an option to create a Business Desk for that site. For example, you saw in Chapter 3, "Creating the Site Foundation," that when we unpacked the Retail PuP package to create the Estore site, we could also unpack the RetailBizDesk application to create the EstoreBizDesk site. The Estore site was placed at port 80, whereas the EstoreBizDesk site was installed at port 81. In short, Business Desk is an IIS application used to manage the database of an e-commerce site, which is another IIS application. Each e-commerce site has its own instance of the Business Desk. The Business Desk for a site need not be installed the very first time while a package is being unpacked. The Business Desk application can be added to a site at any time, as required, using the Site Packager. In fact, for an ideal implementation that aims at scalability and security, it would make more sense to install the Business Desk on a separate machine. The commerce site and its business Desk Application don't need to be on the same machine.

Once a Business Desk application is installed for a site, managers first connect to the application using the path

`http://<machine_name>:<port_number>/<BizDesk_Name>`

where `<machine_name>` is the name of the server, `<port_number>` is the port at which the Business Desk is installed, and `<BizDesk_Name>` is the name of the application.

For the Estore example, I used the following path to first connect to the Business Desk for the Estore site:

`http://Ecommsrv:81/EstoreBizDesk`

The page launched is the Business Desk Client Setup page (see Figure 14.1). It asks for a location in which to install the client software. The Business Desk application on the server (port 81, in our example) can be accessed only through its client software installed on a client machine.

FIGURE 14.1
The Business Desk Client Setup page.

Once a location is specified, the installation program installs the required software on the client machine. After the installation is complete, a file with an `.hta` extension can be found under the folder specified for installation. For my installation, I specified the folder `E:\EstoreMgmt`; therefore, I found the file `Estore ECOMMSRV 81.hta` in that folder. The installation program also creates two shortcuts to this HTA file: one on the desktop and one in the Start menu. The business manager can now access the Business Desk for the site at any time by clicking either of the shortcuts from her workstation.

HTML Application

The file extension `.hta` indicates an HTML Application (HTA) file. An HTA exploits the Internet Explorer (IE) 5.5 Document Object Model (DOM) to present the application and

14

EXTENDING THE
BUSINESS DESK

manipulate information. An HTA is simply a browser instance that hides many of the normal browser features, such as the address bar, the toolbar, and the right-click context menu. If you have experience with building client-side interfaces for a Web browser, you already know how IE's DOM, as compared to other browsers, provides a variety of programmable objects that can be used to build a consistent interface across many pages of your Web application. Without these DOM objects and behavior, it is difficult to accomplish certain types of functionality, such as disabling (graying out) a button, similar to what is easily possible with a client/server application.

Remember that Business Desk is a combination of the IIS application on the server and the HTA on the client side. Therefore, whenever we try to access this Web application from a normal browser window, the `default.asp` page will always attempt to install the Business Desk client (the HTA). So, the only way to access the Business Desk is by launching the HTA. If you open the installed HTA file itself in a text editor, among other things, you will notice the following frame defined:

```
<FRAME SRC='http://ecommsrv:81/EstoreBizDesk/bizdesk.asp' SCROLLING='no'
➡APPLICATION='yes'
        STYLE='HEIGHT: 100%; WIDTH: 100%; BORDER: none' BORDER='0' FRAMEBORDER
        ➡='0' FRAMESPACING='0'>
```

In the HTA file on my workstation, the `SRC` attribute of the `FRAME` element points to the `bizdesk.asp` file in the EstoreBizDesk application. It implies that this file is the default page that is launched inside the HTA. `Bizdesk.asp`, in turn, has a couple more frames. One frame is the left navigation bar generated by `navtree.asp`, and the other significant frame in the Business Desk is the one that welcomes the user (`welcome.asp`) the first time (see Figure 14.2).

The Visual Framework

The leftmost frame that `navtree.asp` generates is called the *navigation pane*. The navigation pane contains the navigation menu of categories and modules. A default installation of Business Desk contains the five categories Analysis, Campaigns, Catalogs, Orders, and Users (refer to Figure 14.2). Categories are used to group modules based on the functionality of the modules. Categories can be expanded or collapsed to access the modules under them. For instance, expanding the Campaigns category would reveal several modules that deal with creating, modifying, managing, and publishing campaigns. A *module* is a collection of ASP pages that implements the purpose of the module. To discuss other visual elements in the Business Desk framework, let's expand the Orders category and click the module Data Codes. Figure 14.3 shows some of the different elements in the Business Desk visual framework.

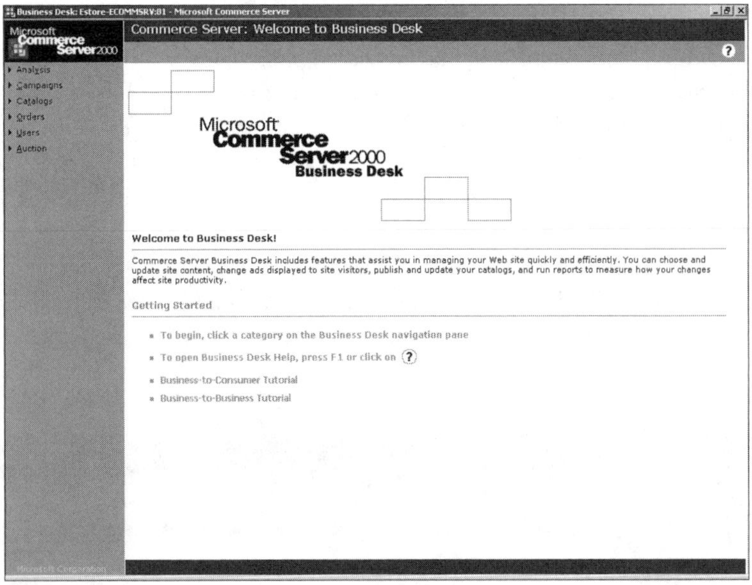

FIGURE 14.2

Two main frames in Business Desk.

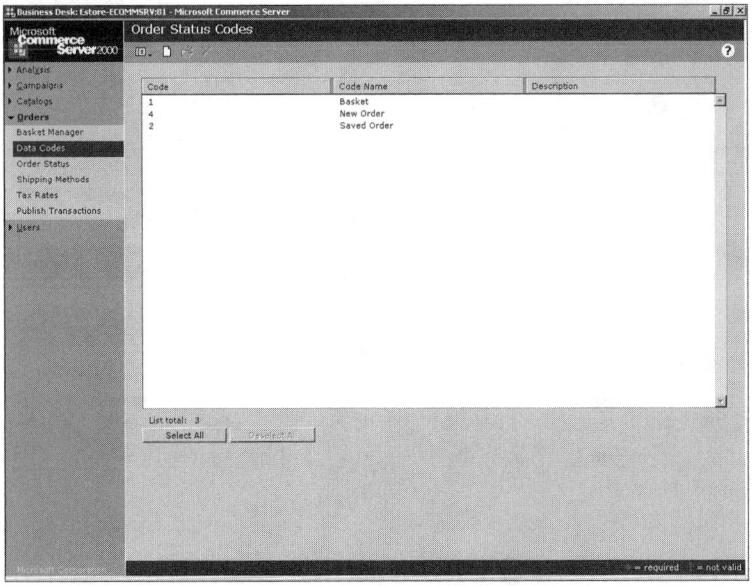

FIGURE 14.3

Example of the Business Desk visual framework.

14

Because you clicked the Data Codes module in the navigation pane, a list of records are fetched and shown in the frame next to the navigation pane. This pane is called the *content pane*, and it is where modules display their interfaces. The pages that modules display in this content pane are divided broadly into two types: list pages and edit pages. A list page is implemented by ASP pages that retrieve records from a data source. In the Data Codes module, the default list of records are fetched from the database table Decode, which stores the status codes of baskets. From a list page, you can choose a record and perform modify or delete operations by choosing the corresponding task icons from the taskbar. Note that the Open Folder icon and the Delete icon are disabled when no record is chosen in the content pane (refer to Figure 14.3). Once a record is chosen, these icons are enabled (see Figure 14.4). Choose a record and click the Open Data Code task icon.

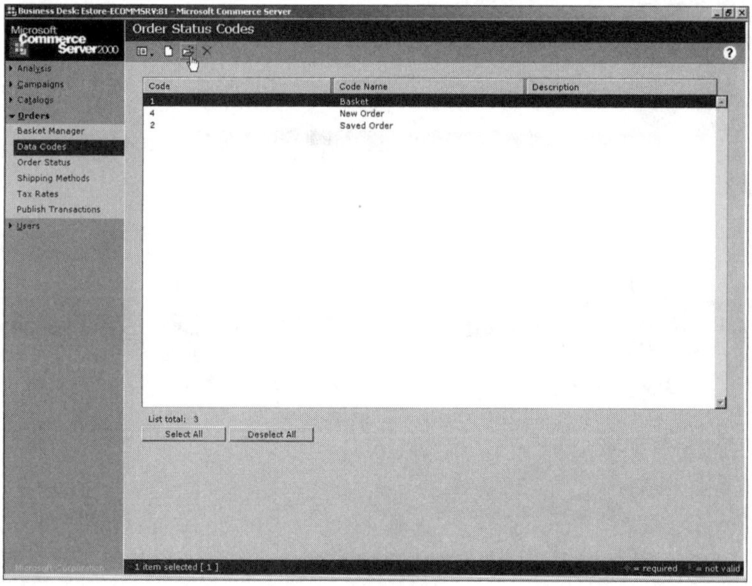

FIGURE 14.4

Opening the edit page for a chosen record.

Once this toolbar button is clicked, the order status code is opened for editing in a separate page (see Figure 14.5). You can see from the figure that I have already used this page to update the description of the status.

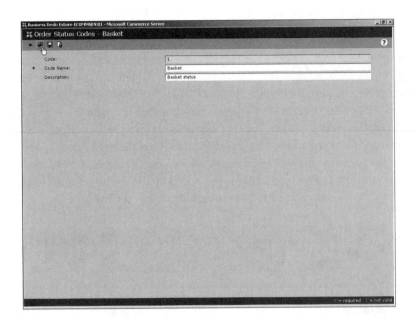

FIGURE 14.5

The edit page in a module.

This is the edit page for the module. It fetches the record chosen from the list page and enables certain fields for modification by the user. You can see that the edit page occupies the entire Business Desk, unlike a list page, which fills up only the content pane next to the navigation pane. This is because the user is not allowed to navigate or return to any other module unless the edit operation is saved or canceled. Similar to the list page, the edit page has its own tasks and corresponding taskbar icons. Typically there is a Save task icon, which saves the changes to the database. There is also a Save and Create New task icon that saves the modified record and launches a form to insert a new record. The two leftmost icons lead to the list page for the module again, which means that the user can go from one task to another only from the list page.

Therefore, clicking the Save and Back to Data Codes List (Alt+K) icon saves the changes to the database and returns to the list page from which the edit page was launched. Observe that if you made changes and clicked the Back to Data Codes List (Alt+B) task icon, you would see an alert asking you to either save the changes or ignore them before returning to the list page. The edit page is generated by an ASP page, and the form changes are posted to a response ASP page that processes the form and updates the database.

14

**EXTENDING THE
BUSINESS DESK**

Once in the list page again, you can take other actions, such deleting an existing order status code or creating a new status code, using the corresponding icons from the taskbar. Each action has its own set of ASP pages to paint the form interface and to process the form to update database tables. Note that the module Data Codes not only deals with order status codes but also enables managers to manage the country and state codes used throughout the site. Therefore, there are other sets of list pages and edit pages corresponding to country and state. Click the View Data Codes List (Alt+V) icon. You will see the other two menus dealing with country/region and state/province codes. Choosing, say, the Country/Region Codes menu brings up the list page for country/region codes, where you can create, modify, or delete these codes. Choosing the State/Province Codes menu brings up the list page for the state/province codes, where the task icons can be used to manage the codes (see Figure 14.6).

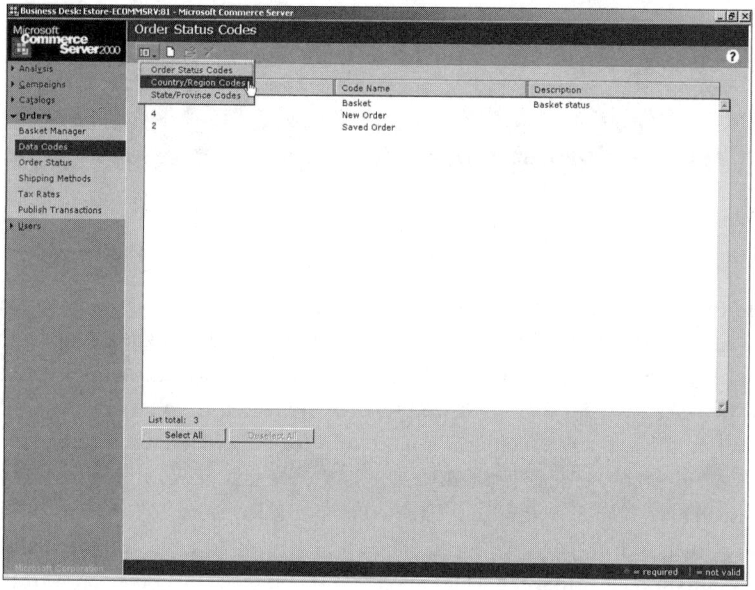

FIGURE 14.6
A task icon with a menu.

This type of a task icon in a module is called *a task menu icon*, as opposed to a *task icon*, which is used for a single action. A task menu icon is used to switch between multiple action pages.

Business Desk Configuration

The five categories and the 23 modules that they contain are provided by Commerce Server. Each module contains various action pages to manage business data in the site's database. How are these categories, modules, and action pages configured? Where are they configured? Is there a standard that third-party developers need to follow in order to create new modules or extend existing modules? You will find the answers to these questions in this section.

A master configuration file exists that defines the available categories and modules. Each module or group of related modules has a module configuration file specifying what categories it belongs to and the action ASP pages that are invoked in clicking the task icons. Both these configuration files are in XML format and are governed by schema definitions. The master configuration file, the individual module configuration files, and the schema definition files are all contained under the `config` directory in the Business Desk installation folder. In my installation, the path to the `config` folder is as follows:

```
E:\EstoreBizDesk\EstoreBizDesk\config
```

The schema that defines a master configuration file is present in the file `bdconfig-schema.xml`. The master configuration file is named `bizdesk.xml` for EstoreBizDesk. Note that the master configuration file could be given any name; it just has to conform to the schema. How does the EstoreBizDesk application then know in which file to look for the master configuration information? It is specified in the `bizdesk.asp` file, which you know is the default page for the Business Desk HTA.

In `bizdesk.asp`, the following statement identifies `bizdesk.xml` as the master configuration file for the application:

```
g_sConfigXML = g_sBDConfigPath & "bizdesk.xml"
```

Loading, parsing, and creating the navigation pane are accomplished by the `LoadObjects()` routine, which is called from `bizdesk.asp`. The routine `LoadObjects()` is actually implemented in `BizDeskObjects.asp`, which is in the `include` folder. The master configuration file is loaded as an `MSXML.DOMDocument` object. Then, this object is parsed to obtain the configuration information for categories, module configurations, modules, and action pages. Several helper routines are defined in `BizDeskObjects.asp` that help in parsing and loading this information into dictionary/simple list objects at the Application scope.

The Master Configuration File

It is now time to open the master configuration file for EstoreBizDesk, `bizdesk.xml`, from the `config` folder and analyze its contents. Here is a listing of the `bizdesk.xml` file provided by Commerce Server:

```
<?xml version = '1.0' encoding='windows-1252' ?>
<config xmlns="x-schema:bdconfig-schema.xml">
```

```xml
<categories>
    <category id="analysis">
        <name>Anal&lt;U&gt;y&lt;/U&gt;sis</name>
        <key>y</key>
        <tooltip>Design, Run, and View Analysis Reports</tooltip>
    </category>
    <category id="campaigns">
        <name>&lt;U&gt;C&lt;/U&gt;ampaigns</name>
        <key>c</key>
        <tooltip>Manage Campaigns</tooltip>
    </category>
    <category id="catalogs">
        <name>Ca&lt;U&gt;t&lt;/U&gt;alogs</name>
        <key>t</key>
        <tooltip>Design and Edit Your Catalogs</tooltip>
    </category>
    <category id="orders">
        <name>&lt;U&gt;O&lt;/U&gt;rders</name>
        <key>o</key>
        <tooltip>Manage Orders</tooltip>
    </category>
    <category id="users">
        <name>&lt;U&gt;U&lt;/U&gt;sers</name>
        <key>u</key>
        <tooltip>Manage Users and Organizations</tooltip>
    </category>
    <category id="auction">
        <name>&lt;U&gt;A&lt;/U&gt;uction</name>
        <key>A</key>
        <tooltip>Manage Auctions</tooltip>
     </category>
    <category id="framework">
        <name>do not delete</name>
        <key>|</key>
        <tooltip>do not delete - used by framework</tooltip>
    </category>
</categories>
<moduleconfigs>
    <moduleconfig id="analysis.xml" category="analysis"/>
    <moduleconfig id="marketing_cmanager.xml" category="campaigns"/>
    <moduleconfig id="catalogs_designer.xml" category="catalogs"/>
    <moduleconfig id="catalogs_editor.xml" category="catalogs"/>
    <moduleconfig id="catalog_sets.xml" category="catalogs"/>
    <moduleconfig id="baskets.xml" category="orders"/>
    <moduleconfig id="application.xml" category="orders"/>
    <moduleconfig id="orders.xml" category="orders"/>
```

```
        <moduleconfig id="shipping_methods.xml" category="orders"/>
        <moduleconfig id="tax.xml" category="orders"/>
        <moduleconfig id="refreshcache.xml" category="orders"/>
        <moduleconfig id="users.xml" category="users"/>
        <moduleconfig id="organizations.xml" category="users"/>
        <moduleconfig id="profiles.xml" category="users"/>
        <moduleconfig id="auction.xml" category="auction"/>
        <moduleconfig id="bdmaster.xml" category="framework"/>
    </moduleconfigs>
</config>
```

From this file, you can see that the following tag indicates that the XML format conforms to the master schema defined in the `bdconfig-schema.xml` file:

```
<config xmlns="x-schema:bdconfig-schema.xml">
```

Also from the file, it is clear that the categories that appear in the Business Desk navigation pane are those defined under the `<categories>` tag. Each category is defined within a `<category>` tag. For instance, the category Order has a category tag with the ID `"orders"`:

```
<category id="orders">
```

The `<name>` tag indicates what will be displayed in the navigation pane. In this case, the following element tells the Business Desk framework to display Orders with the letter *O* underlined:

```
<name>&lt;U&gt;O&lt;/U&gt;rders</name>
```

The next tag, `<key>`, makes "O" the keyboard shortcut (Alt+O) for accessing the module:

```
<key>o</key>
```

The following tag, `<tooltip>`, helps display tooltip information when the cursor is hovering over the module name:

```
<tooltip>Manage Orders</tooltip>
```

Of course, the closing `</category>` tag needs to be present to make the XML well formed. Finally, the `<categories>` tag is closed by the corresponding `</categories>` tag. All the XML must be well formed for Business Desk to read the file successfully.

Continuing with the file, we see the `<moduleconfigs>` tag section. This section defines the various modules grouped under each of the categories. The modules themselves are defined in separate module configuration files, which are named according to the purpose of the modules. One XML file could be used to define many modules, or each module could be defined in individual files. For example, the module Data Codes is defined in the module configuration file `application.xml`. More than one module can be defined in a single module configuration file.

What these modules have in common is that they are grouped under the specific category (say, Orders) by the following tag:

```
<moduleconfig id="application.xml" category="orders"/>
```

If you want to know more about the XML format for the master configuration file, you can open the bdconfig-schema.xml file in a text editor and browse through the definitions.

Module Configuration File

Open the module configuration file application.xml, from the config folder, in a text editor and turn off the Word Wrap feature. From the following tag found in the file, we know that this XML file conforms to a schema:

```
<config xmlns="x-schema:bdmodule-schema.xml">
```

Two main sections are contained in the <config> tags. One is the <actions> section, and the other is the <modules> section. The <actions> section contains individual <action> tags, representing each action ASP page along with the taskbar for that page. For instance, the first <action> tag specifies the ASP page that performs the action of listing records:

```
<action id='application/datacodes_list.asp?type=1' helptopic='cs_ft_orders
➥_CPUS.htm'>
    <name>Data Codes</name>
    <tooltip>Manage Data Codes</tooltip>
    <tasks>
        <task icon='taskviewmenu.gif' id='view' type='menu'>
                <postto action='application/datacodes_list.asp?type=1' formname
                ➥='selectform'>Order Status Codes</postto>
                <postto action='application/datacodes_list.asp?type=2' formname
                ➥='selectform'>Country/Region Codes</postto>
                <postto action='application/datacodes_list.asp?type=3' formname
                ➥='selectform'>State/Province Codes</postto>
                <name>&lt;U&gt;V&lt;/U&gt;iew</name>
            <key>v</key>
                <tooltip>View Data Code Lists</tooltip>
         </task>
        <task icon='tasknew.gif' id='new'>
                <goto action='application/datacodes_edit.asp?type=1'/>
                <name>&lt;U&gt;N&lt;/U&gt;ew</name>
            <key>n</key>
                <tooltip>New Data Code</tooltip>
        </task>
        <task icon='taskopen.gif' id='open'>
            <postto action='application/datacodes_edit.asp?type=1' formname
            ➥='selectform' />
                <name>&lt;U&gt;O&lt;/U&gt;pen</name>
```

```
            <key>o</key>
                <tooltip>Open Data Code</tooltip>
        </task>
    <task icon='taskdelete.gif' id='delete'>
        <postto action='application/datacodes_list.asp?type=1' formname
        ➥='selectform' />
            <name>&lt;U&gt;D&lt;/U&gt;elete</name>
        <key>d</key>
            <tooltip>Delete Data Code</tooltip>
        </task>
    </tasks>
</action>
```

The <action> tag has id and helptopic attributes associated with it. The id attribute of the
<action> tag is the ASP page that gets called. In this case, the ASP page is datacodes_
list.asp, called with a query string type=1. This ASP page is stored under the folder
application at the root of the Business Desk installation folder. The helptopic attribute is
used to specify a help file that will be launched when the user clicks the Help icon while at
this page. If nothing is specified for the helptopic tag, the default Business Desk help topics
are shown when the Help icon is clicked. The <name> and <tooltip> tags specify what should
be shown in the navigation pane and hovering on the cursor, respectively.

The <tasks> section contains individual tasks and associated action pages for the module.
Each task is defined by the <task> tag. The <task> tag has attributes for the icon to be displayed in the taskbar, the ID for the task, and the type of the icon. The tag

```
<task icon='taskviewmenu.gif' id='view' type='menu'>
```

means that the icon taskviewmenu.gif is shown in the taskbar for this task. Commerce Server
has a collection of icons for commonly executed tasks under the folder assets, at the root of
the Business Desk installation folder. Extensions should use similar icons for similar tasks to
maintain consistency across the Business Desk modules.

The second attribute of the <task> tag is id, which is used to identify this task. The value
'view' signifies that the action pages are going to be list pages that are basically for viewing
(read-only) purposes. The attribute type is used to specify whether this task icon should show
a menu of options. A task icon of type 'menu' will show a drop-down list of multiple options,
which we have discussed for this module (refer to Figure 14.6).

In the Data Codes module, this task menu icon has three options. The action page ASP URL
varies, depending on which option the user chooses, as defined by the three <postto> tags:

```
<postto action='application/datacodes_list.asp?type=1' formname='selectform'>
➥Order Status Codes</postto>

<postto action='application/datacodes_list.asp?type=2' formname='selectform'>
➥Country/Region Codes</postto>
```

```
<postto action='application/datacodes_list.asp?type=3' formname='selectform'>
➥State/Province Codes</postto>
```

In the Data Codes module, the same ASP page, `datacodes_list.asp`, is used for processing all three items. Only the query string is modified, depending on needs to be fetched. If the user chooses Order Status Codes from the menu, the ASP page is invoked with the parameter `type=1`. Similarly, for Country/Region Codes, the type is 2, and for State/Province Codes, the type is sent as 3. Incidentally, Commerce Server allows up to 30 menus for an icon. The `<postto>` tag basically posts the form specified in the *formname* attribute, along with the query string attributes. Every task has a `<postto>` or a `<goto>` element to transfer control to an ASP page. The other elements in this "view" task are the `<name>`, `<key>`, and `<tooltip>` tags, whose purpose by now must be obvious.

At the end of the file, the `<task>` tag is closed by the corresponding `</task>` element, terminating the "view" task. You can see from the file that other tasks are defined for new, open, and delete tasks, along with their corresponding icons. Following the closing `</tasks>` tag we have the closing `</action>` tag. This terminates the various task icons and associated action pages while the list page for Order Status is shown.

Similarly, separate `<action>` tags are defined for the list pages for country/region and state/province codes. Therefore, the first set of three `<action>` elements corresponds to the list pages of the three codes (Order, Country, and State) in the database.

The next set of three `<action>` elements define the edit pages for the Data Codes module. Again, the action page used for all the codes is the same file, `datacodes_edit.asp`, with the `querystring` parameter type specifying which code (Order, Country, or State) is being edited. The icons and tasks in these `<action>` elements correspond to the edit page task icons (refer to Figure 14.5):

- Back to Data Codes List
- Save and Back to Data Codes List
- Save Data Code and Save
- Create New Data Code

For example, the task icons and actions for the edit page of Order Status is defined by the following `<action>` element:

```
<action id='application/datacodes_edit.asp?type=1'
        helptopic='cs_ft_orders_CPUS.htm'>
    <name>Data Code Properties</name>
    <tooltip>View Data Code Properties</tooltip>
```

```
<tasks>
    <task icon='taskback.gif' id='back'>
        <postto action='application/datacodes_list.asp?type=1' formname=
        ➡'backform' />
        <name>&lt;U&gt;B&lt;/U&gt;ack</name>
        <key>b</key>
          <tooltip>Back to Data Codes List</tooltip>
    </task>
    <task icon='tasksaveback.gif' id='saveback'>
        <postto action='application/datacodes_edit.asp?type=1' formname=
        ➡'saveform' />
        <name>Bac&lt;U&gt;k&lt;/U&gt;</name>
        <key>k</key>
        <tooltip>Save and Back to Data Codes List</tooltip>
    </task>
      <task icon='tasksave.gif' id='save'>
        <postto action='application/datacodes_edit.asp?type=1' formname=
        ➡'saveform' />
        <name>&lt;U&gt;S&lt;/U&gt;ave</name>
        <key>s</key>
        <tooltip>Save Data Code</tooltip>
    </task>
     <task icon='tasksavenew.gif' id='savenew'>
        <postto action='application/datacodes_edit.asp?type=1' formname=
        ➡'saveform' />
        <name>Save &lt;U&gt;N&lt;/U&gt;ew</name>
        <key>n</key>
        <tooltip>Save and Create New Data Code</tooltip>
    </task>
    </tasks>
</action>
```

At the end of the `<action>` elements for both list and edit pages, the `<modules>` section is defined as follows:

```
<modules>
        <module id='application/datacodes_list.asp?type=1'>
            <name>Data Codes</name>
            <tooltip>Manage Data Codes</tooltip>
        </module>
</modules>
```

The `id` attribute of the `<module>` element points to the default action page invoked when the user clicks the module in the navigation pane. In this case, the action page URL is `'application/datacodes_list.asp?type=1'`, which is nothing but the list page for Order

Status. This is the reason why when the Data Codes module is clicked in the navigation page, order status codes are listed.

In our current discussion, we have only a single module, Data Codes, defined in this file (application.xml). As I have already stated, a single file can contain more than one module as well as the necessary action elements for the defined modules. One good example of such a file is analysis.xml, which defines three modules—Reports, Completed Reports, and Segment Viewer—in the same file.

To know more about the XML schema for a module configuration file, you can open the file bdmodule-schema.xml, located in the config directory.

The List Page

Now that you understand the Business Desk framework and the master and module configurations, we can now drill deep into those action pages that actually do the work of presenting interfaces and processing user input. We will start with the list page for data codes, datacodes_list.asp.

First, you need to understand that interface elements such as forms, text boxes, drop-down boxes, and so on are not designed as the usual HTML elements. Instead, they are IE 5.5 behaviors that are used to implement functionality. These behaviors are called HTML Components (HTCs) and are used to provide ready-made and consistent interfaces to display and manipulate data. Commerce Server provides the following standard HTCs:

- editField
- editSheet
- listBox
- listSheet
- listEditor
- expressionBuilder
- queryBuilder
- dynamicTable
- treeView

If you have worked with the DOM of IE, you will already know that each DHTML control has its own set of methods, properties, events, and validation rules. For example, you can implement a routine to handle the OnClick event of a command button element, change the text color on the button, and so on. The HTCs serve a similar purpose and come as prebuilt DHTML scriptlets with all these characteristics.

XML Data Islands

An HTC can be considered a package in which the required data types, events, properties, and methods are built in. Unlike an HTML element, an HTC is not used directly on the page as an element. Instead, HTCs are behaviors that are instantiated by a DHTML element, usually the DIV element, like this:

```
<DIV CLASS="editField">
```

The DIV element is called the *container* of the HTC. The data to be displayed in these HTCs should come from an XML *data island*, which is data defined in an XML format as shown here:

```
<XML id="dataIslandID">
    XML formatted data here...
</XML>
```

The data in the data island is generated by the ASP page by converting a retrieved ADO recordset into the required XML format. In our Order Status list page, the XML data island on the page sent to the browser would look like this:

```
<xml id='lsCodesData'>
<document recordcount="3">
<record>
<i_Type>1</i_Type>
<i_Code>1</i_Code>
<u_Name>Basket</u_Name>
<u_Description>Basket status</u_Description>
<g_UserIDChangedBy>{0F979C06-F176-4C2A-8D8F-84643BC7F974}</g_UserIDChangedBy>
<d_DateLastChanged>2/3/2001 1:44:28 PM</d_DateLastChanged>
<d_DateCreated>11/9/2000 6:55:39 PM</d_DateCreated>
</record>
<record>
<i_Type>1</i_Type>
<i_Code>4</i_Code>
<u_Name>New Order</u_Name>
<u_Description/>
<g_UserIDChangedBy>{348EF1EB-A778-42BA-AB80-2AC1497C1A2C}</g_UserIDChangedBy>
<d_DateLastChanged>11/9/2000 6:55:39 PM</d_DateLastChanged>
<d_DateCreated>11/9/2000 6:55:39 PM</d_DateCreated>
</record>
<record>
<i_Type>1</i_Type>
<i_Code>2</i_Code><u_Name>Saved Order</u_Name><u_Description/>
<g_UserIDChangedBy>{726A1213-0234-4A7E-A72D-308EBF4FC31F}</g_UserIDChangedBy>
<d_DateLastChanged>11/9/2000 6:55:39 PM</d_DateLastChanged>
<d_DateCreated>11/9/2000 6:55:39 PM</d_DateCreated>
```

14

EXTENDING THE
BUSINESS DESK

```
</record>
</document>
</xml>
```

This is an XML representation of the database records. Now how does the HTC know about the data in the data island and use it to display? The container will have an attribute pointing to the data-island on the page:

```
<DIV CLASS="editField" DataXML= "dataIslandID" >
```

The dataIslandID value of the XML data island in the preceding listing is lsCodesData, standing for the status codes of a basket retrieved from the database.

Metadata Island

Similar to a data island, a *metadata island* is generated for each HTC, depending on the type used in the page. The XML metadata island contains information that allows the HTC to choose data to display from the data island and configuration information specific to the HTC. In order for the HTC to have access to this XML metadata island, the container element should have the attribute to include the metadata island's ID, too:

```
<DIV CLASS="editField" DataXML= "dataIslandID" MetaXML= "meta-dataIslandID">
```

This piece of XML is also produced by the ASP file that generates the list page (in our case, datacodes_list.asp). The metadata island that's generated is shown here (note that meta-dataIslandID is lsCodesMeta in this example):

```
<xml id='lsCodesMeta'>
<listsheet>
<global curpage='1' pagesize='20' recordcount='3' selection='multi' />
<columns>
<column id='i_code' width='25'>Code</column>
<column id='u_name' width='25'>Code Name</column>
<column id='u_description' width='25'>Description</column>
</columns>
<operations>
<newpage formid='sortform'/>
<sort formid='sortform'/>
<delete formid='selectform'/>
</operations>
</listsheet>
</xml>
```

The preceding metadata information is for the listSheet HTC, as specified by the `<listsheet>` element. Further, certain listSheet-specific configuration information, such as page size and multiple-select, is specified in the `<global>` tag. The column IDs i_code, i_name, and u_description are the mappings of the data columns retrieved from the data island to their display label names (Code, Code Name, and Description, respectively).

The data islands, the container DIV element, and the HTC components are delivered to the browser from the generating ASP page.

Action Page Overview

In order to show the list of records in the content pane in the Business Desk HTA, the following steps are performed in an action page (ASP):

1. Retrieve the records in a RecordSet object from the database using ADO by the ASP page on the server.

2. The RecordSet object is converted to an XML data island by the ASP page using routines defined in include files.

3. Generate an XML metadata island specific to the data island and the HTC to be used.

4. Create a DHTML element (typically DIV) in the HTML part of the page with CLASS pointing to the required HTC. The DataXML and MetaXML attributes of the DIV tag should point to the corresponding data islands on the page.

Action Page Details

A few include files need to be included in all the action pages in the Business Desk. These files are present under the include directory in the root installation folder for the Business Desk instance. The BDHeader.asp file just sets the content header, expiry, and buffer characteristics of the HTML stream using the Response object. The BizDeskUtil.asp file is used to include a number of utility files such as DBUtil.asp, ASPUtil.asp, and ActionPageUtil.asp. All these include files contain the necessary helper routines needed by various action pages of the Business Desk. More specific include files need to be added, depending on the purpose of a module. For example, datacodes_list.asp includes application_strings.asp and application_utils.asp, which are specific to this module and are therefore stored under the application/include folder.

Retrieving the Recordset

In the datacodes_list.asp file, a call is made to the routine ProcessListForm(), which is defined in the same file. Remember that this ASP file is called the Data Codes module with a query string parameter type=1 is clicked, meaning we want to list the Order Status codes saved in the database table Decode. The call to the routine BuildDataCodesQuery() builds the SQL query needed to retrieve records from the Decode table. The routine BuildDataCodes Query() is defined in the application_util.asp file, located under the application/include folder. The actual SQL query for retrieving order status codes is built as follows:

```
BuildDataCodesQuery = "Select * from Decode where i_type = 1 ORDER BY "
➥& sOrderBy
```

Here, sOrderBy is the string "u_name_ASC".

In the same routine, you can see how queries for retrieving other status codes (Country and State) are built. Once an SQL query is built, the routine GetRecordset() is called to execute the query and fetch a RecordSet object corresponding to the results. The routine GetRecordset() is defined in application_util.asp.

The GetRecordset() routine sets the CommandText property of an ADODB.Command object to the built SQL query, as follows:

```
g_oCmd.CommandText = sQuery
```

It's obvious that the ADODB Connection and Command objects should have already been defined at a global scope. That's exactly the case—these are defined in the included file DBUtil.asp in the global variables g_oConn and g_oCmd. The Connection and Command objects are gotten by using the routines oGetADOConnection and oGetADOCommand, respectively, which are defined in DBUtil.asp. These functions are actually called by the included file application_util.asp.

Next, an ADO recordset is created by the following statement:

```
Set rs = Server.CreateObject("ADODB.Recordset")
```

Finally, the SQL query is executed and a recordset is returned, as shown here:

```
With rs
    .CursorLocation = AD_USE_CLIENT
    .open g_oCmd,, AD_OPEN_KEYSET, AD_LOCK_PESSIMISTIC
End With
```

Note that all the database-related constants, such as AD_USE_CLIENT and AD_LOCK_PESSIMISTIC, are defined in DBUtil.asp.

ADO to XML

After the ADO recordset is retrieved, the recordset is converted into XML format and stored in the global variable g_xmlCodeListData. The routines used to do the conversion are defined in DBUtil.asp:

- xmlGetXMLFromRS
- xmlGetXMLFromQuery
- xmlGetXMLFromRSEx
- xmlGetXMLFromQueryEx

All these routines can be called from the server-side ASP page, and the resulting XML data island is written onto the downloaded client-side HTML page. Any ASP page can use these routines to generate data islands because the converted format will be the same—ADO to XML. The data island is therefore common to all HTCs. In our example, the routine xmlGetXMLFromRSEx is used to get the XML data for the data island. The routines with "Ex" in their names are used to control the number of records converted to XML. Using the routines that don't have the "Ex" in their names will result in an XML Document element populated with all the records in the ADO recordset.

However, the metadata island is unique because it describes the data in the data island and also gives configuration information unique to the HTC being used on the generated page. Therefore, generating the metadata island is unique to each module. Hence, for the Data Codes module, we have the routine GetXMLCodeListMeta() defined in application_util.asp. The generated XML data island is stored in the global ASP variable g_xmlCodeListMeta.

Both the XML data islands are stored in the global variables in the form of an XMLDOMElement object. Therefore, the purpose of the ProcessListForm() routine is to generate the data islands and store them in the ASP variables.

The HTML content to be delivered to the browser starts at this point in datacodes_list.asp, as shown here:

```
<HTML>
<HEAD>
<LINK REL='stylesheet' TYPE='text/css' HREF='../include/bizdesk.css' ID=
➥'mainstylesheet'>
</HEAD>

<BODY SCROLL='NO'>

<!— #INCLUDE FILE = "./include/application_select.vbs" —>

<% InsertTaskBar g_sTitleText, g_sStatusText %>

<SCRIPT LANGUAGE="VBScript">
...scripts for client-side operations are written here...
</SCRIPT>

<xml id='lsCodesMeta'>
        <%= g_xmlCodeListMeta %>
</xml>

<xml id='lsCodesData'>
        <%= g_xmlCodeListData %>
```

```
</xml>

<DIV ID="bdcontentarea">
    <DIV ID='lsCodes' CLASS='listSheet' STYLE='MARGIN:20px; HEIGHT:80%'
        DataXML='lsCodesData'
        MetaXML='lsCodesMeta'
        LANGUAGE='VBScript'
        OnRowSelect='OnSelectRow()'
        OnRowUnselect='OnUnSelectRow()'
        OnAllRowsUnselect='OnUnSelectAllRows()'
        OnAllRowsSelect='OnSelectAllRows()'>
        <%= L_LoadingList_Text%>
    </DIV>
</DIV>
.....

</BODY>
</HTML>
```

Most of the ASP pages in Business Desk have a very similar format to the one shown here. Hence, a couple items should be noted from this page. It is necessary to link the style sheet used across Business Desk modules as defined in `bizdesk.css`. In case the look and feel of an instance of Business Desk needs to be modified, the changes have to be made to the style sheet to maintain consistency among modules of that instance. Another notable piece of client interface–generating code is the call to the routine `InsertTaskBar`. This routine inserts the proper taskbar for a list page. The `InsertTaskBar` routine should be used while generating a list page because it keeps the navigation pane visible. On the other hand, edit pages should use the routine `InsertEditTaskbar` to prepare the taskbar because this routine hides the navigation pane and makes the edit page occupy the entire workspace. Both these routines are defined in the file `ActionPageUtil.asp`, found in the `include` folder at the EstoreBizDesk root folder.

You have already seen the data islands on the generated result page sent to the browser in the section "XML Data Islands."

Edit Page

An edit page has a framework very similar to what we have discussed so far for a list page, except for a few obvious differences. An edit page allows certain data fields to be modified and saved. Also, the page occupies the entire workspace, and the taskbars are different. The edit page for the Data Codes module is generated by `datacodes_edit.asp`. Here is a snippet from the HTML portion of that file:

```
<HTML>
<HEAD>
<LINK REL='stylesheet' TYPE='text/css' HREF='../include/bizdesk.css' ID=
```

```
➥'mainstylesheet'>

<SCRIPT LANGUAGE = 'VBSCRIPT'>
....

</SCRIPT>
</HEAD>
<BODY SCROLL=no LANGUAGE="VBScript" ONLOAD="esDataCodes.focus()">
    <% InsertEditTaskBar g_sTitleText , g_sStatusText %>

    <xml id='esMeta'>
        <%= g_xmlCodeEditMeta %>
    </xml>

    <xml id='esData'>
        <%= g_xmlCodeEditData %>
    </xml>

    <FORM ID='saveform' METHOD='POST' ONTASK='onSave'>
        <INPUT TYPE='hidden' ID='mode' NAME='mode'>
        <INPUT TYPE='hidden' ID='key' NAME='key'>
        <INPUT TYPE='hidden' ID='group' NAME='group'>

        <DIV ID="editSheetContainer" CLASS="editPageContainer">
            <DIV ID='esDataCodes'
                CLASS='editSheet'
                MetaXML='esMeta'
                DataXML='esData'
                LANGUAGE="VBScript"
                ONCHANGE='setDirty("<%= L_SaveConfirmationDialog_Text%>")'
                  ONREQUIRE='setRequired("")'
                ONVALID='setValid("")'>
                <%= L_LoadingProperties_Text%>
            </DIV>
        </DIV>
    </FORM>

    <FORM ID='backform' METHOD='POST'>
    </FORM>

</BODY>
</HTML>
```

Sure enough, the taskbar is generated by the InsertEditTaskBar routine, as is required for an edit page. The variables g_xmlCodeEditMeta and g_xmlCodeEditData hold the XML-formatted data islands for metadata and data, respectively. Next, note that the editSheet HTC is contained in a DIV element, which is in turn wrapped in a FORM element. The form is posted to the response ASP page as specified in the module configuration file; therefore, there is no ACTION attribute specified for the form. The editSheet HTC uses the configuration and data islands to display the fetched record to the user. Also note that an event handler is defined for the ONCHANGE event of the HTC, in case something is changed in the form before the user saves the changes.

Securing Modules

Business Desk deals with different aspects of managing a site. The sales manager might update discounts and product information. A marketing person might deal solely with private shopper information. Therefore, it is sometimes necessary that certain people have access to certain modules only and not everything. This security can be implemented if the module is available only to specific users or made unavailable to specific users. A module has many actions, but a particular action is made the default. This action is the one that is triggered when the module is clicked in the navigation pane. This action is called the *entrypoint* to the module and is typically a task whose ASP action page is a list page. If we make the entry page inaccessible to a user, the module itself will not be displayed by Business Desk.

This method of security is achieved by modifying the ACL changes to the file in the Windows file system. For example, datacodes_list.asp is the entry page for the Data Codes module. You can right-click the file in Windows Explorer and navigate to the property page. In the Security tab, you could deny or allow access to this file to groups or individual users on the system. Therefore, when the file is not accessible to a user, the module itself is not available to the user in Business Desk.

Building a Module

At this point, I believe you have enough knowledge to put together a new module in the Business Desk for Estore. Let's assume that Estore has an officer responsible for processing and shipping orders. Now recollect that at the end of the shopping cycle, the user gets an order confirmation with the friendly order number on the site. At this point in time, the order is saved with an order_status_code value of 4 (New Order) in the OrderGroup database table. The officer responsible for the orders after this stage should be able to update order_status_code. Traditionally, you would build from scratch a couple of ASP pages to update the table, put these pages on a separate Web site, and give access to the site only to the responsible person. But with the availability of the Business Desk infrastructure, it would be relatively easy to build a module to handle this requirement. Furthermore, this module would be just like any other Business Desk module, thus providing the same consistency visually and operationally.

Design Decisions

The business analysis team of Estore finalizes a decision that there be two custom status codes for orders. One is called *Processed*, indicating that the order information is processed successfully and is waiting to be shipped. The second status is called *Shipped*, to indicate that the order has been shipped successfully. Also, the details available to the individual who is updating the order are just the order number and order status code. The technical team has decided to create a new category and a module under it instead of modifying an existing module (say, Order Status). This decision would make it easy to maintain custom modules as well as share custom scripts. Therefore, the new category is simply called Custom, and the module is named Update Order. With this information in hand, we can go ahead with building the module. Here are the steps required, in brief, to accomplish our objective:

1. Add the required custom order status codes to the database.

2. Create a folder to hold action pages (ASP) for the module.

3. Create a module configuration file to define the tasks, actions, and thumbnail images that will serve as taskbar icons for this module.

4. Update the master configuration file for displaying the new category and the new module under this category.

5. Create the required list and edit action pages in the newly created folder.

6. Restart the Business Desk IIS application so that the configuration files are read again.

7. Modify the action pages (ASP files) until the desired functionality is reached and then modify the module configuration file as needed.

Inserting Order Status Codes

In step 1, we need to insert the order status codes corresponding to the statuses Processed and Shipped. Commerce Server has already provided a Business Desk module called Data Codes to update these status codes. Using the Data Codes module found under the Orders category, insert two new data codes for the order status with the information shown in Table 14.1.

Table 14.1   New Order Status Codes

Code	Code Name	Description
10	Processed	Processed successfully, waiting to be shipped
11	Shipped	Shipped successfully

14

Using the New Data Code (Alt+N) task button in the Order Status list page, we can create the required codes easily. After I insert the codes and sort the list page by code, the list shows the added codes (see Figure 14.7).

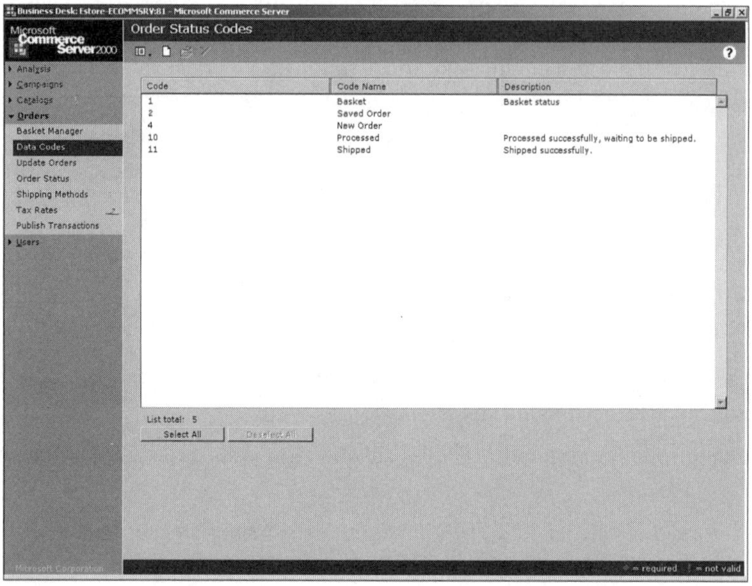

FIGURE 14.7

New order status codes added through the Data Codes module.

Creating the Module Folder

Because we have chosen to have a new module and category, it is best to create a new folder, too, to hold the action ASP pages. Let's call this folder custom. Using Windows Explorer, create the folder directly under the root folder where Business Desk is installed. For example, on my server, the new folder has the following path:

```
E:\EstoreBizDesk\EstoreBizDesk\custom
```

Creating the Module Configuration

We will call the configuration file for our module orderupd.xml. Instead of creating a new XML file and worrying about the syntax and schema, we can use a readily available file to create the configuration for our module. Commerce Server provides you with a few sample files under the SDK folder. The file we are looking for is called module.xml. It is located in the following directory:

```
<MSCS_installation_folder>\SDK\Samples\Management\BizDesk.
```

Copy `module.xml` to the `config` folder under the Estore Business Desk root folder. Rename `module.xml` as `orderupd.xml`. Open `orderupd.xml` in a text editor. From the file, you can see that the `id` and `action` attributes of the `<action>`, `<postto>`, and `<goto>` tags point to ASP pages. Because the ASP pages are under the `custom` folder, the URL should be `custom/<filename>.asp`. Therefore, the first modification is to replace "module/" with "custom/" throughout the file. After doing so, save and close the file.

Now the module configuration is ready, but we need to make some changes to it later.

Updating the Master Configuration

You already know that the master configuration file for the PuP-generated EstoreBizDesk application is `bizdesk.xml`, stored in the `config` folder. I would suggest making a backup of this file before starting to edit it. After doing so, open `bizdesk.xml` in a text editor such as Notepad or Visual InterDev. To create a new category, we need to insert a new `<category>` element in the `<categories>` section. Before the closing `</categories>` tag, insert the new `<category>` element, as shown here:

```
<category id="custom">
    <name>Cu&lt;U&gt;s&lt;/U&gt;tom</name>
    <key>s</key>
    <tooltip>Custom Modules</tooltip>
</category>
```

Note that the letter *s* in "Custom" is underlined. This letter will be used as the keyboard shortcut.

Under the `<moduleconfigs>` section, you will find a lot of individual `<moduleconfig>` elements used to tie together the categories and the modules defined in module configuration files. We need to insert a new `<moduleconfig>` tag for the `orderupd.xml` file in which our module is defined and tie this module to the category Custom created earlier. Here's the tag to do this:

```
<moduleconfig id="orderupd.xml" category="custom"/>
```

Insert this tag before the ending `</moduleconfigs>` tag. Save and close the `bizdesk.xml` file.

Creating List and Edit Pages

The module configuration file is now ready, pointing to the custom folder for ASP action pages. Therefore, we need to create the list and edit pages in the `custom` folder. Again, the SDK of Commerce Server comes in handy by providing us with template files that can be copied over and modified as needed. So now navigate to the `<MSCS_installation_folder>\SDK\Samples\Management\BizDesk` folder and copy the following files to the `custom` folder:

- `list.asp`
- `edit.asp`

14

- response.asp

- strings.asp

Restarting the Biz Desk Application

Any time changes are made to the master or module configuration files, the IIS application has to be restarted to force it to read the files again. To restart the IIS application for EstoreBizDesk, right-click the application under Internet Information Services from the MMC and open the property sheet. Click the Unload button to unload the application and then click the OK button (see Figure 14.8).

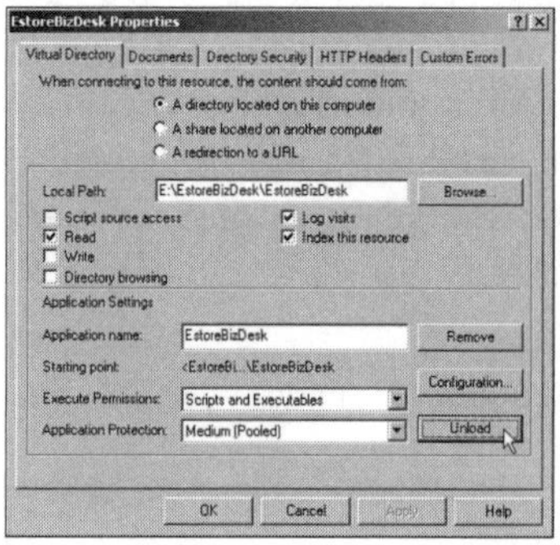

FIGURE 14.8

Unloading the Biz Desk application.

Also, whenever you make some changes to the global.asa file and save the file, the site will automatically sense the change and restart the IIS application for the site.

Therefore, the way you restart a site application depends on what's convenient for you.

After you unload the application and access it again, the Business Desk will restart and load the application afresh. Figure 14.9 shows what appears in my Business Desk after it reloads.

Here you see the category Custom and the module listed under it. Of course, we need a proper name for the module to appear under the category instead of "List Page." Also, the list page itself displays some junk data along with various task icons for New, Delete, Properties, and Find. You might want to choose the lone record listed and click the View Properties (Alt+V) button, which will fetch the default edit page, again with the same junk data. We need to start making modifications to these action pages now.

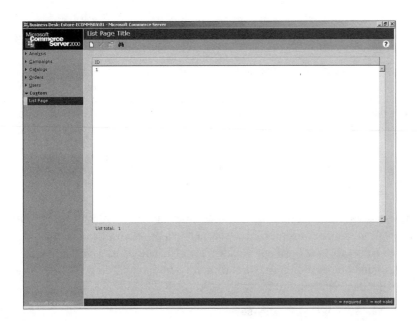

FIGURE 14.9
New category and module.

Modifying the Module Configuration

Our list page should list the order numbers and the order status for each of the orders. Then the user should be able to choose an order and click a toolbar icon to start modifying the order status in an edit page. Because we really have only one action to be taken from the list page, there is no need to have the Delete, New, Properties, and Find icons in the taskbar.

Now let's concentrate on the first `<action>` element in the file `orderupd.xml`, which starts with this:

```
<action id='custom/list.asp' helptopic=''>
```

This is the action that invokes the list page. The list page lists all the orders. Because creating new orders and deleting orders is not being planned for in this module, we can remove all the `<task>` elements and just insert the `<task>` element to open an order from the list:

```
<action id='custom/list.asp' helptopic=''>
    <name>List</name>
    <tooltip>List Page</tooltip>
```

14

EXTENDING THE
BUSINESS DESK

```
<tasks>
  <task icon='taskopen.gif' id='open'>
          <postto action='custom/edit.asp' formname='selectform' />
          <name>&lt;U&gt;O&lt;/U&gt;pen</name>
          <key>o</key>
          <tooltip>Open Order</tooltip>
      </task>
    </tasks>
</action>
```

The second `<action>` element is for the edit page. It starts with this:

```
<action id='custom/edit.asp' helptopic=''>
```

Here again, we know that the user is not going to create any new orders from this module. Therefore, the usual `savenew` task and its associated `<task>` element can be removed from the edit page. Remember that the Save and Create New task icon in an typical edit page saves the current changes and prepares to display a form for a new entry. Therefore remove this task, which starts with the following:

```
<task icon='tasksavenew.gif' id='savenew'>
```

Make sure you remove everything, including the closing `</task>` element for this task. Now the tasks that are left are the `back`, `saveback`, and `save` tasks. Our action page for saving changes is going to be `edit.asp` itself. Therefore, make sure the `action` attribute of the `<postto>` elements in the save and saveback tasks is pointing to `'custom/edit.asp'`. Note that the action for the `back` task should be pointing to `'custom/list.asp'`; this task is invoked by the leftmost arrow icon, which takes the user from an edit page to the initial list page from which the edit page was launched.

Because we have done away with the `savenew` task, we can eliminate the `<action>` tag in the file for the "Save and New" action. Therefore, remove the entire section starting with

```
<action id='custom/edit.asp?savenew=yes' helptopic=''>
```

and ending with the corresponding closing `</action>` tag.

Finally, change the `<module>` element's `name` and `tooltip` values to the display values desired:

```
<module id='custom/list.asp'>
    <name>Update Order</name>
    <tooltip>Update the Status of Orders</tooltip>
</module>
```

My final module configuration file looks like this:

```
<?xml version = '1.0' encoding='windows-1252' ?>
<config xmlns="x-schema:bdmodule-schema.xml">
```

```
    <actions>
        <action id='custom/list.asp' helptopic=''>
            <name>List</name>
            <tooltip>List Page</tooltip>
            <tasks>
        <task icon='taskopen.gif' id='open'>
            <postto action='custom/edit.asp' formname='selectform' />
            <name>&lt;U&gt;O&lt;/U&gt;pen</name>
            <key>o</key>
            <tooltip>Open Order</tooltip>
        </task>
            </tasks>
        </action>
        <action id='custom/edit.asp' helptopic=''>
            <name>Edit</name>
            <tooltip>Edit Page</tooltip>
            <tasks>
         <task icon='taskback.gif' id='back'>
                <goto action='custom/list.asp' />
                <name>&lt;U&gt;B&lt;/U&gt;ack</name>
                <key>b</key>
                <tooltip>Back</tooltip>
            </task>
            <task icon='tasksaveback.gif' id='saveback'>
                <postto action='custom/edit.asp' formname='saveform' />
                <name>Save and Bac&lt;U&gt;k&lt;/U&gt;</name>
                <key>k</key>
                <tooltip>Save and back to List</tooltip>
            </task>
            <task icon='tasksave.gif' id='save'>
                <postto action='custom/edit.asp' formname='saveform' />
                <name>&lt;U&gt;S&lt;/U&gt;ave</name>
                <key>s</key>
                <tooltip>Save</tooltip>
            </task>
            </tasks>
        </action>
    </actions>
    <modules>
        <module id='custom/list.asp'>
            <name>Update Order</name>
            <tooltip>Update the Status of Orders</tooltip>
        </module>
    </modules>
</config>
```

At this point, the Business Desk should show the required task icons in both list and edit pages. Also, the name of the module, Update Order, should appear under the Custom category in the navigation pane. However, we need to make some more modifications before all the actions pages are functional. The next step is to modify the list page `list.asp`.

Modifying the List Page

The list page is the default page (as well as the first page) launched for the module. We want to fetch and show only the order number and status of the orders in the list. Recall from our discussion on list page architecture that the following steps are needed:

1. Retrieve the records from the database using ADO.
2. Convert the ADO recordset to form an XML data island on the generated page sent to the browser.
3. Generate an XML metadata island corresponding to the HTC and the data island generated on the page sent to the browser.
4. Create a `DIV` element as a container for the listSheet HTC and point the `MetaXML` and `DataXML` attributes of `DIV` to the IDs of metadata islands and data islands, respectively.
5. Now the downloaded page will have the listSheet HTC and its required metadata and data islands. IE 5.5 will display the data.

To accomplish these steps, open the file `list.asp` we saved under the `custom` folder. An editor such as Visual InterDev is the preferred tool for working with ASP files because it has good color schemes for analyzing the different parts of code easily. We will work the changes starting from the top of the file and go line by line down the page.

First, uncomment the statement that retrieves the connection string to the Estore database:

```
g_sConnectionString = GetSiteConfigField("Product Catalog", "connstr_db_
➥Catalog")
```

Recall that the connection string is already stored in the Product Catalog site resource.

The next change involves the client-side subroutine `OnRowUnselect()`. You've probably noticed the call to `Main()` and routines such as `Main()` and `deleteItem()` defined in the page. Because we are not going to use the delete task at all, we can simply ignore this code. We will follow the same policy of ignoring instead of deleting code that we don't need. When everything works as intended, after all the changes are done, you can clean up unwanted code.

Continuing with the changes, the following statement needs to be inserted inside the `OnRowUnselect()` subroutine:

```
DisableTask("open")
```

The OnRowUnselect() subroutine gets fired whenever a row in the listSheet is unselected. Because we want to disable the Open task icon when no row is selected, we call the DisableTask() routine to do the job. DisableTask() is defined in the include file ActionPageUtil.asp.

In the client-side routine OnRowSelect(), the key *lookupkey* should be replaced with order_number in the following statement:

```
set xmlNode = window.event.XMLrecord.selectSingleNode("order_number")
```

Throughout the file, placeholders such as *lookupkey* are provided so that it's easy to replace them as needed. The preceding statement parses the XML data referred to by the listSheet. Inside the condition block that checks whether an order was selected, insert the EnableTask routine to enable the Open task icon. Also, once an order is selected, the hidden key order_number in the form selectForm should be set to the value of the order number chosen. Therefore, replace *lookupkey* again with order_number. We will see the selectForm later in the page. Here are the changes required inside the OnRowSelect():

```
if not xmlNode is nothing then
    .....
    .....
EnableTask("open")
.....
.....
selectform.order_number.value = sKeyValue
    .....
    .....
End if
```

By now you know that the list page uses a listSheet HTC to display fetched records. HTCs use XML-formatted data islands for data and metadata. Therefore, we need to build the required metadata and data islands (XML formatted) to be sent along with the page.

So, the next change in the page involves where the XML metadata island is being built on the page. We need to specify the column names in the XML-converted data recordset that we will generate after this. Also, the display labels for these columns need to be specified. Here's what the modified code looks like:

```
<!— product list meta data —>
<xml id='metaxml'>
    <listsheet>
        <global />
        <columns>
            <column id='order_number' width='25'>Order Number</column>
            <column id='u_name' width='25'>Order Status</column>
```

14

```
            </columns>
            <operations>
                <newpage formid='newpageform'/>
                <sort formid='sortform'/>
                <findby formid='findbyform'/>
            </operations>
        </listsheet>
</xml>
```

We have just replaced the dummy column with column names expected to come out of a SQL query. We will soon form a query that will fetch order_number and u_name as the columns in the record. Note that the `<listsheet>` element indicates that a listSheet HTC is going to use this piece of metadata.

We are about to change the code required to access the database to fetch the ADO recordset and convert the recordset to XML format for the data island. The code will replace the junk data (the "1" shown earlier in Figure 14.9). Here is the changed code in the file:

```
<!— XML INSERT recordset HERE —>
<xml id='dataxml'>
<%    const PAGE_SIZE = 20

    'Get a recordset and call an XML conversion routine here:
    g_sQuery = "select order_number, u_name from OrderGroup,decode where
decode.i_code=ordergroup.order_status_code"
    set g_rsQuery = rsGetRecordset(g_sConnectionString, g_sQuery, AD_OPEN
    ➥_KEYSET, AD_LOCK_PESSIMISTIC)
    response.write(xmlGetXMLFromRSEx(g_rsQuery, 0, PAGE_SIZE, -1, null).xml)
%>
</xml>
```

First, we build the SQL query in g_sQuery so as to fetch all orders, with their order number (order_number in OrderGroup) and the status name (u_name in Decode) retrieved. The query is actually a join between the tables OrderGroup and Decode. Next, we execute the query using one of the routines, rsGetRecordset, defined in the included file DBUtil.asp. Then the ADO recordset available in g_rsQuery is converted to an XML form using the routine xmlGetXMLFromRSEx. The resulting XML data is written inside the data island.

Finally, there is one more change to make in list.asp. The hidden key *lookupkey* has to be replaced with the key order_number:

```
<FORM ID='selectform'>
    <INPUT TYPE='hidden' NAME='type' VALUE='open'>
    <INPUT TYPE='hidden' NAME='order_number' VALUE='-1'>
</FORM>
```

This change is required because the form is submitted when the Open Order (Alt+O) task icon is clicked, and hence the key value should be passed to the edit.asp page. Remember that the OnRowSelect() client-side routine dynamically sets the value of the hidden key (order_number) to the order number the user chooses from the list.

Before saving and exiting from list.asp, take a moment to observe the usage of the listSheet HTC on the page:

```
<!— putting ListSheet within this container allows for scrolling without
     losing the task buttons off the top of the screen —>
<div ID="bdcontentarea">

    <DIV ID='lsDiv' CLASS='listSheet' STYLE='HEIGHT: 80%; MARGIN: 20px'
        DataXML='dataxml'
        MetaXML='metaxml'
        LANGUAGE='VBScript'
        ONROWSELECT='OnRowSelect()'
        ONROWUNSELECT='OnRowUnselect()'
        ONALLROWSUNSELECT='OnRowUnselect()'
        ONHEADERCLICK='OnHeaderClick()'
        ONNEWPAGE='OnNewPage()'><%= L_ListPGLoadingList_Text %></DIV>
</DIV>
```

The listSheet HTC is instantiated on the browser page by the container DIV element. The HTC expects DataXML and MetaXML in order to function; these are, in turn, defined as attributes of the container DIV element and point to the respective data islands already generated on the page. Also, observe that the DIV element implements the events of the listSheet HTC, such as OnRowSelect and OnRowUnselect, that have corresponding event-handler routines defined on the page—and you already know what these routines do!

We are now ready to see our changes in the Business Desk. Therefore, save the file and refresh the Business Desk. By now, the Business Desk should be showing the Update Order module under the Custom category. Clicking the Update Order module brings up the list page, which has the orders and status information fetched from the database (see Figure 14.10).

Note that there is only the task icon we need and it is disabled because no record is selected. Before we choose a record to open and update its status, remember that our edit.asp page is not yet ready. However, before doing work on edit.asp, let's take a small detour.

The success of the list page discussed so far came about only after quite a few "gotchas" popped up. Rarely in the software industry do we achieve perfection in the first attempt. So, in our example, what if something goes wrong and Business Desk keeps producing errors? Fortunately, there are quite a few ways to debug your code using the framework provided by Commerce Server. If you run into errors in the new module-creation process, the following section will help you.

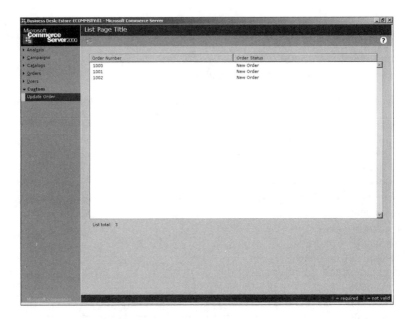

FIGURE 14.10

A successful list page of the new module.

Debugging Business Desk

Traditionally, we debug ASP files with a combination of methods. One method is to have IIS send server-side error messages to the client page. Then we would debug the ASP page that generated the error. In cases of logical errors, where data rendered by an ASP page is not what was expected, we would view the source of the generated HTML file in the browser.

While we're dealing with the Business Desk HTA browser instance, the regular browser interface is not there. Therefore, you cannot really view the source of the generated page by either choosing the appropriate View menu option or by right-clicking the View Source context menu item. If you try to access the Business Desk from a normal browser, you will get an error. Also, even though the server-side error messages are sent out to the HTA browser, they might not be useful because we want to know the entire sequence of events happening in the process.

However, the Business Desk framework makes the aforementioned debugging techniques possible by just flipping a switch in `global.asa`. At the beginning of the `global.asa` file for the EstoreBizDesk application appears the following statement:

```
MSCSEnv = PRODUCTION
```

This means that Business Desk is running in production mode. There is another constant, called `DEVELOPMENT`, defined for the development mode. Both these constants are defined in `global.asa` itself.

Depending on the mode, certain flags are set, as shown here:

```
if MSCSEnv = PRODUCTION then
    ' — production settings
    VERBOSE_OUTPUT              = false     SHOW_OBJECT_ERRORS     = false
AUTO_REDIRECT_ENABLED          = true          FORCE_HTA_ONLY      = true
ALLOW_CONTEXT_MENUS        = false     SHOW_DEBUG_TEXT        = false
else
    ' — development settings
    VERBOSE_OUTPUT          = false
    SHOW_OBJECT_ERRORS      = true
    AUTO_REDIRECT_ENABLED     = false
    FORCE_HTA_ONLY          = false
    ALLOW_CONTEXT_MENUS       = true
    SHOW_DEBUG_TEXT         = true
end if
```

As you can see, in development mode, the settings are such that they will help with the debugging of the application. For instance, setting FORCE_HTA_ONLY to false means that the Business Desk can be accessed from a normal browser window. The option ALLOW_CONTEXT_MENUS, when set to true, will enable the right-click context menu even within the HTA browser. This way, you can take a look at, say, an XML data island generated by an ASP page. If you want to see verbose output as the Business Desk proceeds, you could set VERBOSE_OUTPUT to true.

I am going to set my mode to DEVELOPMENT and then restart the IIS application and close the already-opened Business Desk HTA windows. I'll launch the Business Desk from one of the shortcuts to the HTA. The Business Desk now allows me to right-click and choose View Source to see the HTML source. Also, the tooltips on task icons now display helpful information, such as the action page that will be launched and the form name that is getting posted. Note that if I had set the VERBOSE_OUTPUT option to true, a separate browser window would open and list the entire process of loading objects and provide a detailed lists of tasks accomplished in loading the module.

Modifying the Edit Page

After that small detour, we are now back at work modifying the edit.asp page that will be generating the edit page when the Open Order task icon is clicked. In the edit page, we are going to present both the order number and the current order status as read-only fields. Another drop-down box will list the custom status codes that we added using the Data Codes module. The user will be able to choose a new custom status and save the order.

Here again, we will make the changes line by line, starting from the top of the file. Open edit.asp from the custom folder in a text editor such as Visual InterDev. The first change we need to make in edit.asp involves the declaration of a global variable that we will use to store data for an XML data island. This data island is the one that contains the custom order status

14

EXTENDING THE
BUSINESS DESK

codes required to be displayed by the drop-down box. Here is the first change (an addition), just before the call to the main() statement:

```
dim g_orderstatuses 'population of custom Order Statuses in the drop-down box
```

Next, in the main() subroutine, uncomment the statement that fetches the connection string from the Product Catalog site config resource:

```
sConnectionString = GetSiteConfigField("Product Catalog", "connstr_db_
➥Catalog")
```

Again, in the edit page, we need to change the placeholder *lookupkey* to the actual key being passed, order_number. The change would be inside the main() subroutine:

```
sKeyValue = Request("order_number")
```

Now find the place where the junk value "1" was being shown by the edit page and replace it with the code required to fetch the data chosen by the user in the list page and generate the XML data island. Specifically replace the commented code

```
'Get a recordset and call an XML conversion routine here:
        'sQuery = "your query here"
        'set rsQuery = rsGetRecordset(sConnectionString, sQuery, AD_OPEN_
        ➥KEYSET, AD_LOCK_PESSIMISTIC)
        'g_sDataXML = xmlGetXMLFromRS(rsQuery).xml
g_sDataXML = "<document><record><lookupkey>1</lookupkey></record></document>"
```

with the following lines:

```
'Get a recordset and call an XML conversion routine here:
        sQuery = "select order_number, u_name from OrderGroup,decode where
decode.i_code=ordergroup.order_status_code and ordergroup.order_number=" &
➥sKeyValue
        set rsQuery = rsGetRecordset(sConnectionString, sQuery, AD_OPEN_
        ➥KEYSET, AD_LOCK_PESSIMISTIC)
        g_sDataXML = xmlGetXMLFromRS(rsQuery).xml
```

This change is pretty much similar to the one we did in the list page. Only here, the SQL query fetches the specific order chosen by the user from the list page. We will use the XML-formatted data stored in g_sDataXML later while creating the data island on the page.

With that done, we need one more data island for the drop-down list box to show the custom order status codes from the Decode database table. Therefore, the statements to generate the data island can be inserted just before the End Sub statement for the main() routine:

```
'##########################################################
    'Custom code added to populate Order Status drop down box
    sQuery = "select i_code,u_name from decode where i_type=1 and i_code<>1
    ➥ and i_code<>2 and i_code<>4"
```

```
set rsQuery = rsGetRecordset(sConnectionString, sQuery, AD_OPEN_KEYSET,
 ➥AD_LOCK_PESSIMISTIC)
Do Until rsQuery.EOF
        g_orderstatuses = g_orderstatuses & "<option value='" & rsQuery
        ➥("i_code") & "'>" & rsQuery("u_name") & "</option>"
        rsQuery.MoveNext
Loop
'#############################################################
```

As you can see, the SQL query will fetch the code number and name of all Order Status codes other than Basket (1), New Order (4), and Saved Order (2). Then, in the loop, we iterate the resulting recordset and build the HTML needed for the drop-down (select element) box. At the end of the loop, the variable g_orderstatuses should have a string similar to this:

```
<option value='10'>Processed</option>
<option value='11'>Shipped</option>
```

We will use g_orderstatuses while actually writing out the metadata island XML section for the editSheet HTC.

The next major change to make is in the routine saveItem(), called by main() to save the changes to the database. Remember that the same edit.asp page is called for both displaying the edit page as well as processing the changes posted by the saveform in the edit page. Therefore, until we get to the form generation itself, assume that the name of the select box from which to choose the new status for the order will be sel_name. Here is the modified function, followed by an explanation:

```
function saveItem(sKeyValue)
    saveItem = false
    '
    ' INSERT CODE TO SAVE THE ITEM with lookupkey = sKeyValue HERE
    '
    dim sNewOrderStatus
    dim sConnString,oConn,oCmd,sCommandText
    sNewOrderStatus = Request.Form ("sel_name")
    sCommandText = "update ordergroup set order_status_code=" &
    ➥sNewOrderStatus & " where order_number=" & sKeyValue
sConnString = GetSiteConfigField("Product Catalog", "connstr_db_Catalog")
    Set oConn = oGetADOConnection(sConnString)
    Set oCmd = oGetADOCommand(oConn, AD_CMD_TEXT)
    oCmd.CommandText = sCommandText
    oCmd.Execute
    'if unable to save, set error that will display when taskbar displayed
    If Err <> 0 Then
        setError "", sFormatstring(L_EditPGUnableToSave_Text,
        ➥array(sKeyValue)), "", ERROR_ICON_ALERT
        exit function
```

```
End If

' if item saved with no errors then set saveItem = true
saveItem=true
end function
```

The new status code, as chosen by the user, is accessed by the following statement:

```
sNewOrderStatus = Request.Form ("sel_name")
```

The SQL query that follows thereafter is pretty simple; it updates the OrderGroup table, setting `order_status_code` to the code chosen by the user for the specific order. We then get the ADODB `Connection` and `Command` objects to execute the query. Routines such as `oGetADOConnection` and `oGetADOCommand` are defined in the included file `DBUtil.asp`. After the query is executed, the `Err` object is checked for any errors. If any error occurs, a message such as "Unable to save[1001]" is displayed in the status bar. If there is no error, the function returns success (true). Standard error strings such as "Unable to save the item: [1001]" are defined as constants in `strings.asp`.

Now we come to the metadata and data islands. The island is recognized by the following tag:

```
<xml id='metaxml'>
```

The `<fields>` section in the metadata island is modified to reflect what data is used from the data island to be displayed in which type of control. Here is the modified `<fields>` section in the metadata island:

```
<fields>
    <numeric id='order_number' readonly='yes'
        default='<%= Request("order_number") %>'
           subtype='integer'>
        <name>Order Number:</name>
        <tooltip>Order Number</tooltip>
        <error>Error in order number</error>
        <prompt>Prompt message</prompt>
    </numeric>
    <text id='u_name'  readonly='yes'>
        <name>Current Order Status:</name>
        <tooltip>The status of the order</tooltip>
        <error>You must enter valid text in the required field before
        ➥proceeding.</error>
        <prompt>Enter a status name</prompt>
    </text>
    <select id='sel_name' required='yes' >
        <name>Change Order Status to:</name>
        <tooltip>Change status of the order</tooltip>
        <prompt>Choose a status </prompt>
```

```
        <select id="sel_name">
            <%=g_orderstatuses%>
        </select>
    </select>
</fields>
```

The editSheet HTC will basically display three controls: two text type controls and a drop-down box.

The first control to be displayed by the editSheet is specified by the `<numeric>` tag, whose data comes from the order_number column of a data island. Also, the `readonly` attribute is set to `'yes'`, meaning that the control will display data but not allow it to be edited. Nevertheless, we put in the order number from the posting form selectForm as the default value. These controls could have validations such as `max="35"`. We have a validation called `subtype=` `'integer'`. The `<name>`, `<tooltip>`, and `<error>` elements are obvious. The `<prompt>` tag specifies the text to be displayed in a blank control just before data entry.

The second control embedded in the editSheet is of type `<text>`, and its data comes from the u_name column of the data island. This control is also read-only. The third control is a drop-down list box specified by the `<select>` tag. The actual data to be displayed in this control does not come from the data island. Instead, the data that is embedded here is gotten from the global ASP variable g_orderstatuses. Remember that this variable already has the required data in the required form for a `<select>` element. Now the metadata island is ready.

Immediately thereafter, the data island is built, as shown here:

```
<!— item data: get the data for all the EditSheet groups. —>
<xml id='dataxml'>
    <%= g_sDataXML %>
</xml>
```

Remember that g_sDataXML was populated with the required XML recordset earlier.

Going further down the page, we can observe that the editSheet HTC is included within a FORM element. This form is, of course, the saveform that is posted back to the same ASP page. As a final observation, check out the structure where the editSheet is contained. The editSheet now actually embeds three controls that are defined by MetaXML. Changes in any of the embedded controls trigger the ONCHANGE event of the editSheet. That's when we call setDirty to set a global variable. Similarly, whenever data entered in any of the controls changes from valid to invalid, or vice versa, the event ONVALID is fired. We have the handler setValid() to deal with the event.

Alright, now we can save the edit.asp file and go to the Update Order module again in Business Desk. Choose an order that is in the New Order status and click the Open Order (Alt+O) task icon. In the resulting edit page, change the order status to Processed. Then click

14

EXTENDING THE
BUSINESS DESK

any of the task buttons and save the changes (see Figure 14.11). The list page now would show the order with the modified status.

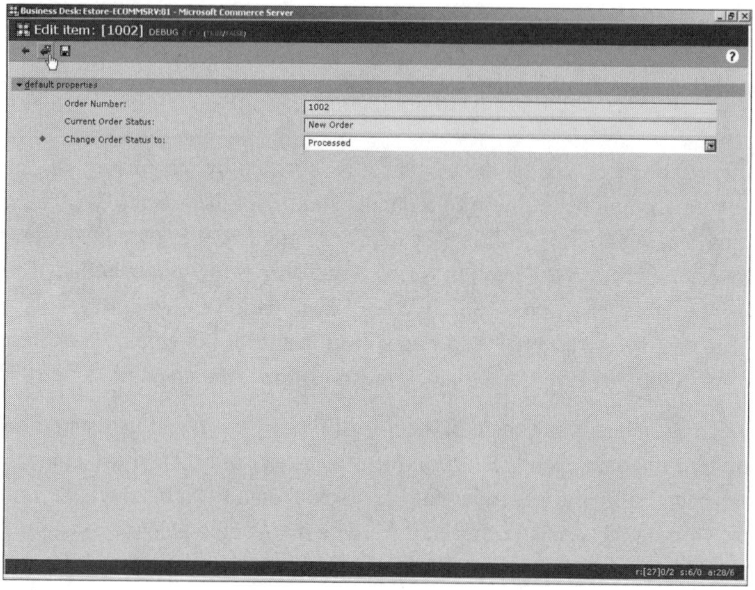

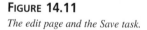

FIGURE 14.11

The edit page and the Save task.

From the edit page, you can see how the editSheet is an element of the `editSheets` collection, as specified by `MetaXML`. Each editSheet can be expanded or collapsed by clicking the name of the editSheet, which in our case is "default properties." Renaming this editSheet and adding another editSheet is left as an exercise for you to tackle on your own.

Summary

From our discussions so far, it is clear that the Business Desk aims at providing a consistent, quick, and secure way to manage the site database. Commerce Server provides the framework and infrastructure to extend or build modules. The Business Desk itself is a combination of the application on the server and the client installation (HTA) that accesses the application from within a customized browser instance. The framework manages the different visual aspects of the Business Desk and discovers the availability of categories, modules, and action pages from the master and module configuration files, which are in a predetermined XML format.

The action pages themselves are ASP pages that retrieve data, convert data into XML islands, and use the HTC behaviors of IE 5.5 to display data. These pages are broadly divided into list and edit pages. In list pages, data records are shown in the browser, exploiting the listSheet behavior. Most of the other actions, such as creating, modifying, and deleting records, are made possible from the task icons on the list pages. The edit pages are used to create or modify records. The HTCs used on these pages are editSheet, editField, listBox, and listEditor. The other components, such as Expression Builder and Query Builder, are used as helper components from edit pages to browse for products or to build logical expressions.

In this chapter, we analyzed an existing module and built a new one. This experience should give you the necessary motivation to extend your Commerce Server Business Desk according to your needs.

For further reference on XML, refer to the following resources:

- `www.xml.com`
- `www.w3c.org`

For further reference on IE 5.5 behaviors and HTCs, refer to `http://msdn.microsoft.com`.

14

EXTENDING THE
BUSINESS DESK

Data Warehouse, Reports, and Prediction

IN THIS CHAPTER

- Introduction to Data Warehousing   486
- Commerce Server Data Warehouse   491

Commerce Server depends on and is very well integrated with many of the .NET servers and DNA components of the Microsoft solution sets. Using SQL Server and Analysis Services, Commerce Server builds a data warehouse for a site that helps managers analyze site data from various dimensions. For example, it is possible to find out how effective a campaign has been in terms of sales. Based on the analysis, the campaign is modified accordingly to be more effective. This cycle of content delivery, analysis of content effectiveness, and fine-tuning content forms a closed loop. You have already seen how content delivery as well as content modification can be done using Business Desk and development tools. Analysis of effectiveness is the main link in this loop because it measures customer behavior, reveals buying trends, and so on. Commerce Server, with the infrastructure provided by SQL Server, Analysis Services, and Biz Desk modules, provides you with an effective data warehouse solution to "close the loop."

Introduction to Data Warehousing

Data warehousing as a concept has gained practical importance in the last decade as a result of the growth in computerized systems. As more and more systems have become automated, the data collected has grown beyond being treated as just an archive. Historical data can be used to reveal trends and buying patterns as well as help predict information based on the historical data sets.

OLTP Versus OLAP

Most of the systems, such as Sales Order, Asset Management, and Human Resources, are used by companies to record business transactions on a daily basis. These systems are used to support individual transactions such as placing an order, processing payroll, or storing inventory levels of a company. These systems are generally referred to as Online Transaction Processing (OLTP) systems. OLTP systems are designed to process daily transactions and are highly scalable to support thousands of concurrent transactions. However, OLTP systems are not designed to take care of the many reporting needs of management. For instance, suppose you try to issue a SQL query to a relational database that holds transaction data in order to find the average purchases made by a customer for each of the weeks in the year. If the database contains, say, tens of thousands of users, the query is going to take a long time to arrive at the results you asked for. Not only that, running a query on an OLTP system when users are accessing it at the same time slows down transactions. If this continues, you might not have any more new users to analyze!

Another reality is that enterprises have large numbers of disparate systems running the operations of different functional areas. These systems could be running on a different platform, use different data structures, and be provided by different vendors. However, managers need to analyze correlated data in a uniform manner. To solve many of the issues in using OLTP for analysis, Online Analytical Processing (OLAP) systems have been designed to enable managers to analyze data in a timely manner and in a way that does not disturb transactions. In OLAP, data is aggregated and stored in predefined dimensions based on expected queries. Therefore, queries to OLAP return results faster than RDBMS queries because data has already been aggregated according to querying needs. To enable the storage of aggregated data in a predetermined way, OLAP uses special structures called *cubes*.

OLAP Structures

A *cube* is a multidimensional structure that has been designed to hold aggregated data based on measures and dimensions. A *measure* is summarized data that we are interested in analyzing. For example, sales, average cost, and units sold are all measures. Measures are most often numbers in OLTP that result from transactions. Although measures alone can be calculated and stored, they don't offer much insight in and of themselves. What does a "units sold" figure mean outside of a context? It has to be viewed along dimensions, such as time (this month, this quarter, this year, and so on) and place (East, South, North, and West units). A *dimension* is an entity that provides more sense to a measure and helps in analysis. A cube can have multiple dimensions and measures.

Each measure is aggregated and stored along dimensions. An aggregation most often refers to a mathematical function performed on the underlying data set, such as SUM, AVG, and so on. Because measures are stored along dimensions, it is easy to read off a measure at the intersection of the dimensions in question. For example, consider the cube shown in Figure 15.1.

This cube is designed to answer sales queries, such as what were the units and the revenues for printers sold this quarter in the West business unit? The cell intersecting these three dimensions of Time, Category, and Location contains the aggregated data for units sold and revenues. Each dimension can have multiple levels in a hierarchical format. For instance, Date has four levels: Year, Qtr, Month, and Day.

Once data is aggregated up to a certain level in the dimension, it is then not too time consuming to roll up for higher levels. For example, if data is aggregated for Year, Qtr, Month, and Day, it is easy to roll up to calculate for the All level of Date, which is the base level. It depends on the designer of the cube to choose the level of aggregation. Also, it is possible to drill down from an aggregation to a lower level of transaction data directly.

After a cube is populated with data, it is then easy to slice or dice the cube to get the information one needs.

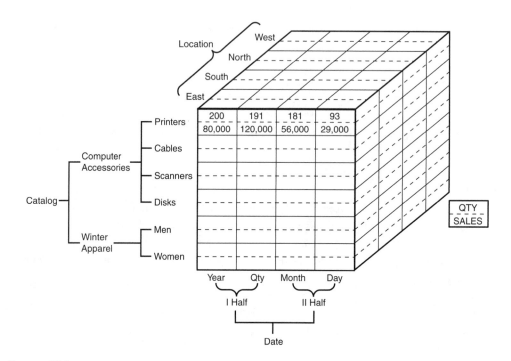

FIGURE 15.1

Conceptual model of a cube.

The Data Store

The source of data for OLAP is usually an intermediate database and not the OLTP system itself. That is, data from the OLTP system is imported into the intermediate database. Then data from the intermediate database is used to populate the cubes in OLAP. The intermediate database is called a *data mart* or *data warehouse*. Some refer to both the OLAP and the data source as the *data warehouse*, whereas others maintain that OLAP is just an analysis provider and hence the intermediate database is the warehouse. Whatever the case may be, it would suffice to understand that in a Commerce Server site, the data source for OLAP is a separate database in SQL Server. For example, in the case of our example site Estore, the data warehouse created is called Estore_dw, which created a database by that name in SQL Server. This database is separate from the site database Estore_commerce. Therefore, transaction data will be imported from Estore_commerce to Estore_dw, which will then be used as a source for the OLAP cubes.

The need for an intermediate data warehouse (DW) database is evident from the fact that sources of transaction data are varied. We can also import the Web log files into the DW database to be able to analyze site usage, user visits, and so on. Therefore, data can be imported from the product database, Web log files, and other external sources so that we get a consolidated data store designed according to the requirements of an organization.

When you're building OLAP cubes, the measures come from a DW table called the *fact table*. The dimensions come from one or more DW tables. For example, if you are trying to build a cube to analyze sales, most likely a table called as Sales would be the fact table because it contains the required transaction numbers. The columns in a fact table, such as Quantity, Sales Amount, and so on are used as measures for the cube. A cube, as you know, can have multiple dimensions. We can measure Sales Amount along many dimensions such as Time, Products, Location, and so on. Data for each of these dimensions come from DW tables, which are conceptually referred to as *dimension tables*.

OLAP Storage

Cube storage also needs to be configured, depending on the performance requirements. A cube can be stored in one of the three modes:

- Multidimensional OLAP (MOLAP)
- Relation OLAP (ROLAP)
- Hybrid OLAP (HOLAP)

In the MOLAP mode, both the aggregated data and a copy of the source data are stored in the OLAP server in multidimensional structures. This provides for the fastest response times to OLAP queries because queries can be resolved from the source data even if a populated cube doesn't have an answer. In the ROLAP mode, both aggregations and source data reside in the relational database. Therefore, this mode is one of the slowest and is generally used for very large data sets that are not accessed frequently (for example, data that belongs to some time period very long ago).

HOLAP is similar to MOLAP in that aggregated data is stored in the multidimensional structure; however, the source data is not copied to the OLAP server. Therefore, if the user query can be answered from the cubes or a cache, the speed of HOLAP is similar to that of MOLAP. If some data is not available (say, a user uses the Drilldown feature on a cell), then the source table is sought.

Multidimensional Expressions

A cube can be sliced across different dimensions to obtain the answer to various questions. Very much similar to a SQL query, multidimensional expressions (MDX) queries allow a client to access Analysis Services to query cubes. Here is an example of a simple MDX:

```
SELECT
{ [Measures].[Units Sold], [Measures].[Sales] } ON COLUMNS,
{ [Time].[Month} ON ROWS
FROM Sales
WHERE ( [LOCATION].[EAST] )
```

This query fetches the units sold and revenues for this month due to sales from the East business unit. Application programs connecting to the cube would use MDX to get result sets. Objects such as the PivotTable and PivotChart are used at the client site to manipulate result sets returned by a query.

Data Mining

One of the new features of Analysis Services in SQL Server 2000 is the capability to build data-mining models. A data-mining model builds relationships between statistical information contained in a supplied data source. The statistical information obtained from historic data is called a *case*, which refers to a collection of records from the transaction system. For example, in the transaction database, customers have many orders, and each order can have many line items. The collection of such information focusing on an entity (such as a customer) is a model that is used to analyze patterns between, say, customer attributes and order information. You could switch the focus to orders instead of customers and construct a different model from the very same physical data. Then your focus will be on purchases instead of user data.

Once a model is built, data is supplied to the model in a process called *training*. Training a model involves using an algorithm that continuously parses data and arrives at conclusions about the classification of data. There are various algorithms based on the type of model being built.

In the Decision Tree Model, data is recursively parsed to split attributes from the root to the leaf of a tree structure. For example, if salary is an attribute in the record set, the algorithm first splits salary values into two groups: one greater than or equal to a certain salary and the other less than a certain salary. The count at each of the groups will be used to arrive at the probabilities of that salary group in a given record set. Next, the groups are again split until there cannot be any more splits. The root of an attribute split is called the *leaf level* of the decision tree. This node contains the distribution information starting from the root and is used to predict information given other customer data columns.

The other model used by Analysis Services is the Clustering Model. Here, the training data is plotted very similarly to a graph. Wherever data groups together, a cluster is formed that can be used to classify prediction data into these clusters.

Data Warehouse Resources

Building a data warehouse and modeling cubes have become specialized areas in information technology. There are a lot of publications related to these areas. Therefore, in this chapter so far, we have just had a bird's-eye view of these subjects. As we move to the next sections, dealing with the Commerce Server data warehouse, you will not be surprised upon seeing terms such as cubes, measures, dimensions, MDX, and so on. However, I recommend that you spend some time with the Analysis Services tutorials to get a much closer look at these structures. The tutorial can be found on your server at

```
C:\Program Files\OLAP Services\Help\Tutorial\tutorial_menu.htm
```

Your file path could be different from the path shown, depending on where you installed Analysis Services on the server. If you thirst for more information on Data Warehouse or OLAP, another resource to seek would be

```
http://www.microsoft.com/SQL/evaluation/features/OLAPServ.asp
```

Commerce Server Data Warehouse

Commerce Server provides the necessary infrastructure to maintain and use a data warehouse for each of your sites. While you are unpacking a site using the Site Packager, Data Warehouse is one of the resources that can be unpacked immediately. You can also add a Data Warehouse resource to the site at any time. The data warehouse is comprised of a SQL Server database, an OLAP database, and the processes needed to import data into these databases. These databases are then used to generate reports and analyze various aspects of your site. For example, after scheduling an ad campaign, you might create sales reports to analyze the impact of the campaign (see Figure 15.2). From the analyses, you might target different users or improve the campaign.

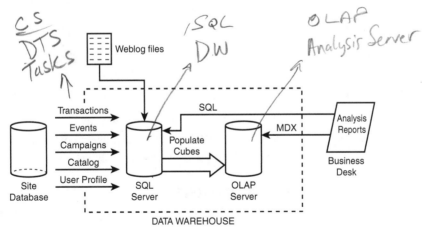

FIGURE 15.2

Data warehouse infrastructure.

SQL Server and OLAP Databases

While creating a site using Site Packager, we usually create the Data Warehouse resource for the site. The name given to the database is used for both the SQL Server and OLAP databases. For example, Estore_dw is the name of the SQL Server database as well as the OLAP database for our example site Estore. You can use the Analysis Manager to access the OLAP database. The SQL Server data warehouse database can be accessed through the Enterprise Manager. Both Analysis Manager as well as Enterprise Manager are available as snap-ins in the Commerce Server Manager MMC, so you can conveniently access them from a single place.

The SQL Server DW database contains tables designed to gather usage data for the site. Even though these tables might appear similar in name to those in the commerce dB, they are not. Further, the DW database contains tables such as Visit, VisitInfo, and UserAgent to collect Web log files data. Data-transformation tasks are designed to import data from the Web files or the commerce dB into these specific DW tables. These tasks are also prebuilt by Commerce Server. We need not modify any of these tables or tasks unless there is an intention to extend the data warehouse.

Therefore, the data that will be imported into the Estore_dw SQL Server database can come from the Commerce Server database, Web log files, and other external files. The types of data include the following:

- Transactions data
- Purchase data
- Events data
- User profile data
- Campaigns data
- Catalog data
- Web log files

There are individual tasks registered with Data Transformation Services (DTS) of SQL Server to import each of these types of data. Once the DW database has imported data, the next step would be to populate the cubes in the OLAP database by exporting data from the DW database.

Cubes, Measures, and Dimensions

The Estore_dw database created in the OLAP server is already provided with about 12 cubes that can be used in different types of analyses. The data source for this database is the Estore_dw database in SQL Server. Therefore, if you click a cube, you can see the fact tables, dimension tables, measures, and levels designed with a cube (see Figure 15.3).

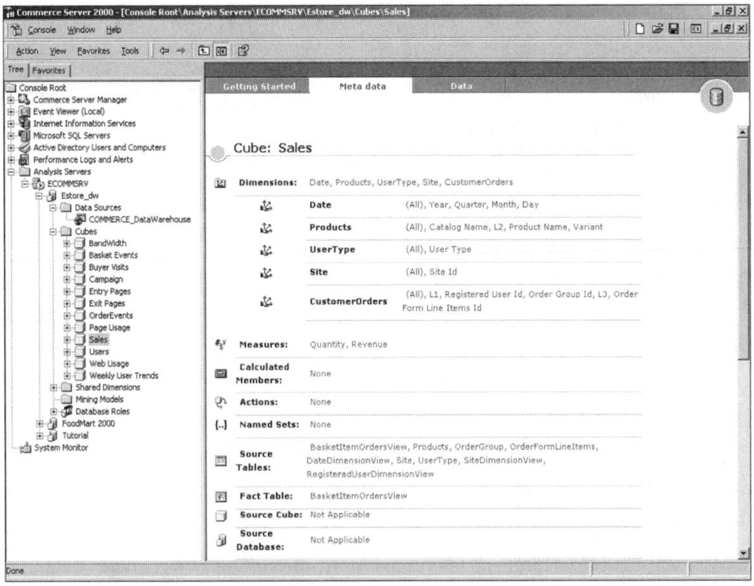

FIGURE 15.3

Metadata of a cube.

Click a cube, and the right pane opens up metadata and data details on the cube. In the Meta Data page, you can see what is being measured using the cube. From the Sales cube (refer to Figure 15.3), it is clear that the measures are Quantity and Revenue. The values for these measures come from the Quantity and Revenue columns, respectively, in the fact table, BasketItem OrdersView. In this case, the fact table happens to be a view that is linked to several other DW tables.

You can also see the dimensions of the cube and the levels in the dimensions. For example, in the Sales cube, the Products dimension has two levels: The first one is called *Catalog Name*, and the second level contains Product Name and Variant information. Note that level 0 for a dimension is the level named *All*, which contains all data for that dimension. Each of the dimensions and levels come from one or more dimension tables in the DW database. For example, the data for the Registered User ID dimension level comes from the Registered UserID column in the RegisteredUserDimensionView table. Another example would be that the Order Group ID dimension level is populated from the OrderGroupID column data of the OrderGroup table in the DW database.

You can look at these dimensions in more detail by clicking a dimension under the Shared Dimensions node (see Figure 15.4).

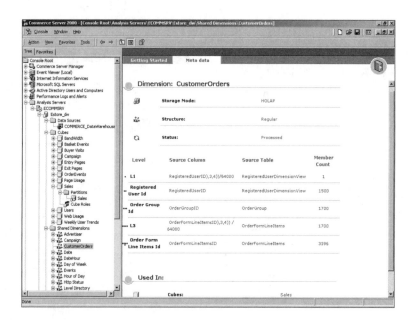

FIGURE 15.4

Metadata of a dimension.

As you can see, the dimension levels are populated with data from different table or view columns in the DW database. Also note that shared dimensions can be used in any cube.

In all, 12 cubes are available by default for each Commerce Server site. These cubes satisfy the queries of various reports available from the Analysis Biz Desk module. Table 15.1 provides a summary of all the cubes and dimensions.

Table 15.1   OLAP Cubes Provided by Commerce Server.

Cube	*Dimensions*
Bandwidth	DateHour
	Day of Week
	Hour of Day
	Site
	SiteUnfiltered
Basket Events	DateHour
	Events
	Products
	RegisteredUser
	Site
	UserType
	SiteUnfiltered

Table 15.1   continued

Cube	Dimensions
Buyer	Visits BuyerType Site UserTypeSiteUnfiltered
Campaign	Advertiser Campaign DateHour Events Page Group Site UserType URI
Entry Pages	Date Site URI
Exit Pages	Date Site URI
Order Events	DateHour Day of Week Events Hour of Day Site UserType Week of Year SiteUnFiltered
Page Usage	Date HTTP Status Is Request Level Directory Site URI Win32Status
Sales	CustomerOrders Date Products Site UserType

Table 15.1   continued

Cube	Dimensions
Users	Date
	Site
	UserType
	SiteUnFiltered
Web Usage	Date
	DateHour
	Day of Week
	Hour by Day
	Referrer
	RegisteredUser
	Site
	UserType
	SiteUnfiltered
	Week of Year
Weekly User Trends	Date
	Site
	Week of Year
	SiteUnfiltered

Logical Schema

We discussed the SQL Server database and the OLAP database in the last two sections. These two databases are the physical databases used by the data warehouse. To insulate us from having to deal with physical databases, Commerce Server has provided a logical schema that can be used by developers. The logical schema offers an abstraction of the physical tables by mapping tables to classes and business categories. In this schema, a *class* is used to model an entity that has individual members. For example, the class OrderFormHeader represents an individual customer order. A *data member* of a class stores some piece of data. For instance, the member billing_currency stores the currency in which the order was billed. The DW table ClsDef stores class definitions, whereas the table MemDef stores member definitions.

A *key* is a single data member or a set of data members that serves as the primary key for an instance of the class. For example, the OrderFormHeader class will have OrderFormHeaderID as well as the inherited OrderGroupID as keys. The DW table ClsKeyDef stores the key definitions. As the inherited key suggests, there can be relationships between classes. For example, one relationship might be that of the OrderGroup class to OrderFormHeader in a one-to-many relationship, meaning that one order group can have many order forms. Similarly, the

OrderFormHeader class has a one-to-many relationship with OrderFormLineItems. A child class always stores within itself the parent class' ID. This ultimately translates into the column ordergroup_id in the OrderFormHeader DW table.

Commerce Server provides the default DW tables and hence the classes by logically grouping the classes into the following business categories:

- Campaigns
- Catalog
- Transactions
- Profile Management
- Web Log Import
- Web Topology

Your product box is supposed to contain colored posters for each of these categories, showing the classes and the relations.

As an example, see Figure 15.5, which illustrates the classes in the Transactions category.

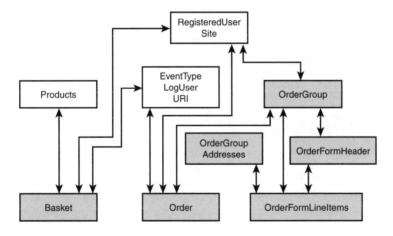

FIGURE 15.5
Data warehouse classes for the Transactions category.

The gray classes in the figure represent classes that are used in more than one category. The logical schema is just a convenient way to view the DW objects instead of looking at them as database tables. Each class is the schema in a table in the DW database. Therefore, the schema can be used to understand the metadata of the DW database. However, Microsoft suggests that modifications of the database should be attempted only after understanding the schema, the relationships, and any connected activities, such as import task changes.

Importing Data

Before reports can be run from the Business Desk Analysis module, we need to make sure that both the DW database and the OLAP cubes are populated with data. Because the DW database is not part of the commerce site, data from the site database should be manually imported into the DW database. Similarly, the Web log files also need to be imported to enable analysis, such as Web Trends and Web Usage. One can use the Data Transformation Services (DTS) of SQL Server to automate these imports and schedule them to happen at off-peak hours.

Commerce Server has already provided the DTS tasks, which are registered with SQL Server. We just need to run these tasks in order to accomplish the import process.

Site Configuration Synchronization

Before we run any other import tasks, we need to run the Site Configuration Synchronization task. This task synchronizes the IIS Application metabase with the data warehouse so that the task of importing Web log files will be successful. Any time you change any Web site–related configuration, the Synchronization task needs to be run before any other task is run.

On your SQL Server machine, expand the Data Transformation Services node and right-click Local Packages (see Figure 15.6).

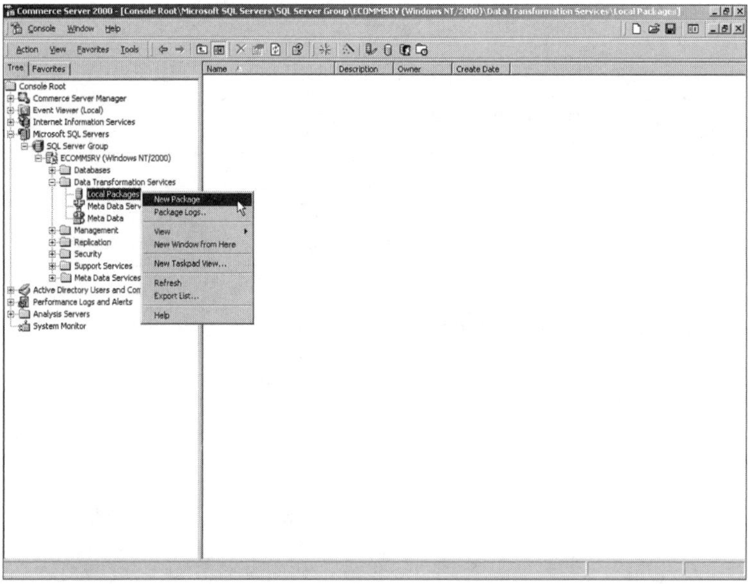

FIGURE 15.6

Creating a new package with DTS.

Choose New Package. In the New Package window, shown in Figure 15.7, you'll find that Commerce Server tasks are listed along with the other tasks in the panel. You just need to click a particular task from the panel to insert the task in the package. The Task menu item can also be used to choose and insert a task.

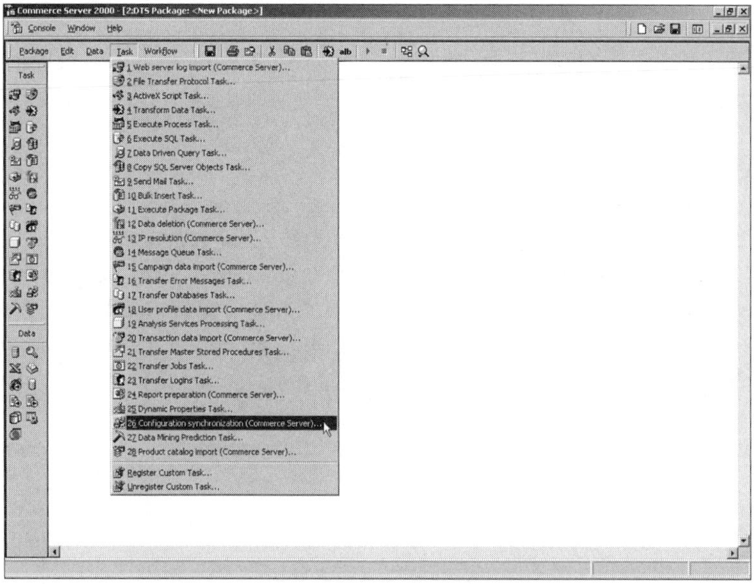

FIGURE 15.7
Commerce Server DTS tasks.

From the Task menu, choose the Configuration Synchronization task. Note that a Commerce Server task is distinguished within parentheses "(Commerce Server)" next to a task name.

In the Synchronize DW Properties dialog box, shown in Figure 15.8, enter a description for the task. Choose Estore as the Site Name setting. This is the site for which data is going to be imported. Click the OK button.

An icon is now created in the workspace. To run the task immediately, right-click the icon and choose Execute Step. After successful execution of the task, a message is popped. Click OK. Now the data warehouse is synchronized with the site configuration.

FIGURE 15.8

Inserting the Synchronization task.

Transaction Data

Next, let's import transaction data from the Estore database. The data warehouse design treats data such as order groups, order forms, and baskets as transaction data. Therefore, the Transaction Data Import task imports the data into the transaction-related class tables in DW. Choose Transaction Data Import from the Task menu. In the Transaction Import Properties dialog box, choose Estore as the site. Also choose the Full Load option if you are importing into the data warehouse for the first time. Subsequently, imports can be done as incremental loads. This applies to all the import tasks. Once the icon is created on the workspace, right-click it and execute the task. After the task has been successfully executed, we'll move on to the next import.

Campaign Data

Campaign information in the Estore database is stored in many tables, such as campaign, campaign_item, lm_master_operations, and so on. To import all this campaign-related data into the DW, click the Task icon and choose the Campaign Data Import task. As usual, choose Estore for the Site Name setting here as well as in all other DTS tasks that have a Site Name property to be set. Now run the task.

User Profile Data

To answer many of the questions related to user behavior, user profile data has to be imported. Choose the User Profile Data Import task. Right-click the task icon in the workspace and click Properties. In the User Import Properties dialog box, a query interval can be specified to prevent locking of data while the import operation processes tens of thousands of users. You can choose the default value of 15 minutes. Then run the task with Full Load.

Product Catalog Data

The next task to be executed is to import catalog information from the Estore database. Dimensions that have products and variants as levels will be populated with data from these tables. Therefore, proper product names or categories will be displayed in generated reports. Choose Product Catalog Import from the Task menu. Run the task from the workspace.

Importing Web Logs

Apart from data in the site database, the Web logs also contain vital information about user behavior and usage trends. The Web Server Log Import task provided by Commerce Server can import log files into the DW database. The only requirement is that the log files should be in the W3C Extended file format. Enabling Web site logging and specifying the format of the log file can be done in IIS from the property page of the site (see Figure 15.9).

FIGURE 15.9
Configuring Web logs for W3C format.

The Enable Logging option is chosen and the selected active log format is the W3C Extended log file format. To know what properties of the HTTP request will be logged, click the Properties button and then click the Extended Properties tab (see Figure 15.10).

FIGURE 15.10
Properties logged by the Web server.

Each checked item is logged in the file for each of the requests. For a successful import of log files into the DW database, the properties URIStem, Date, Time, and Client IP Address should all be selected. Apart from these required properties, you could select other properties, such as

Win32 Status, but this is entirely optional and dependent on what you want to be logged. Any Web server log file in W3C format can be imported into the database. Also, if you are importing from a live IIS site, make a copy of the log files to a different location and then start the import process.

After verifying all this information, you can run the import task. But note that if you change any of the logging information, the Configuration Synchronization task needs to be run before the Import task can be executed.

Now, in the DTS Package screen, choose the Web Server Log Import task from the task menu. In the Import Web Server Logs dialog box, the Commerce Site applications are listed (see Figure 15.11). Therefore, Estore as well as EstoreBizDesk appear.

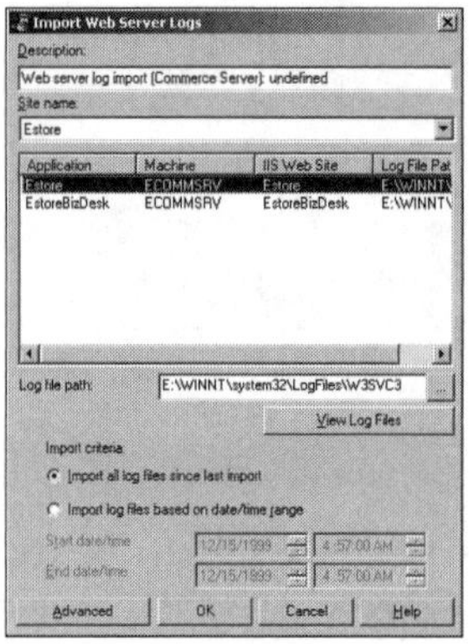

FIGURE 15.11
Choosing the site for importing Web server logs.

Choose Estore and specify the location where log files for the site can be found. In the Import Criteria section, select Import All Log Files Since Last Import. As you can see, you could possibly restrict the import of the log files based on a time range. Now click the Advanced button. Quite a few tabs are available to set the information for the process. We will run through them in the next several sections.

Excludes

In the Excludes tab, choose All for the Filter Excludes By criteria (see Figure 15.12). This list contains many other options. Using the Host option, you will be able to specify hostnames whose requests should be excluded from the import. This is typically required in a scenario where internal hosts are used for testing an application. The file options are File Types and File Expression. Because HTTP commands are for each resource on the page and not a single request, it may not be useful to count all the requests for, say, images on the page.

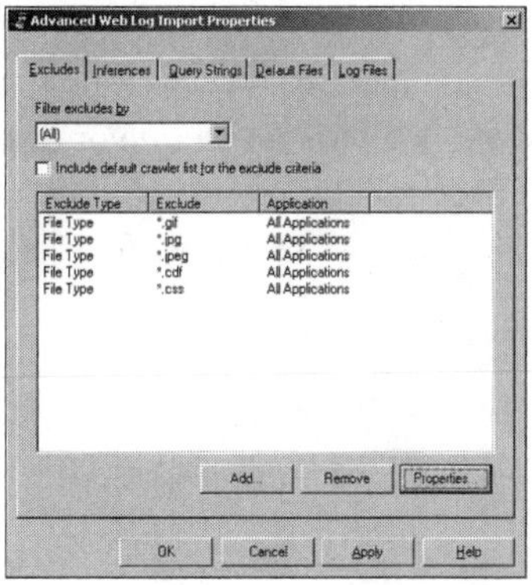

FIGURE 15.12
Exclude filters for Web log import.

The standard file types to exclude include JPG, GIF, CDF, JPEG, and CSS. You can add your own file types, such as JS and INC. This tab also gives you the ability to set the filter on individual applications. You can choose the Properties button and then select or unselect a specific application from this filter criteria.

Inferences

Measuring when a user entered the site and exited is not easy. In order to identify a visitor as a site user, you can specify one or all of the three references for a user in the log file: a Commerce Server cookie, a username in the log file, or an identifier in a custom cookie (see Figure 15.13). Therefore, a user is inferred by these cookies. In order to decide that a user has exited a site, an idle time can be specified in Visit Inferences. Note that Site Server cookies are considered custom cookies.

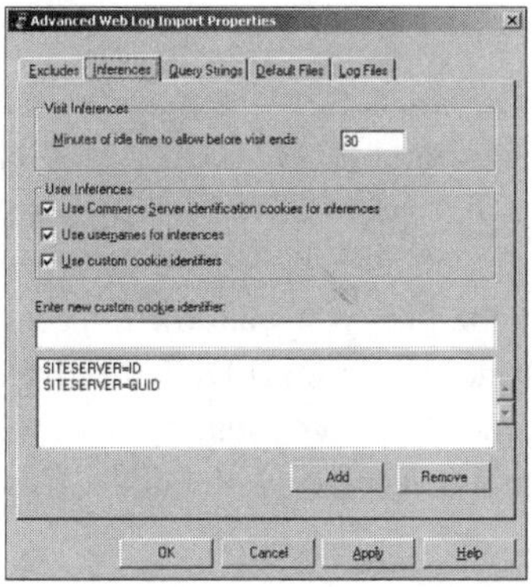

FIGURE 15.13
Setting inferences for a user visit.

Query Strings

The log file contains uniform resource identifiers (URIs) along with the entire query. You can import these query strings to perform analysis on them. For example, if you use the query string ProdSearch in your search page to let users search for a product, importing values for this query string would reveal what users are searching for. Click the Add button in the property page (see Figure 15.14).

FIGURE 15.14

Importing site query strings into the data warehouse.

Type the name of the query string (in this example, **ProdSearch**). You may want to exclude the Biz Desk site from most of the import processes. You can choose a data type for the query string value. Then click the OK button. The query string is now added. You can add as many query strings as you want, up to 256; that's the maximum number the task can import. Also note that if you want to import more query strings, more time will be needed for the import process. Furthermore, if your query string runs across the entire address bar in the browser, be aware that the import process will truncate beyond 512 characters.

Default Files

Use the Default Files tab to add filenames that you consider to be pointing to your default page on the site. A user could hit a site using different addresses, such as www.<sitename>.com or www.<sitename>.com/default.asp, or even be redirected from another page or frame. In all cases, the count of requests for the default page should be incremented in the ultimate analysis. Therefore, to enable that, specify the files you want the import process to treat as the same file. Optionally, you can check the Truncate Top-level Directory from File System Paths option so that the report just lists the filenames instead of starting with the root address. In this example, for the Estore default page we can just accept the default values.

Log Files

The Log Files tab is used to instruct the import process how to handle log files that overlap in time. There are two well-known issues with Web log files in a Web farm. For example, if you are using multiple Web servers in a farm, users could be redirected to different servers during the entire site visit. Therefore, to recognize time overlaps and identify visits as accurately as possible, you can enter a number in the Number of Minutes That Records Must Overlap field. In the Overlap Is Detected field, you specify what action should be taken by the import process, such as Discard Records and Proceed and Stop All Imports.

Another issue with Web log files is the problem of log rotation. Because we can configure the Web server to start on a new log file every hour, day, week, month, and so on, it's possible that the start time is in one log file and the end time of a visit is in another. If such open entry or exit times exist, you can tell the import process what to do in the When Import Is Completed option box. You could make the process store the open visits in the cache (until the timeout) for the next import process to determine the end time. Other options are to discard the open visits and commit the open visits to the database.

Click OK in the Advanced Web Log Properties dialog box. Once you're back in the Import Web Server Logs dialog box, click the View Log Files button to make sure that there are log files to import for the import criteria specified (see Figure 15.15). This means that the log file path should be pointing to the W3SVC folder on the server. The path to that folder is `WINNT\system32\LogFiles\W3SVC3`. Then click the OK button. Right-click the task icon from the workspace to execute the task.

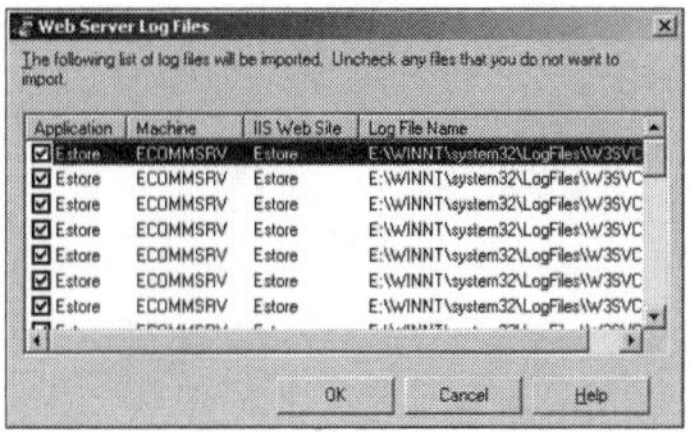

FIGURE 15.15
Web server log files to import.

Now all the required data is imported into the DW database.

Populating the Cubes

The next task is to populate the cubes with the data from the data warehouse. The task to accomplish this is called the Report Preparation task.

Choose the Report Preparation task from the Task menu. Choose the site name and full load for populating the cubes. Then right-click the Report Preparation icon from the workspace to execute the task. This task might take quite a long time, depending on the amount of data, cubes, and dimensions.

15

Workflow Between Tasks

As you might have observed, the data import and cube-population processes need to happen frequently, depending on the analysis needs of an organization. Therefore, these task could be stored in a package and scheduled for execution at, say, 2 A.M. every day. Also, workflow could be inserted in the package so that an external execution could be triggered upon the success, failure, or completion of a task. The external task could be an e-mail to send upon failure, and so on. Similarly, a workflow is configured between tasks so that as soon as one task completes, another task can be triggered to execute.

To configure workflow between two tasks, choose two tasks in the package workspace using Ctrl+click. With two tasks chosen, single click the To task that should be executed after the completion of a From task. For instance, following our example so far, choose the tasks Configuration Synchronization and Transaction Data Import in the workspace. Right-click the Transaction Data Import task and then choose Workflow, On Completion (see Figure 15.16).

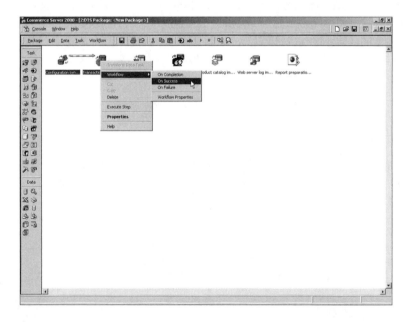

FIGURE 15.16

Configuring workflow between DTS tasks.

An arrow is inserted between two tasks with the head pointing to the Transaction Data Import task. If you right-click the arrow and choose Properties, you can see how the workflow is configured with the source and destination of tasks based on an action precedence, such as Completion (see Figure 15.17). With this type of workflow, you could send e-mail or alerts upon each task failure or at the end of the task to signal success of the entire package using the Send Mail Task option from the Task menu.

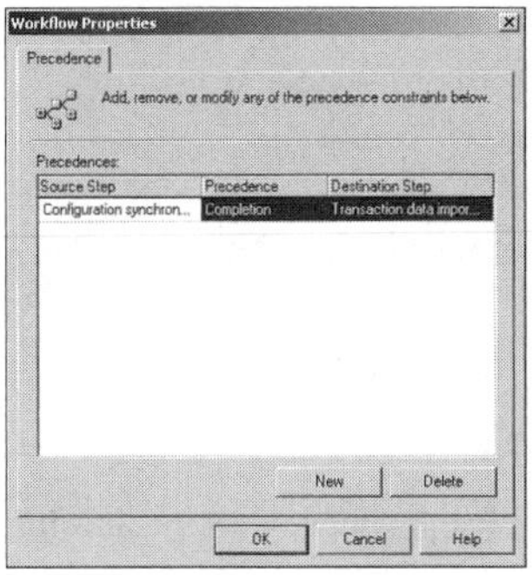

FIGURE 15.17
Details of a DTS workflow.

After configuring tasks and workflow as a DTS package, save the package as, say, *Commerce Server Data Import*. Then schedule it by right-clicking the package under Local Packages in SQL Server (see Figure 15.18).

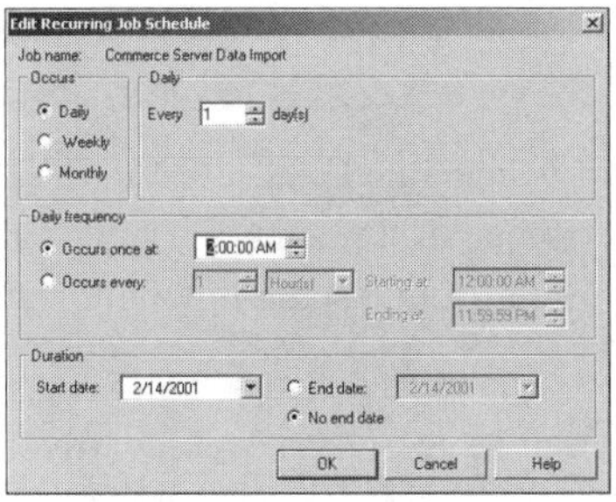

FIGURE 15.18
Scheduling a saved DTS package.

A final note here: If you are planning to save the tasks in a package for scheduling, make sure the import processes do an incremental load and not a full load every time.

Analysis Reports

Commerce Server provides a set of 39 reports that can be used to query the data warehouse to find answers. These reports cover a wide variety of requirements and are categorized as follows:

- Advertising reports
- Diagnostic reports

- Product sales reports
- Query string reports
- User reports
- Visit reports
- Web usage reports

These reports are available under the Reports module in Business Desk. The Reports module's pages issue the query to the data warehouse and display the results, depending on the type of the report. Reports are divided into two types: static and dynamic.

Static and Dynamic Reports

When a dynamic report is run, the most recent data in the data warehouse is used to fetch the results. Therefore, a dynamic report is actually executed at runtime, with only the report definition saved in the database. A static report is generated when run and the results are stored as a snapshot report in the Completed Reports module. There are other differences between static and a dynamic reports.

The output of a dynamic report results in a browser window with the result rows in a PivotTable. Users can move dimensions and measures using the PivotTable and analyze data. Also, they can save the changed dimensions and measures as a new report definition. The data generated by a dynamic report cannot be saved in Business Desk. However, the report can be exported to Excel.

On the other hand, a static report is generated and saved in the Completed Reports module with a timestamp. The report is opened as a plain HTML file in a browser window. Managers cannot create a new report definition using a static report. A static report can be exported to the List Manager module.

Both dynamic and static reports can issue SQL as well as MDX queries to the data warehouse. New static reports and custom dynamic reports can be created by a developer. A manager cannot delete any of these default 39 reports; custom reports created over this can be deleted. The report definitions are stored in the DW database in the table report.

To learn more about these reports, let's start using the Business Desk modules now.

Working with a Dynamic Report

Launch the Reports module by clicking the module under the Analysis category in the Estore Biz Desk. Select Customer Spend Summary, which is a dynamic report under the Sales category. Then from the taskbar, click the Run Customer Spend Summary (Alt+R) button to run the report (see Figure 15.19).

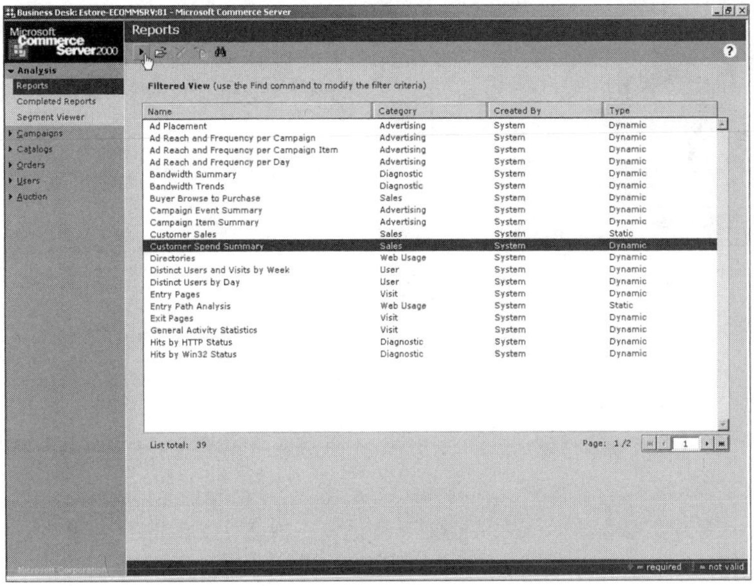

FIGURE 15.19
Running a dynamic report.

The report opens up a new browser window and displays the report in a PivotTable (see Figure 15.20). The PivotTable works in the browser as a client-side component. Therefore, the workstation on which the Business Desk is run should have Office Web Components (OWC) installed to be able to work with PivotTable and PivotChart components.

The report gives the quantity and revenues along the four dimensions of the Sales cube. You could expand the catalogs and find the measures for each month or year for a particular catalog. Catalog Name and Year/Month are called *row fields*. If you have multiple sites, the Site dimension can be used as a filter to slice through the cube. Therefore, Site and Customers in this report are the *filter fields*. The toolbars, such as Move to Row Area, Move to Column Area, and Move to Filter, can be used to move dimensions as required.

FIGURE 15.20

Key components of a generated dynamic report.

Creating a New Report Definition

The default PivotTable can be changed by switching filters and row fields or by adding more dimensions or filters. Each dimension can be dragged and dropped on another dimension to exchange places. Apart from that, the PivotTable field list can be launched via the Field List button next to the Help button on the PivotList toolbar. In the default PivotTable, only the CatalogName dimension level from the Products cube dimension is used as a row field. Suppose we want to know the quantity and revenue per product sold. In the PivotTable field list, expand the Products dimension. Under L2, we have Product Name. Click and drag Product Name and drop it over the Year level in the table. The Product Name dimension level is now added next to Catalog Name, and upon expanding each catalog, we can see the measures calculated for each of the products in the catalogs (see Figure 15.21).

You can make more such changes to the dynamic report, such as changing Site to another site name or adding Registered User ID as a filter. Once you see the result you want, the modified structure can be saved as a different report definition. Just click the Save icon at the left top of the PivotTable. In the dialog box titled Save a Report–Web Page Dialog, give a different name for the report and enter a description. Then click the OK button (see Figure 15.22).

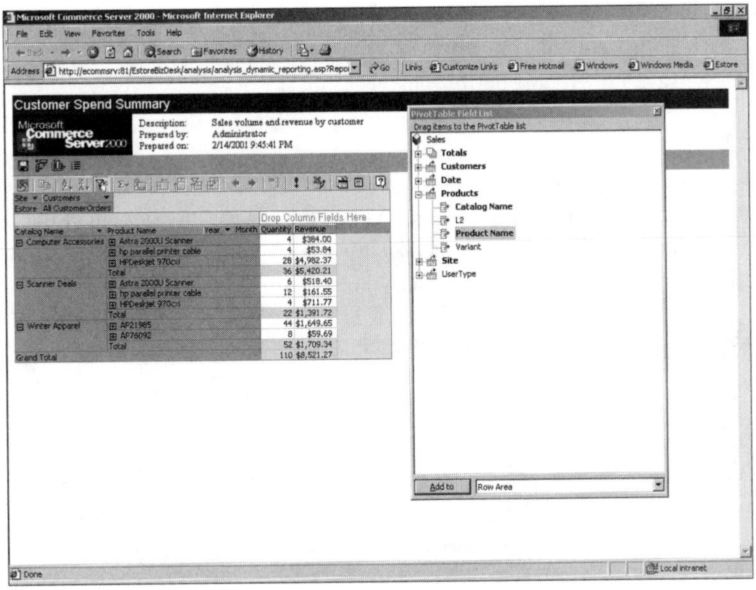

FIGURE 15.21
Modifying dimensions and filters in a dynamic report.

FIGURE 15.22
Saving a report modification as a new definition.

The browser refreshes with the new report definition and the fetched data. Now whenever the modified report is run, it will contain the row and filter fields that were configured. If you go back and click the Reports module in Biz Desk again, you can see that the new report definition has been created. You can create new report definitions out of existing dynamic reports and save the definitions. These reports can be executed whenever you need to analyze the most recent data in the data warehouse. Therefore, by changing the PivotTable of an existing report by adding and removing filters, sorting the displayed data, adding measures, moving fields, changing the data that's detailed and summarized, or pivoting (or manipulating) the columns and rows, you can save new report definitions.

PivotChart

The dynamic reports use another component called the *PivotChart*, which is used to display the report data at the client side using one of 15 available chart formats. Click the Show Chart button in the PivotTable toolbar. A bar chart is shown along with the table (see Figure 15.23). You can use the drop-down list to change the type of chart to Line, Pie, Doughnut, and so on.

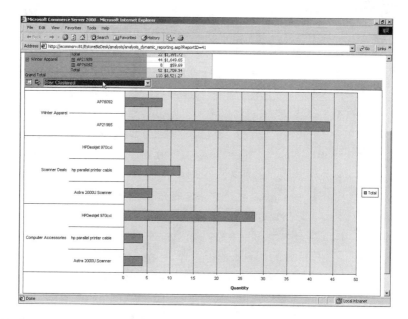

FIGURE 15.23
A bar chart generated by the PivotChart component.

Reports such as these help managers analyze sales data along various dimensions, and they can apply filters as needed. The data can be exported to Excel for any further analysis. Also, there are a few functions, such as Sort Ascending, Sort Descending, Auto-Calc, and Sub-Total, provided in the PivotTable toolbars. These functions can be used for performing quick and simple analysis.

Note from the report that the Winter Apparel catalog does not contain valid product details or the catalog import process failed, because SKUs are shown for products instead of product names. Also notice that only the first measure (that is, Quantity) is shown in the PivotChart. If you want the other measure, Revenue, you have to move it to the first column in measures.

Dynamic reports are designed to access frequently used reports on relatively small data sets and hence are run synchronously with the Biz Desk. The more that purchases are made on the Estore site, the more these purchases are detailed in this report.

Working with Static Reports

A static report is one designed for accessing large amounts of data, and the report itself is run infrequently. For example, you generate a report to find the number of registered users, say, once in two weeks. After the report is run, the results are stored in the Completed Reports module in Biz Desk, from where the reports can be viewed at any time.

You will learn the characteristics of a static report by running the Top Requested Pages report. This report can be found in the Reports module. The arrow button at the bottom of the report list is used to move to the second page to access this report. Select Top Requested Pages from the report list and click the Run Top Requested Pages (Alt+R) task icon. Immediately, the Run a Report dialog box is launched. This form is used to specify filters much the same way we specified filters in the dynamic report. The difference is that in the case of a dynamic report, you can apply filters on the result set using the PivotTable on the Web page. In the case of a static report, however, because the report is a plain HTML file, the filter has to be applied even before the report is generated and saved.

Click the Advanced button in the Run a Report dialog box to see the actual query that is being made (see Figure 15.24).

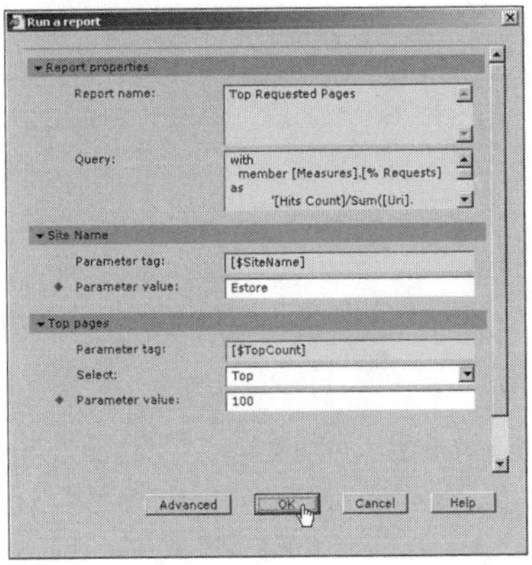

FIGURE 15.24
Specifying report filters for a static report.

Click the OK button. The static report is being generated asynchronously. Therefore, you can go to the module Completed Reports under Analysis in Biz Desk.

Viewing a Completed Report

In the Completed Reports module, you should be able to see the report with the name Top Requested Pages. If the report has not completed execution, the status should be Pending. Time and Date Run distinguish two static reports run from the same report definition, such as Top Requested Pages. Click the saved report and click the Open Top Requested Pages (Alt+O) task icon in the toolbar. The report is opened as an HTML document in the Web browser (see Figure 15.25).

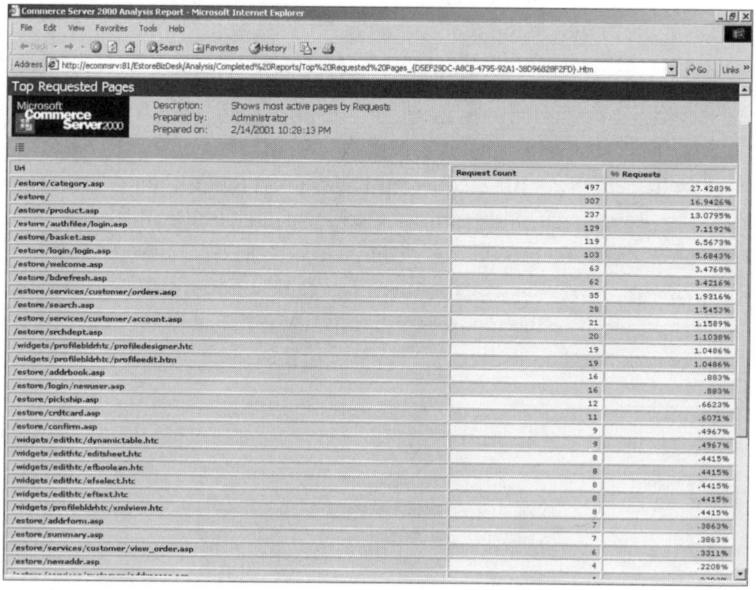

FIGURE 15.25

A static report saved in Completed Reports.

The report can be saved like any other HTML file to a file system.

Exporting to List Manager

Static reports can be used to export lists to the List Manager, which can use these lists for personalization and targeted e-mails. You know that a list can be exported to the List Manager, but a mailable list is one that contains a valid e-mail address in the rcp_email column of the exported rows. So, let's observe the export process by electing to export the results of the New Registered Users static report. Click the Export New Registered Users (Alt+E) taskbar icon. Change the Number of Users filter to All. Set the User Registration Date filter to Last Month. Click the OK button. The Export Report as a List dialog box is launched (see Figure 15.26).

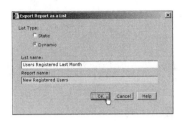

FIGURE 15.26
Exporting a static report to the List Manager.

The list type could be static or dynamic. This needs an explanation because the report definition itself, as you have seen, is static. If the list is chosen as static, the report is run when the OK button is clicked, and the list is exported to List Manager as a static list. A static list won't change.

If the exported list is dynamic, only the report definition (even though it's static) is stored in the list. Therefore, whenever the list is accessed from List Manager, the report is executed to fetch the list of registered users for the previous month. After choosing a dynamic list, click the OK button.

Creating Custom Reports

You have already seen that a custom report definition can be created by modifying an existing dynamic report. However, for reasons such as building an entirely new cube or extending the data warehouse, the site developer can create custom dynamic and static reports to be used with Business Desk. Both static and dynamic reports are stored under the Reports table in the DW database. The Query column in the table contains any SQL or MDX query for a static report, whereas the XMLData column contains the query information to be used in a dynamic report.

Static reports pass the parameters and the query, similar to what you saw in Figure 15.24, to the `ReportRenderer` object, which generates an HTML document with the result set. In the case of dynamic reports, the query is stored in XML format to be used by the PivotTable component to connect to the cube and get the result set. The default reports in the Reports table are generated by the script `CSReports.sql`. For creating new custom reports, the Commerce Server SDK provides four files in the path `<Microsoft Commerce Server>SDK\Samples\Business Analytics\Scripts`. These four files correspond to creating the following types of reports:

- A new dynamic report using SQL
- A new dynamic report using OLAP

- A new static report using SQL

- A new static report using OLAP

These are SQL scripts that are used to insert the definition for the custom report in the Reports table.

A New Dynamic OLAP Report

Assume that you want to analyze more information using the Web Usage report than is available with the default reports. Also, the new report will be a dynamic report that passes on a reference to the cube in the XML-formatted data for the PivotTable. Open the file New dynamic OLAP report script.sql. The comments for Directions give clear instructions on how to use the script. Insert values for the variables @ReportName, @ReportCategory, @ReportCreator, and @CubeName. That is all that is needed to create the report. The modified script has to be run on the Estore_dw data warehouse database.

The report definition will appear in the Reports module. You have to run the report and then modify and save the definition as another report. Here is a snippet of the SQL script needed to create the definition:

```
Declare @Dynamic_MDX tinyint
Select @Dynamic_MDX = 1


— — — — — — — — — — —
— Report Variables
— — — — — — — — — — —


Declare @ReportName [nvarchar] (128)
Select @ReportName = 'New dynamic OLAP report name'

Declare @ReportCategory [nvarchar] (128)
Select @ReportCategory = 'Web Usage'

Declare @ReportCreator [nvarchar] (128)
Select @ReportCreator = 'Gopal Sreeraman'

Declare @CubeName [nvarchar] (128)
Select @CubeName = 'Web Usage'


— — — — — — — — — — —
— Report Definition
— — — — — — — — — — —


Insert Into [dbo].[Report] ([DisplayName], [ReportType], [Category],
➥[CreatedBy], [XMLData])
```

```
Values (@ReportName, @Dynamic_MDX, @ReportCategory, @ReportCreator, '<xml
➥xmlns:x=''urn:schemas-microsoft-com:office:excel''>
 <x:PivotTable>
  <x:OWCVersion>9.0.0.3821</x:OWCVersion>
  <x:DisplayFieldList/>
  <x:FieldListTop>357</x:FieldListTop>
  <x:FieldListLeft>837</x:FieldListLeft>
  <x:FieldListBottom>726</x:FieldListBottom>
  <x:FieldListRight>1024</x:FieldListRight>
  <x:CacheDetails/>
  <x:ConnectionString>Provider=MSOLAP;Data Source=;Initial Catalog=;Client
  ➥Cache Size=25;Auto Synch Period=10000</x:ConnectionString>
  <x:DataMember>' + @CubeName + '</x:DataMember>
 </x:PivotTable>
</xml>' )
```

A SQL query–based dynamic report can be defined using the file New dynamic SQL report
script.sql. As you can see, everything is the same as that for the OLAP report, except that
instead of passing a cube name to the PivotTable, we pass a SQL query in the variable
@SQLQuery. Also, the data access provider for the PivotTable is MSOLAP:

```
<x:ConnectionString>Provider=MSOLAP;Data Source=;Initial Catalog=;Client
➥Cache Size=25;Auto Synch Period=10000</x:ConnectionString>.
```

The connection string for a SQL query would be this:

```
<x:ConnectionString>Provider=SQLOLEDB;Integrated Security=SSPI;Initial Catalog
➥=;Data Source=</x:ConnectionString>
```

Creating Custom Static Reports

The other two SDK files for static reports can be used to insert report definitions in the Reports
table. Open the New static SQL report script.sql file in a text editor. Similar to the
dynamic reports, there's a Report Variables section. The parameterized SQL query is built as
follows:

```
Declare @ReportQuery [nvarchar] (2000)
Select @ReportQuery = 'SELECT [$SelectOrder] UserId rcp_guid,
DateCreated, DateRegistered, Email rcp_email, FirstName, LastName,
➥TelephoneNumber, UserTitle, UserType
Into [$ResultTable] From RegisteredUser, LinkSiteRegisteredUserRel, Site
Where RegisteredUser.RegisteredUserID = LinkSiteRegisteredUserRel.
➥RegisteredUserID
And LinkSiteRegisteredUserRel.SiteID = Site.SiteID And [$SiteName]
And [$DateRange] And [$Expression] [$SimpleValue] Order By rcp_email asc'
```

This query can be modified as required by the site. The report is inserted into the Report
table in the DW database, with the SQL query inserted into the Query column. In this query,

parameters such as [$DateRange] and [$Expression] come from the user selection in the Run a Report dialog box. The query, along with the parameters, is passed to the ReportRenderer object. The dimensions and report filters (parameters) for each of the static reports are stored in the tables ReportDimension and ReportParam, respectively. Notice that the parameter [$ResultTable] is an arbitrary GUID generated by SQL Server as a name for an intermediate temp table for the renderer object to store results.

Once you run the script, the static report is available in the Business Desk Reports module.

Prediction in Commerce Server

We have talked in passing about how a data warehouse can be used in prediction by extrapolating historical data and generating a model out of it. Statisticians are adept at various methods of modeling real-world phenomena such as earthquakes, floods, and torrential rains. Models are common in stock market analysis, where future value of a stock or an index is given as a prediction. There are various other applications of models throughout our life. All these models share a common thing; they feed on large chunks of historical data fed to state-of-the-art algorithms devised to process such data.

The data warehouse is well integrated with Commerce Server, with site data such as Web logs, transactions, and campaigns being pulled frequently into the DW database and populating the OLAP cubes. Therefore, this reservoir of valuable enterprise data can be mined to build prediction models that can be used to better service customers. For example, Web sites give recommendations to users when users are browsing the basket page. The recommendations are products that other users have bought, and they are generated based on filtering algorithms. Also, analysis models can predict missing attributes of an user from the model. If the age of a user is missing, a model can be used to predict the property. Therefore, prediction gives your Web site the power to cross-sell, up-sell, and give friendly product recommendations that can greatly increase the probability of increased revenues.

The Predictor Resource

The resource enabling the predictive capabilities in a Commerce Server site is the *Predictor resource*. The Predictor resource can be installed while you're unpacking a site using the Site Packager at the global level. There can be only one Predictor instance running on the computer. One commerce site can have multiple Predictor resources at the site level, pointing to many Predictor resources on different computers. The resource runs as PredServ.exe. The Predictor is connected with the DW database of the site by default. However, it is also possible to specify an external database using the property pages at the global level.

The Predictor resource connects to the DW database to access data and build various analysis models on the server. A PredictorClient object is then used in an ASP page to load a specific model and ask for predictions to be rendered on the page.

Analysis Models

Using Commerce Server, you can build two types of models: prediction and segment. As the names indicate, a prediction model is built to offer predictions, whereas a segment model is used to classify users based on similar user properties in the underlying statistical data. Prediction models use the Decision Tree Algorithm to construct a dependency network among the various attributes in the data. It relates the probability of one attribute predicting the occurrence of a second attribute based on historical data. Therefore, the model could become a complex network of linked relationships as data keeps growing.

On the other hand, a segment model is based on the concept of *clustering*, which we discussed in the introduction to data warehousing. In this model, the user data in the underlying data mart is plotted. Similar user attributes bring together users forming a segment. A segment can be viewed in the Segment Viewer module of Biz Desk and can also be used by a `PredictorClient` object to classify users.

Data for a Model

Because analysis models are built on large amounts of historical data, it is first necessary to gather all such data needed to build a model. Once data has been imported into the data warehouse, you can build cases out of that data. A *case* is a collection of specifically gathered information about a user, such as user profile attributes, purchase history, products clicked, and so on. Tables are built to gather these types of information from various fact tables that have meaningful data. Most often, the case is based on a database view, compared to a table, which collects information from various fact tables. Many analysis models use tens of thousand of cases to build models. The greater the number of cases in a model, the better the accuracy of prediction using that model. However, cases can also quickly reach a saturation point if used beyond their reasonable incremental contribution to prediction and may burden the system. This is decided based on the type of model, number of cases, and accuracy expected from the model.

The case tables or views themselves are classified based on whether they contain *dense* or *sparse* data. An example of a dense table is shown in Figure 15.27.

In this table, exactly one row is stored for a user; the row contains attributes for the user, such as gender and age. Therefore, each row is a case, and the total cases are equal to the total number of rows in the view or table. User profile information is one good example of why a table should be configured as a dense table.

A sparse table contains more than one row for a single user. This is exemplified in Figure 15.28.

Case ID

LoginName	Gender	Age
Mark21	M	29
Becky02	F	19
LeeMJ	M	39

FIGURE 15.27

A dense table.

Case ID	Pivot Property	Value of Pivot
LoginName	SKU	QTY
Mark21	Z9C099	2
Mark21	M-987	1
Mark21	ABC099	3
Becky02	ABD098	2
Becky02	KM7645	2
LeeMJ	ABD098	4
LeeMJ	Z9c099	2
LeeMJ	YZ877	1

FIGURE 15.28

A sparse table.

As you can see from the example, a sparse table typically gathers transactions for a user. Therefore, there might be many rows for a user corresponding to different transactions. Here, a case is the collection of all such rows for a user. The Pivot property is the item we want to predict, and the value is the quantity of that property. Because data for a sparse table comes from many objects, such as User Profile, Orders, OrderFormLineItems, and so on, the case data source is in fact designed as a database view.

A model can be built out of either one of these types of tables, or both. In the case where both dense and sparse tables are specified for a model, only the dense tables are used.

Even though we have used the examples of user profile and purchase information to build models, it is possible to extend the same concept to build case tables containing properties such as user profile, page requested, and time stayed. We will see all this concretely by analyzing the default model configuration provided by Commerce Server.

The Transactions Configuration

Before we use Predictor to build an analysis model, we need a configuration for that model. A model configuration specifies information such as the name of the configuration, the site to which it belongs, and the underlying dense and/or sparse tables. The configuration itself is stored in the DW database.

Commerce Server includes a default configuration called *Transactions*, which can be used to build models for tasks such as predicting product recommendations. You can see the configuration from the Commerce Server Manager under the Global Resource Predictor, as shown in Figure 15.29.

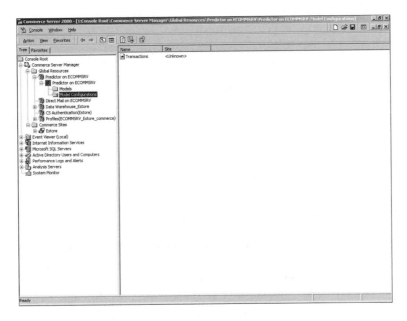

FIGURE 15.29
The default model configuration.

Here are the important DW database tables that store model configuration–related information:

- PredictorModelCfgs
- PredictorDataTables
- PredictorModels

PredictorModelCfgs is a simple table with two columns. The first one, ModelCfgName, stores the name of the configuration, such as Transactions. The second column is called SiteName, to denote that this configuration is specified for a particular site.

If you open PredictorDataTables, you'll seen that this table stores information about the source data tables for this model configuration (see Figure 15.30).

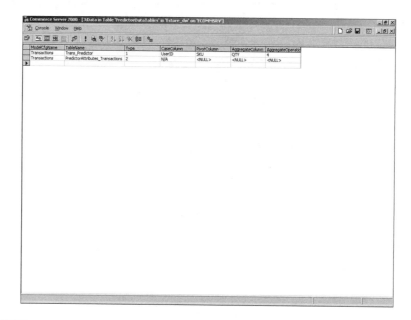

FIGURE 15.30

The PredictorDataTables table for a model configuration.

By default, the Trans_Predictor View object is given as the source for the model. The Type column specifies what type of source the table is, where 0 means a dense table, 1 denotes a sparse table, and 2 is used for an attributes table, which is optionally created for each model manually. The other columns in this table are obvious: CaseColumn identifies the column name in the table to be treated as a case ID. PivotColumn is the column about which we make predictions, and AggregateColumn is the value of the pivot column. The AggregrateOperation column specifies what operation is to be performed on AggregateColumn. Here are the possible values:

- 0 for SUM
- 1 for MAX
- 2 for MIN
- 3 for AVG
- 4 for COUNT

It is up to the configuration schema designer to decide what the quantity represents; if AggregateColumn is sales quantity, it would make sense to use SUM. If the column stores page hit frequency, COUNT could be used to aggregate for a particular time period.

If you do not have the Product_Attributes table so far, its okay. This is because a blank Product_Attributes_<configuration name> table is created only when you build a model based on a configuration. The Product_Attributes table has a Type setting of 2, meaning that it is an attribute table. An attribute table can be used to indicate which attributes should be used to build the model and which are to be predicted. This table is optional; by default, all attributes in the data table are used for prediction as well as to be predicted. Apart from that, the Distribution column in this table can be used to tell the Predictor how to statistically link the data in the table. By default, with nothing entered in this attributes table, the mode is Discrete-Autodetect. You can force Predictor to use other types, such as Normal (Gaussian) Distribution, Continuous, and Discrete Distributions. For example, string values could be just related as discrete distributions, such as "NY" and "GA". On the other hand, values such as unit cost can be represented as a continuous curve with a start value, and each additional cost treated as a positive or negative delta over the previous cost.

All you need to know is that if we don't fill up this attributes table, the data distribution is going to be Autodetect; the algorithm uses the appropriate type of distribution. An attribute table has the naming convention of PredictorAttributes_<model configuration name>.

Finally, let's see what the data table contains. Opening the Trans_Predictor view shows that it contains various values imported during the Transactions Import task (see Figure 15.31).

As you can see, this is a sparse table (view) with many rows for a single user, with each row representing a product bought by the user, along with the quantity.

Building a Predictor Model

An analysis model can be built from the Commerce Server Manager by right-clicking a model configuration and choosing the Build command. The Predictor expects to have a minimum of 200 cases before it thinks its worth it to build a model. It will give an error if you attempt to build a model with less than those required number of cases.

Even though you may have run all the data import tasks, the data table still might not contain very many cases if your server is still in development or just went to test production. As you know, a *case* is a collection of all rows for a case ID. In the Trans_Predictor table, because UserID is the case ID for the model, you need to have at least 200 distinct user IDs in the table.

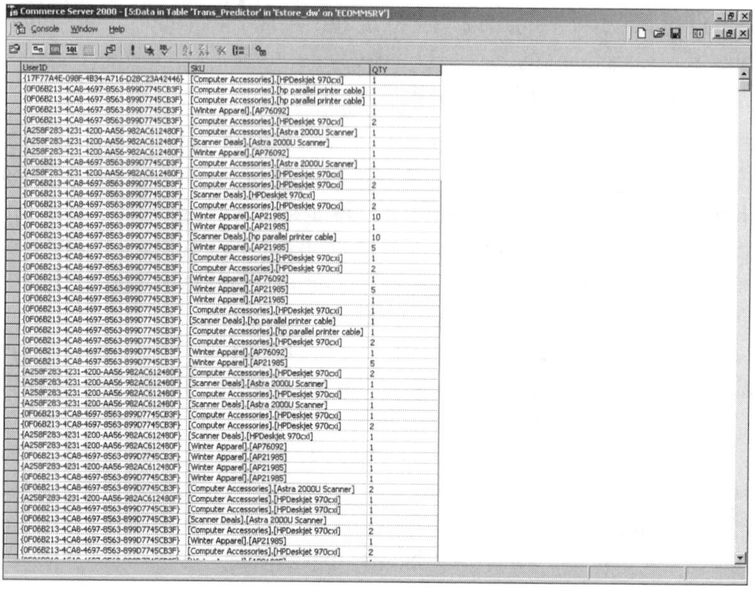

FIGURE 15.31
Data in the Trans_Predictor case view for the Transactions model.

Because that may not be feasible in development or test situations, you could insert those additional cases into the table yourself. You may skip the next section, "Test Data Preparation," if you have more than the required number of cases.

Testing the Data Preparation

Trans_Predictor is a view based on the DW tables OrderGroup, OrderFormLineItems, and RegisteredUser. We don't want to mess up the data in these tables. Therefore, what we will do is create a table called Trans_Predictor_Tmp for building the model and import all the data from Trans_Predictor. Then we will populate Trans_Predictor_Tmp with additional cases. Note that we need to modify the TableName column in PredictorTables to point it to the new table. Here are the steps in detail:

1. To create a new table and import from Trans_Predictor, run the following query in the Estore_dw database:

```
Select * into Trans_Predictor_Tmp from Trans_Predictor
```

The new table is created and populated with existing site data.

2. To simulate the required number of cases in Trans_Predictor_Tmp, a script such as the following could be run on the SQL Server DW database:

```
declare  @usercount int
declare @sku nvarchar(25)
declare @guid uniqueidentifier

select @usercount = 1
while(@usercount <=500) — Insert 500 Users
begin
    select @guid = NEWID()
    declare @itemtmp int

    select @itemtmp = 1
    while(@itemtmp <= 5) — 500 users buy 5 items from 5 different
    ➥catalogs
    begin
        select @sku = '[Catalog' + CAST(@itemtmp as varchar(3)) + '].
        ➥[SKU' + CAST(@itemtmp as varchar(3)) + ']'
            Insert Trans_Predictor_Tmp(UserID,SKU,QTY) values (@guid ,
            ➥@sku,@itemtmp)
        select @itemtmp = @itemtmp + 1
    end

    select @usercount = @usercount + 1 — Next User ID
end
```

3. Update the PredictorDataTables table in the DW database with the following query:

```
Update PredictorDataTables
Set TableName='Trans_Predictor_Tmp'
Where TableName='Trans_Predictor'
```

Building the Model

Using the Commerce Server Manager, expand the global resource Predictor on the server for which you are building the model. Click Model Configurations. In the right pane, right-click Transactions and choose Build. In the Model Build Properties dialog box, give a name for this model instance (see Figure 15.32).

Choose a Build Priority setting depending on the resources available on the server. The build process is resource intensive and takes time. It will be faster if the data warehouse database is on the same computer as the Predictor resource. Next, specify the model type as Prediction. Click the Next button.

In the next screen, shown in Figure 15.33, leave the Sample Size setting at the default value. A value of –1 indicates that all data (or up to 20,000 cases, whichever is less) will be used for building the model. The Measured Accuracy Sample Fraction field is used to specify what percentage of data is used to score the model versus build the model. Accept the default of 0.4, which means 40 percent of the data is used for scoring and 60 percent is used for building the model.

15

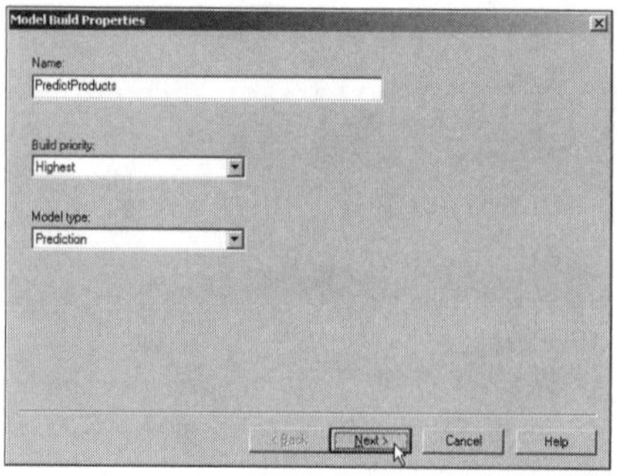

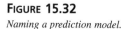

FIGURE 15.32

Naming a prediction model.

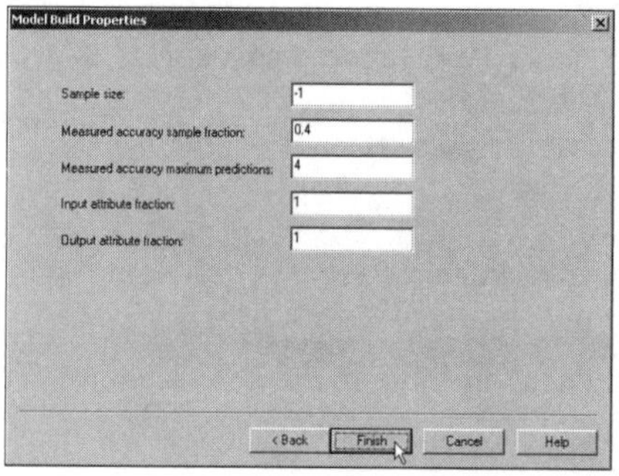

FIGURE 15.33

Properties used in building a model.

Measured Accuracy Maximum Predictions should be changed to 4—this is the number of recommendations we are going to give on a page. The Input Attribute Fraction field is used to specify what percentage of the attributes should be used as input for prediction. Leave this at 1 to indicate that all attributes will be used. Similarly, accept the value of 1 for Output Attribute Fraction to include all attributes as part of the predicted set.

Finally, click the Finish button to start building the model. The status bar indicates task progress. After the task is successfully completed, the model is ready for making predictions for the site.

About the Scores

In the Commerce Server Manager, you can see that there are two scores assigned after the model is built. These are Recommend Score and Data Fit Score. These scores are also stored in the PredictorModels DW database table. The algorithms used to arrive at these scores are a little involved. However, here's all you need to know from these scores: The higher the recommend score (that is, closer to 1), the higher the quality of predictions returned. This score depends on the Measured Accuracy Maximum Predictions number that is set while building the model, and this value should closely match the maximum recommendations to be asked from any site page. The Data Fit score indicates the quality of predicting missing properties. In our example, we did not build a model to predict properties. Therefore, the attributes in the model are skewed rather than being in the same segment. Therefore, the Data Fit score is negative.

Using the `PredictorClient` Object

To get predictions on a site page, the `PredictorClient` object is instantiated, configured with certain context values and inputs, and then asked for a certain number of predictions. In the retail site Estore, the code needed for predictions is already included in the `basket.asp` page. We will use that to illustrate and achieve the predictions generated by the model.

Initializing the `PredictorClient` Object

Recall that the `InitPredictor` routine defined in `global_predictor_lib.asp` is called at application startup. In this function, change the name of the model to the one we created:

```
Const strModelName = "PredictProducts"
```

The next statement is used to fetch the connection string to the DW database:

```
connstr_db_dw = GetDWConnectionString()
```

A few lines down, the `PredictorClient` object is instantiated as follows:

```
Set objPredictor = Server.CreateObject("Commerce.PredictorClient")
```

Next, the `LoadModelFromDB` method of the `PredictorClient` object is used to load the analysis model:

```
objPredictor.LoadModelFromDB strModelName, connstr_db_dw
```

Quite a few properties can be set for `PredictorClient`. One of them is `fpPopularityPenalty`, which indicates what penalty should be applied to already popular products, thus preventing them from being recommended. A value of 0 means no penalty, whereas 1 means the product won't be recommended:

```
objPredictor.fpPopularityPenalty = 0.8
```

Another property that is set in this routine at the global level is `fpDefaultConfidence`. Each attribute is assigned a probability of "not missing" from the prediction. If that value is less than this value, that attribute will not be in the recommended list. A value of 0.0 indicates no restriction on confidence, whereas 100.0 indicates that the attribute should have had a 100-percent probability if "not missing" in the model:

```
objPredictor.fpDefaultConfidence = 0.0
```

This initialized instance of the `PredictorClient` object is available to all site pages through the following application variable:

```
Application("MSCSPredictor")
```

In the Basket Page

You must have already noticed the bold text *Recommendations* in the basket page on the site. This was displayed just to remind us that recommendations have to be configured and developed for the site.

At the beginning of the `basket.asp` file, two constants are defined as follows:

```
Const PREDICTOR_PIVOT_COLUMN = "SKU"
Const PREDICTOR_AGGREGATE_COLUMN = "QTY"
```

You definitely know what these columns mean.

Next, a dictionary is created to hold the input cases for the prediction and a simple list is created to hold the properties asked for prediction. The function `htmRenderPredictions` is where the prediction-related code can be found:

```
Set dCase = GetDictionary()
Set slToPredict = GetSimpleList()
```

Because for product recommendation we use SKU as the pivot column in the DW data table, only that is given as the property to predict:

```
slToPredict.Add PREDICTOR_PIVOT_COLUMN
```

The input case is built as key/value pairs for the products and their quantities currently in the basket. For example, the dictionary would contain

```
dCase("QTY([Catalog1].[Product1])")=2
dCase("QTY([Catalog2].[Product2])")=1
```

and so on for each of the products in the basket. This is done by the following loop:

```
For Each sOrderFormName in oOrderFormDisplayOrder
        Set oOrderForm = mscsOrderGrp.value.OrderForms.Value(sOrderFormName)
        For Each dItem in oOrderForm.Items
            strPropName = PREDICTOR_AGGREGATE_COLUMN & "([" & dItem.product_
            ➥catalog & "].[" & dItem.product_id & "])"
            lQuantity = CLng(dItem.quantity)
            dCase(strPropName) = lQuantity
        Next
    Next
```

Now set the value of maximum predictions to 3, because that is the maximum number of recommendations we want to give on this page:

```
lMaxPredictions = 3
```

Next, the `Predict` method of the `PredictorClient` object is called, passing the case dictionary, properties to predict, and maximum predictions required:

```
oPredictor.Predict dCase, slToPredict, arPredictedProps, arPredictedVals,
➥lMaxPredictions
```

The resulting predictions are returned in the array `arPredictedProps`, which is iterated to write the predicted product names as hyperlink text to the basket page:

```
For i = 0 To UBound(arPredictedProps)
    strHREF = PredictedPropToHREF(arPredictedProps(i))
    htmContent = htmContent & strHREF & "<BR>"
Next
```

I am eager to see the recommendations now. Therefore, I'll restart the Estore IIS application because we modified the `InitPredictor` function in the global file `global_predictor_lib.asp`. Then I'll log in to Estore and browse my basket page. The recommendations are shown in Figure 15.34.

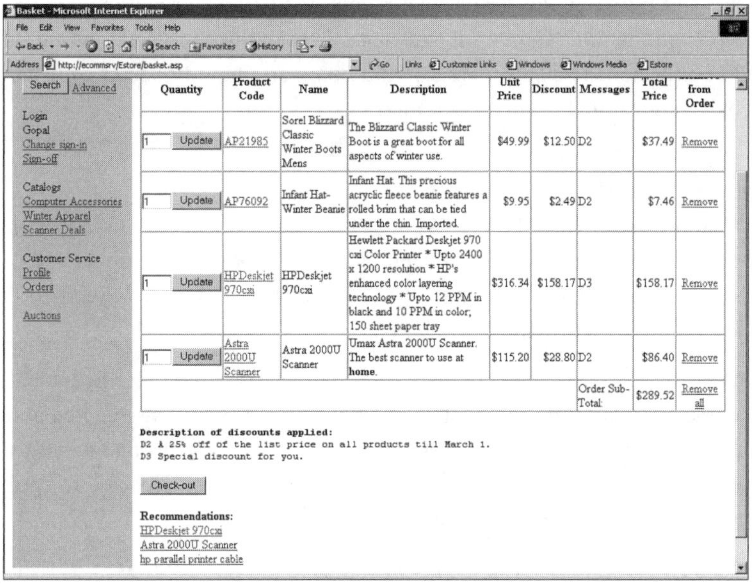

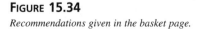

FIGURE 15.34

Recommendations given in the basket page.

The number of products recommended depends on the maximum recommendations requested, the number of unique products, quality of the model, and so on.

You can use the Model Viewer from Commerce Server Manager to view the network diagram and the decision tree for the Prediction model. Right-click a model (say, PredictProducts) and then choose View Model. For more information on how to use the Model Viewer, consult the accompanying documentation or the Help menu.

Segment Models

Although prediction models are ideal to get product recommendations for cross-sell support, segment models can be used to analyze why certain cases are huddled around each other. In a segment model, cases with similar attributes and values are grouped into segments using the clustering method of data mining. Using a segment model, a manager can compare two segments and find the differences and similarities between users. Accordingly, he can initiate new marketing programs targeted toward segments. Segment models can be used to analyze a hierarchy of segments.

We will use the Transactions configuration again for generating a segment model. Right-click Transaction in Model Configurations in the CS MMC. Choose Build. Name the model **PurchaseSegment** and set the Model Type to Segment. Click the Next button. Because we are not going to use a segment model for product recommendations, accept the default values in the next screen. Note that the Number of Segments field defines the maximum number of clusters that would be formed. The buffer size should be given liberally because clustering is also a resource-intensive algorithm. Finally, click the Finish button.

Segment Viewer

The Segment Viewer module can be found under the Analysis category in Business Desk. Click the module. The segment we just created is listed. Choose the segment and click the Open Model (Alt+O) task icon. The Segment Viewer shows the PurchaseSegment model in a hierarchical fashion (see Figure 15.35).

The Segment Viewer can be used to compare one segment with the other to evaluate common or different characteristics of the segments. All segments are finally aggregated at the root level Population. In our example, we see that Segment 0 contains attributes that occur frequently together. This data is due to our test run. In a real scenario, data is expected to be distributed more evenly, and segments would differ by few attributes.

Using the Launch Report (Alt+P) task icon, you can generate the report as an HTML page and launch it in a new browser window. It is also possible to export the segment as a list to the List Manager using the Export Segment to List (Alt+X) task icon. Recall that any list can be imported in the List Manager, but only valid "mailable" lists can be used for direct mail purposes.

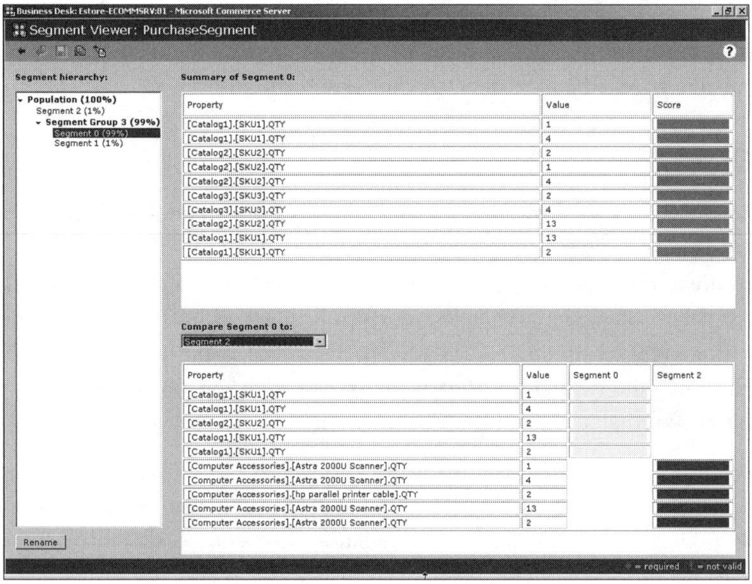

FIGURE 15.35
The Segment Viewer module.

Commerce Server provides objects such as `PredictorServiceAdmin`, `PredictorService SiteAdmin`, and `PredModelBuilder`. These objects can be used to programmatically build, retrieve, rename, and delete models and model configurations. Also, they can be used to programmatically start, stop, pause, and resume model builds. If you want, say, a Web-based interface for doing these activities, the Predictor objects might be of help.

Tips on Extending the DW

The data warehouse schema should satisfy many of the analysis needs of a commerce site. In spite of that, there could be some unique requirements, such as a new cube, different report requirements, or analysis models. Going through this entire chapter will give you a better idea of what is involved before attempting any changes to the data warehouse. Following are the key points to remember:

- Be careful not to remove existing schema definitions because many cubes, import tasks, and reports might be using them. If you need to re-create the original schema, run the `csdwschema.sql` script on an empty database.

- Define class, member, and key definitions using the logical schema. Be familiar with the data warehouse meta-model in order to add new objects.

- Using the Users module in Business Desk or the Profile resource in the CS MMC, you can export attributes of a user profile. New export attributes and new query strings are automatically handled by the data warehouse schema.

Summary

Commerce Server provides data warehouse and analysis infrastructure conveniently integrated with the site. It is possible to import data effectively from Web log files and the site database into the data warehouse relational database. Then the gathered data can be exported to populate prebuilt OLAP cubes. Static and dynamic reports in Biz Desk are used to access the data warehouse and generate reports for analysis. Static reports can be exported to List Manager for targeting content. Using the Predictor resource, analysis models can be built to provide the site with cross-sell and predictive capabilities. Segment models are used to cluster data and compare segments.

In this chapter, you saw how to import data into the data warehouse, customize reports, and build analysis models to add product recommendations.

Integration with BizTalk Server

IN THIS CHAPTER

- **About BizTalk Server**   534
- **Messaging Manager Objects**   535
- **Integration Between Commerce Server and BizTalk Server**   536
- **Building a Partner Site**   537
- **Exchanging Catalogs with Partners**   539
- **Scenario 2: Partner Has Different Infrastructure**   545
- **Scenario 1: Partner Has Similar Infrastructure**   553
- **Fulfilling Orders Through Partners**   557

Long before the advent of the World Wide Web, large organizations had private networks through which they conducted electronic transactions with their trading partners. Electronic Data Interchange (EDI) was affordable only to a few companies, as it required a lot of capital and effort in building the infrastructure. Private networks were used for exchanging documents such as requisitions, bids, purchase orders, shipment routing slips, invoices, and payment information. This greatly boosted the "time to market" for these businesses and gave them a competitive advantage over paper document–based companies. To support the development of electronic transactions, international standards bodies such as ANSI X12 and UN/EDIFACT were evolved. For example, a Purchase Order Acknowledgement is specified by the standard EDI X12 855.

The WWW has made it possible for almost anyone with an Internet presence to engage in electronic transactions with partners. The wave that made Business-to-Consumer (B2C) retail sites a reality is now necessitating the next wave of Business-to-Business (B2B) transactions on the Web. With advancement in encryption techniques and Internet standards, midsize to large companies have already started considering the Web as a reliable channel for conducting business with partners. XML-based standards have been created and are being accepted widely. To fuel the growth of the B2B market, Microsoft has delivered a solution called BizTalk Server, an important member of the .NET family of Enterprise Servers. This solution involves tools, frameworks, and services that help companies to achieve Enterprise Application Integration (EAI) and conduct B2B transactions. BizTalk Server 2000, when integrated with Commerce Server 2000, gives a commerce site the ability to exchange catalogs with partners and send customer orders to different partners for fulfillment.

About BizTalk Server

Apart from delivering BizTalk for the B2B market, Microsoft has also emerged with a platform-independent application framework for EAI and B2B based on Internet standards such as XML, Simple Object Access Protocol (SOAP), HTTPS, and so on. The framework known as BizTalk Framework 2.0 provides for interoperable and reliable messaging for BizTalk Server 2000. BizTalk acts as a standard gateway for exchanging business documents on the Internet, and it ensures data integrity, security, and once-only delivery mechanisms. In addition to its B2B services, BizTalk enables enterprises to manage transactions that even span weeks or months, not just a few minutes. These EAI capabilities include the ability to draw business processes as XLANG diagrams and convert them to XLANG schedules using the BizTalk Orchestration Designer. XLANG is language based on Extensible Markup Language (XML). BizTalk also offers the ability to create document specifications and tools to track business documents that are in the exchange channels.

An important part of BizTalk is the Messaging Manager, which handles the receipt and transfer of documents. A queuing system is used to exchange messages between applications and partners, both local and remote. Receiver applications or scripts are integrated with the queues to process documents. Even though discussing BizTalk in its entirety is beyond the scope of this book, we will look briefly at the necessary information one needs to know in order to integrate Commerce Server with BizTalk Server. Specifically, we will take a look at important Messaging Manager objects.

Messaging Manager Objects

The following list presents a brief overview of the Messaging Manager objects:

- *Document definitions.* A document definition is created to point to a specification usually in a BizTalk server–specific XML schema. For example, a definition for a purchase order could point to POSchema.XML. Then inbound and outbound purchase orders could be validated against the definition.

- *Organizations.* In BizTalk, you create organizations to represent partners. A default organization called the *Home* organization is automatically created and represents, of course, your business. Furthermore, applications can be defined for an organization. Therefore, documents can be exchanged between applications of the same organization (within your business in the case of Home) or between your applications and those of your partners.

- *Channels.* Channels are the central objects in Messaging Manager. A channel identifies the *source* of documents in an interchange, which can be an organization, an application within your organization, or even an XLANG schedule. Channels also relate document definitions to inbound and outbound documents on the channel.

- *Messaging ports.* Messaging ports define the destination for documents that are processed by a channel. A destination can be an organization, an application within your organization, or even an XLANG schedule. Using messaging ports, you identify the destination address, the method used to transport the document (HTTP, file, SMTP, and so on), and the security for the interchange.

- *Application Integration Component (AIC).* An AIC is a pipeline component that BizTalk calls to process and deliver documents. Similar to a Commerce Server pipeline component, an AIC implements the IPipelineComponent interface. A Scriptor can be used to prototype some functionality either to process documents before sending or to receive documents for an application in the channel.

Integration Between Commerce Server and BizTalk Server

Figure 16.1 illustrates the idea of business transactions on the Web.

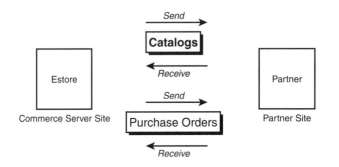

FIGURE 16.1

Typical B2B interaction between business partners.

Based on the diagram, you can imagine how the exchange of catalogs and purchase orders can be done. Using the EstoreBizDesk, we would export a catalog as, say, XML and then somehow send it over to the partner. When the partner receives the catalog, it is imported into the system. The transfer of purchase orders (POs) is even more complex. If we need to send orders on the site to product suppliers, components such as MakePO and POtoFile need to be inserted in the checkout pipeline. The generated PO would then somehow be sent to the supplier. The reverse would be the case for fulfilling orders, but Estore has to enter the orders in the database as received from a partner.

When agreements are set between you and your partners, BizTalk can be used to reliably exchange catalogs and purchase orders between both the organizations electronically. The "somehow" of document interchange has now been turned into a reliable framework of electronic transactions, without the intervention of traditional exchanges. By integrating your Commerce Server site with BizTalk, it is possible to exchange catalogs with partners and fill partners' orders as well as send orders to be filled by partners.

The agreement between you and a partner could be based on many aspects of this infrastructure. Both of you would use BizTalk to exchange documents, or your partner might not use BizTalk but might agree to an XML-based schema for document transfer. Many combinations of scenarios are possible. Figure 16.2 provides an illustration of two scenarios.

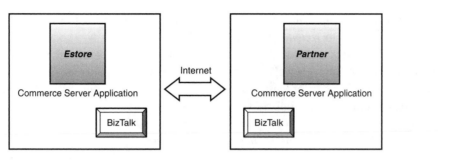

Scenario 1. Commerce Server integrated with BizTalk on both sides.

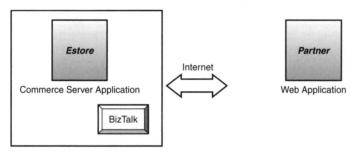

Scenario 2. Commerce Server integrated with BizTalk on one side.

FIGURE 16.2

Two scenarios for document exchange.

In Scenario 1, both parties have a similar infrastructure, such as using Commerce Server and BizTalk. In this case, it is possible to integrate both the parties very well with only a little effort. For example, an order made at Estore can be automatically sent to the commerce database of the partner site. On the other hand, Scenario 2 depicts a different environment at the partner's side. Due to the openness of the platform, BizTalk can still be used to reliably send the document in an agreed-upon format to the partner's applications. In our integration examples, we will have a chance to look at these scenarios and configure solutions for both. These are just sample scenarios; as mentioned earlier, there might be many combinations possible in the real world.

Building a Partner Site

Before we get on with the integration examples, we need a partner application that will interact with our Estore site. While in reality, you and your partner could be millions of bandwidths away on the Internet, for development purposes, we will create a commerce site called Partner on the same machine as that of Estore.

Typically, the entity supplying products is the *supplier*, whereas the entity selling those products to consumers is the *retailer*. In current-day business complexity, a company can act as both supplier and retailer for similar or different products and services. We will assume the latter and hence treat Estore as well as Partner as retailers that are partners. Therefore, you need to create a commerce site for Partner by unpacking the Retail package using Site Packager. Then you need to install BizTalk Server on the same machine. Finally, you need to configure and integrate the Estore commerce site with BizTalk to send catalogs to Partner. Figure 16.3 provides the illustration for our development architecture.

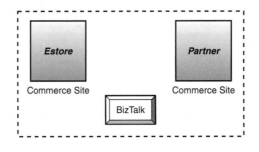

FIGURE 16.3
The development environment on a single machine.

Note that as of this writing, Commerce Server cannot connect to BizTalk installed on a different machine. This may be fixed in Service Pack 1 for CS2K. Therefore, be sure to look for CS2K SP1 and the details of fixes on the CS2K site at `http://www.microsoft.com/commerceserver`.

Unpacking a Retail Site

You have already seen in detail the process of creating the retail site Estore using Site Packager in Chapter 3, "Creating the Site Foundation." Use a similar procedure to create the Partner site and its Business Desk. The following list is an overview of the important steps required (for more details, refer to Chapter 3):

1. Create the folders Partner and PartnerBizDesk using Windows NT Explorer.

2. Create two IIS applications called Partner and PartnerBizDesk. These point to the folders created in step 1. Take care to create these sites on unoccupied ports. For this example, I created Partner on port 86 and PartnerBizDesk on 87.

3. Use Site Packager to unpack the Retail and RetailBizDesk applications into the Partner and PartnerBizDesk sites, respectively. Remember to create virtual directories under Partner and PartnerBizDesk similar to what we did for Estore and EstoreBizDesk in Chapter 3.

4. Connect to the PartnerBizDesk application and install the Biz Desk client.

Installing BizTalk Server

Now that we have both sites ready for some B2B transactions, the next step is to install BizTalk Server. Follow the instructions in the BizTalk documentation to install the product. For more information, refer to www.microsoft.com/biztalk.

Check the Windows Event Viewer to see whether everything is working fine in BizTalk. The installation comes with an MMC-based administration console called BizTalk Server Administration. You may want to add this snap-in to the Commerce Server Manager MMC for the sake of convenience. Using the BizTalk administrator, we can view the queues and the documents in the queue.

After I installed the Partner site and BizTalk Server, my Commerce Server MMC looks like what's shown in Figure 16.4.

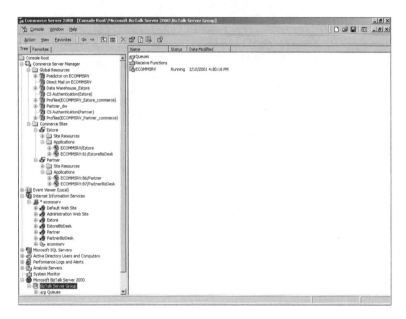

FIGURE 16.4
After BizTalk Server and the Partner site are installed.

Exchanging Catalogs with Partners

Now we will integrate the Commerce Server site Estore with BizTalk server to send a catalog to the Partner site. Here are the steps, in brief, required to accomplish it:

1. Configure AppDefaultConfig for Estore.

2. Create BizTalk Messaging Manager objects for this exchange, such as document definitions, organizations, channels, and messaging ports.

3. Using the Catalog Editor module of EstoreBizDesk, send a catalog to the Partner site.

Configuring AppDefaultConfig

In order to enable integration between a Commerce Server site and BizTalk, you need to modify a few BizTalk-related properties in the AppDefaultConfig resource for the site. Modify the
configuration of Estore's AppDefaultConfig site resource, in the property page shown in Figure
16.5, to the values shown in Table 16.1.

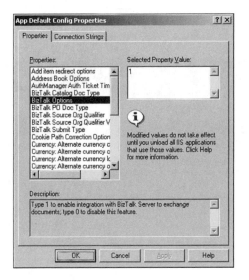

FIGURE 16.5

Modifying the AppDefaultConfig properties for Estore.

TABLE 16.1 BizTalk Properties for Estore Site

Property	Property Value	Description
BizTalk Catalog Doc Type	Catalog	This is the name of the document definition we will use in BizTalk to define a catalog document for exchanges.
BizTalk Options	1	Change this setting from 0 (disabled) to 1 (enabled) for integration with BizTalk.

TABLE 16.1 continued

Property	Property Value	Description
BizTalk PO Doc Type	PurchaseOrder	This is the name of the document definition we will use in BizTalk to define a purchase order document for exchanges.
BizTalk Source Org Qualifier	Estore	Provide an alias for this site in BizTalk.
BizTalk Source Org Qualifier Value	Sender	This is the alias value for this site in BizTalk.
BizTalk Submit Type	1	Type **1** to enable asynchronous submission of documents to BizTalk. A value of 0 makes submissions synchronous.

After modifying AppDefaultConfig for the site, unload the Estore application or run IISReset from the command line.

Creating Messaging Manager Objects

Using the Start, Programs, Microsoft BizTalk Server 2000 menu, launch the BizTalk Messaging Manager. If a Configuration Options dialog box appears on launch, dismiss it by clicking the Cancel button. The BizTalk installation, by default, installs the Messaging Manager application under Default Web Site. If your default Web site is running on a port other than the default port (80), you need to specify that information to the Messaging Manager. Using the Tools, Options menu, specify the correct port number and server name where the Messaging Manager Web application is installed (see Figure 16.6).

Recall that Estore is on port 80 throughout the examples in this book. The default Web site is now on port 90. BizTalk installs its application, such as Messaging Manager and BizTalk Tracking, as virtual directories under the default Web site. That's the reason why in Figure 16.6 the BizTalk Server application path is specified as ECOMMSRV:90.

Creating the Source Organization

In the left pane, click Organizations to search for all organizations. Then click the Search Now button. The Home organization is fetched in the pane on the right. Double-click it. In the General tab, rename the Home organization to Estore (see Figure 16.7).

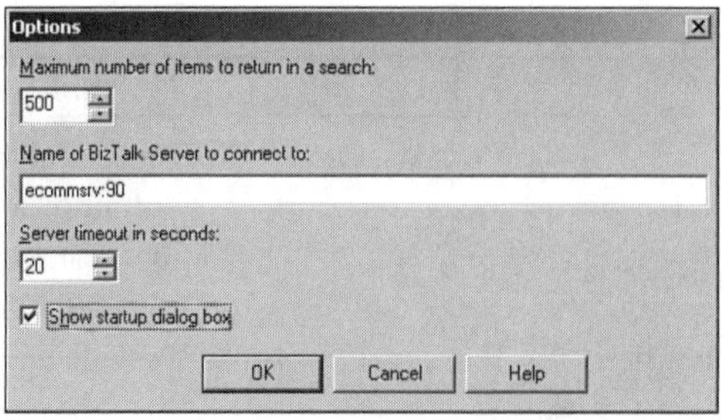

FIGURE 16.6

Configuring the BizTalk application server.

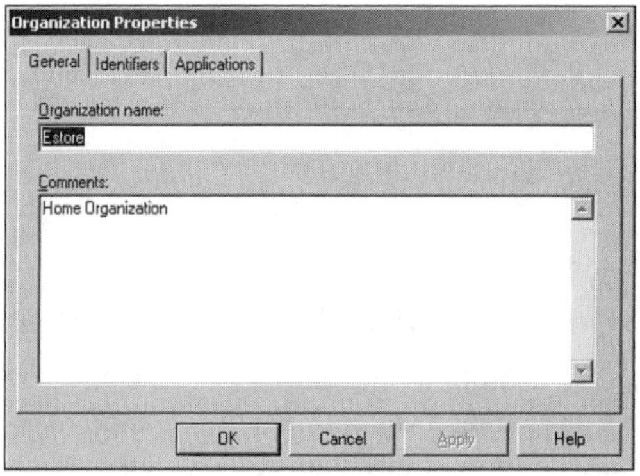

FIGURE 16.7

The Home organization for Estore.

In the Identifiers tab, click the Add button. In the Identifier Properties dialog box that comes up, choose the Custom option button and enter **Estore**. In the Qualifier text box, enter **Estore**. In the Value box, enter **Sender** (see Figure 16.8). Remember that the qualifier and its value should be exactly the same as what was specified in the AppDefaultConfig property for Estore for the properties BizTalk Source Org Qualifier and BizTalk Source Org Qualifier Value, respectively. Check the Set as Default check box and then click the OK button.

In the Applications tab, click the Add button. Enter **Catalog** and click the OK button (see Figure 16.9). Click the OK button in the Organization Properties dialog box. Now we have made the necessary changes for the Home organization, Estore. Therefore, the source organization for the document interchange will be Estore.

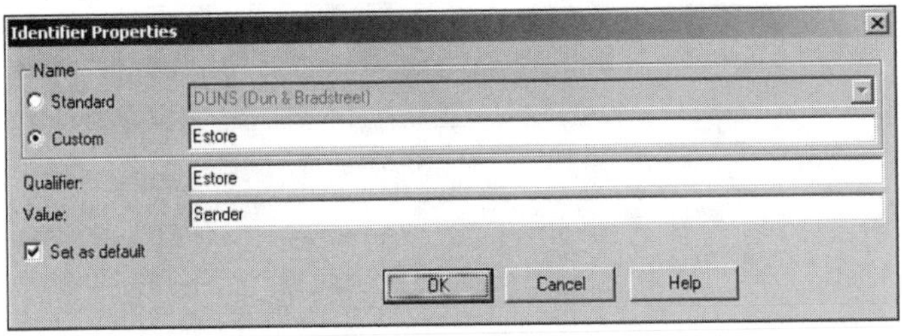

Identifier Properties

Name
- Standard: DUNS (Dun & Bradstreet)
- Custom: Estore

Qualifier: Estore

Value: Sender

☑ Set as default

[OK]   [Cancel]   [Help]

FIGURE 16.8

Setting the organization qualifier and value.

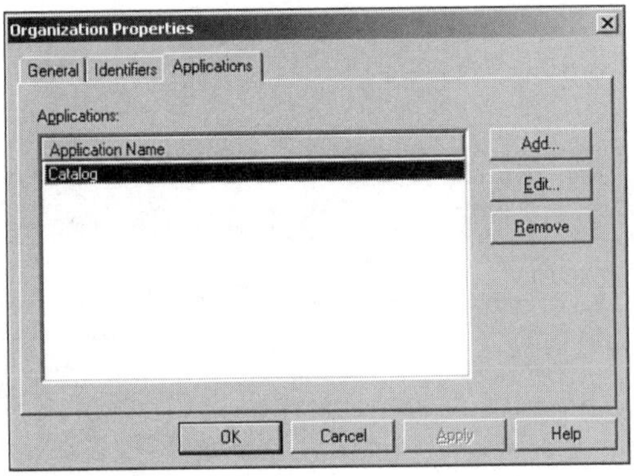

Organization Properties

General | Identifiers | Applications

Applications:

Application Name
Catalog

[Add...]
[Edit...]
[Remove]

[OK]   [Cancel]   [Apply]   [Help]

FIGURE 16.9

Adding the Catalog application to the Estore organization.

Creating the Destination Organization as Partner

Next we need to create a destination organization with BizTalk for the Partner site. From the File menu in Messaging Manager, choose New, Organization. In the New Organization dialog box, enter **Partner** for the organization name and then enter any appropriate comments (see Figure 16.10).

In the Identifiers tab, click the Add button. Choose the Custom option and enter **Partner**. In the Qualifier box, enter **Partner** and in the Value edit box enter **Receiver**. Click the OK button (see Figure 16.11).

Click the OK button on the New Organization dialog box to save the organization to the Messaging Manager database.

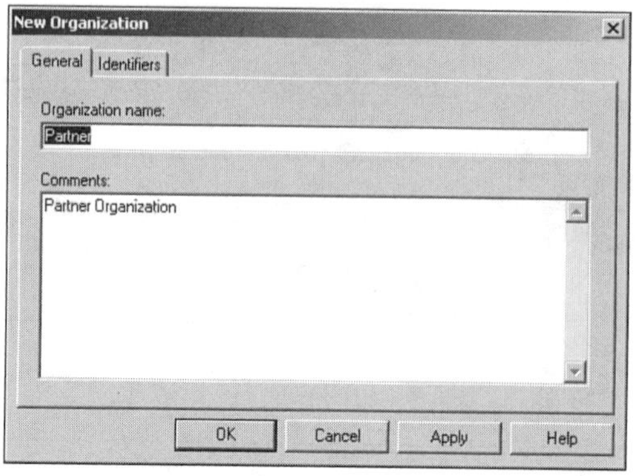

FIGURE 16.10
Creating an organization for Partner.

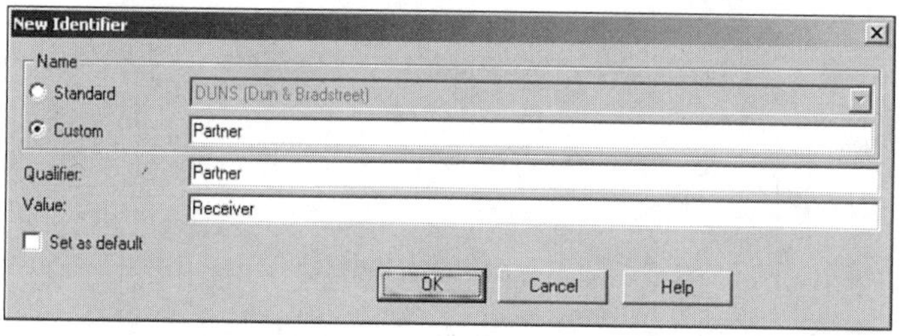

FIGURE 16.11
Setting the qualifier and value for the Partner organization.

Creating a Document Definition

Let's now create the document definition for catalogs. A document definition points to an XML schema. When the definition is used in a channel for inbound and outbound documents, those documents are validated against the schema. You already know that Commerce Server catalogs can be imported or exported in XML formats based on the schema defined in the file CatalogXMLSchema.xml. First, we need to make this file available in the BizDesk repository.

Copy the CatalogXMLSchema.xml file from the Microsoft Commerce Server install folder to the following folder:

```
<Microsoft BizTalk Server Install folder> \BizTalkServerRepository\DocSpecs
➥\Microsoft
```

To create a new document definition, choose New, Document Definition from the File menu. In the New Document Definition dialog box, enter the document definition name **Catalog**.

Check the Document Specification check box. Click the Browse button and then double-click the Microsoft folder in the dialog box. Select a document specification from the WebDAV directory. Choose `CatalogXMLSchema.xml` and then click the Open button. Finally, click the OK button in the New Document Definition dialog box (see Figure 16.12). If you get an error message saying that no repository was found, check the server path. I gave the path as `http://localhost:90` because BizTalk Server applications are installed under the default Web site, which is running on port 90.

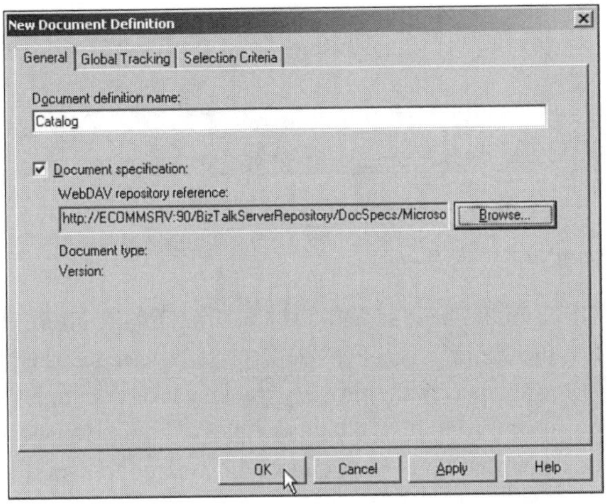

FIGURE 16.12
The document definition for Catalog.

Scenario 2: Partner Has Different Infrastructure

Now let's assume Scenario 2, which we discussed earlier. We will work through this scenario before coming back to Scenario 1, where both parties have a similar infrastructure. In Scenario 2, the partner does not have a matching infrastructure but agrees to open up a secured directory where Estore can drop its XML-formatted catalogs.

Creating a Messaging Port

The next step in the process is to create a messaging port to the destination organization, Partner. The messaging port will specify the transport method, the address at the destination, and any security information required. From the File menu in BizTalk Messaging Manager, click New, Messaging Port, To an Organization. Alternatively, simply press the Ctrl+R key combination. In the New Messaging Port dialog box, enter the name **CatalogPortToPartner** and then enter appropriate comments for this port (see Figure 16.13).

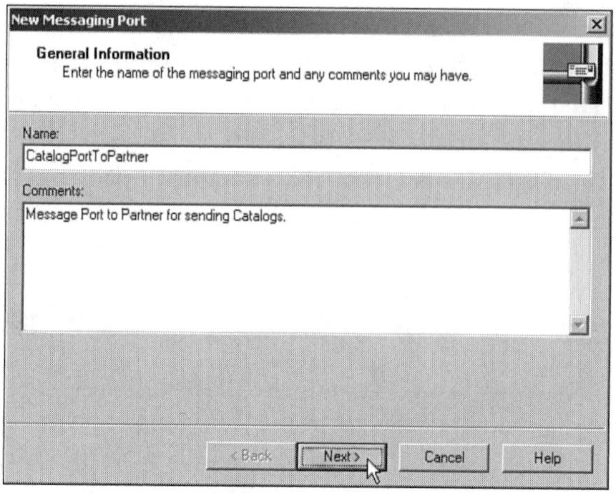

FIGURE 16.13

The messaging port for sending catalogs to Partner.

Now click the Next button. In the next screen, Destination Organization, choose the Organization option. For the Name box, click the Browse button and then choose Partner as the organization. We now need to specify the primary transport for document interchange at this port. In the Primary Transport group box, click the Browse button for the Address field. In the Primary Transport dialog box that comes up, choose File as the transport type (see Figure 16.14).

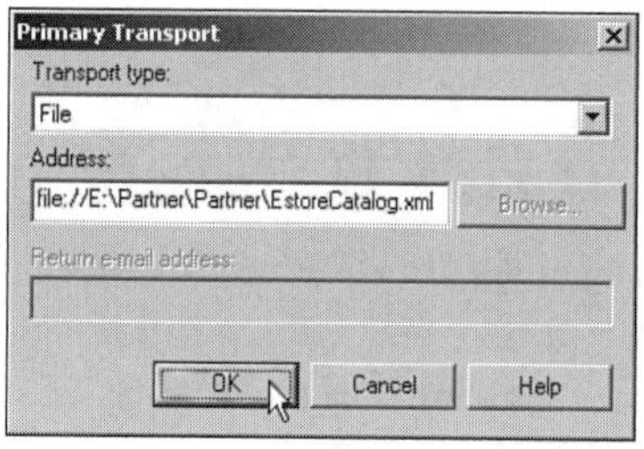

FIGURE 16.14

Specifying the main transport method.

Because our scenario is such that the partner organization may not have BizTalk or Commerce Server (or both), we assume that there is an agreement to drop off the catalog at a secured place where the partner has access. The location could be one of your partner's servers or Estore's own, which is accessible by the partner. As you can see, there are quite a few options, such as File, SMTP, HTTP, and HTTPS, that can also be used. We will choose File as the transport type for this example. In the real world, File may be realistic only in the simplest of scenarios, where two departments within the same organization want to exchange documents. We have chosen File just to simplify the example.

In the Address box, type the full path to the catalog file (for example, `file://E:\Partner\Partner\EstoreCatalog.xml`). Click the OK button, followed by the Next button. Ignore the next screen, Envelope Information—we will not bother with envelopes for now. Choose Partner/Receiver as the organization identifier (see Figure 16.15).

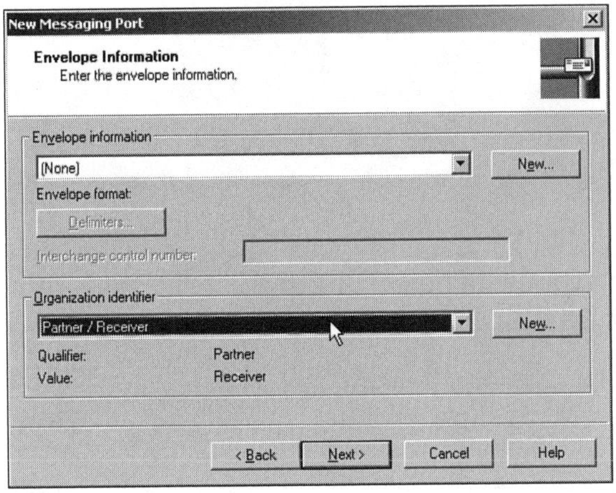

FIGURE 16.15
The Envelope Information screen.

Click the Next button. In the Security Information screen, we need not bother with Encoding, Encryption, and Signature. In a real-world implementation, you would have a digital certificate that is used to encrypt the catalog being sent. In that case, you would choose the encryption type as, say, S/MIME and browse to choose a certificate present in the BizTalk repository. For this example, we are not going to be bogged down with security aspects. Make sure that the check box Create a Channel for This Messaging Port is checked and that the channel type is From an Application. Then click the Finish button (see Figure 16.16).

Creating a Channel

The messaging port is created for Partner, and automatically the New Channel Wizard is launched to connect this port to a channel. In the New Channel dialog box, enter **CatalogChannelToEstore** for the name and add an appropriate comment for this channel. Then click the Next button (see Figure 16.17).

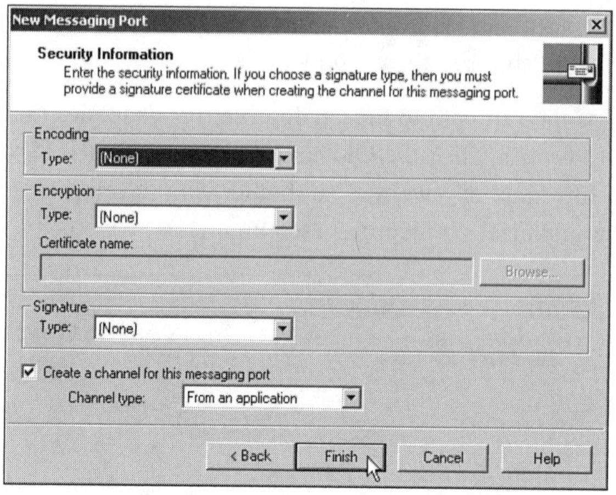

FIGURE 16.16

Finishing the creation of the messaging port.

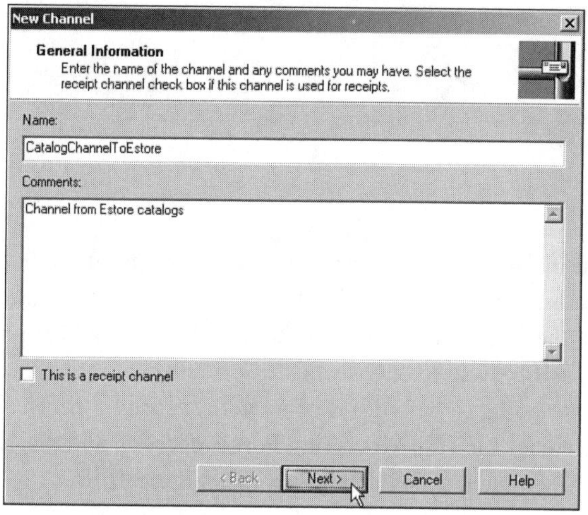

FIGURE 16.17

The channel for sending Estore catalogs to the Partner port.

In the next screen, Source Application, make sure the name of the application is Catalog and the organization identifier chosen is Estore/Sender (default). Then click the Next button (see Figure 16.18).

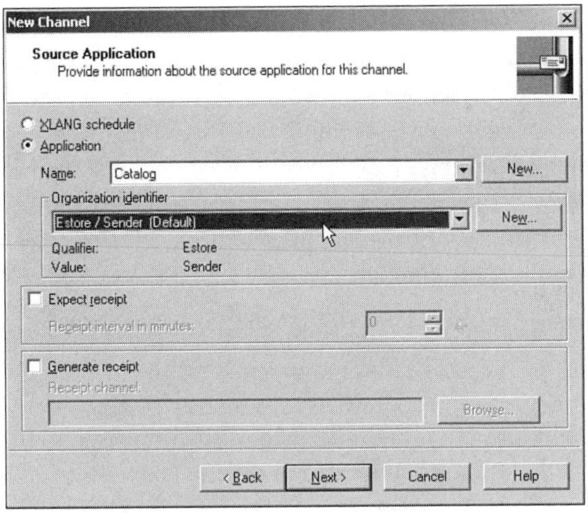

FIGURE 16.18
Choosing the Catalog application of Estore.

The next screen is used to specify the definition for an inbound document on this channel. For the Inbound Document Definition Name box, click the Browse button and choose Catalog in the Select a Document Definition box. We won't go into verifying the signature of the documents. Just click the Next button (see Figure 16.19).

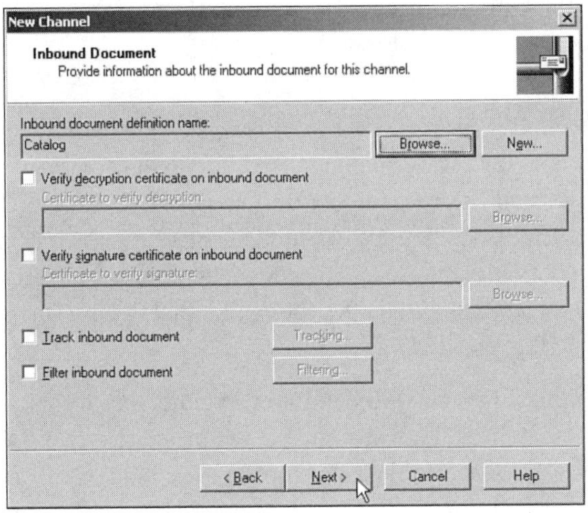

FIGURE 16.19
Specifying the document definition for inbound documents.

The next screen is for specifying the definition of an outbound document. Choose Catalog again and click the Next button. In the Document Logging screen, accept the default selections and then click the Next button again. In the Advanced Configuration screen, click the Advanced button. In the Overriding Messaging Port Defaults dialog box, you can see that the primary transport component used is BizTalk SendLocalFile. Click the Properties button. In the BizTalk SendLocalFile Properties dialog box, we need to enter the authentication information for accessing the file. Enter the username and password needed to access the file for the operation. Also, choose an option specifying whether the catalog file should be overwritten, appended, or created new every time (see Figure 16.20).

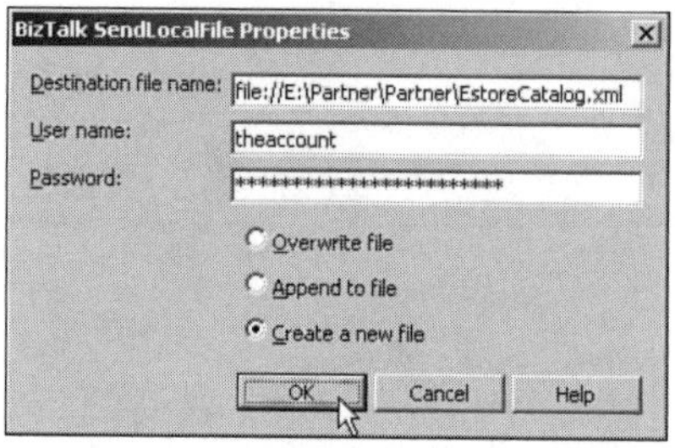

FIGURE 16.20
Specifying access for the catalog drop-off.

Click the OK button. Click the OK button again in the Override Messaging Port Defaults dialog box. Finally, click the Finish button in the Advanced Configuration screen. A channel is created from the Catalog application of Estore.

Sending the Catalog

Now that we have configured BizTalk and integrated it with the commerce site Estore, we just need to push the catalog from Estore using the Business Desk for Estore. So, from the Catalog Editor module in EstoreBizDesk, click the catalog Computer Accessories. In the task bar, click the Send Catalog button or press the Alt+S key combination. The partner we added as an organization in BizTalk is now available in the Select Vendor dialog box. Choose Partner and then click the OK button (see Figure 16.21).

The export process is initiated successfully and if everything goes well, the catalog XML file should have been created at the address specified in the messaging port. In a real-life scenario, it is up to the partner to make use of this XML-formatted catalog. If the partner has Commerce Server and Biz Desk, the XML file can be directly imported using the Catalog Editor. Otherwise, some other application needs to process the file before integrating the catalog with the Partner site.

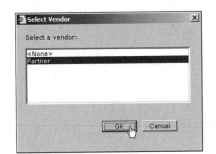

FIGURE 16.21
Choosing a vendor to send in Catalog Editor.

But don't import the XML file in Partner, yet, because we will discuss in the next scenario a method to automatically push the catalog to the partner's database.

Tips for Troubleshooting

If there were any problems when you ran through this example, check the user privileges used for the target file. Also make sure the AppDefaultConfig properties match exactly those defined in BizTalk. For example, the BizTalk Catalog Doc Type parameter is Catalog, which should be exactly the same for the Document Definition Name parameter in BizTalk. Also consult the Event Viewer to know more about the nature and type of error.

The Vendor Picker

As I said before, if no vendors appeared in the Business Desk, it means configuration mismatches have occurred between Commerce Server and BizTalk. For example, document definitions may not have been created yet in BizTalk or the Home organization's qualifier may not be exactly the same in both servers. The ASP file responsible for fetching the vendors from BizTalk is dlg_VendorPicker.asp, which can be found under the following folder:

```
E:\EstoreBizDesk\EstoreBizDesk\Catalogs\Editor
```

The function sVendorsAsOptions() builds the list of available vendors. Here are the key statements in this function:

```
Function sVendorsAsOptions ()

    ....
....

    'Get the CatalogToVendorAssociation object
    GetCatalogVendorObject oCatalogVendor
    ....
.....
```

```
'Send catalog or assign a vendor to a catalog?
Select Case g_sMode
Case MODE_SEND
    sInputDocumentName = g_MSCSAppConfig.GetOptionsDictionary("").Value
    ➡("s_BizTalkCatalogDocType")
Case MODE_ASSIGN
    sInputDocumentName = g_MSCSAppConfig.GetOptionsDictionary("").Value("s
    ➡_BizTalkOrderDocType")
End Select
.....
.....
    Set rsVendors = oCatalogVendor.GetVendorList(sSourceAliasQualifier,
    ➡sSourceAliasValue, sInputDocumentName)
    Set oCatalogVendor = Nothing
    If Not IsObject (rsVendors) Then Exit Function

    Do Until rsVendors.EOF
        sVendorsAsOptions = sVendorsAsOptions & _
                        "<DIV QUALIFIER='" & rsVendors("qualifier") & "'
                        ➡VALUE='" & rsVendors("value") & "'>" &
                        ➡rsVendors("orgname") & "</DIV>" & vbCR
        g_nVendors = g_nVendors + 1
        rsVendors.MoveNext
    Loop
    ....

End Function
```

A `CatalogToVendorAssociation` object is created. This object, provided by Commerce Server, is used to retrieve the list of available vendors from BizTalk as well as to set associations between vendors and catalogs. The input document definition names that have been set in BizTalk are fetched for both catalogs and purchase orders. If the Send Catalog button is clicked in the Catalog Editor list page, the mode would be MODE_SEND; the other case of clicking the Browse button in the Catalog Editor list page to pick a vendor is represented by the mode MODE_ASSIGN. This corresponds to the document types Catalogs and Purchase Orders, respectively. Only when these document types are defined will the organizations (vendors) appear in both the vendor pickers.

The `GetVendorList()` method of the `CatalogToVendorAssociation` object connects to the BizTalk database to fetch vendors that have the required document types. Other methods of this object, such as `SpecifyVendorForCatalog` and `UnspecifyVendorForCatalog`, can be used to programmatically assign or disassociate vendors and catalogs.

Having seen how to send a catalog using BizTalk to a partner, we will move on to Scenario 1, where both parties have CS2K running on their sites. Estore will have BizTalk integrated, but additionally the partner may also have BizTalk Server integrated with its copy of CS2K.

Scenario 1: Partner Has Similar Infrastructure

If you launch the Partner site in a browser now, it typically will represent a freshly created retail site, with no catalogs installed. The Catalog Editor module of PartnerBizDesk also will confirm that there are no catalogs defined in the Partner site's database. In Scenario 1, we will assume that the partner has at least a Commerce Server infrastructure. In this case, instead of specifying a file as the transport type, we will use an AIC to directly push the catalog to the partner's catalog database. We already know that AIC is a pipeline component, and we can use Scriptor to prototype this component.

Modifying the Messaging Port

We will modify the messaging port and channel created for Scenario 2. In BizTalk Messaging Manager, search for messaging ports. Double-click the CatalogPortToPartner port in the Results pane. In the Destination Organization screen, click the Browse button for Primary Transport. In the Primary Transport dialog box, choose Application Integration Component from the drop-down list for Transport Type. Then click the Browse button for Component Name. In the Select a Component dialog box, choose BizTalk Scriptor and then click the OK button (see Figure 16.22).

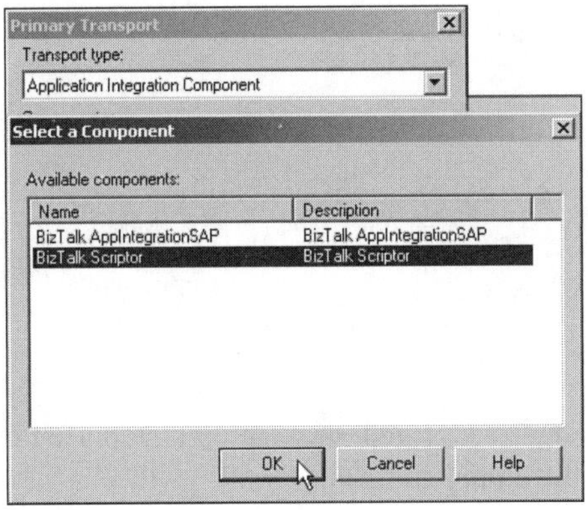

FIGURE 16.22

Changing the primary transport to an AIC, the Scriptor.

Click the OK button again in the Primary Transport dialog box. Then click the Finish button in the Destination Organization screen.

Next we need to change a few properties of the associated channel to incorporate the port changes.

Modifying the Channel

From the Messaging Manager, search for channels to find CatalogChannelToEstore, which we created earlier. Double-click the channel and keep clicking the Next button until the Advanced Configuration screen is shown. In the Advanced Configuration screen, click the Advanced button, which launches the Override Messaging Port Defaults dialog box. Here, we can see that the primary transport component has been changed to BizTalk Scriptor. Click the Properties button in this dialog box. We now see the familiar Scriptor interface (see Figure 16.23).

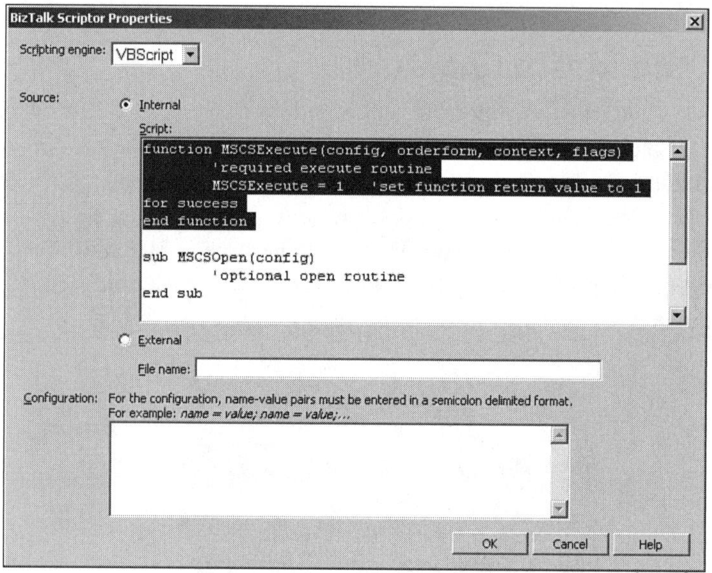

FIGURE 16.23
Modifying the script in the BizTalk Scriptor.

Modify the MSCSExecute function such that the catalog is imported programmatically into the partner's database. Here is the complete listing:

```
function MSCSExecute(config, orderform, context, flags)
    'required execute routine

strXML = orderform.Value("working_data")

Dim fso, objFile
Set fso = CreateObject("Scripting.FileSystemObject")
tmpdrive = "E:\temp\"          'Drive for storing the temp file
tmpDate = cstr(Date)           'Time and Date for naming temp file
```

```
tmpime = cstr(Time)
tmpFilename = tmpDate & tmpime & ".xml"
tmpFileName = Replace(tmpFileName , "/", "")
tmpFileName = Replace(tmpFileName , ":", "")
tmpFileName = tmpdrive & tmpFileName
tmpFileName = Replace(tmpFileName , " ", "") 'Form a proper file name

'Write the XML catalog to the temp file

Set objFile= fso.CreateTextFile(tmpFileName , True)
objFile.WriteLine(strXML)
objFile.Close

'Create AppConfig and CatalogManager objects

set objAppcfg = createobject("commerce.appconfig")
set objCatalogmanager = createobject("commerce.catalogmanager")

'Initialize AppConfig to the Partner site's database
objAppcfg.initialize("Partner")
set objOptDict = objAppcfg.getoptionsdictionary("")
sConnstr = objOptDict.s_CatalogConnectionString
objCatalogmanager.initialize sConnstr, true

'Import the XML catalog in the temp file to the database

objCatalogmanager.importxml tmpFilename ,TRUE, FALSE


    MSCSExecute = 1    'set function return value to 1 for success
end function
```

From this sample code, you can see that the catalog is imported in the XML format directly into the database of the Partner site using the ImportXML method of the CatalogManager object.

Click the OK button in the BizTalk Scriptor Properties dialog box. Then click the OK button again in the Override Messaging Port Defaults dialog box. Finally, click the Finish button in the Advanced Configuration screen. Now the channel is modified for the required operation.

Sending the Catalog

Using the CatalogEditor module, send the ComputerAccessories catalog to Partner. After successful execution, it can be verified at the Partner site, as well from PartnerBizDesk, that the ComputerAccessories catalog has been successfully sent to Estore's partner. If the catalog was not sent successfully, see the following section on troubleshooting to get some ideas.

Tips for Troubleshooting

Similar to our earlier discussion on troubleshooting, look at the Event Viewer for most of the errors that could occur during the process, because failure could be due to many reasons. For example, when I executed the Scenario 1 example, the process failed to push the catalog to Partner. From the Event Viewer, I found that there was a simple error—the product definitions in the Estore catalogs were modified and therefore different from the fresh product schemas of Partner (see Figure 16.24).

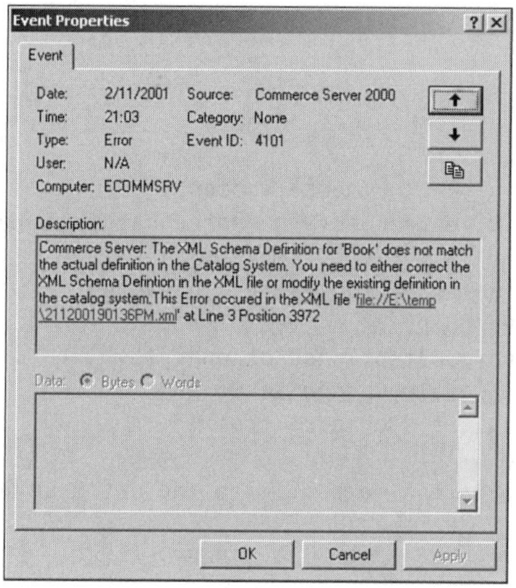

FIGURE 16.24
Logged errors in the Event Viewer.

By comparing the product definitions of both sites using the Catalog Designer module in the respective Biz Desks, we can solve this problem by ensuring that the schemas do not clash. You would remove properties from Estore product definitions that are not found in Partner product definitions, and so on. Once both the product schemas are exactly the same, the catalog will be imported into the Partner catalog system successfully. For more information on errors due to schema differences, refer to "Importing and Exporting Catalogs" in Chapter 6, "Catalog Management."

If there are any errors with the BizTalk processing, such as the catalog not matching the `CatalogXMLSchema.xml` definition, the document would still be in the suspended queue (see Figure 16.25).

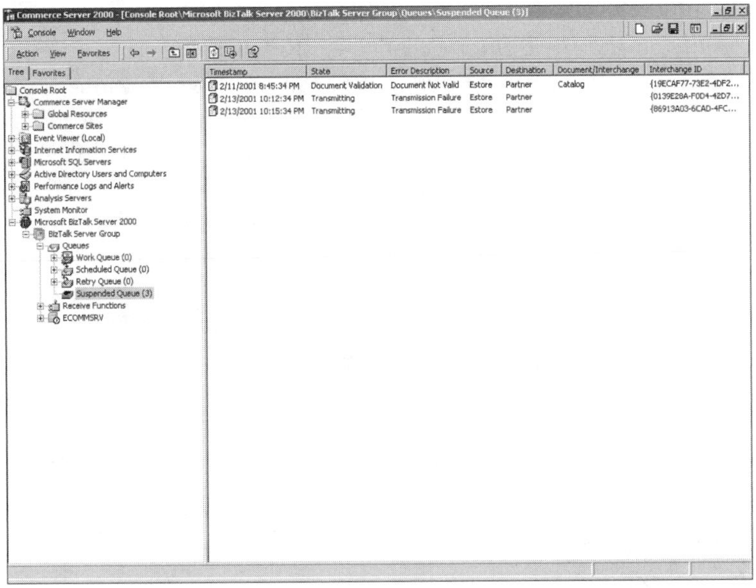

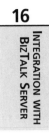

FIGURE 16.25
Unsuccessful documents in the suspended queue.

Note that the tight integration allows us to push the catalogs to a partner's database directly. It is also possible to push catalogs using the BizTalk Server, after which the partner's receiving application would process the queue. The file `ReceiveStandard.asp` at the root of a solution site can be used to submit documents using the `BizTalk.Interchange` object.

Fulfilling Orders Through Partners

The right partnership means everything in business. A strong and amicable relationship is the base on which many business partnerships are built. Apart from the stronger relationship between you and your partner, what if both of your systems are also strongly integrated? This would be the ideal scenario every company yearns for. With the ability to automatically send orders on your site to suppliers, the integration between Commerce Server and BizTalk proves again that the interchange of business documents can be a breeze. The solution sites are already loaded with the necessary integration code to spawn site orders to different vendors. We will use the example of a purchase order to demonstrate how B2B sites could be built to take advantage of BizTalk and exchange most of the business documents electronically using the Internet.

We will continue with the example sites Estore and Partner, businesses that have a relationship with each other. Because we have already configured BizTalk and Estore for the integration aspects, this time we will assume that Estore is the retail site that sells Partner's products. When a user on Estore confirms an order, the order is automatically split based on catalogs of vendors and submitted to BizTalk. BizTalk takes care of routing the order to the supplier. In our setting, an order on Estore for Partner's products will be split as a separate order and sent to Partner's order database to be filled. Figure 16.26 illustrates the idea.

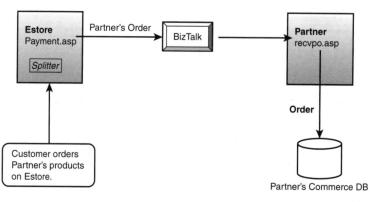

FIGURE 16.26
Integrating with Partner for order fulfillment.

Integrating with Partner for Order Fulfillment

This example for order integration depends on the configuration and BizTalk objects we created for exchanging catalogs. Both `payment.asp` in Estore and `_recvpo.asp` in Partner are ready to do their job.

Configuring AppDefaultConfig Properties

We are again using Estore as the sender of a document. Even though we have already set the required configuration properties earlier, make sure that the properties for BizTalk PO Doc Type have values such as PurchaseOrder, and so on, as per the data given earlier in Table 16.1.

Creating Messaging Manager Objects

We will be using the object configurations we set earlier because of the assumption that Estore will again be the sender—only this time the document is a purchase order. Therefore, we just add to the existing organization configuration, but we need to create new document definitions, messaging ports, and channels.

Modifying the Organizations

Similar to how we created an application called Catalog for exchanging catalogs, we will create an application for Estore to transmit purchase orders. In the Messaging Manager, search for
Organizations. In the Results pane, double-click Estore. In the Organization Properties dialog
box, click the Applications tab. Then click the Add button and enter the application name
PurchaseOrder in the New Application input box (see Figure 16.27).

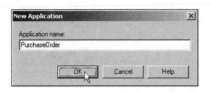

FIGURE 16.27
Adding an application for purchase orders.

Click the OK button. Then click the OK button again in the Organization Properties dialog box.

Creating a Purchase Order Definition

The next step is to create a document definition for a purchase order. The purchase order will
be based on the schema defined in POSchema.xml; therefore, the schema file should be made
available to BizTalk. Copy POSchema.xml from the root folder for your Estore site to the
BizTalk folder:

```
E:\Microsoft BizTalk Server\BizTalkServerRepository\DocSpecs\Microsoft
```

From the File menu in Messaging Manager, choose New, Document Definition. Enter
PurchaseOrder as the document definition name. Check the Document Specification check
box; then click the Browse button. Choose POSchema.xml from the list. Click the Open button.
Then click the OK button in the New Document Definition dialog box to create the purchase
order definition (see Figure 16.28).

Creating the Messaging Port

We will now create the port to be used to deliver the purchase order. From the Messaging
Manager's File menu, choose New, Messaging Port, To an Organization. In the New Messaging
Port dialog box, enter **PoPortToPartner** as the name for this port. Enter an appropriate description for this port and click the Next button. In the Destination Organization screen, choose
Organization. Click the Browse button for the Name box. Choose Partner as the organization. In
the Primary Transport section, click the Browse button. In the Primary Transport dialog box
that's launched, select HTTP as the Transport Type setting (see Figure 16.29).

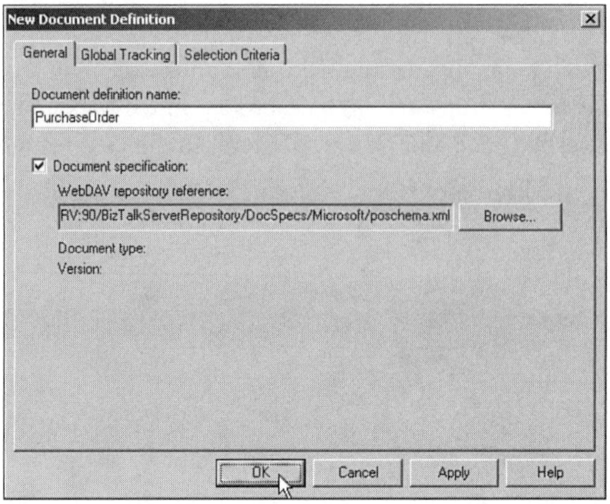

FIGURE 16.28

The document definition for a purchase order.

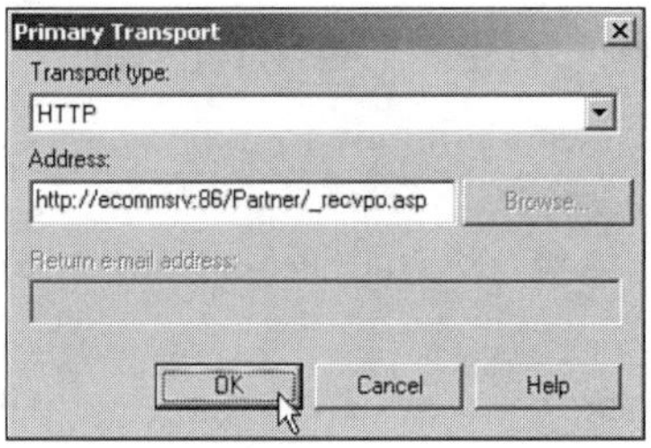

FIGURE 16.29

Specifying the order-processing file for Partner.

In the Address box, enter the address of the file _recvpo.asp on the Partner site. Here's an example:

```
http://ecommsrv:86/Partner/_recvpo.asp
```

Click the OK button and then click the Next button. In the Envelope Information screen, change the Organization Identifier setting to Partner/Receiver (see Figure 16.30).

Click the Next button in the wizard. In the next screen, Security Information, accept all the defaults. Make sure Create a Channel for This Messaging Port is checked. Also ensure that the channel type chosen is From an Application. This option will enable you to create the channel to the port immediately. Now click the Finish button. The New Channel Wizard is launched immediately.

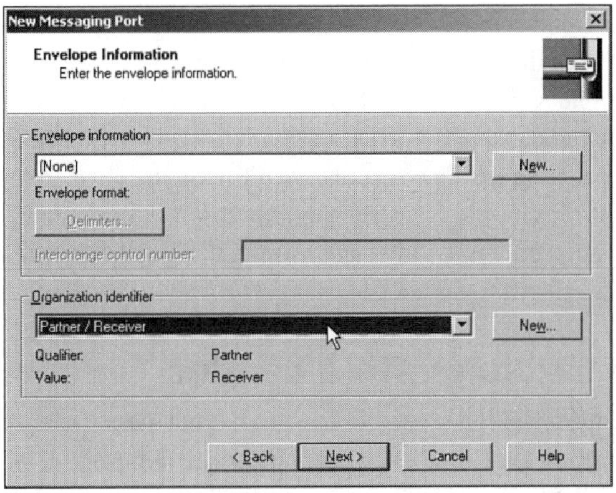

FIGURE 16.30
Choosing Partner/Receiver for receiving the purchase order.

Creating the Channel for PurchaseOrder

Enter **POChannelToPartner** as the name of the channel and click the Next button. In the next
screen, Source Application, choose the Application option. Change the name of the application
to **PurchaseOrder** and choose Estore/Sender as the Organization Identifier setting (see
Figure 16.31).

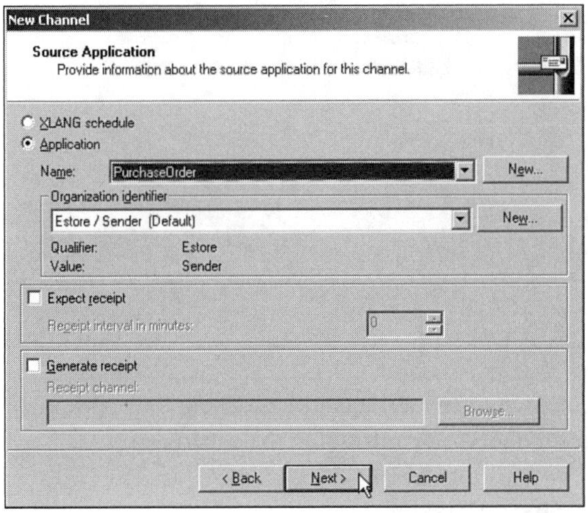

FIGURE 16.31
The PurchaseOrder application for Estore/Sender.

The next screen is Inbound Channel. Click the Browse button and choose PurchaseOrder as the document definition. Click the Next button and then choose PurchaseOrder as the outbound document definition name. Click the Next button and accept the defaults in the Document Logging screen. Finally, click the Finish button in the Advanced Configuration screen to finish creating the PO channel. Note that the _reccpo.asp file on the Partner site will be accessed using the proxy account. If that file is accessible only through some other account, you might have to click the Advanced button in Advanced Configuration and use the Properties button to set the username and password to access the file.

Associating a Catalog with a Vendor

In Business Desk, the term *vendor* is used to represent a business partner. Vendors are defined as organizations (other than the Home organization) in BizTalk Messaging Manager, as you have already seen. The first step in integrating with BizTalk for orders is to associate a catalog with a vendor. The vendor ID will be part of the product information on the OrderForm object. While processing the order, the Splitter component in the checkout.pcf pipeline will bundle a collection of items for each vendor. Ultimately, payment.asp processes the OrderForm objects and submits the order for a vendor using BizTalk.

Using the EstoreBizDesk module Catalog Editor, open the Computer Accessories catalog. In the edit page for the catalog, click the Browse button for Vendor ID. In the Select Vendor dialog box, choose Partner and click the OK button (see Figure 16.32).

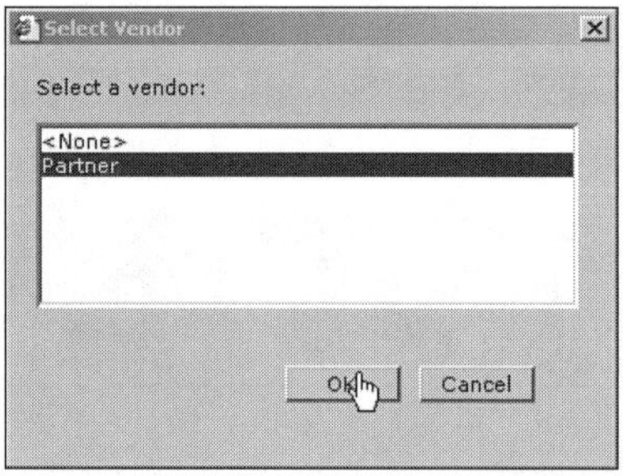

FIGURE 16.32
Associating a vendor with a catalog.

Now save the catalog and return to the catalog lists. Using the appropriate task bar button, publish the catalog changes to the site by refreshing the catalog cache.

The Checkout Pipeline

Recall from Figure 16.26 that the Splitter component is the one that actually creates the grouping of items in the order form based on the vendor of the product catalog. It stores this grouping in dictionaries on the order form. After the order has been processed by the pipeline, payment.asp creates an OrderForm object for each of the item groups and sends it to the BizTalk interchange.

The checkout.pcf pipeline in Estore already has the Splitter component in one of its stages (see Figure 16.33).

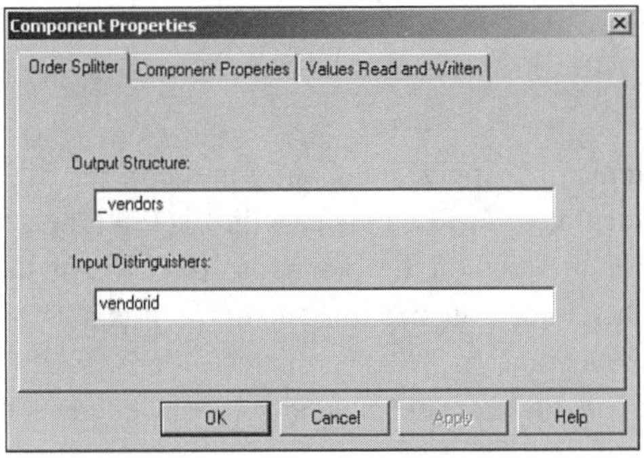

FIGURE 16.33
The splitter for splitting orders based on catalog vendors.

From the Component Properties dialog box of the Splitter, we can see that the grouping is based on vendorid in the Input Distinguishers field. The Output Structure setting, _vendors, will ultimately contain a simple list of dictionaries with key/value pairs, such as those shown in Table 16.2.

TABLE 16.2   The Contents of the _vendors Simple List

Key	Value
Vendor 1	Item0,Item4
Vendor 2	Item2,Item3

The keys are distinct vendor IDs, whereas the item indexes in the order that belong to the vendor's catalog form the values. Therefore, the OrderForm object's items are grouped based on the vendors.

Sending the Order to BizTalk

After the checkout pipeline has run, the order form will contain the _vendors collection with information on items that need to be bundled into a separate order, one each per vendor. If the checkout pipeline was successful, the order form is saved to the database with an Order status, which we already discussed in Chapter 10, "Business Flows and Pipelines." SaveBasketAsOrder is the routine in `payment.asp` that does this. After the `SaveAsOrder()` method of the `OrderGroup` object is called, the `InvokeBizTalk` subroutine is called:

....

```
Call mscsOrderGrp.SaveAsOrder()

' Submit appropriate OrderForms using BizTalk
Call InvokeBizTalk(mscsOrderGrp)
```

....

In the `InvokeBizTalk` routine, the AppDefaultConfig property for BizTalk integration is tested. If this commerce site is integrated for PO transfer with BizTalk, the `OrderForm` object in the order group is iterated through based on the _vendors collection on the order. If `VendorID` is `"default"`, it represents the Home organization; therefore, it is not considered. For all other vendors in the _vendors collection, an XML-formatted order is built using the routine `GetXMLForVendorItems`. Note that `GetXMLForVendorItems` generates the XML from the order form based on the `POSchema.xml` definition.

The generated XML order for a vendor is sent to BizTalk using the routine `SubmitUsingBizTalk`. Here is a snippet of the `SubmitUsingBizTalk` function that actually submits the formatted order to BizTalk:

```
Function SubmitUsingBizTalk(ByVal sXML, ByVal sVendorName, ByVal sDestQual, _
➥ ByVal sDestQualValue)
    Dim sSubmitType
    Dim sDocName, sSourceQualifierID, sSourceQualifierValue, sDestQualifierID, _
    ➥ sDestQualifierValue
    Dim oDBConfig, oOrg, sID, sName, sDef, oInterchange, oRes

        sSubmitType = dictConfig.s_BizTalkSubmittypeQueue
    sDocName = dictConfig.s_BizTalkOrderDocType

    sSourceQualifierID  = dictConfig.s_BizTalkSourceQualifierID
    sSourceQualifierValue  = dictConfig.s_BizTalkSourceQualifierValue

    Set oInterchange = Server.CreateObject("BizTalk.Interchange")

    oRes = oInterchange.Submit(iBIZTALKOPENNESS, _
                        sXML, _
                        sDocName, _
                        sSourceQualifierID, _
                        sSourceQualifierValue, _
                        sDestQual, _
                        sDestQualValue)
End Function
```

The actual submission is done using the Submit method of the `BizTalk.Interchange` object. The destination qualifier and qualifier values are obtained from the order form itself.

Upon submission to BizTalk, the channel processes the submitted document. The channel POChannelToPartner, in our example, sends the XML-formatted order along with other query string parameters to the `_recvpo.asp` file on the Partner site.

Receiving the Order

As you know, `_recvpo.asp` is the file that is designated to accept the XML order at the Partner site. First, the routine `ParseRequestForm` is used to parse the query string and get the XML order. Here is a snippet of code that does this:

```
Function ParseRequestForm()
....
....

' Get the post entity body
        '
        EntityBody = Request.BinaryRead (Request.TotalBytes )

        ' Convert to UNICODE
        '
        Set Stream = Server.CreateObject("AdoDB.Stream")
        Stream.Type = 1                    'adTypeBinary
        stream.Open
        Stream.Write EntityBody
        Stream.Position = 0
        Stream.Type = 2                    'adTypeText
        Stream.Charset = CharSet
        PostedDocument = PostedDocument & Stream.ReadText
        Stream.Close
        Set Stream = Nothing
....
....
ParseRequestForm = PostedDocument

End Function
```

Therefore, `ParseRequestForm` should return the XML string that represents the order for the vendor. Then, the obtained XML order is converted to an `OrderForm` dictionary using the following routine:

```
Set objXMLTransforms = Server.CreateObject("Commerce.DictionaryXMLTransforms")
    sFilePath = Server.MapPath("\" & MSCSAppFrameWork.VirtualDirectory) &
    ➥"\poschema.xml"
```

```
Set xmlSchema = objXMLTransforms.GetXMLFromFile(sFilepath) ' Can also be
➥read from WebDAV
Set mscsOrderForm = objXMLTransforms.ReconstructDictionaryFromXML(szXML,
➥xmlSchema)
```

Finally, an `OrderGroup` object is created and a new `OrderForm` object is added to it:

```
Set mscsOrderGrp = GetOrderGroup(m_userid)
Call mscsOrderGrp.AddOrderForm(mscsOrderForm)
```

The value for m_userid is set to a constant value of {00000000-0000-0000-0000-000000000000}.

Then a pipeline is run on the order form by the following statement:

```
Call RunOrderPipeline(mscsOrderGrp).
```

The pipeline that is executed is the `recvpo.pcf` pipeline, which is similar to the `total.pcf` Plan pipeline for the site (see Figure 16.34).

FIGURE 16.34

The recvpo.pcf pipeline in Partner.

If the order has any kind of errors, a failure HTTP status of 500 is sent to the requesting BizTalk Server, which would log the error and put the document in the suspended queue.

The pipeline itself is pretty similar to the other Plan pipelines we have already come across, except for a couple of Scriptor insertions that take care of small processing needs. For example, the component `Scriptor:MyTotal` in the Order Total stage sets the shipping, handling, and tax charges to zero:

```
function MSCSExecute(config, orderform, context, flags)
    'set tax/ship/handling to 0... add stages to compute if desired
    orderform.value("_cy_shipping_total") = 0
    orderform.value("_cy_handling_total") = 0
    orderform.value("_cy_tax_total") = 0
    orderform.value("_cy_total_total") = orderform.value("_cy_oadjust_
    ➥subtotal")
    orderform.value("saved_cy_total_total") = orderform.value("_cy_total_
    ➥total")
    MSCSExecute = 1
end function
```

The Partner site can customize the page to process the order again through a Purchase pipeline or add the relevant stages in the `recvpo.pcf` pipeline.

After the pipeline is run successfully without any errors, the order is saved to the Partner's database with an Order status:

```
sOrderID = mscsOrderGrp.SaveAsOrder(sTrackingNumber)
```

Testing the Integration

Now restart the IIS application for the Partner site. To test the integration for purchase orders, browse the Estore site and add products from the Computer Accessories catalog. Finally, check out the basket and confirm the purchase. The order confirmation is successfully displayed on Estore. Now you can verify the order from the Partner's commerce database as well as use the PartnerBizDesk module Orders (see Figure 16.35).

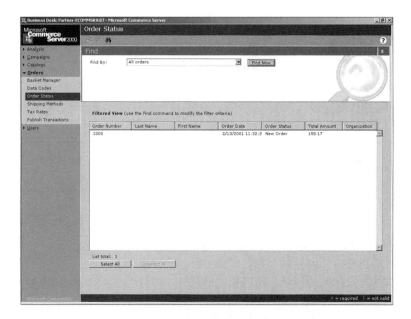

FIGURE 16.35
A purchase order made on Estore that's sent to Partner.

Summary

The Commerce Server infrastructure makes Web applications easy to build and deploy. By integrating with BizTalk, commerce sites can take advantage of the B2B services provided by BizTalk Server. BizTalk Server offers reliable and secure document interchange between business partners. Commerce Server integrates with BizTalk for exchanging catalogs with partners and sending orders on the site to partners for fulfillment.

You saw that the first step in integrating both products is to configure the AppDefaultConfig properties of the Commerce Site for BizTalk options. These very same integration values are used in the creation of BizTalk Messaging Manager objects, such as organizations, messaging ports, channels, and document definitions. Once these items are integrated, the Business Desk module Catalog Editor can be used to send catalogs to vendors, either as directory drop-offs or as direct database drop-offs. We used the AIC to write a Scriptor that imports the catalog into the database. Similarly, the solution sites already have the Splitter component in the checkout pipeline and the `payment.asp` page for submitting vendor orders to BizTalk. Also, Partner has the `_recvpo.asp` file to accept orders.

Appendixes

IN THIS PART

A Commerce Server Objects: A Quick
   Reference   571

B Pipeline Components: A Quick Reference   591

C Retail Store Helper Routines: Where to
   Find What   603

D Migrating from Site Server 3.0 to Commerce
   Server 2000   613

Commerce Server Objects: A Quick Reference

IN THIS APPENDIX

- List of Commerce Server Objects 572
- Methods and Properties of Frequently Used Objects 578

Although there are many tools and utilities readily provided by CS2K that can be used conveniently, many sites require programmatic access to the underlying CS2K infrastructure. This appendix gives you a quick reference to the COM objects supplied with Commerce Server 2000. For additional information about these objects, refer to the "Object Reference" section under "Programmer's Reference" in the Commerce Server documentation.

List of Commerce Server Objects

This section lists all the COM objects, along with a description of their usage and a broad classification in a commerce site application.

TABLE A.1 A Comprehensive List of CS2K Objects and Their Purpose Based on Their Broad Classifications

Object	Purpose	Broad Classification
CatalogManager	One of the most important objects in the Catalog API. Used to work with the entire catalog system for activities such as defining, creating, deleting, and importing catalogs and products.	Catalog Management
CatalogSets	Use this object to create, update, delete, or retrieve different catalog sets for different users.	Catalog Management
CatalogToVendorAssociation	Use this object to retrieve vendors from BizTalk as well as associate vendors with catalogs.	Catalog Management
Category	Mainly used to manage parent/child relationships between categories. Also used to add or remove products in a category.	Catalog Management
Product	Used mainly to work with variants and products in a catalog.	Catalog Management
ProductCatalog	One of the most important objects in the Catalog API. Used to create, retrieve, update, or delete categories and products in a catalog. Also used to perform free-text and specification searches on catalogs.	Catalog Management

TABLE A.1   continued

Object	Purpose	Broad Classification
ProfileObject	The core component to retrieve or update a profile instance.	User Management
ProfileService	Mainly used to create, retrieve, or delete ProfileObject objects.	User Management
AuthManager	Used universally across pages to authenticate, authorize, and manage user information in tickets.	User Management
OrderForm	The central object that holds the order and item information in memory. Accessed using the OrderGroup object.	Order Management
OrderGroup	The main object used to work with baskets, orders, and OrderForm objects.	Order Management
OrderGroupManager	Used to delete OrderGroup objects and to search for orders and baskets in the database.	Order Management
SimpleFindResultInfo	Used to specify the criteria that will be used by OrderGroup-Manager's SimpleFind and SimpleDelete methods to return result sets.	Order Management
SimpleFindSearchInfo	Used to specify the search criteria that will be used by OrderGroupManager's SimpleFind and SimpleDelete methods to query the database and delete order group entries, respectively.	Order Management
MicroPipe	Used to execute a single pipeline component directly from an ASP page.	Pipeline
MtsPipeline	Used to execute a nontransacted pipeline.	Pipeline

TABLE A.1   continued

Object	Purpose	Broad Classification
MtsTxPipeline	Used to execute a transacted pipeline.	Pipeline
OrderPipeline	Used to execute the CSF pipelines.	Pipeline
PooledPipeline	Used to execute a nontransacted pipeline consisting of components that can take advantage of COM+ object pooling.	Pipeline
PooledTxPipeline	Used to execute a transacted pipeline of components that are enabled for COM+ object pooling.	Pipeline
AppFrameWork	Mainly used for simple functions such as to get query strings and form values in an ASP page.	ASP User Interface
DataFunctions	A highly utilitarian object that's used for locale-based formatting, conversion between data types, and validating data values in site pages.	ASP User Interface
EuroDisplay	Used to format and convert between multiple currency values.	ASP User Interface
Page	Contains a lot of methods for displaying and processing forms.	ASP User Interface
AsyncRpt	Used to render or export a static report asynchronously.	Biz Desk
BizDeskSecurity	Used to determine whether a user has access to a specific Business Desk module or action page.	Biz Desk
ListManager	The central object in list-management activities, such as adding users, exporting and importing lists, generating lists from analysis reports, and retrieving lists.	Biz Desk
ReportRenderer	Used to render or export a static report synchronously.	Biz Desk

TABLE A.1 continued

Object	Purpose	Broad Classification
AppConfig	Used to retrieve a commerce site's configuration information.	Configuration
GlobalConfig	Used to create or delete site-configuration information in the administration database. Also contains a lot of functions to convert between, say, Array and SimpleList. Use this object to get a list of sites in the Commerce Server administration database.	Configuration
SiteConfig	This object is very similar to the GlobalConfig object, but it has more functions to import and export site resources.	Configuration
SiteConfigReadOnly	Used to return site-configuration information from the administration database.	Configuration
ContentList	Provides access to private data stored in ContentList and shared data stored in ContentListFactory. Passes through the CSF pipeline for filtering, scoring, and selecting content items. Created by the ContentListFactory object.	Content Selection Framework
ContentListFactory	Along with the ContentList object, this object gives efficient access to content items that are to be scored and selected for delivery on a site.	Content Selection Framework
ContentListSchema	Used to manipulate the schema of a ContentListFactory object that holds records of content items.	Content Selection Framework
ContentSelector	Used on an ASP page to run a CSF pipeline and return the selected content items, formatted, to the page.	Content Selection Framework

Table A.1   continued

Object	Purpose	Broad Classification
ExpressionEval	Use this object to programmatically connect to the evaluation store, load expressions, and evaluate expressions in a specified evaluation context.	Content Selection Framework
ExpressionStore	The object used to manipulate the expression store in the commerce database.	Content Selection Framework
ExprEvalContext	This object is used to create a context such as a user profile, using whichever multiple expressions will be evaluated.	Content Selection Framework
ExprFltrQryBldr	Used to convert an expression in an XML format to a SQL query string.	Content Selection Framework
RowCollection	Use this object to access rows of data in the ContentList object that holds a list of content items.	Content Selection Framework
AdminEventLog	Use to programmatically write informational, error, or warning message to the Event Log.	Site Administration
AdminFiles	A simple object that provides read-only access to files on the server.	Site Administration
AdminSite	Provided for backward compatibility only. This object is for accessing a Site Server 3.0 Commerce Edition site's configuration information.	Site Administration
AdminWebServer	Used to get the Web sites on a server and to obtain commerce sites under a Web site.	Site Administration
PredictorServiceAdmin	Used to retrieve available analysis models and model configurations.	Site Administration
PredictorServiceSiteAdmin	Used to manage analysis models and model configurations.	Site Administration

TABLE A.1   continued

Object	Purpose	Broad Classification
PredModelBuilder	This object can be used to programmatically manage the creation of analysis models using multiple threads.	Site Administration
Shipping	Use this object to obtain a preview of the shipping cost of an order that is split into individual shipments.	Site Administration
ShippingMethodManager	This object is used to programmatically create, retrieve, and delete shipment methods in the database. This object is used by Shipping Methods in BizDesk.	Site Administration
Auction	The only object to be used to provide an auction framework to a site.	Site Functionality
CacheManager	A key object in improving the performance of a commerce site. Used to manage caches in LRUCache or Dictionary objects.	Site Functionality
LRUCache	Supports storage of name/value pairs in memory. Uses the Least Recently Used algorithm to cache values.	Site Functionality
MessageManager	Used to load in memory error strings that can be in multiple languages.	Site Functionality
PredictorClient	Use this on an ASP page to load analysis models and ask for predictions.	Site Functionality
StandardSManager	Provided for backward compatibility with Site Server 3.0 Commerce Edition. Use the AuthManager object, instead, to deal with the creation, retrieval, and setting of shopper IDs.	Site Functionality

TABLE A.1 continued

Object	Purpose	Broad Classification
DBStorage	Used to map an OrderForm or Dictionary object to the database for transferring data between the object and the database.	Utility
Dictionary	A general-purpose object for storing and retrieving name/value pairs in memory. The values are of the Variant type.	Utility
DictionaryXMLTransforms	This object is used to transform data between dictionary and XML formats using an XML Data Reduced (XDR) schema.	Utility
GenID	Used to generate a GUID.	Utility
SimpleList	Used to maintain an array of Variant types in memory.	Utility

Methods and Properties of Frequently Used Objects

This section lists select methods and properties of the most frequently used Commerce Server objects.

AuthManager

TABLE A.2 Methods of the *AuthManager* Object

Member	Method/Property	Description
GenerateEncryptionKey	Method	Generates an encryption key to use for encrypting cookie data.
GetProperty	Method	Used to retrieve a custom property from a ticket.
GetURL	Method	Used to get a server-encoded URL string.
GetUserID	Method	Gets the user ID from the current ticket.

TABLE A.2   continued

Member	Method/Property	Description
GetUserIDFromCookie	Method	Gets the user ID from a cookie.
Initialize	Method	Called first to initialize AuthManager.
IsAuthenticated	Method	Gets information about whether a user is currently authenticated.
Refresh	Method	Used to update the cache maintained for site-configuration properties.
SetAuthTicket	Method	Used to set an MSCSAuth ticket for a registered user.
SetProfileTicket	Method	Used to set an MSCSProfile ticket for an anonymous user.
SetProperty	Method	Used to set a custom property in the current ticket.
SetUserID	Method	Used to change the user ID property in the current ticket of the user.
UnInitialize	Method	Clears the cache holding the configuration for a site.
URLArgs	Method	Used to get a URL-encoded query string of passed name/value pairs.
URLShopperArgs	Method	Used to get a URL-encoded query string of passed name/value pairs and append the ticket if it's set.

CacheManager

TABLE A.3   Methods and Properties of the *CacheManager* Object

Member	Method/Property	Description
AppURL	Property	Contains the full URL of the IIS application.
CacheObjectProgId	Property	Determines the type of objected returned by the GetCache method.
LoaderConfig	Property	A reference to a dictionary object that will be the configuration for the Loader component.

TABLE A.3   continued

Member	Method/Property	Description
LoaderProgId	Property	Contains the Prog ID of the component used to populate the cache.
RefreshInterval	Property	Specifies the time in seconds for the interval between automatic cache refreshes.
RetryInterval	Property	Specifies the number of seconds to wait before retrying to refresh a cache after an earlier attempt has failed.
WriteConfig	Property	A reference to a Dictionary object that will be the configuration property for the Writer component.
WriterProgId	Property	Contains the Prog ID of the component used to write events from the cache back to the database.
GetCache	Method	Retrieves either the Dictionary or LRUCache object for the specified cache name.
RefreshCache	Method	Issues an immediate synchronous refresh of the cache.

MessageManager

TABLE A.4   Methods and Properties of the *MessageManager* Object

Member	Method/Property	Description
DefaultLanguage	Property	The default language in which the message will be added or retrieved unless specified.
AddLanguage	Method	Adds a string to identify a message set associated with a locale.
AddMessage	Method	Adds a message text under a message key to be stored in MessageManager.
GetLocale	Method	Gets the locale associated with a message set.
GetMessage	Method	Gets the message text associated with the message key.

CatalogManager

TABLE A.5   Methods and Properties of the *CatalogManager* Object

Member	Method/Property	Description
Catalogs	Property	Contains a read-only recordset of all catalogs in the database.
CategoryDefinitions	Property	Contains a recordset of the names of all the categories defined in the database.
CustomCatalogs	Property	Contains a read-only recordset of all the custom catalogs in the database.
ProductDefinitions	Property	Contains a read-only recordset of the names of all the product definitions in the catalogs.
Properties	Property	Contains a read-only recordset of all the properties in a specified product catalog.
AddDefinitionProperty	Method	Adds a property to a definition.
AddDefinitionVariantProperty	Method	Adds a variant property to a definition.
AddPropertyValue	Method	Adds a value to the list of defined values for this property. Only applies to enumerations.
CreateCatalog	Method	Used to create a specific catalog in the database.
CreateCategoryDefinition	Method	Creates a new category definition.
CreateProductDefinition	Method	Creates a new product definition.
CreateProperty	Method	Creates a new property.
DeleteCatalog	Method	Deletes a catalog.
DeleteDefinition	Method	Deletes a product or category definition.
DeleteProperty	Method	Deletes a property.
ExportCSV	Method	Used to export a catalog as a CSV file.

A

TABLE A.5   continued

Member	Method/Property	Description
ExportXML		Used to export a catalog as an XML file.
FreeTextSearch	Method	Used to perform a free-text search on catalogs.
GetCatalog	Method	Returns a reference to a specified ProductCatalog object.
GetDefinitionProperties	Method	Returns the properties of a specified product or category definition.
GetPropertyAttributes	Method	Returns all the attributes of a specified property.
GetPropertyValues	Method	Returns a list of appropriate values for an enumeration property.
ImportCSV	Method	Used to import a catalog from a CSV file.
ImportXML		Used to import a catalog from an XML file.
Initialize	Method	Initializes the CatalogManager object before calling any other method.
Query	Method	This method is used to query on columns of product, categories, or variants.
RemoveDefinitionProperty	Method	Removes the specified property or variant property from a definition.
RemovePropertyValue	Method	Removes a defined value from an enumeration property.
RenameDefinition	Method	Renames a definition.
RenameProperty	Method	Renames a property.
SetDefinitionProperties	Method	Used to change the properties of a category or product definition.
SetPropertyAttributes	Method	Changes the attributes of a property.

OrderForm

TABLE A.6   *OrderForm* Object Keys and Methods

Member	Method/Property	Description
Order.Items	Property	A SimpleList object of products in the order.
Item.SKU	Property	The SKU of a particular product in the order.
Item.list_price	Property	The list price of a particular item.
Item.quantity	Property	The quantity of a particular product SKU.
Item._product_*	Property	Database information about the product. * is a placeholder for any database column.
Item._n_unadjusted	Property	The number of unadjusted items available in the order.
Item._iadjust_regularprice	Property	The default list price of a product.
Item._iadjust_currentprice	Property	The current price of the product after accounting for price adjustments for the product.
Item.placed_price	Property	The final price of the product after accounting for adjustments in product level and order level.
Item._tax_included	Property	A flag to indicate that tax is already included in the price of the product.
Item._cy_tax_total	Property	The total tax to be paid on the product.
Item.delete	Property	A flag to indicate that this product is no longer available in the database and can be deleted from the order.
Order._Basket_Errors	Property	A SimpleList object containing all the errors generated during a pipeline execution for checking out a basket.
Order._Purchase_Errors	Property	A SimpleList object containing all the errors generated during a pipeline execution for purchase processing.

TABLE A.6   continued

Member	Method/Property	Description
Order._oadjust_subtotal	Property	The subtotal of the order.
Order._cy_shipping_total	Property	The shipping total for the order.
Order._cy_handling_total	Property	The handling total for the order.
Order._cy_tax_total	Property	The tax total for the order.
Order._cy_total_total	Property	The total cost of the order.
Order.shopper_id	Property	The shopper ID of the shopper.
Order._cc_*	Property	* represents the expiry year, expiry month, type, name, or number related to the credit card.
Order._payment_auth_code	Property	The authorization code after the specified payment information, such as paying by credit card, is processed.
Order.bill_to_*	Property	The billing address information for the order.
Order.ship_to_*	Property	The shipping address information for the order.
Order.shipping_method	Property	The shipping method for the order.
Order.order_id	Property	The generated GUID for the order.
AddItem	Method	Adds an item to the Items simple list of the OrderForm object.
ClearItems	Method	Clears the Items simple list in the OrderForm object.
ClearOrderForm	Method	Clears all entries in the OrderForm object.

OrderGroup

TABLE A.7   Methods and Properties of the *OrderGroup* Object

Member	Method/Property	Description
LogFile	Property	The location of the log file for pipelines run using the RunPipe method.
SavePrefix	Property	Order form keys with this prefix will not be saved to the database.

TABLE A.7 continued

Member	Method/Property	Description
Value	Property	A Dictionary object that contains order group–level key/value pairs.
AddItem	Method	Adds an item to the specified order form or a default `OrderForm` object.
AddItemsFromTemplate	Method	Adds previously saved order group line items to a new order group.
AddOrderForm	Method	Adds an `OrderForm` object to the `OrderGroup` object.
AddXMLAsOrderForm	Method	Adds an order form saved as XML back to the order group.
AggregrateOrderFormValues	Method	Computes the sum of a specified key in all order forms and stores this information in a specified key in the order group.
Clear	Method	Clears all entries in the order group, including order forms and address dictionaries.
GetAddress	Method	Used to get a specified address dictionary.
GetItemInfo	Method	Gets a reference to a specified item in a specified order form.
GetOrderFormAsXML	Method	Used to convert an `OrderForm` object into an XML string.
GetOrderFormValue	Method	Gets the value of the specified key in the specified order form.
Initialize	Method	Initializes the `OrderGroup` object with the user ID of the user.
LoadOrder	Method	Used to load a specified order group from storage.
LoadTemplate	Method	Used to load a specified order group template from storage.
LoadBasket	Method	Used to load the basket of the current user. If the basket is not found, this method returns a new empty basket for the user.

A

COMMERCE
SERVER OBJECTS:
A QUICK

TABLE A.7   continued

Member	Method/Property	Description
PurgeUnreferencedAddresses	Method	Removes all addresses from the addresses dictionary that are not referenced for shipping or billing.
PutItemValue	Method	Puts a value in a specified line-item key of a specified order form.
PutOrderFormValue	Method	Puts a value in a specified key of a specified order form.
RemoveItem	Method	Removes an item from a specified order form or from the default order form.
RemoveOrderForm	Method	Removes an OrderForm object from the OrderGroup object.
RunPipe	Method	Used to execute the pipeline for each of the order forms in the order group.
SaveAsBasket	Method	Saves the order to a database with a Basket status.
SaveAsOrder	Method	Saves an order to the database with an Order status.
SaveAsTemplate	Method	Saves an order to the database with a Template status.
SetAddress	Method	Adds an address to the Addresses dictionary of the OrderGroup object.
SetAddressFromFields	Method	Sets an address in the Addresses dictionary directly from a Fields object.
SetShippingAddress	Method	Sets a shipping address for a specific item or all items of an order form.

ProfileService

TABLE A.8   Methods and Properties of the *ProfileService* Object

Member	Method/Property	Description
Errors	Property	Collection of errors that occurred during the last ProfileService operation.
BindAs	Method	Specifies the username and password to access profile objects.

TABLE A.8 continued

Member	Method/Property	Description
CreateProfile	Method	Used to create a specific `ProfileObject` object.
DeleteProfile	Method	Used to delete a specific `ProfileObject` object using a primary key.
DeleteProfileByKey	Method	Used to delete a specific `ProfileObject` object using a particular profile key.
GetProfile	Method	Retrieves a particular `ProfileObject` object using the primary key for the profile object.
GetProfileByKey	Method	Retrieves a particular `ProfileObject` object using any profile key for the profile object.
GetProfileDefXML	Method	Retrieves, as XML, the name of the schema or the schema itself of a profile definition.
Initialize	Method	Used to connect to the database and populate profile cache with all profiles.
UnBind	Method	Resets the user credentials supplied for accessing profiles.

ContentSelector

TABLE A.9 The Method of the *ContentSelector* Object

Member	Method/Property	Description
GetContent	Method	Executes the pipeline specified in the passed context dictionary. Returns the selected items in an HTML or XML string.

AppConfig

TABLE A.10 Methods of the *AppConfig* Object

Member	Method/Property	Description
DecodeStatusCode	Method	Decodes the specified status code.
GetCountryCodeFrom CountryName	Method	Returns the country code for the specified country name.

TABLE A.10 continued

Member	Method/Property	Description
GetCountryNameFrom-CountryCode	Method	Returns the country name for the specified country code.
GetCountryNamesList	Method	Returns an alphabetical list of country names.
GetOptionsDictionary	Method	Gets all the site-configuration options as key/value pairs in a dictionary.
GetRegionCodeFrom-CountryCodeAndRegionName	Method	Returns the region code for the specified country code and region name.
GetRegionNameFrom-CountryCodeAndRegionCode	Method	Returns the region name for the specified country code and region code.
GetRegionNamesListFrom-CountryCode	Method	Returns an alphabetical list of region names for the specified country code.
Initialize	Method	Initializes the AppConfig object for a commerce site.
RefreshCache	Method	Refreshes the AppConfig object cache.

Category

TABLE A.11 Properties of the Category Object

Member	Method/Property	Description
AncestorCategories	Property	Contains a recordset of category names that exist anywhere above this category and that directly or indirectly contain this category in the hierarchy. This property is read-only.
CatalogName	Property	Contains the name of the catalog of which this category is a member.
CategoryName	Property	Gives the name of this category.
ChildCategories	Property	A read-only recordset of all child categories directly below this category.

TABLE A.11   continued

Member	Method/Property	Description
DescendantProducts	Property	Contains all products that exist anywhere below this category. Accessing this property on the root category returns every product in the entire catalog. This property is read-only.
GetCategoryProperties	Property	Contains a recordset containing the property values for this category. This property is read-only.
ParentCategories	Property	Contains a recordset containing the names of the Category objects that are parent categories to this category. This property is read-only.
Products	Property	Contains the products that exist within this category but not within descendant categories. This property is read-only.
RelatedCategories	Property	Contains a recordset that describes all the categories and product families that have relationships to this category. This property is read-only.
RelatedProducts	Property	Contains a recordset that describes all the product variants and product families that have relationships to this category. This property is read-only.

MtsPipeline

TABLE A.12   Methods of the *MtsPipeline* Object

Member	Method/Property	Description
Execute	Method	Runs the components in the configuration file as loaded by the LoadPipe method.
LoadPipe	Method	Used to load a pipeline configuration file (PCF) into the pipeline.
SetLogFile	Method	Used to identify a file to be used by the object for logging its operations.

ProfileObject

TABLE A.13 Methods and Properties of the *ProfileObject* Object

Member	Method/Property	Description
Fields	Property	This is a read-only `Fields` collection. It can be used to access data in profile properties.
GetProfileXML	Method	Used to retrieve the profile schema and/or the profile data that's in XML format.
Update	Method	Saves any changes made to a profile instance to the underlying data storage.

Pipeline Components: A Quick Reference

IN THIS APPENDIX

- Reference by Type or Pipeline and Stage   592
- Reference by Component Names   600

This appendix contains a quick reference to the pipeline components, their purpose, and the stages and pipelines in which the components are normally used. The keys read and written, along with the purpose and stage affinity of a component, should most often be all you need to know when developing a pipeline using a component. You can use the File, Save Values Read and Written menu item in the Pipeline Editor to know what keys are read and written by each component in a pipeline. Also, from a component's property sheet, you can get the same information from the Values Read and Written tab. For additional information about a component, refer to the section "Pipeline Component Reference" under "Programmer's Reference" in the Commerce Server documentation.

Reference by Type of Pipeline and Stage

This section contains a listing of components based on the pipelines they are used in and their stage affinities. The purpose of each component is also given. Also specified is whether a component is provided for backward compatibility only. In that case, the backward compatibility refers to a Site Server 3.0 Commerce Edition pipeline component that could be used with a Commerce Server 2000 pipeline. If two components differ only due to the improved currency precision in Commerce Server 2000, use the one with the currency precision because it will save you from manually formatting currency values. For example, you would use RequiredItemAdjustPriceCy instead of RequiredItemAdjustPrice. The components with high currency precision have "Cy" in their name.

Sometimes you might come across an individual component used in Site Server whose functionality has been replaced by a new CS2K component. In this case, too, it is preferable to use the recent component to take advantage of the new functionality. For example, use Query-CatalogInfo (new in CS2K) instead of QueryProdInfoADO (which existed in Site Server).

Order Processing Pipeline

TABLE B.1   Stages and Components of OPP

Stage	Component	Purpose
Product Info	QueryCatalogInfo	Queries the database to retrieve information about each item in the order. If an item is not found in the product catalog, this component marks the item as deleted in the OrderForm object.
	QueryProdInfoADO	Provided for backward compatibility only. Typically used to run SQL queries against a database to fetch product information. Use QueryCatalogInfo instead.

TABLE B.1   continued

Stage	Component	Purpose
	RequiredProdInfo	Deletes the items that are marked as deleted by the previous component.
Shopper Information	DefaultShopperInfo	Copies the shopper profile from the context dictionary to the order form.
Item Price	DefaultItemPriceCy	Sets the item._cy_iadjust_ regularprice key to the value retrieved by the Product Info stage. This component is for backward compatibility only because many components look at this key.
	DefaultItemPrice	Provided only for backward compatibility. Instead, use the recent component DefaultItemPriceCy.
	RequiredItemPriceCy	Verifies that the key item._cy_ iadjust_regularprice is initialized with a value.
	RequiredItemPrice	Provided only for backward compatibility. Instead, use the recent component RequiredItemPriceCy.
Item Adjust Price	RequiredItemAdjustPriceCy	Verifies that the item price is current and has not changed.
	RequiredItemAdjustPrice	Provided only for backward compatibility. Instead, use the recent component RequiredItemAdjustPriceCy.
	SaleAdjust	Provided for backward compatibility. Use OrderDiscount instead.
	ItemPromo	Provided only for backward compatibility. Use components such as OrderDiscount instead to apply discounts.
Inventory	FlagInventory	Verifies that items are in stock and generates an error if they are not. This component also sets the item._ inventory_backorder key if Disallow Backorder is checked in the configuration property sheet.

B

PIPELINE
COMPONENTS: A
QUICK REFERENCE

TABLE B.1 continued

Stage	Component	Purpose
	LocalInventory	Sets the item._inventory_backorder key to the difference between the total ordered quantity of an item and the value in item._product_local_ inventory, which contains the stock quantity.
Order Initialization	RequiredOrderInitCy	Creates an order ID and writes to the order form. This component also initializes values such as order subtotal, total, shipping total, and tax total to NULL values.
	RequiredOrderInit	Provided only for backward compatibility. Instead, use the recent component RequiredOrderInitCy.
Order Check	RequiredOrderCheck	Verifies that the order contains at least one item.
Order Adjust Price	RequiredOrderAdjustPriceCy	Computes the effective price of each item, taking into account discounted and nondiscounted quantities.
	RequiredOrderAdjustPrice	Provided only for backward compatibility. Instead, use the recent component RequiredOrderAdjustPriceCy.
	OrderDiscount	Applies discounts scheduled in Campaign Manager to the items in the basket.
	DBOrderPromoADO	Provided for backward compatibility. Use OrderDiscount and ScoreDiscounts instead.
Order Subtotal	DefaultOrderSubtotalCy	Sums up the total cost of each item and arrives at the order subtotal.
	DefaultOrderSubtotal	Provided only for backward compatibility. Instead, use the recent component DefaultOrderSubtotalCy.
	RequiredOrderSubtotalCy	Verifies that the order subtotal, order._cy_oadjust_subtotal, is set and has a value other than the initial value of NULL.

TABLE B.1 continued

Stage	Component	Purpose
	RequiredOrderSubtotal	Provided only for backward compatibility. Instead, use the recent component RequiredOrderSubtotalCy.
Shipping	DefaultShippingCy	Initializes the shipping total, order._cy_shipping_total, for the order to zero.
	DefaultShipping	Provided only for backward compatibility. Instead, use the recent component DefaultShippingCy.
	FixedShipping	Applies a fixed cost to the shipping total as specified in the component's property page. This component is provided for backward compatibility.
	LinearShipping	Provided for backward compatibility only. Use other shipping components.
	ShippingDiscountAdjust	Used to provide free shipping by setting order._cy_shipping_total to zero.
	TableShippingADO	Retrieves shipping charges from a database to set the shipping total.
	ShippingMethodRouter	Runs components to calculate the shipping total in a multiple-shipment order.
	RequiredShippingCy	Checks whether the shipping total, order._cy_shipping_total, has been set for the order.
Handling	FixedHandling	Applies a fixed cost to the handling total, order._cy_handling_total, as specified in the component's property page.
	DefaultHandlingCy	A placeholder component that initializes the handling total, order._cy_handling_total, to zero.
	DefaultHandling	Provided only for backward compatibility. Instead, use the recent component DefaultHandlingCy.

B

**PIPELINE
COMPONENTS: A
QUICK REFERENCE**

TABLE B.1   continued

Stage	Component	Purpose
	LinearHandling	Provided for backward compatibility only. Use other handling components.
	TableHandlingADO	Retrieves the handling charges from a database to set the handling total, `order._cy_handling_total`.
	RequiredHandlingCy	Checks whether the handling total, `order._cy_handling_total`, has been set for the order.
	RequiredHandling	Provided only for backward compatibility. Instead, use the recent component `RequiredHandlingCy`.
Tax	DefaultTaxCy	Initializes the tax total, `order._cy_tax_total`, to zero.
	DefaultTax	Provided only for backward compatibility. Instead, use the recent component `DefaultTaxCy`.

	SampleRegionalTax	A sample component for calculating tax for multiple-shipment orders. You might want to use a custom component for calculating taxes. Note that the following components are also available, purely as examples, for backward compatibility:
		`SampleCanadaTax`
		`SampleJapanTax`
		`SampleUSTax`
		`SampleVATTax`

	RequiredTaxCy	Verifies that the tax computations have been completed for the order by looking at the keys `order._cy_tax_total` and `order._cy_tax_included`.
	RequiredTax	Provided only for backward compatibility. Instead, use the recent component `RequiredTaxCy`.
Order Total	DefaultTotalCy	Computes the order total from the subtotal, shipping, handling, and tax totals. If one of the four values is missing, an error is generated.

TABLE B.1 continued

Stage	Component	Purpose
	DefaultTotal	Provided only for backward compatibility. Instead, use the recent component DefaultTotalCy.
	RequiredTotalCy	Makes a final check to see whether the values in the form have been tampered with by malicious entities.
	RequiredTotal	Provided only for backward compatibility. Instead, use the recent component RequiredTotalCy.
Payment	ValidateCCNumber	Checks whether the entered credit card number has a valid date and number format. However, it does not check whether the card account exists.
	DefaultPayment	Initializes the payment authorization key to a value of FAITH, a simple string.
	RequiredPayment	Ensures that the payment authorization key is not NULL.
Accept	SaveReceipt	Saves the order to the database using the DBStorage object.
	MakePO	This component takes a template file and merges the file with order form values. It writes the merged text value to a key in the order form. This key can be used by POtoFile.
	SQLItemADO	Use this component to run a database query for each item in the order.
	SQLOrderADO	Use this component to run a database query once for an entire order.
	POtoFile	This component reads from a key in the order form, typically created by MakePO. The key is specified using the property page of the component. This component also saves the text to a file.

Content Selection Framework Pipeline

TABLE B.2   Stages and Components of CPP

Stage	Component	Purpose
Load Context	InitCSFPipeline	Creates dictionaries and initializes values for use throughout the pipeline.
	LoadHistory	Retrieves a history string from one of the following sources: user profile, cookie, or a Session object.
Filter	FilterContent	Applies filters stored in order.FilterRequire and order.FilterExclude dictionaries to the list of content so that items can be eliminated at an early stage.
Initial Score	AdvertisingNeed-OfDelivery	Sets the NOD of each content item. An item with an NOD greater than 1 indicates lagging delivery, whereas an NOD less than 1 indicates that the goals for the item delivery have been exceeded.
Scoring	EvalTargetGroups	Applies a multiplier to each content item based on target expressions.
	HistoryPenalty	Applies a penalty score to reduce the likelihood of recently delivered content items.
	ScoreDiscounts	In the context of discounts, this component applies a multiplier to each item depending on discount rules.
Select	SelectWinners	Selects and returns winning content items up to the requested number.
Record	IISAppendToLog	Using this component at this stage would record the selected items as a QueryString object in the IIS log.
	RecordEvent	The winning items are recorded in a dictionary for future CSF use.
	RecordHistory	The winning items are recorded in a history string for future CSF use.
	SaveHistory	The winning items are recorded in one of three places: User Profile object, an ASP session object, or an HTTP cookie.
Format	FormatTemplate	Returns the content items as HTML or XML strings.

Direct Mailer Pipeline

TABLE B.3   Stages and Components of DMP

Stage	Component	Purpose
Throttle	ThrottleDMLPerformance	This component simply generates a delay between messages. The delay is set by the DML service in the key context.delay_msec.
Preprocess Recipient	VerifyRecipientData	Checks for a valid e-mail address and determines the formatting of the message body.
Filter	None	This stage can be used to include custom components or a scriptor to provide functionality such as opt-out and domain name filtering.
Create Cookies	CreateUPMCookie	Using the context and order dictionaries as inputs, this component creates cookie information and stores it in the order.Cookie dictionary.
Compose E-mail	ComposeDMLMessage	Creates the message body and uses the cookie string if it is a personalized e-mail message.
	AddAttachments	Adds attachments to the message body using the Collaborative Data Objects (CDO).
Send E-mail	VerifyMessageBody	Verifies that the message body is not blank and that the correct number of attachments are present.
	SendPrecomposedMessage	Sends an e-mail using the CDO of Windows and writes the e-mail count back to the pipeline.
PostProcess Recipient	None	Use a Scriptor or other custom components in this stage.

B

PIPELINE COMPONENTS: A QUICK REFERENCE

Other Pipeline Components

Table B.4   General Pipeline Components

Stage/Pipeline	Component	Purpose
Any/Any	`Scriptor`	Used to prototype functionality quickly.
Any/OPP	`MoneyConvertor`	Provides conversion of key values between currency and integer values.
Any/Any	`SendSMTP`	Used to send e-mails with the help of an SMTP server. This component can access order form keys set in the Configuration tab.
Any/Any	`Splitter`	Normally used to split orders based on vendors, catalogs, or shipment methods.
None/None	`StepWiseShipping`	Not used directly in a pipeline. This component is called by `ShippingMethodRouter` to calculate the shipping total.

Reference By Component Names

Table B.5   List of Pipeline Components

Pipeline Component	Used in Pipeline...	Stage Affinity
`AddAttachments`	Direct Mailer	Compose E-mail
`AdvertisingNeedOfDelivery`	Content Selection	Initial Score
`ComposeDMLMessage`	Direct Mailer	Compose E-mail
`CreateUPMCookie`	Direct Mailer	Create Cookies
`DBOrderPromoADO`	Order Processing	Order Adjust Price
`DefaultHandlingCy`	Order Processing	Handling
`DefaultItemPriceCy`	Order Processing	Item Price
`DefaultOrderSubTotalCy`	Order Processing	Order Subtotal
`DefaultPayment`	Order Processing	Payment
`DefaultShippingCy`	Order Processing	Shipping
`DefaultShopperInfo`	Order Processing	Shopper Information
`DefaultTaxCy`	Order Processing	Tax
`DefaultTotalCy`	Order Processing	Order Total
`EvalTargetGroups`	Content Selection	Score

TABLE B.5   continued

Pipeline Component	Used in Pipeline...	Stage Affinity
ExecuteProcess	Any	Any
FilterContent	Content Selection	Filter
FixedHandling	Order Processing	Handling
FixedShipping	Order Processing	Shipping
FlagInventory	Order Processing	Inventory
FormatTemplate	Content Selection	Format
HistoryPenalty	Content Selection	Score
IISAppendToLog	Event Processing	Record
InitCSFPipeline	Content Selection	Load Context
ItemPromo	Order Processing	Adjust Price
LinearHandling	Order Processing	Handling
LinearShipping	Order Processing	Shipping
LoadHistory	Content Selection	Load Context
LocalInventory	Order Processing	Inventory
MakePO	Order Processing	Accept
MoneyConverter	Order Processing	Any
OrderDiscount	Order Processing	Order Adjust Price
POtoFile	Order Processing	Accept
QueryCatalogInfo	Order Processing	Product Info
QueryProdInfoADO	Order Processing	Product Info
RecordEvent	Event Processing, Content Selection, and Order Processing	Record in CSP and EPP; Receipt in OPP
RecordHistory	Content Selection	Record
RequiredHandlingCy	Order Processing	Handling
RequiredItemAdjustPriceCy	Order Processing	Item Adjust Price
RequiredItemPriceCy	Order Processing	Item Price
RequiredOrderAdjustPriceCy	Order Processing	Order Adjust Price
RequiredOrderCheck	Order Processing	Order Check
RequiredOrderInitCy	Order Processing	Order Initialization
RequiredOrderSubtotalCy	Order Processing	Order Subtotal
RequiredPayment	Order Processing	Payment

B

PIPELINE
COMPONENTS: A
QUICK REFERENCE

TABLE B.5   continued

Pipeline Component	Used in Pipeline...	Stage Affinity
RequiredProdInfo	Order Processing	Product Info
RequiredShippingCy	Order Processing	Shipping
RequiredTaxCy	Order Processing	Tax
RequiredTotalCy	Order Processing	Order Total
SaleAdjust	Order Processing	Item Adjust Price
SampleRegionalTax	Order Processing	Tax
SaveHistory	Content Selection	Record
SaveReceipt	Order Processing	Accept
ScoreDiscounts	Content Selection	Scoring
Scriptor	Any	Any
SelectWinners	Content Selection	Select
SendPrecomposedMessage	Direct Mail	Send E-mail
SendSMTP	Any	Any
ShippingDiscountAdjust	Order Processing	Shipping
ShippingMethodRouter	Order Processing	Shipping
SimpleCanadaTax	Order Processing	Tax
SimpleJapanTax	Order Processing	Tax
SimpleUSTax	Order Processing	Tax
SimpleVATTax	Order Processing	Tax
Splitter	Order Processing	Any
SQLItemADO	Order Processing	Accept
SQLOrderADO	Order Processing	Accept
TableHandlingADO	Order Processing	Handling
TableShippingADO	Order Processing	Shipping
ThrottleDMLPerformance	Direct Mailer	Throttle
ValidateCCNumber	Order Processing	Payment
VerifyMessageBody	Direct Mailer	Send E-mail
VerifyRecipientData	Direct Mailer	Preprocess Recipient

Retail Store Helper Routines: Where to Find What

As you have seen throughout this book, site pages use helper routines defined in other ASP files that act as libraries of routines. These library files are included in the ASP page that uses routines from the included library file. This appendix gives you a handy reference to most of the helper routines that come along with the solution site Retail. These libraries are listed under functional categories for your convenience.

TABLE C.1   Catalog Routines

File	Routines	Description
Include/global_catalog_lib.asp	InitCatalogManager InitCatalogSets DictGetCatalogAttributes dictGetRSFields	Initialization of product catalog
Include/catalog.asp	sUserCatalogsAsString mscsUserCatalogsetID mscsUserCatalogs mscsUserCatalogsFromID GetPriceAndCurrency mscsGetCategoryObject rsFreeTextSearch mscsGetProductList mscsGetSubCategoriesList EnsureUserHasRightsToCatalog GetCatalogForUser htmRenderCategoryPage htmRenderCategoriesList htmRenderProductsTable htmRenderCatalogList RenderSearchResults RenderSearchResultRow RenderCategoryURL RenderProductURL RenderCatalogURL RenderCategoryLink RenderProductLink RenderCatalogLink	Functions related to retrieving, rendering, and searching catalogs
Include/cataloglib.asp	GetCategoriesRs GetProductsRs GetProductDetailRs GetProductVariantsRs BuildPropSearchClause GetCatalog GetRootProducts	Functions for manipulating catalog objects

TABLE C.2   User Profile–Related Routines

File	Routines	Description
Include/global _profile_lib.asp	InitProfileService InitAuthManager OGetProfile listGetProfileSchema oGetOpenConnectionObject AddGroupAndPropertySchemas dictGetProfileSchemaForAllProfileTypes	Initialization and retrieval functions for user profile objects and services
Include/std_ access_lib.asp	GetUserInfo EnsureAccess EnsureAuthAccess IsFormLoginRequired CheckPartnerServiceAccess IsPersistentCookieAllowed SGetUserIDForNewGuestUser GetAuthManagerObject	Functions related to determining user access
Include/std_ profile_lib.asp	GetProfileService UpdateUserProfile EnsureUserProfile GetNewGuestUserProfile GetCurrentUserProfile GetProfileFromDB EnsureUpToDateUserProfile GetUserProfileByLoginName rsGetProfile rsGetProfileByKey	Functions to retrieve, check, and update the user profile
Include/ addr_lib.asp	GetUserAddresses GetOrganizationAddresses GetAddresses GetAddressType IsZipCodeValid LookupRegion	Functions to help with addresses in an Address Book
Include/global_ addressbook_ lib.asp	GetShipToAddressFieldDefinitions GetAddressFieldDefinitions GetAddressBookAddressFieldDefinitions	Initialization functions for the Address Book functionality

C

RETAIL STORE
HELPER ROUTINES:
WHERE TO FIND

TABLE C.3   HTML Presentation Routines

File	Routines	Description
Include/global _ui_lib.asp	GetSiteStyles GetStyles	Initialization of HTML styles used by global _main_lib.asp
Include/html _lib.asp	RenderText RenderTextBox RenderPasswordBox RenderLink RenderCheckBox RenderRadioButton RenderHiddenField RenderSubmitButton RenderResetButton RenderImageButton RenderForm RenderListBox RenderListBoxFromSimpleList RenderListBoxFromArray RenderImage RenderUnorderedList RenderUnorderedListFromSimpleList RenderListFromSimpleList RenderTable RenderTableHeaderRow RenderTableDataRow RenderTableRow RenderElement GetRepeatStyle InsertLineBreaks InsertParagraphBreaks InsertBlankSpace Bold Italic BRTag Ptag RenderPreFormattedText Tag	Functions to format HTML content

TABLE C.3 continued

File	Routines	Description
Include/global _forms_lib.asp	dictGetPropertySchema GetFormDefinitions GetLoginFieldDefinitions GetPasswordFieldDefinition GetPurchaseOrderFieldDefinitions GetRegistrationFieldDefinitions	Functions to build various forms across the site
Include/form_lib.asp	IsFormSubmitted GetSubmittedFieldValues GetFieldsErrorDictionary BMatchesPattern HtmRenderFillOutForm	Common functions for rendering forms and accepting form submits

TABLE C.4 Order and Payment Processing Routines

File	Routines	Description
Include/std _ordergrp_lib.asp	GetOrderGroup GetLineItemsCount LoadBasket GetAnyLineItem GetAnyOrderForm SetKeyOnOrderForms GetErrorCount RemoveEmptyOrderForms GetOrderGroupManager AddDiscountMessages	Functions to access instances of the OrderGroup and OrderForm objects
Include/payment.asp	CatchErrorsForPaymentPages CheckOut SaveBasketAsOrder InvokeBizTalk SubmitUsingBizTalk EnsureSupportForPaymentMethod GetXMLForVendorItems GetPaymentMethodsForUser GetDefaultPaymentMethodForUser GetPaymentPageFromPaymentMethod GetPaymentMethodDisplayName htmRenderPaymentOptionsForUser	Functions for payment processing and BizTalk integration

TABLE C.4   continued

File	Routines	Description
Include/global _creditcards.asp	GetCreditCardNamesList GetCreditCardFieldDefinitions GetCreditCardCodesList	Initialization of a credit card form for display
Include/std _pipeline_lib.asp	GetPipelineLogFile RunMtsPipeline	Functions to run a pipeline

TABLE C.5   Other Routines Used

File	Routines	Description
Include/analysis.asp	Analysis_LogAddToBasket Analysis_LogSubmitOrder Analysis_LogEvent Analysis_LogRemoveFromBasket Analysis_ConstructKeyValueString Analysis_ConstructPRID	Functions for logging and analysis used by most of the site files
Include/global _cache_lib.asp	InitCacheManager	Initialization of caches for the site
Include/global _csf_lib.asp	InitCSF	Initialization of CSF contexts for advertising and discounts
Include/global _data_lib.asp	InitDataFunctions GetDWConnectionString oGetBizDataObject oGetGenIDObject	Initialization information for data warehouse, data functions, and biz data
Include/global _internationalization _lib.asp	InitAltCurrencyDisp GetCountryNamesList GetCountryCodesList GetBillToCurrencyFieldDefinition GetBillToCurrenciesListValues	Functions to help with internationalization or localization
Include/global _messagemanager _lib.asp	GetMessageManagerObject GetXMLFromFile	For dealing with MessageManager
Include/global _predictor_lib.asp	InitPredictor	Initialization of the PredictorClient object

TABLE C.5 continued

File	Routines	Description
Include/global _siteconfig_lib.asp	GetINIString GetINIFileName GetRootPath JoinWebFarm GetSiteConfigObject GetComputerName GetCommerceSiteName GetConfigDictionary GetAppConfigObject GetSitePages GetSecurePagesDictionary InitPageSets GetBaseURL GetMachineBaseURL iGetWebServerPort IsActiveDirectoryPresent sGetActiveDirectoryDefaultNamingContext GetCommerceSiteInstallPoint InitSitePipelines GetPaymentMethodsForSite	Functions to initialize and deal with a variety of site configurations, such as page groups, Active Directory, and pipelines
Include/global _siteterms_lib.asp	oGetSiteTermOptions bIsSiteTerm sGetReferenceString	Initialization of site terms
Include/header.asp	None	Sets Response header and a reference to a nontransactional pipeline
Include/helper.asp	IsValid DebugTrace DumpTrace RaiseError SetErrSource SetStatus GetVirtualPath BuildGetRequest NumVal val	Utility functions

C

TABLE C.5 continued

File	Routines	Description
Include/setupenv.asp	SetupPage	Calls the main() routine in all site pages
Include/std _util_lib.asp	GetAddressPage DoubleQuote GetListItemIndex GetArrayFromList ConvertListToArray FormatOutput GetDictionary SortDictionaryKeys GetRegExp GetSimpleList GetObjectInstanceDictionary GetQualifiedName IsBitValueSet IsNumberInRange GetRecordCount CreateSet IsEntityInSet IsEntityInList IsEntityInArray GetDiscountDescription htmRenderCurrency GetFileSystemObject GetKeyValue GetErrorSource RsToDict	Utility functions
Include/std _url_lib.asp	GetTicketInUrlArg GenerateURL GenerateURL GetTicketLocation AddURLArguments GetRequestStringRange GetRequestString	Functions to get a ticket and generate URL strings
Include/std _string_lib.asp	BooleanToString StringToBoolean Space RemoveBlankItemsFromArray sChopOffRight sChopOffLeft	Functions to deal with strings

TABLE C.5 continued

File	Routines	Description
Include/std _dates_lib.asp	GetMonthNamesList GetMonthCodesList GetYearsListItems GetYearsListValues	Functions for date information
Include/std _cookie_lib.asp	CorrectRequest GetCorrectedCookiePath GetCorrectedHostName GetRequestType SetTestCookie GetIISApplicationName	Functions for working with cookies
Include/std _cache_lib.asp	CacheFragment LookupCachedFragment LookupCachedObject CacheObject	Functions to retreive and update site caches
Include/txheader.asp	None	Twin of header.asp (has a reference to a transactional pipeline for use in site pages)

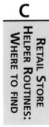

C

RETAIL STORE
HELPER ROUTINES:
WHERE TO FIND

Migrating from Site Server 3.0 to Commerce Server 2000

D

IN THIS APPENDIX

- SSCE Features That Migrate to CS2K   614
- SSCE Features That Migrate to Other Products   615
- SSCE Features That Do Not Migrate   615
- Getting Ready to Migrate   615
- Migration Approaches   620

If your e-commerce site runs using the Site Server 3.0 Commerce Edition (SSCE), it's time to think about moving the site to Commerce Server 2000 (CS2K). CS2K is not just a version upgrade of SSCE; rather, it's an altogether different platform and product. However, CS2K allows you to migrate the commerce site built with SSCE. Some features of SSCE you can migrate to CS2K, but others need to be moved to a different Microsoft product for you to continue using their functionality. A few other SSCE features need to be altogether discarded because they are no longer supported in any of the current Microsoft products. In this appendix, you will see the list of SSCE features that need to be migrated, the process of migration, and the tools provided by CS2K for the migration process.

SSCE Features That Migrate to CS2K

Table D.1 shows a mapping of SSCE features with CS2K features, giving you an idea of what can be migrated from SSCE to CS2K.

TABLE D.1   SSCE and Corresponding CS2K Features

SSCE Features	CS2K Features
Site Foundation Wizard (SFW)	Site Packager and Site Builder Wizard (SBW)
Starter Sites	Solution Sites
Site Manager application	Business Desk application
Online Store	Catalog System and database
Personalization and Membership	User Profiles in the Profile System
Ad Server/Ad Manager	Content Selection Framework and the Campaigns Manager biz desk module
Analysis: Custom Import and Usage Import	Analysis: Data Warehouse, DTS Tasks, and Custom Import
Analysis: Report Writer	Business Desk Analysis and Reports
Predictor	Predictor Resource
Content Deployment and Content Replication	Some features incorporated in Site Packager
Site Vocabulary	Site Terms
Rule Builder	Expression Builder
Pipelines	Pipelines
Direct Mail	Direct Mail
Product Search	Catalog System Search

SSCE Features That Migrate to Other Products

Table D.2 provides you with a quick look at some of the SSCE features that are now incorporated into other Microsoft products.

TABLE D.2   SSCE Features in Other Microsoft Products

SSCE Features	Microsoft Products
Posting Acceptor	Microsoft WebDAV
Commerce Interchange Pipeline	Microsoft BizTalk Server 2000
Search: Crawl, Index Knowledge Manager	Microsoft SharePoint Portal
Content Deployment and Content Replication	Some aspects handled in Microsoft Application Center 2000

SSCE Features That Do Not Migrate

Here are the SSCE features that don't readily migrate into any of the latest products:

- Web-based Pipeline Editor
- Content Analyzer
- Tag Tool
- Publishing Wizard
- Active Channel Multicaster (Push)

Getting Ready to Migrate

Now that you've seen the list of features that migrate, let's discuss briefly the key migration points.

SFW/SBW to Site Packager

In SSCE, the Site Foundation Wizard and Site Builder Wizard were used to build a starter site and the infrastructure needed for the site. In CS2K, you use the Site Packager and unpack a packed solution site on which to base your development. The unpacking process takes care of installing the ASP pages and the global and site resources as well as creating the database for the initial site. Also, you don't need to set up the DSN, as was necessary in SFW/SBW.

Starter Site to Solution Site

In SSCE, you used the SBW to choose a type of site based on one of the sample sites, such as clocktower, market, mspress, or vc. You also had the choice to create a custom site. Then, using the SBW, you created the locale, site style, promotions, and products. You used to specify the features that the site should have, such as enabling Product Searching, specifying when to ask for user registration, and defining the depth of product departments.

In CS2K, you choose one of the solution sites available: Blank, Retail, or SupplierActive-Directory. These solution sites are available as packages called PuP files. You use the Site Packager to unpack a solution site. To add products and promotions or manage orders, you use the Business Desk modules. To change the locale, site style, or other site configuration options, you use the Commerce Server Manager, an MMC-based administration tool. While unpacking a solution site, you can choose to unpack the site's corresponding business desk application that would be used to manage the site.

When you are migrating from SSCE to CS2K, you can unpack the `Blank.PuP` package to create a blank site. This site has just a `default.asp` page and the `global.asa` file. Then you can begin mapping the functionality and start building additional pages for the site.

Site Manager to Business Desk

The Site Manager Web application was used in SSCE to manage product catalogs, users, and orders. In CS2K, all this and much more can be accomplished from the user-friendly interfaces provided by business desk modules.

Online Store to Catalog System

SSCE provided a collection of database tables and a set of management pages to manage product catalogs. You created departments, products, variants, and so on, based on predefined schemas. In CS2K, the catalog system provides a powerful infrastructure to define your own schemas and populate catalogs. You can integrate the catalogs by importing from or exporting to external sources using XML and CSV formats. The Catalog System API offers a collection of COM objects you can use to programmatically manage the catalog database.

You can move your product catalogs from SSCE to CS2K using more than one method. You can export the products from the SSCE database in a CSV format using Data Transformation Services. From the Catalogs module in business desk, you can then import the CSV file into the CS2K catalog database. Of course, you need to create definitions for properties and products. Also, the SSCE departments need to be mapped to the categories in CS2K.

A more convenient way to export the SSCE product catalog is to use XML to format the exported data. The XML file needs to have the categories, products, and variants for a catalog, satisfying the schema specified in the `CatalogXMLSchema.xml` file found under the CS2K installation folder.

Another way to automate the catalog-migration process is to use the Catalog API COM objects and do so programmatically. To do this, you need to have a clear understanding of how catalogs, categories, products, and variants are organized in CS2K. Then, using the COM objects, such as CatalogManager and ProductCatalog, you create properties, categories, products, variants, and relationships in order to create a catalog in the database. Your source database would of course be the SSCE products database. The Commerce Server 2000 Resource Kit contains a script called `migrateCatalog.vbs` that can be customized and used to migrate SSCE catalogs to CS2K.

P&M to User Profiles

The Personalization and Membership server in SSCE was used to authenticate site visitors. You used to map a P&M instance with an IIS site. In CS2K, you use the Profile Service to maintain user profiles and authenticate site visitors against a profile data store. The user profile can be aggregated from multiple data sources, such as an Active Directory and an SQL Server.

The CS2K SDK contains the necessary resources for you to migrate users in an SSCE Membership directory to CS2K's user profile system. The Membership Migration tool is available under the folder <Microsoft Commerce Server Installation Folder>, SDK, Tools, Membership Migration

The Membership Migration tool uses the following objects:

- `MigrationMainObj`
- `MigrationReadObj`
- `MigrationWriteObj`
- `MigrationModifyObj`
- `MigrationLogObj`

These objects are specially provided for reading the users, attributes, and groups created in the SSCE Membership directory and moving them to the CS2K's profile store. As you already know, CS2K's profile store could be an SQL Server database or an Active Directory. Membership migration can take place in two ways using the SDK tools: You can migrate users from SSCE to CS2K on demand when users log in to the site, or you can migrate all users in a batch mode. The file `login.asp` in the SDK can be used to do on-demand migration when users log in. This file can be found under the Client subfolder.

To perform batch migration of the membership directory to the CS2K profile store, including the mapping of groups, subgroups, and attribute schemas, use the `Client.exe` program in the bin/release subfolder. Note that the source code for the Client.exe program as well as for all the migration objects can be found under the same MembershipMigration SDK directory. There is another utility called ProfileBuilder.exe, under the ProfileBuilder subfolder, that can be used for the migration (see Figure D.1)

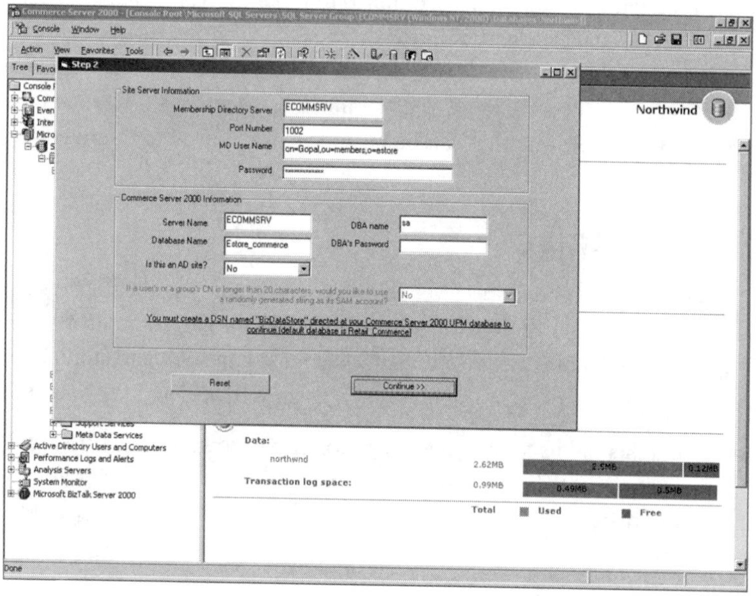

FIGURE D.1
Step 2 in the ProfileBuilder tool.

Ad Server/Ad Manager to CSF/Campaigns Manager

In CS2K, the Campaigns Manager module in Business Desk is used to schedule and run ad campaigns on the site. You specify the number of requests or clicks for an ad, the valid dates, and other ad-related information using the Campaigns Manager module. In an ASP page, the ContentSelector object is used to get ads to be displayed using the CSF and CSF pipelines.

Use the adservermigration.exe tool to migrate ad details, schedules, and rules to the CS2K Campaigns database. The tool is available under the SDK folder <Microsoft Commerce Server Installation Folder>, SDK, Tools, Migration, Ad Server. Note that SSCE rules have to be created as CS2K expressions using the Expression Builder in the business desk modules.

Analysis: Data Import and Reports

SSCE uses the analysis database to generate reports from the Report Writer tool. Tools such as Custom Import and Usage Import were used to import different types of site data into the analysis database. In CS2K, a data warehouse is provided with prebuilt OLAP cubes and an SQL Server database to populate the cubes. First, you import site and usage data into the SQL Server data warehouse database, using many of the pre-built data transformation tasks (DTS). Then, the OLAP cubes are populated with data in the data warehouse database. You then use the Reports module in business desk to generate analysis reports.

Predictor

CS2K offers the Predictor resource, whose services can be used to build one of two analysis models: prediction or segment models. You use the PredictorClient object in an ASP page to request for predictions by loading a prediction model. You use the Segment Viewer module in business desk to analyze user clusters using the segment models. After the CS2K site goes into production, you import transaction data into the data warehouse. The analysis models are then built using the Predictor resource.

Content Deployment and Replication

SSCE offered different tools for managing content deployment and replication among multiple servers. In CS2K, you manage some of the deployment processes using the Site Packager to pack a site to be deployed and unpack the site at a target server. As you have already seen, not all features of Content Deployment and Replication are available with Site Packager. However, some of the SSCE features are now available with Microsoft Application Center.

Site Vocabulary and Rule Builder

Whereas SSCE had the Site Vocabulary editor to support maintaining a standard vocabulary for the site, CS2K has the Site Terms application, accessible from the Commerce Server Manager. Note that the Tag Tool is no longer available to tag content with the site terms.

The Rule Builder has been replaced with the Expression Builder in CS2K. The Expression Builder is available in modules such as Target Expression and Campaign Expression in the business desk for the site.

Pipelines

It is suggested that you use the CS2K pipeline components while developing pipelines. However, if you need to migrate pipelines and components, CS2K supports running pipelines in SSCE mode. The CS2K pipelines support the SSCE version of components for backward compatibility. Improved currency versions of components have been introduced in CS2K as well as functionally different components, as compared to components in SSCE. The components in the CS2K pipelines may look for values in certain keys and also can take advantage of using COM+ object pooling. These are some of the reasons why you should rewrite SSCE pipeline components in accordance with CS2K components.

Direct Mail

In CS2K, you use the Campaigns Manager module in business desk to schedule and run direct mails. The List Manager module is used to build "mailable" lists that can be built from a variety of sources, such as SQL Server, analysis reports, or a flat file. The Direct Mailer pipeline is used to process recipients.

Search

SSCE had Search and Build Servers to build catalogs and distribute them on search servers. The crawl and indexing features are now moved to a new product that is yet to be released. Searching a product in the database is now made powerful in CS2K's catalog system using the COM objects in the Catalog API. It is possible to perform free text searches and specification searches in the catalogs. Also, the Knowledge Manager in SSCE is made available in the new product, SharePoint Portal Server.

B2B Pipelines

You might have used any of Receive or Transmit pipelines in SSCE to receive or send orders over the Internet. In CS2K, the complete integration with BizTalk Server should provide a more powerful and better infrastructure to exchange catalogs and orders with business partners.

Migration Approaches

Because migration to CS2K can be a fairly involved process, it is best to plan for a parallel migration process. The old SSCE site can still be serving your customers while you plan and implement the CS2K site in parallel. Once you have migrated, functionality by functionality, from SSCE to CS2K, you can then test the CS2K site and flip the switch to make CS2K your live site. This way, there's no interruption to the existing services.

Again, consider visiting the Microsoft CS2K site regularly for updated information, not only on SSCE migration but also for CS2K features and fixes.

Summary

A lot of planning is certainly involved to migrate from your SSCE site to a CS2K site. I suggest that first you go through the entire book and understand the CS2K functionality. Then, with the help of this appendix, the product documentation, and the SDK tools, you can slowly migrate to a full-fledged CS2K site.

INDEX

A

accept stage, checkout pipelines (Estore), 317-320

accessing

catalogs (Catalog.asp file), 89-91

profiles, 195

action pages (Business Desk)

records list, displaying in content pane, 459

recordsets

conversion to XML, 460-462

retrieving using ADO, 459-460

Active Directory, authentication filter, 212-215

ad cache, advertising campaigns, 367

Ad Server (SSCE), evolution to Campaigns Manager (CS2K), 618

AddAttachments component, Direct Mailer pipeline, 599

AddDefinitionProperty method, CatalogManager object, 581

adding

ASP pages for auctions (Auction Manager), 388-390

pipelines

COM components (Pipeline Editor), 257-258

stages (Pipeline Editor), 257-258

purchase order application, 559

AddItem method, OrderGroup object, 283, 585

additem.asp page, product page (Estore), 279-285

AddLanguage method, MessageManager object, 580

AddMessage method, MessageManager object, 580

AddOrderForm method, OrderGroup object, 585

Address profile, 198

addresses, basket pipelines (Estore), 300-301

addrform.asp file, billing/shipping addresses, 104

AdminEventLog object, 576

AdminFiles object, 576

administration

e-Commerce store
  components, 18
  responsibilities, 60
Commerce Server Manager
  (CSM)
    general resources, 20-21
    global resources, 20-21
    site-specific resources,
      20-21
return on investment (ROI),
  performance analysis, 60
AdminSite object, 576
AdminWebServer object, 576
**ADO (Active Data Objects)
recordsets**
converting to XML (Recordset
  object), 460-462
retrieving (Recordset object),
  459-460
**ADODB Connection,
global.asa file, 79**
advertising
campaigns
  ad creation (Campaign
    Manager), 374
  ad display options
    (Campaign Manager),
    375-376
  ad scheduling (Campaign
    Manager), 374
  ad targeting (Campaign
    Manager), 375
  creating (Campaign
    Manager), 373-376
  goals, 223
  site-wide discounts,
    224-232
  targeted discounts,
    233-247
  targeted e-mails, 224
  troubleshooting
    (Campaign Manager),
    381-383

elements
  ad cache, 367
  ad properties, 366
  advertising.pcf file, 367
  customers, 366
  goals, 366
  house ads, 367
  items, 366
  paid ads, 367
design sheet example,
  367-369
events, recording delivery,
  383-384
infrastructure, design sheet
  example, 367-369
Internet Advertising Bureau
  (IAB), 364
management of (Business
  Desk Reference Table
  module), 369-372
metadata, defining, 369-372
online, Year 2000 revenue
  statistics, 364
pipelines, advertising.pcf file,
  378-381
**advertising.pcf file (CSP),
345-350**
advertising campaigns, 367
ContentSelector object,
  378-381
**AdvertisingNeedOfDelivery
component**
content selection framework
  pipeline, 598
initial score stage, 354
Amazon.com
Barnes & Noble reaction, 15
click-and-mortar store
  example, 15
Analysis Manager (CSM), 57
**analysis modules (Business
Desk), 63**

**analysis reports, data ware-
house queries, 507-508**
custom output, 515-518
dynamic output, 508-513
static output, 508, 513-515
**Analysis Services (SQL Server
2000)**
data mining models, 490
data warehouses, help tutorials,
  490-491
**AncestorCategories property,
Category object, 588**
anonymous users
authentication filter, applying,
  212-215
catalog sets, viewing, 188-190
cookie-less browsing, 200
registering
  (GetCurrentUserProfile
  function), 201-203
treatment of, 189-190
user profiles, MSCSProfile
  ticket, 192
**ANSI X12 standards body,
534**
AppConfig object, 575
methods
  DecodeStatus, 587
  RefreshCache, 588
**AppDefaultConfig proper-
ties, BizTalk Server, 540-541**
AppFrameWork object, 574
Application Center 2000, 23
**Application Integration
Component (AIC), BizTalk
Server, 535**
**Application OnStart event
handler, 81**
applications
names (global.asa file), 78
restarting after new module
  configuration (Business
  Desk), 468

sites
  configuration settings, 76-77
  initializing, 74-82
applying authentication filter for user logons, 212-215
AppURL property
  CacheManager object, 579
  LoaderConfig object, 579
ASP (Active Server Pages) pages, debugging (Business Desk), 476-477
ASP User Interface objects
  AppFrameWork, 574
  DataFunctions, 574
  EuroDisplay, 574
  Page, 574
associating catalogs with vendors, 562
asynchronous processing, software performance optimization, 36
AsyncRpt object, 574
ATL Pipeline Component Wizard (Visual C++), registering, 422-423
ATL Pipeline Wizard (Visual C++), order-level Visa discount component
  building, 423-440
  compiling, 439-440
  registering, 438
Auction Manager, 386
  bid pages, 391-392
  creating, 386-390
Auction object, 577
  instantiating, 385
  message strings, adding, 385
auctions
  Auction object, instantiating, 385
  bid pages (Auction Manager), 391-392
  creating (Auction Manager), 386-390

Estore, ASP page additions, 388-390
message strings, adding (Auction object), 385
modules, configuration modifications (Business Desk), 386-390
authenticating user profiles (MSCSAuth ticket), 203-205
authentication filter (Active Directory), user logons, applying, 212-215
AuthManager object, 573
  methods
    GenerateEncyptionKey, 578
    GetProperty, 578
    GetURL, 578
    GetUserID, 578
    GetUserIDFromCookie, 579
    Initialize, 579
    IsAuthenticated, 579
    Refresh, 579
    SetAuthTicket, 579
    SetProfileTicket, 579
    SetProperty, 579
    SetUserID, 579
    UnInitialize, 579
    URLArgs, 579
    URLShopperArgs, 579

B

B2B transactions (business-to-business)
  BizTalk Server
    frameworks overview, 534
    Messaging Manager, 535
    Orchestration Designer, 534
    protocols, 534
    XLANG, 534

channels
  creating (Messaging Manager), 547, 550
  modifying (Messaging Manager), 554-555
document exchanges, 536-537
examples, 536
illustrated diagram, 536-537
messaging ports
  creating (Messaging Manager), 545-547
  modidying (Messaging Manager), 553
model
  FedEx example, 14
  order processing pipeline, 21
partner sites
  building (BizTalk Server), 537-539
  catalog exchanges, 539-545, 550-552, 556-557
  order fulfillment, 557-567
role of suppliers, 538
Web, tools overview, 534
B2C model (business-to-consumer), 14
  Calyx & Corolla example, 14
  order processing pipeline, 21
  sites, building, 40
back ends
  e-Commerce stores
    Customer Relationship Management (CRM), 18
    Enterprise Resource Planning (ERP), 18
    importance of, 18
  as Web site element, 74
Bandwidth cube (OLAP), 494
banner files, advertising campaigns, modifying, 378-381
Barnes & Noble, reaction to Amazon.com competition, 15

Basket Events cube (OLAP), 494

basket.asp page
   CheckBasket routine, 287
   Estore, 286-288
   InitializeBasketPage routine, 287

basket.pcf pipeline, 289
   addresses, setting, 300-301
   Check-out button, 298
   item adjust price stage, 293
   item price stage, 292-293
   order adjust stage, 293, 296-297
   order check stage, 292
   order initialization stage, 292
   order subtotal stage, 294
   order summary, 303
   product info stage, 289-291
   shipping methods, 302-303

baskets (Estore)
   additem.asp pages, 280-285
   basket.asp pages, 286-288

bid pages for auctions (Auction Manager), 391-392

Bids Manager, 386

billing addresses, specifying (addrform.asp file), 104

BindAs method, ProfileService object, 586

BizDeskSecurity object, 574

BizTalk Server (B2B markets), 23, 534
   AppDefaultConfig properties, configuring, 540-541
   catalogs
      document definitions, creating, 544-545
      sending, 550-552, 556-557
      troubleshooting exchanges, 551-552, 556-557
   Enterprise Application Integration (EAI), 534
   frameworks overview, 534
   installing, 539
   integration with Commerce Server, 536-537
   Messaging Manager, 535
      Application Integration Component (AIC), 535
      channel creation, 547, 550
      channel modification, 554-555
      channel objects, 535
      document definition objects, 535
      launching, 541
      messaging port creation, 545-547
      messaging port modification, 553
      messaging ports, 535
      organization objects, 535
   Orchestration Designer, 534
   orders, fulfilling, 557-567
   organizations
      destination, creating, 543
      source, selecting, 541-542
   partner sites, building, 537-539
   protocols, 534
   vendors, fetching, 551-552
   XLANG, 534

browsing catalogs
   Estore simulation, 163-168
   via category (category.asp file), 91-93, 99-100

building
   modules (Business Desk), 464-468
   partner sites, B2B transactions (BizTalk Server), 537-539
   pipeline components
      Visual Basic, 403-415
      Visual C++, 422-440
   prediction model, 523-526

business
   Calyx & Corolla, e-commerce evolution, 13-14
   Internet
      growth of, 12
      technological evolution, 12

business analytics systems, 22

Business Desk, 22
   action pages
      records list display overview, 459
      recordset conversion to XML, 460-462
      recordset retrieval using ADO, 459-460
   analysis features, 60
   applications, restarting after new module configuration, 468
   architecture, 442-443
      action pages, 459-462
      edit pages, 462-464
      HTA files, 443-444
      list page, 456
      master configuration file, 448-452
      module configuration file, 452-456
      module security, 464
      visual framework, 444-448
      XML data islands, 457-458
      XML metadata islands, 458-459
   ASP files, debugging, 476-477
   auction modules, configuration modifications, 386-390
   catalogs
      creating, 64-71, 147-148
      property definitions, 120-123
   clients
      installation requirements, 60
      setup, connecting, 61
   Client Setup page, 443
   client-side functionality, 60

Completed Reports module,
data warehouse analysis,
513-515
configuring, 448-456
desktop shortcuts, 62
development mode, 476-477
e-Commerce stores, 60
edit pages
creating, 467
HTML code snippet,
462-464
modifying, 477-482
extended features, 442
frames
content pane, 446
modules, 444-448
navigation pane, 444
HTA files, 443-444
HTML Components (HTC), 61
installation, 61
interface
module pane, 62
navigation pane, 62
Internet Explorer requirement, 32
launching, 62
list pages
creating, 467
modifying, 472-475
modules, 60
analysis, 63
building, 464-468
campaign, 63
Campaign Manager,
224-247
Catalog Expressions,
244-247
catalogs, 63
configuration modifica-
tions, 469-472
master configuration file,
448-452
updating, 467
module configuration file,
452-456

orders, 63
users, 63
objects
AsyncRpt, 574
BizDeskSecurity, 574
ListManager, 574
ReportRenderer, 574
organizations, linking to user
profiles, 208-212
path connections, 442-443
production mode, 476-477
Reference Tables module,
advertising maintenance,
369-372
Reports module, data warehouse analysis, 508-513
Segment Viewer module,
530-531
server-side functionality, 60
site installations, 442-443
**business requirements
(project planning), ques-
tions for analysis, 26-27**
Buyer Visits cube (OLAP), 495

C

**C2C model (consumer-to-
consumer), eBay exam-
ple, 15**
Cache Manager
caches
creating, 94-95
retrieving, 95-96
testing, 96-97
CSF
Advertising, 345-348
Discounts, 347-348
CacheManager object
methods
GetCache, 580
RefreshCache, 580

properties
AppURL, 579
CacheObjectProdId, 579
LoaderConfig, 579
LoaderProgId, 580
RefreshInterval, 580
RetryInterval, 580
WriteConfig, 580
WriterProgId, 580
**CacheObjectProgId property,
CacheManager object, 579**
caches
catalogs, refreshing, 140
creating (Cache Manager),
94-95
DefaultPageCache, 94
dynamic site content, 94-96
FTSearchPageCache, 94
ProductListCache, 94
ProductPageCache, 94, 97
QueryCatalogInfoCache, 94
retrieving (Cache Manager),
95-96
SearchDeptPageCache, 94
ShippingManagerCache, 94
StaticSectionsCache, 94
StepSearchPageCache, 94
testing (Cache Manager),
96-97
Calyx & Corolla
B2C model, 14
IT infrastructure, electronic
commerce example, 13-14
**campaign data, importing to
data warehouses, 500**
**Campaign Manager (Business
Desk module), 63, 224-247**
advertisements, delivery of,
383-384
advertising campaigns
ad creation, 374
ad display options,
375-376
ad scheduling, 374

ad targeting, 375
creating, 373-376
troubleshooting, 381-383
site-wide discount example,
224-232
targeted discount example,
233-247
**campaigns (marketing),
223-247**
advertising
*ad creation (Campaign
Manager), 374*
*ad dislplay options
(Campaign Manager),
375-376*
*ad scheduling (Campaign
Manager), 374*
*ad targeting (Campaign
Manager), 375*
*creating (Campaign
Manager), 373-376*
*troubleshooting
(Campaign Manager),
381-383*
elements
ad cache, 367
ad properties, 366
advertising.pcf file, 367
customers, 366
goals, 366
house ads, 367
items, 366
paid ads, 367
e-mail
*creating (Direct Mailer),
330-338*
*dynamic lists (Direct
Mailer), 334-335*
*opt-out lists (Direct
Mailer), 337-338*
*personalized (Direct
Mailer), 333-337*
*testing (Direct Mailer),
331-333*

goals, 223
site-wide discounts, 224-232
targeted discounts, 233-247
targeted e-mails, 224
**Catalog Editor module
(Business Desk), 64-71**
**Catalog Expressions module
(Business Desk), 244-247**
**catalog helper routines,
Retail solution site, 604**
Catalog Management objects
CatalogManager, 572
CatalogSets, 572
CatalogToVendorAssociation,
572
Category, 572
Product, 572
ProductCatalog, 572
**catalog sets, user profiles,
displaying, 220, 223**
**Catalog.asp file, functions,
89-91**
CatalogManager object, 572
functions,
InitCatalogManager, 76
methods
*AddDefinitionProperty,
581*
CreateCatalog, 581
*CreateCategoryDefinition,
581*
*CreateProductDefinition,
581*
DeleteCatalog, 581
DeleteDefinition, 581
ExportCSV, 581
ExportXML, 582
FreeTextSearch, 582
GetCatalog, 582
ImportCSV, 582
ImportXML, 582
Initialize, 582
Query, 582

properties
Catalogs, 581
CategoryDefinition, 581
CustomCatalogs, 581
ProductDefinitions, 581
**CatalogManager object
(COM), 162**
**CatalogName property,
Category object, 588**
catalogs
accessing (Catalog.asp file),
89-91
anonymous users, viewing,
188-190
B2B transactions
*exchanging on partner
sites, 539-545*
*sending to partner sites,
550-552, 556-557*
*troubleshooting exchanges,
551-552, 556-557*
browsing
*relationships, 168-170,
173*
simulation, 163-168
*via categories
(category.asp file),
91-93, 99-100*
caches, refreshing, 140
categories, creating, 133-135
channels
*creating (Messaging
Manager), 547, 550*
*modifying (Messaging
Manager), 554-555*
COM objects
CatalogManager, 162
CatalogSets, 162
Category, 163
Product, 163
ProductCatalog, 162
creating, 133, 147-148
creating (Catalog Editor
module), 64-71

custom, creating, 143, 146

definition types

    categories, 130-133

    products, 127-130

    properties, 120, 123-125

document definitions, creating
(BizTalk Server), 544-545

e-Commerce stores, cross-
marketing opportunites, 16

exporting

    CSV format, 148, 152-153

    XML format, 148-152

expressions, targeted discounts, creating, 244-247

importing in CSV format,
153-156

messaging ports

    *creating (Messaging
Manager), 545-547*

    *modifying (Messaging
Manager), 553*

online versus printed, 118

overview, 119

printed versus online, 118

product variants, 156

    creating, 157-160

    viewing, 160

products

    creating, 135-138

    details, viewing, 97

    simple searches, 138

schemas, 119

search types

    free text, 174-176

    specification, 174-184

sets, creating, 141-143

SKUs, 118

vendors

    associating, 562

    checkout pipeline, 562-563

**catalogs modules (Business
Desk), 63**

**Catalogs property,
CatalogManager object,
581**

CatalogSets object, 162, 572

**CatalogtoVendorAssociation
object, 572**

categories (catalogs)

browsing (category.asp file),
91-93, 99-100

creating, 131-135

Category object, 163, 572

properties

    AncestorCategories, 588

    CatalogName, 588

    ChildCategories, 588

    DescendantProducts, 589

    ParentCategories, 589

    RelatedCategories, 589

    RelatedProducts, 589

**category-to-category
relationship (catalogs),
168-170, 173**

**category-to-product relation-
ship (catalogs), 168-170,
173**

**category.asp file, catalog
browsing, 91-93, 99-100**

**CategoryDefinition property,
CatalogManager object,
581**

**CGI (Common Gateway
Interface), 12**

**channel objects (BizTalk
Server), 535**

channels

creating (Messaging
Manager), 547, 550

modifying (Messaging
Manager), 554-555

purchase orders, creating,
561-562

**Check-out button, basket
pipelines (Estore), 298**

**CheckBasket routine,
basket.asp page, 287**

**checkout pipelines (Estore),
312**

accept stage, 317-320

inserting order level Visa
discount component, 413

payment stage, 314-317

purchase check stage, 313-314

vendor orders, 562-563

Visa discount

    reporting, 414-415

    testing, 415

**ChildCategories property,
Category object, 588**

**Clear method, OrderGroup
object, 585**

click and mortar stores, 15

**Client Tools for SQL Server
2000 (Business Desk), 60**

**clients, connecting (Business
Desk), 61**

**clustering data warehouses,
519**

**COM (Component Object
Model), 401**

catalog objects

    CatalogManager, 162

    CatalogSets, 162

    Category, 163

    Product, 163

    ProductCatalog, 162

components

    *Content Selection Pipeline,
260-262*

    *Direct Mailer Pipeline,
271-273*

    Plan Pipeline, 267-269

    Product Pipeline, 265, 267

    *Purchase Pipeline,
270-271*

interfaces, 401-402

language support

    C, 401

    Java, 401

    SmallTalk, 401

Visual Basic, 401
Visual C++, 401
pipeline components, 402
  adding (Pipeline Editor),
    257-258
  currency values, 276
  deleting (Pipeline Editor),
    257-258
  IDispatch, 403
  IPersistStreamInit, 403
  IPipelineComponent, 403
  IPipelineComponentAdmin,
    403
  IPipelineComponent
    Description, 403
  MtsPipeline, 255
  MtsTxPipeline, 255
  OrderGroup, 255
  OrderPipeline, 255
  PooledPipeline, 255
  PooledTxPipeline, 255
  summary table listing,
    273, 275
resources, Microsoft Web site,
  402

**Commerce Server 2000
(CS2K), 614-615**
administration resources,
  20-21
advertising infrastructure,
  364-366
Business Desk, 22
  analysis features, 60
  client installation
    requirements, 60
core systems
  business analytics sys-
    tem, 22
  product catalog system, 22
  profiling system, 22
  targeting system, 22
features summary, 20-24
fixes, downloading from
  Microsoft Web site, 538
forerunners, 19

installing, 32
  multiple-server scenario,
    34-35
  single-server scenario,
    32-33
integration with BizTalk
  Server, 536-537
Microsoft evaluation copy,
  downloading, 32
Microsoft.NET platform, 23
pipelines
  B2B model, 21
  B2C model, 21
  function of, 21
Retail solution site, 40
Site Packager, 21
site types, 20
SSCE migrated features,
  614-618
SupplierActiveDirectory solution site, 40

**Commerce Server Manager
(CSM)**
Analysis Manager, 57
Estore Web site, resources,
  viewing, 57
general resource administra-
  tion, 20-21
global resource administra-
  tion, 20-21
MMC application, 41
nodes, expanding, 56
site-specific resource
  administration, 20-21
**Common Gateway Interface.
  See CGI**
**Completed Reports module
(Business Desk), static
output, 513-515**
**Component Object Model.
  See COM**
components (pipelines)
Content Selection Framework
  AdvertisingNeedOfDeliver
    y, 598
  EvalTargetGroups, 598

  FilterContent, 598
  FormatTemplate, 598
  HistoryPenalty, 598
  InitCSFPipeline, 598
  LoadHistory, 598
  RecordEvent, 598
  RecordHistory, 598
  SaveHistory, 598
  ScoreDiscounts, 598
  SelectWinners, 598
Direct Mailer
  AddAttachments, 599
  ComposeDMLMessage,
    599
  CreateUPMCookie, 599
  SendPrecomposedMessage,
    599
  ThrottleDMLPerformance,
    599
  VerifyMessageBody, 599
  VerifyRecepientData, 599
General
  MoneyConvertor, 600
  Scriptor, 600
  SendSMTP, 600
  Splitter, 600
  StepWiseShipping, 600
information, viewing (Pipeline
  Editor), 592
Order Processing
  DBOrderPromo, 594
  DefaultHandling, 595
  DefaultItemPrice, 593
  DefaultItemPriceCy, 593
  DefaultOrderSubtotal, 594
  DefaultPayment, 597
  DefaultShipping, 595
  DefaultTaxCy, 596
  DefaultTotalCy, 596
  FixedHandling, 595
  FixedShipping, 595
  FlagInventory, 593
  ItemPromo, 593
  LinearHandling, 596
  LinearShipping, 595
  LocalInventory, 594

MakePO, 597
OrderDiscount, 594
POtoFile, 597
QueryCatalogInfo, 592-593
QueryProdInfoADO, 592
RequiredHandling, 596
RequiredItemAdjustPriceCy, 593
RequiredItemPrice, 593
RequiredItemPriceCy, 593
RequiredOrderAdjustprice, 594
RequiredOrderCheck, 594
RequiredOrderInit, 594
RequiredOrderInitCy, 594
RequiredOrderSubtotal, 595
RequiredPayment, 597
RequiredProdInfo, 593
RequiredTax, 596
RequiredTotal, 597
SaleAdjust, 593
SampleRegionalTax, 596
SaveReceipt, 597
ShippingDiscountAdjust, 595
ShippingMethodRouter, 595
SQLItemADO, 597
TableHandlingADO, 596
TableShippingADO, 595
ValidateCCNumber, 597
compose e-mail stage, Direct Mailer pipeline, 342
ComposeDMLMessage component, Direct Mailer pipeline, 599
config folder (Business Desk)
application.xml file, 452-456
bizdesk.xml file, 449-452
Configuration objects
AppConfig, 575
GlobalConfig, 575
SiteConfig, 575
SiteConfigReadOnly, 575

configuring
Business Desk, 448-456
clients (Business Desk), 61
site applications, 76-77
confirm.asp file, order confirmation pages, 112
connecting Business Desk
client setup, 61
paths, 442-443
constraint clauses, catalog specification searches, 181-184
Content cache (CSF)
Advertising, 345-348
Discounts, 347-348
content pane (Business Desk), 446
Content Selection Framework. *See* CSF
Content Selection Pipelines. *See* CSPs
ContentList object, 575
ContentListFactory object, 575
ContentListSchema object, 575
ContentSelector object, 575
advertising.pcf file, 378-381
banner files, modifying, 378-381
GetContent( ) method, 349-350, 587
pipeline stages
filter, 344
format, 345
initial score, 344
record, 345
score, 344
select, 345
context profiling, 218-219
cookie-less browsing, 200-201
cookies
deny settings, 200-201
non-persistent, 192

persistent, 192
placement on local machines, 189-190
core systems (Commerce Server 2000), 22
crdtcard.asp page, 310-312
create cookies stage, Direct Mailer pipeline, 341
CreateCatalog method, CatalogManager object, 581
CreateCategoryDefinition method, CatalogManager object, 581
CreateDMLMessage component, 342
CreateProductDefinition method, CatalogManager object, 581
CreateProfile method, ProfileService object, 587
CreateUPMCookie component, 341
Direct Mailer pipeline, 599
creating
advertising campaigns (Campaign Manager), 373-376
auctions (Auction Manager), 386-390
caches (Cache Manager), 94-95
catalogs, 133
Catalog Editor module (Business Desk), 64-71
custom, 143, 146
product variants, 158-160
sets, 141-143
summary steps, 147-148
categories for catalogs, 133-135
e-mail address sources (List Manager), 327-330
e-mail campaigns (Direct Mailer), 330-338

IIS Web sites, 41-43

product definitions for
catalogs, 127-138

property definitions for
catalogs, 123-125

**credit card processing, pay-
ment.asp file, 110-112**

**CS Authentication, global
level resource (Site
Packager), 55**

**csapp.ini file, site application
configuration file, 76-77**

**CSF (Content Selection
Framework), 344**

Advertising cache, 345-348

ContentSelector object

*GetContent( ) method,
349-350*

pipeline stages, 344-345

Discounts cache, 347-348

objects

ContentList, 575

ContentListFactory, 575

ContentListSchema, 575

ContentSelector, 575

ExpressionEval, 576

ExpressionStore, 576

ExprEvalContent, 576

ExprFltrQryBldr, 576

RowCollection, 576

overview, 344

**CSPs (Content Selection
Pipelines), 350, 396**

advertising.pcf file, 350, 367,
378-381

COM components, 260-262

discounts.pcf file, 350

filter stage, 353-354

format stage, 358

initial score stage, 354

load context stage, 351-352

record stage, 357-358

scoring stage, 354-357

select stage, 357

stages, 260-262

**CSV (Comma Separated
Values), catalogs**

export formats, 148, 152-153

import formats, 153-156

cubes (OLAP)

Bandwidth, 494

Basket Events, 494

Buyer Visits, 495

dimensions, 487

viewing, 493-494

fact tables, 489

measures, 487

metadata details, viewing,
492-493

multidimensional expressions
queries (MDX), 489-490

Order Events, 495

Page Usage, 495

populating, 498-507

storage

*hybrid OLAP (HOLAP),
489*

*multidimensional OLAP
(MOLAP), 489*

*relation OLAP (ROLAP),
489*

Web Usage, 496

Weekly User Trends, 496

**custom catalogs, creating,
143-146**

**custom reports, data
warehouse analysis**

creating, 515-518

dynamic OLAP output,
516-517

static SQL output, 517-518

**CustomCatalogs property,
CatalogManager object,
581**

**Customer Relationship
Management (CRM), 18**

customers

advertising campaigns, 366

e-Commerce stores, registration of, 17

explicit targeting, 219

personalization

catalog sets, 220, 223

e-Commerce stores, 17

predicitve targeting, 220

profiling system, 22

targeted discounts, creating
based on age, 233-247

targeting strategies, 218

Web sites, personalization
strategies, 218

**customizing e-mail order
confirmation, 396-400**

D

data codes, list pages

Business Desk, 456-459

HTCs, 456

**Data Codes module, order
status codes, inserting, 465**

**data fit scores, prediction
model, 526-527**

data islands (XML), 457-458

data marts (OLAP), 488-489

data mining models, 490

**data sources, profiles,
mapping, 212**

data stores (OLAP), 488-489

data warehouses

analysis models, dense versus
sparse data tables, 519-521

analysis reports, 507-508

custom output, 515-518

dynamic output, 508-513

static output, 508, 513-515

cubes

Bandwidth, 494

Basket Events, 494

Buyer Visits, 495

*dimensions, viewing,
493-494*

*metadata details, viewing,
492-493*

Order Events, 495
Page Usage, 495
Web Usage, 496
Weekly User Trends, 496
data categories
  campaigns, 500
  product catalogs, 500
  transactions, 500
  user profiles, 500
databases
  data types, 492
  OLAP, 492
  populating, 498-507
  SQL Server, 492
global level resource
  (Site Packager), 54
help tutorials, Analysis
  Services (SQL Server 2000),
  490-491
OLAP (Online Analytical
  Processing), 486-487
  cubes, 487-490
  data sources, 488-489
OLTP (Online Transaction
  Processing), 486-487
prediction models, 518
  building, 523-526
  data fit scores, 526-527
  *Decision Tree algorithm,
    519*
  installing, 518
  *recommend scores,
    526-527*
  *Transactions configura-
    tion, 521-523*
segment models
  clustering, 519
  generating, 530
  *Segment Viewer module,
    530-531*
  uses, 530
Site Packager, 491
tables, logical schemas,
  496-497
use guidelines, 531-532

databases
  data warehouses
    data types, 492
    OLAP, 492
    SQL Server, 492
  Direct Mailer, available tables,
    325
  populating (data warehouses),
    498-507
DataFunctions object, 574
**DBOrderPromo component,
  order processing pipeline,
  594**
DBStorage object, 578
debugging
  ASP files (Business Desk),
    476-477
  pipelines, 416
    *dumping OrderForm
      object contents, 416-417*
    *logging object activity,
      418-419*
    *Micropipe object execu-
      tion, 419-421*
**Decision Tree algorithm, data
  warehouses, 519**
**DecodeStatus method,
  AppConfig object, 587**
**default files, Web logs,
  importing to data ware-
  houses, 504**
**Default ShopperInfo compo-
  nent, order processing
  pipeline, 593**
default.asp file
  home pages, 82-83
  include files
    environment setup, 86
    header file, 84
    *HTML rendering routines,
      85*
    layout pages, 87-89
    site constants, 84
    standard libraries, 85-86

**DefaultHandling component,
  order processing pipeline,
  595**
**DefaultItemPrice component,
  order processing pipeline,
  593**
**DefaultItemPriceCy compo-
  nent, order processing
  pipeline, 593**
**DefaultLanguage property,
  MessageManager object,
  580**
**DefaultOrderSubtotal com-
  ponent, order processing
  pipeline, 594**
DefaultPageCache, 94
DefaultPayment component
  order processing pipeline, 597
  payment stage, 317
**DefaultShipping component,
  order processing pipeline,
  595**
**DefaultTaxCy component,
  order processing pipeline,
  596**
**DefaultTotalCy component,
  order processing pipeline,
  596**
definition types (catalogs)
  categories, 130-133
  products, 127-130
  properties, 120-125
**DeleteCatalog method,
  CatalogManager object,
  581**
**DeleteDefinition method,
  CatalogManager object,
  581**
**DeleteProfile method,
  ProfileService object, 587**
deleting pipelines
  COM components (Pipeline
    Editor), 257-258
  stages (Pipeline Editor),
    257-258

delivery of advertisements, recording, 383-384

deploying pipeline components in production environments (Visual Basic), 422

DescedantProducts property, Category object, 589

designing
advertising campaigns, 367-369
modules, decision objectives (Business Desk), 465

destination organizations, partner sites, creating (BizTalk Server), 543

detecting returning customers, user profiles, 206-208

development mode (Business Desk), 476-477

dialog boxes
App Default Config Properties, 77
New Channel (Messaging Manager), 547, 550
New Messaging Port (Messaging Manager), 545-547
Override Messaging Port Defaults (Messaging Manager), 554-555
Primary Transport (Messaging Manager), 553
Unpack Site, 44

Dictionary object, 578

DictionaryXMLTransforms object, 578

dimensions, OLAP cubes, viewing, 493-494

Direct Mailer, 22
components
ComposeDMLMessage, 342
CreateUPMCookie, 341
FilterRecipient, 340

SendPrecomposedMessage, 342
ThrottleDMLPerformance, 339
VerifyRecipientData, 340
databases, available tables, 325
DMLService.exe , 324
e-mail campaigns
address formats (List Manager), 327-330
creating, 330-338
dynamic lists, 334-335
opt-out lists, 337-338
personalized pages, 333-337
testing, 331-333
features, 326-327
global-level resource, 53-54, 324
jobs
listing, 342
stopping, 343
troubleshooting, 343
launching, 342
pipelines, DMLPipe.pcf, 339-342
system elements, 326-327

Direct Mailer Pipeline, 259
COM components, 271-273
SMTP, 271-273
stages, 271-273

Discounts cache (CSF), 347-348

discounts.pcf file (CSP), 350

displaying advertisements (Campaign Manager), 375-376

Distributed interNet Applications Architecture. See DNA

DMLPipe.pcf file, 339
compose e-mail stage, 342
create cookies stage, 341
filter recipient stage, 340

postprocess recipient stage, 342
preprocess recipient stage, 340
send e-mail stage, 342
throttle stage, 339

DMLService.exe, global-level resource, 324

DMLService.exe (Direct Mailer), 324

DNA (Distributed interNet Applications Architecture), 56

document definition objects (BizTalk Server), 535

document definitions
catalogs, creating (BizTalk Server), 544-545
purchase orders, creating, 559

downloading
Internet Explorer, 32
Retail solution site, 40
SupplierActiveDirectory solution site, 40

dumping OrderForm object contents, 416-417

dynamic content, starter sites, caching, 94-96

dynamic information interchange, 12

dynamic lists, e-mail campaigns (Direct Mailer), 334-335

dynamic OLAP reports, data warehouse analysis, 516-517

dynamic reports, data warehouse analysis, 508-513

E

e-Commerce stores
Business Desk
analysis features, 60
client installation requirements, 60

client-side functionality, 60
server-side functionality, 60
campaigns
   site-wide discounts,
      224-232
   targeted discounts,
      233-247
catalogs, creating (Business
   Desk), 64-71
components
   back ends, 18
   catalogs, 16
   management of, 18
   online catalogs, 16
   order transactions, 17
   personalization features, 17
   shopper registration, 17
   shopping carts, 16
   system diagram, 18
   targeted marketing, 17
customer profiling
   context, 218-219
   explicit, 218-219
   implicit, 218-219
marketing
   campaigns, 223
   targeted e-mails, 224
personalization
   catalog sets, 220, 223
   targeted marketing, 218
pipelines
   component/stage summary
      table, 273-275
   Content Selection, 259-262
   currency components, 276
   Direct Mailer, 259,
      271-273
   Event Processing, 259
   function of, 250
   Order Processing, 250,
      259, 263-265
   .pcf (Pipeline
      Configuration File), 250
   Pipeline Editor, launching,
      251

return on investment (ROI), 18
targeting
   explicit, 219
   expressions, 219
   predictive, 220
URL, browsing, 63-64

e-mail
addresses, importing from flat
   text file (CSV), 328, 330
campaigns, troubleshooting
   (Direct Mailer), 343
Direct Mailer lists, 327-330,
   343
order confirmation, customizing, 396-400
product campaigns
   creating (Direct Mailer),
      330-338
   dynamic lists (Direct
      Mailer), 334-335
   opt-out lists (Direct
      Mailer), 337-338
   personalized pages (Direct
      Mailer), 333-337
   testing (Direct Mailer),
      331-333
targeted marketing, 17
   Direct Mailer, 22
   List Builder, 22

eBay, C2C model, 15
EDI (Electronic Data
Interchange), 15, 534
development of, 534
standards bodies
   ANSI X12, 534
   UN/EDIT, 534

edit pages
creating (Business Desk), 467
HTML code snippet, 462-464
modifying (Business Desk),
   477-482

electronic commerce. See
also e-Commerce stores
Calyx & Corolla, IT infrastructure, 13-14
click-and-mortar stores, 15

partnerships
   business-to-business para-
      digm (B2B), 14
   business-to-consumer
      paradigm (B2C), 14
   consumer-to-consumer
      paradigm (C2C), 15
potential of, 13-14
private networks, high cost
   of, 15

Electronic Data Interchange.
See EDI
EnsureAccess( ) subroutine,
MSCSAuthManager object,
191-192
Enterprise Application
Integration (EAI), 534
Enterprise Resource Planning
(ERP), 18
entrypoints, modules, access
security (Business Desk),
464
EPP (Event Processing
Pipeline), 359-360
error handling in pipelines,
294-296
Estore
auctions
   ASP pages additions,
      388-390
   bid page additions,
      391-392
B2B partner site,
   AppDefaultConfig property
   configuration, 540-541
basket pages, 289
   addresses, setting, 300-301
   Check-out button, 298
   item adjust price stage,
      293
   item price stage, 293
   order adjust stage, 293,
      296-297
   order check stage, 292
   order initialization stage,
      292

order subtotal stage, 294
order summary, 303
product info stage,
    289-291
shipping methods, 302-303
catalogs, simulated browsing,
    163-168
checkout pages, 312
    accept stage, 317-320
    payment stage, 314-317
    purchase check stage,
        313-314
Direct Mailer pipelines, 339
    compose e-mail stage, 342
    create cookies stage, 341
    filter recipient stage, 340
    postprocess recipient
        stage, 342
    preprocess recipient stage,
        340
    send e-mail stage, 342
    throttle stage, 339
e-mail campaign
    creating (Direct Mailer),
        330-338
    dynamic lists (Direct
        Mailer), 334-335
    opt-out lists (Direct
        Mailer), 337-338
    order confirmation,
        customizing, 396-400
    personalized pages (Direct
        Mailer), 333-337
    testing (Direct Mailer),
        331-333
order-level Visa discount
    component
    building, 404-440
    compiling, 411, 439-440
    inserting in checkout.pcf
        pipeline, 413
    modifying configuration
        interface, 408-411
    registering, 411-413, 438

reporting the discount,
    414-415
setting configuration
    values, 413
setting read and write
    values, 411
testing, 415
pipelines
    error handling, 294-296
    global initialization,
        278-279
product page
    additem.asp page,
        279-285
    basket.asp page, 286-288
total pages, 304
    CopyFields stage, 307-309
    handling stage, 306
    Inventory stage, 309-310
    order stage, 307
    shipping methods,
        304-306
    summary page stage,
        310-312
    tax stage, 306
Estore Web site
anonymous users, 188
    persistent cookies,
        189-190
EstoreBizDesk application,
    41-43
resources, viewing, 57
SQL Server database
    objects, 57
EuroDisplay object, 574
EvalTargetGroups compo-
    nent, content selection
    framework pipeline, 598
event handlers, Application
    OnStart, 81
Event Processing Pipeline
    (EPP), 259, 359-360
Event Viewer, catalog
    exchanges, trouble-
    shooting (BizTalk Server),
    556-557

events, advertising, recording
    delivery of, 383-384
exchanging catalogs (B2B
    transactions), 539-545
Exclude filters, Web logs,
    importing to data ware-
    houses, 502
Execute method, MtsPipeline
    object, 589
executing Micropipe object
    for pipeline debugging,
    419-421
explicit profiling, 218-219
explicit targeting, 219
ExportCSV method,
    CatalogManager object,
    581
exporting
    catalogs
        CSV format, 148, 152-153
        XML format, 148-152
    static reports (List Manager),
        514-515
ExportXML method,
    CatalogManager object,
    582
Expression Evaluator, 219
expression evaluators,
    global.asa file, 78
ExpressionEval object, 576
expressions
    catalogs, targeted discounts,
        creating, 244-247
    targeting (Expression
        Evaluator), 219
ExpressionStore object, 576
ExprEvalContent object, 576
ExprFltrQryBldr object, 576
eXtensible Markup
    Language. See XML

F

fact tables, OLAP cubes, 489
FedEx (B2B model), 14
fetching vendors (BizTalk
    Server), 551-552
Fields property, ProfileObject
    object, 590
filter recipient stage, Direct
    Mailer pipeline, 340
filter stage (CSPs), 353-354
FilterContent component
    content selection framework
        pipeline, 598
    filter stage, 353-354
FilterRecipient component,
    340
FixedHandling component,
    order processing pipeline,
    595
FixedShipping component,
    order processing pipeline,
    595
FlagInventory component,
    order processing pipeline,
    593
flat text files, e-mail
    addresses, importing,
    328-330
folders, modules, creating
    (Business Desk), 466
format stage (CSPs), 358
FormatTemplate component
    content selection framework
        pipeline, 598
    format stage, 358
forms, user registration,
    value validation, 201-203
free text searches (catalogs),
    174-176
FreeTextSearch method,
    CatalogManager object,
    582
FTSearchPageCache, 94
fulfilling orders (B2B transac-
    tions), 557-567

G

GenerateEncyptionKey
    method, AuthManager
    object, 578
generating
    tickets, 198-199
    user profiles, 192-194
GenID object, 578
GetAddress method,
    OrderGroup object, 585
GetCache method,
    CacheManager object, 580
GetCatalog method,
    CatalogManager object,
    582
GetContent method
    Content Selector object,
        349-350
    ContentSelector object, 587
GetFormsDefinition( ) func-
    tion, global.asa file, 81
GetItemInfo method,
    OrderGroup object, 585
GetLocale method,
    MessageManager object,
    580
GetMessage method,
    MessageManager object,
    580
GetProfile method,
    ProfileService object, 587
GetProfileXML method,
    ProfileObject object, 590
GetProperty method,
    AuthManager object, 578
GetShippingMethods( )
    method, OrderGroup
    object, 302-303
GetSitePages( ) function,
    global.asa file, 78
GetSiteStyles( ) function,
    global.asa file, 79
GetURL method,
    AuthManager object, 578

GetUserID method,
    AuthManager object, 578
GetUserIDFromCookie
    method, AuthManager
    object, 579
GetUserInfo( ) subroutine,
    MSCSAuthManager object,
    190
global level resources,
    solution sites (Site
    Packager), 53
    CS Authentication, 55
    Data Warehouse, 54
    Direct Mailer (DM), 53-54
    Predictor, 54
    Profiles Service, 54
global.asa file, 78
    ADODB connection, 79
    expression evaluators, 78
    GetFormsDefinition( )
        function, 81
    GetMessageManagerObject( )
        function, 80
    GetSitePages( ) function, 78
    GetSiteStyles( ) function, 79
    InitAltCurrencyDisp( )
        function, 80
    InitCacheManager( ) function,
        80
    InitCatalogManager( )
        function, 80
    InitCSF( ) function, 81
    InitDataFunctions( )
        function, 80
    InitPredictor( ) function, 81
    InitProfileService( )
        function, 79
    InitSitePipelines( )
        function, 79
    instantiation functions, 74-76
    partial code snippet, 74-76
    pipelines, 79
    site and application names, 78
GlobalConfig object, 575

H

handling stage, total pipelines (Estore), 306

hardware, technical requirements (project planning)
horizontal scaling, 29
load balancing, 30
minimum requirements, 28-29
vertical scaling, 29

helper routines, Retail solution site
catalog category, 604
HTML presentation category, 606-607
miscellaneous category, 608-611
order/payment processing category, 607-608
user profiles category, 605

HistoryPenalty component, content selection framework pipeline, 598

home pages
Catalog.asp file, 89-91
default.asp file (starter sites), 82-83
include files, 84-89

horizontal scaling, hardware technical requirements (project planning), 29

Host Integration Server, 23

house ads, advertising campaigns, 367

HTA files (HTML Application), 443-444

HTCs (HTML Components), 61, 456
data codes list pages, 456
XML data islands, 457-458
XML metadata islands, 458-459

HTML (Hypertext Markup Language), 12
home page template, layout1.asp file, 87-89
presentation helper routines, Retail solution site, 606-607

HTML Application. *See* HTA files

HTML Components. *See* HTCs

hybrid OLAP (HOLAP), 489

Hypertext Markup Language. *See* HTML

I

IDispatch (COM), 403

IDL (Interface Definition Language), 402

IIS (Internet Information Server) Web sites
creating, 41-43
post-unpacking stage, 56-57

implicit profiling, 218-219

ImportCSV method, CatalogManager object, 582

importing
catalogs (CSV format), 153-156
data to data warehouses, 498-507
e-mail addresses, flat text file (CSV), 328-330
Web logs, data warehouses, 501-505

ImportXML method, CatalogManager object, 582

include files, default.asp file
environment setup, 86
header file, 84
HTML rendering routines, 85
layout pages, 87-89

site constants, 84
standard libraries, 85-86

include/const.asp file, 84

include/header.asp file, 84

include/Html_lib.asp file, 85

information interchange
dynamic, 12
static, 12

InitAltCurrencyDisp( ) function, global.asa file, 80

InitCacheManager( ) function, global.asa file, 80

InitCatalogManager( ) function, global.asa file, 76, 80

InitCSF( ) function, global.asa file, 81

InitCSFPipeline component
content selection framework pipeline, 598
load context stage, 351-352

InitDataFunctions( ) function, global.asa file, 80

initial score stage (CSPs), 354

Initialize method
AuthManager object, 579
CatalogManager object, 582
OrderGroup object, 585
ProfileService object, 587

InitializeBasketPage routine, basket.asp page, 287-288

initializing site applications, 74-82

InitPredictor( ) function, global.asa file, 81

InitProfileService( ) function, global.asa file, 79

InitSitePipelines ( ) function, 79, 278-279

installing
BizTalk Server, 539
Business Desk, 61
clients, 60, 442-443
servers, 442-443

Commerce Server 2000, 32
multiple-server scenario, 34-35
single-server scenario, 32-33
Pipeline Component Wizard (Visual Basic), 404
instantiating Auction object, 385
Interface Definition Language (IDL), 402
interfaces (COM), 401-402
Internet Advertising Bureau (IAB), online advertising reports, 364
Internet business
growth of, 12
technological evolution, 12
Internet Explorer
Business Desk, client installation requirements, 60
downloading, 32
software requirements, project planning, 32
Internet Information Server. *See* IIS
Inventory stage, total pipelines (Estore), 309-310
IPersistStreamInit (COM), 403, 434-435
IPipelineComponent (COM), 403
Activate method, 431-432
Apply method, 432, 434
Execute method, 427-429
IPipelineComponentAdmin (COM), 403, 435-438
IPipelineComponentDescription (COM), 403, 437
IsAuthenticated method, AuthManager object, 579
item adjust price stage, basket pipelines (Estore), 293
item price stage, basket pipelines (Estore), 292-293

ItemPromo component, order processing pipeline, 593
items
advertising campaigns, 366
shopping basket, adding (_additem.asp file), 101-104

J-K-L

Java, COM support, 401

launching
Business Desk, 62
Direct Mailer, 342
Messaging Manager, 541
Pipeline Editor, 251
layout1.asp file, 87-89
LDAP (Lightweight Directory Access Protocol), 19
LinearHandling component, order processing pipeline, 596
LinearShipping component, order processing pipeline, 595
linking user profiles to organizations (Biz Desk), 208-212
List Builder, 22
List Manager
e-mail address sources, 343
e-mail list formats, 327-330
static reports, exporting to, 514-515
list pages
creating (Business Desk), 467
data codes
Business Desk, 456
HTCs, 456
modifying (Business Desk), 472-475

ListManager object, 574
load balancing, hardware technical requirements (project planning), 30
load context stage (CSPs), 351-352
LoadBasket method, OrderGroup object, 281-282, 585
LoaderProgId property, CacheManager object, 580
LoadHistory component, content selection framework pipeline, 598
LoadOrder method, OrderGroup object, 585
LoadPipe method, MtsPipeline object, 589
LoadTemplate method, OrderGroup object, 585
LocalInventory component, order processing pipeline, 594
log files, Web logs, importing to data warehouses, 504-505
LogFile property, OrderGroup object, 584
logging object activity, pipeline debugging, 418-419
logical schemas, data warehouse tables, 496-497
LRUCache object, 577

M

MakePO component, order processing pipeline, 597
managing e-Commerce stores
BizDesk (Commerce Server 2000), 22
Business Desk tool, 60
components, 18

mapping data sources to profiles, 212

marketing campaigns
goals, 223
site-wide discounts, 224-232
targeted discounts, 233-247
targeted e-mails, 224

master configuration file
Business Desk modules, 448-452
new modules, updating (Business Desk), 467

Membership Migration tool (CS2K), 617-618

MessageManager object, 577
message strings in Auction object, 385
methods
AddLanguage, 580
AddMessage, 580
GetLocale, 580
GetMessage, 580
properties, DefaultLanguage, 580

Messaging Manager (BizTalk Server), 535
Application Integration Component (AIC), 535
catalogs, vendor associations, 562
channels
creating, 547, 550
modifying, 554-555
purchase orders, 561-562
document definitions, purchase orders, 559
launching, 541
messaging ports, 535
creating, 545-547
modifying, 553
purchase orders, 559-560
objects
channels, 535
document definitions, 535
organizations, 535

messaging ports
BizTalk Server, 535
creating (Messaging Manager), 545-547
modifying (Messaging Manager), 553
purchase orders, creating, 559-560

metadata, advertising, defining, 369-372

metadata islands (XML), 458-459

methods
AppConfig object
DecodeStatus, 587
RefreshCache, 588
AuthManager object
GenerateEncyptionKey, 578
GetProperty, 578
GetURL, 578
GetUserID, 578
GetUserIDFromCookie, 579
Initialize, 579
IsAuthenticated, 579
Refresh, 579
SetAuthTicket, 579
SetProfileTicket, 579
SetProperty, 579
SetUserID, 579
UnInitialize, 579
URLArgs, 579
URLShopperArgs, 579
CacheManager object
GetCache, 580
RefreshCache, 580
CatalogManager object
AddDefinitionProperty, 581
CreateCatalog, 581
CreateCategoryDefinition, 581
CreateProductDefinition, 581

DeleteCatalog, 581
DeleteDefinition, 581
ExportCSV, 581
ExportXML, 582
FreeTextSearch, 582
GetCatalog, 582
ImportCSV, 582
ImportXML, 582
Initialize, 582
Query, 582
ContentSelector object, GetContent, 587
MessageManager object
AddLanguage, 580
AddMessage, 580
GetLocale, 580
GetMessage, 580
MtsPipeline object
Execute, 589
LoadPipe, 589
SetLogFile, 589
OrderGroup object
AddItem, 585
AddOrderForm, 585
Clear, 585
GetAddress, 585
GetItemInfo, 585
Initialize, 585
LoadBasket, 585
LoadOrder, 585
LoadTemplate, 585
PutItemValue, 586
RemoveItem, 586
RemoveOrderForm, 586
RunPipe, 586
SaveAsBasket, 586
SaveAsOrder, 586
SaveAsTemplate, 586
SetAddress, 586
SetShippingAddress, 586
ProfileObject object
GetProfileXML, 590
Update, 590
ProfileServuce object
BindAs, 586
CreateProfile, 587

DeleteProfile, 587
GetProfile, 587
Initialize, 587
UnBind, 587
MicroPipe object, 573
pipelines, debugging, 419-421
**Microsoft Application Center
2000, SSCE migrated
features, 615**
**Microsoft BizTalk Server
2000, SSCE migrated
features, 615**
**Microsoft SharePoint Portal,
SSCE migrated features,
615**
Microsoft Web site
COM resources, 402
Commerce Server 2000
evaluation copy, 32
Retail solution site, 40
*SupplierActiveDirectory
solution site, 40*
Commerce Server fix
downloads, 538
Internet Explorer, down-
loading, 32
.NET platform resources, 23
SQL Server resources, 31
Windows 2000
hot fixes, 31
service packs, 31
**Microsoft WebDAV, SSCE
migrated features, 615**
Microsoft.NET, 23
**middle tiers as Web site
element, 74**
migrating SSCE
ad information to Campaigns
database (CS2K), 618
database reports to Business
Desk Reports module
(CS2K), 618

features
*to Commerce Server 2000,
614-618*
*to other Microsoft
products, 615*
membership to CS2K Profile
Service (Membership
Migration tool), 617-618
**miscellaneous helper
routines, Retail solution
site, 608-611**
**MMC (Microsoft
Management Console), 41**
modifying
banner file (ContentSelector
object), 378-381
edit pages (Business Desk),
477-482
list pages (Business Desk),
472-475
module configuration
(Business Desk), 469-472
modules (Business Desk)
analysis, 63
auction category, 386-390
building, 464-468
campaign, 63
catalogs, 63
configuration file
creating, 466-467
modifying, 469-472
design decisions, building
process, 465
edit pages, creating, 467
folders, creating, 466
list pages, creating, 467
master configuration file,
448-452
module configuration file,
452-456
orders, 63
security, 464
task icons, 447-448
users, 63
visual framework, 444-448

**MoneyConvertor component,
General pipeline, 600**
**MSCSAdoConnection object,
79**
**MSCSAuth object, signed-in
users, 192**
MSCSAuthManager object
EnsureAccess( ) subroutine,
191-192
GetUserInfo( ) subroutine, 190
SetAuthTicket method,
203-205
SetProfileTicket method,
198-199
MSCSProfile cookie, 189-190
anonymous users, 192
**MSCSProfileService object,
CreateProfile method,
193-194**
MtsPipeline object, 255, 573
methods
Execute, 589
LoadPipe, 589
SetLogFile, 589
**MtsTxPipeline object, 255,
574**
**multidimensional expressions
queries (MDX), OLAP cube
queries, 489-490**
**multidimensional OLAP
(MOLAP), 489**
**multiple servers, installing,
34-35**

N - O

**navigation pane (Business
Desk), 444**
**New Channel dialog box
(Messaging Manager), 547,
550**
**New menu commands,
Unpack Site, 44**

New Messaging Port dialog
  box (Messaging Manager),
  545-547
Nielsen/Netratings, person-
  alizaiton results, 218
nodes, expanding
  (Commerce Server
  Manager), 56
non-persistent cookies, 192

objects
  AdminEventLog, 576
  AdminFiles, 576
  AdminSite, 576
  AdminWebServer, 576
  AppConfig, 575
  AppFrameWork, 574
  AsyncRpt, 574
  Auction, 577
  AuthManager, 573
  BizDeskSecurity, 574
  CatalogManager, 572
  CatalogSets, 572
  CatalogToVendorAssociation,
    572
  Category, 572
  ContentList, 575
  ContentListFactory, 575
  ContentListSchema, 575
  ContentSelector, 575
  DataFunctions, 574
  DBStorage, 578
  Dictionary, 578
  DictionaryXMLTransforms,
    578
  EuroDisplay, 574
  ExpressionEval, 576
  ExpressionStore, 576
  ExprEvalContent, 576
  ExprFltrQryBldr, 576
  GenID, 578
  GlobalConfig, 575
  ListManager, 574
  LRUCache, 577
  MessageManager, 577

MicroPipe, 573
MtsPipeline, 573
MtsTxPipeline, 574
OrderForm, 573
OrderGroup, 573
OrderGroupManager, 573
OrderPipeline, 574
Page, 574
pipelines, debugging, 418-419
PooledPipeline, 574
PooledTxPipeline, 574
PredictorClient, 577
PredictorServiceAdmin, 576
PredictorSiteServiceAdmin,
  576
PredModelBuilder, 577
Product, 572
ProductCatalog, 572
ProfileObject, 573
ProfileService, 573
ReportRenderer, 574
RowCollection, 576
Shipping, 577
ShippingMethodManager, 577
SimpleFindResultInfo, 573
SimpleFindSearchInfo, 573
SimpleList, 578
SiteConfig, 575
SiteConfigReadOnly, 575
StandardSManager, 577
Office 2000 Web Controls,
  client installation require-
  ments, 60
OLAP (Online Analytical
  Processing), 486-487
  cubes
    Bandwidth, 494
    Basket Events, 494
    Buyer Visits, 495
    dimensions, 487
    fact tables, 489
    hybrid OLAP (HOLAP),
      489
    measures, 487

multidimensional
  expressions queries
  (MDX), 489-490
multidimensional OLAP
  (MOLAP), 489
Order Events, 495
Page Usage, 495
populating, 498-507
relation OLAP (ROLAP),
  489
Web Usage, 496
Weekly User Trends, 496
data sources for data stores,
  488-489
data warehouses, database
  access, 492
OLTP (Online Transaction
  Processing), 486-487
online advertising
  Commerce Server, fundamen-
    tal elements, 364-366
  Internet Advertising Bureau
    (IAB), 364
  Year 2000 revenue statistics,
    364
Online Analytical Processing.
  See OLAP
online catalogs, e-Commerce
  stores, 16
online stores (SSCE),
  evolution to catalog system
  (CS2K), 616-617
Online Transaction
  Processing. See OLTP
OPPs (Order Processing
  Pipelines), 396
  InitSitePipelines ( ) function,
    278-279
opt-out lists, e-mail
  campaigns (Direct Mailer),
  337-338
Orchestration Designer
  (BizTalk Server), 534

order adjust stage, basket pipelines (Estore), 293, 296-297

order check stage, basket pipelines (Estore), 292

order confirmation page, confirm.asp file, 112

Order Events cube (OLAP), 495

order initialization stage, basket pipelines (Estore), 292

Order Management objects
OrderForm, 573
OrderGroup, 573
OrderGroupManager, 573
SimpleFindResultInfo, 573
SimpleFindSearchInfo, 573

order modules (Business Desk), 63

order processing helper routines, Retail solution site, 607-608

Order Processing Pipelines, 250, 259
OrderForm object, 263-265
templates
Plan Pipeline, 267-269
Product Pipeline, 259, 265-267
Purchase Pipeline, 259, 270-271

Order Processing Pipelines. See OPPs

order stage, total pipelines (Estore), 307

order subtotal stage, basket pipelines (Estore), 294

order summary, basket pipelines (Estore), 303

order-level Visa discount component, pipeline components
building (VB), 404-415
building (Visual C++), 423-440

compiling (VB), 411
compiling (Visual C++), 439-440
inserting in checkout.pcf pipeline (VB), 413
modifying configuration interface (VB), 408-411
registering (VB), 411-413
registering (Visual C++), 438
reporting the discount (VB), 414-415
setting configuration values (VB), 413
setting read and write values (VB), 411
testing, 415

OrderDiscount component, order processing pipeline, 594

OrderForm object, 255, 573
Order Processing Pipeline, 263-264
Context dictionary, 264
error collections, 265
pipelines, debugging, 416-417
properties, 583-584

OrderGroup object, 573
AddItem method, 283
GetShippingMethods( ) method, 302-303
LoadBasket method, 281-282
methods
AddItem, 585
AddOrderForm, 585
Clear, 585
GetAddress, 585
GetItemInfo, 585
Initialize, 585
LoadBasket, 585
LoadOrder, 585
LoadTemplate, 585
PutItemValue, 586
RemoveItem, 586
RemoveOrderForm, 586
RunPipe, 586
SaveAsBasket, 586

SaveAsOrder, 586
SaveAsTemplate, 586
SetAddress, 586
SetShippingAddress, 586
ParseRequestForm( ) method, 565-567
properties
LogFile, 584
SavePrefix, 584
Value, 585
RunPipe method, 288
SaveAsBasket method, 283
SaveAsOrder( ) method, 563-565
SaveBasket method, 285
SaveBasketAsOrder( ) method, 563-565
SetAddress( ) method, 300-301

OrderGroupManager object, 573

OrderPipeline object, 255, 574

orders
B2B transactions, fulfilling, 557-567
basket pages, basket.asp pages, 286-288
e-Commerce stores, billing/ shipping transactions, 17
pipelines, error handling, 294-296
product pages, additem.asp pages, 279-285
vendors
receiving, 565-567
sending, 563-565

organization objects (BizTalk Server), 535

organizations
destination, creating (BizTalk Server), 543
source, selecting (BizTalk Server), 541-542
user profiles, linking to (Biz Desk), 208-212

Organizations profile, 198
  users, linking to, 208-212
Override Messaging Port
  Defaults dialog box
  (Messaging Manager),
  554-555

P

Page object, 574
Page Usage cube (OLAP), 495
paid ads, advertising campaigns, 367
ParentCategories property,
  Category object, 589
partner sites
  B2B transactions, building
    (BizTalk Server), 537-539
  catalogs
    exchanging, 539-545
    sending, 550-552, 556-557
  channels
    creating (Messaging
      Manager), 547, 550
    modifying (Messaging
      Manager), 554-555
  messaging ports
    creating (Messaging
      Manager), 545-547
    modifying (Messaging
      Manager), 553
  orders, fulfilling, 557-567
payment pages, payment.asp
  file, 110-112
payment processing helper
  routines, Retail solution
  site, 607-608
payment stage, checkout
  pipelines (Estore), 314-317
.pct templates (pipelines)
  Content Selection, 259-262
  Direct Mailer, 259, 271-273
  Event Processing, 259
  Order Processing, 259,
    263-265

performance (software)
  asynchronous processing, 36
  caching, 36
  separation of static and
    dynamic content, 36
  session management, 36
persistent cookies, 192
  local machines, placing,
    189-190
  MSCSProfile, 189-190
personalization
  catalog sets, 220, 223
  customers, 17
  portal sites, 218
  profiling
    context, 218-219
    explicit, 218-219
    implicit, 218-219
  strategies, 218
  targeted marketing, 218
Personalization and
  Membership Server (SSCE),
  evolution to Profile Service
  (CS2K), 617-618
personalized pages, e-mail
  campaigns (Direct Mailer),
  333-337
pickship.asp file, shipping
  methods, 105-108
Pipeline Component Wizard
  (Visual Basic)
  installing, 404
  order-level Visa discount
    component
    building, 404-415
    compiling, 411
    inserting in checkout.pcf
      pipeline, 413
    modifying configuration
      interface, 408-411
    registering, 411-413
    reporting the discount,
      414-415
    setting configuration
      values, 413

    setting read and write
      values, 411
    testing, 415
pipeline components
  Content Selection Framework
    AdvertisingNeedOfDelivery,
      598
    EvalTargetGroups, 598
    FilterContent, 598
    FormatTemplate, 598
    HistoryPenalty, 598
    InitCSFPipeline, 598
    LoadHistory, 598
    RecordEvent, 598
    RecordHistory, 598
    SaveHistory, 598
    ScoreDiscounts, 598
    SelectWinners, 598
  Direct Mailer
    AddAttachments, 599
    ComposeDMLMessage,
      599
    CreateUPMCookie, 599
    SendPrecomposedMessage,
      599
    ThrottleDMLPerformance,
      599
    VerifyMessageBody, 599
    VerifyRecepientData, 599
  General
    MoneyConvertor, 600
    Scriptor, 600
    SendSMTP, 600
    Splitter, 600
    StepWiseShipping, 600
  information, viewing (Pipeline
    Editor), 592
  Order Processing
    DBOrderPromo, 594
    DefaultHandling, 595
    DefaultItemPrice, 593
    DefaultItemPriceCy, 593
    DefaultOrderSubtotal, 594
    DefaultPayment, 597
    DefaultShipping, 595
    DefaultShopperInfo, 593

DefaultTaxCy, 596
DefaulttotalCy, 596
FixedHandling, 595
FixedShipping, 595
FlagInventory, 593
ItemPromo, 593
LinearHandling, 596
LinearShipping, 595
LocalInventory, 594
MakePO, 597
OrderDiscount, 594
POtoFile, 597
QueryCatalogInfo, 592
QueryProdInfoADO, 592
RequiredHandling, 596
RequiredItemAdjustPriceCy,
   593
RequiredItemPrice, 593
RequiredItemPriceCy, 593
RequiredOrderAdjustPrice,
   594
RequiredOrderCheck, 594
RequiredOrderInit, 594
RequiredOrderInitCy, 594
RequiredOrderSubtotal,
   595
RequiredPayment, 597
RequiredProdInfo, 593
RequiredTax, 596
RequiredTotal, 597
SaleAdjust, 593
SampleRegionalTax, 596
SaveReceipt, 597
ShippingDiscountAdjust,
   595
ShippingMethodRouter,
   595
SQLItemADO, 597
TableHandlingADO, 596
TableShippingADO, 595
ValidateCCNumber, 597
Pipeline Configuration files
(.pcf), 250

Pipeline Editor
  basket pipeline (basket.pcf),
    288-289
    Check-out button, 298-303
    item adjust price stage,
      293
    item price stage, 292-293
    order adjust stage, 293,
      296-297
    order check stage, 292
    order initialization stage,
      292
    order subtotal stage, 294
    product info stage,
      289-291
  checkout pipeline
    (checkout.pcf), 312
    accept stage, 317-320
    payment stage, 314-317
    purchase check stage,
      313-314
  launching, 251
  pipelines
    COM components, adding,
      257-258
    COM components,
      deleting, 257-258
    information, viewing, 592
    properties, 255, 257
    stages, adding, 257-258
    stages, COM components,
      252-255
    stages, deleting, 257-258
    stages, viewing, 251
  total pipeline (total.pcf), 304
    CopyFields stage, 307-309
    handling stage, 306
    Inventory stage, 309-310
    order stage, 307
    shipping, 304-306
    summary page stage,
      310-312
    tax stage, 306

Pipeline objects
  MicroPipe, 573
  MTSPipeline, 573
  MtsTxPipeline, 574
  OrderPipeline, 574
  PooledPipeline, 574
  PooledTxPipeline, 574
pipelines
  baskets (basket.pcf), 288-303
  checkout (checkout.pcf),
    312-320
  COM components, 402
    adding, 257-258
    building in Visual Basic,
      403-415
    building in Visual C++,
      422-440
    deleting, 257-258
    deploying to production
      environments (Visual
      Basic), 422
    IDispatch, 403
    IPersistStreamInit, 403
    IPipelineComponent, 403
    IPipelineComponentAdmin,
      403
    IPipelineComponentDescri
      ption, 403
    order-level Visa discount,
      404-415, 423-440
    summary table listing,
      273-275
  COM objects
    MtsPipeline, 255
    MtsTxPipeline, 255
    OrderGroup, 255
    OrderPipeline, 255
    PooledPipeline, 255
    PooledTxPipeline, 255
  Content Selection, 21, 259,
    396
    COM components,
      260-262
    stages, 260-262

CSF
  filter stage, 344
  format stage, 345
  initial score stage, 344
  record stage, 345
  score stage, 344
  select stage, 345
CSPs
  filter stage, 353-354
  format stage, 358
  initial score stage, 354
  load context stage,
    351-352
  record stage, 357-358
  scoring stage, 354-357
  select stage, 357
currency components, 276
debugging, 416
  dumping OrderForm
    object contents, 416-417
  logging object activity,
    418-419
  Micropipe object execu-
    tion, 419-421
Direct Mailer, 259, 271-273
  DMLPipe.pcf, 339-342
e-mail order confirmation,
  customizing checkout.pcf
  pipeline, 396-400
error handling, 294-296
Event Processing, 259
Event Processing Pipeline
  (EPP), 359-360
function of, 250
global initialization,
  InitSitePipelines ( ) function,
  278-279
order processing
  B2B model, 21
  B2C model, 21
Order Processing Pipelines
  (OPPs), 259, 396
Pipeline Editor, launching,
  251
properties, setting, 255-257

stages
  adding, 257-258
  COM components,
    252-255
  deleting, 257-258
  summary table listing,
    273-275
  viewing, 251
templates
  Content Selection,
    259-262
  Direct Mailer, 259,
    271-273
  directory location, 259
  empty, 259
  Event Processing, 259
  Order Processing, 259,
    263-265
  test, 259
  totals (total.pcf), 304-312
PivotChart, report displays,
512-513
Plan Pipeline
  COM components, 267-269
  stages, 267-269
planning projects
  business requirements, 26-27
  overview, 26
  technical requirements, 27-32
po.asp page, 310-312
PooledPipeline object, 255,
574
PooledTxPipeline object, 255,
574
populating databases for
data warehouses, 498-507
portals, personalization
options, 218
postprocess recipient stage,
Direct Mailer pipeline, 342
POtoFile component, order
processing pipeline, 597

prediction models
  building, 523-526
  data warehouses, 518
    Decision Tree algorithm,
      519
    sparse versus dense data
      tables, 519-521
  scores
    data fit scores, 526-527
    recommend scores,
      526-527
  Transactions configuration,
    521-523
predictive targeting, 220
Predictor resource
  data warehousing, installing,
    518
  global level resource (Site
    Packager), 54
  PredictorClient object
    initializing, 527-530
    instantiating, 527
  Transaction configuration,
    521-523
PredictorClient object, 577
  initializing, 527-530
  instantiating, 527
PredictorServiceAdmin
  object, 576
PredictorServiceSiteAdmin
  object, 576
PredModelBuilder object, 577
preprocess recipient stage,
  Direct Mailer pipeline, 340
Primary Transport dialog box
  (Messaging Manager), 553
private networks
  EDI, development of, 534
  high cost of, 15
product catalog data
  export formats, 22
  importing to data warehouses,
    500

product definitions (catalogs), 127-130
product info stage, basket pipelines (Estore), 289-291
Product object, 163, 572
product page (Estore)
additem.asp page, 279-285
basket.asp page, 286-288
Product Pipeline, 259
COM components, 265-267
stages, 265-267
product variants (catalogs)
classifications, 156-160
creating, 157-160
viewing, 160
product-to-product relationship (catalogs), 168-170, 173
ProductCatalog object, 162, 572
ProductDefinitions property, CatalogManager object, 581
production mode (Business Desk), 476-477
ProductListCache, 94
ProductPageCache, 94, 97
products
catalog relationships
category-to-category, 168-170, 173
category-to-product, 168-170, 173
product-to-product, 168-170, 173
catalogs
creating, 135-138
detailed views, 97
simple searches, 138
planning
business requirements, 26-27
overview, 26
technical requirements, 27-32

site-wide discounts, applying, 224-232
targeted discounts, applying, 233-247
Profile Editor, 196
ProfileObject object, 212, 573
methods
GetProfileXML, 590
Update, 590
properties, Fields, 590
profiles
accessing, 195
Address, 198
data sources, mapping, 212
definitions, 212
entities, examples, 194
Organization, 198
ProfileObject object, 212
ProfileService object, 212
properties, setting, 198
storage locations, 194
system architectural disgram, 194
UserObject
database table schema, 195-196
definitions, 196
ProfileService object, 212, 573
global level resource (Site Packager), 54
methods
BindAs, 586
CreateProfile, 587
DeleteProfile, 587
GetProfile, 587
Initialize, 587
UnBind, 587
profiling, 22
context, 218-219
explicit, 218-219
implicit, 218-219
projects, planning
business requirements, 26-27
overview, 26
technical requirements, 27-32

properties
CacheManager object
AppURL, 579
CacheObjectProgId, 579
LoaderProgId, 580
RefreshInterval, 580
RetryInterval, 580
WriteConfig, 580
WriterProgId, 580
CatalogManager object
Catalogs, 581
CategoryDefinition, 581
CustomCatalogs, 581
ProductDefinitions, 581
Category object
AncestorCategories, 588
CatalogName, 588
ChildCategories, 588
DescendantProducts, 589
ParentCategories, 589
RelatedCategories, 589
RelatedProducts, 589
LoaderConfig object, AppURL, 579
MessageManager object, DefaultLanguage, 580
OrderForm object, 583-584
OrderGroup object
LogFile, 584
SavePrefix, 584
Value, 585
pipelines, setting (Pipeline Editor), 255-257
ProfileObject object, Fields, 590
profiles, setting, 198
property definitions (catalogs), 120-125
public networks
lower costs, 15
Secure Multipurpose Internet Mail Extensions (SMIME), 15
Secure Sockets Layer (SSL), 15
XML technology, 15

PuP file extension (Site Packager), 21
purchase check stage, checkout pipelines (Estore), 313
purchase orders
    application, adding, 559
    channels, creating, 561-562
    document definitions, creating, 559
    messaging ports, creating, 559-560
Purchase Pipeline, 259
    COM components, 270-271
    stages, 270-271
PutItemValue method, OrderGroup object, 586

Q-R

Query method, CatalogManager object, 582
query strings, Web logs, importing to data warehouses, 504
QueryCatalogInfo component, order processing pipeline, 592
QueryCatalogInfoCache, 94
QueryProdInfoADO component, order processing pipeline, 592

receiving vendor orders, 565-567
recommend scores, prediction model, 526-527
record stage (CSPs), 357-358
RecordEvent component
    content selection framework pipeline, 598
    record stage, 357-358
RecordEvents.pcf file (EPP), 359-360

RecordHistory component, content selection framework pipeline, 598
recording delivery of advertisements, 383-384
recordsets (ADO)
    converting to XML for Business Desk action pages, 460-462
    retrieving for Business Desk action pages, 459-460
Reference Table module (Business Desk), advertising maintenance, 369
    content sizes, 369
    industry codes, 369
    page groups, 370
    target groups, creating, 370-372
Refresh method, AuthManager object, 579
RefreshCache method
    AppConfig object, 588
    CacheManager object, 580
refreshing caches for catalogs, 140
RefreshInterval property, CacheManager object, 580
registering
    ATL Pipeline Component Wizard, 422-423
    customers, 17
    user profiles, GetCurrentUserProfile function, 201, 203
RelatedCategories property, Category object, 589
RelatedProducts property, Category object, 589
relation OLAP (ROLAP), 489
RemoveItem method, OrderGroup object, 586
RemoveOrderForm method, OrderGroup object, 586

Report Writer (SSCE), evolution to Business Desk Reports module (CS2K), 618
ReportRenderer object, 574
Reports module (Business Desk), dynamic output, 508-513
RequiredHandling component, order processing pipeline, 596
RequiredItemAdjustPriceCy component, order processing pipeline, 593
RequiredItemPrice component, order processing pipeline, 593
RequiredItemPriceCy component, order processing pipeline, 593
RequiredOrderAdjustPrice component, order processing pipeline, 594
RequiredOrderCheck component, order processing pipeline, 594
RequiredOrderInit component, order processing pipeline, 594
RequiredOrderInitCy component, order processing pipeline, 594
RequiredOrderSubtotal component, order processing pipeline, 595
RequiredPayment component, order processing pipeline, 597
RequiredProdInfo component, order processing pipeline, 593
RequiredTax component, order processing pipeline, 596

RequiredTotal component, order processing pipeline, 597

restarting applications after new module configurations (Business Desk), 468

Retail solution site

B2C site construction, 40

downloading, 40

helper routines

catalogs, 604

HTML presentation, 606-607

miscellaneous, 608-611

order/payment processing, 607-608

user profiles, 605

profiles

Address, 198

Organization, 198

UserObject, 198

resources

global level (Site Packager), 53-55

selecting (Site Packager), 47-49, 52

site level (Site Packager), 53-55

unpacking (Site Packager), 44-52

retrieving caches (Cache Manager), 95-96

RetryInterval property, CacheManager object, 580

return on investment (ROI), 18

adinistrator responsibilities, 60

returning customers, detecting, 206-208

routines (helper), Retail solution site

catalog category, 604

HTML presentation category, 606-607

miscellaneous category, 608-611

order/payment processing category, 607-608

user profiles category, 605

RowCollection object, 576

RunPipe method, OrderGroup object, 288, 586

S

SaleAdjust component, order processing pipeline, 593

SampleRegionalTax component, order processing pipeline, 596

SaveAsBasket method, OrderGroup object, 283, 586

SaveAsOrder method, OrderGroup object, 586

SaveAsTemplate method, OrderGroup object, 586

SaveBasket method, OrderGroup object, 285

SaveHistory component, content selection framework pipeline, 598

SavePrefix property, OrderGroup object, 584

SaveReceipt component, order processing pipeline, 597

scheduling advertisements (Campaign Manager), 374

schemas (catalogs), 119

ScoreDiscounts component, content selection framework pipeline, 598

scoring stage (CSPs), 354-357

Scriptor component, General pipeline, 600

SearchDeptPageCache, 94

searching catalogs

free text searches, 174-176

products, 138

specification searches, 174-184

Secure Sockets Layer. *See* SSL

security, Business Desk modules, 464

segment models, data warehouses

clustering, 519

generating, 530

Segment Viewer module, 530-531

uses, 530

Segment Viewer module (Business Desk), 530-531

select stage (CSPs), 357

selecting resources for solution sites (Site Packager), 47-49, 52

SelectWinners component

content selection framework pipeline, 598

select stage, 357

send e-mail stage, Direct Mailer pipeline, 342

sending

catalogs, B2B transactions, 550-552, 556-557

MSCSAuth ticket, user registration, 203-205

vendor orders, 563-565

SendPrecomposedMessage component, 342

Direct Mailer pipeline, 599

SendSMTP component, General pipeline, 600

server clusters (SQL Server), 31

session management, software performance optimization, 36

SetAddress method, OrderGroup object, 586

SetAddress( ) method, OrderGroup object, 300-301

setadrs.asp page, 300-301

SetAuthTicket method

AuthManager object, 579

MSCSAuthManager object, 203-205

SetLogFile method,
MtsPipeline object, 589
SetProfileTicket method
   AuthManager object, 579
   MSCSAuthManager object,
   198-199
SetProperty method,
AuthManager object, 579
sets (catalogs), creating,
141-143
setship.asp page, 302-303
SetShippingAddress method,
OrderGroup object, 586
setting pipeline properties
(Pipeline Editor), 255-257
Setup_env.asp file, 86
SetUserID method,
AuthManager object, 579
shipping addresses, specifying (addrform.asp file), 104
shipping methods
   basket pipelines (Estore),
   302-303
   specifying (pickship.asp file),
   105-108
   total pipelines (Estore),
   304-306
Shipping object, 577
ShippingDiscountAdjust component, order processing
pipeline, 595
ShippingManagerCache, 94
ShippingMethodManager
object, 577
ShippingMethodRouter com-
ponent, order processing
pipeline, 595
shoppers. See customers;
user profiles
shopping carts
   anonymous users versus registered users, 16
   items, adding (_additem.asp
   file), 101-104
   registered users versus anonymous users, 16

SimpleFindResultInfo object,
573
SimpleFindSearchInfo object,
573
SimpleList object, 578
simulated browsing (cata-
logs), 163-168
single-servers, installing,
32-33
Site Administration objects
   AdminEventLog, 576
   AdminFiles, 576
   AdminSite, 576
   AdminWebServer, 576
   PredictorServiceAdmin, 576
   PredictorSiteServiceAdmin,
   576
   PredModelBuilder, 577
   Shipping, 577
   ShippingMethodManager, 577
Site Builder Wizard (SSCE),
evolution to Site Packager
(CS2K), 615
Site Configuration
Synchronization, data
warehouses, 498-500
Site Foundation Wizard
(SSCE), evolution to Site
Packager (CS2K), 615
Site Functionality objects
   Auction, 577
   LRUCache, 577
   MessageManager, 577
   PredictorClient, 577
   StandardSManager, 577
site level resources, solution
sites (Site Packager), 53
   App Default Config, 55
   Campaigns, 55
   Transactions, 55
Site Manager (SSCE), evolu-
tion to Business Desk
(CS2K), 616

Site Packager (Commerce
Server 2000), 21
   data warehouse resources, 491
   Predictor resource, installing,
   518
   .PuP file extension, 21
   Select Resources screen,
   47-53
   solution sites
      changes, examining, 56-57
      unpacking, 44-52
Site Server Commerce
Edition. See SSCE
site-wide discounts, creating,
224-232
SiteConfig object, 575
SiteConfigReadOnly object,
575
SKUs (Stock Keeping Units),
118
   product variants, 156
      creating, 157-160
      viewing, 160
SmallTalk, COM support, 402
SMTP (Simple Mail Transfer
Protocol), 271-273
soft goods versus hard
goods, 16
software
   performance optimization
      asynchronous processing, 36
      caching, 36
      separation of static and
      dynamic content, 36
      session management, 36
   technical requirements
   (project planning)
      Internet Explorer, 32
      minimum requirements,
      30-31
      SQL Server, 31
      Windows 2000, 31

solution sites
post-unpacking stage
(Site Packager), 56-57
resources
global level, 53-55
selecting, 47-52
site level, 53-55
Retail, unpacking, 44-52
source organizations, selecting (BizTalk Server), 541-542
specification searches (catalogs), 174-184
Splitter component, General pipeline, 600
SQL Server 2000, 23
data warehouses, database access, 492
Estore databases, 57
server clusters, 31
service packs, 31
software requirements, project planning, 31
SQLItemADO component, order processing pipeline, 597
SSCE (Site Server Commerce Edition), 614-615
AD Server, evolution to Campaigns Manager (CS2K), 618
migration features to
Commerce Server 2000, 614-618
other Microsoft products, 615
online store concept, evolution to catalog system (CS2K), 616-617
Personalization and Membership Server, evolution to Profile Service (CS2K), 617-618
Report Writer, evolution to Business Desk Reports module (CS2K), 618

Site Builder Wizard, evolution to Site Packager (CS2K), 615
Site Foundation Wizard, evolution to Site Packager (CS2K), 615
Site Manager, evolution to Business Desk (CS2K), 616
Starter Site, evolution to Solution Site (CS2K), 616
SSL (Secure Sockets Layer), 15
stages
Content Selection Pipeline, 260-262
Direct Mailer Pipeline, 271-273
pipelines
adding (Pipeline Editor), 257-258
COM components (Pipeline Editor), 252-255
deleting (Pipeline Editor), 257-258
summary table listing, 273-275
viewing (Pipeline Editor), 251
Plan Pipeline, 267-269
Product Pipeline, 265-267
Purchase Pipeline, 270-271
StandardsManager object, 577
Starter Site (SSCE), evolution to Solution Site (CS2K), 616
starter sites
applications
configuration settings, 76-77
initializing, 74-82
billing addresses, specifying (addrform.asp file), 104
catalogs, product details, 97
dynamic site content, caching (Cache Manager), 94-96

elements
back ends, 74
middle tiers, 74
user interfaces, 74
home pages
Catalog.asp file, 89-91
default.asp file, 82-89
names (global.asa file), 78
order confirmation page, confirm.asp file, 112
order summary page, summary.asp file, 108-109
payment pages, payment.asp file, 110-112
shipping addresses, specifying (addrform.asp file), 104
shipping methods, selecting (pickship.asp file), 105-108
shopping basket, items, adding, 101-104
static information interchange, 12
static reports, data warehouse analysis, 508
exporting to List Manager, 514-515
launching, 513-514
static SQL reports, data warehouse analysis, 517-518
StaticSectionsCache, 94
std_access_lib.asp file, 85
std_cache_lib.asp file, 85
std_cookie_lib.asp file, 85
std_profile_lib.asp file, 85
std_url_lib.asp file, 85
std_util_lib.asp file, 85
StepSearchPageCache, 94
StepWiseShipping component, General pipeline, 600
Stock Keeping Units. *See* **SKUs**
stopping Direct Mailer jobs, 343
summary page stage, total pipelines (Estore), 310-312

summary.asp file
order summary pages,
108-109
payment options, 303
**SupplierActiveDirectory
solution site**
B2B site construction, 40
downloading, 40
**suppliers, B2B transaction
roles, 538**

T

**TableHandlingADO compo-
nent, order processing
pipeline, 596**
tables, data warehouses
logical schemas, 496-497
sparse versus dense analysis,
519-521
**TableShippingADO compo-
nent, order processing
pipeline, 595**
**targeted discounts, creating
based on age, 233-247**
targeted e-mails, 224
targeted marketing, 17
**TargetGroups component,
scoring stage, 354-357**
targeting
advertisements (Campaign
Manager), 375
explicit, 219
expressions (Expression
Evaluator), 219
predicitive, 220
systems, 22
**task icons (Business Desk
modules), 447-448**
**tax stage, total pipelines
(Estore), 306**

**technical requirements
(project planning), 27**
hardware
horizontal scaling, 29
load balancing, 30
*minimum requirements,
28-29*
vertical scaling, 29
software
Internet Explorer, 32
*minimum requirements,
30-31*
SQL Server, 31
Windows 2000, 31
testing
caches (Cache Manager),
96-97
email campaigns (Direct
Mailer), 331-333
**throttle stage, Direct Mailer
pipeline, 339**
**ThrottleDMLPerformance
component, 339, 599**
tickets
EnsureAccess( ) subroutine,
192
generating, 198-199
MSCSAuth, user profile
authentication, 203-205
user profiles
*MSCSAuth (signed-in
users), 192*
*MSCSProfile (anonymous
users), 192*
*sending to local machines,
189-190*
total.pcf pipeline, 304
CopyFields stage, 307-309
handling stage, 306
Inventory stage, 309-310
order stage, 307
shipping methods, 304-306
summary page stage, 310-312
tax stage, 306

transactions
e-Commerce store orders, 17
importing to data warehouses,
500
Predictor resource, 521-523
site level resource (Site
Packager), 55
troubleshooting
advertising campaigns
(Campaign Manager),
381-383
catalog exchanges (BizTalk
Server), 551-552, 556-557
Direct Mailer jobs, 343

U

UN/EDIT standards body, 534
**UnBind method,
ProfileService object, 587**
**UnInitialize method,
AuthManager object, 579**
**Unpack Site command (New
menu), 44**
**unpacking solution sites (Site
Packager), 44-52**
**Update method,
ProfileObject object, 590**
**updating master configura-
tion file for new modules
(Business Desk), 467**
**URLArgs method,
AuthManager object, 579**
**URLs (Uniform Resource
Locators), browsing, 63-64**
**URLShopperArgs method,
AuthManager object, 579**
**user interfaces as Web site
element, 74**
User Management objects
AuthManager, 573
ProfileObject, 573
ProfileService, 573

user modules (Business Desk), 63
user profiles
anonymous, 188
persistent cookies, 189-190
treatment of, 189-190
authenticating (MSCSAuth ticket), 203-205
catalog sets, displaying, 220, 223
context profiling, 218-219
cookie-less browsing, 200
explicit profiling, 218-219
generating, 192-194
helper routines, Retail solution site, 605
implicit profiling, 218-219
importing data to data warehouses, 500
logons, authentication filter, 212-215
MSCSAuthManager object
EnsureAccess( ) subroutine, 191-192
GetUserInfo( ) subroutine, 190
MSCSPProfile object, GetNewGuestUserProfile function, 193-194
MSCSProfileService object, CreateProfile method, 193-194
organizations, linking to (Biz Desk), 208-212
purpose of, 188
registration forms, GetCurrentUserProfile function, 201-203
returning customers, detecting, 206-208
site-wide discounts, creating, 224-232
targeted discounts, creating based on age, 233-247

tickets
generating, 198-199
MSCSAuth (signed-in user), 192
MSCSProfile (anonymous user), 192
sending to local machines, 189-190
UserObject profile
database table schema, 195-196
definitions, 196
properties, viewing (Profile Editor), 196
Utility objects
DBStorage, 578
Dictionary, 578
DictionaryXMLTransforms, 578
GenID, 578
SimpleList, 578

V

ValidateCCNumber component
order processing pipeline, 597
payment stage, 316-317
validating forms, user registration values, 201-203
Value property, OrderGroup object, 585
vendors
catalogs
associating, 562
checkout pipeline, 562-563
fetching (BizTalk Server), 551-552
orders
receiving, 565-567
sending, 563-565

VerifyMessageBody component, Direct Mailer pipeline, 599
VerifyRecepientData component, Direct Mailer pipeline, 340, 599
vertical scaling, hardware technical requirements (project planning), 29
viewing catalogs
product details, 97
product variants, 160
virtual marketplace
B2B model, 14
B2C model, 14
C2C model, 15
EDI, 15
WANs, 15
VisaDiscountComp.cls, COM interfaces
IPersistDictionary, 406-408
IPipelineComponent, 406-408
IPipelineComponentAdmin, 406-408
IPipelineComponentDescription, 406-408
ISpecifyPipelineComponent, 406-408
Visual Basic
COM support, 401
Pipeline Component Wizard, installing, 404
pipeline components
building, 403-415
deploying to production environments, 422
order-level Visa discount, 404-415
Visual C++
ATL Pipeline Component Wizard, registering, 422-423
C support, 401
COM support, 401

pipeline components
building, 422-440
order-level Visa discount,
423-440
visual framework (Business Desk)
content pane, 446
modules, 444, 447-448
task icons, 447-448
navigation pane, 444

W

W3C (World Wide Web Consortium) Web site, 483
WANs (wide area networks), EDI technologies, 15
Web browsers
cookies, deny settings, 200-201
HTML, 12
Web logs, importing to data warehouses, 501-502
default files, 504
Exclude filters, 502
log files, 504-505
query strings, 504
Visit Inferences, 503
Web sites
Amazon.com, click-and-mortar store example, 15
business
growth of, 12
technological evolution, 12
CGI technology, 12
click-and-mortar stores, 15
Commerce Server 2000, type options, 20
dynamic information interchange, 12
e-commerce, potential of, 13-14

elements
back end, 74
middle tier, 74
user interfaces, 74
IIS
creating, 41-43
post-unpacking stage, 56-57
marketing campaigns, 223-247
Microsoft
COM resources, 402
Commerce Server 2000 evaluation copy, 32
Internet Explorer downloads, 32
.NET platform resources, 23
SQL Server resources, 31
Windows 2000 resources, 31
personalization
catalog sets, 220, 223
customer loyalty, 218
portals, 218
profiling, 218-219
pipelines
Content Selection, 259-262
Direct Mailer, 259, 271-273
Event Processing, 259
Order Processing, 259, 263-265
static information interchange, 12
targeting
explicit, 219
expressions, 219
predictive, 220
W3C (World Wide Web Consortium), 483
XML.com, 483

Web Usage cube (OLAP), 496
Weekly User Trends cube (OLAP), 496
wide area networks (WANs), 15
Windows 2000
hot fixes, 31
service packs, 31
software requirements, project planning, 31
WriteConfig property, CacheManager object, 580
WriterProgId property, CacheManager object, 580

X-Y-Z

XML (eXtensible Markup Langauge), 15
ADO recordsets, converting for Business Desk action pages, 460-462
catalogs, export formats, 148-152
data islands (Business Desk), 457-458
metadata islands (Business Desk), 458-459
Web resources
W3C Web site, 483
XML.com Web site, 483
XML.com Web site, 483

Yahoo!, e-commerce business model, 15